Educating All Children

American Academy of Arts and Sciences

136 Irving Street
Cambridge, MA 02138-1996
Telephone: (617) 576-5000
Fax: (617) 576-5050
email: ubase@amacad.org
Visit our website at www.amacad.org

Educating All Children: A Global Agenda

Joel E. Cohen, David E. Bloom, and Martin B. Malin, editors

American Academy of Arts and Sciences
Cambridge, Massachusetts

The MIT Press
Cambridge, Massachusetts
London, England

"Universal Basic and Secondary Education." © Joel E. Cohen, David E. Bloom, and American Academy of Arts and Sciences. 2006.

"Global Educational Expansion and Socio-Economic Development: An Assessment of Findings from the Social Sciences," Emily Hannum and Claudia Buchmann. Reprinted from *World Development* 33 (3) Pp. 1–22, © 2004, with permission from Elsevier.

This book was set in ITC Galliard by Anne Read.
Printed and bound in the United States of America.

Library of Congress Cataloging-in-Publication Data
Educating all children: a global agenda / Joel E. Cohen, David E. Bloom, and Martin B. Malin, editors.
  p. cm.
Includes bibliographical references and index.
ISBN-13: 978-0-262-53293-8 (pbk. : alk. paper)
ISBN-13: 978-0-262-03367-1 (hardcover : alk. paper)
ISBN-10: 0-262-53293-X (pbk. : alk. paper)
ISBN-10: 0-262-03367-4 (hardcover : alk. paper)
1. Educational equalization—Developing countries. 2. Education—Developing countries—Finance. I. Cohen, Joel E. II. Bloom, David E. (David Elliot), 1955– III. Malin, Martin B. IV. American Academy of Arts and Sciences.

LC213.3.D44E38 2006
379.2'6091724—dc22
                                                            2006026545

The views expressed in this volume are those held by each contributor. They do not necessarily represent the position of the Officers and Fellows of the American Academy of Arts and Sciences.

10 9 8 7 6 5 4 3 2 1

Contents

Section IV: Costs

Section V: Consequences

ACKNOWLEDGMENTS

This volume presents work of the project on Universal Basic and Secondary Education (UBASE) of the American Academy of Arts and Sciences. The project has, for the past five years, sponsored and reviewed research on the rationale, the means, and the consequences of providing basic and secondary education of quality to all children between the approximate ages of 6 and 17. The collaborations that have made this volume possible have been both extensive and intensive. Our gratitude to those who have given their time, talent, and financial support is deeply felt.

The UBASE project has received generous financial support from several sources. Many of those who have offered or facilitated such support have also contributed significantly to the project's content. The project received major support from the William and Flora Hewlett Foundation and particular encouragement from Paul Brest, Marshall Smith, and Tamara Fox. John S. Reed, the Golden Family Foundation, Paul Zuckerman, the Zlinkoff Fund, an anonymous donor, and the American Academy of Arts and Sciences also provided generous support. Leslie Berlowitz, the Academy's chief executive officer, supported and encouraged the development of the UBASE project from the outset. Her leadership and vision have been indispensable.

Our deepest intellectual debts are to the UBASE project authors, Aaron Benavot, Eric Bettinger, Melissa Binder, Henry Braun, Claudia Buchmann, Javier Corrales, Paul Glewwe, Emily Hannum, Anil Kanjee, Michael Kremer, Julia Resnik, and Meng Zhao. In the course of writing and revising their papers, they taught us much of what we can claim to know about what it would take to provide an education of high quality to every child in the world, and what the consequences would be.

Members of an advisory committee to the UBASE project provided valuable guidance on peer review and other matters for which we are grateful. The committee consisted of Nancy Birdsall, Joan Dassin, Howard Gardner, George Ingram, Kishore Mahbubani, Katherine Namuddu, Kenneth Prewitt, John S. Reed, Jeffrey Sachs, Gene Sperling, Paul Zuckerman, and Leslie Berlowitz.

Nearly all of the chapters in the volume were discussed at workshops with members of topic-specific working groups. We thank the workshop participants for their rich insights and suggestions. Workshop participants included: María Inés Aguerrondo, Farida Allaghi, Abhijit Banerjee, Albert Beaton, Leslie Berlowitz, Eric Bettinger, Melissa Binder, David E. Bloom, Cecilia Braslavsky, Henry Braun, Barbara Bruns, Chip Bury, David Canning, Claudio de Moura Castro, Colette Chabbott, Kai-Ming Cheng, Michael Clemens, Joel E. Cohen, Javier Corrales, John Craig, William K. Cummings, Oeindrila Dube, Tamara Fox, Juan Enrique Froemel, Paul Glewwe, Kira Gnesdiloff, Rangachar Govinda, Andy Green, Donald Green, Merilee Grindle, Silvina Gvirtz, Emily Hannum, Stephen Heyneman, Margaret Honey, George Ingram, Dean Jamison, Shireen Jejeebhoy, Emmanuel Jimenez, Anil Kanjee, Julie Kennedy, Elizabeth King, Michael Kremer, Robert LeVine, Deborah Levison, Maureen Lewis, Denise Lievesley, Stanley Litow, Angela Little, Cynthia Lloyd, Edilberto Loaiza, Marlaine Lockheed, Colin Maclay, George Madaus, Charles Magnin, Kishore Mahbubani, Martin Malin, Alain Mingat, Albert Motivanergs, Lynn Murphy, Francois Orivel, Laura Ruiz Pérez, Ryan Phillips, Kenneth Prewitt, Lant Pritchett, Jeffrey Puryear, Francisco Ramirez, Laura Salganik, Joel Sherman, Gene Sperling, Robert Spielvogel, Camer Vellani, Daniel Wagner, David Weil, Robin Willner, Annababette Wils, Cream Wright, and Kin Bing Wu.

The work of the UBASE project also underwent external review. We thank the following reviewers for their constructive and generous comments: Alaka Basu, Jere Behrman, Eric Bettinger, John Boli, William Cummings, Joan Dassin, Christopher Dede, David Figlio, Tamara Fox, Howard Gardner, Sherry Glied, Tamara Ortega Goodspeed, Emily Hannum, Mohsen A. Khalil, Patel Kinshuk, Anjini Kochar, Robert LeVine, Keith Lewin, Denise Lievesley, Thomas Lindh, Cynthia Lloyd, Colin Maclay, Michael O. Martin, Andrew Mason, John Meyer, Kurt Moses, Albert Motivans, Ina V.S. Mullis, Richard Murnane, Brendan O'Flaherty, Roy Pea, David Post, Kenneth Prewitt, Jeffery Puryear, Janet Ward Schofield, T. Paul Schultz, Erkki Sutinen, Michael Teitelbaum, Michael Trucano, Miguel Urquiola, Jan Vandemoortele, and Annababette Wils. We also thank four anonymous reviewers who provided comments at the request of MIT Press.

Our thinking was also influenced by those who participated in a working group on the "Goals of Education," whose work will be published in a separate volume. Members of this group included: Mallam Zaki Abubakar, Mallam Bala Ahmed, David E. Bloom, James Carroll, Mohamed Charfi, Kai-ming Cheng, Joel E. Cohen, William Cummings, David Hansen, George Ingram, Beryl Levinger, Claudia Madrazo, Martin Malin, Kishore Mahbubani, Deborah Meier, Mary Joy Pigozzi, Stephen Provasnik, Vimala Ramachandran, Mohamed Redissi, John S. Reed, Fernando Reimers, Gowher Rizvi, Richard Rothstein, Laura Salganik, Martin Sleeper, Adam Strom, Margot Stern Strom, Marcelo Suarez-Orozco, and Camer Vellani.

When planning the project, we received helpful advice from: Robert McCormick Adams, Kate Auspitz, Jorge Balán, Francis Bator, Jeffrey Boutwell, Harvey Brooks, Don Bundy, Nathan Glazer, Edward Glynn, William T. Golden, Patricia Graham, Linda D. Harrar, Suzanne Grant Lewis, John Holdren, Heather Joshi, Jerome Kagan, Carl Kaysen, Nathan Keyfitz, Jennifer Leaning, Noel McGinn, Tom Merrick, Joyce Moock, Anthony G. Oettinger, Rakesh Rajani, Larry Rosenberg, Henry Rosovsky, Corinne Schelling, Bruce Scott, Wendy R. Sheldon, Adele Simmons, Steven Sinding, Neil J. Smelser, Marshall Smith, J. Joseph Speidel, and Raymond Vernon.

We join the volume's contributors in acknowledging the research support and comments of Ashley Bates, Kate Bendall, Jonathan Borowsky, Diana Bowser, Indu Bhushan, Anna Cederberg, Victoria Collis, Jane Frewer, Juan Guzman, Michael Hand, Sidney Irvine, Jón Torfi Jónasson, Ruth Levine, Sangeetha Madhavan, Andrew Mason, Christopher Modu, Juan Manuel Moreno, Darren Morris, Richard Murnane, Joan M. Nelson, Nina Ni, António Nóvoa, Pai Obanya, David Post, Edward Reed, Erin Riley, Larry Rosenberg, Ernesto Schiefelbein, Jaypee Sevilla, Yasemin Soysal, David Steven, Duncan Thomas, Meghan Tieu, Mark Weston, and Heidi Williams. Aaron Benavot acknowledges the generous support of the International Bureau of Education during his chapter's completion.

Larry Rosenberg provided invaluable research support to David E. Bloom and helpful comments on all aspects of the UBASE project. Joel E. Cohen acknowledges with thanks the assistance of Priscilla K. Rogerson and the hospitality of William T. Golden during this work. American Academy staff members Anthony Baird, Phyllis Bendell, James DiFrancesca, Jennifer Gray, Leigh Nolan, Carolyn Yee, and Corinne Schelling helped to keep the project on track. Anne Read provided production assistance. Kathy Garcia compiled the index. A special note of thanks is due to Helen Anne Curry, whose project coordination, copy-editing, and intellectual contributions were indispensable.

This volume has been a collective effort from start to finish. It has been a tremendous privilege to work with each of those named above in producing this work. We thank the Academy for making this collaboration possible.

Joel E. Cohen	David E. Bloom	Martin B. Malin
Rockefeller and Columbia Universities	*Harvard University*	*American Academy of Arts and Sciences*

Figure 2: Percentage of Students of Secondary School Age Not Enrolled in School

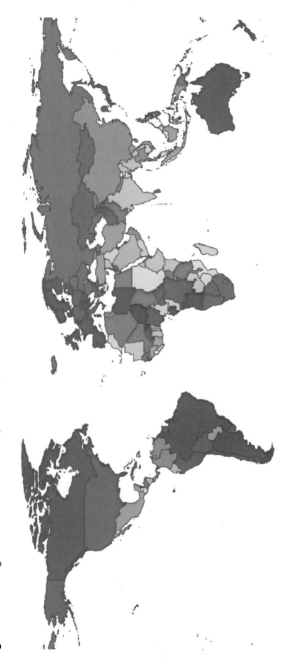

Percent unenrolled

0 - 5
6 - 10
11 - 15
16 - 20
21 - 25
26 - 30
31 - 35
36 - 40
41 - 45
46 - 50
51 - 55
56 - 60
61 - 65
66 - 70
71 - 75
76 - 80
81 - 85
86 - 90

Maps are based on data calculated by Bloom from UNESCO online data. See chapter one, Appendix A.

Figure 1: Percentage of Students of Primary School Age Not Enrolled in School

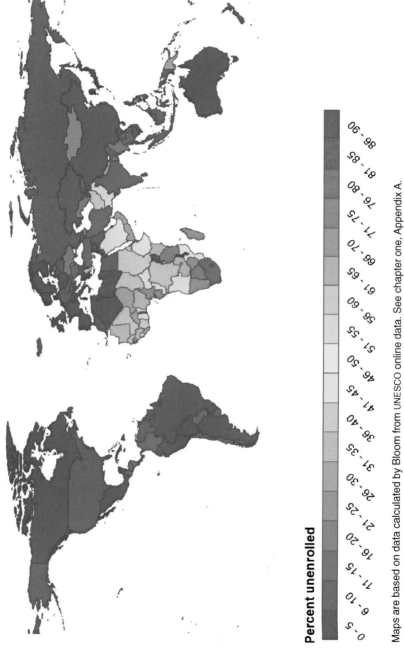

Percent unenrolled

0 - 5
6 - 10
11 - 15
16 - 20
21 - 25
26 - 30
31 - 35
36 - 40
41 - 45
46 - 50
51 - 55
56 - 60
61 - 65
66 - 70
71 - 75
76 - 80
81 - 85
86 - 90

Maps are based on data calculated by Bloom from UNESCO online data. See chapter one, Appendix A.

Cohen et al. / Educating All Children: A Global Agenda
ISBN-13: 978-0-262-03367-1 (hc. : alk. paper)—978-0-262-53293-8 (pbk. : alk. paper)

 American Academy of Arts and Sciences
Cambridge, Massachusetts

The MIT Press
Cambridge, Massachusetts
London, England

The Way Forward for Universal Education

GENE SPERLING

The second Millennium Development Goal (MDG) set by the United Nations—that all children should receive a primary education by 2015—is simultaneously perhaps the world's most important, ambitious, and pathetic global goal.

It is important because, as this book documents, education is a critical foundation for virtually all of the world's major humanitarian and development goals. While education has long been considered essential to raising lifetime earnings in both developed and developing nations, one of the most significant insights over the last two decades has been the power of education to improve health outcomes. In particular, improved education for girls tends to result in smaller and healthier families, as well as in lower infant and maternal mortality rates. Growing evidence also shows that girls who are still in school in their teens are less likely to be infected with HIV and that a curriculum that includes HIV/AIDS education can affect beliefs and behavior that reduce the occurrence of AIDS.

Education, health, and development certainly interact. As this volume details, not only can education improve health outcomes, but sound health and nutrition practices in school can increase attendance and learning at school. Yet the benefits of education do not end here. The ability to read, write, and do elementary math is essential if more women are to benefit from micro-enterprise opportunities, engage effectively in the democratic process, develop their full individual potential, and model for their children the importance of knowledge and learning. The same can be said for boys and men, particularly those who are poor and living in remote rural areas.

This goal is ambitious, because today there are approximately 115 million children who are not in school and some 150 million more who are likely to drop out before they complete primary school. About 50 percent of girls in Africa will not complete a primary education, and sixty-six poor nations are off track to provide primary education for all by the year 2015. School fees remain a critical obstacle to putting all children in school. While the recent experiences of Uganda, Kenya, and Tanzania provide overwhelming evidence that eliminating school fees can dramatically increase the demand for education, UNESCO's latest data show that as many as 86 of 100 nations they were able to survey still charge either formal or informal fees. While such fees raise the costs of attending school for all children, it seems to be a particular deterrent for girls, those living in extreme poverty, and children who have been orphaned or otherwise negatively impacted by the spread of HIV/AIDS. To realize the goal of universal basic education, these and other vulnerable children—such as those with disabilities or those in living in refugee situations, conflict zones, or fragile states—will need additional assistance to help them overcome the barriers needed to realize the full benefits of a quality education.

Yet, this goal is in some ways pathetic. If anyone has, like me, ever addressed a group of children on the issue of education in poor nations, two questions they ask are: Why we are aiming for *only* primary education, and why we are aiming *only* for 2015? Not only children find this puzzling. Many who were involved in creating this goal in Dakar at the World Education Forum—months before it was incorporated as an MDG—agreed to use the term "primary education" because they thought it was a proxy for basic education—usually defined as eight years of schooling. Thus, many were disappointed when they learned that multinational institutions consistently defined primary education as consisting of only five to six years of schooling—an amount well below what most experts believe is needed to achieve a true basic education in developing nations.

One point missed too frequently, but not in this book, is that even if one aims only for universal primary education, the achievement of that goal would create significant new costs for secondary education. A 100 percent attendance rate in sixth grade would dramatically drive up the demand for, and therefore the costs of, education in the seventh and eighth grades. One of this book's most significant contributions is that, rather than shying away from the important issue of secondary education, it confronts it head on and boldly. Equally important, this book does not fall prey to the problem of thinking of secondary education in a zero-sum context. The book stresses a greater focus on secondary education not at the expense of seeking universal primary education, but as an addition to it.

As the global community further understands the potential for education to act as a social vaccine for HIV/AIDS, it should indeed become clear that an education that ends at the beginning of a youth's teenage years is increasingly unsatisfactory. The costs and practicality of reaching universal secondary education—ten to twelve years of education—may be unachievable in the near future, but hopefully this volume will help move those who aspire to universal education at least to agree that achieving universal primary education will not suffice. Eight years of education should be considered a minimum target, and universal secondary education should be understood as a longer-term goal.

THE WAY FORWARD

If important, ambitious, and pathetic are the three words that define the Millennium Development Goal for education, the three words that should define the way forward—and I believe characterize this volume—are *rigor, realism, and heart.*

We need rigor in the analyses and recommendations of advocates and experts. This careful attention will ensure that much-needed expansions of enrollment and resources result in educational achievement. Those who are serious about achieving the Millennium Development Goal for education understand that the problem is not just access to school, but actual learning through the completion of a quality basic educational curriculum. While a child may gain important social benefits from simply attending school, universal basic education is dramatically diminished and its aims are frustrated when young people find themselves in classrooms with no textbooks, huge class sizes (sometimes as large as 100 students), and inadequately trained, underpaid teachers (who too often rely on rote learning). Efforts to increase enrollment and ensure that learning is taking place in the classroom must go hand-in-hand. Poor and rich nations must make significant advancements to ensure accountability for learning, not just enrollment.

While greater steps must be taken to expand the things we know work—eliminating fees, making schools girl-friendly and close-by, and establishing well-designed school lunch programs, for instance—we must also expand our knowledge of other areas: What are the best ways to quickly scale up the numbers of teachers without sacrificing professionalism? What are the most effective curriculums for different ages to discourage behavior that leads to HIV infection? How can education officials introduce widespread evaluations and testing without overburdening the system's resources or detracting from real learning by encouraging teachers to teach to the test? How can countries and the international community take concrete steps to garner the additional resources that will be required to pay the recurrent costs for the teachers who are needed to reach universal enrollment while improving learning outcomes? This volume is a very positive step forward for applying rigor to this enterprise.

We need realism about the circumstances and incentives both parents and governments face if we want to reach the goal of universal basic education. Realism starts with understanding that in poor nations, which lack legally enforced compulsory education, parents are the ultimate decision-makers as to whether children attend school. We must recognize that, although it is almost always best for a child to receive an education, parents who deal with extreme poverty and who often face direct costs (e.g., fees) and opportunity costs (lost income and lost help with chores, such as gathering water and firewood) of sending their children to school, that decision may not be clear-cut. We do know, however, that when we look at policies that align the interests of parents with those of their children—such as eliminating fees, keeping schools close-by, and lowering opportunity costs by providing financial assistance tied to school attendance—parents will choose to send their children to school even when cultural norms may push the other way.

We must be equally realistic about the role of politics and government. It is easy for academics to make recommendations that assume complete flexibility as to the timing of major education reforms or that political leaders can easily push aside pressing political constraints in favor of more rational long-term investments in education. Contributors to this volume have sought to deal with these political constraints and to incorporate them in their findings.

Realism means recognizing the following political truths. First, massive investment in the learning and skills of very young children will likely help the economy and political fortunes of a head of state's successor's successor. When a leader takes such a bold step it is rare and often driven by a desire to leave a noble legacy. Second, while careful planners might prefer cautious expansion of education and methodical reform, strategic advances only take place at critical moments of political opportunity, such as the first year of a new presidential administration. When such moments arrive, those seeking to slow down this process can easily create a slow train to nowhere. Scholars, policy experts, and advocates alike must recognize the importance of devising policy responses and financing mechanisms that allow donors and national governments to seize and capitalize on these rare windows of opportunity. This may mean a greater focus on devising quick-response mechanisms that, while not the best choice compared to careful long-term planning, would allow large expansions in coverage with as few growing pains as possible. For example, when a head of state makes a bold commitment to eliminate fees—as recently occurred in Kenya—leading to more than a million new enrollees in a single year, the international community must be willing to work quickly with national officials to help recruit, train, and fund new teachers on an accelerated basis to ensure that dramatic expansion in enrollment does not lead to exploding class sizes and declining quality.

Realism also should compel us to understand how long-term uncertainty about financial assistance is a major deterrent to the more sweeping expansions needed to reach universal education. Perhaps the greatest challenge going forward will be strengthening the global compact on education that encourages poor nations to take bold action to eliminate school fees, bring more children into schools, and all the while improve school quality, by expanding the pools of qualified teachers, improving school infrastructure and curricula, and making other changes.

Nations need reliable funding streams to be able to commit to large increases in recurrent costs like teachers' salaries, but international aid is generally distributed in cycles of only a few years. Finance ministers of developing nations—wary of "aid shock" when aid funding is suddenly cut—are reluctant to significantly expand the numbers of teachers if they cannot guarantee that they will be able to pay them down the line. Britain's Chancellor of the Exchequer, Gordon Brown, and Department for International Development head, Hillary Benn, therefore made a historic step forward when they not only committed $15 billion dollars to support universal education, but also stressed that it would be available to be disbursed in ten-year cycles to avoid this problem. Expanding on such efforts will require a strengthening of our global compact on education.

Donor nations need confidence that there will be high levels of monitoring and financial accountability, and developing governments must have the confidence that if they take on significant recurrent costs associated with increasing quality and expanding their teacher corps, they will not be hung out to dry after only a few years. The Education for All-Fast Track Initiative (FTI) has created a critical foundation for such a global compact between developing nations and donors, with twenty developing nations meeting the criteria to qualify as partners in the initiative, but there is a need to strengthen—not replace—FTI with dramatically more long-term funding.

Finally, we cannot address this issue without heart. Listening to our hearts does not mean that we soften the call for rigor, but rather that we remember that this issue is about the lives of children, not commodities or consumer products. Moving slowly with universal education comes at the cost of losing more and more childhoods and futures each year. We may never see a child dying from lack of education on television, but the evidence is clear that children die from the ramifications of no or inferior education all the time. Rigor therefore must be a call for high standards and evidence, not an excuse for passivity and timidity. When President Clinton once chose to attempt to secure a Middle East peace agreement that he knew had a high probability of failure, he told his staff that the issue was so important that there could only be two outcomes, "either we will succeed or get caught trying." With the hopes, health, and futures of the world's poorest children on the line, this is not a bad motto for the goal of universal education as well.

Universal Basic and Secondary Education*

JOEL E. COHEN, DAVID E. BLOOM, MARTIN B. MALIN, AND HELEN ANNE CURRY

O ver the past century, three approaches have been advocated to escape the consequences of widespread poverty, rapid population growth, environmental problems, and social injustices. The *bigger pie* approach says: use technology to produce more and to alleviate shortages. The *fewer forks* approach says: make contraception and reproductive health care available to eliminate unwanted fertility and to slow population growth. The *better manners* approach says: eliminate violence and corruption; improve the operation of markets and government provision of public goods; reduce the unwanted after-effects of consumption; and achieve greater social and political equity between young and old, male and female, rich and poor (Cohen, 1995). Providing all the world's children with the equivalent of a high-quality primary and secondary education, whether through formal schooling or by alternative means, could, in principle, support all three of these approaches.

Universal education is the stated goal of several international initiatives. In 1990, the global community pledged at the World Conference on Education for All in Jomtien, Thailand, to achieve universal primary education (UPE) and greatly reduce illiteracy by 2000. In 2000, when these goals were not met, it again pledged to achieve UPE, this time at the World Education Forum in Dakar, Senegal, with a target date of 2015. The UN Millennium Development Conference in 2000 also adopted UPE by 2015 as one of its goals, along with the elimination of gender disparities in primary and secondary education by 2015.

---

* Portions of this chapter were published previously in *Finance and Development* 42 (2) (June 2005).

Educational access increased enormously in the past century. Illiteracy fell dramatically and a higher proportion of people are completing primary, secondary, or tertiary education than ever before. Despite this progress, huge problems remain for providing universal access and high-quality schooling through the secondary level of education. The UPE goal looks unlikely to be achieved by 2015 at the current rate of progress. An estimated 299 million school-age children will be missing primary or secondary school in 2015; of these, an estimated 114 million will be missing primary school. These statistics suggest that providing every child between the approximate ages of 6 and 17 with an education of high quality will require time, resources, and colossal effort. Should the international community commit the necessary economic, human, and political resources to the goal of universal education? If so, how should it deploy these resources, and how much will it cost?

This volume reviews research related to the achievement of universal primary and secondary education globally: the current state of education, the quality and quantity of available data on education, the history of education and obstacles to expansion, the means of expanding access and improving education in developing countries, estimates of the costs, and the potential consequences of expansion. This research implies that achieving universal primary and secondary education is both urgent and feasible. Achieving it will require overcoming significant obstacles, developing innovations in educational practices, and spending more money on education.

THE CURRENT SCENE

Current educational data indicate that the world has made significant progress in education, though shortfalls and disparities remain.

The Good

Over the past century, formal schooling spread remarkably, as measured by the primary gross enrollment ratio (GER)—the ratio of total primary enrollment, regardless of age, to the population of the age group that officially belongs in primary education. In 1900, estimated primary GERs were below 40 percent in all regions, except that in northwestern Europe, North America, and Anglophone regions of the Pacific, collectively, the ratio was 72 percent (Williams, 1997: 122). Within the past few years, the estimated global primary net enrollment ratio (NER)—the number of pupils in the official primary school-age group expressed as a percentage of the total population in that age group—reached 86 percent (Bloom, chapter one, Appendix A). The NER is a stricter standard (i.e., it gives lower numbers) than the GER, so the achievement is all the more remarkable. Secondary-school enrollment shows similar progress. The number of students enrolled in secondary school increased eight-fold in the past 50 years, roughly from 50 million to 414 million (calculations by Bloom, based on UNESCO online data).

Measures distinct from enrollment round out this picture. Over the twentieth century, literacy tripled in developing countries, from 25 percent to 75 percent. The average years of schooling in these countries more than doubled between 1960 and 1990, increasing from 2.1 to 4.4 years (Bloom and Cohen, 2002). That figure has risen further since 1990. This growth in enrollment and literacy was supported by more global spending on primary and secondary education than at any previous time. According to Glewwe and Zhao (chapter seven), developing countries spent approximately $82 billion on primary schooling in 2000; Binder, in chapter eight, estimates that spending for secondary education in developing countries in 2000 was $93 billion per year. Although the data and methods of estimation underlying these figures differ, they both indicate large expenditures.

As access to education and literacy increased, global monitoring of students, schools, and educational systems also increased. Developing countries are participating in international measurements of educational status in greater numbers (Braun and Kanjee, chapter four). More statistical measures of schooling have been defined (for example, net and gross enrollment ratios, attendance rates, completion rates, average years of attainment, and school life expectancy). Though not all are well supported by reliable, internationally comparable, comprehensive data, several organizations are working toward this goal. The UNESCO Institute of Statistics, Montreal, maintains the highest-quality data (for example, UNESCO, 2000, 2004).

The Bad

This progress is considerable, but large deficits remain. Roughly 323 million children are not enrolled in school (23 percent of the age group 6–17); roughly 30 percent of these children are missing from primary school, the rest from secondary school (Bloom, chapter one). In developing countries, 15 percent of youth aged 15 to 24 are illiterate, as are about one in every four adults (UNESCO, 2005).

Moreover, enrollment does not necessarily mean attendance, attendance does not necessarily mean receiving an education, and receiving an education does not necessarily mean receiving a good education. High enrollment ratios may give the mistaken impression that a high proportion of school-age children are being well educated. Some 75–95 percent of the world's children live in countries where the quality of education lags behind—most often far behind—the average of OECD countries, as measured by standardized test scores (Bloom, chapter one). That standard may not be universally appropriate. However, it is uncontested that educational quality is too often poor.

In addition, indicators of educational quality are scarce. Though participation in international and regional assessments of educational quality has increased, countries most in need of improvements are least likely to participate. As a result, important comparative data on quality continue to be lacking for the developing world. The problem of inadequate or missing data is pervasive. Bloom, and Braun and Kanjee examine in their respective chapters why it is so difficult to gather and assess basic facts about who is learning what, where, when, and how.

The Ugly

Gross disparities in education separate regions, income groups, and genders. The populations farthest from achieving UPE are typically the world's poorest. Net primary enrollment ratios have advanced in most of the developing world but remain low in Sub-Saharan Africa. Figures 1 and 2 illustrate the sometimes-dramatic disparities between countries in school enrollment at the primary and secondary levels.

Girls' education falls short of boys' education in much of the world. Although enrollment rates sometimes do not differ greatly, many more boys than girls complete schooling, especially at the primary level. Although we know that gender, proximity to a city, and income level interact in influencing educational deficits, a systematic global analysis remains to be done of how much each contributes to differences in children's educational opportunities and achievements. In India in 1992–93, the enrollment rate of boys aged 6–14 exceeded that of girls by 2.5 percentage points among children of the richest households; the difference in favor of boys was 24 percentage points among children from poor households (Filmer, 1999). The study also shows that wealth gaps in enrollment greatly exceeded sex gaps in enrollment. The boys from rich

Figure 1: Percentage of Students of Primary School Age Not Enrolled in School

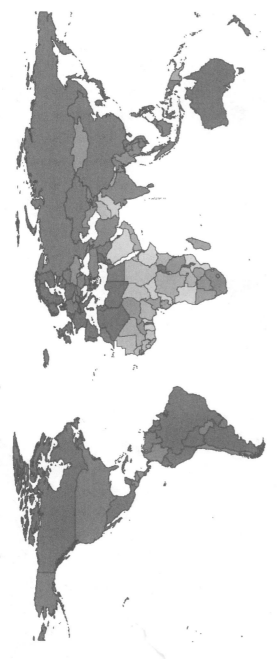

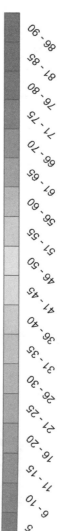

Percent unenrolled

0 - 5
6 - 10
11 - 15
16 - 20
21 - 25
26 - 30
31 - 35
36 - 40
41 - 45
46 - 50
51 - 55
56 - 60
61 - 65
66 - 70
71 - 75
76 - 80
81 - 85
86 - 90

Maps are based on data calculated by Bloom from UNESCO online data. See chapter one, Appendix A.

Figure 2: Percentage of Students of Seconday School Age Not Enrolled in School

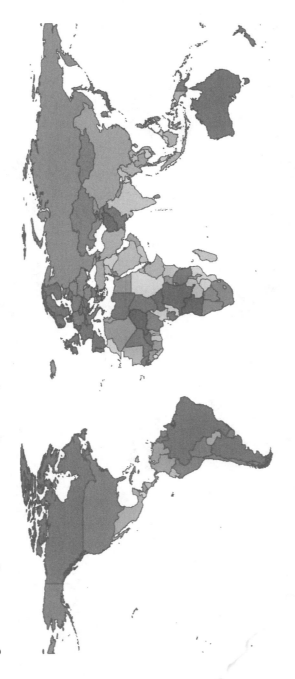

Percent unenrolled

0 - 5
6 - 10
11 - 15
16 - 20
21 - 25
26 - 30
31 - 35
36 - 40
41 - 45
46 - 50
51 - 55
56 - 60
61 - 65
66 - 70
71 - 75
76 - 80
81 - 85
86 - 90

Maps are based on data calculated by Bloom from UNESCO online data. See chapter one, Appendix A.

households had enrollment rates 34 percentage points higher than those of boys from poor households; the gap in favor of rich girls compared to poor girls was 55.4 percentage points.

Developing countries differ widely in spending on primary education, ranging from $46 per student per year in South Asia and $68 in Sub-Saharan Africa to $878 in Europe and Central Asia (see Table 1). Spending per student in secondary education shows a similar range, from $117 per student per year in South Asia and $257 in Sub-Saharan Africa to $577 in Latin America and the Caribbean (Binder, chapter eight).

Table 1: Recent Public Current Expenditures on Primary Schooling in Developing Countries

Region	Public Spending per Student (U.S. $)	Total Public Spending (millions U.S. $)	Fraction of Population with Public Spending Data*
South Asia	46	6,910	0.98
Sub-Saharan Africa	68	6,100	0.98
East Asia and Pacific	103	21,200	0.96
Latin America and the Caribbean	440	28,200	0.90
Middle East and North Africa	519	14,200	0.60
Europe and Central Asia	878	5,210	0.22
All developing regions	151	81,800	0.88

Source: Glewwe and Zhao, chapter seven.
*Public spending figures are more reliable in regions where public spending data are available for a higher fraction of the population.

CHALLENGES

Closing the gap between the current state of global education and the goal of providing all children with high-quality primary and secondary education schooling requires meeting several distinct challenges.

• Educate the roughly 97 million children of primary-school age who are not currently enrolled in school (Bloom, chapter one). As a majority of these students are female and most live in absolute poverty, the underlying conditions that create disparities in educational access will likely need to be addressed.

- Educate the 226 million children of secondary-school age not in school. Improved access to primary education fuels the demand for secondary education. As more and more children attend school, more and more teachers—who should have at least a secondary education—will also be needed (UNESCO, 2006).

- Develop the capacity to educate the 90 million additional children 5–17 years old in developing countries in the next 20 years (United Nations, 2004).

- Improve the quality of primary and secondary education, assessed according to constructive goals and clear standards.

- Provide policymakers with clear, empirically supported rationales for why education matters. Achieving these goals requires a realistic appraisal of the obstacles that have thus far prevented educational opportunity for all children. It requires fresh thinking about what the goals of education should be, and how best to pursue those goals. And it demands an assessment of the costs, which are likely to be significant, as well as an assessment of the consequences of educational expansion and the returns on this investment, which are essential to securing societal and political support.

The contributors to this volume consider these and other questions and lay the groundwork for the development of new policies to achieve universal basic and secondary education.

WHY UNIVERSAL PRIMARY AND SECONDARY EDUCATION?

Although education is not available to hundreds of millions of children, neither are health care, adequate nutrition, employment opportunities, and other basic services available to these children or their families. Why should universal primary and secondary education be a development goal of high priority?

Several rationales support the pursuit of universal primary and secondary education. Education provides economic benefits. Education builds strong societies and polities. Education reduces fertility and improves health. Education is a widely accepted humanitarian obligation and an internationally mandated human right. These rationales are commonly offered for universal primary education, but many benefits of education do not accrue until students have had 10 or more years of education. Completion of primary education is more attractive if high-quality secondary education beckons.

Economic Benefits

As Hannum and Buchmann report in their chapter on the consequences of educational expansion, extensive sociological and economic studies have found that education generally enables individuals to improve their economic circumstances. Although the benefits of education for the individual are clear, the aggregate effects on economic growth are more difficult to measure and remain a matter of dispute (Krueger and Lindahl, 2001; Pritchett, 1997; and Bloom and Canning, 2004).

It is clear, however, that more education contributes to a demographic transition from high fertility and high mortality to low fertility and low mortality, and Bloom and colleagues (2003) find this change is associated with accelerated growth. When fertility rates fall, the resulting demographic transition offers countries a large working-age population with fewer children to support, although only for a transient interval before population aging begins. In this interval, the large fraction of the population that is of working age offers an exceptional opportunity for high economic growth (Bloom et al., 2003).

Women who attend school, particularly at the secondary or tertiary level, generally have fewer children than those who do not. An increase by 10 percent in primary GERs is associated with an average reduction in the total fertility rate of 0.1 children. A 10 percent increase in secondary GERs is associated with an average reduction of 0.2 children (Hannum and Buchmann, chapter nine). In Brazil, women with a secondary education have an average of 2.5 children, compared to 6.5 children for illiterate women. In some African societies, total fertility is reduced only among girls who have had 10 or more years of schooling (Jejeebhoy, 1996).

Education contributes to reduced fertility through numerous pathways. Maternal education can lead to increased use of contraceptives. Education can enable women more easily to work outside the home and earn money. This improvement in status leads to empowerment and increased decision-making authority in limiting fertility. Educated women tend to delay marriage and childbearing, perhaps because of the increased opportunity costs of not participating in the paid labor force. Education and income may also become intertwined in a virtuous spiral: as incomes grow, more money is available to finance the spread of education, which leads to further increases in income.

Strong Societies and Polities

Although the evidence is not definitive, education has been shown to strengthen social and cultural capital. Absolute increases in educational attainment can shift disadvantaged groups, such as ethnic minorities or females, from absolute deprivation to relative deprivation compared to more advantaged groups. Educated citizens may be more likely to vote and to voice opposition. Among states, higher enrollment ratios at all levels of education correspond to increases in indicators of democracy (Hannum and Buchmann, chapter nine). If the content of the education encourages it, education can promote social justice, human rights, and tolerance. As the percentage of the male population enrolled in secondary school goes up, the probability of civil conflict goes down (Collier and Hoeffler, 2001). These desirable effects depend on the content of education and do not flow from the fact of education per se (Cohen, forthcoming).

Health

Controlling for income, educated individuals have longer, healthier lives than those without education. Children who are in school are healthier than those who are not, though causation could flow in either direction or both.

Many effects of education on health are indirect effects through increased income. Education increases economic status, and higher-income individuals have better access to health care services, better nutrition, and increased mobility. Education also has direct impacts on health, unrelated to income. It can provide vital health knowledge and encourage healthy lifestyles. For example, the offspring of educated mothers have lower child and infant mortality rates and higher immunization rates, even when socioeconomic conditions are controlled statistically (as discussed by Hannum and Buchmann, chapter nine).

Improved health may in turn enhance education. For example, as Kremer and Bettinger discuss in their chapters, randomized evaluations of school-based health programs in Kenya and India suggest that simple, inexpensive treatments for basic health problems such as anemia and intestinal worms can dramatically increase the quantity of schooling students attain. Bloom reviews research on the reciprocal relationship between health and education in chapter ten.

A Basic Human Right

Universal education is justified on ethical and humanitarian grounds as right, good, and fair. Education enables people to develop their capacities to lead fulfilling, dignified lives. High-quality education helps people give meaning to their lives by placing them in the context of human and natural history and by creating in them an awareness of other cultures. Article 26 of the United Nations' Universal Declaration of Human Rights, adopted in 1948, asserts: "Everyone has the right to education." It maintains that primary education should be free and compulsory. The Convention on the Rights of the Child, which entered into force in 1990, obliges governments to make universal primary education compulsory and also to make different forms of secondary education accessible to every child.

OBSTACLES

The rationales for continued educational expansion are powerful, but the barriers too are numerous and formidable. The cost to governments of providing universal primary and secondary schooling, discussed later in this introduction and in chapters seven and eight, are significant. The cost of education to individuals and families is sometimes a strong disincentive. Because governments face competing demands for the allocation of state resources, education is often pushed down the list of priorities. And even if financial resources for education were plentiful, then politics, corruption, culture, poor information, and history among other factors would conspire to block or slow the achievement of access to high-quality education for all children.

Economic Disincentives

Millions of children have access to schooling but do not attend. Some families may place greater value on the time children spend in other activities, such as performing work for income or handling chores so other household members are free to work in market activities. In developing countries, a troubled household economic situation may more often be a deterrent to enrollment than lack of access to a school (Glewwe and Zhao, chapter seven). For example, in Ghana, almost half of parents, when asked why their children were not in school, answered, "school is too expensive" or "child needed to work at home"; another 22 percent believed that education was of too little value (World Bank, 2004).

Economic barriers disproportionately harm girls. Some parents perceive the costs—direct, indirect, and opportunity costs—of educating daughters to be higher than that of educating sons (Herz and Sperling, 2004).

Political Obstacles

Education competes for scarce national resources with many worthy projects such as building roads, providing medical care, and strengthening a country's energy system. Limited resources can hamper educational expansion in many ways, as Javier Corrales describes in chapter three. Organized interest groups may divert funding from education to their own causes. When social crises, such as crime, unemployment, or civil war, demand the time and resources of the government, citizens are perhaps unlikely to focus on education. Popular demand for education is frequently weakest in poor regions or countries where it is most needed.

Directing adequate funds to education requires a national commitment to education that many countries lack. Government decisions guided by the short-term interests of those in power are unlikely to reflect the importance of education, as educational returns accrue over much longer time horizons. When politicians devote funds to education, the funding sometimes flows to political supporters rather than to programs and regions where it is most needed. Moreover, a limited capacity to oversee the implementation of education programs and the limited political status of education ministries within many governments may blunt reforms as they are enacted.

Corruption

As with any large public sector, the education sector is rife with opportunities for corruption. When funds are diverted for private gain at any level, educational expansion and improvement may be harmed. At the highest levels of government, corruption can affect the allocation of funds to the education budget; at the ministry level, it can influence the distribution of funds to individual schools; and at the school level, it can involve the diversion of money from school supplies, the payment of bribes by parents to ensure their children's access to or success in school and by teachers to secure promotions or other benefits (Meier, 2004).

International donors may be deterred by a recipient's history of poor spending accountability, and may curtail funding or impose accountability measures that are themselves costly. The loss of financial resources is always harmful. It is most detrimental at the local level, where the poorest children may be denied access to education because they are not able to afford bribes or where systems of merit—both for students and teachers—are distorted through the widespread use of bribes to secure advancement (Chapman, 2002). Heyneman (2003) argues that if pervasive corruption leads to the public perception of education as unfair or not meritocratic, then this distrust of the school system may lead to distrust of the leaders it produces. As a result, he says, a country's "sense of social cohesion, the principal ingredient of all successful modern societies," may be undermined.

Lack of Information

Reliable, internationally comparable, useful data on many aspects of primary and secondary education are lacking. For example, the mechanisms that keep children out of school are poorly understood in quantitative (as opposed to qualitative) detail. Most routine data focus on measures of "butts-in-seats" (in the expressive language of Lant Pritchett) such as enrollment, attendance, and completion. As Bloom points out in chapter one, data on educational processes, such as pedagogical techniques and curricula, and on learning outcomes, are inadequate.

Political incentives sometimes work against accurate reporting on even basic quantitative measures. In Uganda, enrollment was historically under-reported because schools were required to remit private tuition receipts to the government in proportion to the number of students they reported. When schools became publicly funded on the basis of enrolled pupils, the incentive for schools to report higher numbers resulted in a leap in official enrollments (Bloom, chapter one). In addition, governments may be reluctant to publish potentially unflattering data on their school systems for fear of political consequences (Corrales, chapter three).

Failing to provide data on education feeds a vicious circle. Lack of accurate data impairs the formulation of effective education policy; citizens lack the information they need to hold their school administrators and elected officials accountable; unaccountable officials have few incentives to collect information that would help them to improve the system. Improving educational data could help to transform this vicious circle into a virtuous one by providing necessary information to citizens, administrators, and officials to monitor and improve the quality of schooling.

Historical Legacies

The history of efforts to expand education provides a rich source of models and lessons. These historical legacies can also present impediments to those who underestimate their importance. Benavot and Resnik examine in chapter two the emergence of compulsory education laws, the transformation of diverse educational frameworks into formal school systems, the problems of inequality that have arisen, and the role played by international organizations in creating an increasingly interconnected global education system.

Despite the apparent uniformity in contemporary schooling, past educational models took many forms and motivations for educational expansion varied widely. Because national contexts differ, international organizations seeking to facilitate educational expansion need to be attuned to this varied history if their interventions are to succeed. Solutions that ignore the history of education in a particular country are likely to be less effective than solutions tuned to context. For example, when leaders advocated the decentralization of public schools in Latin American countries in the 1980s, they ignored the specific social and political purposes for which those schools had been founded, which included ending severe socio-economic segregation. Decentralization led to a growth of private schools and renewed fragmentation along socio-economic lines, which exacerbated the social divide that school centralization was initially intended to correct.

Though the past must not be ignored, it is not always a useful guide to present educational reform. Corrales notes that past state motivations to provide education—to consolidate national identity, win citizen loyalty, or neutralize rival political groups—were most prominent when nationalist, revolutionary, and totalitarian ideologies drove political development. Today, these rationales are less relevant.

MEETING THE CHALLENGE

To overcome the obstacles described above and to achieve universal basic and secondary education, many steps are necessary. These include: clarifying what constitutes an education of high quality, improving the implementation of assessments to measure progress toward those goals, evaluating rigorously educational innovations to determine the most effective strategies for making progress, and adopting effective technology in classrooms and schools. These efforts must be directed not only at increasing access to education in the poorest and most remote regions, but also at improving the quality of what is learned.

Defining Goals

Assessments and evaluations presume goals for what education should accomplish. Goals must be clearly laid out so that the success of programs can be continuously monitored (Bloom and Cohen, 2002). What are the goals of education, and who should decide these goals? What relative weight should be given to the views of children, parents, teachers, education officials, policymakers, religious leaders, business leaders, and the community at large? More policy attention to these questions is needed and should be encouraged by international organizations.

Who should decide what students learn may differ in different localities. Sometimes the goals and content of education are determined by localities within nations, sometimes nationally. In either case, international economic requirements and international comparative educational assessments can powerfully influence national decisions about the goals of education within a country. National and international officials should therefore be sensitive to ongoing public and political discussions at the local level.

Proposed educational goals include readiness for the local or global labor market; health knowledge and healthy behavior; the creation (or sustaining) of a more cohesive society; the capacity to adapt to continual change and to learn under conditions of freedom; assisting youth to fulfill their physical, emotional, social, spiritual, and intellectual potential; providing the competencies children need for their lives and livelihoods; enabling students to interact in socially heterogeneous groups and act autonomously; addressing the needs of the world's poorest children and youth, those the global economy has left behind; teaching tolerance rather than hatred; and opening people's minds rather than controlling them. (See Charfi and Redissi, 2003; Cheng, 2003; Delors, 1998; Ingram, 2004; Levinger, 2004; Reimers, 2004; Rogers, 1969; Rychen and Salganik, 2001; Salganik and Provasnik, 2004; and Strom et al., 2004. For a comprehensive view, see Cohen, 2006; Cohen, forthcoming.)

Bloom and Cohen (2002) characterized the goals of education in terms of skills, knowledge, and attitudes.

Skills. They proposed that the skills taught should include reading with understanding, writing with clarity, and speaking with confidence.

The choice of language or languages in which these skills are practiced is likely to be a national or local issue. The skills taught should also include numeracy, that is, the ability to read and understand the kinds of quantitative information encountered in daily life, plus the ability to compute as required in the contexts of daily life. These fundamental skills with words and numbers differ from the specialized disciplinary skills of literary and mathematical analysis.

Additional skills worthy of attention include peaceful ways to manage and resolve, where possible, conflicts and differences within and between social groups. The conflicts and the means of resolving them will differ culturally (e.g., compromise vs. consensual discussion vs. majority vote vs. appeal to tradition), but the skills of dealing peacefully with conflict have widespread value. Other important skills include being productive and finding satisfaction in personal life and work.

Knowledge. The knowledge provided by education must be about both the self and others (Bloom and Cohen, 2002). In human terms, others might include the family, the local community, other communities and cities, the nation state, other countries and cultures, and humankind. In nonhuman terms, others might include other living species and the major nonliving components of the Earth. "Other" also refers to other times, including the sources and limitations of our understanding of past and future. These domains of knowledge can be approached through the perspectives of the natural sciences, the social sciences, and the arts and humanities. For example, understanding the self in scientific perspective provides a vehicle for instruction in health and human biology and behavior.

Attitudes. The attitudes to be provided by education must also refer both to the self and to others—though here the goals of a universal education are liable to provoke controversy, according to Bloom and Cohen (2002). How will schools balance the values of individuality and of collective concern, of innovation and conformity, of initiative and obedience, of competitiveness and cooperation, of skepticism and respect? The industrial model of classroom education, with students sitting silently and obediently at desks arranged on a grid and listening to an authoritative teacher, with classes starting promptly when the bell rings, conveys a different set of values and attitudes than many alternative modes of education.

The goals—and related delivery—of education around the world will shape the kinds of people we and our children will live among. There is as much at stake in defining and ensuring a quality education for every child as there is in defeating terrorism, reducing poverty, and spreading justice, dignity, and democracy. Also at stake are the inventiveness and civility of the people among whom we will live, and the richness of our own opportunities to learn from them.

Assessing Progress

Although assessment is often seen as a tool to measure the progress of individual students, it also allows individuals, communities, and countries to track the quality of schools and educational systems. In theory, if policymakers have access to reliable information on educational quality in specific schools and make this information available to the aware public, then students and parents may be better able to choose among educational options and demand education of higher quality. For example, the Southern African Consortium for Monitoring Education Quality is a regional learning assessment study introduced by UNESCO and now governed by the 14 southern African participating governments. It aims to identify within-country disparities in education as a guide to where interventions might be needed.

To be successful, educational assessment must overcome a central dilemma, as Braun and Kanjee observe in chapter four. If there are no consequences attached to a test, then it will do little to motivate healthy change within the educational system; however, if the result is highly consequential, then it may engender unproductive or undesirable outcomes such as narrowing the curriculum or "teaching to the test." Where assessments are tied to funding decisions, those responsible for the quality of education—teachers, administrators, and state officials—may oppose the release or even the creation of such data.

The development of reliable and useful assessments requires institutional capacity, technical expertise, and money, all likely to be scarce in developing countries. Braun and Kanjee advocate that developing countries be encouraged to participate in international assessments as "associates," without requiring that results be released internationally. They argue that this interim arrangement will promote the generation of much-needed data, give developing countries access to expertise, and build local capacity to develop, administer, and analyze tests, while avoiding the political consequences to participating countries of possible poor performance.

Nationally and regionally developed assessments should also be encouraged, as international assessments may not be optimal for all countries. National assessments focused on country-specific curricula or regional approaches provide information more relevant to the needs of some countries than the information provided by international assessments, which are largely based on OECD models.

Innovation and Evaluation

Assessments enable citizens and governments to track the outcomes of schools and educational systems, but offer only limited insight into the specific educational practices that lead to improved or worsened outcomes. Other means are needed to identify these effects.

Many traditional practices in education have never been evaluated by scientific experimentation to measure quantitatively what they contribute to educational outcomes. Would students learn arithmetic or history less effectively if they were not required to be in their seats by the time the school bell rang? Nor have many educational innovations been rigorously evaluated in comparison to traditional practices. Does a student who learns touch-typing from a computer learn any better, or at a significantly lower cost, than a student who learns from a traditional teacher or by self-instruction from a printed book?

As Bettinger discusses in chapter five, one reliable means of getting answers to questions like these—namely, randomized controlled experimentation, the gold standard for evaluating treatments in medicine—is now finding use in education. Such experiments make possible valid comparisons among pedagogical techniques and systems of management because randomization establishes equivalent participant and nonparticipant groups for comparison. Randomized controlled experiments can, therefore, produce the most credible assessment of programs, including their cost-effectiveness. With more reliable information, leaders can focus efforts and resources on the programs that have been found to be most effective.

In chapter six, Kremer reviews his own and others' earlier randomized evaluations of school-based health programs. He concludes, for example, that deworming can be an extremely cost-effective way of boosting attendance as evidenced in a study in Kenya. A study in Delhi, in which students received deworming medication and vitamin A supplements, found similar results, offering hope that the program may be effective in a range of settings.

Unfortunately, randomized evaluations remain underutilized guides. Randomized experiments can be expensive and time-consuming. They require technical sophistication to plan, implement, and analyze properly. However, such experiments may be no more expensive or more time-consuming than other rigorous data collection activities, as Bettinger notes in chapter five. More likely, randomized evaluations are underused because it can be politically difficult to deliver a program to only a small set of students or schools while withholding it from a comparison group of students or schools. However, when budgetary constraints make it difficult or impossible to reach all members of a population in a given year, randomly selecting which groups receive the program in year 1, year 2, et cetera, may be the fairest way to implement the program and simultaneously permit measurements of the program's impact.

Incorporating New Technologies

Information and communication technologies have enormous potential to facilitate universal high-quality education. But to date, efforts to utilize information technology have yielded mixed results. The problem often lies with the implementation.

As its cost decreases, information technology (IT) in classrooms is spreading even to some of the poorest, most remote, and most sparsely populated areas. This technology can increase both the quantity and the quality of education, in part through distance education. Distance learning can provide education to those without access to traditional schools. It can benefit those who would like to learn on a non-traditional schedule, such as during evenings after work. Distance learning can improve the quality of instruction for those already in school. For example, the Indira Gandhi National Open University (http://www.ignou.ac.in/) in India broadcasts lectures to classrooms across the country and claims more than one million students. Students can respond by email.

Information technology can be a tool for both students and teachers. It can facilitate a transition from rote memorization to more learner-centered education in which students actively gather information, grasp new ideas, and creatively display what they have learned. In principle, IT can enhance learning in a wide range of subjects. One area of particular interest includes gender, sex, and health, because technology can allow students to explore these areas with relative anonymity (Maclay, 2004). Teachers can also benefit from IT through the use of computer-based teaching aids and curricula and online professional development. It can also facilitate communication among colleagues in different communities, allowing them to share materials and ideas.

There are obstacles to the continued expansion of IT in primary and secondary education. Many involved in education oppose the diversion of resources to IT, citing competing priorities such as textbooks and basic supplies. Moreover, political leaders may focus on visible short-term gains such as buying computers at the expense of long-term investments such as maintaining the computers and providing adequate training for their use. Successful implementation entails costs, particularly for proper training. Practitioners recommend that 30–40 percent of a budget for IT should be allocated to training (Maclay, 2004).

Improving Both Quantity and Quality

Quality of education is a major problem now and will still be a problem in 2015. At first sight, it would appear obvious that there is a trade-off between the quantity of education and its quality. The rush to achieve more "butts in seats" could reasonably be expected to undermine the quality of education, as more students are placed in already crowded classrooms and resources are spread more thinly. However, Glewwe and Zhao suggest that improving the quality of education may be a necessary precondition for achieving universal primary and secondary coverage (chapter seven). Improving quality increases the incentives to parents to send their children to school. The quality of education may compete with the quantity of education when a country is trying to extend the reach of primary education from 20 percent of school-aged children to 60 percent of school-aged children, but higher quality may facilitate a country's efforts to educate the 40 percent of school-aged children who are least accessible.

COSTS AND FINANCE

What would it cost to achieve universal primary and secondary education? Assuming education will be largely delivered through schools, educating all children will require additional money for schools, teachers, teacher training, materials and equipment, administration, assessments, randomized evaluations, and overcoming economic disincentives to families. Cost estimates are crude at best. Studies of educational costs generally ignore the burden borne by those who seek or provide education outside of schools. It is also difficult to measure the cost of ignorance.

Cost Estimates for Universal Primary and Secondary Education

Estimates by the World Bank, UNICEF, and UNESCO of the annual costs of achieving UPE by 2015 range from $6.5 billion to $35 billion per year, over and above the approximately $82 billion that developing countries spend each year on primary education. These investigations focus on the cost of increasing the number of places for students in schools. However, as Glewwe and Zhao discuss in chapter seven, the number of places available is often not the limiting factor. Parents may choose to keep their children out of school for various reasons. The true cost of UPE will include the cost of implementing policies that influence parental decisions and boost the demand for primary education. Future cost estimates should reckon the cost of providing other improvements necessary to encourage students to attend school—such as meals, tuition subsidies to families, higher quality and more reliable teaching, and reductions in rates of repetition and non-completion. The spending necessary to implement such improvements would likely increase the cost of UPE a significant amount.

The cost of achieving universal secondary education will be greater than that for UPE because more children in this age bracket are not in school and secondary education is more expensive per pupil. In chapter eight, Binder presents pioneering estimates. According to her analysis, if a gradual approach is taken between now and 2015, the annual additional cost would likely be between $27 billion and $34 billion. If an instantaneous expansion of secondary education is sought, the cost could rise to $62 billion annually, at least under current policies. This high-estimate cost could fall to $47 billion if policymakers adopted the practices of countries most successful in making schooling available to students, getting students to attend school, and helping them learn while they are in school. The best (albeit unlikely) scenario, including a sharp drop in repetition rates, would reduce the additional annual cost of an instantaneous expansion of secondary education to $28 billion. Binder notes that the biggest expansion of secondary education will be needed in the poorest countries, where the average per-student yearly cost is $126, compared with $244 in low-income countries and $884 in upper-middle-income ones.

The estimated total cost for universal primary and secondary education combined ranges from a low of $34 billion to a high of $69 billion per year (setting aside the "instantaneous" expansion of secondary education mentioned above)—a huge amount of money, but certainly not beyond the ability of the world to fund. If investments in education promote economic growth in the poorer countries as anticipated, the share of income devoted to primary and secondary education could be expected to decline.

Financing Universal Education

How much do countries have to spend? The low- and middle-income countries, with a population of 5.3 billion, had a combined gross national income (GNI) of nearly $7 trillion in 2003 (with an average annual per capita income of just over $1,300) (World Bank, 2005). The incremental cost of $34–$69 billion per year for them would be about 0.5–1.0 percent of their GNI.

If the richer countries shared the cost, the burden on the poorer countries would, of course, be less. The GNI of the high-income countries was $29.4 trillion of the world's $36.4 trillion; an extra $70 billion per year would be roughly 0.25 percent of their income. The OECD reported that official development assistance (ODA) in 2003 was $69 billion, the highest ever in nominal and real terms. At only 0.25 percent of high-income countries' combined GNI, it was well short of the average of 0.33 percent achieved in 1980–92 and of the United Nations' ODA target of 0.7 percent. The incremental cost of $34–$69 billion per year could consume up to the entire pie of recent ODA.

As public funds are limited, it is natural to ask: Is education the best use of the marginal dollar of government expenditure in a developing country? Should that dollar be spent on education rather than health, physical infrastructure, applied research, cash grants, or land purchases for the poor? Unfortunately, we know no convincing answers to these questions, even if "the best use" is interpreted narrowly to mean economically efficient. Credible models to evaluate the trade-offs for human well-being between education and other sectors of public investment are lacking. The same lack of knowledge applies to the trade-offs and complementarities among primary, secondary, and tertiary (higher) education.

REMAINING WORK AND NEW QUESTIONS

Many questions important to the achievement of universal basic and secondary education remain to be addressed by scholarly, policy-oriented research.

- Goals and values: What should be the goals of basic and secondary education of high quality? Which, if any, of these goals should be universal? What does "universal" mean? What happens when educational goals conflict? Who decides these questions, and by what process do they decide? How should the quality of decisions about educational goals be evaluated? How can national and international discussions of the goals of education best be encouraged?

- Incentives: In developing countries where schools are physically available and parents choose not to enroll their children, what policies will substantially increase the willingness of parents to enroll their children in school, and what will implementation of those policies cost? Answering this question is crucial to estimating realistically the costs of attaining universal primary and secondary education.

- Finance: What financing strategies make the most sense under different circumstances, and what financing mixes are best matched with particular country characteristics? What are the implications of "basket funding" for education (i.e., channeling all education support to local authorities, rather than earmarking funds for specific programs, such as teachers' salaries, construction and maintenance of buildings, or provision of school lunches)?

- Role of business: Under what circumstances do local and multinational businesses demand and support better education for large numbers of children? What are the actual and potential activities of firms (local, national, multinational) in supporting and providing education to their employees, families, and communities? What are the actual and potential partnerships of firms and governments in providing and financing education? What are the benefits and drawbacks of business involvement?

- Future trends: How will the costs and financing of primary and secondary education be affected by future trends such as continuing rapid population growth in some developing countries, population aging, infectious diseases including HIV/AIDS, the globalization of economic activity, migration, economic growth, and changing economic inequality between nations?

- Learning out of school: What is the status (extent, effect, and cost) of non-school-based learning (e.g., professional apprenticeships and religious study)? What data could be gathered to assess that status more effectively?

- Teachers: How can shortages of qualified teachers be overcome? How can motivation and continuing education for teachers be assured? Hanushek (2005) argues that only selection and retention of the teachers most effective at raising students' test scores will result in an improvement in the corps of teachers. How generally does this conclusion apply? Are its implications relevant in countries where many students remain out of school? If this conclusion is confirmed, what are the best means of selecting effective teachers? What incentives are most effective in retaining good teachers?

- Development: Given a marginal dollar to invest in development, how should it best be allocated among education, public health, jobs, physical infrastructure (roads, bridges, and harbors), grants to the poor, purchase of land for the poor, scientific and educational research, and other means of promoting social and economic development?

- Case studies: How should case studies be selected so as to provide a systematic view of countries that have achieved, or failed to achieve, universal primary and secondary education? What generalizations can validly be drawn from case studies?

- Research: What can be done to encourage greater local capacity for research on the extension of education to all children? What can be done to facilitate the development of a knowledge base on the necessary steps? When a knowledge base is available, how can it be adapted to local needs and put to use most effectively?

- Remittances: What roles do remittances from expatriates play in supporting education in developing countries?

- Schools and technologies: How are models for imparting knowledge changing? Will the Western model of schooling (e.g., buildings, classrooms, teachers, schedules) be the model for future education in developing countries? Will alternative models exploit new information technologies and opportunities and a post-industrial vision of learning? For example, how can technologies for distance education be used most effectively? What cost-effective new technologies for distance education can be developed and implemented?

- Inequalities: How do differences of income, gender, and residence (urban vs. rural) interact to produce inequalities in educational access and achievement? What are effective points of intervention to reduce these inequalities?

- Employment: Secondary education is more likely to attract students if there are jobs for graduates. What characteristics of the labor market make secondary education a sound investment? What is the relationship between the demand for labor and the demand for education?

- Quality-quantity interactions: What are optimal trajectories to high-quality mass education for countries starting at any combination of educational and economic development?

- Private education: What are the forms, costs, curricula, and achievements of private education globally? What institutions and incentives are necessary to facilitate the collection of useful comparative data on private education globally?

- Decentralization: What are the benefits and disadvantages of the decentralization of formal education? Which responsibilities and activities are best decentralized and which are not? Under what circumstances and toward what end should decentralization be undertaken?

- Learning: When many children never finish primary school, how can a basic level of learning—reading and numeracy—be best achieved in a short time? What components are important to ensure learning? How can learning be measured?

Plans to achieve universal education should incorporate investments in research required to find the answers to these questions, as well as the answers derived from the best available evidence. They should also include unconventional approaches. In a best-case scenario, educational plans will resemble an experimental design, so that innovations can be evaluated, adapted, and changed based on outcomes. Educational plans should include audit mechanisms to ensure accountability at every level of operation from the local to the international. They should include innovation in two-way information systems, both to solicit feedback from participants in educational systems at every level and to provide all participants with information about the performance of the educational systems they support.

CONCLUSIONS

The goal of providing high-quality primary and secondary education to all the world's children is as inspiring and formidable a challenge as any extraterrestrial adventures—and far more likely to enrich and improve life on earth, even in ways that may be difficult to anticipate today. Because many benefits of education do not accrue until students have had 10 or more years of education, and because primary education is more attractive if high-quality secondary education may follow, international conventions and national governments should adopt formally the goal of universal secondary education of high quality.

Universal, high-quality primary and secondary education is achievable by the middle of the 21st century, though probably not at the current rate of progress. What is needed now? No single magic bullet will bring high-quality primary and secondary education to all the world's children. Rather, at least five complementary, interacting changes are needed (Cohen and Bloom, 2005):

- open discussions, nationally, regionally, and internationally, on what people want primary and secondary education to achieve—that is, the goals of education;

- a commitment to improving the effectiveness and economic efficiency of education in achieving those goals, whether through formal schooling or other means; this improvement would be driven by reliable data on what children learn, careful experiments with alternative pedagogical techniques and technologies, and comparative studies of the countries that perform best, region by region, within any given level of funding and material resources;

- a commitment to extending a complete, high-quality secondary education to all children;

- international recognition of the diverse character of educational systems in different countries, and adaptation of aid policies and educational assessment requirements to local contexts; and

- more money and higher priority for education—especially an increase in funding from rich countries for education in poor countries.

Achieving universal primary and secondary education of high quality is likely to require enhanced political will to apply tested approaches combined with new interventions, carefully evaluated and widely reported.

References

Bloom, David E. 2004. "Universal Education and Human Progress." In *Wide Angle Discussion Guide 2*. New York: Educational Broadcasting Corporation.

Bloom, David E., and David Canning. 2004. "Reconciling Micro and Macro Estimates of the Returns to Schooling." Working Paper of the Project on Universal Basic and Secondary Education. American Academy of Arts and Sciences, Cambridge, MA.

Bloom, David E., David Canning, and Jaypee Sevilla. 2003. *The Demographic Dividend: A New Perspective on the Economic Consequences of Population Change*. Santa Monica: RAND Corporation.

Bloom, David E., and Joel E. Cohen. 2002. "Education for All: An Unfinished Revolution." *Daedalus* 131 (3): 84–95.

Chapman, David. 2003. "Corruption and the Education Sector." Sectoral Perspectives on Corruption Series, USAID/MIS, November.

Charfi, Mohamed, and Mohamed Redissi. 2003. "Teaching Tolerance and Open-Minded Approaches to Understanding Sacred Texts." Working Paper of the Project on Universal Basic and Secondary Education. American Academy of Arts and Sciences, Cambridge, MA.

Cheng, Kai-Ming. 2003. "Questioning Education: Challenges from a Changing Society." Working Paper of the Project on Universal Basic and Secondary Education. American Academy of Arts and Sciences, Cambridge, MA.

Cohen, Joel E. 1995. *How Many People Can the Earth Support?* New York: W. W. Norton.

———. 2006. "Goals of Universal Basic and Secondary Education." *Prospects: Quarterly Review of Comparative Education* (UNESCO) 36 (3), September.

———, ed. Forthcoming. *Education for All, But for What?: International Perspectives on the Goals of Primary and Secondary Education*.

Cohen, Joel E., and David E. Bloom. 2005. "Cultivating Minds." *Finance and Development* 42 (2) (June): 8–14.

Collier, Paul, and Anke Hoeffler. 2001. "Greed and Grievance in Civil War." World Bank, October. http://www.worldbank.org/research/conflict/papers/greedgrievance_23oct.pdf.

Delors, Jacques, et al. 1998. *Learning: The Treasure Within: Report to UNESCO of the International Commission on Education for the Twenty-first Century*, 2nd Pocket edition. Paris: UNESCO Publishing.

Hanushek, Eric A. 2005. "Why Quality Matters in Education." *Finance and Development* 42 (2) (June): 15–20.

Herz, Barbara, and Gene B. Sperling. 2004. "What Works in Girls' Education: Evidence and Policies from the Developing World." New York: Council on Foreign Relations.

Filmer, D. 1999. "The Structure of Social Disparities in Education: Gender and Wealth." In *Engendering Development Through Gender Equality in Rights, Resources, and Voice*, World Bank Background Paper, World Bank, Washington, DC. Cited in: Birdsall, Nancy, Ruth Levine, and Amina Ibrahim. 2005. *Toward Universal Primary Education: Investments, Incentives, and Institutions*. UN Millennium Project, Task Force on Education and Gender Equality. Sterling, VA: Earthscan.

Heyneman, Stephen P. "Education and Corruption." Mimeo. Vanderbilt University, September. http://www.corisweb.org/article/articlestatic/537/1/334/.

Ingram, George. 2004. "Quality Education – What is it and Who Decides?" Commentary prepared for a workshop of the Project on Universal Basic and Secondary Education. American Academy of Arts and Sciences, Cambridge, MA, May.

Jejeebhoy, Shireen J. 1996. *Women's Education, Autonomy, and Reproductive Behaviour: Experience from Developing Countries*. New York: Oxford University Press.

Krueger, Alan B., and Mikael Lindahl. 2001. "Education for Growth: Why and For Whom?" *Journal of Economic Literature* 39 (December): 1101–1136.

Levinger, Beryl. 2004. "Quality Education: The Work of Optimists." Commentary prepared for a workshop of the Project on Universal Basic and Secondary Education. American Academy of Arts and Sciences, Cambridge, MA, May.

Maclay, Colin. 2004. "The Use of Information and Communication Technologies in the Delivery of Education in the Developing World." Paper prepared for the Project on Universal Basic and Secondary Education. American Academy of Arts and Sciences, Cambridge, MA, August.

Meier, Bettina. 2004. "Corruption in the Education Sector: An Introduction." Working Paper, Transparency International, July.

Pritchett, Lant. 1997. "Where Has All the Education Gone?" World Bank Policy Research Working Paper 1581.

Reimers, Fernando. 2004. "Teaching Global Values." Working Paper of the Project on Universal Basic and Secondary Education. American Academy of Arts and Sciences, Cambridge, MA.

Rogers, Carl R. 1969. *Freedom to Learn: A View of What Education Might Become.* Columbus, OH: Charles E. Merrill Publishing Co.

Rychen, Dominique Simone, and Laura Hersh Salganik, eds. 2001. *Defining and Selecting Key Competencies.* Göttingen: Hogrefe and Huber Publishers.

Salganik, Laura, and Steven Provasnik. 2004. "Defining Education Quality for Universal Basic and Secondary Education." Working Paper of the Project on Universal Basic and Secondary Education. American Academy of Arts and Sciences, Cambridge, MA.

Strom, Margot Stern, Martin Sleeper, and Adam Strom. 2004. "Goals of Universal Primary and Secondary Education." Commentary prepared for a workshop of the Project on Universal Basic and Secondary Education. American Academy of Arts and Sciences, Cambridge, MA, May.

UNESCO. 2000. *Education for All 2000 Assessment: Statistical Document.* Prepared for the International Consultative Forum on Education for All, World Education Forum, Dakar, Senegal, April 26–28. http://unesdoc.unesco.org/images/0012/001204/120472e.pdf.

UNESCO-UIS. 2004. *Global Education Digest 2004: Comparing Education Statistics Across the World.* Montreal: UNESCO-UIS.

UNESCO. 2005. *Education for All: Literacy for Life.* Paris: UNESCO Publishing.

UNESCO-UIS. 2006. *Teachers and Educational Quality: Monitoring Global Needs for 2015.* Montreal: UNESCO-UIS.

United Nations. 2004. *World Population Prospects: The 2004 Revision.* http://esa.un.org/unpp.

Williams, James H. 1997. "The Diffusion of the Modern School." In *International Handbook of Education and Development: Preparing Schools, Students and Nations for the Twenty-First Century,* ed. William K. Cummings and Noel F. McGinn. Oxford: Pergamon, Elsevier Science.

World Bank. 2004. "Books, Buildings and Learning Outcomes: An Impact Evaluation of World Bank Support to Basic Education in Ghana." World Bank, Washington, DC.

World Bank. 2005. *World Development Indicators 2005.* Washington, DC: World Bank.

Section I: Basic Facts and Data

CHAPTER I

Measuring Global Educational Progress

DAVID E. BLOOM

T he 1990 World Conference on Education for All at Jomtien pledged to achieve universal primary education by 2000. By the turn of the century, progress toward this goal in low- and middle-income regions ranged from a 97 percent primary education completion rate in East Asia/Pacific to 51 percent in Sub-Saharan Africa—the latter an increase of just 1 percentage point over 1990 levels (World Bank, 2003). The second Millennium Development Goal (MDG), on universal primary education, extended the deadline to 2015, and official estimates state that up to 32 developing countries may realize the target by this date, in addition to the 37 that have already done so (World Bank, 2003).[1]

Although there has been some progress at the primary level, secondary education has historically received relatively little international funding or attention. For example, between 1965 and 1995 the Inter-American Development Bank (IDB) lent over a billion dollars for the development of primary schooling, but made no investment at the secondary level (Bloom, 2004). However, as the international labor market increasingly demands more sophisticated skills than primary schooling provides, there is grow-ing recognition that secondary education is a vital stimulus for develop-ment.[2] Further, as more children complete primary schooling, demand for

---

[1] *Towards Universal Primary Education* (UN Millennium Project, 2005) is a very useful new study that focuses on the measures needed to reach two of the Mil-lennium Development Goals—those on universal primary education and gen-der equality in education.

[2] "It is now generally recognized that, for economic growth to take place, a high proportion of the population has to have received secondary education" (Delors, 1996).

secondary education naturally increases among students and their parents. As a result, an exclusive concentration on primary education is neither desirable nor feasible.

Equal attention must be directed toward the quality of education offered. In theory at least, all parties—parents, students, employers, taxpayers—have a greater interest in whether a student has been effectively educated than in the time a student has spent in the schooling system. At present, three of the four indicators selected to monitor progress toward the second MDG—net enrollment, attainment of fifth grade schooling, and completion of primary schooling—focus entirely on the quantity of education available. Although the fourth, the literacy rate for 15 to 24 year olds, is an important indicator of the quality of education, data in this area are notoriously inconsistent (Puryear, 1995).

This chapter surveys and assesses the basic data available to inform any effort to achieve universal education. The study analyzes and reviews the nature and quality of information available to measure and assess primary and secondary education, focusing on the information needed to help achieve a quality universal education for all children through these educational levels.

The chapter also provides an overview of selected, currently available indicators. It focuses on three categories: enrollment, quality, and educational attainment. Without enrollment, there is no formal education to speak of. Quality is necessary, because without it schooling is an empty shell. And completion is essential, as succeeding in today's world requires ever-higher levels of knowledge and training. The section presents descriptive analyses of a selection of existing cross-country datasets and identifies the major trends and patterns that relate to the achievement of universal basic and secondary education (UBASE). The section also explores the covariates and determinants of educational development, gender differences and the pace at which they are changing, and projections for a number of educational indicators.[3]

---

[3] This essay is restricted to the indicators that most directly facilitate assessment of the state of primary and secondary education. There are other indicators that are important (such as financing of education and the political environment in which decisions are made), but which receive little or no attention. The issue of finance, in particular, is beyond the scope of this study. A serious treatment of educational finance would have to first ensure data comparability. Among the issues to be resolved (with difficulty, given the current state of the data) are: the use of local versus internationally comparable currencies, real versus nominal figures, and current expenditures versus capital expenditures versus total expenditures.

The final section summarizes the chapter and explores policy implications—with respect both to the future of the global system of educational data collection and the achievement of UBASE.

Part 1: Education Data—What are Available, What are Needed

"The world has only limited information with which to monitor and evaluate one of its major investments."
—Puryear, 1995

Public investment in education typically accounts for 10 to 25 percent of a country's public spending. In some countries, the education ministry is the largest employer. Despite the magnitude of this investment, astonishingly little can be confidently asserted about education systems. Examining the nature and quality of existing data on education, tracing the evolution of educational indicators, and asking questions about how data can be developed are important foundations for the realization of universal basic and secondary education. Robust measurement systems are vital to effective goal setting. This issue is particularly pressing for policymakers and researchers concerned with education quality.

As this study shows, educational statistics are underdeveloped. Little investment has been made in this area, in comparison to the vast amount of money spent on educational provision. The availability and quality of data on basic indicators of progress (e.g., enrollment, completion of schooling) are far from ideal. Equity indicators are particularly lacking; although there are considerable data on gender differences in education, there are little systematic data on urban/rural disparities, and little on racial and ethnic divides. In this, there is a marked contrast between education and other areas of social policy. Economic and demographic indicators, for example, are relatively robust in comparison to their educational counterparts.

Within countries, the collection and aggregation of many quantitative educational statistics, including enrollment, are open to misinterpretation and corruption. Differences of application are common from country to country, as are missing data. Meanwhile, it is unclear whether currently available information meets the needs of all involved groups. Parents and students, with strong personal interests in schooling, are as vital to educational decision making as governments and transnational organizations but may lack adequate information on which to base their choices. The same types of information that are used for cross-national comparisons, if replicated within a country to compare sub-national regions, would be useful to parents and students. This data would shed light on the ability of a country's education system to educate students of different backgrounds and from different regions.

This section investigates the basic facts about education around the world, and the nature, temporal and geographic scope, quality, comparability, and accuracy of existing data that underpin this information. It opens with a discussion of the type of indicators that *could* be collected about education given plentiful resources and capacity, and develops a conceptual framework that splits available data into input, process, output, and outcome measures. This framework is used to provide a critical analysis of the quality of existing measures. A large number of deficits are identified, and the section concludes by asking what difference these deficits make in progress toward universal basic and secondary education. Would better information improve the quantity and quality of education? If so, what changes in the creation and use of educational data would generate this improvement?

WHAT COULD BE COLLECTED?

"Achieving [the UN Millennium Development Goal for education] will require a level of international resources and commitment not yet seen; it will also require better tools for monitoring educational progress."
—Lloyd and Hewett, 2003

Measures that assess progress in education can be divided into four basic types:[4]

---

[4] Some measures span more than one category. In particular, the distinction between inputs and processes is not always clear-cut. In addition, some measures, such as attainment and completion rates, can be considered either inputs or outputs. These rates are inputs in the sense that they are closely related to duration of schooling and reflect the amount of time that students spend in school. They can also measure output, as they reflect the accomplishments of an education system in passing students through a prescribed set of educational steps (sometimes measured, validated steps). In this chapter, the Bruns et al. 2003 data on completion rates, which appear to be output measures, are just a different way to assess inputs. They measure, over a long period of time, a country's efforts to expose its students to a given level of education.

Inputs, or measures of investments in the educational system, such as money and time (of students or teachers);

Processes, or measures of the functioning fabric of the system, such as qualifications of teachers, or lesson quality;

Outputs, or measures of direct results of the education process, such as literacy and numeracy levels, or specific competencies gained; and

Outcomes, or measures of long-term effects or consequences of the education process, such as the rate of return on schooling, or the effects of education on innovation or governance.

Most of the education indicators that are available for a comparative international assessment of education are input measures. Among these are enrollment data from UNESCO and attainment and completion data from Barro and Lee (2000) and Cohen and Soto (2001).[5]

Process measures, which show how countries use their inputs, are scarce and in some instances—think of the educational content and pedagogical style of a history, math, science, or literature curriculum—difficult to quantify. Information on the types of schools in an educational system should be more tractable, but cross-country cultural and economic differences bedevil analysis. Understanding differences in accreditation would be useful, but for similar reasons has proven daunting.[6]

Outputs—particularly those that focus on the quality of what an education system produces—are measured, but data are somewhat unreliable and sparse. Literacy rates are available, but differing standards across countries make comparisons somewhat problematic. In recent years, more countries have begun to participate in standardized tests, but only a small fraction of these are developing countries. Outputs are attractive measures of an education system, but some of the most important outputs of schooling "[reside] in the mind, which is relatively resistant to direct observation and precise analysis" (Puryear, 1995). All the same, the more straightforward output measures (such as literacy rates and standardized test scores) are extremely important in assessing the quality of learning.

---

[5] Average years of schooling are also reported, but this measure is not used in this study.

[6] I do not mean to imply that processes have not been studied extensively. Indeed, a considerable number of cross-country studies have taken place and been documented. Stigler and Hiebert (1999) review ideas from around the world, as do various articles in recent editions of *Comparative Education Review*.

Finally, it is especially important to distinguish between outputs and outcomes. If a cadre of students is successfully educated to a given level, does this have the predicted impact on individuals, economies, and societies? Outcomes are the least straightforward class of indicators to obtain, as understanding the effect of the education system on health or government corruption, for example, requires extensive analysis, not just measurement.

Hence, the framework of this analysis rests heavily on input measures, with considerable attention given to attainment and completion rates. This is unfortunate, because it is difficult to assess a system's overall operation when the best data do little to reflect the overall quality of a country's efforts.

Input Measures

Inputs are indicators of investment in the educational system. Combined with outcome and output measures, input measures allow high-level decisions to be made about investment in education. How much should be spent? On what should this money be spent, and by whom? What proportions of expenditure should be directed at different levels of education and at different priorities within each level?

A considerable proportion of primary and secondary education is purchased publicly by societies, under the assumption that education is a public good. However, some countries, such as South Korea, have expanded educational access through heavy reliance on private schools, and every country has some privately financed education. Private money is also used within public school systems, for transport, books, and other school equipment. In theory, it should be possible to provide figures for public and private expenditure per student at different levels of education, as well as aggregate figures at the national level. Accounts could be provided to show the proportion of investment directed toward administration, school infrastructure and supplies, staffing, and staff development.

As described below, data of this quality are available from very few countries and are not in a format that allows easy comparison between countries, although UNESCO's International Standard Classification of Education (ISCED) has taken steps to address this problem. Reliable data on even the most basic expenditures are often hard to come by. In Uganda, for example, Puryear (1995) reports that the Ministry of Finance believed the country had around 85,000 primary teachers, while the Ministry of Education estimated there were 140,000. These gaps in data make certain questions difficult to address, i.e., whether there is a straightforward relationship between the money spent on education and the outputs or outcomes achieved, or whether the proportion of public to private investment has any impact on results.[7]

Time is also an important input, particularly in developing countries, where the opportunity cost of time spent in school rather than as part of the labor force is often key in the decision to enroll a child in school or to continue education. This decision in turn may be influenced or overturned during the course of childhood by changed circumstances at the family, regional, or national level. Compulsory schooling limits the ability of students and their parents to choose whether to invest time in education or not; in either case, the cost remains real. Participation data are perhaps the most widely used education indicators; for example, they provide the measures of progress toward the second Millennium Development Goal.[8] Enrollment figures, however, can mask problems with attendance, and attendance indicators may conceal other issues, including grade repetition. In Uganda, enrollment was historically under-reported because parents paid schools per child enrolled, and a proportion of this income was payable from the school to the government. However, after schools became publicly funded on the basis of enrolled pupils, the incentive for schools to report higher numbers led to a leap in official enrollment levels (and perhaps in over-reporting).[9]

---

[7] The difficulty of this particular question is illustrated by the contradictory results of available studies on the subject. Barro and Lee (2001), for example, find that more resources improve educational performance, as measured by international test scores, while Hanushek (1995) finds no strong relationship with spending, and Woessman (2000) maintains that, if anything, higher spending corresponds to poorer student performance.

[8] Data on participation are discussed extensively in this chapter. More precise definitions of the various measures appear at the appropriate points in this discussion, but, briefly, "enrollment" means that a child has been registered for school, "attainment" refers to a child's attendance at a particular level for at least some time, and "completion" refers to a child's having finished a particular level of education.

[9] The strength of the incentive to distort enrollment rates very likely affects the amount of distortion. It would be interesting, in this and similar cases, to investigate whether there is any feasible and credible means to impute more accurate data by taking such incentives into account.

As with levels of funding, an increase in participation does not necessarily indicate an improvement in the quality of schooling. Indeed, at the community level, as opposed to the individual level, there may be a trade-off between educational quantity and quality, because an increase in the number of students in the system may mean that teachers, classrooms, and other elements vital to a quality education are spread more thinly. Accurate data in this area could be used to determine the extent of such trade-offs and to compare the effectiveness of various educational systems in managing expansion.

Process Measures

Process measures have a quite different purpose from input measures. They are intended to provide the detailed information needed for effective management of the education system and should be useful for managers at all levels—from teachers with managerial responsibilities, to education ministers, and, given education's great importance, to heads of state. Schools are complex organizations surrounded by sizeable bureaucracies. Management of a school is a far from trivial undertaking, and many developed countries are facing new challenges in managing schools and school systems (OECD, 2001; OECD, 2004). Process data provide governments with the information they need as they develop policy to improve educational systems and recommend teaching methodologies. These data enable educational authorities to assess the performance of institutions and to set investment priorities. Finally, within schools, they enable head teachers to make decisions about issues such as staff performance. Measures of management practices, and of process measures more broadly, are predictably less established in developing countries with countries suffering, in the worst case, from near-total breakdown of management feedback systems.

The relationship between process and output measures is not necessarily straightforward. Woessman (2000), for example, suggests that smaller class sizes actually correspond to lower student performance. Similarly, Nabeshima (2003), in a study of schools in East Asia, finds that teachers' qualifications play a significant role in students' achievement in science but a much smaller role in math, and that the effects of class size are ambiguous.[10] Nabeshima also finds teacher autonomy to be of uncer-

---

[10] This study, however, did not include very large classes such as those seen in Africa—the effect of class size may be more significant in this context.

tain value. Whether or not these counterintuitive and rather controversial findings are justified, they should make us wary of assuming that a particular educational action will lead to the expected consequences for an individual or a society.

Output Measures

Output data measure what the educational process is producing and, when combined with input data on time, money, and participation, are key to understanding the value of a country's education system. Output data measure the immediate quality and quantity of learning purchased publicly or privately.

Output measures could include any gauge of educational achievement, including literacy, numeracy, competencies of any type, and examination results. In theory, these are hard and relatively tangible indicators. Examination systems, for example, provide benchmark outputs for one level of education and thus implicitly indicate the minimal level of accomplishment that can be expected of students entering the next level. They offer students, parents, and employers a simple measure of educational achievement, and allow comparisons across and between generations. Literacy and numeracy rates, meanwhile, offer a vital measure of competencies that are basic building blocks for all future educational achievement.

Internationally comparable data are especially important in this area, because cross-country comparisons naturally occur and result in pressure for improvement of educational standards. Cross-country comparison tables provide an effective mechanism for monitoring progress and creating accountability, as has been shown by the use of existing international comparators.

In practice, however, available output indicators are less robust than they seem, as discussed at length in the following section. There is no accepted international definition of literacy (Puryear, 1995), for example, and grade inflation can undermine the consistency of an examination system. The more robust systems, such as the Trends in International Mathematics and Science Study (TIMSS) and the International Adult Literacy Survey (IALS), cover relatively few developing countries, and countries are not required to make the results public. More broad-based statistical systems, meanwhile, suffer from acute problems of comparability, consistency, and accuracy. The 1998 UNESCO Statistical Yearbook, for example, repeatedly warns users to exercise caution when comparing data across countries (World Bank, 2000).

Outcome Measures

Outcome data are both the hardest measures to track and the most important educational indicators for individuals and societies. The measurement of outcomes includes evaluating whether and how education creates stocks of human capital, and the returns, accruing to either individuals or society, realized on investment in education. Without adequate outcome measures, it is impossible to make fundamental decisions about the value that societies should place on education and the importance it should be given in a world of competing priorities.

The most commonly collected outcome measure attempts to capture increased earning capacity on entering the labor force (see Bloom and Canning, 2004). However, education can have many outcomes beyond direct economic advantage. Education is widely believed to have a positive impact on a range of key issues, including public health and birth rates. In a recent overview of the consequences of increased education, Hannum and Buchmann (this volume) find:

> Countries with better-educated citizens indeed have healthier populations, as educated individuals make more informed health choices, live longer, and have healthier children. The populations of countries with more educated citizens are likely to grow more slowly, as educated people tend to marry later and have fewer children. Second, educational opportunities enhance, but do not necessarily ensure, the future economic security of the world's most vulnerable children.

Broader outcome measures would include indicators such as the competitiveness of businesses, social and economic equality, foreign direct investment, and enrollment in higher education.

Too often, findings about the non-economic impact of education suffer from being both too general and too specific. On the one hand, they tend to suggest that education in general is a social good, but offer little or no insight on whether some types of education are a greater good than others. On the other, they are often based on limited and small-scale studies, which suffer from problems related to data quality, rigor, and establishing causality.

Ease Versus Applicability

A categorization of the types of indicators used to assess education leads to the recognition of a very rough trade-off between ease of measurement and the applicability of the contribution that data make to a reliable and rich picture of education offered. The measures are categorized as follows:

INPUT MEASURES	OUTPUT MEASURES
Enrollment rates	Literacy rates
Average years of schooling	Numeracy rates
Duration of schooling	Standardized test scores
Attainment rates	Any other measures of
Completion rates	competency
Budgets, salaries, and modes of funding	
Hours per day (per teacher)	
Drop-out and repetition rates	
Total hours in class per student per year	
Infrastructure of schools	
Number of schools	
PROCESS MEASURES	**OUTCOME MEASURES**
Type of schools	Rate of return on educational investment
Mathematics and science content	Improvements in public health
Civics, history, and ideology content	Lowering of the birth rate
Arts and humanities content	Impact on governance, corruption, etc.
Books per capita	Competitiveness of businesses
Teacher training standards	Social and economic equality
Student/teacher ratios	Foreign direct investment
Administration/teacher ratios	Enrollment in higher education
Accreditation practices	
Administrative organization	

Although inputs are among the easiest indicators to measure and offer some information about the quantity of education available, they are insufficient for assessing the quality of education. Processes are describable in general terms but are often difficult to quantify and compare. Real outputs and outcomes from education are sometimes hard to capture and in some instances can only be assessed indirectly. The most reliable datasets cover relatively few developing countries, and those countries that are furthest from achieving universal education are also those with the least available information on the current state of their education systems. These problems can be more clearly seen in the discussion of what data are currently collected and the exploration of their quality.

WHAT IS COLLECTED?

> *"Studies have typically relied on school-enrollment ratios or adult literacy rates that do not correspond to the stock of human capital that influences current decisions about fertility, health and so on."*
> —Barro and Lee, 1996

This section sets out current education indicators, examines the way they are gathered, and discusses strengths and weaknesses in the available data (see Table 1 for some basic information about each indicator).

This section first provides an outline of the measures of educational access collected by UNESCO—the primary source of global education data. It then looks at attainment and completion information that can be gleaned from UNESCO and other related datasets.[11] It also examines a number of indicators of educational quality. These measure literacy—the International Adult Literacy Survey (IALS), the Progress in International Reading Literacy Study (PIRLS), and the Program for International Student Assessment (PISA); numeracy—the Trends in International Mathematics and Science Study (TIMSS) and PISA; and science—TIMSS and PISA. Although they offer encouraging possibilities for benchmarking between countries, these measures cover only a limited number of countries. They have little to say about those parts of the world that are furthest from reaching universal education.[12]

Indeed, taken together, the indicators discussed in this chapter are weak with respect to the provision of universal education. Data on gender equity are substantial, but comparisons that highlight racial and ethnic disparities and the different circumstances faced by urban and rural students are scant. Because these differences are likely to be great, the lack of data on them significantly impedes any complete understanding of the resources and actions required to extend a high-quality education to all.

---

[11] Demographic and Household Survey data may also be of some use in assessing educational access and attainment. Detailed discussion of these data, however, is beyond the scope of this study.

[12] This study focuses on the three most widely cited studies of educational outputs. There are, of course, many others, which are not reviewed here, in the interest of tractability. A useful compendium of studies on cross-national surveys appears in Porter and Gamoran (2002).

UNESCO Data

UNESCO is the primary international source of information about education at all levels. UNESCO's Institute for Statistics (UIS), founded in 1999, collects and organizes information on pre-primary, primary, secondary, and tertiary education, and provides data on education expenditure and students studying overseas. This overview focuses on the three categories that are most relevant to UBASE: primary indicators, secondary indicators, and education expenditure data.

In 2003, UNESCO initiated a new annual digest of education statistics (UNESCO-UIS *Global Education Digest* 2003, 2004, 2005). Data are collected according to the International Standard Classification of Education (ISCED), which acts as "an instrument suitable for assembling, compiling, and presenting statistics of education both within individual countries and internationally" (UNESCO, 1997). The current classification is known as ISCED 1997 and is named after the year of its adoption. ISCED provides a standard classification for different levels of education, which aims to offer international comparability between education systems that define levels of education in different ways. There are seven ISCED levels (ISCED 0–6), of which three cover primary and secondary education:

- ISCED 1 – Primary education, which is defined as education that gives "students a sound basic education in reading, writing and mathematics" along with an elementary understanding of other key subjects. This stage normally lasts for six years.
- ISCED 2 – Lower-secondary education, which is designed to complete the implantation of basic skills with the aim of laying "the foundation for lifelong learning and human development on which countries may expand, systematically, further educational opportunities." This level normally ends after a total of nine years of schooling and often coincides with the end of compulsory education.
- ISCED 3 – Upper-secondary education, which typically starts at 15 or 16 years of age, and usually involves more specialization than at ISCED 2.

When this report was drafted, UNESCO presented data for three years, 1998/1999,1999/2000, and 2000/2001.[13] For the primary level

---

[13] The 2005 *Global Education Digest*, the most recent published since this chapter was drafted, presents 2002/2003 data.

Table 1: Databases Measuring the Quantity and Quality of Education

Database	UBASE-related Indicators Included	Years for which Data are Collected	Years for which Data are Projected	Countries Included	How to Obtain
UNESCO	Primary GER, Secondary GER, GER by gender, Primary NER, Secondary NER	1970–2005, although different indicators cover differing ranges of years	None	200+	http://www.uis.unesco.org/
Barro and Lee	Completion rate, Attainment rate	1960–2000 (five-year intervals)	None	129	http://www.worldbank.org/researc h/growth/aer96bl.htm http://www.worldbank.org/researc h/growth/ddbarle2.htm
Cohen and Soto	Completion rate, Attainment rate	1960–2000 (ten-year intervals)	2010	95	via OECD
Bruns, Mingat, and Rakotomalala	Completion rate	1990–2000	2010–2050	155	Book contains a CD that includes all of the data.
International Adult Literacy Survey (IALS)	Literacy	1994, 1996, 1998	None	About 30	http://www.nald.ca/nls/ials/introduc.htm
Progress in International Reading Literacy Study (PIRLS)	Reading ability	2001, 2006 (forthcoming)	None	35 (in 2001)	http://nces.ed.gov/surveys/pirls
Program for International Student Assessment (PISA)	Reading ability; math and science understanding	2000, 2003, 2006 (forthcoming)	None	41 (in 2003)	http://www.pisa.oecd.org/
Trends in International Mathematics and Science Study (TIMSS)	Math and science understanding	1995, 1999, 2003	None	49 (in 2003)	http://timss.bc.edu/timss2003.html

(ISCED 1), UNESCO provides data on a number of input and process measures:

- The education system – theoretical entrance age, theoretical duration of study, starting ages, and finishing ages for compulsory education
- Enrollment – numbers of students enrolled, with the proportion of girls and a gender parity index and the proportion educated privately; and gross and net enrollment ratios
- Teaching staff – the numbers of teaching staff, percentage of trained teachers, and the pupil/teacher ratio
- Attainment – the proportion of students repeating a year, the survival rates at grades 4 and 5, and a measure of the number of students in the last grade of primary education

At the secondary level (ISCED 2 and 3), it publishes data on a similar set of measures:

- The education system – theoretical entrance age and the theoretical duration of study
- Enrollment – enrollment in all programs, with the proportion of girls and a gender parity index; enrollment in general programs and technical or vocational programs; and gross and net enrollment ratios
- Teaching staff – the numbers of teaching staff, percentage of trained teachers, and the pupil/teacher ratio
- Attainment – the proportion of students repeating a year and the proportion of students making the transition from primary to secondary levels

UNESCO also publishes data covering outputs from the educational system:

- Literacy – literacy rates and illiterate population, including figures for men and women
- Education stocks – percentage distribution of population aged 15 plus or 25 plus, by gender, with educational attainment according to the following categories: no schooling, primary incomplete, primary complete, lower secondary education, upper secondary education, and post-secondary[14]

---

[14] As discussed earlier, this analysis treats attainment and completion as inputs to the education system.

Finally, the following financing data are available:

- Total public expenditure on education, as a percentage of GDP and of total government expenditure
- Current versus capital public expenditure on education

UNESCO data are compiled from information provided by governments or other relevant authorities. Questionnaires are sent to the UNESCO National Commissions, who forward them to the relevant national authorities (Ministries of Education, Ministries of Finance, the National Library, etc.), or are downloaded from the UNESCO website. The instructions give definitions of all indicators and require that local authorities conform to UNESCO standards in reporting data. The questionnaires are completed by national experts and then returned to UNESCO. At this stage, UNESCO uses national statistical or educational publications to cross check figures, as well as to ensure that there have been no changes in the structure of the country's education system since the last questionnaire was entered into the database. If any inconsistencies in the data presented by the national authorities are noted, UIS contacts the country for clarification. Despite this careful and labor-intensive process, UNESCO has historically faced difficulty collecting any information from some countries, and the quality of information provided by many other countries has been questioned. In some instances, it has proved difficult to ensure comparability of data across countries.

In its discussion of education statistics, the Task Force on Higher Education convened by UNESCO and the World Bank highlighted some of the difficulties of earlier years:

In the 1998 Statistical Yearbook, UNESCO authors repeatedly warn users of the need to take care when exercising comparisons between countries, and especially across groups of countries. Many of the differences between nations are detailed in charts that demonstrate differing years of educational entry, different years of schooling offered at the various levels, and different requirements about compulsory education. Readers are warned of particular issues, such as the counting of full-time and part-time teachers, which may vary across nations and have a strong and potentially misleading impact on data about pupil/teacher ratios (World Bank, 2000).

Puryear, meanwhile, focused on the quality of data reported by countries in the 1980s and early 1990s, suggesting that, at that time, twenty to thirty countries suffered "disastrous problems" in generating reliable education statistics, while another fifty suffered "significant gaps and weaknesses in this area." Statistics from five of the world's nine largest countries were then believed to be seriously deficient, while UNESCO staff told him that statistics from nearly half of UNESCO's member countries were unreliable (Puryear, 1995). Since its foundation, UIS has worked to rectify these problems. As a result of intensive work with national and international users and producers of education statistics, it claims that response rates have improved and that indicators (whose definitions are frequently reviewed) are more timely and comparable. Problems still remain, however.

It is possible to examine the nature of the data collected and ask whether UNESCO's efforts are directed toward generating the right kind of indicators. UNESCO defends its focus on relatively simple enrollment-rate measures by pointing out that the development of more complex indicators is often beyond the capacity of poorer countries, many of which struggle to provide UNESCO with even basic information. It argues that progress toward measuring educational processes, outputs, and outcomes must be complemented by "a parallel strategy...that improves and exploits education data which are more readily available and comparable." UNESCO believes these data can provide valuable insights into countries' educational systems and the characteristics of these systems that are amenable to policy change. "This information can inform policies that create more effective, equitable and efficient educational systems... Reporting on the widening of access to education," it suggests, "needs to be alongside an examination of whether this has been achieved at the expense of the quality of the education being received" (UNESCO-UIS, 2003).

In the past, however, critics wondered whether UNESCO's approach did, in fact, lead to indicators useful to policymakers or other audiences. Although the establishment of UIS has improved the quality and relevance of data collected, Puryear (1995) earlier accused UNESCO of adopting a "collect and file" mentality, rather than showing a commitment to "understand and use." As a result, UNESCO presented policymakers with a crude set of statistics that seemed more precise than they were, instead of more developed indicators that would enable policymakers to base their decisions on firm evidence. Behrman and Rosen-zweig, meanwhile, underline the tendency for UNESCO data to be used without a clear understanding of the data's limitations. They point out that data they describe as fictional or made-up (i.e., data points from earlier years or inferences) were often used by researchers and policy makers as if these data were as valid as empirical observations (Behrman and Rosenzweig, 1994).

Input Measures: Enrollment

At the time this report was drafted, data availability was problematic; for example, there were numerous countries for which UNESCO did not provide a figure for the primary gross enrollment ratio[15] (arguably the most fundamental input indicator), and the data for secondary education were even more sparse. However, in the newest version (2005) of the *Global Education Digest,* these particular data are essentially complete. UNESCO now publishes both primary and secondary gross enrollment ratios for 96 percent and 95 percent, respectively, of countries with at least 100,000 people.[16] These figures cover 99 percent of all school-age children.

The corresponding figures for net enrollment ratio are much lower, particularly at the secondary level, where there are no data for China, India, Pakistan, or Russia. Commenting on the challenge of calculating net enrollment rates, UNESCO at one point remarked that "it is of concern that [many countries] are unable to provide the data to calculate the indicator [at the primary level] because the building blocks of the indicator (year of age, gender, and grade) represent fundamental information required to manage educational systems" (UNESCO-UIS, 2003). Survival rates, which measure those who reach the fifth year of education, cannot be calculated in numerous countries, and the usefulness of measures of primary completion is bedeviled by a lack of comparability across countries. UIS has stated that it is committed to exploring with countries

---

[15] The gross enrollment ratio for a given level of education is the number of children of any age who are registered in school at that level of education, divided by the total population of the appropriate age, expressed as a percentage. This number can be higher than 100 percent. The net enrollment ratio for a given level of education (used more extensively in this chapter) is the number of children of the appropriate age for that level of education who are registered in school at that level, divided by the total population of children of the appropriate age.

[16] That is, UNESCO publishes a figure for at least one of the last several years.

whether ISCED level 1 should be used as a common standard for measuring primary completion or whether the completion of a fixed number of years of schooling should be used as a standard international benchmark.

Although UNESCO receives more data than in the past, questions still arise about the quality of the information that countries provide. One possible way of evaluating UNESCO data is to compare these data with findings from survey-based instruments such as USAID's Demographic and Health Surveys (DHS) or the World Bank's Living Standards Measurement Study.[17] *Global Education Digest* compares official Kenyan data, as provided to UNESCO, with two DHS surveys in Kenya, and surveys conducted by ILO and UNICEF. Official data show 5 percent of children out of school in 1990, with 35 percent out of school in 1999. DHS surveys show 26 percent of children out of school in 1993, compared to 13 percent in 1998. The ILO and UNICEF surveys show around 26 percent of children out of school in 1998 and 2000 respectively. These highly contradictory findings cannot be reconciled. As UNESCO comments, "further analysis is needed in order to understand why different sources produce such different results" (UNESCO-UIS, 2003). Lloyd and Hewett also compare DHS data with UNESCO data, across Sub-Saharan Africa. They argue:

> UNESCO provides an incomplete and sometimes potentially biased picture of progress towards the millennium education goal with the current data derived from country management information systems. Comparisons with data from DHS suggest that fewer children ever attend school than the UNESCO estimates suggest, but a higher percentage of those who do attend eventually complete grade four. Furthermore, gender gaps in school participation are likely to be smaller than implied by UNESCO enrolment estimates (Lloyd and Hewett, 2003).

UNESCO, meanwhile, detailed a number of problems with survey data, including the timing of fieldwork in the school year, which result in inconsistent estimates of school participation, sampling biases, and cul-

---

[17] UNICEF makes such comparisons. In its effort to determine how many primary-school-age children do not attend school, it found that survey data suggest that the number is 121 million—considerably higher than other published estimates. UNICEF pointed out that even data collected via surveys may underestimate the number of children who are not in school, because parents may be unwilling to say that their children are not in school (UNICEF, 2003).

tural biases. It argued that international surveys do too little to take account of country-specific conditions and that these efforts "should also be balanced alongside more long-term goals of building capacity within countries to monitor their own educational systems"[18] (UIS, 2003).

Some, such as Bruns, Mingat, and Rakotomolala (2003), have attempted to strengthen UNESCO data by complementing these with data from other sources. Using a recent dataset designed to assess progress toward the Millennium Development Goal of universal primary completion by 2015, Bruns et al. analyze completion rates of primary education in 155 developing countries between 1990 and 2000. They also provide projections for 2015. Bruns and her coauthors collect completion data directly from national education ministries where possible. Only when these data were not available do they rely on data from previous years. Still, the data set is not perfect: the methodology is complicated by differing lengths of the primary education cycle, which lasts for six years in nearly half the countries studied, but differs in the remainder, ranging from three years to ten years. There are also limitations in the accuracy of the data. First, because primary completion rates were not reported in all countries, these must be estimated from the number of students enrolled in the last year of primary school, subtracting the number likely to repeat. Second, dropout rates were not available for many countries, so the completion rates tend to be overestimates. Third, population data are not always accurate, especially for countries for which there were no recent census data, or for countries that recently experienced dislocations such as war or mass migration. However, the study is the most direct effort to date to measure progress toward universal primary completion, and to provide a basis for future monitoring.[19]

---

[18] UIS's work in capacity building includes strengthening National Education Statistical Information Systems (NESIS). Set up in 1991, this program aims to build statistical capacities in Sub-Saharan Africa. UNESCO and UNICEF are also currently working to draw together administrative and survey data.

[19] The completion rate data contained in Bruns, Mingat, and Rakotomalala (2003) are not used in the statistical analysis of this study. Bruns et al. use a definition of completion rate different from that of the Barro-Lee and Cohen-Soto indicators (though not different from that used by UIS, which supplied some of the data used by Bruns). Bruns et al. write, "The primary completion rate is a flow measure of the annual output of the primary-education system. It is calculated as the total number of students successfully completing (or graduating from) the last year of primary school in a given year, divided by the total number of children of official graduation age in the population." By contrast,

Input Measures: Education Stocks

Indicators derived from the current education system provide a snapshot of how that system is performing and whom it is serving at a particular time, but they say little about the educational stocks that have accumulated in the population over time. UNESCO reports data in this area, providing figures for the percentage of population with no schooling, incomplete primary, complete primary, incomplete secondary, complete secondary, and tertiary education. In addition, a number of composite indicators exist, which attempt to strengthen UNESCO's figures by filling in missing observations. This chapter discusses datasets created by Barro and Lee (2000) and Cohen and Soto (2001), two distinct approaches to devising composite indicators for these measures. The UNESCO, Barro-Lee, and Cohen-Soto datasets are important efforts to build the foundations of knowledge about the most fundamental elements of global educational development.[20]

Barro and Lee and Cohen and Soto define completion rate as the percentage of people in the total population of a certain age (either 15+ or 25+) that have completed primary education. Thus, Bruns et al. are analyzing a considerably younger population—typically, 11 year-olds—rather than the 15+ and 25+ populations used for other datasets. Although the measure calculated and used by Bruns et al. is important, it cannot be compared directly with Barro-Lee or Cohen-Soto indicators. Indeed, as should be expected, the primary completion rates reported by Bruns are much higher than those reported by Barro and Lee or Cohen and Soto. To ensure that information from Bruns et al. is statistically consistent with that contained in the primary sources for this chapter, I correlated the 1990 and 2000 data against the Barro-Lee and Cohen-Soto datasets. The correlation is high. Despite the difference in definition for completion rate, countries that have low completion rates in Bruns et al. tend also to have low completion rates in both Barro-Lee and Cohen-Soto (and conversely).

[20] Krueger and Lindahl (2001) conducted several analyses of the information content of country-level education data. For example, they compared average years of schooling in the Barro-Lee data with measures of average education in Kyriacou (1991), and reported simple correlations of 0.86 in levels (for 68 countries in 1985) and 0.34 (for the same countries for changes from 1965–85). Unfortunately, this is not a clear cut comparison insofar as the Barro and Lee and Kyriacou data sets both rely on the same underlying enrollment data, and because the Barro-Lee data refer to the population aged 25 and over whereas the Kyriacou data refer to the workforce. The same concern applies to Barro and Lee's (1993) comparisons of their data with those of Kyriacou and Psacharopoulos and Ariagada (1986). Krueger and Lindahl (2001) also analyzed data derived from the World Values Survey and concluded that measurement error was particularly prevalent for secondary and tertiary levels of

A comparison of results from the Barro-Lee and Cohen-Soto datasets uncovers significant inconsistencies within these indicators, including what are inferred to be negative enrollment rates for certain country–age group combinations, as well as some implausible decadal changes. The review also discusses significant discrepancies between the two datasets. These discrepancies cloud, in some cases considerably, any understanding of trends and patterns in primary and secondary education at the national level. The inconsistencies are worrying, and particularly so where these concern the 15–24 year-old cohort, because information about this group should provide a more up-to-date indicator of the education system's current performance.[21] Examination of these two key datasets suggests that available indicators may be less than robust. The snapshot of current progress toward universal basic and secondary education that follows, and the examination of trends and developments, is, as a result of data limitations and errors, incomplete and tentative.

Barro and Lee produced a series of reports on measures of educational attainment; their latest paper provides figures for the proportion of

---

school. Schooling data derived from the World Values Survey were, in principle, independent of schooling data in Barro and Lee, but those data only referred to 34 countries and required numerous assumptions about the age at entry into primary and secondary school, and the absence of grade repetition.

Krueger and Lindahl (2001) also explored the implications of measurement error in education for estimates of the effect of schooling on the growth of national income (Pritchett (1997) addressed similar issues). Consistent with the econometric result that the coefficients of regressors that are measured with error (i.e., additive white noise, uncorrelated with the true value of the regressor in question, with any other regressors, or with the equation's disturbance term) will be biased toward zero, they found evidence that measurement error in education severely attenuates estimates of the effect of the change in schooling on GDP growth. Correcting econometrically for measurement error is consequential insofar as it leads to larger estimates of the effect on income per capita of schooling.

[21] I devote considerable effort in this study to analyzing the educational attainment rates of the 15–24 year age cohort. Achievements in that age group reflect recent changes in the education system and are thus, potentially, an excellent indicator of progress or lack thereof. However, I am aware of the limitations of such a focus. In particular, high retention rates result in many younger members of this group continuing to attend primary school; although their education may be progressing, these students will not be counted as having completed primary education. This is particularly a problem in Africa, and hence with the data on Africa. Because I also look at trends over time, it is possible to use these rates to assess progress.

the population who successfully completed each of seven levels of schooling (no formal education, attended primary, completed primary, attended secondary, completed secondary, attended tertiary, completed tertiary), standardized according to ISCED 97. It also presents figures for average years of schooling. Data are provided at five-year intervals between 1960 and 1995, with projections for 2000, for the adult population aged 25 and over and aged 15 and over. Complete information is provided for 142 countries, with at least one observation presented for another 35. Data are constructed using UNESCO and other census data as a benchmark. 354 observations are available for educational attainment for the population aged 15 and over, spread across 141 countries during the period 1960–1995 (an average of 2.5 survey observations per country, instead of the ideal 8). 375 observations provide data for the population aged 25 and over in the same period, spread across 142 countries (2.6 survey observations per country). An estimation method is therefore needed to supply a considerable number of missing observations. The authors use the perpetual inventory method, where information on enrollment (gross enrollment ratios, adjusted for repeaters) and the age structure of the population is used to estimate flows of enrolled population. These flows are then used, in conjunction with known attainment levels, to determine levels for subsequent years. In this manner, full estimates of educational attainment are obtained for most countries from the established figures of one or more years, and from the reasonably complete data on school enrollment ratios.[22]

Cohen and Soto (2001) present a new dataset on educational attainment and completion rates, based on data compiled by national sources, OECD,[23] and UNESCO. They also reported average years of schooling. In contrast to Barro and Lee, their primary concern was to minimize extrapolations from school enrollment data to keep data as close as possible to those directly available from national censuses. Cohen-Soto data split the population into age groups for ten-year intervals from 1960–2000. Missing observations are filled in using backward or forward extrapolation.

---

[22] A definition of the perpetual inventory method, used in the more typical financial context, appears at http://forum.europa.eu.int/irc/dsis/coded/info/data/coded/en/gl008546.htm.

[23] In 1997, and in collaboration with the OECD, UNESCO launched the World Education Indicators (WEI) pilot program, which now covers 19 middle-income countries, including China, Brazil, and India (UNESCO/OECD, 2000). These countries comprise over 70 percent of the world's population.

School enrollment data are used as a last resort, whereas Barro and Lee use enrollment data to fill missing observations in the first instance. Data cover 95 countries, with 119 censuses available (an average of 1.3 per country); 28 countries do not have any censuses available.

Potential problems with Cohen-Soto (as well as Barro-Lee) imputation methods include their lack of accounting for immigration, emigration, and the impact of epidemics. These affect the assumptions of stable population growth and mortality rates. Also, the authors are not confident of their numbers for African countries and exclude them from subsequent econometric analysis in growth models. Krueger and Lindahl (2001), in critiquing Barro-Lee imputation methods, note various problems that stem from UNESCO data: the difference between beginning-of-year registration and ultimate attendance, the varying definitions of secondary schooling across countries, and the compounding of errors through the use of the "perpetual inventory method" of constructing the data.

Although the Barro-Lee and Cohen-Soto datasets provide similar figures for some countries, numerous and substantial discrepancies between the figures for individual countries in each dataset undermine confidence in the data. Additionally, relatively simple calculations of attainment rates for the 15–24 year-old cohort yielded some implausible results, especially in the Barro and Lee dataset (discussed in detail below). This section explores the extent of these irregularities and discusses the possible consequences.

Figures 1 and 2 compare the Barro-Lee and Cohen-Soto data on attainment rates for the population aged 25+. If the two datasets were in perfect agreement, the points on the scatterplot would fall exactly on the one-to-one line through the figure (with an R-squared value of 1). As Figure 1 shows, at the primary level, the Barro-Lee and Cohen-Soto datasets are in agreement for most countries. However, there are discrepancies of over 10 percentage points between the datasets for five countries in the Latin America/Caribbean region, for six countries in Sub-Saharan Africa, and for Jordan, Myanmar, and Indonesia. At the secondary level, Figure 2 shows that although the datasets are in agreement for countries with lower attainment rates, inconsistency increases as attainment rate increases. The figures for the developed world are particularly inconsistent, with discrepancies of over 20 percentage points for eight countries. Figures for most developing countries are in rough

Figure 1: Comparing Datasets: Primary Attainment Rates, Population Age 25+

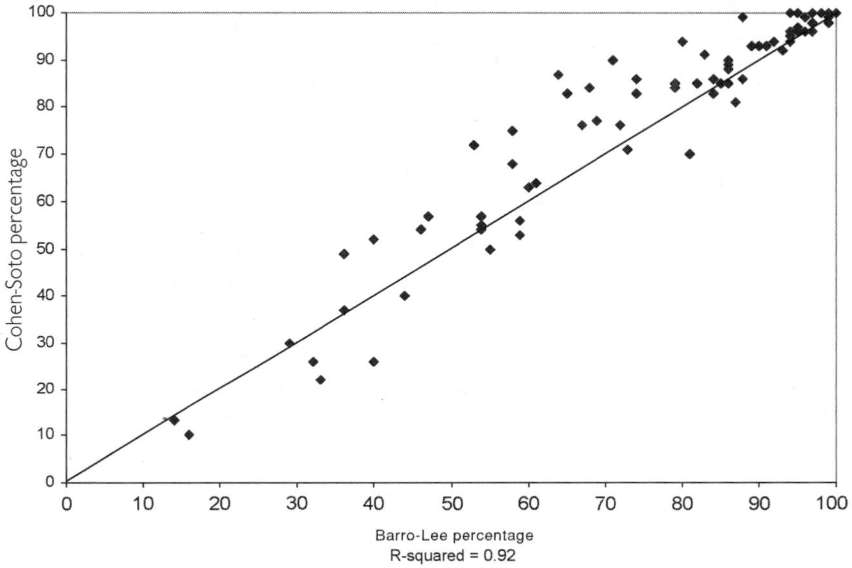

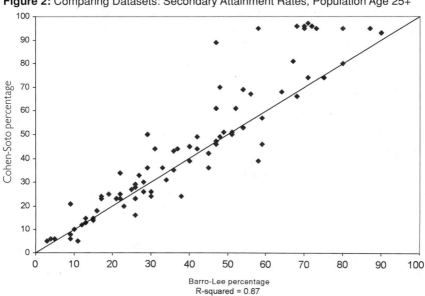

Sources: Barro and Lee (2000) and Cohen and Soto (2001).

Figure 2: Comparing Datasets: Secondary Attainment Rates, Population Age 25+

Sources: Barro and Lee (2000) and Cohen and Soto (2001).

agreement, although there are discrepancies of over 10 percentage points in seven countries.[24]

This study also calculated the attainment figures for the cohort aged 15–24 years. These were calculated by extrapolating from the figures reported by Barro and Lee and Cohen and Soto for the 15+ and 25+ age groups in each country, using the size of each country's population, reported by the United Nations Population Division for each five-year age group for five-year intervals since 1950. Parallel calculations were performed on both datasets to yield the attainment figures by gender and the completion rates for primary education.[25] Although these calculations are straightforward, the accuracy of the results depends on the accuracy of the population figures.[26] Discrepancies between datasets are in some cases larger, and are found more frequently, between the extrapolated figures than between the attainment data in the datasets. For example, for primary attainment in the Dominican Republic, estimates differ by 9 percentage points for the 25+ group but by 45 percentage points for the 15–24 cohort. Among the estimates of secondary attainment in developed countries, there are differences of more than 50 percentage points between the datasets for Denmark and France in the 15–24 year-old cohort.

Additionally, there are discrepancies in the estimates for secondary attainment in Colombia, Guyana, and Malaysia of 13, 7, and 0 percentage

---

[24] The complete, country-level data on primary and secondary attainment from the Barro-Lee and Cohen-Soto datasets are available on the UBASE website, http://www.amacad.org/projects/ubase.aspx.

[25] These data—primary and secondary attainment, primary completion, and attainment by gender—calculated for the 15–24 year-old cohort are available in full on the UBASE website, http://www.amacad.org/projects/ubase.aspx.

[26] As an example of these calculations: In Argentina in 2000, Barro and Lee give secondary attainment rates of 51.2 percent for the 15+ age group and 44.6 percent for the 25+ age group. From the UN figures, the 15+ population is 26.8 million, and the 25+ population is 20.2 million, so the 15–24 population is 6.6 million. To determine the number of people in that age group with secondary level attainment, I calculate how many in the 15+ and 25+ age groups have secondary attainment, by multiplying the attainment rate by the population size. For the 15+ group, this is 51.2 percent of 26.8 million (13.7 million): for the 25+ age group, the result is 9.0 million. By subtracting, I find that 4.7 million people have secondary attainment in the 15–24 year age group. Dividing by the population size of 6.6 million gives a secondary attainment rate of 71 percent.

points respectively in the 25+ age group, but of 28, 34, and 68 percentage points respectively in the 15–24 age group (with figures higher in the Cohen-Soto dataset). The figures for South Africa are still more inconsistent: 19 percentage points higher in Barro and Lee's estimate in the 25+ age group, but 85 percentage points higher in Cohen and Soto's estimate in the 15–24 age group.

Another, more significant irregularity appears in the secondary attainment data from Barro and Lee. In Singapore in 2000, the secondary attainment rate reported for the 25+ population is 59 percent. For the 15+ population, the figure given (but not shown in the Appendix of that paper) is 45 percent. It seems unlikely that secondary attainment rates would have decreased in Singapore in the most recent generation, and indeed they did not do so in 1960, 1970, 1980, or 1990. The 25+ population in 2000 in Singapore was approximately five times larger than the 15–24 population. Following the methods described above, I calculated a secondary attainment rate in the 15–24 cohort of -32 percent, which is by definition impossible. This leads to the conclusion that the underlying data are incorrect, though the population data in Singapore for 2000 seem unlikely to contain large errors. Although a negative attainment value for the 15–24 year-old cohort was detected only in Singapore, there may nevertheless be errors in the data for other countries, which were not detected because they led to low positive values for this age group rather than to negative values. There is no obvious way to distinguish such results, and they would routinely be included in calculations of regional and world averages, distorting the results. These considerations cast doubt on the validity of the Barro and Lee data for attainment rates.[27]

In the data for primary completion rates for the 25+ group, there are a number of significant differences between the two datasets, as Figure 3 shows. In developing countries, discrepancies are particularly large for Guyana (31 percentage points higher in the Cohen-Soto dataset) and Thailand (35 percentage points higher in the Cohen-Soto dataset). Data

---

[27] I did not examine the parallel question regarding completion data for secondary education. Secondary completion data for the 15+ age group are necessarily (and correctly) skewed downward, because, in most countries, students do not complete secondary education until approximately age 17. Therefore a small portion of the 15+ age group, rising to approximately one-third in the 15–24 cohort, cannot reasonably be expected to have completed secondary education. However, this caveat does not affect the calculation of secondary attainment rates in the 15–24 age group.

Figure 3: Comparing Datasets: Primary Completion Rates, Population Age 25+

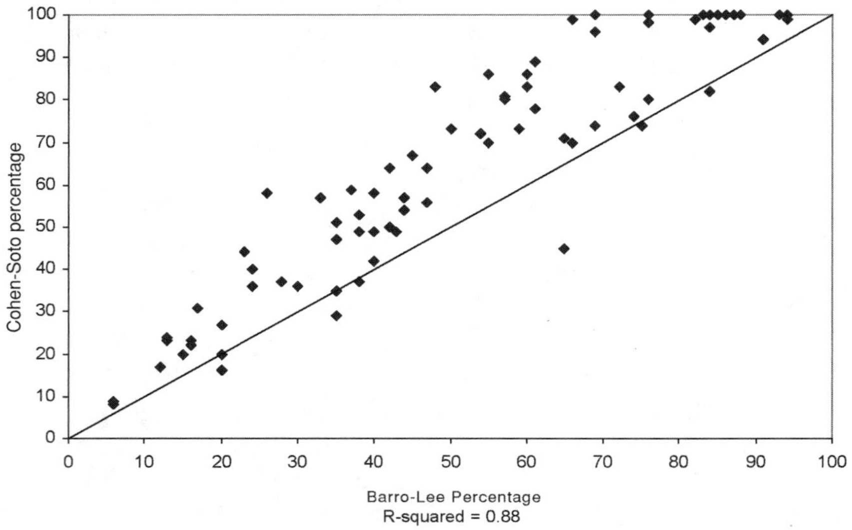

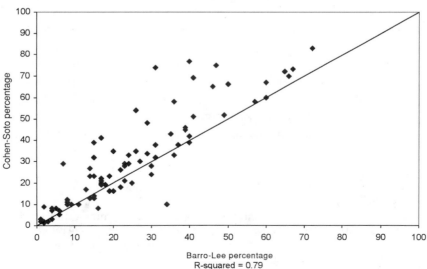

Sources: Barro and Lee (2000) and Cohen and Soto (2001).

Figure 4: Comparing Datasets: Secondary Completion Rates, Population Age 25+

Sources: Barro and Lee (2000) and Cohen and Soto (2001).

for secondary education are compared in Figure 4, which shows that estimates are substantially higher in the Cohen-Soto dataset for several developing countries, notably Hungary (by 28 percentage points), Guyana (by 24 percentage points), Trinidad and Tobago (by 24 percentage points), and Zimbabwe (by 22 percentage points). There are also major inconsistencies among developed countries, with estimates over 20 percentage points higher in the Cohen-Soto dataset for five countries, the largest of which is in the United Kingdom (43 percentage points).

In general, the data from the Barro-Lee and Cohen-Soto datasets on trends in primary and secondary attainment in the 25+ age group are more consistent between sources.[28] However, some of the shifts from one decade to the next are large and difficult to believe. Because membership in the 25+ population does not vary dramatically from one decade to the next, changes in these figures should be relatively minor. Kuwait seems to have decreased its primary attainment rate by 8 percentage points during the 1970s, perhaps related in some unexpected fashion to the first oil price shock. In the Barro-Lee dataset for primary attainment, Senegal and Sri Lanka have particularly unlikely patterns, and Mozambique's pattern in the Cohen-Soto dataset is questionable. The pattern for secondary attainment in Barbados in the Barro-Lee dataset is quite obviously incorrect. Additionally, there are a few discrepancies between datasets. Notably, the Barro-Lee figures for primary attainment in El Salvador are 8, 18, -2, and 3 percent for each decade. The figure of -2 may be explained by the civil war in El Salvador in the 1980s. However, the Cohen-Soto dataset gives corresponding figures of 5, 9, 16, and 12 percent.

Despite their many gaps and inconsistencies, input indicators currently provide the broadest international coverage of any available measures. Nevertheless, input indicators only provide part of the story; to assess education systems' effectiveness, output indicators must be considered.

Output Measures: Testing of Educational Quality

Work to measure education quality across countries has principally been carried out by the International Association for the Evaluation of Educational Achievement (IEA) and the OECD.

---

[28] These decadal trend data from both datasets on primary and secondary attainment are available on the UBASE website, http://www.amacad.org/projects/ubase.aspx.

IEA was set up in 1958 "to conduct large-scale comparative studies of educational achievement, with the aim of gaining a more in-depth understanding of the effects of policies and practices within and across systems of education."[29] Although its membership is dominated by developed countries, it does have a number of developing country members, including four African countries—Botswana, Kenya, Nigeria, and South Africa. Member and non-member countries are able to join IEA studies, but a considerable degree of institutional sophistication is needed for participation. Countries must appoint a National Study Center, a National Research Coordinator, and a National Committee with expertise in curricula and educational policymaking and in the technical design and implementation of the study. Countries are required to meet all costs incurred in their national study and to contribute to costs incurred internationally. IEA has conducted 15 cross-national studies since its inception. Its current major studies include the Trends in International Mathematics and Science Study (TIMSS 1995, TIMSS 1999, TIMSS 2003, and the planned TIMSS 2007) and the Progress in International Reading Literacy Studies (PIRLS 2001, and the planned PIRLS 2006). These tests had a number of forerunners, such as the First International Science Study and the First International Mathematics Study (Husén, 1967; Walker, 1976). The contribution from countries to participate in these assessments is relatively modest. TIMSS 2003, for example, which has funding from the United States National Center for Education Statistics, the National Science Foundation, the World Bank, and the United Nations Development Programme, requires a donation over a three-year period of $40,000 per year for one grade level and $60,000 per year for two grade levels.

TIMSS represents IEA's most sustained attempt to measure mathematical and scientific achievement. It is directed at children in the fourth and eighth grades (or the grades with the greatest proportions of 9 year-old and 13 year-old students, respectively). In 1995, 42 countries participated in the eighth-grade study and 27 in the fourth-grade study. In 1999, 26 of the original countries took part in a second assessment of eighth-grade achievement and were joined by 12 additional countries. 53 countries and regions took part in the 2003 study,[30] including sub-

---

[29] As described by UNESCO, at http://portal.unesco.org/education/en/ev.php-URL_ID=34283&URL_DO=DO_TOPIC&URL_SECTION=201.html.

[30] In 2003, 30 low- and middle-income countries participated: Argentina, Armenia, Botswana, Bulgaria, Chile, Egypt, Estonia, Ghana, Hungary, Indonesia,

national units with distinct educational systems (Flanders, the Basque Country, England, the state of Indiana in the United States, etc.). This feature differentiates TIMSS from the UNESCO data-collection system (IEA *TIMSS*, 2003). The study reported at the end of 2004.

At the heart of the study are the TIMSS tests, which ask students a number of multiple choice and open-ended questions. For mathematics, the tests are framed by a content domain (numbers, algebra, measurement, geometry, and data) and a cognitive domain (knowing facts and procedures, using concepts, solving routine problems, and reasoning). According to the IEA, "The content domains define the specific mathematics subject matter covered by the assessment, and the cognitive domains define the sets of behaviors expected of students as they engage with the mathematics content." For science, the tests are similarly framed by a content domain (life science, chemistry, physics, earth science, and environmental science) and cognitive domain (factual knowledge, conceptual understanding, and reasoning and analysis). TIMSS also asks students, teachers, and school principals to complete questionnaires about "the contexts for learning mathematics and science" (IEA *TIMSS*, 2003).

It is not possible to test all students on all content, as IEA estimates that a full test would take seven hours at the eighth-grade level and five and a half hours at the fourth-grade level. Eighth grade students therefore answer only a subset of TIMSS questions that takes 90 minutes to answer; fourth grade students answer a set of questions designed to take 65 minutes. Each student has an additional 15–30 minutes to answer the accompanying questionnaire. Countries are expected to test a sample of at least 4,500 students to ensure that enough students take each part of the test. Responses to each part are then combined to provide an overall picture of the country's performance, in a format that allows accurate comparison with the performance of other countries (IEA *TIMSS*, 2003). Tests are prepared in English, but then must be translated (into 43 languages in 2003) and modified for cultural reasons. Training manuals support the testing procedure, and further procedures are required to ensure quality control and consistent scoring, especially for open-answer questions. The study ranks performance in mathematics and science, and

Iran, Jordan, Latvia, Lebanon, Lithuania, Macedonia, Malaysia, Moldova, Morocco, Palestinian Authority, Philippines, Romania, Russian Federation, Saudi Arabia, Serbia, Slovakia, South Africa, Syria, Tunisia, and Yemen.

tracks improvements over time (through comparisons with earlier versions of the test) and differences in performance by gender. Responses to the questionnaire are used to assess student attitudes toward each subject, the way national curricula are developed, the proportion of time in school dedicated to each subject, and the main pedagogical methods employed. Findings from TIMSS 1999 are discussed in more detail in Section 2.[31]

The organization of PIRLS is similar, in many regards, to TIMSS. It assesses reading achievement at the fourth-grade level, or the grade that contains the largest proportion of 9 year-old children. Perhaps most significantly, "the target grade should represent that point in the curriculum where students have essentially finished learning the basic reading skills and will focus more on 'reading to learn' in the subsequent grades" (IEA, 2003: 286). PIRLS also collects information on the home, school, and national context within which children learn to read. The first assessment was conducted in 2001, and follows earlier IEA studies in the area in 1970 and 1991. A second assessment is currently being developed for 2006. 35 countries participated in the study in 2001, while various developing and middle-income countries[32] have expressed interest in participating in 2006.

The assessment framework for 2001 focused on three aspects of reading: processes of comprehension, purposes for reading, and reading behaviors and attitudes. PIRLS developed eight passages and accompanying comprehension questions, and students responded to two passages each in a test lasting 80 minutes. An additional 15–30 minutes were allocated to the student questionnaire. Tests were prepared in English and translated into 31 languages; the extensive translation effort included statistical checks to detect elements within the test that did not perform comparably in translation. As with TIMSS, PIRLS provides rankings of reading achievement, disaggregated by gender, and an assessment of contextual issues such as the role of home activities in fostering literacy, the nature of curriculum and school organization, the methods used to teach reading and the support provided by schools, and information on students' attitudes and reading habits.

---

[31] Results for TIMSS 2003 are now available; however, at the time this chapter was drafted, TIMSS 1999 was the most recent available study.

[32] These include Albania, Belarus, Bulgaria, China, Czech Republic, Hungary, Indonesia, Iran, Latvia, Lithuania, Macedonia, Moldova, Morocco, Nicaragua, Poland, Romania, Russian Federation, Slovakia, Slovenia, South Africa, and Zimbabwe.

PIRLS and TIMSS test basic skills as a student moves through the school system. PISA—run by OECD—takes a different but complementary approach, emphasizing competencies at the end of compulsory education. OECD describes the assessment as "forward-looking: rather than focusing on the extent to which these students have mastered a specific school curriculum, it looks at their ability to use their knowledge and skills to meet real life challenges" (Adams and Wu, 2002: 15). PISA is to be run every three years. Numerous developing and middle-income countries were involved in PISA 2000 and 2003.[33] Each country tested between 4,500 and 10,000 students.

PISA surveys reading, mathematical, and scientific literacy. In 2000, the primary focus was on reading. Mathematics was the primary focus in 2003, and science will be the focus in 2006. Multiple choice, short answer, and extended response questions are included. A student and school questionnaire are also used, although not all countries took up this option in 2000. Used to make international comparisons of reading, mathematics, and science, the questionnaires also allow PISA to report on the impacts of engagement, family background, and school characteristics on learning. The study disaggregates a range of factors that it believes explain differential performance between countries and schools, and attempts to quantify their relative importance. OECD suggests these factors include socioeconomic background, school resources, school policy and practice, and classroom practice, though it suggests that further research and analysis are needed to identify more precisely how these factors operate. OECD maintains that its approach will provide policymakers, parents, and students with more accurate information about what educational policies and practices work and why, as well as the extent to which countries are able to develop educational systems that make the most effective use of continually limited resources.

Prospects for International Comparisons

The development of indicators such as PIRLS, TIMSS, and PISA, which allow comparisons across international education systems, is relatively

---

[33] These include Albania, Argentina, Brazil, Bulgaria, Chile, China, Czech Republic, Hungary, Indonesia, Latvia, Macedonia, Mexico, Peru, Poland, Romania, Russian Federation, and Thailand. Serbia, Slovakia, Tunisia, Turkey, and Uruguay joined the study for PISA 2003, though several former participants, including China, did not participate.

recent. Each is, to at least some extent, a cooperative venture among governments or other relevant educational authorities, and requires considerable commitment from participating countries. This is both a strength and a weakness. On the one hand, the commitment required suggests that participants expect to receive results that will be immediately relevant to the development of their educational systems. There is unlikely to be any tendency to "file and forget" these indicators, and there will be ongoing pressure from participants to increase relevance and applicability. On the other hand, those countries that are furthest from achieving universal education are also likely to be those with the least incentive to participate. They lack resources and capacity, and may also find more unwelcome evidence of their educational failings. These disincentives will not disappear quickly, and researchers and policymakers will likely continue to be hampered by a lack of data.

The participation of some developing countries in these assessments shows the potential to gradually increase the reach of international assessments. Recent research in the developing world suggests "a global trend toward greater use of assessment" (Braun and Kanjee, this volume), but also concedes that participation in studies like TIMSS and PIRLS is "a political decision...not taken lightly...because of concern about the consequences of poor performance" (Braun and Kanjee, this volume). Although assessments are unlikely ever to be conducted in states that face catastrophic educational deficits or widespread systemic breakdown, many countries may choose to adopt these assessment systems as they increase investment in their educational systems. It is to the advantage of donors to encourage participation, so as to evaluate the effectiveness of their investments.

Unfortunately, any move toward greater use of international assessments will have to take into account concerns about the information content of assessments, at least as they are currently conducted. Braun and Kanjee (this volume) point out that assessment data are not necessarily very reliable and may not have been gathered in valid ways. Factors unrelated to the education system itself, such as uneven participation in exam-preparation courses within countries, can affect results, and some students may not perform well on standardized tests even if they possess the relevant information.

Gradstein and Nikitin (2004) note other significant problems with using standardized tests as measures of school quality. For a given country, mastery of foreign languages or knowledge of history could be a more important focus of the education system and therefore a better indicator of quality than measures of literacy, science, and math. They add, "Schooling may instill social norms, develop work habits, and inculcate values…As has been noted in the literature, these factors may have various beneficial effects, such as on crime reduction, better informed fertility choices, political participation, etc" (2004: 3).

DOES IT MATTER?

"Not everything that can be counted counts, and not everything that counts can be counted."
—Albert Einstein

Commentary on the current shortcomings of international educational data can be separated into three types. Puryear identifies the first of these as an ideological belief that education is unquantifiable and that attempts to measure it "miss the point of what education is all about" (1995: 87). Although education is hard to measure, as the above analysis would suggest, it seems that this particular objection to measuring the quantity and quality of schooling is being eroded by mounting evidence of a relationship between education and development. Moreover, the difficulty in quantifying educational inputs and outputs does not mean that the endeavor is useless. Indeed, what has already been learned from tracking the consequences of increased education indicates that there are good returns on investment as well as private and public returns to health, gender equity, and income.

A second argument is that a lack of capacity and expertise is partially responsible for the variable quality of educational data. Lievesley (2001) points out that international statisticians are "constrained in what they can do about the quality of the data they receive." She explores the importance of capacity building to improve statistical skills in developing countries, and their potential to raise the quality of international data. As UNESCO argues, "The development and implementation of new indicators require time and national expertise, and these resources have to be balanced against those that support more immediate requirements for data. Trade-offs are inevitable, especially when many countries are still struggling to produce even the most basic monitoring information about their educational systems" (UNESCO, 2003). The UNESCO Institute for Statistics is developing several new indicators in the areas of literacy, adult education, measures of primary completion, early childhood, life skills, and out-of-school children.

Third, many argue that comparisons of educational inputs, processes, outputs, and outcomes across countries can be politically embarrassing and unpopular. In some cases this situation may lead to pressure to inflate statistics when they are provided for studies. For example, Jean Drèze and Amartya Sen (1995) refuse to use official data in their analysis of economic development in India, partly because of the incentive to government employees to report exaggerated figures. They compare data from the census and a National Sample Survey that suggest that only 40–42 percent of rural girls between ages 5 and 14 attend school, although official statistics state a gross enrollment rate of 98–99 percent. These points suggest that incentives work against the production of high-quality data on education.

Pressure to focus more resources on data and data analysis comes from a number of sources, including policymakers, investors, and those who use the educational system, and works through a number of pathways. Leaders and policymakers need data to make the case for educational investment and to direct that investment toward types of education that will have the greatest impact on an individual or society's future. Likewise, efforts to set goals for educational development at national and international levels require data both to set reasonable goals and to measure progress toward meeting these goals.

Data are essential to developing sound investment policies. Education programs may require evaluations of the effectiveness of new and existing investment in education, whether the investment is provided at a national level or contributed by international donors. In addition, more effective process information about the educational system allows limited resources to be deployed to greatest effect.

Demand can also come from the users of educational systems and the taxpayers who largely fund them, as internationally comparable data allow pressure to build for reform and increase accountability. Parents and students may also demand the publication of information that allows them to make informed choices among educational options offered.

Although most primary and secondary education continues to be purchased by governments, using public money, the chain of consumption is extended. It includes the state and its citizens, as well as parents and students. These groups have overlapping roles and interests in both the quantity and the quality of education, but none has absolute and clear responsibility for making decisions about when and whether to purchase education. Better information about the quality of education available helps all three groups in their decision making. For governments, accurate and comparable data enable robust assessment of the cost-effectiveness of the school system and evaluation of inputs and processes, and they provide for citizens some measure of how successfully taxes are being deployed. For parents and students, information about the quality of education may, depending on the design of the local system, help them to exercise choices that provide an impetus to improve quality across the board.

From the perspective of achieving universal basic and secondary education, a small set of indicators may be the most useful and applicable:

- Inputs: indicators of financing available for education (and its distribution); attendance figures at all stages of primary and secondary education to allow for trends in access to be accurately monitored
- Process: indicators that provide policymakers with a greater understanding of how schools can most effectively support desired learning; outputs class sizes and teacher qualifications, for example, are important indicators that are relatively easy to measure
- Outputs: measures of educational completion; international benchmarks of educational quality, especially focusing on the development of basic "building block" skills (reading, mathematical, and scientific literacy) and the development of desired competencies
- Outcomes: analyses showing the degree to which universal access will improve the health of a population, lower the birth rate, and enhance the economic prospects of poor children (Hannum and Buchmann, this volume; Bloom and Canning, 2004; and World Bank, 2000)

Of course, better information on educational outcomes will continue to provide a broad context for efforts to achieve UBASE by allowing governments, parents, and students to better understand the impact education has on individual lives and the effect that full primary and secondary schooling is likely to have on countries as they become increasingly highly skilled and knowledge rich.

Finally, it is important to recognize that even pervasive problems in the data on education do not make such data worthless—far from it. First, even very rough data can be useful if they shed some light on the concept they are intended to measure. For example, enrollment rates are clearly connected with countries' experiences in giving children access to education. Large disparities between one country and another likely indicate genuine differences. All of the indicators discussed in this chapter are useful for understanding the state of education, and they shed light on the direction in which countries need to move if they are to improve the quantity and quality of education. The disquieting problems cited above suggest that one should be cautious in reaching specific or narrow conclusions. Nevertheless, many of the trends indicated by these data are so overwhelming as to be indisputable.

Part 2: The Current State of Education Worldwide

This section sets out a snapshot of current global, regional, and national access to, engagement with, and outcomes from primary and secondary education. It examines three of the core sets of indicators of educational quantity, including both input and output measures, currently available to policymakers: UNESCO enrollment data and the Barro-Lee and Cohen-Soto datasets on educational attainment and completion.[34] It also analyzes recent progress toward achieving universal access to basic and secondary education, regionally and by gender, and considers some of the instruments designed to measure educational quality that are currently available and the insights these have provided.

First, I examine current net enrollment rates at the primary and secondary levels, using UNESCO data. This fundamental input measure is compared between countries and regions, to identify areas where progress toward universal enrollment is relatively strong and areas that lag behind the rest of the world.[35] Enrollments are also analyzed for gender disparity, to identify regions where girls continue to have significantly reduced access to education.

---

[34] As noted, despite the problems detailed above regarding the Barro-Lee and Cohen-Soto data, these datasets can still be useful, but conclusions derived from them must be handled with caution.

[35] Net enrollments (see footnote 15 for definition) are limited in the information they can offer, however. Net enrollment data may still include a large number of repeaters; for example, in Brazil, 26 percent of primary school children repeated their grades in 1997, and on average, Brazilian students repeat over two years of classes, which accounts for around one third of the average total time spent in school in the mid-1990s (Bloom and Cohen, 2002). Second, enrollment is an input, and therefore not necessarily linked to any educational outputs and long-term outcomes. Many children may be present to register at the start of the school year but never return to school again.

To enrich the global picture of education, the section examines data and trends in educational attainment (i.e., the percentage of children that have attended at least some of a given level of education), and completion of educational levels. It uses data from Barro and Lee and Cohen and Soto, which are described alongside other key indicators in Table 1. As a result of problems arising between the Cohen-Soto and Barro-Lee datasets, the snapshot of current worldwide progress toward universal access to primary and secondary education as presented here is necessarily partial and tentative.

Attainment and completion information, taken from the Barro-Lee dataset for 2000, and Cohen-Soto for 2001, with further comparisons against recent UNESCO information[36] is analyzed using methods similar to those used for UNESCO enrollment data. First, regional comparisons produce a basic picture of lagging and leading regions and countries, with respect to attainment and completion at the primary and secondary levels. Second, an analysis of gender disparity using Barro-Lee data adds to the enrollment-based information on gaps in educational access between boys and girls.

Series data for attainment and completion are further manipulated to produce information about trends in average attainment and completion rates since 1960, although much of this material is patchy and fraught with problems. The analysis later focuses specifically on trends in, and predictions for, low-income and low-attainment countries, where much work must be focused if universal access to basic and secondary education of good quality is to become a reality.

However, attainment and completion data do not measure skills obtained in school, and in particular give no indication of differences between countries in the quality of education available. This section therefore also includes information on the acquisition of core skills, as measured by the TIMSS 1999 and PIRLS 2001 programs at the primary level, and evidence of literacy, numeracy, and scientific understanding in 15 year-olds from the PISA 2000 dataset.

These data on quality contain some insights and provide greater context, particularly for some countries in developing regions where quantitative indicators suggest excellent progress toward universal education, at least at the primary level. However, the small-scale nature of these studies, and their concentration amongst OECD and developed countries, means that global

---

[36] Percentage distribution of population by educational attainment, UNESCO Institute for Statistics, December 2002.

conclusions on quality of education are impossible to develop, because most of the developing world is not represented within these studies of quality.

NEW ESTIMATES

Before focusing on education trends in specific countries and regions, it is helpful to first estimate the overall level of global educational access. A description of how the estimates for current and 2015 enrollment levels were made can be found in Appendix A. My calculations suggest that, judging by official enrollment statistics and UN population data, roughly 97 million children of primary school age and 226 million children of secondary school age (15 percent and 30 percent of the children in the world of those age groups, respectively) do not attend school.

A separate set of calculations leads me to estimate that if enrollment rates continue to change at the pace they did between 1990 and 2002, then, in 2015, 114 million children of primary school age will not be enrolled in school and 185 million of secondary school age will not be enrolled (17 percent and 24 percent of the relevant populations, respectively).[37]

An overall assessment of the quality of education can be made across a sample of 113 countries, using recent data and projecting data for 2015. The primary-age population for these countries in 1998 is approximately 640 million. Of this population, only about 33 to 34 million (5 percent) live in countries that score at or above the OECD level, using either TIMSS science or TIMSS math scores as the baseline. Using PIRLS as the baseline, approximately 155 million children (24 percent) live in countries scoring at or above the OECD level.

---

[37] The finding that recent rates of improvement in primary enrollment do not lead to predicted improvement in 2015—indeed, I foresee a worsening of the problem—probably results from offsetting factors such as rapid population growth in countries that are off track to meet education goals. In a positive direction, one would expect recent improvements to lead to fewer (or at least a lower percentage of) non-enrolled students in 2015. In the other direction, countries with fast-growing populations are often those with a range of socioeconomic problems and that have struggled with primary enrollment over many years; absent major changes, these struggles will continue. These factors combine to more than offset progress in other countries. The modest improvement predicted for secondary education may stem from the fact that secondary education enrollment rates are currently much lower than primary enrollment rates. In recent years, it has been easier to make significant progress where there is a further distance to the desired goal.

Projections for 2015 show a virtually unchanged quality divide. The relevant population grows to around 655 million children of primary school age. With TIMSS science as the baseline, about 32 million (5 percent) live in countries scoring at or above OECD levels (taking into account the fact that the OECD level will rise over time, as well). For TIMSS math and PIRLS, the numbers are approximately 28 million (4 percent) and 155 million (24 percent), respectively.[38]

NET ENROLLMENT

Overview

UNESCO data on net enrollments in primary education show that although total global progress toward universal access, as evidenced by this fundamental measure, is strong, several regions and many individual countries lag the rest of the world, some significantly. In some cases, equality of access to primary education is also a serious concern, particularly in those countries and regions where overall enrollment levels are relatively low.

Further, many of the countries where the most progress needs to be made are also those where the under-15 population is growing most rapidly; this places an even greater burden on systems and resources. Using only enrollment statistics and demographic projections, it appears that if

---

[38] To arrive at these estimates, I first regress country test scores on life expectancy and primary net enrollment. Life expectancy figures are from UN data, and test scores are from the organizations cited in this document. Using this regression, I generate a larger set of fitted values for countries with known net enrollment rates and life expectancies but in which students had not taken the standardized tests. For the sake of comparison, I fit all values, even for countries that had taken the test (so that I did not compare incompatible true values and fitted values). I then average the fitted scores for countries within the OECD, generating a "high quality" score. Using population data from the UN, I find the relevant population for each country (assuming primary schooling age of 6–11). Finally, I count the number of children living in countries where fitted values are at or above the OECD average, in an attempt to quantify the quality divide between rich and poor countries. Using the original regressions, projected net enrollment rates, and projected life expectancy figures, I make the same calculations for 2015. Projected life expectancy figures are from the UN. Projected net enrollment rates are calculated under the assumption that the change in enrollment rates between 1990 and 2000 is a good predictor of future change. In the case where 1990 or 2000 data are unavailable, the nearest year(s) possible are used in the calculation.

universal primary education is to be achieved by 2015, primary schools in developing countries will have an estimated 110 million more primary-age children to absorb than they did in 2000/2005—an increase of roughly one fifth. Sub-Saharan Africa and South Asia, the two regions with the lowest current enrollment figures, will account for the lion's share of this increase.

Access to secondary education is poor throughout most of the developing world, particularly in those regions where primary-level enrollments are low. Transfer rates between primary and secondary education in many countries appear to be low, which suggests two possible scenarios. First, many countries may be still be focusing on the delivery of universal primary education, which may limit secondary school infrastructure and resources. The sharp decline in data available for secondary-level enrollments supports this possibility. Second, the drop in primary as compared to secondary enrollments may occur where survival rates in primary education are poor, and registration at the primary level cannot be equated with any significant educational attainment. This possibility indicates the importance of using data beyond enrollment figures, including attainment rates, (especially) completion rates, and quality indicators where these are available, to develop a picture of outputs and outcomes.[39]

Data

The table in Appendix B uses UNESCO data to compare net enrollment at the primary and secondary levels. It also compares net enrollments by gender and calculates the extent of gender disparity in access to education where this occurs. Figures are for the most recent year available between 1998/99 and 2004/05. Data are available for 170 countries at the primary level, and 151 at the secondary level. Unlike other tables in this chapter, unweighted country averages are used.[40]

---

[39] Indeed, relying solely on net enrollment ratios is far from the ideal way to determine transfer rates from primary to secondary education because, by definition, this indicator does not count students who are out of the age range of a specific level of education. The best way to study transfer rates would be to examine the experience of specific cohorts of students, but I do not have data to support such a study. One personal communication from UNESCO suggests that transition rates in at least some countries are considerably higher than is implied by a comparison of primary and secondary net enrollment rates.

[40] It would be better to use weighted averages, but inconsistencies across countries in the designation of age groups for primary and secondary education, and the varied years for which the data are available, make weighting problematic.

Data for net enrollment rates are patchy. This lack of information is particularly marked at secondary level, across all regions and countries. One source suggests that the lack of data for India masks dropout rates of over 50 percent and the poorest rates of education among girls in South and East Asia (*Times of India*, 2004).

This section discusses regional and national data. Variation within countries is likely to be significant, as the poor, those living in rural areas, and disadvantaged ethnic groups are likely to have much lower enrollment rates than the population as a whole. Data on these variations, to the extent they exist, are available only from national agencies. Although such national data will be useful to policymakers seeking to expand access to education, they are beyond the scope of this study.

Primary Education

Globally, average net enrollment at the primary level is high. 86 percent of children[41] of primary school age are registered in school; within this population there is a 2-percentage-point gender disparity in favor of boys. Enrollment is strongest in the developed countries, where the average is 95 percent, with no gender disparity. Among developing world regions the strongest regions are Latin America/Caribbean, at 92 percent with a 1-percentage-point disparity in favor of boys; East Asia/Pacific, at 90 percent with a 2-percentage-point disparity in favor of boys; and Eastern Europe/Central Asia, at 90 percent with a 1-percentage-point disparity in favor of boys.

The picture is considerably less promising in Middle East/North Africa (an average of 85 percent net enrollment in primary school), South Asia (79 percent), and particularly in Sub-Saharan Africa (70 percent). 12 of the 15 countries in the sample that have overall primary enrollment rates below 60 percent are in Sub-Saharan Africa, and average access to school falls as low as 36 percent in Burkina Faso and 38 percent in Niger. No recent figures (1998/99 or later) are available for the Democratic Republic of Congo, Sierra Leone, or Uganda, so these countries are not included in the analysis.

The relationship between poor overall access to primary education and high levels of gender disparity is strong. The same three regions with the lowest enrollment rates have the greatest disparities in access between

---

[41] This figure is based on the unweighted average of the table in Appendix B. The more detailed analysis described above shows that 85 percent are unenrolled.

boys and girls, rising to a high of 6 percentage points on average in Sub-Saharan Africa. Some of the largest gender disparities are in countries where overall access to primary education is near or below 60 percent. These include Chad, (where the gender gap among enrolled students favors boys by 23 percentage points), Benin (22 percentage points), and Guinea-Bissau (16 percentage points). UNESCO reports that in 11 countries girls are 20 percent less likely to start school than boys; 7 of these countries are located in Sub-Saharan Africa (UNESCO, 2003). As the data table in Appendix B shows, among the 11 countries with the largest gaps in access, all in favor of boys, only 4 have total average enrollment rates of at least 70 percent.[42]

The UNESCO data may well hide even larger gender disparities. Herz and Sperling (2004), citing other sources, offer an array of figures that document the extent to which girls in South Asia and Sub-Saharan Africa, especially in poor and rural areas, fail to complete even the earliest grades. Further, the figures show that even when girls do complete early grades, they often emerge with very minimal skills.

Within every region there is considerable variation, both in overall enrollments at the primary level, and in terms of equality of access to education.

For example, in the Middle East/North Africa region, total enrollment levels and equality of access are highly variable. Although some countries, including Algeria, Jordan, Palestine, and Tunisia, have high overall registration in primary education and little gender disparity, others have high total enrollment but limited access for girls. Iraq falls in the latter category, with 98 percent enrollment for boys versus 83 percent for girls. According to a UNESCO report on progress in Arab states, gender parity in education has only been achieved to date in Bahrain, Jordan, Lebanon, Palestine, and the United Arab Emirates (UNESCO-UIS, 2002).

In South Asia, where overall enrollment figures are highly variable, ranging from 92 percent in the Maldives and 88 percent in India, to 70 percent in Nepal and 59 percent in Pakistan, equality of access to primary education is extremely mixed. Enrollment of girls exceeds that of boys in Bangladesh by 4 percentage points, but Pakistan, Nepal, and India have

---

42 These countries are: Togo (91 percent with a 16-percentage-point gender disparity), Yemen (72 percent with a 25-percentage-point gender disparity), Liberia (70 percent with an 18-percentage-point gender disparity), and Iraq (91 percent with a 15-percentage-point gender disparity).

disparities in favor of boys at the primary level of 18, 9, and 5 percentage points, respectively. As in Sub-Saharan Africa, figures for Pakistan and Nepal show that the relationship between relatively low enrollment and poor access to primary education for girls is strong. According to UNESCO estimates, 104 million children of primary school age are not enrolled in education, and 75 percent of these live in Sub-Saharan Africa and South Asia (UNESCO, 2003).

Secondary Education

Sixty-four percent of all children of secondary school age are enrolled in secondary education; this is 22 percentage points lower than at the primary level. (An additional 6 percent of secondary-school-age children are enrolled in primary school.) As with primary education, enrollments are highest in developed countries at 86 percent, where there is also a high transition rate from primary to secondary (a fall of 8 percentage points). In the developing world, levels of enrollment are generally extremely low. With the exception of Eastern Europe/Central Asia, where the average enrollment rate is 85 percent, more than one of every four children of secondary school age living in a developing country is not registered. In Sub-Saharan Africa (28 percent enrollment) and South Asia (48 percent), more than half of all secondary-school-age children are not enrolled.[43] A recent UNESCO report suggests that 19 of the 26 countries with less than 30 percent secondary-level enrollment are in Sub-Saharan Africa (UNESCO, 2003).

The contrast between enrollment at the primary and secondary levels is stark in many developing regions. In Sub-Saharan Africa, there is a gap of 42 percentage points between the two figures, and South Asia has a 31-percentage-point difference. The transfer from primary to secondary education is also far from smooth in East Asia/Pacific (a 34-percentage-point fall) and Latin America/Caribbean (23 percentage points), two regions with strong primary-level enrollments overall.

Many fewer countries provide data to UNESCO on enrollments at the secondary level than at the primary level; for example, Bangladesh and the Maldives are the only countries in South Asia to do so.

Within Sub-Saharan Africa, where overall registration is lowest, there are no data available for several countries, even for some with high enroll-

---

[43] Because of missing data at the secondary level, the figure for South Asia does not include enrollment in India or Pakistan.

ments at the primary level, including Gabon and Rwanda. In countries where data are available, the transfer to secondary education appears to be weak (although the cautions cited earlier about using enrollment rates as indicators of transfer are relevant here), even where access to primary education is relatively high. For example, an 82 percent primary registration rate in Tanzania contrasts with a 5 percent enrollment figure in secondary school, a decline of 77 percentage points. In Senegal, the difference is 69 percentage points. The results are similar in many countries, including Madagascar, Lesotho, Togo, Congo, Liberia, and Mauritania.

Gender disparity is, at the secondary level, much less marked than for the primary level, except where low overall enrollment masks gender disparity. UNESCO notes that considerable progress in gender equality was made in the 1990s; for example, Algeria, Malawi, Mauritania, Nepal, Niger, Pakistan, Rwanda, Sierra Leone, and Tunisia all gained over 0.2 points on the gender parity index[44] (UNESCO, 2003). However, total numbers of enrolled students are much smaller. Data show that on average in Sub-Saharan Africa, only about one in every four girls is enrolled in secondary education. Among all countries in the world, gender disparity in favor of boys is highest in Yemen, at 26 percentage points. However, at the secondary level there are also marked examples where more girls are enrolled in school than boys, a list led by Guyana (with a difference of 34 percentage points).

There is considerable variation in enrollment rates within every developing world region. In Latin America/Caribbean, eight countries—Anguilla, Argentina, Barbados, Chile, Cuba, Dominica, Grenada, and Saint Kitts and Nevis—have secondary enrollments above 80 percent. By contrast, 50 percent or more of all secondary-school-age children in the Dominican Republic, Ecuador, El Salvador, Guatemala, and Nicaragua are not registered in secondary school, although primary-level enrollment is above 80 percent in all five of these countries. This region also includes six of the eleven highest gender disparities in favor of girls at the secondary level, suggesting that completion of basic education and successful transition to secondary school is elusive to many boys.

East Asia/Pacific, which also has generally high primary enrollment levels, presents a similar picture. Niue is the only country with average secondary-level enrollment over 80 percent, and fewer than 50 percent

---

[44] The gender parity index is defined as the ratio of female to male values of a given indicator.

of secondary-school-age children in Cambodia, Laos, Myanmar, Papua New Guinea, and Vanuatu are registered in secondary school, although primary enrollments are above 80 percent in all except Papua New Guinea (where primary enrollment is 74 percent). Cambodia, Laos, and Papua New Guinea also have the highest gender disparity of access in the region in favor of boys, at 11, 6, and 6 percentage points respectively. These are not the highest rates of gender disparity, however, as Mongolia, the Philippines, and Tonga report gender disparities in favor of girls of 11, 11, and 10 percentage points, respectively.

EDUCATIONAL ATTAINMENT—CURRENT POSITION

Overview

The Barro-Lee and Cohen-Soto datasets show that attainment[45] in primary education is widespread, but some regions and countries lag behind. Leaders and laggards are the same as for net enrollment data. In most regions, data extrapolated from Barro-Lee and Cohen-Soto suggest that developing regions are making some progress toward universal primary education. By contrast, but also in common with net enrollment, attainment rates at the secondary level are low throughout the developing world, particularly in regions that lag for other indicators.

Gender disparity in attainment is strong at both the primary and secondary levels, and for the 15–24 year-old cohort as well as the 25+ population. Strong attainment gaps in favor of boys are most common in developing regions where disparity is strongest in enrollments, particularly East Asia/Pacific and South Asia, although small group sample sizes may affect regional averages in some cases (notably Eastern Europe/Central Asia).

Data

Both the Barro-Lee and Cohen-Soto data on primary- and secondary-level attainment for the 25+ population were considered in this analysis. The samples are not identical; Barro and Lee include 104 countries and Cohen and Soto, 95. In addition, a comparison was also made of extrapolated data for the 15–24 year-old cohort on primary and secondary attainment, using the Barro-Lee and Cohen-Soto datasets for the 15+

---

[45] Attainment is defined as having participated in some education at a given level. It does not imply completion.

and 25+ populations.[46] These data are not analyzed except at the regional level, owing to considerable discrepancies and inconsistencies. Even at the regional level, great caution must be exercised in interpreting the results because of data problems discussed above.

Figure 5 uses data from the Barro-Lee dataset to compare primary attainment between regions, for both the 25+ population and the 15–24 year-old cohort. Figure 6 makes similar comparisons for secondary attainment.

Figure 7 considers regional patterns of gender disparity in primary and secondary attainment for the 25+ population, using information from the Barro-Lee dataset. An additional table, available online, compares extrapolated data for the 15–24 year-old cohort on gender disparity at the primary and secondary levels, using the Barro-Lee datasets for the 15+ and 25+ populations.

Primary Education

At the global level, the datasets broadly agree on attainment levels in primary education among the 25+ population, with roughly three in four people worldwide having spent some time in school at the basic level. Extrapolation for the 15–24 year-old cohort further suggests that this indicator of educational access is rising at the global level, although the datasets do not agree on how sharp this increase is.[47]

As shown in Figure 5, attainment at the primary level is strongest in developed countries, reaching near-universal participation in some basic education among the 15–24 year-old population. In the developing world, attainment rates are highly variable, and follow a similar pattern to net enrollment (see the data table in Appendix B); Latin America, Caribbean, East Asia/Pacific, and Eastern Europe/Central Asia all have relatively high levels of attainment, and the Middle East/North Africa, South Asia, and Sub-Saharan Africa regions lag. Regionally, extrapolation for the 15–24 year-old cohort shows considerable improvements over the total population in attainment for all developing regions.[48]

---

[46] Full country-level comparison tables for both datasets, for primary and secondary attainment in both the 25+ population and the 15–24 year-old cohort, are available online at http://www.amacad.org/projects/ubase.aspx.

[47] Barro-Lee data suggest 81 percent have some attainment; Cohen-Soto data suggest 95 percent.

[48] An exception is the Barro-Lee data for Sub-Saharan Africa, which suggest little change.

Figure 5: Primary Attainment, Year 2000 (Barro and Lee Data)

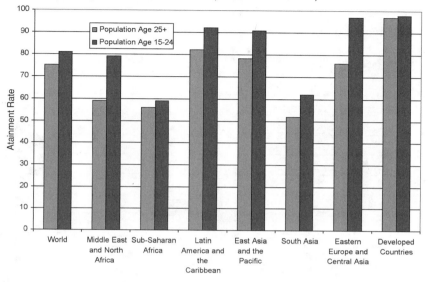

Source: Barro and Lee (2000), with data extrapolated for population age 15–24.

The Barro-Lee dataset shows widespread gender disparity in attainment rates in primary education in the 25+ population (see Figure 7), but also in the extrapolated data for the 15–24 year-old cohort. This large disparity is in sharp contrast to the narrow gap in favor of boys observed globally for net enrollments shown in the data table in Appendix B. Disparity is negligible in the developed countries, but Figure 7 shows particularly weak levels of female participation in some basic education in South Asia (38 percent), Middle East/North Africa (47 percent), and Sub-Saharan Africa (48 percent). There is also a marked disparity in East Asia/Pacific, where male primary attainment is 21 percentage points higher than that of females, although both male and female figures are much higher than in these other regions. Data weaknesses make even regional analysis for the 15–24 year-old cohort inadvisable.

Secondary Education

As with net enrollment data, secondary-level attainment shows a sharp decline globally compared with primary education, according to both datasets. Figure 6 shows that while three in four of the 25+ population have participated in some basic education, fewer than one in two has participated in secondary education. Although data suggest some improvement among the 15–24 year-old group, global figures stand at just over 50 percent of the cohort.

Figure 6: Secondary Attainment, Year 2000 (Barro and Lee Data)

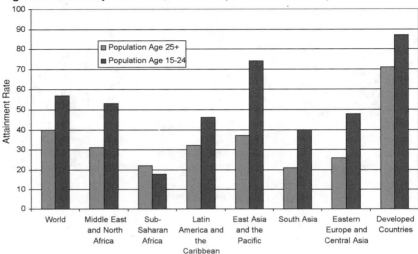

Source: Barro and Lee (2000), with data extrapolated for population age 15–24.

Figure 7: Gender Disparity in Primary and Secondary Attainment (Population Age 25+, Year 2000)

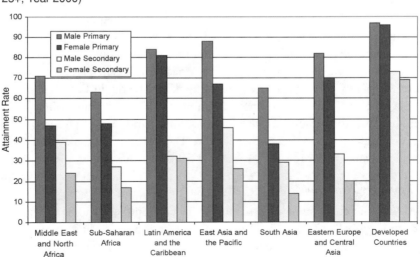

Source: Barro and Lee (2000).

In every region of the developing world, secondary attainment is extremely low for the 25+ population, particularly in Sub-Saharan Africa and South Asia. Barro-Lee data also find that only 71 percent of all adults over age 25 have participated in some secondary education. Extrapolated data suggest this has improved dramatically in some regions, particularly East Asia/Pacific, but that the situation is stagnant, or worsening, in Sub-Saharan Africa.

The Barro-Lee dataset shows strong gender disparity for the 25+ and the 15–24 year-old populations in terms of secondary-level attainment, similar to the disparity it shows for primary education, as shown in Figure 7. Although extrapolated data show that participation in secondary schooling rises by almost 20 percentage points for the younger cohort, the gender gap in favor of boys remains constant at 20 percentage points.

EDUCATIONAL COMPLETION—CURRENT POSITION

Overview

Patterns of regional leaders and laggards in completion[49] at the primary and secondary levels are broadly similar to patterns of both net enrollment and attainment. Further, data for primary-level completion suggest significant recent improvement, with the exceptions of South Asia and Sub-Saharan Africa. Improvements in secondary-level completion rates are hard to assess, given that many in the 15–24 year-old cohort are not yet old enough to have graduated.

Patterns of gender disparity in completion rates broadly mirror those observed for attainment and enrollment. Disparity tends to be strongest in favor of boys in East Asia/Pacific and South Asia.

Data

As with the attainment data, the Barro-Lee and Cohen-Soto datasets on primary- and secondary-level completion for the 25+ population were compared, regionally, and by country,[50] and data were extrapolated on primary completion for the 15–24 year-old cohort, using both datasets.

---

[49] Completion is defined as having finished a given level of education.

[50] As is the case with attainment data, the samples are not identical: Barro-Lee data include 104 countries and Cohen-Soto include 95.

These data are not analyzed except at the regional level, owing to considerable discrepancies and inconsistencies.[51]

Figure 8 uses data from the Barro-Lee dataset to compare primary
attainment between regions, for both the 25+ population and the 15–24
year-old cohort. Figure 9 shows secondary completion for the 25+ population.

Figure 10 considers regional patterns of gender disparity in primary
and secondary completion for the 25+ population, using information
from the Barro-Lee dataset. An additional table, available online, compares extrapolated data for the 15–24 year-old cohort on gender disparity
at the primary level, using the Barro-Lee datasets for the 15+ and 25+
populations.[52]

Primary Education

At the global level, Barro-Lee data show that roughly one person in two
over age 25 has completed primary education (see Figure 8); Cohen-
Soto data show higher overall figures, at 66 percent. When data are
extrapolated for the 15–24 year-old cohort, both datasets suggest rises in
primary completion, Barro-Lee to 66 percent, and Cohen-Soto to 82
percent.

Completion rates are, by definition, lower than attainment rates.[53]
However, similar patterns are discernible for primary-level completion in
the 25+ population as for enrollment and attainment. Broadly, Eastern
Europe/Central Asia, East Asia/Pacific, and Latin America/Caribbean
lead the developing world, while South Asia, Sub-Saharan Africa, and to a
lesser extent, the Middle East/North Africa lag.

Extrapolation for the 15–24 year-old cohort produces some extreme
differences between the datasets at regional level, but progress in completion rates is observable for most cases. In particular, both datasets suggest
improvement of at least 20 percentage points in Middle East/North

---

[51] Full country-level comparison tables for both datasets, for primary completion
in both the 25+ population and the 15–24 year-old cohort (primary only), are
available online, at http://www.amacad.org/projects/ubase.aspx.

[52] The country-level data on gender disparity in both attainment and completion
are available online, at http://www.amacad.org/projects/ubase.apsx.

[53] A student is considered to have "attained" a level of education by virtue of
having begun to study at that level, whereas "completion" requires finishing
the level. Anyone who has completed a level education has also attained it, but
not vice versa.

Figure 8: Primary Completion, Year 2000 (Population Age 25+)

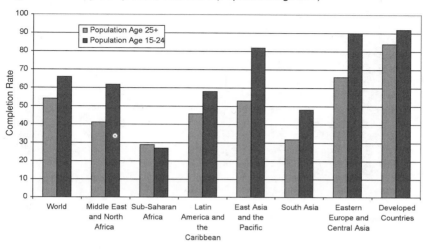

Source: Barro and Lee (2000), with data extrapolated for population age 15–24.

Africa,[54] and both figures for Eastern Europe/Central Asia indicate that primary-level completion has reached near-universal levels among the younger group.

As with attainment, Barro-Lee data show strong gender disparity in completion levels for primary education—13 percentage points in the 25+ population. Extrapolated data for the 15–24 year-old cohort show no improvement at the global level. Once again, although the disparity is negligible in developed countries and Latin America/Caribbean, gaps in favor of boys are particularly strong in South and East Asia, as well as the Middle East/North Africa.

Secondary Education

Global completion rates at the secondary level for the 25+ population are extremely low, at 24 (Barro-Lee) or 28 (Cohen-Soto) percent. In developed countries, completion of secondary education is placed at 49 (Barro-Lee) or 66 (Cohen-Soto) percent of the total population. As with other quantitative indicators, Sub-Saharan Africa and South Asia lag the rest of the world, as shown in Figure 9.

---

[54] Extrapolated completion rates for Middle East/North Africa are 62 (Barro-Lee) and 77 percent (Cohen-Soto).

Figure 9: Secondary Completion, Year 2000 (Population Age 25+)

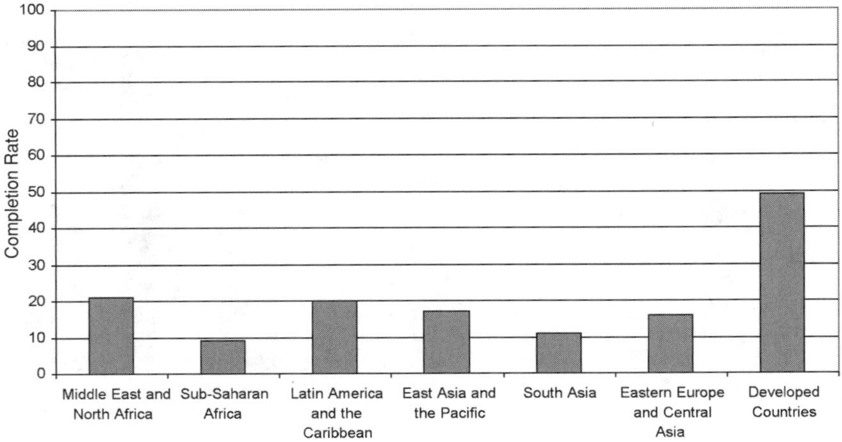

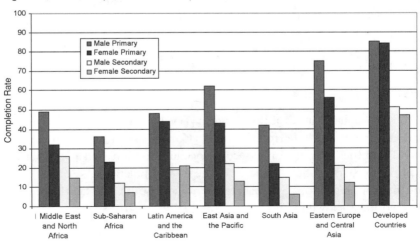

Source: Barro and Lee (2000).

Globally, gender disparity in completion is less marked for secondary than primary education among the 25+ population, and it mirrors the weak gaps in favor of boys for secondary-level attainment, as shown in Figure 10.

Figure 10: Gender Disparity in Primary and Secondary Completion (Population Age 25+, Year 2000)

Source: Barro and Lee (2000).

TRENDS IN ATTAINMENT AND COMPLETION

Trends in attainment and completion rates tend to mirror trends in enrollment. Regional leaders and laggards remain much the same.[55]

Data

The analysis considered data from the Barro-Lee and Cohen-Soto datasets relating to trends in primary and secondary attainment and completion. Trend data on primary and secondary attainment between 1990 and 2000 for the 15–24 year-old cohort were calculated. A selection of these calculations are used in the figures below, and full tables are available online. Additional analyses considered primary and secondary attainment and completion rates for each decade from 1960 and 1990; these tables are available online.

Figure 11 presents data for low-income countries, showing changes in primary attainment rates, for the 15–24 year-old cohort over the decade 1990–2000.

Figure 12 uses the percentage-point increase in primary- and secondary-level attainment from 1990 to 2000 to project attainment in 2015 for the 25+ population.

Tests run for both datasets, and for both attainment and completion rates, suggest reasonably high positive correlations with the share of the population that lives in urban areas.

Trends in Attainment Levels, 1990–2000

Primary-level attainment rates in developed countries, East Asia/Pacific, and Latin America/Caribbean were already very high in 1990, and most countries showed no change or only a very small improvement throughout the subsequent decade. Figure 11 shows percentage-point increase or decrease in primary attainment over the period for developing countries. In the Middle East/North Africa region, improvements at the primary level were slightly larger and several countries had improvements of over 10 percentage points. The largest improvements in primary attainment overall are seen in South Asia, although there is disagreement between datasets over the scale of progress. The Eastern Europe/Central Asia

---

[55] Goujon and Lutz (2004) present a new methodology for assessing a population's educational achievements over time. They account for demographic change and the future effect of educational achievement on fertility rates.

Figure 11: Changes in Primary Attainment, 1990–2000

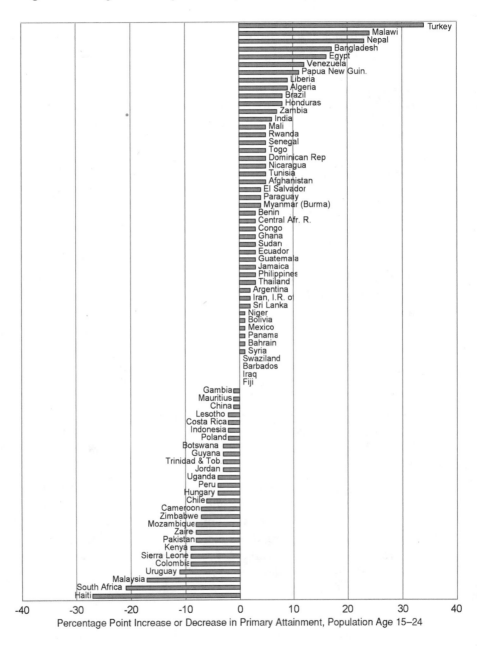

Source: Data extrapolated from Barro and Lee (2000).

dataset is small, but overall there appears to be a slight decrease in primary attainment.

In Sub-Saharan Africa, progress is patchy; some countries show significant increases or decreases, and others show little or no change. According to the Barro-Lee data, 16 of 26 countries in Sub-Saharan Africa show increases or decreases of 5 percent or less in primary attainment rates between 1990 and 2000. Among the remaining countries, a few show large improvements but seven countries show decreases in attainment, with the greatest decrease in South Africa at 21 percentage points.

At the secondary level, more countries in the developed group, East Asia/Pacific region, and Latin America/Caribbean region show some improvement, but there are also some significant decreases in attainment, in Kuwait (18 percentage points, Barro-Lee) and Hong Kong (27 percentage points, Barro-Lee). There are large discrepancies between datasets for a number of countries in these regions, and although there are large (and likely improbable) decreases in attainment in West Germany and Switzerland according to Cohen-Soto, and in Singapore according to Barro-Lee, in each of these countries the other dataset suggests little or no change, precluding reliable conclusions.

The Eastern Europe/Central Asia dataset shows moderate improvements at the secondary level. In both South Asia and Sub-Saharan Africa, improvements in secondary attainment are weaker than in primary attainment.

Trends in Attainment Levels, 1960–2000

Attainment at the primary level has in general improved steadily since 1960. The two datasets are generally in agreement, increasing confidence in the data. Most developed countries, with high levels of attainment, show low levels of progress. In Eastern Europe/Central Asia, Turkey stands out as making larger improvements than other countries in the region. Improvements appear to be greatest in the Middle East/North Africa and East Asia/Pacific. Improvement is mixed in Sub-Saharan Africa.[56]

---

[56] For example, very little improvement is seen in Mali and Niger—both countries improve by 11 percentage points (Barro-Lee) and 9 percentage points (Cohen-Soto) over the period measured. At the other end of the range, substantial percentage point improvements have taken place in Kenya (44 points (Barro-Lee) and 55 points (Cohen-Soto)) and Zambia (49 (Barro-Lee) and 41 (Cohen-Soto)) over the period measured.

The trends in secondary attainment over the forty-year period show a different pattern, with the highest overall gains in developed countries and somewhat lower improvements in other regions. The least improvement occurs in Sub-Saharan Africa. Among the developed countries, Finland and Korea achieve total improvements of over 60 percentage points in both datasets during the period measured. However, the data for Australia, Canada, Denmark, New Zealand, and West Germany all show very large (and likely improbable) discrepancies between datasets.

In developing countries, gains are observable in East Asia/Pacific, Middle East/North Africa, and Latin America/Caribbean, although a few countries show very low levels of progress: Myanmar shows a total improvement of 7 percentage points (Barro-Lee) and 16 percentage points (Cohen-Soto) over the period measured, and Haiti and Guatemala show total improvement of approximately 10 percentage points in both datasets.

Gains in South Asia are also substantially lower than in developed countries, ranging from 24 percentage points (Barro-Lee) in Sri Lanka, to a 2-percentage-point decline in Afghanistan. The weakest improvements are in Sub-Saharan Africa, where 14 countries show total gains of less than 10 percentage points in both datasets. A few countries in this region do show large improvements, with the highest figures in Zimbabwe (total percentage-point improvement of 32 (Barro-Lee) and 30 (Cohen-Soto) over the period measured).

Figure 12: Attainment in 2015 at Current Rate of Change (for Population Age 25+)

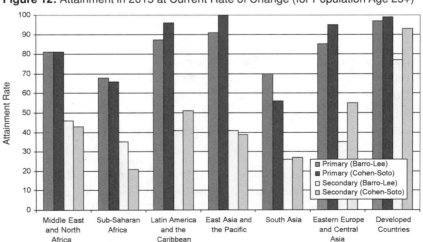

Source: Barro and Lee (2000) and Cohen and Soto (2001).

Figure 12 shows projected primary and secondary attainment rates for the 25+ population in 2015, based on progress by country during the 1990s. This information shows the slow rate at which improvements in this key quantitative indicator of universal basic and secondary education affect education stock in the total population.

Trends in Completion Levels, 1990–2000

As with attainment levels, many countries saw increased primary- and secondary-level completion during the 1990s. There were few increases in completion rates in the developed world, presumably due to high levels of completion before 1990. For some developing countries, increases were extremely high, which at face value suggests a decade of significant progress; however, discrepancies between datasets make firm conclusions very hard to draw.[57]

Comparisons suggest that information generated from the datasets does not agree consistently on which countries and regions had worsening completion rates over the 1990 to 2000 period.[58] The most positive and definite point that can be made about the two tables is that there are many fewer countries where either or both sets of data indicate declining levels of primary completion for the 15–24 year-old cohort than countries where one or both indicate progress in completion rates.

Trends in Completion Levels, 1960–2000

As with similar attainment data, average completion rates for all countries at the primary level for each decade from 1960 to 1990 among the 25+ population show reasonably steady progress over the period. Both Barro-Lee and Cohen-Soto suggest a slight stagnation between 1980 and 1990. Data for individual countries show much more significant advances and stagnations. Thailand shows relatively slow progress (Cohen-Soto) and negative development (Barro-Lee) in the 1960s and 1970s, but a large leap in the 1980s—31 (Barro-Lee) and 60 (Cohen-Soto) percentage

---

[57] For example, Barro-Lee records a 5-percentage-point improvement in primary completion rates over the decade in Bangladesh, compared with a 46-percentage-point improvement according to Cohen-Soto. Similarly, for Venezuela, Barro-Lee suggests a 52-percentage-point improvement in primary level completion, while Cohen-Soto finds just 19.

[58] For example, while Barro-Lee suggests a decrease in primary completion rates of 44 percentage points for Singapore, Cohen-Soto finds an improvement of 7 percentage points.

points—with further increases in the 1990s. These data, along with others in the table, not only show significant discrepancies between datasets, but also suggest decadal changes that are too extreme to be plausible, given that the information is for the 25+ population, not individual cohorts.

On a worldwide basis, trends in secondary-level completion from 1960 to 1990 are similar to those trends seen in primary education. The average steady upward trend for all countries is similar to progress in primary and secondary attainment.

Although discrepancies in the data and between datasets make it hard to draw firm conclusions, the data suggest that progress toward higher secondary completion rates may be particularly slow in some parts of Sub-Saharan Africa.[59] Tentative though this evidence is, it fits with the picture of Sub-Saharan Africa lagging the rest of the developing world— on every indicator from enrollments to trends in completion rates.

INDICATORS OF EDUCATIONAL QUALITY

Overview

Although TIMSS, PIRLS, and PISA are all limited by the small number of countries included in the studies and their strong bias toward the developed world, they do offer some useful evidence about the quality of educational outputs for three core skills at the primary and secondary level.

All three indicators suggest that the quality of educational outputs is generally higher in developed countries. Recent studies by both Barro and Lee and Hanushek and Kimko find a positive relationship between test scores and growth rates of real per capita GDP (cited in Barro and Lee, 2000). PISA data suggest that 43 percent of variations among countries' mean scores for reading, numeracy, and scientific understanding at the secondary level can be predicted on the basis of their GDP per capita (OECD/UNESCO-UIS, 2003). This correlation is further supported by the TIMSS and PIRLS data in Tables 2 and 3.

With the exception of Eastern Europe/Central Asia, relatively low levels of literacy, numeracy, and scientific understanding are demonstrated in all developing countries included in the dataset. This gap is particularly

---

[59] For example, Cohen-Soto data suggest improvements in secondary level attainment rates for Kenya at between 2 and 6 percentage points each decade, but improvements in completion rates between 0 and 1 percentage point.

striking in the PIRLS and PISA data available for Latin America/Caribbean countries, where mean performances in tests are poor, compared with enrollment and attainment rates.

Data

Table 2 sets out mean scores on standardized tests in science and math for Grade 8 equivalent students in 38 countries. 45 percent of these countries are in the developed world, 32 percent are from Eastern Europe/Central Asia, and 10 percent each are from East Asia/Pacific and Middle East/North Africa. No country in South Asia is included, and from Latin America/Caribbean and Sub-Saharan Africa, only Chile and South Africa respectively have participated. Mean scores are ranked from highest to lowest, and for math, gender disparity in achievement is also recorded.

Table 3 sets out mean scores on standardized tests in reading for Grade 4 equivalent students in 35 countries. 49 percent of these countries are in the developed world, 34 percent are from Eastern Europe/Central Asia, and 8 percent each are from Latin America/Caribbean and Middle East/North Africa. No country in Sub-Saharan Africa, South Asia, or East Asia/Pacific (other than those in the developed world group) is included. Mean scores are ranked from highest to lowest, and gender disparity in achievement is also recorded.

These data are compared with results from PISA 2000, a study that tested between 4,500 and 10,000 15 year-old students in 43 countries (OECD/UNESCO-UIS, 2003). PISA includes assessment in three core forms of literacy—reading, numeracy, and scientific understanding—as well as background questionnaires on issues including family background and attitudes toward study.

Of the countries included in this study, 28 are members of the OECD, and of those that are not, three—Hong Kong, Israel, and Liechtenstein—are in the developed world group. 21 percent of the PISA sample is from Eastern Europe/Central Asia, 12 percent from Latin America/Caribbean, and 5 percent from East Asia/Pacific. No country in South Asia, Middle East/North Africa, or Sub-Saharan Africa is included.

Of the world's 10 most populous countries, TIMSS includes four (the United States, Indonesia, Russia, and Japan), PIRLS includes two (the United States and Russia), and PISA includes five (the United States, Indonesia, Brazil, Russia, and Japan). China will be included in future PISA studies. This gives a sense of the limited scope of these test-based

Table 2: TIMSS Math and Science Test Scores (with Gender Differences for Math)

Math			Science	
Country	Score	M – F	Country	Score
Singapore	604	2	Taiwan	569
Korea, Rep of	587	5	Singapore	568
Taiwan	585	NA	Hungary	552
Hong Kong	582	-2	Japan	550
Japan	579	8	Korea, Rep of	549
Belgium (Flemish)	558	-4	Netherlands	545
Netherlands	540	5	Australia	540
Slovakia	534	5	Czech Republic	539
Hungary	532	6	England	538
Canada	531	3	Finland	535
Slovenia	530	1	Slovakia	535
Russian Federation	526	1	Belgium (Flemish)	535
Australia	525	2	Slovenia	533
Finland	520	3	Canada	533
Czech Republic	520	17	Hong Kong	530
Malaysia	519	-5	Russian Federation	529
Bulgaria	511	0	Bulgaria	518
Latvia	505	5	United States	515
United States	502	7	New Zealand	510
England	496	19	Latvia	503
New Zealand	491	-7	Italy	493
Lithuania	482	3	Malaysia	492
Italy	479	9	Lithuania	488
Cyprus	476	-4	Thailand	482
Romania	472	-5	Romania	472
Moldova	469	3	Israel	468
Thailand	467	-4	Cyprus	460
Israel	466	16	Moldova	459
Tunisia	448	25	Macedonia	458
Macedonia	447	0	Jordan	450
Turkey	429	2	Iran	448
Jordan	428	-7	Indonesia	435
Iran	422	24	Turkey	433
Indonesia	403	5	Tunisia	430
Chile	392	9	Chile	420
Philippines	345	-15	Philippines	345
Morocco	337	17	Morocco	323
South Africa	275	16	South Africa	243

Note: Scores are for students in Grade 8, for most countries.
Source: Data are from TIMSS 1999. http://timss.bc.edu.

indicators of educational quality in capturing a global picture of the out-puts of education, particularly with regards to the developing world and its poorest regions in South Asia and Sub-Saharan Africa.

TIMSS Results

Mean math scores (Table 2) show a striking division between quality of educational outputs at the primary level in developed and developing countries. Of the top 10 countries for math, 7 are from the developed world group, and developing countries form the whole bottom 10. There is a difference of 170 points (from a total possible score of 800) between average test scores for the top and bottom 10 countries. These results are significant, both statistically and practically. Scores from the 95th percentile of the lowest-scoring nation, South Africa, roughly corre-spond with scores from the 5th percentile of the highest-scoring nation, Singapore (these scores are 485 and 464, respectively) (IEA, 2000). The results are similar for science, although the gap between average scores for the top and bottom 10 countries is slightly narrower, at 150 points. Four countries have average test scores of below 400 for math (Chile, Morocco, the Philippines, and South Africa), and three have sub-400 averages for science (Morocco, the Philippines, and South Africa).

In both subjects, developed countries in East Asia score particularly well; they represent the entire top 5 for math, and 4 of the top 5 for sci-ence. This dominance is also observed at the secondary level in the PISA assessments, where students in Hong Kong, Japan, and Korea display the highest overall performances in both math and science (OECD/UNESCO-UIS, 2003). Malaysia also ranks relatively well for math, at 16th, 86 points behind Singapore's mean score and ahead of several developed countries including England, New Zealand, and the United States. Other scores for East Asia/Pacific countries are much lower; in particular, Indonesia is in the bottom 5 countries for math and the bottom 10 for science.

Performance for countries in the Eastern Europe/Central Asia region is extremely mixed. Although the Czech Republic, Hungary, Slovakia, and Slovenia all rank in the top 15 countries in math and science with scores in the mid- and low-500s, Macedonia, Moldova, Romania, and Turkey are all in the bottom 15 for both subjects with scores in the mid-and low-400s. In math, there is a difference of 105 points between Slova-kia's mean score and Turkey's, and in science the gap is 119 between Hungary and Turkey.

The few countries included in the TIMSS program from other developing world regions score relatively poorly in both subjects, always within the bottom 10 countries. The bottom 4 countries are identical across science and math rankings. Further, there is a wide spread of scores within the bottom 5 countries. In math, for example, there is a difference of 128 points between Indonesia and South Africa's mean scores, and the gap is even wider for science.

Gender disparity in math scores is markedly in favor of boys in most countries, reaching a high of 25 percentage points in Tunisia, and is extremely distinct in some developed countries as well, including England at 19 percentage points and Israel at 16 percentage points. The pattern of better achievement in math among males generally continues at the secondary level.[60] In a few countries girls score better on average than boys, but the difference is less striking, except in the Philippines, where the gap is 15 percentage points in favor of girls (OECD/UNESCO-UIS, 2003).

PIRLS Results

Table 3 shows a similar (although slightly less marked than for math and science) contrast in quality of educational outputs at the primary level for reading between developed and developing countries. Six of the top ten countries are in the developed world group, and 9 of the bottom 10 are developing countries. The gap between the mean test score for Sweden, the top-ranked country, and Belize at the bottom of the list, is 234 points (where the total possible score is 800 points), and three countries (Belize, Kuwait, and Morocco) have an average reading score below 400.

Mean scores in Eastern Europe/Central Asia countries are, as with TIMSS scores for math and science, extremely mixed, ranging from 551 in Bulgaria (the 3rd ranked country), to 442 in Macedonia (29th), a gap of 109 points. Some countries that score relatively well in math and science show similar results for reading, including Bulgaria, the Czech Republic, Hungary, Latvia, Lithuania, and Russia, while others, notably Macedonia and Turkey, rank consistently in the bottom 10 for all three subjects, with average scores in the mid- and low-400s.

As with TIMSS scores, countries taking part in PIRLS from other developing regions all score relatively poorly for reading skills, ranking in the

---

[60] For example, the 7-percentage-point disparity in favor of boys observed in TIMSS scores for the United States is repeated at age 15 in the PISA math assessment (OECD/UNESCO-UIS, 2003).

Table 3: PIRLS Reading Test Scores and Gender Differences

Country	Overall Score	Gender Diff. (M – F)	Country	Overall Score	Gender Diff. (M – F)
Sweden	561	-22	Greece	524	-21
Netherlands	554	-15	Slovakia	518	-16
England	553	-22	Iceland	512	-19
Bulgaria	551	-24	Romania	512	-14
Latvia	545	-22	Israel	509	-22
Canada	544	-17	Slovenia	502	-22
Lithuania	543	-17	Norway	499	-21
Hungary	543	-14	Cyprus	494	-24
United States	542	-18	Moldova	492	-25
Italy	541	-8	Turkey	449	-19
Germany	539	-13	Macedonia	442	-21
Czech Republic	537	-12	Colombia	422	-12
New Zealand	529	-27	Argentina	420	-18
Scotland	528	-17	Iran	414	-27
Singapore	528	-24	Kuwait	396	-48
Russian Federation	528	-12	Morocco	350	-20
Hong Kong	528	-19	Belize	327	-27
France	525	-11			

Note: Scores are for students in Grade 4, for most countries.
Source: Data are from PIRLS 2001. http://timss.bc.edu.

bottom 6 places in the table. Scores for the 2 countries included in both TIMSS and PIRLS are also similarly placed relative to others, in the low-400s for all three subjects. Poor scores in reading skills for all three Latin America/Caribbean countries included are particularly notable, because this is a developing region where access to (see the table in Appendix B), and attainment of (see Figure 5) primary education are high. However, completion rates (see Figure 8) are lower than enrollment and attainment rates for this region, which, combined with the small amount of evidence provided by PIRLS data, suggests that the quality of education in some countries in this region may be limited.

Gender disparity in mean reading scores at the primary level is universally, and in many cases very strongly, in favor of female students. There is no relationship between position in the ranking and the extent of girls' ascendancy in this subject. As with math and science, a pattern of disparity continues at the secondary level; PISA data also show significantly better performance by females across its sample for reading, rising to a gap of 58 percent in Albania (OECD/UNESCO-UIS, 2003). In many cases where data are available for both PIRLS and PISA, gender disparity in reading attainment tends to widen between primary and secondary levels.

Conclusion

The picture of progress toward UBASE offered by these data remains blurred and partial, and forecasting achievement of the Millennium Development Goal is all but impossible. Inconsistencies in basic data generate difficulties in understanding education systems; these difficulties are exacerbated by the limited range of available indicators, particularly of processes and outcomes.

The Barro-Lee and Cohen-Soto datasets, via their measurement of the 25+ and 15+ populations, give an indication of overall progress in education, but an assessment of the stocks of educational attainment and completion within the adult population does not in itself contribute to a clearer understanding of universal access to, and completion of, primary and secondary education. The Barro-Lee and Cohen-Soto data show very high intersource discrepancies, as well as internal inconsistencies that emerge when data are manipulated to produce figures for a particular cohort. Using these data to identify progress toward universal attainment and completion at the primary and secondary levels, and to assess the extent of gender disparity for these measures, is hazardous. Although firm conclusions are hard to draw, observable general regional patterns confirm that progress toward UBASE remains weakest in South Asia and Sub-Saharan Africa.

Enrollment data, too, have their weaknesses. First, UNESCO data rely heavily on country estimates, which can lead to poor-quality information where schools are funded on the basis of total enrollments. Further, information is not always available for the most recent school year, may be contaminated by students repeating grades, and includes those who register but never spend time in school. More important, enrollment does not measure any outcome of an educational system, so it needs to be considered alongside other data in order to provide even a rudimentary picture of progress or the current situation.

A combination of enrollment and completion data on a cohort-by-cohort basis could provide an effective measure of progress in getting children into and through school, but would still lack important information on the quality of education. Indicators like TIMSS, PIRLS, and PISA currently provide estimates of quality, but only for a limited group of countries, and with very few reference points for the developing world. The information that is available for the developing world suggests that the quality of educational outputs in these countries, including those that have high levels of net enrollment, is generally poor by comparison with the developed world. Increasing the scope of these indicators could be extremely useful in sharpening the picture of disparity in educational quality.

Higher quality input measures and more widespread output statistics are necessary, but not sufficient, for making well-informed policy decisions to improve educational quality. One missing and necessary link is data on educational processes. Effective policy depends upon not only a sound foundation of knowledge but also political will and resources. Data linking education inputs to economic, health, and other developmental outcomes are necessary for the continued mobilization of scarce resources for education.

Part 3: Implications for the Future

FINDINGS

Primary and secondary education—in both developed and developing countries—have been the object of substantial, if insufficient, data collection efforts. These data are examined in this chapter using a taxonomy of inputs, processes, outputs, and outcomes. This taxonomy provides a more detailed view than the usual educational quality–educational quantity distinction and also demonstrates the striking lack of data on processes and outcomes. Even after decades of effort, most education indicators focus on inputs, with an extreme dearth of process measures. These input measures have serious problems with comprehensiveness, comparability, accuracy, and reliability. Output measures, too, are in short supply. In particular, assessing the quality of education has been difficult, and most developing countries have no internationally comparable data on quality.

Relevant, timely, accurate, and reliable data are essential underpinnings of evidence-based policymaking. Such policymaking is more rational and transparent than decision making based on power, influence, and hunches. Good data, in conjunction with careful analyses, not only point the way to effective policies, they are also be a powerful safeguard against unintended consequences of interventions to promote educational access and quality.

Unfortunately, in the area of primary and secondary education, the promise of evidence-based policymaking will not be realized without substantial changes in the nature and quality of the data collected.

Having examined the data at hand, I find that despite their limitations, the UNESCO, Barro-Lee, and Cohen-Soto datasets suggest three main conclusions about global progress toward universal basic and secondary education.

First, more children are being enrolled in primary education, although not all of these children are actually going to school or receiving a quality education. Although primary enrollment has reached near-universal levels in some developing regions, secondary level access remains weak throughout the developing world. Attainment and completion figures are low outside the developed world at both primary and secondary levels.

Second, although some developing regions, particularly Latin America/Caribbean and East Asia/Pacific, show progress toward improving access to education, others, particularly Sub-Saharan Africa and South Asia, lag on every measure.

Third, more girls are gaining access to education, but gender disparity remains strong in many developing countries. Equality of access is particularly poor at the elementary level in South Asia and in Africa, but also in East Asia/Pacific despite higher overall levels of access.

These basic indicators of progress in educational expansion are further refined by the TIMSS and PIRLS measures of educational quality. Although data are scant, it appears, as noted above, that the quality of education remains poor in most developing countries when compared with the developed world.

For the moment, though, some of the most straightforward estimates—such as the fact that more than 225 million secondary-school-age students do not attend school—should be enough to motivate Herculean efforts to address the world's education problems.

OBSERVATIONS ON DATA

Inconsistencies, both between the Barro-Lee and Cohen-Soto datasets and within each when data are extrapolated for the 15–24 year-old cohort, impair the ability to draw any firm conclusions from these data. These problems create significant concerns about the quality of data that are currently available for assessing progress toward universal basic and secondary education. Other datasets, including the work of Bruns et al. (2003), may provide a clearer picture for policymakers in the future.

A comparison of countries based on indicators of educational quality is problematic for a different reason. At present, few developing countries take part in TIMSS, PIRLS, and other standardized tests. Those that do participate tend to score much lower than OECD countries, but it is difficult to build a clear global picture of educational quality based on so few participants.

Data on educational processes could theoretically facilitate generalizations across countries or regions regarding the conditions that produce high-quality education. The fragmentary state of these data makes any conclusions difficult.

Overall, more work is necessary on the mechanisms linking inputs, processes, and outputs to down-the-line consequences.

QUALITY VS. QUANTITY

It appears that when defining educational development plans and strategies, developing countries must decide whether to emphasize the quantity or quality of education. Duraisamy et al. (n.d.) provide a detailed case study of educational expansion in Tamil Nadu, India. They show that expansion had a deleterious effect on quality and suggest that better management of public schools and the use of private resources (both allowing new private schools and encouraging private funds to help public and private schools) can partially mitigate this effect. The authors point out that such a policy would also require redirecting public funds toward schools in poor areas, where parents lack funds.

Various paths toward improving quality and quantity are possible. For example, initial emphasis could be on universal access, with the possibility that quality may suffer. If class sizes increase, facilities may become overburdened, and teachers' effectiveness may decrease. Another alternative—prioritizing high quality in the early phases—would likely make universal access more difficult. The introduction of fees for texts or supplemental materials, or increased investment in existing schools[61] and

---

[61] Heyneman (2004) points out the enormous range of non-salary expenditures that countries make in schools. In general, countries that spend more achieve higher quality; however, the efficiency of such investments varies widely across countries.

teaching staffs without expanding their size, may come at the expense of serving new populations.

One could imagine the stimulation of virtuous cycles in which quality improvements also facilitate expansion. Kremer et al. (1997) document that supplying textbooks and uniforms is associated with lower dropout rates and with additional students being attracted to a school. Such measures, moreover, may be less expensive than lowering student-teacher ratios. Similarly, investment in new schools can both reduce existing classroom crowding, likely improving quality, and provide capacity to absorb new students.

Mingat and Tan (1998) find that countries (in reasonably homogeneous income strata) vary widely in the quality-quantity trajectories they pursue. They also state that countries that focus on quality do so mainly by increasing the teacher-pupil ratio at the expense of access. They find that achieving higher teacher-pupil ratios seems not to be valuable (at least, when a country's ratio is similar to those already in place in most developing countries), which means that there is little to be gained by de-emphasizing access.[62] However, Behrman and Birdsall (1983) point out that quality does seem to matter from the standpoint of earnings gains. The possibility that there are quality thresholds below which increased quantity is meaningless remains largely unexplored.

An examination (not reported herein) of more up-to-date information than that given by Mingat and Tan (1998) is consistent with this view. Cross-country regression analysis shows no association between educational quality (i.e., test scores) and access/quantity (i.e., primary or secondary enrollment rates), controlling for the general state of development (i.e., income per capita or life expectancy). The policy implication of this result is that access should not be sacrificed for improved teacher-pupil ratios. Unlike Mingat and Tan, this analysis does not find any evidence of a negative association between teacher-pupil ratios and school enrollment rates.

The paucity of data on educational quality inhibits meaningful inferences about the tradeoff between educational quality and quantity. This information could be extremely useful in helping countries to circumvent

---

[62] Put another way, there is a trade-off between access and teacher-pupil ratios (negatively sloped iso-income curves), but there is no trade-off between access and test scores (flat iso-income curves) because the higher teacher-pupil ratios do nothing to boost test scores.

the barriers to long-run improvements in quality and quantity and to identify the best short- and medium-run steps along the way.[63]

OBSTACLES TO BETTER DATA

This analysis of existing methods for assessing progress toward universal basic and secondary education suggests that recognition of the importance of statistics and indicators has increased over the past decade. Nevertheless, three major obstacles remain.

First, continued capacity building is required in many developing countries where data compilation remains difficult. The availability of key quantitative measures, such as net enrollments, for the developing world has improved since Jomtien and the foundation of UIS in 1999 and will continue to grow. Indeed, UIS suggests that much of the information missing from its datasets is now for OECD countries.

Second, as noted, governments and school systems often face disincentives to provide accurate information. In some cases, schools may inflate data such as enrollments in order to meet political or financial targets. For example, comparison of Demographic and Health Surveys and UNESCO data shows the latter produce consistently higher enrollment estimates (Lloyd and Hewett, 2003). In many Sub-Saharan African countries, the difference may be due to political pressure on administrations.

These two issues lead to a third: the tension between useful information at the country level and data that are useful for a global picture. If developed countries, with near-universal access to education, believe that published global educational information is out of date or measures only the most basic facets of education, they may reasonably prioritize their efforts elsewhere. At the same time, if developing countries believe that global educational information is increasingly focused on more complex issues of quality, they may naturally decide to focus any data-related efforts on their own primary areas of concern: access and equity.

---

[63] An excellent compendium of issues and new thinking on the trade-off between quality and quantity in secondary education, emphasizing the need for each country to craft solutions that are appropriate for its own circumstances, is Chapter 3 of World Bank (2005).

GETTING BETTER DATA

Broadening the Scope of the Data

At present, measurement of educational systems on a global level focuses on access and completion, and to a lesser extent on competencies. There is little emphasis on other key inputs (such as budgets, length of school day, and school infrastructure) and processes (such as types of schools, curricular content, and accreditation/oversight practices).

Work toward achieving a broader perspective on educational inputs and results is already taking place in some regions. For example, the work of the Partnership for Educational Revitalization in the Americas (PREAL) in Latin America includes the presentation of data on public expenditure per student, as well as a regional comparison of a range of other indicators. The recent PREAL report card for Central America and the Dominican Republic included scores for testing, equity (including access for poor students and rural populations as well as by gender), decentralization of the educational system, teacher training and incentives, educational standards, and assessment (PREAL, 2003).

Institutionalizing Commitment to Progress in Data Quality

Capacity building is still needed in some developing countries to create the ability to deliver high-quality information on education, but national political considerations provide powerful disincentives to focus on the delivery of educational indicators. However, education is one of the largest public investments made by any administration. On those grounds alone, it is vital that evaluation be accurate and timely.

The disparate interests of various national governments impede international agencies in their efforts to improve international data quality. There is continued improvement; key organizations, such as the World Bank and the UNESCO Institute for Statistics, are working together to develop a universal standard for reporting and measurement, focusing their efforts and resources on working with countries.[64] On the other

---

[64] The UNESCO Institute for Statistics, for example, is working on the Fast Track Initiative of Education for All, which aims to improve data for participating countries through a program for building statistical capacity. It has also produced a data quality framework, working in cooperation with the World Bank and the International Monetary Fund. Another effort to improve education data internationally is the publication, *The OECD Handbook for Internationally Comparative Education Statistics: Concepts, Standards, Definitions and Classifications.*

hand, there is a danger here. Because the World Bank and other donors have encouraged or required that countries meet certain standards, they may tacitly encourage countries to misrepresent their accomplishments when results are less than hoped for. Placing these institutions in the role of ensuring statistical integrity is problematic.

AVENUES FOR FURTHER RESEARCH:
NEW DATA AND NEW VIEWS OF EXISTING DATA

Further data-oriented research might yield important new insights relevant to universal basic and secondary education. Examples are:

- A study of the differences within individual countries. What patterns and trends are evident, and what, if anything, do they tell policymakers beyond what is already obvious?
- A study of countries or states that have improved education enormously—such as Cuba, Kerala (India), and Sri Lanka—without the economic successes that typically accompany educational achievement.
- A study of whether there is a trade-off between improving educational quality and increasing its quantity. The quality of children's experiences in the classroom depends on various process-level factors, including student-teacher ratios, teacher training, pedagogical styles, curricular relevance, the adequacy of school facilities and their maintenance, and attention to health and safety. Some work that defines and assesses data on these factors has been carried out by Duraisamy et al (n.d.), Heyneman (2004), Jones and Gingrich (1968), and Kremer et al. (1997).
- A study of how various levels of education relate to countries' needs at different stages of development. In particular, it would be useful to assemble data to test further the conclusion of Jamison and Lau (1982) that higher levels of basic and secondary education correlate well with improved productivity.

FINAL REFLECTIONS

Ten years ago, as noted above, Puryear observed that the world had developed little capacity to determine the worth of its huge investment in education. Annual public expenditure on education (including tertiary level) is now approximately $1.5 trillion, of which approximately $250 billion is spent in developing countries (UNESCO, 2000). In this review of some of the major available datasets on education, it appears that Puryear's 1995 assessment still rings true. There are significant gaps in data on enrollment, attainment, and completion. There are huge deficiencies in the measurement of educational quality. Process indicators are severely lacking. Consistency across and within datasets is disturbingly low. Variations in reporting across education systems, such as differences in what age groups belong to what education level, further complicate analysis.

Happily, recent efforts by the UNESCO Institute for Statistics are blowing a much-needed fresh wind through national agencies and independent researchers who report, gather, and analyze educational data. UIS has made significant strides toward overcoming the historic lack of coordination, underfunding, conflicting incentives, collect-and-file-mentality, and lack of dialog with end users that have long characterized the field of educational data. There is reason to hope that analysts who have at times in the past operated under the illusion that they are using reliable data will soon have genuinely reliable data at hand.[65]

Despite their longstanding limitations, the available data do seem to be strong enough to support some general statements and provide a basis for spotting issues and identifying policy directions. Evidence-based policymaking requires much more complete and reliable data, however. Not having these data constitutes a missed opportunity to capitalize on the enormous investment the world makes in education and impedes recognition of education's importance in the overall process of development.

---

[65] Other recent efforts to gather and analyze data include The Global Education Database, which is compiling data from UNESCO and Demographic and Health Surveys, and the World Bank EdStats website, which compiles data from different sources and provides information on enrollment and attainment by household characteristics.

Appendix A

METHOD FOR CALCULATING THE
CURRENT NUMBER OF UNENROLLED CHILDREN

The method described below was used to estimate the number of children of primary and secondary age who are not currently enrolled in school.

The number of primary-school-age children for each country is calculated assuming a homogeneous population distribution. Using the average of 2000 and 2005 population data from *World Population Prospects: The 2004 Revision* (UN, 2004) for children in the 5–9, 10–14, and 15–19 age groups, I divide the total for each age group by 5. The resulting number represents the population of a one-year age group. Using UNESCO data for the starting and ending ages of primary education, I find the number of primary-school-age children by summing the population figures for the one-year age groups that correspond to the years of primary school. (For example, to determine the number of students in a primary age range of 6 to 11, I multiply 4 times the figure for a one-year age group of the 5–9 population and add this to 2 times a figure for a one-year age group of the 10–14 population.) The population of secondary-school-age children is calculated using the same approach.

The most recent available net enrollment rates (NER) and gross enrollment rates (GER) from UNESCO[1] are used for both primary and secondary data. To estimate missing NER, I use a regression of NER on GER, per capita GDP, and under-5 mortality rates, because NER is highly correlated with these indicators (correlations for primary school are respectively: 0.73, -0.69, 0.47; for secondary school, they are: 0.94, –0.84, 0.63). Per capita GDP data and under-5 mortality rates are taken from *World Development Indicators 2005* (World Bank, 2005). For countries without per capita GDP and/or mortality data, regressions using

---

[1] http://www.uis.unesco.org/ev.php?URL_ID=5187&URL_DO=DO_TOPIC& URL_SECTION=201

only GER and the other available data are used. (Thus, if only GER and per capita GDP are available, a regression of NER on GER and per capita GDP is used. Similarly, if only GER and mortality rates are available, a regression of NER on GER and mortality is used. Finally, if neither per capita GDP nor mortality is available, a regression of NER on GER is used to estimate NER.) All estimated NERs are capped at 100 percent, and are capped to be lower than reported GER.

I estimate the number of enrolled primary-age children by multiplying the most recent available primary NER by the population of primary-age children. Perhaps because the various data sets are from different years or simply because of inaccurate data, the estimated enrolled primary-age population for some countries is larger than UNESCO's reported total primary school enrollment. To correct for this overestimation, for any country whose estimated primary-age enrollment is more than 1 percent larger than the reported primary school enrollment, I multiply the reported primary school enrollment by the average ratio of estimated-to-reported primary-age enrollment for all other countries to estimate enrolled primary-age students. This correction is also used for secondary data.

I estimate the number of unenrolled children of primary age by subtracting the number of primary-age enrolled students from the population of primary-age children.

To account for the 19 small countries without any available NER or GER data, the final world number for unenrolled children is increased proportionally by the percentage that children age 5–9 from these countries represent of the total world population of children age 5–9.

For any country with primary but not secondary enrollment data, a regression of secondary enrollment rates on primary enrollment rates and per capita GDP is used to estimate secondary enrollment rates.

The number of secondary-age students enrolled in school is calculated by adding the estimated number of students in secondary school to the number of secondary-age students in primary school.

To calculate the number of secondary-age children in secondary school, I multiply the secondary NER by the population of secondary-age children, and then adjust these calculations using the same methodology used for primary-age children. Making the assumption that students enrolled in primary school who are not primary school age are of secondary school age, I calculate the number of secondary-age children in primary education by subtracting the primary NER [number of students of primary age in primary school/population of primary-school-age children] from the primary GER [number of all students in primary school/population of primary-school-age children] and multiplying this difference by the population of primary-school-age children.

As with the calculations for primary-age children, the number of unenrolled secondary-age students is calculated by subtracting the number of enrolled students from the total number of children who are secondary school age. In the secondary school calculations, this number is negative for some countries, which cannot be correct. There are various possible explanations for this result. First, the simplifying assumption of a homogeneous population distribution within age groups may not hold. Furthermore, the assumption that students in primary school who are not primary age are by default secondary age may be incorrect (as some may be younger than primary age or older than secondary age), and it would lead to an overestimation of the number of secondary-age students enrolled in primary school. Thus, large differences between primary gross and net rates may lead to inaccurate estimates of enrolled secondary-age students; one cannot determine the age of students enrolled in primary school who are not of primary age. Finally, and in my judgment most important, inaccurate data may account for the observed discrepancy.

Because the true number of unenrolled children cannot be negative, any negative value is adjusted to zero. This adjustment, which applies to nine countries, results in a change of less than 1 percent in the estimate of the number of unenrolled secondary-age children (and approximately three-quarters of the total adjustment is due to the figures from Brazil). Nevertheless, the fact that the unadjusted estimate is negative for some countries (and thus stands out in the calculations) suggests that there may be less-visible data problems with other countries.

METHOD FOR CALCULATING THE
NUMBER OF UNENROLLED CHILDREN IN 2015

The method described below was used to project the number of unenrolled children of primary and secondary age in 2015.

The number of students of primary school age for each country is calculated using the same approach as the calculations for current number of students (described above), with the projected 2015 population data from *World Population Prospects: The 2004 Revision* (UN, 2004) substituted for the 2000/2005 data.

Using a linear projection of available NER and GER since 1990—taken from *World Development Indicators 2005* (World Bank, 2005)—for each country, I forecast 2015 NER and GER for both primary and secondary education. For countries with only one available data point, this data point is used as the 2015 rate. To project NER for countries without any NER data, I predict 2015 NER from the projected 2015 GER, per capita GDP, and under-5 mortality rates. To avoid the increasing uncertainty that would be introduced by using regression coefficients based on 2015 estimates, I use the coefficients from the NER on GER, per capita GDP, and under-5 mortality rates regression described above for the current-enrollment calculations. Thus, I assume that the relationship between NER and GER, per capita GDP, and under-5 mortality for 2005 would remain the same for 2015.

To avoid unrealistic projected GERs that would in some instances result from countries experiencing rapid changes in enrollment and/or those with limited data, I cap projected 2015 GER at the higher value of 120 for primary (and 100 for secondary) and the latest available GER. Projected NER is limited to values between 0 and 100, as numbers beyond this range are by definition impossible.

I estimate the number of unenrolled primary- and secondary-age children using the same methodology as before, except that I do not adjust for the difference between estimated enrollment numbers and reported enrollment numbers (as there are no reported 2015 numbers). Any negative value for the number of unenrolled students is set to zero.

To account for the 34 countries without any available NER or GER data, the final world value for unenrolled primary-age students is increased proportionally by the share of the world population age 5–9 that children from these countries represent. Similarly, the share of world population age 15–19 represented by these countries is used for secondary school calculations.

Appendix B

Table A.1: Primary and Secondary Net Enrollment, Total and by Gender, for most recent year (1998–2005)

	Primary				Secondary			
	Total	Male	Female	Gender Gap (M–F)	Total	Male	Female	Gender Gap (M–F)
World (simple average)	86	87	85	2	64	63	64	-1
Region (simple average)								
East Asia and the Pacific	90	91	89	2	56	54	56	-2
Eastern Europe and Central Asia	90	90	89	1	85	84	85	0
Latin America and the Caribbean	92	93	92	1	69	66	71	-5
Middle East and North Africa	85	87	82	5	55	57	53	4
South Asia*	79	81	76	5	48	45	51	-6
Sub-Saharan Africa	70	72	66	6	28	30	27	4
Developed Countries	95	95	95	0	86	85	87	-2
Country								
Albania	95	96	94	2	77	76	78	-2
Algeria	95	96	94	2	67	65	69	-4
Andorra	89	88	90	-2	71	69	74	-5
Angola	61	66	57	9	–	–	–	–
Anguilla	95	94	96	-2	99	100	97	3
Argentina	–	–	–	–	81	79	84	-5
Armenia	94	95	93	2	83	82	85	-3
Aruba	99	100	98	2	75	72	79	-7
Australia	97	96	97	-1	87	86	88	-2
Austria	90	89	91	-2	89	89	89	0
Azerbaijan	80	81	79	2	76	77	75	2
Bahamas	86	85	88	-3	76	74	77	-3
Bahrain	90	89	91	-2	87	84	90	-6
Bangladesh	84	82	86	-4	44	42	47	-5
Barbados	100	100	100	0	90	90	90	0
Belarus	94	95	94	1	85	83	86	-3
Belgium	100	100	100	0	97	97	98	-1
Belize	99	98	100	-2	69	67	71	-4
Benin	58	69	47	22	19	26	12	14
Bolivia	95	95	95	0	71	72	71	1

Table A.1 continued

	Primary				Secondary			
	Total	Male	Female	(M–F)	Total	Male	Female	(M–F)
Botswana	81	79	83	-4	54	50	57	-7
Brazil	97	98	91	7	75	72	78	-6
Bulgaria	90	91	90	1	87	88	86	2
Burkina Faso	36	42	31	11	9	11	7	4
Burundi	57	62	52	10	9	10	8	2
Cambodia	93	96	91	5	24	30	19	11
Canada	100	100	100	0	94	94	94	0
Cape Verde	99	100	98	2	58	55	61	-6
Chad	61	72	49	23	12	17	6	11
Chile	85	85	84	1	81	80	81	-1
China**	95	94	95	-1	–	–	–	–
Colombia	87	88	87	1	55	53	58	-5
Comoros	55	59	50	9	–	–	–	–
Congo, Republic of the	54	55	53	2	–	–	–	–
Costa Rica	90	90	91	-1	53	50	55	-5
Côte d'Ivoire	61	67	54	13	21	27	15	12
Croatia	89	90	89	1	87	86	87	-1
Cuba	96	96	95	1	86	86	86	0
Cyprus	96	96	96	0	93	91	94	-3
Czech Republic	87	87	87	0	90	89	92	-3
Denmark	100	100	100	0	96	94	98	-4
Djibouti	36	40	32	8	21	25	17	8
Dominica	81	83	79	4	92	86	98	-12
Dominican Republic	96	99	94	5	36	30	41	-11
Ecuador	100	99	100	-1	50	50	51	-1
Egypt	91	93	90	3	78	80	76	4
El Salvador	90	90	90	0	49	48	49	-1
Equatorial Guinea	85	91	78	13	–	–	–	–
Eritrea	45	49	42	7	22	25	18	7
Estonia	95	95	94	1	88	87	90	-3
Ethiopia	51	55	47	8	18	23	13	10
Fiji	100	100	100	0	76	73	79	-6
Finland	100	100	100	0	95	94	95	-1
France	99	99	99	0	94	93	95	-2
Gabon	78	79	78	1	–	–	–	–
Gambia	79	79	78	1	33	39	27	12
Georgia	89	89	88	1	78	77	78	-1
Germany	–	–	–	–	88	88	88	0
Ghana	63	64	62	2	36	39	33	6
Greece	99	99	99	0	86	85	87	-2
Grenada	84	89	80	9	99	100	99	1

Table A.1 continued

	Total	Primary Male	Primary Female	(M–F)	Total	Secondary Male	Secondary Female	(M–F)
Guatemala	87	89	86	3	30	30	29	1
Guinea	65	73	58	15	21	28	13	15
Guinea-Bissau	45	53	37	16	9	11	6	5
Guyana	99	100	98	2	75	58	92	-34
Honduras	87	87	88	-1	–	–	–	–
Hong Kong, SAR	98	98	97	1	74	72	75	-3
Hungary	91	91	90	1	94	94	94	0
Iceland	100	100	99	1	86	84	88	-4
India	88	90	85	5	–	–	–	–
Indonesia	92	93	92	1	54	54	54	0
Iran, Islamic Republic of	86	88	85	3	–	–	–	–
Iraq	91	98	83	15	33	40	26	-14
Ireland	96	95	97	-2	83	80	87	-7
Israel	99	99	99	0	89	89	89	0
Italy	99	100	99	1	91	91	92	-1
Jamaica	95	94	95	-1	75	74	77	-3
Japan	100	100	100	0	99	99	100	-1
Jordan	92	91	93	-2	80	79	81	-2
Kazakhstan	91	92	91	1	87	87	87	0
Kenya	66	66	66	0	25	25	24	1
Kuwait	83	82	84	-2	77	75	79	-4
Kyrgyzstan	89	91	88	3	–	–	–	–
Lao People's Democratic Republic	85	88	82	6	35	38	32	6
Latvia	86	86	85	1	88	88	88	0
Lebanon	91	91	90	1	–	–	–	–
Lesotho	86	83	89	-6	22	18	27	-9
Liberia	70	79	61	18	18	23	13	10
Lithuania	91	91	91	0	94	94	94	0
Luxembourg	90	90	91	-1	80	77	83	-6
Macao, China	87	88	86	2	74	71	78	-7
Macedonia, TFYR	91	91	91	0	81	82	80	2
Madagascar	79	78	79	-1	11	11	12	-1
Malawi	100	–	–	–	29	32	26	6
Malaysia	93	93	93	0	70	66	74	-8
Maldives	92	92	93	-1	51	48	55	-7
Mali	44	50	39	11	–	–	–	–
Malta	96	96	96	0	87	86	88	-2
Marshall Islands	76	77	75	2	65	64	66	-2
Mauritania	68	68	67	1	16	18	14	4
Mauritius	97	96	98	-2	74	74	74	0
Mexico	99	99	100	-1	63	61	64	-3

Table A.1 continued

	Total	Primary Male	Female	(M–F)	Total	Secondary Male	Female	(M–F)
Mongolia	79	78	80	-2	77	72	83	-11
Morocco	90	92	87	5	36	38	33	5
Mozambique	55	58	53	5	12	14	10	4
Myanmar	84	84	85	-1	35	36	34	2
Namibia	78	76	81	-5	44	39	50	-11
Nauru	81	80	82	-2	–	–	–	–
Nepal	70	75	66	9	–	–	–	–
Netherlands	99	100	99	1	89	88	89	-1
Netherlands Antilles	88	86	91	-5	63	60	67	-7
New Zealand	100	100	100	0	93	93	95	-2
Nicaragua	85	86	85	1	39	36	42	-6
Niger	38	45	31	14	6	7	5	2
Nigeria	67	74	60	14	29	32	26	6
Niue	99	99	98	1	94	95	93	2
Norway	100	100	100	0	96	96	97	-1
Oman	72	72	72	0	69	69	70	-1
Pakistan	59	68	50	18	–	–	–	–
Palau	96	98	94	4	–	–	–	–
Palestinian Autonomous Territories	91	91	91	0	84	82	86	-4
Panama	100	100	99	1	63	60	66	-6
Papua New Guinea	74	79	69	10	24	27	21	6
Paraguay	89	89	89	0	51	50	53	-3
Peru	100	100	100	0	69	70	68	2
Philippines	94	93	95	-2	59	54	65	-11
Poland	98	98	98	0	91	90	93	-3
Portugal	100	100	99	1	85	81	89	-8
Qatar	94	95	94	1	82	80	85	-5
Republic of Korea	100	100	100	0	88	88	88	0
Republic of Moldova	79	79	79	0	69	68	70	-2
Romania	89	89	88	1	81	79	82	-3
Russian Federation	90	89	90	-1	–	–	–	–
Rwanda	87	85	88	-3	–	–	–	–
Saint Kitts and Nevis	–	–	–	–	97	94	100	-6
Saint Lucia	99	99	100	-1	76	68	85	-17
Saint Vincent and the Grenadines	90	90	90	0	58	56	61	-5
Samoa	98	99	96	3	62	59	65	-6
Sao Tome and Principe	97	100	94	6	29	32	26	6
Saudi Arabia	54	55	54	1	53	54	52	2
Senegal	69	71	66	5	–	–	–	–
Serbia and Montenegro	96	96	96	0	–	–	–	–
Seychelles	100	100	99	1	100	100	100	0

Table A.1 continued

	Total	Primary		(M–F)	Total	Secondary		(M–F)
		Male	Female			Male	Female	
Slovakia	86	85	86	-1	88	88	88	0
Slovenia	93	94	93	1	93	93	94	-1
South Africa	89	89	89	0	62	59	65	-6
Spain	100	100	99	1	96	94	98	-4
Sudan	46	50	42	8	–	–	–	–
Suriname	97	96	98	-2	64	54	74	-20
Swaziland	75	75	75	0	32	29	36	-7
Sweden	100	100	99	1	99	99	100	-1
Switzerland	99	99	99	0	87	89	84	5
Syrian Arab Republic	98	100	96	4	43	44	41	3
Tajikistan	94	97	91	6	83	90	76	14
Thailand	85	87	84	3	–	–	–	–
Togo	91	99	83	16	27	36	17	19
Tonga	100	100	100	0	72	67	77	-10
Trinidad and Tobago	91	91	90	1	72	69	75	-6
Tunisia	97	97	97	0	64	61	68	-7
Turkey	86	89	84	5	–	–	–	–
Turks and Caicos Islands	73	74	73	1	79	78	80	-2
Uganda	–	–	–	–	16	17	16	1
Ukraine	84	84	84	0	85	84	85	-1
United Arab Emirates	83	84	82	2	71	70	72	-2
United Kingdom	100	100	100	0	95	93	97	-4
United Republic of Tanzania	82	83	81	2	5	5	4	1
United States	92	92	93	-1	88	88	89	-1
Uruguay	90	90	91	-1	73	70	77	-7
Vanuatu	94	93	95	-2	28	27	28	-1
Venezuela	91	90	91	-1	59	55	64	-9
Viet Nam	95	98	92	6	65	–	–	–
Yemen	72	84	59	25	35	47	21	26
Zambia	68	69	68	1	23	25	21	4
Zimbabwe	79	79	80	-1	34	35	33	2

* Due to lack of data, this secondary education average does not include data from India or Pakistan.

** Primary net enrollment data for China from UNESCO 2006 EFA Global Monitoring Report.

Sources: UNESCO online data, http://www.uis.unesco.org (Statistical Tables, accessed March 2006).

References

Adams, Ray, and Maragaret Wu, eds. 2002. *PISA 2000 Technical Report*. Paris: Organisation for Economic Co-Operation and Development (OECD).

Barro, Robert J., and Jong-Wha Lee. 1993. "International Comparisons of Educational Attainment." *Journal of Monetary Economics* 32: 363–394.

———. 1996. "International Measures of Schooling: Years and Schooling Quality." *The American Economic Review* 86 (2): 218–223.

———. 2000. "International Data on Educational Attainment Updates and Implications." National Bureau of Economic Research Working Paper no. w7911. Cambridge, MA: NBER.

———. 2001. "International Data on Educational Attainment: Updates and Implications." *Oxford Economic Papers* 53: 541–563.

Behrman, Jere, and Nancy Birdsall. 1983. "The Quality of Schooling: Quantity Alone Is Misleading," *American Economic Review.* 73 (5): 928–47.

Behrman, Jere R., and Mark R. Rosenzweig. 1994. "Caveat emptor: Cross-country Data on Education and the Labor Force." *Journal of Development Economics* 44 (1): 147–171.

Bloom, David E. 2004. "Beyond the Basics: Patterns, Trends and Issues in Secondary Education in Developing Countries." Paper prepared for the World Bank.

Bloom, David E., and David Canning. 2004. "Reconciling Micro and Macro Estimates of the Returns to Schooling." Working Paper of the Project on Universal Basic and Secondary Education. American Academy of Arts and Sciences.

Bloom, David E., and Joel E. Cohen. 2002. "Education for All: An Unfinished Revolution." *Daedalus* 131 (3): 84–86.

Bruns, Barbara, Alain Mingat, and Ramahatra Rakotomalala. 2003. *Achieving Universal Primary Education by 2015: A Chance for Every Child*. Washington, DC: World Bank.

Cohen, Daniel, and Marcelo Soto. 2001. *Growth and Human Capital: Good Data, Good Results*. Paris: OECD.

Delors, Jacques. 1996. *Learning: The Treasure Within*. Report to UNESCO of the International Commission on Education for the Twenty-First Century. Paris: UNESCO.

Drèze, Jean, and Amartya Sen. 1995. *India: Economic Development and Social Opportunity*. Delhi: Oxford University Press.

Duraisamy, P., Estelle James, Julia Lane, and Jee-Peng Tan. n.d. "Is There A Quantity-Quality Trade-Off As Enrollments Increase? Evidence from Tamil Nadu, India." Washington, DC: The World Bank. http://econ.worldbank.org/docs/466.pdf.

The Times of India. 2004. "Few Indian Girls Get to Complete School." February 10. http://timesofindia.indiatimes.com/articleshow/486576.cms, accessed June 2004.

Filmer, Deon, and Lant Pritchett. 1999. "The Effect of Household Wealth on Educational Attainment." *Population and Development Review* 25 (1): 85–120.

Goujon, Anne, and Wolfgang Lutz. 2004. "Future Human Capital: Population Projections by Level of Education." In *The End of World Population Growth in the 21st Century: New Challenges for Human Capital Formation and Sustainable Development*, ed. Wolfgang Lutz, Warren C. Sanderson, and Sergei Scherbov. London: Earthscan.

Gradstein, Mark, and Denis Nikitin. 2004. "Educational Expansion: Evidence and Interpretation." World Bank Policy Research Working Paper 3245.

Hanushek, Eric A. 1995. "Rationalizing School Spending: Efficiency, Externalities and Equity, and their Connection to Rising Costs." Pp. 59–91 in *Individual and Social Responsibility*, ed. Victor Fuchs. Chicago: University of Chicago Press.

Herz, Barbara, and Gene B. Sperling. 2004. "What Works in Girls' Education: Evidence and Policies from the Developing World." New York: Council on Foreign Relations.

Heyneman, Stephen P. 2004. "International Education Quality." *Economics of Education Review* 23: 441–452.

Husén, T., ed. 1967. *A Comparison of Twelve Countries: International Study of Achievement in Mathematics*, vols. 1 and 2. Stockholm: Almquist & Wiksell.

International Association for the Evaluation of Educational Achievement (IEA). 2000. *Trends in Mathematics and Science Study (TIMSS) 1999: International Mathematics Report*. Chestnut Hill: Boston College International Study Center.

———. 2003. *Progress in International Reading and Literacy Study (PIRLS) 2001 International Report: IEA's Study of Reading Literacy Achievement in Primary Schools*. Chestnut Hill: Boston College International Study Center.

————. 2003. *Trends in Mathematics and Science Study (TIMSS) Assessment Frameworks and Specifications 2003*. Chestnut Hill: Boston College International Study Center.

Jamison, Dean, and Lawrence J. Lau. 1982. *Farmer Education and Farm Efficiency*. Baltimore: Johns Hopkins University for World Bank.

Jones, Gavin, and Paul Gingrich. 1968. "The Effects of Differing Trends in Fertility and of Educational Advance on the Growth, Quality, and Turnover of the Labor Force." *Demography* 5 (1): 226–248.

Kremer, Michael, Sylvie Moulin, David Myatt, and Robert Namunyu. 1997. "The Quality-Quantity Tradeoff in Education: Evidence from a Prospective Evaluation in Kenya." Working Paper. Massachusetts Institute of Technology.

Krueger, Alan B., and Mikael Lindahl. 2001. "Education for Growth: Why and For Whom?" *Journal of Economic Literature* 39 (December): 1101–1136.

Kyriacou, George. 1991. "Level and Growth Effects of Human Capital." Working paper. C. V. Starr Center, NYU.

Lievesley, Denise. 2001. "Making a Difference: a Role for the Responsible International Statistician?" *The Statistician* 50 (4): 367–406.

Lloyd C.B., and P.C. Hewett. 2003. "Primary Schooling in Sub-Saharan Africa: Recent Trends and Current Challenges." Population Council Working Paper no. 176.

Mingat, Alain, and Jee-Peng Tan. 1998. "The Mechanics of Progress in Education: Evidence from Cross-Country Data." World Bank Policy Research Working Paper.

Nabeshima, Kaoru. 2003. "Raising the Quality of Secondary Education in East Asia." World Bank Policy Research Working Paper 3140. http://econ.worldbank.org/files/29919_wps3140.pdf.

Organisation for Economic Co-Operation and Development (OECD). 2001. *New School Management Approaches*. Paris: OECD.

————. 2004. *Education at a Glance 2004*. Paris: OECD.

OECD/UNESCO Institute for Statistics (OECD/UNESCO-UIS). 2003. *Literacy Skills for the World of Tomorrow: Further Results from PISA 2000*. Paris: OECD/UNESCO-UIS.

Partnership for Educational Revitalization in the Americas (PREAL). 2003. *Time to Act: A Report Card on Education in Central America and the Dominican Republic*. Washington, DC: PREAL Task Force on Education Reform in Central America.

Porter, Andrew C., and Adam Gamoran, eds. 2002. *Methodological Advances in Cross-national Surveys of Educational Achievement*. Washington, DC: National Academy Press.

Pritchett, Lant. 1997. "Where Has All the Education Gone?" World Bank Policy Research Working Paper 1581.

Psacharopoulos, G., and A. M. Ariagada. 1986. "The Educational Composition of the Labor Force: an International Comparison." *International Labor Review* 125: 561–574.

Puryear, Jeffrey M. 1995. "International Education Statistics and Research: Status and Problems." *International Journal of Educational Development* 15 (1): 79–91.

Stigler, James W., and James Hiebert. 1999. *The Teaching Gap: Best Ideas from the World's Teachers for Improving Education in the Classroom*. New York: Free Press.

United Nations. *UN World Population Prospects: The 2002 Revision*. New York: United Nations.

United Nations Educational, Scientific and Cultural Organization (UNESCO). 2003. *Gender and Education for All: The Leap to Equality*. Paris: UNESCO.

———. 2002. *Approved Programme and Budget, 2002–2003*. Paris: UNESCO.

———. 2001. *International Expert Meeting on General Secondary Education in the Twenty-first Century: Trends, Challenges and Priorities*. Paris: UNESCO.

———. 2000. *World Education Report 2000*.

UNESCO-UIS. 2005. *Global Education Digest 2005: Comparing Education Statistics Across the World*. Montreal: UIS.

———. 2004. *Education Statistics 2004 – Regional Report on South and East Asia*. Montreal: UIS.

———. 2003. *Global Education Digest 2003: Comparing Education Statistics Across the World*. Montreal: UIS.

———. 2002. *Arab States Regional Report*. Montreal: UIS.

———. 1997. *International Standard Classification of Education (ISCED) 1997*. Montreal: UIS.

UNESCO/OECD World Education Indicators Programme. 2000. *Investing in Education: Analysis of the 1999 World Education Indicators*. Paris, France: OECD.

United Nations Children's Fund (UNICEF). 2003. *The State of the World's Children 2004: Girls, Education and Development*. New York: UNICEF.

United Nations Millennium Project. 2005. *Towards Universal Primary Education: Investments, Incentives, and Institutions*. Task Force on Education and Gender Equality. London: Earthscan.

Walker, D.A. 1976. *The IEA Six-Subject Survey: An Empirical Study of Education in Twenty-One Countries*. Stockholm: Almquist & Wiksell.

Woessman, Ludger. 2000. "Schooling Resources, Educational Institutions, and Student Performance: The International Evidence." Kiel Institute of World Economics Working Paper no. 983.

World Bank. 2005. *Expanding Opportunities and Building Competencies for Young People: A New Agenda for Secondary Education*. Washington, DC: World Bank.

———. 2003. "Millennium Development Goals." The World Bank Group. http://www.developmentgoals.org/Education.htm, accessed June 2004.

———. 2000. *Peril and Promise: Higher Education in Developing Countries*. Washington, DC: The Task Force on Higher Education and Society.

Section II: Historical Legacies, Political Obstacles

Lessons from the Past: A Comparative Socio-Historical Analysis of Primary and Secondary Education

AARON BENAVOT AND JULIA RESNIK

The foremost policy aim of educational elites and international organizations dedicated to education is to enable every young child in the world to exercise his or her right to a quality education by means of national frameworks of universal schooling. The notion of education as a basic human right, initially laid out in Article 26 of the 1948 Universal Declaration of Human Rights, has been reiterated in numerous international covenants and conventions (UNESCO, 2000). Because children cannot secure access to a quality education for themselves, state officials, regional authorities, and local communities are morally obligated to establish the means by which universal access to education becomes a reality. Moreover, the idea of education as a fundamental human right is increasingly supplemented by a view that underscores the intrinsic value of education as an experience that enhances each and every individual's capabilities and freedoms (Sen, 1999). Thus, educational expansion can be understood as a form of development in and of itself, which moves beyond conventional ideas about the impact of education on economic and national development. Undoubtedly, the worldwide circulation of these moral, legal, and social imperatives concerning education has helped to justify the tremendous allocation of resources, by national governments and international agencies alike, to provide education for all (UNESCO, 2002; 2003/4).

This chapter explores the historical bases of the idea of universal education and of efforts to realize this goal, as well as the conditions that facilitated (or hindered) these in different times and places. It seeks to move beyond existing avenues of scholarly inquiry and sketches out an alternative strategy for a comparative historical study of universal education. By identifying key analytical components of the contemporary conception of mass schooling and examining their historical emergence, this chapter focuses on the diverse antecedents of existing models of universal education and revisits the unique pathways and divergent outcomes of past models. We liken our strategy to standing over a rich and flavorful "educational" broth, in which the initially distinct and numerous ingredients have settled to the bottom of the pot. We wish to stir up and reexamine the savory (and often forgotten) ingredients lying at the base of the soup cauldron, which are perceived as having fused together into a standard framework of universal education. By doing so, we hope to raise new questions and ideas, which are relevant to current policy debates on universal education.

Viewed from a world-historical perspective, the long-term trend towards universal education can be characterized as follows: Under varying economic, cultural, and political conditions, public mass schooling expanded and underwent initial consolidation in the West during the late eighteenth and early nineteenth centuries. The idea that young people needed to undergo special forms of socialization and training in public schools, rather than at home or through religious institutions, gained favor. The public increasingly viewed school-based experiences as important because the parameters of adult life were not fixed at birth and because social progress depended on the actions, choices, and inclinations of a society's members. The rhetoric and realities of mass public education were later selectively adapted in non-European and colonial education systems during the nineteenth and twentieth centuries. Over time, education in general, and compulsory mass schooling in particular, underwent significant institutionalization owing to the decisions of independent nation-states and the declarations of international associations and organizations. Transnational networks and international organizations played a particularly influential role in the development of mass schooling in Asia, Africa, and Latin America, especially after World War II, insofar as they impelled modernizing elites to facilitate the circulation, emulation, and adoption of Western educational models and the adaptation of these models to local contexts. Overall, the expansion of national education systems, the diffusion of comparative accounts of schooling, and the diverse activities of international organizations laid the groundwork for the emergence of a relatively uniform model of mass, state-sponsored schooling. They also contributed to the convergence of basic educational realities in much of the world today.[1]

Existing historical explorations of the idea of universal education and of educational expansion can be broadly classified into two major paths of inquiry. The first concentrates on the history of educational ideas—in this case, universal education and mass schooling—and surveys the writings of leading educational, religious, and political thinkers who, at different times and places, championed the spread of formal education to young children of different social and cultural backgrounds in increasingly inclusionary terms. A second path of inquiry involves cross-national research on educational expansion and formalization. This substantial body of work spans academic disciplines, investigates alternative theoretical explanations, encompasses different levels of analysis and employs a range of research designs (see Meyer et al., 1977; Craig, 1981; Archer, 1979; Heidenheimer, 1981; Boli et al., 1985; Rubinson and Ralph, 1984; Benavot and Riddle, 1988; Fuller and Rubinson, 1992; Meyer et al., 1992; Jónasson, 2003; Clemens, 2004).[2]

The present chapter follows a third path of inquiry. It sketches a historical geography of the diverse, often context-specific, meanings and institutional forms of education, and explores the different historical trajectories along which these elements developed. This approach involves two essential steps: first, a delineation of analytical issues concerning the comparative institutionalization of mass schooling; and second, an examination of their historical emergence, including a description of the diverse meanings they embodied in different contexts and an outline of their evolution. In principle, this approach deconstructs existing conceptions of the

---

[1] Mass schooling can be examined on at least two levels. First, it can be understood as an evolving reality of schools, teachers, pupils, curriculum, educational laws, statutes, and so forth. Second, it can be seen as a social construct or model that conceives, accounts for, theorizes and, more often than not, celebrates this reality, especially its contribution to desirable societal outcomes (e.g., economic development, nation building, social equality, political revitalization) and individual-level transformations (e.g., literacy acquisition, skill enhancement, rational behavior, value changes). Although developments at each level are intertwined and mutually reinforcing, we believe that it is analytically advantageous to keep them separate.

[2] The details and limitations of these two paths of inquiry are discussed in Benavot and Resnik 2006.

development of a uniform, undifferentiated model of mass schooling (Boli et al., 1985; Ramirez and Boli, 1987; Meyer et al., 1992). Although some historical elements of universal education eventually fused into a relatively standard model of free, compulsory mass schooling, others remained inextricably bound to particular times and places and, in a sense, have been lost to all but a few specialists in educational history.

The comparative historical strategy employed in this chapter, though "unconventional," complements recent scholarship in the field of comparative education. For example, in his historical survey of primary education in Africa, Kenneth King (1990: 216) discusses the importance of "untangling the threads that led to the formation of state systems." Recent work by William Cummings (2003) also emphasizes the need to examine variations that eventually coalesced into more standardized forms in modern education systems. Notions of "culture-specific diversification" and "domestic reflections on education," as discussed by Juergen Schriewer and Carlos Martinez (2003), are certainly relevant to the historical approach employed below.

On its own, a comparative analysis of key historical processes and institutional forms has considerable academic merit. Moreover, we reason that this strategy represents a potentially informative contribution to ongoing policy debates concerning universal basic and secondary education (UBASE). If, as we shall argue, much of the institutional diversity in educational history has either been ignored or forgotten in contemporary discourse, then revisiting past meanings and forms of education should, at least in theory, broaden the conceptual basis upon which alternative policies and intervention strategies are evaluated. Having said this, the present chapter does not presume to provide a comprehensive comparative history of mass schooling (a daunting, if not impossible task). At this juncture, we highlight several important analytical elements in the history of mass schooling, as a point of departure for further work.

In order to identify key analytical topics and issues for the present comparative historical survey of mass schooling, we cast a wide—albeit far from all-encompassing—net over relevant written documents, books, and essays. The present chapter focuses on a select set of these issues, which have been classified into four categories: *compulsory schooling and its prolongation, the transformation of diverse educational frameworks into formal school systems, inequality and equity issues, and the institutionalization of the global education system.* These categories are not meant to exhaust all relevant (or possible) thematic issues. The changing nature of educational goals and aims, the curricular contents of public schooling (Benavot and Braslavsky, 2006), gender inequality, educational financing, teaching training and licensing, minority and immigrant education, and non-formal education are important analytical topics, for which comparative histories will need to be developed in the future.

LEGAL-INSTITUTIONAL CONDITIONS

Compulsory Schooling and its Prolongation

Compulsory school legislation represents both an important enabling condition and a significant political intention in national attempts to universalize access to basic education. Whether by decree, proclamation, statute, law, or constitutional provision, government authorities set forth a legal basis for the establishment of systems of publicly funded, state-administered schools. Historically, newly independent nation-states often enacted legal provisions for compulsory schooling as they sought to consolidate their authority and control over a given territory and population. Many political leaders came to view the building of a national system of public secular schools as a conscious strategy to weaken the influence of religious institutions in local communities and to empower the state in its pursuit of industrialization and national unity. By compelling attendance in public secular schools, governments ensured that young children would receive instruction in basic literacy and numeracy as well as in "appropriate" (i.e., non-religious) moral precepts and political principles.

Colonial administrations established compulsory school laws and educational ordinances in dependent colonies, sparsely populated territories, and semi-autonomous regions even though, as was often the case, the resources needed to provide school spaces for all school-age children were insufficient.[3] Although unrealistic in scope, the enactment of compulsory school rules symbolized the importance and desirability of formalizing socialization frameworks for the young. In addition, they legitimated and bolstered efforts by missionaries and other private groups to construct and expand school buildings. Certainly, colonial policies supporting modern (in this case, Western) schooling were one means of

---

[3] While the lack of implementation or enforcement of compulsory laws was not exclusive to non-independent political entities, it was much more pervasive than in independent countries.

securing native support for other government policies. Overall, the passage of compulsory school laws evinced the political intentions of public authorities, even if the laws were limited by design and infeasible to realize. They also forged a social contract between colonial administrations, religious groups, local communities, parents, and children. Below, we discuss key issues regarding the establishment, substance, and prolongation of compulsory schooling laws. We emphasize the lack of uniformity concerning the intentions and design of compulsory enrollment statutes throughout history, to say nothing of their actual impacts on the lives and routines of families and school-age children.

The Timing and Passage of Compulsory School Legislation

Today, over 90 percent of the world's countries have legally binding rules requiring children's school attendance (UNESCO, 2002; Benavot, 2002). The first such laws were enacted about 200 years ago in Prussia and Denmark (Soysal and Strange, 1989). Prior to these first laws, however, proclamations obligating parents to provide for the education of their children, not necessarily in schools, circulated in various European and North American communities such as Weimar, Massachusetts, Brunswick, and Gotha (Ramirez and Boli, 1993). Nordic families were urged by King and Church alike to educate their children in fundamental religious precepts, moral virtues, and the rudiments of reading and writing. Such proclamations—normative rather than legally binding—underscored the pivotal roles that religious authorities and families played in the early spread of literacy in Europe (Maynes, 1985; Graff, 1987; Mitch, 1992; Vincent, 2000).

The establishment of compulsory mass schooling is best understood as an extended historical process, initially limited in geographical scope, in which education of the young moved out of the home and church and into the public sphere of differentiated schools. Ramirez and Boli (1993) describe this process as the institutionalization of Western models of socialization and propose three distinct stages of development. *Compulsory education* was a part of the Reformation movement to enhance religious piety and individual faith among Protestant families. It developed in the seventeenth century, mainly in Denmark, Norway, Sweden, and certain German principalities and North American colonies. *Mass schooling* was part of a movement to weaken family socialization and home-based instruction by establishing community schools with largely religious and fairly standardized curricula that emphasized the development of literacy, biblical knowledge, and moral character. It emerged in the eighteenth century, mainly in Norway, various Swiss cantons, Dutch provinces, and German *Länder*. Lastly, *compulsory mass schooling*, in which the nation-state became the central—if not the sole—initiator, guarantor, and administrator of an inter-connected system of schools, emerged in nineteenth century Europe and the Americas. Children of specified ages were legally compelled to attend state-authorized schools for a stipulated number of days and weeks each year.

Most scholarly research focuses on the third stage, analyzing historical and comparative patterns in the development of compulsory mass schooling (e.g., Soysal and Strange, 1989; Ramirez and Ventresca, 1992; Mangan, 1994; Cummings, 2003). Historical case studies describe, in considerable detail, political developments that influenced the establishment or revision of compulsory education statutes in, for example, Thailand (Jumsai, 1951), Iraq (Clark, 1951), the Philippines (Isidro et al., 1952), Indonesia (Hutasott, 1954), South Korea (Central Education Research Institute, 1967), Prussia and Austria (van Horn Melton, 1988), Bavaria (Schleunes, 1989), and the United States (Glenn, 1988). Cross-national studies, on the other hand, analyze variations in the timing of compulsory schooling laws. For each country, a particular date is chosen to reflect either the creation of a national education system (Soysal and Strange, 1989) or the intentions of a government or governing body to require all children within defined age categories to attend school (Ramirez and Ventresca, 1992). Despite slight differences in the exact years used by researchers to designate the establishment of compulsory schooling in each country (and keeping in mind that laws and administrative rules were often rescinded, re-instated, or revised), the following basic patterns can be summarized:

- Several German states were the forerunners in passing compulsory education laws, beginning in the eighteenth century and continuing through the early nineteenth century.
- Almost all European countries—earlier in Western Europe, later in Eastern Europe—enacted compulsory school laws during the nineteenth century and the first three decades of the twentieth century.
- Although the United States never passed a federal law compelling school enrollment, individual states made provisions for compulsory schooling in state constitutions and/or legal statutes. Massachusetts

passed its first compulsory attendance law in 1852, followed by states in the Northeast, Midwest, and the far West. In total, 33 states passed compulsory school laws during the nineteenth century; 17 states, mainly from the South, did so in the twentieth century. Interestingly, many western territories passed compulsory attendance laws prior to achieving statehood, in anticipation of subsequent settlement (Richardson, 1984; 1986).

• Most Southern and Central American countries passed compulsory school statutes fairly early during the nineteenth and twentieth centuries, although the term free and compulsory education was used "more as utopian projects than as any reflection of reality" (Garcia Garrido, 1986: 19).[4] Indeed, primary enrollment rates in the first half of the twentieth century were much lower in Latin America than in Europe or North America (Benavot and Riddle, 1988).

• About 80 percent of the 60 countries that were independent in 1945 had enacted compulsory attendance laws.

• Between 1945 and 2004, 125 former colonies and non-self-governing territories became independent in Asia, Africa, Europe, and parts of the Americas; 85 percent of these new states had passed compulsory school laws by 2000. As in the case of the United States, a significant number of former colonies had already passed educational ordinances that addressed pupil attendance prior to achieving independence.

Beyond these descriptive patterns, the literature addresses several analytical issues. For example, comparative analyses discovered an interesting link between the date of independence and the date at which compulsory schooling rules were enacted (Ramirez and Boli, 1982). Based on information for over 55 countries, it appears that the lag between these two dates shortened in each successive wave of national independence. Whereas for countries that became independent in the nineteenth cen-

---

[4] Exemplifying the recurrent proclamations regarding compulsory schooling in Latin America, Garcia Garrido mentions the Paraguyan case: "Since independence in 1811, compulsory primary education was decreed by Rodrigo de Francia in 1828, by Lopez in 1844, by the Constitution of 1870, by the Law of 1887, by the Compulsory Education Law of 1909, by the subsequent law of 1924, by the Constitution of 1940 and, lastly, by the current Constitution of 1967" (Garcia Garrido, 1986: 19). Although utopian proclamations in favor of mass schooling were voiced and passed by political leaders, well beyond the boundaries of the Americas, the disjuncture between the ideal and reality was apparently acute in Latin American educational history.

tury, the mean lag period from independence until the passage of a compulsory schooling rule was between 25 to 50 years, this lag was reduced to less than 6 years during the first half of the twentieth century. Following World War II, newly independent countries typically passed a compulsory education law within about a year of becoming independent, although some countries, as previously noted, have yet to do so. Ramirez and Boli argue that this pattern illustrates that the ideology of compulsory education was not inherent in the formation of nation states during the eighteenth and nineteenth centuries, but became increasingly part of the nation-state model during the twentieth century. In recent decades, compulsory education has become closely intertwined with the array of activities undertaken by national governments. As Ramirez and Boli note, "The link between the state and education is complete and taken for granted" (1982: 29).

Other studies have examined the relationship between the extent of educational expansion and the timing of compulsory school legislation. Comparative evidence in Europe (Soysal and Strange, 1989) and across nations (Ramirez and Ventresca, 1992) indicates a weak association between these two variables. In some cases (e.g., Prussia, Denmark, Sweden, Japan), the adoption of compulsory school laws initiated a period of enrollment expansion. In others, mainly in South America, laws supporting compulsory education were enacted but rarely enforced. In the latter contexts, enrollment rates in elementary schools were limited at the time of formal enactment and remained relatively low throughout the nineteenth and early twentieth centuries. In still other cases (e.g., Swiss cantons, France, most U.S. states), systems of mass schooling were already well in place when compulsory schooling legislation was passed. Even today, several countries lacking compulsory school laws (e.g., Singapore, Oman, Saudi Arabia) have achieved very high enrollment rates. Overall, it appears that pressures on new states to pass compulsory school laws following political independence have increased sharply over time. These expectations are only indirectly related to the actual (and future) expansion of a country's education system. Their impact on other features of educational modernization (e.g., teacher training, public financing of education, the building of schools) remains under-studied.[5]

---

[5] A state's commitment to educational expansion should be examined through measures beyond the passage of compulsory school legislation, important as

Furthermore, historical evidence suggests that the political, social, and institutional meanings associated with the establishment of compulsory schooling varied significantly over time and place. In France, for example, the passage of such laws reflected an ongoing struggle between the Catholic Church and the state, while in Prussia and Scandinavian countries where the state mobilized Protestant churches to create national churches, support for mass schooling was ensured (Soysal and Strange, 1989; Schleunes, 1989). In Japan, compulsory education, long in gestation, owed much to comparisons to industrial leaders such as the United States and military competitors such as China (Japanese National Commission for UNESCO, 1958). In Ecuador, the compulsory attendance law of 1871 was meant to overcome the lack of interest in education among parents, on the one hand, and strongly rooted colonial prejudices against girls' schooling, on the other (Uzcategui, 1951). In dependent Indian States (i.e., Baroda, Kolhapur, Mysore) and parts of British India, the passage of compulsory school laws coincided with a "rising tide of nationalist opinion" (Saiyidain et al., 1952: 21). In Sri Lanka, the legislation to make education free and compulsory was intended to reduce child labor in coffee, rubber, and coconut plantations, and to create conditions for enrollment expansion (Little, 1998). In many Arab states, compulsory education laws reflected initial attempts to redress long-standing gender disparities in enrollment and attendance (UNESCO, 1956a). In the western territories of the United States, the passage of such laws anticipated actual settlement, crystallizing a blueprint for future development (Richardson, 1986). In short, although the establishment of compulsory school laws increasingly accompanied nation-state formation, the meanings and intentions of such legal provisions reflected diverse configurations of local political, economic, and cultural conditions.

The historical record suggests that political authorities employed widely different rationales to enact compulsory school laws. In some cases, the establishment of compulsory education addressed narrowly defined educational problems; in others, it was employed as a strategy to "solve" or defer solving long-standing economic, cultural, or social problems. In India, for example, the impact of several early initiatives towards

---

this legislation may be. The public financing of building schools, the percentage of a nation's domestic product allocated to education, and other indicators of state investment in mass schooling may be better predictors of subsequent educational expansion.

compulsory education under British rule remained highly localized, even after the country became independent. According to Weiner (1991: 4–5), the Indian state was unable, or unwilling, to deal with pervasive low school enrollments and endemic child labor. He argues that this was not due to the country's precarious economic situation, but rather to deeply rooted beliefs among the Indian middle class about social order and hierarchy, the importance of education in reinforcing social class distinctions, and "concerns that 'excessive' and 'inappropriate' education for the poor would disrupt social arrangements" (Weiner, 1991: 5).

The Particularities of Compulsory School Laws

Below, we briefly discuss the contents of select compulsory attendance laws, with the aim of exposing forgotten, yet potentially interesting, historical particularities. We first examine the compulsory school ordinances passed in the Northwest Territories ceded to the Dominion of Canada by the Hudson Bay Trading Company in 1870. Settled in far flung trading posts, peopled by diverse populations of Indians, whites, and Métis, and served by religious missionaries representing Catholic, Methodist, and Anglican churches, the huge expanses of the Northwest Territories had little to speak of in the way of mass schooling (Kach and Mazurek, 1993). Nevertheless, during the last quarter of the nineteenth century, several compulsory education ordinances were enacted. In 1875, the earliest ordinance devised an initial blueprint for school expansion that, in effect, disenfranchised foreign immigrants and Native Americans and set forth demanding preconditions for the creation of schools. Subsequent ordinances, which sought to provide a stronger basis for school expansion, established school districts and separate school boards for Protestants and Catholics, each of whom was responsible for teacher certification, curricular guidelines, and school inspections. The ordinance of 1892 abolished the emergent framework of schools controlled by religious authorities in favor of a system of publicly supported and administrated schools. Though this ordinance best exemplifies a modern, inclusionary legal statute for mass compulsory schooling, it carried important caveats in its rich details:

- "In every School District, where there are at least fifteen children of School age, resident within a radius of one mile and a half from the School House, it shall be compulsory for the Trustees of such District to keep the school open all year (section 186).

- "In every School District, where there are at least ten children of School age, it shall be compulsory for the Trustees of such District to leave their school in operation at least six months in every year (187).
- "Every parent, guardian or other person, resident in School District having control of any child or children, between ages seven and twelve years, shall be required to send such child or children to School for a period of at least twelve weeks in each year...(188).
- "It shall be the duty of the Trustees of every School District...after being notified that any parent or guardian...neglects or violates the provisions of the above section, to make complaint of such neglect to a Justice of the Peace...(189).
- "It shall be the duty of the Justice of the Peace to ascertain...the circumstances of any party complained of for not sending his or her child to School...and he shall accept any of the following as a reasonable excuse:
  1. That the child is under instruction in some other satisfactory manner;
  2. That the child has been prevented from attending School by sickness or any unavoidable cause;
  3. That there is no School open...not exceeding two and one half miles, measured according to the nearest passable road from the residence of the child;
  4. That such a child has reached a standard of education of the same or of a greater degree than that attained in the School of the School District within which such child resides (190)." [6]

These statutes are noteworthy in many respects. First and foremost, they formalized a web of social and institutional relationships between local communities, political bodies, elected officials, educational authorities, the legal system, and, naturally, parents, teachers, and children. For example, the establishment of compulsory schooling compelled action from multiple parties: the trustees of each school district were required to build, maintain, and operate schools; parents and guardians were required to send all their 7–12 year old children to school (barring officially recognized mitigating circumstances); school officials and commu-

---

[6] Ordinance of Northwest Territories, 1892, An Ordinance to Amend and Consolidate as Amended the Ordinance Respecting Schools, sections 186-190, quoted in Kach and Mazurek (1993: 170ff).

nity members were asked to report non-compliant parents; and judges were responsible for determining the reasons for, and consequences of, non-attendance. Second, the 1892 ordinance highlights the many contingencies associated with compulsory schooling. The establishment of schools depended on local population concentrations and age distributions; the length of the school term depended on the size of the school-age population; parental obligations were contingent on residential location (in relation to schools) and the provision of alternative educational opportunities at home. Third, these statutes underscore inequalities in school provisions—note the varying length of the school year and school session by district. Fourth, these statutes illustrate that compulsory education was not just a circumscribed relationship between the state (or territorial authority) and families with children, but an issue in which the wider community had a stake, for example, in ensuring parental compliance. Lastly and significantly, legislators who passed these statutes clearly acknowledged alternative avenues of educational provision, through home based instruction, private tutoring, or "some other satisfactory manner." Given the geographical and climatic realities of northern Canadian communities, the importance (and perhaps the practical necessity) of home-based instruction is understandable.

A realistic approach to free and compulsory education, one that acknowledges the widely diverse material and cultural conditions of the communities to be covered by educational statutes, was also apparent in the 1950s, when newly independent nations began passing and implementing compulsory school legislation. In Pakistan, for example, authorities encouraged different provinces to develop their own multi-year schemes to establish compulsory education in gradual stages, taking into account historical ordinances as well as the actual distribution of school facilities, classrooms, qualified teachers, attendance patterns, and the possibility of regular supervision and enforcement (Huq, 1954). Burma and Cambodia employed pilot projects and provisional solutions, especially in relation to existing religious and private schools, as a mechanism for enlarging the scope and coverage of compulsory education (UNESCO, 1954). Owing to harsh economic conditions and limited public budgets, many countries introduced special measures to help fund and maintain primary schools—for example, village-based financing (Laos), or obligatory parental contributions to school budgets in the form of cash, material, or labor (Philippines). To encourage parents to send their children to school, and to improve the well being of enrolled pupils, primary schools in Mauritius provided free milk and yeast each day to pupils (UNESCO, 1954: 68). Additional strategies intended to boost public support for compulsory education and to increase regular pupil attendance included curricular reforms in public schools, changes in languages of instruction, and teacher involvement in community life.

Nevertheless, public authorities knew they were fighting a protracted, uphill battle to institutionalize mass schooling and compel attendance. As a result, early compulsory attendance statutes included many categories of exemptions based on conditions such as geographical location, physical and mental disabilities of children or parents, access to home instruction, agricultural cycles, and household poverty levels.

In short, though there are few instances of newly independent countries having directly opposed the basic principle of free and compulsory schooling, political leaders openly acknowledged that material and cultural conditions in their countries made it virtually impossible to implement this principle in practice. A close examination of the contents of compulsory school legislation illustrates the degree to which diverse social realities were acknowledged and considered, even as the principle was being institutionalized and as political leaders envisioned the development of elaborate public school systems.

International Organizations' Impacts on Compulsory Education in Newly Independent Countries

On December 10, 1948, the United Nations adopted the Universal Declaration of Human Rights (UDHR). Article 26 of the Declaration stated emphatically: "Everyone has the right to education. Education shall be free, at least in the elementary and fundamental stages. Elementary education shall be compulsory...."[7] Signatories of the UDHR committed them-

---

[7] When the term fundamental education was used in the UDHR, it meant the right to education for illiterate adults and others who were denied the opportunity to receive a full elementary education during their youth. The term was first used by the Preparatory Commission of UNESCO in preparing documents for UNESCO's 1st General Conference held in November 1946. Despite some uncertainty over the term, there was considerable consensus that fundamental education meant an education that would provide for the acquisition of literacy and other essential knowledge, including skills and values needed to fully participate in society (UNESCO, 2000). The definition of fundamental education is very similar to today's concept of basic education. The main difference is that

selves to the goal of providing school places for all children and were
expected to implement legislation making schooling compulsory. By compelling attendance in school, political authorities sought to enable each
child to exercise his or her right to education. Depending on the nature
of educational provisions, governments were under considerable international pressure to either stipulate the minimum duration of school attendance and the age groups to be enrolled or to establish laws prolonging
the duration of compulsory schooling. Where compulsory education was
well established and included primary education, the extension of the
school-leaving age into post-primary or secondary education was
expected. Where only part of the primary cycle was mandatory, compulsory education was to be prolonged to include the full length of the primary cycle. Where no compulsory school laws existed, there was pressure
to pass such laws and, in doing so, to expand access to primary education.

The positions and declarations adopted by member states attending
regional UNESCO conferences on Free and Compulsory Education in the
1950s (Bombay 1952, Cairo 1955, Lima 1956) reflected the results of
this international pressure. The Bombay conference recommended compulsory education for no less than seven years, whereas the Cairo and
Lima conferences recommended compulsory education for a minimum
of six years. (In Latin America, it was understood that this did not necessarily apply to rural areas, where the duration was often only three years.)
All regional conferences recognized the legal obligation of states to
expand provisions for primary education—compulsory attendance was
unrealistic unless schools were available and essentially free (i.e., no
tuition, although fees for school books were allowed). Even when the
financial means to provide school spaces for all school-age children were
insufficient, governments enacted compulsory school laws to crystallize

---

the former term emphasizes the immediate needs of community while the latter
term conceives of education as preparation for life-long learning. In operational
terms, fundamental education was mainly understood as community education
(e.g., adult literacy programs, agricultural and health education). Fundamental
education and adult education were considered two aspects of the French term:
popular education. In the early 1960s, especially with the independence of former colonies, international focus on adult education—a more established term
among UN member states—widened to include literacy and the learning needs
of adults who had not received any formal education during childhood. In general, attention shifted away from fundamental education and emphasis on the
eradication of illiteracy increased.

their commitment to free and universal education. In short, although quite a few former colonies had passed limited educational ordinances prior to independence (e.g., India, Philippines, Iraq, Malaya), there is little doubt that international organizations played a leading role in the passage of compulsory attendance legislation in newly independent states.

The Prolongation of Compulsory Education

In the 1950s, international policy discussions on compulsory schooling typically revolved around the establishment of an inclusive law that defined the minimum number of years that children would be required to attend school and, when possible, the extension of this period. In practice, this meant that countries were encouraged to define two age boundaries: first, the entry age, when parents were expected to enroll their children in school; and second, the minimum exit age, when children could leave school and either remain at home or enter the labor market.

Interestingly, few comparative historical studies have examined the social, political, and economic forces affecting changes in the duration (as distinct from the timing) of compulsory schooling. Nevertheless, initial evidence suggests that different sets of factors affected long-term changes in the age boundaries of compulsory education. On the one hand, the entrance age boundary became more fixed over time. To the degree that evolving conceptions of childhood and child development, women's labor force participation, and the availability of certified teachers influenced this boundary, compulsory education incorporated younger and younger children. On the other hand, the exit age changed more frequently (to include older and older youth) and was more influenced by the passage of child labor laws, the demand for youth labor, changing norms regarding marriage and family formation, the expansion of secondary schooling, and budgetary constraints.

In 1927, the International Labour Office asked the International Bureau of Education (IBE) to carry out an international survey of the duration of compulsory schooling, to inform new policies for raising the school-leaving age (IBE, 1932). Table 1 compares the results from this survey with present-day figures on the duration of compulsory schooling for over 42 education systems. During the 70-year interval between 1930 and 2000, the vast majority of education systems (68 percent) made no change to the entrance age of compulsory schooling. By contrast, 85 percent of systems raised the exit age of compulsory education, usually by 1 or 2 years, but in some cases by 3 or 4 years. In addition, it can be

Table 1: Long-term Trends in the Age Boundaries of Compulsory Schooling, 1930–2000

Country	Ages entering and leaving compulsory schooling, circa 1930	Ages entering and leaving compulsory schooling, circa 2000
Austria	6–14	6–15
Belgium	6–14	6–18
Denmark	7–14	7–16
England	5–14	5–16
Finland	7–15	7–16
France	6–13	6–16
Greece	6–12	6–15
Iceland	7–14 (towns)/10–14 (country)	6–16
Ireland	6–14	6–15
Italy	6–12	6–15
Luxembourg	7–14	6–15
Netherlands	6–13	6–17
New Zealand	7–14	6–16
Norway	7–14	6–16
Portugal	7–11	6–15
Spain	6–14	6–16
Sweden	7–14	7–16
Albania	6–12	6–14
Bulgaria	7–14	7–15
Czechoslovakia/Czech Rep.	6–14	6–15
Estonia	8–16	7–15
Hungary	6–15	7–16
Latvia	7–14	7–15
Lithuania	7–12	7–16
Poland	7–14	7–18
Romania	5–14	7–16
USSR/ Russian Federation	8–15	6–15
Argentina	6–14	6–15
Brazil	7–14	7–14
Costa Rica	7–14	6–15
Ecuador	6–14	6–14
Guatemala	7–14	6–15
Haiti	6–14	6–15
Mexico	6–14	6–15
Paraguay	7–14	6–14
Uruguay	6–14	6–15
China	6–14	6–14
Egypt	Not compulsory	6–14
India	6–11	6–14
Japan	6–14	6–15
Tunisia	Not compulsory	6–16
Turkey	7–12	6–14

Sources: *Bulletin of the International Bureau of Education* (1932) 23 (2): 51–53; and Table 4 in UNESCO-EFA *Global Monitoring Report (2003/4) Gender and Education for All.* Paris: UNESCO.

assumed that for many countries in the 1930s, especially in Eastern Europe, Latin America, and Asia, laws stipulating the entrance and exit ages of compulsory schooling reflected intentions more than realities, with few enforcement mechanisms in place. Today, even in cases when the age parameters of compulsory schooling have changed little since 1930, the disjuncture between legal statutes and educational realities has been significantly reduced. Finally, the systems compared in Table 1 show a certain degree of institutional convergence. Over time, cross-national variation in the entrance and exit ages of compulsory education has been reduced.

Analyses of contemporary patterns of compulsory schooling, involving a greater number of national education systems, reveal several interesting patterns. First, among the 90 percent of countries having passed compulsory attendance laws, considerable variation is apparent in the duration of compulsory schooling. In some countries, pupils are expected to attend school for only 4–5 years (e.g., São Tomé, Equatorial Guinea, Bangladesh, Nepal, Vietnam, Iran), while other countries compel attendance for as long as 12–13 years (e.g., Netherlands, Saint Kitts, Germany, Belgium, Brunei). Second, there appears to be a fairly strong association between a country's income level and the duration of compulsory education (Benavot, 2002). Third, in recent decades, the mean duration of compulsory schooling (which typically begins at age 5 or 6) has increased by a full year, from a global average of 7.2 years (86 countries) in 1965 to 8.2 years (169 countries) in 2000. During this period, European and North American countries mandated, on average, between 8 to 10 years of compulsory education. In other regions, the mean duration was as follows: 8.3 years in Latin America and the Caribbean, 7.9 years in the Middle East and North Africa, 7.8 years in Asia and the Pacific, and 7.2 years in sub-Saharan Africa. In all world regions, except Sub-Saharan Africa, the trend over time has been to prolong compulsory schooling. In Sub-Saharan Africa, by contrast, there has been a decline in the mean duration of compulsory education, especially since 1995, reflecting the inability of countries in this region to mobilize the necessary financial resources to pay for, and enforce, 7 or 8 years of compulsory schooling.

Conclusion

Although discussions of compulsory schooling today are overwhelmingly taken for granted, the establishment of compulsory mass schooling involved different logics, interests, and approaches. When former colonies established a legal framework for compulsory attendance following independence, they drew upon different historical experiences and rationales. Typically, the political authorities in newly independent nations moved quickly to adopt the legal and ideological garb of compulsory education. The laws they passed were not only rich in content, but also full of qualifications and exemptions. In retrospect, they reveal the rather realistic and sanguine approach of supporters of compulsory mass schooling to the implementation process and its chances for success. These supporters explicitly built many accommodations and contingencies into the process, which was to be carried out over a prolonged period. These historical realities should be revisited as discussions turn to contemporary strategies to achieve universal basic education.

SYSTEMIZATION PROCESSES

The Formation of National School Systems

A distinctive feature of modern education is its systemic character. From an analytical perspective, the transformation of disparate educational frameworks into an organized, interconnected system involved at least two processes: the formation of a national system of schools and the standardization of educational forms. In Europe, the creation of national education systems entailed a drawn-out process whereby most—if not all—types of education were placed under one umbrella and administered through an integrated state bureaucracy. This process parallels the "unification" of a state education system, as discussed by Archer (1979: 174): "...the incorporation or development of diverse establishments, activities and personnel under a central national and specifically educational framework of administration." In such systems, government authorities, typically located in a central ministry, oversaw all state-regulated schools through the licensing and inspection of school institutions, the recruitment, training, and certification of teachers, the determination of curricular contents, and the development of nationally recognized qualifications. Thus, the extent of centralization in educational governance is a key analytical feature of the formation of national education systems.

In addition, various processes of standardization accompanied the growth of national school systems. Schools at different educational levels—pre-primary, primary, secondary, and higher education—were classified into standard, hierarchical categories. Increased standardization of curricula, examinations, and certification enabled the articulation and coordination of different educational levels. The actual level of standardization depended, to a large extent, on the extent of centralization within the educational system. Nevertheless, far from being the outcome of innocuous bureaucratic decisions and directives, standardization often touched upon salient social, cultural, and political tensions. Among other things, authorities had to determine the status of religious schools as well as the role of private or voluntary associations in educational affairs. Thus, the formation of national education systems created at least two difficult dilemmas for state administrators, one dealing with the relationship between religious and secular education, and the other involving the relationship between public and private education. Although the two dilemmas are interrelated (most private schools were also religious ones), for the purpose of clear analysis, we prefer to deal with them separately. The public versus private dilemma stresses the role and authority of the state in the finance, governance, and regulation of education, while the religious versus secular dilemma focuses on the conflict over worldviews and values (Western, Christian, Muslim, Buddhist, etc.).

We characterize early models of national education systems and address three core dilemmas that have accompanied systemization in the past: 1) the extent of centralization or decentralization in educational governance; 2) the tension between public schools and private schools; and 3) the tension between religious education and secular education.

Early Models of National Education Systems

The first major national education systems in Europe—Prussian and French—included an expanding framework of secular public schools based on compulsory school laws and a strong state administrative apparatus.[8] These distinctive features have defined the foundations of many education systems throughout the world ever since. In addition, the education systems of England, the United States, the Soviet Union, and Japan constituted basic models that influenced educational systemization in different world regions. Below we briefly describe these early national education systems.

---

[8] The educational reform in Piedmont (Italy) in 1729 is considered by many as the first attempt to build a state education system in Europe. We prefer to focus on the Prussian and French cases because of their formative influences on later education systems.

In Prussia, under King Frederick II (1740–1786), the state came to assume an active and expansive role in the mobilization of society for economic, technical, and scientific progress. This involved the establishment of state-authorized schools, the development of a common state-mandated curriculum, and the creation of an administrative structure to oversee and inspect state-financed schools. The 1794 General Code specified the details of this system and represented a move towards both systemization and the affirmation of the state as the central authority responsible for national education (Maynes, 1985; Cummings, 1997). By the 1830s, Prussia had built an extensive national network of public elementary schools, providing education for most children until the age of 14, as well as an elaborate system of elite secondary schools. As public institutions, schools were authorized and inspected by the state, teachers were trained and licensed by the state, and the curriculum was developed by state officials and regulated by national examinations (Green, 1990: 3).

Whereas the creation of the Prussian education system was an integral part of the state formation process, in France, the state was already well consolidated and, as early as the seventeenth century, a central state apparatus had emerged. This extremely centralized administration was the foundation for the education system created by Napoleon, who placed schools under the authority of a central university, regional academies, departments, and local communes. The early systemization of education in France owed much to the power and authority of this centralized royal bureaucracy, even though the emphasis was on elite educational institutions in the form of lycées and *grandes écoles* (Durkheim, 1977). Popular education, by contrast, was limited and largely under the auspices of the Catholic Church. The creation and incorporation of elementary schools into the French education system occurred only after the Revolution. In 1833, François Guizot established a national system of basic education following the model shaped in the Napoleonic era. *Loi Guizot* (the Guizot Law) extended state control over teacher licensing and school inspection, and attempted to expand primary schooling to each of the French communes. Only with the Ferry law in 1882, however, did elementary education become free and compulsory in France (Ringer, 1979; Garnier, Hage, and Fuller, 1989; Cummings, 1997).

These early national education systems can be understood as conscious strategies to address three critical needs in nascent states: 1) the need to shape citizens' loyalty through the inculcation of ideologies of nationhood, 2) the need to provide the state with trained public administrators and military personnel, and 3) the need to mobilize society for economic purposes and industrial development.

In Prussia, expanding public schooling served to consolidate a nation, create a public administration, and further economic development. In France, the systemization of education not only aimed to address these purposes, but also to undermine the power of the Catholic Church and enhance citizens' loyalty to the state. Both the Prussian and French models of systemization were extremely influential in other parts of Europe and in South America and were adapted in different ways in nascent state structures by dominant social classes (Green, 1990: 4).

The creation of a national education system in England was late in coming (almost 100 years after France and Prussia), despite extensive industrialization. Political factors, especially the decentralized nature of the English state, accounted in part for the absence of mass compulsory schooling and the late timing of educational systemization (Green, 1990: 309). In contrast to continental Europe, political transformations in England brought an end to absolutism by the seventeenth century. During the subsequent two centuries, England established a relatively stable ruling class and experienced few external military threats, social revolutions, or problems related to economic backwardness similar to those faced by elites on the continent (Green, 1990: 312). Thus, nation building and economic development were not the main driving forces for the creation of a national education system in England.

Many members of the English elite feared that educating the commoner would contribute to political malcontent and revolutionary outbursts as had occurred in France, and preferred the spread of elitist "public" schools, which aimed at nurturing knowledgeable and refined gentlemen. Other segments of the elite sought to broaden notions of citizenship, including political enfranchisement, and viewed the education of the masses as a focal point for their reform efforts. During the late nineteenth and early twentieth centuries, the enactment of a series of legal provisions increased the educational responsibilities of the central state as well as local governments. These changes led to the creation of new educational institutions serving the children of common English citizens, effectively supplementing existing institutions that had long served the offspring of political and economic elites. Nevertheless, the English education system, which was based on deeply rooted principles of charity and local initiative, was not nearly as well coordinated and integrated as continental education systems (Green, 1990: 310–11).

One important motivating factor in the establishment of education systems in Europe was the incorporation of distinct ethnic and cultural groups within an integrated national territory. This often meant the imposition of a national language and a dominant culture with which the ruling elite identified (Bendix, 1969; Breuilly, 1982; Gellner, 1983; P. Anderson, 1991). Elites often banned or restricted local languages and dialects in order to create national "imagined communities" (B. Anderson, 1983). In France, the move to linguistic homogenization succeeded in eliminating dialects such as Breton and Patois; in Spain, however, this initiative made few inroads with the Catalan and Basque languages, which were later revived and bolstered. Homogenization weakened many local and ethnic traditions, but these traditions continued to act as a source of social and economic inequalities, especially in relation to educational opportunities. Citizens belonging to cultural groups or geographical regions in which the official language was not completely rooted remained at a disadvantage.

In the United States, individual states, rather than the federal government, had sovereign power over education. No national education system developed, although certain federal regulations required territories to make educational provisions as a condition of entry into the Union (Tyack, 1976). Between 1830 and 1870, northern states developed systems of public schools, financed from public sources and administered by state and county boards of education (Green, 1990). The moral "crusade" of the common-school movement during this period, suffused with religious and ideological themes, resulted in the very high enrollments of young children in community-built and publicly funded schools (Tyack, James, and Benavot, 1987). In fact, outside of the South, school enrollment rates were actually higher in predominantly rural and agricultural states than in more urban ones (Meyer et al., 1979; Walters and O'Connell, 1988; Baker, 1999). As the government planned and established settlements in the Western territories, they sold or rented public lands in order to raise funds for the building of local schools (Richardson, 1986). Overall, despite the lack of a centralized bureaucracy, the educational structures created in United States, based on mass compulsory schooling and extensive public spending, approximated a national education system (Green, 1990).

In the Soviet Union, the creation and expansion of a national education system emerged out of the Bolshevik Revolution (Matthews, 1982). Key principles of Soviet education, established in 1918, continued to influence educational patterns until the breakup of the Soviet Union. In particular, Soviet authorities developed mass educational institutions to improve literacy levels, enhance meritocratic principles, and pursue industrial development (Cummings, 2003: 27–29). The structure of Soviet education followed highly rational, hierarchical, and bureaucratic lines of authority, which extended from the central ministry through various regional and district levels until they reached school directors, classroom teachers, and pupils. As part of an explicit strategy of national development, the education system expanded to support collective state objectives. Given these ideological concerns, the state fully subsidized education and public authorities prepared detailed plans for human resource development and manpower utilization. Central planning, which accentuated the needs of the national economy and the state above those of individual pupils, permeated the system (Grant, 1979; Whittacer, 1991; Eklof and Dneprov, 1993). The Soviet model strongly influenced the education systems of Communist block countries, many of which adopted substantial features of Soviet ideology and practice. Other communist countries (Cuba, Vietnam, and China) also borrowed heavily from the Soviet model (Noah, 1986), even though the Soviet presence itself was less pervasive.

In Japan, following the abolition of feudalism and the Meiji Revolution of 1868, educational reform was a key element in the reorganization of national institutions and the creation of a central bureaucracy. The Meiji leaders sought to use education as a means of enhancing national solidarity, training a technically competent labor force, and developing a more future-oriented elite (Cummings, 1980; Westney, 1987; Shimahara, 1979). Several statutes issued during the last decades of the nineteenth century resulted in the consolidation of existing elementary schools, which included ordinary, girls', village, paupers', private, and infants' schools. They also created a centralized educational administration, a national system for the production of textbooks, and uniform finance and personnel policies (Japanese National Commission for UNESCO, 1958). As a consequence, the new regulations appreciably reduced inter- and intra-regional differences in per student expenditures in public schools. This centralized approach brought about considerable uniformity in resource allocation and administrative procedures (Cummings, 1980).

In the cases of the Soviet Union, Japan, and China (Hawkins, 1974), the creation of a national education system resulted from major political transformations and the rupturing of ancient regimes. The centralized and hierarchical organization of the newly constituted education systems reflected the basic governmental structures that emerged in the wake of these social revolutions (i.e., highly centralized, strong bureaucracies).

National Education Systems in Postcolonial States

Newly independent countries, with different histories of colonial rule and economic dependence, built systems of schooling that were fundamentally shaped by powerful external and internal political processes (Clignet and Foster, 1964; King, 1990; Carnoy and Samoff, 1990). Governments in the West typically used the formation of national education systems to further state consolidation, economic improvement, and nation building. Postcolonial states faced additional challenges, including the legacies of colonial education, the transformation of uneven and highly dependent economies, and the creation of national political identities from disparate ethnic affinities brought together under colonial partitions (Altbach and Kelly, 1984).

The education systems established in Africa and Asia struggled with English, French, Portuguese, German, and Dutch colonial legacies that lasted well into the twentieth century. Latin American states, best viewed as "old" dependencies in relation to the new states of Africa and Asia, also confronted patterns of educational stagnation (with the exception of Argentina). European colonialism may have created a relatively educated, even modernizing, elite, but it also bequeathed weak and uneven infrastructures for the development of mass education (Coleman, 1965). Scholars have commented on the diminished influence of Portugal on education in its colonies. During colonial times, the English-speaking world had a pervasive influence on the Portuguese colony of Mozambique; until the mid-1920s, Protestant mission schools outnumbered Catholic ones in Mozambique (Nóvoa et al., 2002), and the former were seen as endangering Portuguese colonial authority (Cross, 1987). As early as the 1930s, Brazil had already detached itself from Portugal and did not consider the imperial power a point of reference in educational matters (Nóvoa et al., 2002).

Following independence, government authorities in many African and Asian countries expanded education as a means of facilitating national solidarity and economic development. Inspired by socialist and egalitarian ideals, and seeking to harness the widespread support of populist independence movements, national leaders and intellectuals envisioned optimistic scenarios that linked educational expansion with national development ingrained in African values (Makulu, 1971: 34). These progressive ideals, however, encountered colonial legacies in which the educational philosophy and structures of European countries had been uncritically transferred to their colonies (Coleman, 1965: 37). The transfer of educational models was even reinforced by the fact that local elites would continue to get their education in Europe. Foreign languages of instruction, imported cultural values, and elite-oriented schools rooted in colonial policies conditioned subsequent developments in the newly formed national education systems.

Religious organizations and colonial administrations had not only created schools with strong exogenous orientations, they had also actively hindered the activities of indigenous educational institutions. Many traditional educational frameworks experienced severe dislocation, as they were unable to compete with the programs and positions offered by mission schools and colonial authorities. Others were dismantled or "eliminated" when colonial authorities suspected them of inculcating nationalism or fomenting rebellion (Carnoy, 1974; Di Bona, 1981).

Although the educational legacies of European colonialism were far reaching, many scholars in postcolonial states have moved beyond blaming current conditions of educational malaise on past colonial policies. For example, Gauhar (1981: 64) contends that the "deplorable" state of education in many African countries is the responsibility of their own leaders; many children are deprived access to schools, sharpening ethnic divisions, and others become alienated from native values and worldviews. Khan (1981: 17–21) claims that the basic nature of formal education in Muslim areas has changed little since independence, apart from its quantitative expansion. In the long shadow of unmet targets to achieve free and universal education, enrollment rates in primary education have increased slowly, whereas secondary and higher education enrollments have increased more quickly. Eager to ensure their children's mobility, elite groups pressured governments to increase access to secondary and higher education, even though teaching standards and student academic expectations in such institutions were often poor.

Nation building was a critical concern of the Latin American education systems created in the aftermath of independence. The ideology of constructing a nation reflected a shift from an exclusionary policy in colonial times to a more inclusionary one after statehood (Rama, 1983: 15–16). Spanish and Portuguese authorities secured their domination in part by excluding the descendants of the conquered race from cultural resources and valued knowledge. By ensuring the continued illiteracy of indigenous peoples in the language used for official and market transactions, authorities maintained political control over "the broad masses of the socially inferior." Colonial educational policies focused primarily on strengthening the elite Latin American universities, which typically emphasized legal and theological training.

After independence, education was viewed as a means of enhancing political participation and was used as a prerequisite for citizenship (e.g., illiterates were disqualified from voting). Expanding educational opportunity reflected the "sacred responsibility of governments to educate the sovereign for the full exercise of his rights," and education was, in theory, accessible for all (Rama, 1983: 17). Notwithstanding this modern participatory discourse, educational developments on the ground remained stagnant. A highly unequal supply of schools clearly favored the urban proletariat over the rural masses. Despite the relatively high esteem accorded to education, demand varied greatly among social groups. This can be explained partly by the underdevelopment of democratic institutions in Latin America (Gale, 1969: 105).

Rama (1983) suggests that three interrelated elements—state action, educational demand, and the degree of educational differentiation—evolved into a limited number of core educational models in Latin America. When restrictive state policies were combined with a demand for education among the upper classes and a fraction of the middle class, then an *exclusive* model emerged. When the upper and middle classes came to predominate, and were confronted with state policies favoring integration, then a *segmentary* model resulted. When the middle classes and popular classes joined to demand education, but the state, representing the dominant groups, restricted participation and limited aspirations for social mobility, then a *classist* model emerged. And finally, when the middle class and popular classes joined together and called on the state to increase educational opportunities to alleviate social inequalities, then a *universalist* model resulted. Variations of these models have featured prominently in the development of Latin American education systems.

Among Latin American states, a sense of national unity took centuries to create. And yet, this national unity has left many minority cultures completely marginalized, especially groups such as the Quechua and Araya-speaking Indians in the altiplano of Bolivia, the Incas of Peru, and indigenous peoples in Mexico (Chiapas), Colombia, and Ecuador.

Nation building and national solidarity were prime objectives for educational expansion in Southeast Asia (e.g., Indonesia, Singapore, Malaysia, Philippines, and Thailand). Owing to strong regional loyalties and a plurality of ethnic groups, issues of social integration and national unity were critical concerns. In addition, colonial educational legacies in this region (with the exception of independent Siam) differed significantly from other regions. To begin with, most countries in southeastern Asia had centuries-old educational traditions. Special pagoda schools existed in Buddhist monasteries. In Hindu areas, the *padepokan* served not only as a meeting place for villagers, but also as a center of learning and religious instruction. Later, with the introduction of Islam, young Muslim boys in Indonesia and Malaysia acquired simple literacy skills in the *pesantren*, *surau*, or Koranic classes. In other settings, temple priests became the main instructors in small village schools. Christian missionaries, who arrived in the region with the influx of European traders, established mission schools that provided rudimentary education to some children. Moreover, colonial education policies in the region, especially in the British colonies, followed a laissez-faire policy, allowing different ethnic groups to develop separate educational institutions. In Malaysia, for instance, there were Malay, Chinese, and Tamil vernacular schools, as well as English medium schools, which were run mainly by Christian missions (Wong, 1973: 129–39).

Finally, following independence, many states in this region actively sought ways to integrate the diverse array of preexisting schools into their emergent national education systems. Instead of closing or prohibiting religious schools, including missionary ones, new governments employed different strategies to adapt them to national purposes. In Burma, for instance, three systems of education were melded into one uniform system following independence. In Malaysia, government policies towards school curricula became a means of integrating diverse schools into a more uniform education system (Wong, 1973). The Malaysian government ended separate vernacular schools (Chinese, Tamil, etc.) and replaced them with a single type of primary school. English medium schools remained open, although the government instructed these schools to reorganize their curricula with a stronger emphasis on Malaysian content. In Singapore, parents were encouraged to send their children to English medium schools rather than Chinese medium schools, in part because interethnic interaction was greater in the former.

This broad characterization of the formation of national education systems informs our discussion of three issues that accompanied systemization: centralization versus decentralization, private education versus public education, and religious education versus secular education.

Centralization and Decentralization in National Education Systems

Archer (1979) argues that the basic structure of an educational system—centralized versus decentralized—had important effects on the nature of school provisions. A centralized bureaucracy was better positioned to engineer education systems by ensuring clearer ties and better coordination among various parts of the system. Centralization promoted, for example, closer linkages among teacher training programs, intended curricular policies, and national systems of examinations. Decentralized education systems, on the other hand, involved less explicit controls and oversight of educational purposes, practices, and processes, and thus facilitated more heterogeneous outcomes. As we have discussed, nations that developed strong state structures created more centralized educational bureaucracies, whereas nations with weak state structures or those organized into federal polities tended to construct more decentralized education systems. Historically, Prussia, France, Spain, Portugal, and much of Scandinavia best exemplify the more centralized systems; England, the United States, Switzerland, and Belgium are prominent examples of more decentralized systems. As Green (1990: 311) maintains, "...forms of national [education] systems reflected the nature of the state which created them."

Since the end of the 1970s, a neo-liberal discourse that stresses the value of decentralization has pervaded national policies of educational governance. Concepts such as efficiency, local participation, power delegation and devolution, de-concentration, school autonomy, and parental choice have circulated extensively in national and international policy fora (see Bray, 1999; Whitty et al., 1998; Dutercq, 2001). In the early 1990s, a survey of developed countries found that after a decade of policies focused on decentralization, the concentration of educational power and decision-making authority had been re-allocated across central, intermediate, and local levels, creating new modes of governance and regulation (Rideout and Ural, 1993). While centralized governance is still relatively strong in France, it has been significantly reduced in Sweden and Norway (Lauglo, 1990; Hutmacher, 2001).

Despite the historical development of distinct models of educational governance in Europe and North America, rooted in varying state formation processes and socio-political conditions, recent trends suggest a growing convergence among countries. On the one hand, nations with highly centralized systems, such as France and Sweden, have incorporated some degree of educational decentralization by means of deregulation, the devolution of central power, and greater school autonomy (for other European examples, see Brock and Tulasiewicz, 2000). On the other hand, countries with historically decentralized education systems, such as Britain and the United States, have increased centralization by adopting national laws, creating national goals and standards, or using national funds to equalize local district expenditures. Converging on the middle, most education systems are establishing various policies of decentralized governance, even in the area of curricula (Astiz et al., 2002).

The centralization-decentralization distinction has considerably less analytical value when examining postcolonial education systems, in contrast to European and North American systems. Centralized educational structures predominated when newly independent nations first established national school systems. The reasons for this vary, but many argue that the exigencies of political independence movements, which brought together diverse—even antagonistic—ethnic and cultural groups to oppose colonial occupation, left an indelible mark of centralistic power. In addition, continental models of educational governance that favored centralization—particularly in France, Spain, and Portugal—significantly conditioned educational developments in many former colonies (Makulu, 1971: 59; Waggoner and Waggoner, 1971: 17; Gale, 1969: 15).

In recent years, most decentralization policies in less-developed states have been recommended or instigated by international organizations. Rather than being adapted to local institutional or political conditions, these policies often come "ready made." In the highly indebted countries of Latin America, decentralization measures have been imposed by loan organizations to reduce public expenditures, especially education costs. The actual implementation of decentralization policies varies by national context. For example, in Argentina and Chile, decentralization in educational governance has meant a shift in the locus of control, from national to regional (or provincial) governments, whereas in Brazil, it has meant a shift from state governments to local authorities.

In all these cases, decentralization reforms took place within different regulatory frameworks and under different market conditions (Narodowski and Milagros, 2002).

Supporters of educational decentralization in Latin America marshal an ambitious range of rationales and objectives to advance their reforms: improvements in basic education, the mobilization of local actors, increased equity, greater school autonomy, and teacher empowerment. However, they tend to ignore or minimize the specific conditions in which the reforms are supposed to be implemented. For example, with limited budgets and tight financial restrictions, stagnating teacher salaries, and little systematic monitoring of educational outcomes, the success of decentralization policies is questionable. Paradoxes abound, some of which contradict the spirit of the reforms themselves. For instance, many teachers in the poorer provinces of Argentina and Brazil are unable to understand or carry out the curricular directives sent by government authorities, resulting in schools turning to private institutions to implement the school "autonomy" projects. Or, in the cases of El Salvador and Nicaragua, where educational regulations are minimal, financial resources are offered to individuals to establish self-managed schools (Braslavsky and Gvirtz, 2000).

In short, initial analyses of decentralization reforms in Latin America indicate that as authorities dramatically reduce public funding of education, private institutions (some partially supported by the state) begin to blossom. Middle- and upper-class parents gain access to private schools and leave deteriorated public schools to the poor. As a result, social and class inequalities in educational access deepen. Evidence suggests that decentralization reforms have adversely impacted the educational opportunities of children from lower socioeconomic strata.

In the past, many political authorities viewed educational centralization as a powerful means for creating national citizens, largely by subverting individuals' loyalties to local entities in competition with the emergent nation-state. By removing young children from parochial socialization frameworks, and by placing them in state-oriented educational or training contexts, political loyalties to the state (and the nation) were assured (Cohen, 1979: 113). In light of this, it is important to consider whether the economic and organizational discourses supporting decentralized governance may inadvertently undermine the political outcomes to which state-directed, mass education systems have contributed in the past.

The Tension between Private Schools and Public Education

The principle that national education systems should provide free and compulsory education is deeply engrained in the modern world. In other words, it is widely believed that every child should have access to formal education in state-sponsored, public schools (Green, 1990: 3). The development of public financing of elementary schools by nation states was a long, drawn-out process. Notwithstanding compulsory education statutes, European states did not immediately assume responsibility for the financing of schooling, and supporters of public finance confronted powerful private-school networks. Prussia and France succeeded in financing elementary schooling at a relatively early stage, and public funding encouraged families to withdraw their children from private institutions. By 1861, public elementary schools in Prussia outnumbered private schools by a ratio of 34 to 1 (Green, 1990: 3). In France, the Jules Ferry Law of 1881 rendered elementary education free. As a result, the state began to financially support private schools, a strategy of increasing control over these institutions (Reisner, 1927: 41). In the 1960s, the Guermeur and Debré Law organized and reinforced the state financing of private (mainly Catholic) schools, while demanding strict conformity to the national curriculum. These laws engendered different relationships between private schools and the state.

In England, until 1833, educational establishments were organized on a purely voluntary basis. They ranged from dame and charity schools at the primary level, owned and run by private individuals; through endowed public schools, which were founded, financed, and regulated by individual bequests; to the university colleges, which continually asserted their independence from state intervention or control (Vaughan and Archer, 1971: 209). Private sponsors funded and governed the elite system of English "public" schools, many of which trace their history back several hundred years (Walford, 1984).

A different set of issues confronted former colonies. In Southeast Asia, private schools, mainly mission schools, provided a general education in British Malaya, Singapore, and the Borneo territories. In these and other parts of Asia, private schools existed at the primary level, but played a much more significant role at the secondary level. Private schools were independent and relied solely on school fees, although they were subject to governmental regulations and were expected to follow the same curriculum as the public state schools (Wong, 1973: 49–50).

In the Philippines, the private sector dominated education at the secondary level (79 percent of enrollments in 1975) but less so at the primary level (only 5 percent of enrollments). The strong demand for education among Filipino elites accounted in part for the considerable investment of private capital in secondary educational institutions. Schools, colleges, and universities operated as profit-making stock corporations and even declared dividends in their stocks. The extensive private-education sector in the country has done little to ensure high standards for quality in all private schools, many of which suffer from poorly trained teachers and run-down facilities and equipment (Wong, 1973: 77).

Contemporary Patterns

In recent decades, the vast majority of education systems have accommodated various forms of private schooling at the primary and secondary levels (Cummings and Riddell, 1994) though world regions vary significantly in the degree to which they rely on the private sector at each level (see Table 2). Private schooling has generally been more prevalent at the secondary level than at the primary level. World regions vary significantly.

Table 2: The Mean Percentage of Private Primary and Secondary Enrollments, by World Region, circa 1980

	Percentage of primary enrollments in private schools	Percentage of secondary enrollments in private schools	Range
Developed countries	14.3	18.6	1–98
Latin America	17.5	29.5	0–76
Sub-Saharan Africa	24.9	30.3	0–99
North Africa/Middle East	9.1	10.9	0–61
Asia	11.8	27.3	0–93

Source: Cummings and Riddell, 1994.

Although types of private schooling vary significantly, schools can be classified by their legal standing vis-à-vis the state and by their mode of finance. Specifically, we can ask whether a state has passed regulations or laws legalizing private schooling and, if so, under what conditions they are allowed to exist (i.e., the extent of state regulation). We can also ask what proportions of school budgets are derived from private sources or from governmental ones. Combining this information determines the overall parameters of private schooling at each educational level. Generally, private schools that are legally recognized and largely financed through public funds belong to the national education system. These private schools incorporate the national curriculum and must submit to national supervision.

States with highly centralized education systems tend to fully subsidize education and to discourage private schooling. France, Russia, China, and Japan best exemplify this tendency. In former communist countries, education was considered an important investment for attaining collective state-defined goals. Thus, the state fully subsidized education and prepared detailed plans both for human resource development and manpower utilization. In contrast, states supporting decentralized education systems tend to admit private schools in parallel to the public-school network. England and the United States are prototypes of this modality.

Interest in the privatization of primary and secondary education has flourished in recent years. As weak economic growth or sluggish international trade creates fiscal crises, governments look for ways to reduce public expenditures, including the centralized funding of public education. In other contexts, government officials believe that the quality and effectiveness of education can be enhanced through privatization and greater competition (and choice) among providers. As part of a broad shift from state-based to market-based development strategies, international organizations such as the World Bank and the IMF have actively supported moves by developing countries to privatize (and decentralize) education.

In Latin America, the move towards privatization (and the support of religious education) has been especially pronounced. According to Albornoz (1993), the Venezuelan government adopted a market discourse, in which people should be "trained" rather than "educated," and spoke about "the cost of education and its usefulness" in private-sector terms. Reforms in favor of private schools in Argentina and Chile have also relied on market-based discourses in their efforts to increase efficiency and reduce state costs. Recent studies suggest that private schooling has indeed expanded (Narodowski and Milagros, 2002). In Latin America, with its long history of class and institutional hierarchies, school labels such as *colegios* and *escuelas* articulate not only the private-sector–public-sector dichotomy, but also deep social inequalities (Albornoz, 1993).

In sum, decentralization policies, administrative school autonomy, voucher systems, and school competition reopen an old question about the value of public school versus private school—a question whose implications for ensuring free, high quality basic education are still being assessed.

The Tension between Religious Institutions and Secular Education

Religion and education have a long, intertwined history. Early educational frameworks trained religious officials and members of the clergy. Over the years, religious leaders have taught and circulated their ideas, philosophies, and dogmas through education. Schools have been responsible for inculcating skills necessary for reading sacred texts and for keeping records of religious activities. Moral education and religious instruction have imbued the curricular contents of many secular schools. All major world religions have established schools to sustain religious movements and to ensure "accurate" interpretations of key religious doctrines.

Historically, the creation of national education systems entailed, in no small measure, the differentiation of education from other societal institutions, particularly religious ones. A public education system typically meant a secular system, which often resulted in hostile and antagonistic attitudes towards religion by state builders and modernizing elites. The extent to which, and the ways by which, the ties unraveled between educational and religious institutions varied considerably over time and place. They still do. Whereas in some countries the two institutions are wholly separated, in theory if not in practice, in other countries, religion continues to influence the education of young children. In Saudi Arabia and Israel, for example, religious education is an integral branch of the national education system. In France, by contrast, religious schools that do not adopt the official curriculum remain private institutions outside of the public system. In Spain, despite a constitutional prohibition against a state religion, the country's dominant Roman Catholic Church continued to enjoy preferential treatment by the government (Callahan, 1992).

The historical struggle between religious and state authorities over the control of education is illustrated in its most extreme form in France. After the revolution, republicans were determined to build a new society by educating and socializing the young. The Republic prohibited religious teaching in schools and subsequently forbade priests to serve as teachers (Cummings, 1997). In 1801, the concordat between Napoleon and the Pope reinstated teaching privileges for church officials and reestablished state recognition of the Church as an educational authority.

During much of the nineteenth century, primary education was in the hands of Christian schools and other congregations (Reisner, 1927: 34). Despite centralized control and a strong bureaucracy, French authorities delayed legal measures concerning compulsory education until 1882, mainly due to ongoing conflicts with the Church. The Ferry Law of 1882 resulted in the secularization of the primary school curriculum. For a state in which the official separation between state and church took place relatively early, a significant portion of education is still in the hands of religious authorities (Schneider, 1982: 10).

In Spain, the church had an overwhelming influence on social life, including educational frameworks. In 1939, Franco re-established Roman Catholicism as the state religion and required all pupils (even non-Catholics) to learn about religion in school. Although Spain's new constitution (1978) separated church and state, classes in religion remained and the state continued its subsidy of ecclesiastical schools, attended by one third of the children (Callahan, 1998). Attempts by the Socialist party to liberalize education did little to reduce the influence of the Roman Catholic Church.

In Belgium, as in France, the state-religion conflict over education persisted well into the twentieth century, and produced two parallel education systems based on the constitutionally guaranteed freedom of education. In addition to a public system operated by the state and the communities, there was a "free" system organized by the Catholic Church. After 1884, under a Catholic government, a protracted process ended in the equalization of the "free" schools with the community schools. In 1914, the equalization of state support for all elementary schools was legally confirmed (Schneider, 1982: 10). In Prussia, the law of 1810 made education a secular activity (Green, 1990: 3). Although religion was not forbidden, only certified teachers could provide religious education in public schools (Cummings, 1997). The Soviet Union pursued an extreme model of separating state-sponsored education from religious influences. After the revolution, all schools supported by the Orthodox Church were abolished.

In the United States, both the strong moral and religious orientations of the citizenry and a fear of state interference in religious affairs influenced the differentiation of religion and education. Many early settlers came to America to establish "God's kingdom on earth," where individuals could communicate directly with God, rather than through the intervention of church officials. The ability to read the Bible was an essential element in personal communion; thus, the early Puritan settlements placed a strong emphasis on literacy and schooling. The U.S. Constitution enshrined the principle of separation of church and state, but also asserted that education was the responsibility of local communities, who often tangibly and prominently displayed their religious sensibilities. Because schools in the United States received funds from public sources, the principle of separation of church and state led to a second distinctive feature—the elimination of religious and moral content from the formal school curriculum. Over time, religious values in the public school curriculum were transformed into civic values (Cummings, 1997). Nevertheless, only after *Brown v. Board of Education* (1954) were religious influences, mainly Protestant values, minimized in public schools (Tyack, James, and Benavot, 1987).

Our analysis of the religion-education nexus in postcolonial states concentrates on non-Christian countries and refers to three historical periods: the precolonial, colonial, and postcolonial periods. In general, colonial governments did little to encourage the development of non-Christian religious education in the territories under their control. After independence, state authorities typically confronted two different types of religious schooling—Christian mission schools and local religious schools (e.g., Muslim, Buddhist, Confucian, Hindu)—and developed different strategies to integrate them in their education systems. Depending on political intentions and the demands of an expanding national education system, different accommodations were struck with existing mission schools and local institutions of religious education. In Muslim countries, for example, there were concerted efforts put towards the "Islamization" of emergent school systems through the integration of Islamic culture and education into official curricula. Islamic education was also reinforced in the Muslim countries that emerged from the collapse of the Soviet Union. In Uzbekistan, for example, authorities began to reconsider secular Soviet traditions in light of growing enthusiasm for Islamic learning and practice (Bureau for Policy and Program Coordination, 2004). The recent revitalization of Islamic education in Turkey further exemplifies the evolution of the relationship between secular and religious education in Muslim countries (see Guven, 2004).

As previously noted, prior to the introduction of Christianity in Asia and Africa, well-developed Confucian and Muslim educational frameworks had existed (Monroe, 1927; Lee, 2000). In Africa, before Islam swept much of the continent, indigenous systems of education were closely involved in child socialization. Even today, indigenous education remains widespread and diffuse, albeit with little institutional power. African families and communities expose their young children to myriads of African languages, part of a strong matrix of indigenous experiences that these children bring with them when they enter the public school system. Only in North Africa and the Nile Valley have indigenous languages been displaced by a powerful language of international currency (Arabic). In any case, the significance of the indigenous cultural values transmitted by African languages should not be minimized (Brock-Utne, 2000).

Islamic education, which developed concurrent to the spread of Islam in Africa and subsequently in parts of Asia, involved the expansion of Koranic schools and *madrassas* (centers of higher learning). In Koranic schools, traditionally located in small rooms attached to mosques, teachers taught young children to read and memorize Koranic verses in Arabic, regardless of the pupils' mother tongue. In many contexts, Koranic schools became an important avenue for the acquisition of literacy (Anzar, 2003) and served as powerful socializing mechanisms, inculcating regional and communal identities (Morgan and Armer, 1988; Fafunwa, 1982). Today, children continue to attend Koranic schools, in most cases before or after their attendance at a regular public school. Nevertheless, although Islamic education has expanded over the years, the percentage of children educated in such institutions remains relatively low. In Indonesia, for example, Islamic schools enroll between 10–15 percent of the school age population (about 40 percent of the pupils are girls). In Bangladesh, about 10 percent of all pupils participate in the religious education system. In Pakistan, as of 2000, 1.2 million students attended religious schools, as compared to 15.7 million in secular schools.

Islamic centers of higher learning flourished centuries before the arrival of Christian missionaries and Western colonialism (Tibawi, 1972). The first organized *madrassa* was established in Egypt in 1067. *Madrassas* provided two types of education: scholastic theology to produce spiritual leaders, and worldly knowledge to produce government administrators for the expanding Islamic empire (Anzar, 2003). The curriculum included grammatical inflections, syntax, logic, arithmetic, algebra, rhetoric and versification, jurisprudence, scholastic theology, Islamic laws, and the traditions and commentaries of the Prophet. *Ijtihad*, or independent reasoning, was a special feature of the *madrassas*, and it contributed to advancements in science, medicine, technology, and philosophy, especially in Andalusia, Spain. In the aftermath of Muslim defeats, the pursuit of worldly knowledge at most *madrassas* was curtailed, and the focus of study returned to the basics of theology (Anzar, 2003). The emphasis on a broad Islamic education, which included the shaping of character within an Islamic worldview, gave way to a narrowly defined religious education—namely, the study of religion and the inculcation of religious mores (Esposito, 1995: 406, cited in Zia, 2006). When *madrassa* students (usually male) completed their studies, they received a "license" allowing them to practice as a teacher, *imam*, or *alkali*, depending on their area of specialization (Mathews and Akrawi, 1949; Fafunwa, 1982). Today, new economic and political forces affect the demand for *madrassas*. In Pakistan, for example, several factors—including the government's inability to meet the educational demands of young males, deteriorating economic conditions, open financial support for religious education by Saudi Arabia and Kuwait, and Western forays into Afghanistan—have played a role in the development of the present *madrassa* system (Anzar, 2003). Contemporary *madrassas* continue to evolve between two poles: on the one hand, institutions with an exclusive emphasis on Islamic teaching (e.g., in Pakistan and parts of Indonesia), and on the other, institutions that balance the teaching of religious and secular subjects (e.g., Egypt, Bangladesh and Indonesia).

When Western missionaries arrived in Africa around the mid-nineteenth century, the first Christian missions on the continent were established. English-speaking missionaries arrived in Nigeria in 1844, in Uganda after 1877, and in Congo-Leopoldville after 1878. Because "Christianity is a religion of the book," education became an important means for preaching and teaching the gospel. In addition, the building of mission schools improved relations between missionaries and colonial authorities, as both were concerned with "civilizing" local Africans, especially through the promotion of European values (Bray et al., 1986: 7). During the height of European colonialism before World War I, religious missions, supported and aided by colonial administrations, provided most education (Connell, 1980: 315). The main purpose of the missions was to save souls, therefore they attempted to Christianize (civilize) without necessarily Westernizing (Yates, 1984). Later, colonial administrations expanded government schools, although the growth in enrollments varied considerably depending on the imperial power (Benavot and Riddle, 1988). Colonial systems of education were conscious, systematic attempts to educate Africans away from their indigenous cultures (Fafunwa, 1982).

The relationship between Christian mission schools and colonial governments varied from one region to the next. In some instances, colonial governments banned mission schools completely. In most cases, however, mission schools and colonial administrations divided the tasks of education, which resulted in different norms. In practice, this usually meant that Christian missions provided primary education for the "natives," and the government provided post-primary schools for the children of the European settlers. Reading, writing, and arithmetic were the basic pillars of the colonial curriculum, in addition to religion (Morgan and Armer, 1988). The limited scope of this school curriculum remained largely unchanged despite increased government involvement in educational affairs. In the decades prior to World War II, the British Empire promoted common schooling in its colonies, especially in Africa (Whitehead, 1981). In the French colonies, education was essentially a means of producing a native aristocracy who propagated French ideals and upheld the French way of life. In British colonies, there was a greater tendency to "adapt" education to African realities. While British education embodied (at least superficially) the ideals of partnership and adaptation, French education stood for association and assimilation (Fafunwa, 1982). In Portuguese colonies, education aimed at evangelizing and civilizing Africans, as well as providing cheap manual labor. Missionary education for Africans was poor and ineffective, in sharp contrast to the education provided to white settlers or assimilated Africans (Cross, 1987).

African parents were initially reluctant to send their children to the mission and government schools, but did so in greater numbers beginning in the early twentieth century (Knight, 1955; Connell, 1980: 314; Kelly, 2000). The mounting pressure of the new social order induced Africans to seek out mission schools. The acquisition of reading, writing, and basic Western knowledge in "bush," "village," or "out" schools became vital for sharing in the progress that the colonizers promised (Connell, 1980: 315). Under European colonialism, many traditional education systems disappeared—first shadowed by ever-increasing mission schools and later pushed out by the more extensive education systems of colonial governments.

National education systems became an important tool for shaping the character of new nations following independence. Government attitudes towards mission schools ranged from eradication to accommodation. In most states, education became a secular responsibility, although the ideological commitment to secularization varied. In much of Africa, the public partnerships that had enabled church-based educational frameworks came to an end, and many mission schools were banned outright (Makulu, 1971: 14). African leaders at the UNESCO-sponsored conference held in Addis Ababa in 1961 declared, "If it is to fulfill its many functions satisfactorily, education in Africa must be African, that is, it must rest on a foundation of a specifically African culture and be based on special requirements of African progress in all fields" (ECA/UNESCO, 1961: v). Among other things, creating a truly African education system meant limiting foreign (Western) influences and asserting state control over private and mission schools.

The tendency to accommodate traditional educational frameworks was much more pronounced in Southeast Asia. Most governments decided to take advantage of previously existing (mainly religious) institutions and found ways to integrate religious education into their national systems. In the Philippines and Indonesia, educational provisions were significantly strengthened without destroying relatively autonomous mission schools. Over time, however, the curricula, practices, and teacher qualifications of the latter converged with those of the public schools. In Thailand, despite strong government control, the private education system continued to flourish (Wong, 1973).

Historical Bridges between Religion and Modern Education

Because mass schooling first emerged in Christian areas, it could plausibly be asserted that Christian values are most compatible with modern educational forms. Nevertheless, European and U.S. educational history underscores the overt tensions between Christianity and modern secular education. Since World War II, different forms of accommodation between religious authorities and public administrations have evolved. Among non-Christian religions, many perceive Confucianism, Taoism, and Hinduism as more compatible with modern education than Islam, which is often depicted as relatively antagonistic towards "modern" sensibilities and educational values. Below, we consider whether, and how, postcolonial states integrated traditional and religious values in their national education systems and question the implications this may have had for contemporary policies of universal education.

For most commentators, Japan confirms the positive effects of accommodating traditional religious values in modern educational forms. Since the Meiji Revolution, when Japan imported Western educational forms and suffused them with traditional Japanese values, educational and material conditions have improved significantly. Nevertheless, it is worth recalling that American administrators forced Japan to remove all religious content from the curriculum after World War II, as it was thought to have contributed to Japanese imperialism and "aggression." In recent decades, by contrast, explanations of the superior performance of Japanese pupils (especially in relation to U.S. pupils) in international achievement studies tend to highlight the successful integration of traditional cultural values and modern educational practices (Fuller et al., 1986).

At the beginning of the twentieth century, China experimented with the integration of religious and Western values. The Nationalist government, established in 1901, sought to produce scholarly gentry through the incorporation of Western educational practices and approaches. Concurrently, the Nationalist government promoted Confucianism to bolster and legitimate its political power. Chinese traditions encouraged an unquestioning trust in authority and conformity with collective goals. Under the slogan "Chinese learning as the essence and Western learning for its utilitarian purposes," educational facilities increased rapidly in China before 1949 (Kwong, 1979; 1988). Nevertheless, the educational successes of the anti-religious Communist regimes leave little reason to draw an unambiguous positive assessment of the role of religion in Chinese education.

In the 1960s, after a wave of de-colonization, many scholars believed that Western forms of schooling could not be mixed with indigenous African education in the ways envisioned by African leaders (Coleman, 1965: 53). The historical record does not support this assessment. For example, in many Muslim areas where the penetration of Christian missions was minimal, a considerable number of Islamic schools remained in place (Matthews and Akrawi, 1949). While some of these schools continued to concentrate on Koranic verses by way of rote learning, others, notably in Tunisia, taught an elementary-school course in Arabic, with French as a second language, which was comparable to that offered in the public sector. In select schools in Algeria and Tunisia, quality secondary education in a traditional Arabic culture was available (notably in the College Sadiki in Tunis). In addition, higher studies could be pursued in a wide spectrum of Islamic universities in the Middle East (Morgan and

Armer, 1988). Findings from the Islamic region of north Nigeria (Kano) suggest that the two education systems—one modern and the other (*Islamiyya*) integrating Western and Koranic curricula—have successfully accommodated each other. In both systems, enrollments and achievement levels have increased (Morgan and Armer, 1988).

In West Africa, too, despite opposition from the traditionalists, "internal" reforms to Islamic education (i.e., the introduction of modern secular subjects from within) have been more successful than those attempted by colonial authorities (Fisher, 1969). From a liberal point of view, Islamic education is problematic because it assumes a primacy of religious beliefs and an ambivalent position toward other religions or non-religious ideologies (Zia, 2006). Some argue that a reformed Islamic education system, in which the traditional and the modern are melded, could have been used to mobilize the Muslim masses for enhanced development (Anzar, 2003). Though Western colonial authorities historically ignored the Muslim education system, Muslim leaders had opportunities to address the extreme stances taken by Islamic religious leaders that further isolated and marginalized the Islamic education system. Instead of finding creative links between Islam and secularization, as had been found in earlier Muslim periods, young cadres of religious leaders insisted on total adherence to their fundamental visions of Islam. Their unwillingness to reform the curriculum in *madrassas* has created new obstacles in today's Muslim societies. A curriculum such as that found in most Arab countries, which encourages submission, obedience, subordination, and compliance rather than critical thinking and creativity, does not promote the increase of knowledge and capital in these societies (Arab Human Development Report, 2003: 53).

Finally, many European education systems are now reexamining the relationship between state secular education and religious sensibilities. Especially in countries with large numbers of Muslim immigrants such as Germany, Britain, and France, public debates on the separation between state and church have reopened. In the past, they involved the adherents of Catholicism, Protestantism, or Judaism; today, the parents of Muslim and Sikh children demand that state schools recognize their freedom of religious expression. In France, Catholic organizations are among the most vociferous defenders of secularism in the education system, seeking to avoid a new ideological struggle around religion similar to those of the past. Discussions concerning the right of Muslims to wear traditional clothes in public schools have also emerged in Spain.

Conclusion

Policies that advance localization and decentralization as strategies for improving the efficiency of national education systems were conceived and consolidated in the West. They aimed at replacing large, stable, but cumbersome state bureaucracies with more flexible, effective, responsive modes of educational governance. When applied to centralized education systems, decentralization measures in some instances reduced state expenditures but may also have had socially regressive effects, especially when pursued in badly funded or highly unequal systems. In Latin America, the movement towards decentralization brought about a "renaissance" of private and religious education, but class inequalities in educational access apparently increased. These developments illustrate how key aspects of the systemization process (i.e., centralization or decentralization, secularization, and privatization) have important implications for social inequalities and equity issues.

In Muslim areas, and in parts of Africa, the secular versus religious dilemma represents a totally different picture. Western education is still perceived as "imported" foreign education, promoted first by Christian missionaries and later by colonial governments. Modern education represents a force that has previously undermined indigenous traditions, Muslim culture, and Muslim educational frameworks. When former colonies achieved independence, secular education gained supremacy and many mission schools were dismantled. African states and Islamic countries, often supported by foreign aid programs and international organizations, later launched ambitious universal education campaigns. Although educational spending and enrollments have increased, these have rarely produced the impressive socioeconomic developments that international experts predicted. Economic growth, still heavily dependent on primary commodities, has been illusive. Many elites view modern education as having facilitated social unrest through increased unemployment, dissonance between traditional and modern values, and intergenerational conflict.

Moreover, Islamic education, although a relatively small proportion of all education, continued to expand in many Muslim societies. In the past, colonial governments and Muslim heads of state attempted to undermine Islamic education systems. International agencies also ignored them. In many Asian countries, however, different accommodations between traditional values and modern educational practices have proved much more successful. Muslim scholars wonder whether, and how, modern education and traditional forms of Muslim learning can be accommodated. Can Islamic educational institutions be reformed and thereby pave the way for the advancement of Muslim societies and economies? We think that there is much to be gained from examining how countries accomplished this challenging task in the past.

INEQUALITY AND EQUITY ISSUES

The Historical Legacies of Elitist and Democratic Education

Schools (or equivalent educational frameworks) have existed in many ancient civilizations, including Egypt, China, Rome, and Greece (Cohen, 1979). The basic function of these schools was to socialize and train an elite class who would govern and administer the country or empire. The education of elite classes entailed the acquisition of knowledge and skills related to warfare, diplomacy, religion, and politics. Additional emphasis was placed on the development of character, virtue, and refinement. These educational frameworks were expected to instill loyalty to the central power and to construct a clear status boundary between the literate, cultured elite and the illiterate commoners.

Schools devoted to the consolidation and reproduction of elites through the education of the children of privileged or propertied classes have a long history in Europe (Ringer, 1979; Bourdieu, 1996; Cookson and Percell, 1985; Cummings, 2003). In Germany, the education of the cultured upper middle class, in contrast to the business-oriented upper middle class, stressed personal cultivation, probity, and social courtesy. The education of French elites emphasized linguistic proficiency, academic distinction, and devoted service to the state, either in administrative or military affairs. The English public schools, which were the principal training ground for the attainment of elite status, inculcated a sense of honor, faith, entitlement, and privilege, together with a willingness to serve and defend the country and British Empire. In practice, membership in European elite classes, whether political, economic, or cultural, meant receiving a classical academic education involving a rigorous program of humanistic, and sometimes scientific, studies at a selective institution or boarding school.

Although private institutions had served the children of dominant classes in the United States since the founding of the early colonies, democratic and egalitarian views permeated the historical development of schooling (Bailyn, 1960; Cremin, 1970; Tyack, 1974; Kaestle, 1983). These views led to educational notions such as widespread but locally controlled schools, education as a means for creating literate (Bible reading) and morally upright citizens, and "having the rich and the poor educated together." These notions not only reflected important ideological legacies of the nation's founding fathers, but also were considered indispensable for the survival of the republic (Ulich, 1967). Such ideas, supported by strong Protestant principles, infused the common school movement in the nineteenth century, and had important consequences for the spread of schooling in both rural and urban areas. By the end of the nineteenth century, enrollment in elementary schools (public and private) was almost universal. The expansion of secondary education in the United States was unprecedented, with enrollment rates increasing from 7 percent of the youth population in 1890 to 80 percent in the 1960s (Ulich, 1967: 242–3). The American high school was the first entirely free secondary school in the world (Green, 1990: 17). By the end of the twentieth century, the provision of post-primary educational opportunities in the United States outranked all other countries, with the possible exception of Japan (Cummings, 1997).

Nevertheless, race, ethnicity, and immigrant status strongly affected access to, and completion of, secondary and higher education in the United States. Notwithstanding egalitarian conceptions and doctrines of equal opportunity, many of which became the object of U.S. Supreme Court rulings, racial and ethnic inequalities in educational outcomes continued unabated throughout the twentieth century. Many American educators questioned whether a strategy of equal educational opportunity was sufficient to substantially reduce educational inequalities. Only through compensatory measures, they maintained, would real progress in access to secondary and higher education be attained (Cummings, 1997).

From Elitist to Popular Education in Europe

The meritocratic ideal—that individuals, whatever their origins, should be given opportunities to carry their talents to full realization through education—was late in coming to Europe (Ringer, 1979; Maynes, 1985). So, too, was the related notion that national progress depends on the extent to which a society provides educational services that enable all its citizens to develop their talents and capabilities. Traditional European forms of secondary education, provided in a gymnasium, lycée, "public," or grammar school, represented an advanced stage of liberal education and a narrow gateway to higher social and occupational statuses. Indeed, throughout Europe, academic secondary schools began as institutions serving universities, with the purpose of preparing upper-class youth for study in higher education. Thus, securing meritocratic ideals meant, in practical terms, that secondary education would need to be democratized, thereby reducing, even eliminating, the class advantages of elite children (Sutton, 1965). Moreover, institutions of secondary education were firmly entrenched in rigid selection mechanisms. These had produced bifurcated structures: on the one hand, a variety of academic-oriented secondary education systems, including preparatory classes for secondary schools, were mainly reserved for the children of higher status families or those who could afford to pay tuition fees; on the other hand, short-term and typically terminal programs provided access to primary (and some post-primary) education for the children of the popular classes.

From a historical perspective, the shift from elitist to more inclusive education systems involved several, not always sequentially organized, transformations. Many countries made an early transition by broadening access to primary schools while simultaneously increasing the number of traditionally elitist secondary schools. In some areas, selective secondary schools, which had exclusively served the aristocracy, began catering to the needs of the growing bourgeoisie and urban middle classes. Another important turning point was the alteration of secondary education entrance examinations, especially the degree to which meritocratic criteria supplanted class-based ones. Many European countries began developing new national entry examinations with stronger academic or IQ-like elements. Pupils who succeeded in these exams were allowed to enroll in elite secondary schools. Children who were unsuccessful, or who chose not to sit for the exams, could remain in school for several additional grades or enroll in vocational programs or tracks, both of which were considered less desirable alternatives.

In the aftermath of World War II, especially with the ascendance of the United States as the major economic and political superpower, intergovernmental organizations such as UNESCO and OECD began articulating progressive American ideas and lent their support to principles of equal educational opportunity. The use of highly selective entry examinations came under severe criticism as an obstacle to the "democratization" of secondary education. In many countries, an array of observation and counseling procedures eventually replaced these exams. The new procedures were meant not to select pupils, but to classify them according to their abilities, interests, and achievements at the conclusion of an extended period of compulsory education.

The prolongation of compulsory education by two to four years (see Table 1) not only extended formal schooling, but served, at least in theory, to universalize access to (lower) secondary education. In many instances, the supply of grammar schools, lycées, and gymnasiums was too limited to meet the increasing demand for secondary education. Moreover, the traditional curriculum, stressing classical languages and academic subjects, was called into question because it contained subject emphases of less value to heterogeneous student populations. Initiatives to expand and diversify secondary education systems gained momentum, including the reinvigoration or addition of various types of vocational and technical education to existing classical and modern curricula (Resnik, 2001).

Significantly, the post-World War II transformation of secondary education occurred during a particularly activist and dynamic period in European political history. The move to ensure greater educational opportunities and reduce social inequalities corresponded to political developments in Western Europe, in particular the ascension to power of democratic socialist parties (Wittrock et al., 1991). Led by cadres of political leaders imbued with strong modernizing visions and a post-war "trenches" feeling of solidarity, many European governments launched large-scale educational reforms including the extension of compulsory education, the establishment of more inclusive school types, and the massive expansion of secondary school enrollments. Though the pace and outcomes of these changes varied from country to country, the transformation of secondary education became a central target of reformists' plans. Indeed, the shift to mass secondary education involved not only a structural change, but also a major social shift. States that had historically created sharp institutional (and class) divisions between primary and secondary education moved to construct a more integrated and less class-based tripartite system involving primary, lower-secondary, and upper-secondary education.

In the wake of these reform initiatives, three basic types of European education systems emerged (Schneider, 1982):

- The Scandinavian comprehensive school (Norway, Denmark, Sweden, and Finland). School reforms in Scandinavia led to the joining of primary and middle schools into a nine-year basic (and compulsory) program of comprehensive schooling. The new system (nine years of primary education and three to four years of post-primary education) was legally institutionalized in Sweden (1962), Finland (1970), and Denmark (1975).

- The mixed systems found in Great Britain, France, and Italy. Specific equivalents to the comprehensive schools were legally implemented without, however, relegating the compulsory education of all pupils to one type of basic school.
- The traditional systems found in Austria, Belgium, the Netherlands, and in most German *Länder* and Swiss cantons. Legislated reforms created a less comprehensive integration of secondary schools and specific national patterns of subdivided systems dominate in these countries. The tripartite system usually included the classic, modern, and technical secondary schools, which form separate tracks.

Expanding Secondary Education in Postcolonial States

Two "American" principles—one, that societies should avoid "wasting talent" and two, that secondary education should be open to all academically capable youth, regardless of social background—not only took root in Europe after World War II, but also gained support in education systems throughout the world. Social science experts, as well as intergovernmental organizations, were instrumental in the circulation of these emergent "democratic" conceptions of secondary schooling. Although the transformation of secondary education in the United States and Europe followed in the wake of a long period of primary education consolidation and universalization, in Africa, Asia, and Latin America, widespread illiteracy, low quality instruction, and educational wastage in primary schools remained salient problems when secondary schooling became the object of reform (Rama, 1983).

Furthermore, colonial legacies had contributed to idiosyncratic educational structures in many developing countries. During the colonial era, educational frameworks in Africa and Asia were institutionally segmented, elitist, and racially divided; most contributed to furthering Western hegemony and domination over native populations. In many African colonies, for example, indigenous children learned rudimentary skills in mission or village "bush" schools, but few passed the rigorous examinations for entrance into upper-elementary or secondary grades. At the same time, colonial authorities actively developed modern academic and technical education for the children of European settlers. Such schools nurtured an elite, racially exclusive group with a shared culture and ideology, who held a monopoly over high-level skills taught in academic schools (King, 1990).

Following independence, African and Asian governments were exposed to two types of pressures: the commitment of their leaders to weaken or dismantle the educational vestiges of colonial rule and the pressure from international agencies to expand education as a condition for socioeconomic development. Certain educational structures were democratized—massive efforts were undertaken to advance free and compulsory primary education (UNESCO, 1958). However, governments rarely transformed the underlying principles and policies that had governed secondary education during the colonial period. In former French and Belgian colonies, for example, a reluctance to break away from policies that had originated under French rule limited the conceptualization and design of educational reforms (Johnson, 1987). More often than not, the elitist character of secondary education remained virtually unchanged: literary and academic instruction continued to be emphasized over practical training or market skills; rote learning continued to dominate classroom interactions; and schooling remained driven by examinations (Khan, 1981). The educational standards of former imperial powers cast long shadows over the curricular contents and educational qualifications in African and Asian secondary schools (World Bank, 2005). Most newly independent regimes lacked the necessary resources to implement major changes to secondary education. Others have argued, however, that retaining the educational status quo served the interests of newly empowered elites (Gauhar, 1981; Khan, 1981). In Muslim countries, the children of elites attended Western schools, while Koranic schools and *madrassas* attracted those unable to pay the high school fees. Unequal access to schools of varying quality not only aggravated economic and class divides in these countries, but also nurtured greater antipathy toward the West, mostly among the have-nots who attended poor public schools (Mernissi, 1992; Zia, 2006).

As in Africa and Asia, secondary education in Latin America mirrored European institutions, which were predominantly elitist and academic in character. Due to the long-term politicization of education and the historical emphasis on higher education (both public and private), Latin American countries developed extremely unequal educational structures in which university sectors flourished (enrollment rates approximated those in Europe) while primary education languished. Secondary schools mainly served as highly selective institutional channels for university entrance and the attainment of elite status. Although universal education was legislated in most Latin America countries, the laws were unevenly applied. Children in urban areas enjoyed vastly superior educational opportunities and mobility prospects than those residing in rural areas. The rising social demand for education, the need to elicit support from politically dominant groups to meet these demands, and the limited resources with which educational reforms were implemented led many Latin American states to view educational reform as a necessary first step to reduce social inequalities. Parties representing middle classes called for an extension of secondary education and greater access to higher education, even though inequalities in elementary education were rampant (Rama, 1983).

Over time, educational developments in some postcolonial states created new problems. In countries that vigorously expanded access to primary education, many school graduates faced a severe shortage of secondary schools as well as a dearth of job opportunities or training programs in the labor market. These problems were accentuated as the overall social demand for education increased (Johnson, 1987). In Muslim countries where secondary education had been expanded, "armies of educated unemployed youth" reflected the unmet needs of the professional labor market (Khan, 1981). Ethiopia and countries in Francophone Africa encountered similar problems (Germa, 1982; Johnson, 1987). In short, although many viewed the expansion and transformation of secondary education as a universal mandate relevant to all less-developed school systems, educational realities on the ground undermined the realization of this mandate in most postcolonial states.

During the 1970s and 1980s, international agencies encouraged developing countries to adopt new types of educational innovations based on human capital models and neoliberal approaches to education. These included the restructuring and diversification of schools, a greater curricular emphasis on practical education, policies to upgrade teacher training and qualifications, and the introduction of new technologies and pedagogical approaches. Initially rejected by many national educational authorities, especially in Francophone Africa, such innovations were perceived as "neo-colonial" attempts by international powers to impose new forms of "second-class" education. Still, initial modifications diminished the elite character of secondary education. For example, some countries established programs in agricultural, craft, and technical training and in lifelong learning. Others incorporated new teaching methods, indigenous languages, and community leaders into the structure and content of their education systems (Johnson, 1987).

In sum, many postcolonial states have committed themselves ideologically in recent decades to the transformation and expansion of traditional secondary schools to serve more diverse educational, social, and economic purposes. Although an increasing number of states adhere to this policy position, actual reforms to secondary education sectors have been limited and uneven. Private secondary schools have grown to satisfy unmet demand among advantaged social classes. More often than not, this expansion has not increased democratization but instead increased segmentation of different social strata.

Despite the many differences in the massification of secondary education in Africa, Asia, and Latin America, several common characteristics may be observed. First, universal access to and completion of primary education have yet to be achieved. Second, the limited extension of secondary education mainly serves elite groups and advantaged social classes. Third, reforms to secondary education have rarely improved social mobility or social and economic conditions for the vast majority of the population. Educational principles circulated by intergovernmental organizations played an influential role in reforming national educational policies, but patterns of educational expansion at the primary, secondary, and tertiary levels, historically unbalanced in postcolonial states, continue to generate substantial social and spatial inequalities.

HIERARCHY, DIVERSIFICATION, AND COMPREHENSIVENESS IN SECONDARY EDUCATION

The historical transformation of secondary education involved at least three interrelated shifts: 1) the expansion of the purposes of secondary schooling; 2) the establishment of new selection mechanisms (or the discontinuation of old ones) to ease the transition between primary and secondary education; and 3) the development of diversified programs of study, curricular offerings, and/or school types, which address the heterogeneous interests and needs of expanding student populations. Our previous discussion concentrated on the first two shifts; we examine the third shift below. Historical initiatives to reshape and diversify the contours of secondary schooling encompassed a wide range of structural and programmatic reforms (Kandel, 1930). We discuss several prominent examples in the movement towards diversification.

Incorporating Science and Vocational Training: England and Germany

Secondary education in England traditionally entailed an intellectually demanding program of academic studies in the classical languages, history, geography, and the humanistic evolution of Western civilization. Revisions to the academic curriculum in England were slow in coming (Goodson, 1987). Although England was the most advanced industrial society, scientific and technological studies, vocational training, and apprenticeship were almost completely disregarded. The privileged economic situation of the British Empire, as well as their confidence in the ability of grammar schools to create an elite class of cultured gentlemen imbued with an ethos of honor, service, and entitlement, provided little impetus for educational innovation. Moreover, as the Taunton Commission[9] (1864–8) later explained, England had produced a bevy of outstanding inventors, engineers, and industrialists, most of whom had little or no formal education. The country's laissez-faire reliance on self-made men to carry its economy forward partly explains its historically weak emphasis on science instruction, both pure and applied. Indeed, as late as 1800, there were virtually no facilities for technical or industrial education in England, and interest in science-oriented instruction in secondary schools was minimal.

Things began to change as the preeminence of British industries deteriorated in the later part of the nineteenth century, especially due to growing competition in overseas markets. Political leaders and academic elites alike increasingly recognized that science and technology play influential roles in national life. Oxford and Cambridge established professorships and study programs in the natural and physical sciences. The study of science, primarily academic in nature, gained visibility at all levels of the English education system. Schools increasingly encouraged the teaching of technical subjects, also based on a textbook approach.

An even more significant step towards technical education developed among institutes providing further education to adult workers, typically

---

[9] The Taunton Commission on secondary education publicized the lack of grammar schools in many towns and recommended the establishment of rate-aided secondary schools and increasing girls' access to secondary education.

after work hours. In the early nineteenth century, the first "Mechanics Institutes" were founded (in Glasgow, Edinburgh, Haddington, and London) with the aim of "instructing artisans in scientific principles of the arts and manufactures" and "diffusing useful knowledge." These institutes not only offered classes in general education, they also established a tradition of emphasizing scientific and technical education over practical craft instruction. This tradition was to persist well into the twentieth century. Overall, the tendency to associate secondary education with academic studies (mainly the classics) and technical education with further education for adults contributed to the weak status of science education and the slow development of vocational education in English schools.

German history offers a richly contrasting model of incorporating science instruction and vocational training into public schools. Much earlier than other countries, German leaders viewed science and technology as key factors for industrial development and created a complex and well-integrated framework of vocational secondary education. Vocational programs were seen not only as preparing working-class children for entrance into the labor market, but also as an effective means for their moral socialization and civic training. General "improvement" schools, whose sessions were first held on Sundays and evenings, were introduced in order to supplement the "imperfect" general education of working-class boys and girls. Legislation compelled industrial employers to allow workers under the age of 18 to attend such "improvement" schools (Beckwith, 1913). Over the course of the nineteenth century, German authorities established a variety of industrial schools: supplemental schools for young workers, middle-technical and trade schools for master tradesmen and lower grade technicians, and highly advanced and scientifically oriented technical high schools for the leaders of industries. These industrial schools were funded and supported by private individuals, guilds, trade unions, merchants' associations, and towns.

A central aspect of vocational education that emerged in Germany was the formalization of an elaborate system of training and apprenticeships. The system encouraged young adolescents (apprentices) to acquire practical vocational training in industrial workshops, rather than in school, within the parameters set forth in legally binding contracts. When combined with limited school-based courses, this dual system became the cornerstone of a German model that mediated the transition of young people from the completion of compulsory education into various occupational statuses in the labor market.

Overall, industrial and technical education in Germany evolved concurrently with the spread of universal schooling. Indeed, vocational education was central to the movement to extend compulsory schooling. Industrial education in German secondary schools was fundamentally linked to
the preeminence of scientific and technological studies in German institutions of higher education. Although the gymnasium privileged high-status
classical studies, the *Ober-realschule*, with its strong scientific bias, was also
highly regarded. In contrast to England, scientific and technological studies in Germany were not considered an "unsuitable" education for respect-
able citizens. The German state viewed technical education and apprenticeship programs as moral education and technical training for young
people destined for industrial positions. Nevertheless, scholars have commented that vocational education in Germany typically reinforced pater-
nalistic attitudes by government officials and strengthened existing social
divisions (the *stande*) in German society. Immediately after their completion of compulsory education, pupils from lower social strata entered
the world of work through apprenticeship programs, thereby foregoing
opportunities to enter institutions of higher learning and, through them,
to improve their socioeconomic status.

The contrasting English and German approaches to vocational education paralleled developments in other parts of Europe. In some countries,
such as France and Italy, the status of technical and vocational education
was marginalized in relation to academic secondary education. In other
countries, such as Switzerland and Austria, key aspects of the German
model were adopted and vocational education and training became integral, relatively high-status components of post-primary schooling. During the 1900–1945 period, the introduction of new vocational and technical education programs slowed. Continued reliance upon on-the-job
training and a corresponding skepticism about the benefits of textbook-
based technical instruction contributed to the indifference towards the
application of scientific research in secondary schools (Evans, 1982).

After World War II, however, vocational education experienced a
period of relative rejuvenation in Europe. Many governments expanded
vocational, technical, and further education programs as well as instruction in the pure and applied sciences at tertiary-level institutions. Shortages of trained manpower and the cost of industrial weakness in the face
of increased competitiveness justified official policies in support of these
programs. In addition, interest in the industrial application of research

and development grew markedly, increasing the demand for middle- and high-level scientists, technologists, and technicians. Current and future workers became interested in obtaining vocational education and training (VET) qualifications because their salary and promotion prospects were increasingly tied to these (Evans, 1982: 227–8).

In short, the expansion and diversification of secondary education in post-World War II Europe was greatly influenced by the development of vocational education frameworks, on the one hand, and the incorporation of science and technology subjects in previously humanities-dominated school curricula, on the other. Although their historical circumstances differed, most European governments become convinced of the benefits of vocational education and training and developed policies in support of VET. Many parents and academics, however, held less sanguine views about the benefits of VET. In any case, popular demands to improve equality in educational opportunity were often used by the supporters of vocational education to defend its status in a reformed secondary education sector.

Comprehensive Schooling in the United States

Emerging in the late nineteenth century and flourishing in the years following World War I, the comprehensive high school embodied a uniquely American vision of post-primary education. It sought to encapsulate democratic values and pragmatic principles by combining the academic, college-preparatory purposes of small, often private, academies with a broad set of curricular offerings that addressed the interests and occupational aspirations of an increasingly diverse student population (Commission on the Reorganization of Secondary Education, 1918). The model of the comprehensive high school had roots in psychological studies on human intelligence (e.g., Thorndike's multifaceted approach), in Dewey's (1916) pragmatic educational philosophy (e.g., schools should train pupils to use their wits and talents in order to better serve society), and in utilitarian views of education's relationship to the labor market (e.g., vocational courses, which enable more manually inclined pupils to realize their potentialities, serve both the individual and the industrializing economy) (Schmida, 1964).

The comprehensive high school not only reflected an anti-elitist, egalitarian ideal in which academically and socially diverse students studied a common core of curricular subjects, but also fostered the "elective principle," allowing students to choose from a wide range of course offerings (Vaizey, 1965). In addition to Latin, biology, history, and physical education, high schools offered "practical" subjects such as shop, home economics, basket weaving, or driver's training (Ulich, 1967). This curricular structure, better adapted to the heterogeneity of talents and abilities among the youth population, called into question the relevance of the humanities-oriented academic programs found in Europe (Sutton, 1965: 60). It also problematized the practice of selecting and channeling students into separate academic and vocational secondary schools at a relatively young age. Emerging studies on human multiple intelligences opposed selection mechanisms and favored fully articulated counseling systems (Conant, 1959). Far from being elitist institutions targeting a small portion of school-age children, U.S. high schools became inclusive institutions that sought to accommodate large segments of students interested in both academic and vocational studies (Cummings, 1997).

Although comprehensive schooling "softened" the sharp distinction between academic and vocational studies by transforming between-school hierarchies into intra-school ones, it did not eliminate it entirely. Vocational programs in the United States, directed at pupils of lower socioeconomic status who had difficulties performing in academic programs, continued to bear the stigma of a "second class" education. Although comprehensive high schools contributed to the unprecedented growth of secondary education in the United States by offering more diverse courses to heterogeneous populations, they continued to act as powerful mechanisms of social stratification (Kerckhoff, 1995). Overall, secondary education in the United States confronted a much weaker elitist tradition and considerably less intellectual opposition to vocational education than in England. The comprehensive high school reflected a pragmatic, instrumental view of education in which vocational subject matter could be easily integrated in an ever-expanding array of course offerings.

Secondary Education Reform in Post-war Europe

In the aftermath of World War II, European states needed to reconstruct not only their economies and polities, but also their education systems. American involvement in European reconstruction via massive aid programs in the Marshall Plan and through its growing influence in international organizations, mainly UNESCO and OECD, provided an auspicious context for spreading U.S.-based educational principles (e.g., equality of educational opportunity, expanded secondary education) and models of schooling (e.g., comprehensive high schools). The growing predominance of U.S. social science communities, in which leading scholars extolled the virtues of human capital and modernization theories that linked education and economic growth, also impacted educational reforms in Europe. A dearth of scientific and technological education incited Western European education systems to promote programs in these areas, especially following the Sputnik affair in 1957.

The above conditions, together with an activist political leadership, resulted in the passage of substantial educational reforms, which sought to foster more egalitarian, more comprehensive, and less hierarchical secondary education systems. Although the timing, scope, and implementation of these reforms varied from country to country, the following elements were integrated (in some form or another) into most educational initiatives:

- A prolongation of compulsory education into secondary education;
- Attempts to blur the hierarchy between academic and non-academic studies (art, informatics, dance, etc.) by greater diversification of subject offerings;
- A tendency towards establishing comprehensive secondary schools; and
- An increase of science-oriented studies at all educational levels and in most programs of study.

In addition, there were concerted attempts to sustain and improve vocational education. Vocational education was transformed into vocational education and training (VET) with the addition of new training programs that emphasized modern skills and competencies. In some countries, improvements to VET occurred at the upper-secondary level, in others, at the post-secondary level. In almost all cases, VET programs increased their emphasis on general education subjects and reduced restrictions for graduates who wanted to enter post-secondary institutions. Expanding education in general, and retooling VET programs in particular, tapped into deeply held convictions that such policies would meet the demand for moderately and highly skilled employees in European labor markets and would help sustain economic growth (Resnik, 2001).

Overall, three basic patterns of vocational and technical education emerged in Western Europe:

- After completing full-time compulsory education, pupils receive instruction in a specific craft from the age of 11 or 12 (e.g., the Netherlands and Belgium, in the past).[10]
- After completing full-time compulsory education, pupils are provided with compulsory part-time vocational education (e.g., the *Berufsschule* in Germany and Switzerland).
- Pupils study in general education frameworks until 15 or 16, after which they take courses specifically directed towards the acquisition of qualifications needed for a chosen career (e.g. France, Italy, Sweden, and the United Kingdom).

Differences in European education and training systems derived from the historical traditions of national structures, practices, and institutional cultures (Green, 1997: 178). Patterns of vocational education and training resulted specifically from the inter-relationship of national labor market structures and education systems (Ashton and Green, 1996). Some convergence in European secondary education systems became apparent as almost all countries established three types of secondary programs: a general or academic program, a broadly vocational or technical program, and a vocational program that prepared students for particular occupations (Green, Wolf, and Leney, 1999).

Such secondary school divisions have led to social stratification. (Due to space and time restrictions, we have defined these as outside the bounds of the present article.) Research has demonstrated that access to differentiated secondary-level programs in Europe and elsewhere is correlated with students' origins (Blossfeld and Shavit, 1993). Children from minority and immigrant groups are often channeled to vocational tracks and schools. Examples of this include Moroccan and Algerian students in France, Turkish students in Germany, Pakistani and Indian pupils in Britain, Indonesians in the Netherlands, and Muslims in Canada (Eldering, 1996; Zine, 2001).

In recent decades, intensifying global economic competition has further strengthened the official view that education and training are critical factors in increasing economic performance and competitive advantage (Green, 1997: 173). Because they are unable to compete with the signifi-

---

[10] In recent years, the Netherlands and Belgium have extended compulsory education to ages 17–18 and have adopted a system that approximates the second pattern listed (IBE, 2003).

cantly lower wage levels of many jobs in less-developed countries, European states have instead concentrated on value-added, knowledge-based production and services, which necessitate higher-level skills and extensive worker flexibility (Finegold and Soskice, 1988, cited in Green, 1997: 182). Many countries have undertaken strategies to strengthen vocational education, especially work-based programs leading to certification that involve contextualized learning in firms (Lerman, 2001). Spain recently implemented a new VET policy (Bonal, 2001), and Sweden initiated a new tertiary-level VET policy during the 1990s (Lindell, 2004). The British government promoted a "Skills Revolution" (Pring, 2004) within the framework of new vocational education and training programs (Avis, 2004), while the Netherlands increased the status of work-based learning (van de Stege, 2003). In addition to VET, all governments have advanced policies to extend individual learning and skill enhancement beyond secondary education through various forms of lifelong learning and adult education, which are based in communities, workplaces, or the academy (Green, 1997: 177).

Vocational Education in the Postcolonial States

The vocational versus general education controversy in African countries and other postcolonial states can be traced back to the colonial period. The main objectives of education supplied by colonial governments were twofold: first, to provide educational services of high standards to expatriates' children; and second, to train local elites to fill administrative, commercial, and teaching jobs in colonial administrations (Kelly and Altbach, 1978). By and large, colonial schools closely mirrored their counterparts in Europe—bookish, academic, and designed to prepare pupils for rigorous examinations. Native populations in European colonies were taught basic skills (i.e., reading, writing, and arithmetic) in mission schools or government-aided village schools. In some instances, schools provided instruction in practical or technical skills, typically farming and crafts production (Fafunwa, 1982).

Influential reports seeking to reform education in European colonies began circulating after World War I. The Phelps-Stokes Fund, representing the interests of several British and American missionary bodies, appointed a group called the African Education Commission (AEC) to tour Africa and make recommendations for the improvement of mission-based education. In 1922, the same year that Lord Lugard published his statements on indirect rule, the AEC published a plan to reform African education, recommending that it be adapted to "community needs." Because African economies were predominantly agricultural, the AEC reasoned, school curricula should emphasize the dignity, importance, and skills associated with agricultural labor.[11]

The British Colonial Office, persuaded by many AEC recommendations, commissioned its own policy reports, the first of which was published by the Advisory Committee on African Education in 1925 (Mayhew, 1938). This report maintained that "education should be adapted to the mentality, aptitudes, occupations and traditions of the various peoples, conserving as far as possible all sound and healthy elements in the fabric of their social life." The adaptation of education—more practical, vocational, and suited to native needs—would mitigate the destabilizing impact of social and economic changes to traditional life under European colonialism. Subsequent reports underscored the need to expand educational opportunities and also reiterated the importance of adapting the structure and content of government-aided schools to local realities (Fafunwa, 1982; Bray et al., 1986). In Asia, too, initial efforts towards vocational education were introduced during the first half of the twentieth century (Tillak, 2002).

After World War II, many national leaders in newly independent countries advanced arguments in favor of vocational education. Leaders in India, China, Tanzania, and Ghana, to name but a few, called for the diversification of school curricula and establishment of vocational education programs as means to enhance agricultural production, stem migration to urban areas, curb the number of unemployed school leavers, and transform work-related attitudes among youth.

Institutional support for vocational and technical education also gained momentum. The Addis Ababa Plan for African Educational Development, adopted in 1961, emphasized the need to orient secondary education to economic and technological development, which required a shift in enrollments from general education to vocational and technical education (Maté, 1969). UNESCO (1974; 1979a) and other intergovernmental

---

[11] According to the AEC plan, the education of native Africans would also entail a strong cultural element: it should seek to civilize them (convince them to abstain from "barbaric" indigenous practices) while sustaining the distinction between European and African cultures. In the words of the AEC, education should combine "the self-confidence of culture with the simplicity of Africans."

organizations endorsed similar recommendations, as a 1979 UNESCO statement exemplifies: "technical and vocational education is a prerequisite for sustaining the complex structure of modern civilization and economic and social development...the rapid technological and educational changes of the last decade require new, creative, and efficient efforts in technical and vocational education to improve education as a whole for social, economic and cultural development" (1979a). An influential World Bank sector policy paper on education characterized school curricula as excessively theoretical and abstract, weakly tied to local conditions, and insufficiently concerned with developing skills for, and positive attitudes towards, manual work (World Bank, 1974). The notion that vocational education could help overcome shortages in skilled manpower, enhance productivity, and contribute to economic growth diffused rapidly to developing countries through regional conferences and special commissions (Gimeno, 1981; Parmers, 1962; Porter, 1970).

Beginning in the 1960s, international agencies targeted vocational education and training for substantial institutional funding. At the time, the World Bank was the largest source of international financial support for VET and invested substantial sums in projects involving vocational and diversified secondary schools (see Table 3). While the percentage of VET funds allocated to secondary-level programs declined between 1963–76 and 1977–88 (dropping from 54 percent to 20 percent), the absolute amount of investments between these two periods increased. (A growing interest in non-formal education involved programs to enable out-of-school youth to acquire vocational or technical skills applicable for formal wage employment or self-employment.) Overall, with generous international financing and widespread belief in the economic legitimacy of VET, many Asian, African, and Latin American countries initiated prevocational, vocational, and technical education or training programs in the 1960s and 1970s.

Nevertheless, disappointment and disillusion over vocational education outcomes proliferated (Chapman and Windham, 1985; Wong, 1973: 36–40; Psacharopoulus and Loxley, 1985; Psacharopoulos, 1987). Many critiques of VET programs in postcolonial states recalled themes first articulated by Foster (1965) in his seminal work on the "vocational school fallacy." Foster maintains that academic schools in Ghana were actually perceived as vocational because they led to the most desirable jobs in the modern sector (e.g., clerical jobs, government positions). Vocational education, he argues, was likely regarded as inferior because it was orientated towards less attractive vocations. In addition, vocational training, especially when directed towards wage employment, would not by itself produce jobs. Although it might redistribute who gets existing jobs and eventually contribute to increased productivity and employment opportunities, without changes in labor market conditions, benefits of vocational training were unlikely. Beginning in the late 1970s, internal evaluations of projects supported by the World Bank highlighted the acute problems engendered by diversifying curricula and supporting vocational education: VET programs necessitated high capital and operating costs; low salaries made it difficult to recruit qualified teachers; prevocational courses in diversified schools were under-enrolled due to "cultural biases" against technical subjects; many technical and diversified school graduates postponed entering the labor market and instead entered tertiary-level institutions; among those who entered the labor market, many were unable to find jobs in their fields of training; links between VET programs and community or business needs were often inappropriate or nonexistent; and many VET curricula were poorly designed (World Bank, 1991: 71ff). As a result, the World Bank increased educational investments in primary education and general secondary education and simultaneously reconfigured its support for VET projects to those that were increasingly privatized, concentrated at the post-secondary level, and more closely linked to specific industrial sectors and skill demands (World Bank, 1991). Since the 1970s, and more intensively during the past decade, UNESCO has also actively promoted technical and vocational education, through initiatives such as the International Project on Technical and Vocational Education (UNEVOC), various reports and international meetings[12] and the establishment of an International Center in Bonn (2000).

The controversy over vocational education and training—whether it should be conceived as curricular diversification in general secondary schools, as separate schools training students for labor market positions, as a broad educational strategy to inculcate job-relevant or life-related skills among young people, or as non-formal frameworks providing status-enhancing skills to out-of-school youth—continues unabated (Lillis

---

[12] In Seoul, Korea, the Second International Congress on Technical and Vocational Education was held in 1999. In Moscow, Russia, An Expert Meeting on Information and Communication Technologies in Technical and Vocational Education and Training was held in 2002.

and Hogan, 1983; Psacharopoulos, 1987, 1990; Gill et al., 2000). Social scientists have raised difficult questions about the effectiveness and efficiency of VET programs in developing countries: Can national policy makers accurately predict changing labor market structures, manpower requirements, and occupational skill demands in order to tighten the links between educational programs and labor markets? Can relevant VET curricula be designed, and can qualified teachers be trained and employed? Can the governments of developing countries afford the higher costs and outlays associated with VET programs, especially under conditions of austerity? Do employers actually prefer VET graduates to general education graduates? Can educational programs, by themselves, alter economic structures and patterns of unemployment or underemployment? Based on findings from accumulated research conducted over recent decades, there is little evidence of unequivocal, affirmative responses to these questions (see Lewin, 1993; Tillak, 2002). In the wake of many failed VET reforms, the relative effectiveness of VET programs seems to depend on relatively scarce and highly contingent conditions being met, such as a country's level of development, clear linkages with existing labor markets, institutional configurations of the national education system, the quality of teacher training, and employer preferences.

Furthermore, as previously discussed, the bias towards academic studies and the perception that vocational education entails an inferior, "second-class" education have deep historical roots in postcolonial states. The introduction of formal school structures during the colonial period significantly affected social-class formation, conceptions of "modernization," and definitions of what counts as valid knowledge and, consequently, valid schooling (Lillis and Hogan, 1983). In many settings, colonial experiences created strong biases and negative attitudes towards vocational education (Beckford, 1972; Abdulah, 1981; Rabo, 1986). Although elite secondary education seemed to contradict the populist, democratic spirit of newly independent nations, many older elites who had been educated in colonial systems viewed the vocationalization of secondary education as eroding academic standards (Sutton, 1965: 75). In addition, those in power were disinclined to dismantle education systems that privileged their children's achievements and futures (Heyneman, 1971). Although government functionaries may have been willing to pay lip service to practical skill training or revitalized agricultural education, they continued to support regressive policies favoring higher education. This orientation towards the elite resulted in persistent educational inequalities (Gauhar, 1981; Khan, 1981).

Formative historical experiences molded public conceptions of appropriate or inappropriate education. For example, Caribbean countries were overwhelmingly partial to a grammar-school-type education and correspondingly averse to technical education, reflecting attitudes consistent with their British heritage and related to their slavery experience (Lewis and Lewis, 1985: 35). Only when the public (especially parents) became critical of the high failure rates of children in the traditional academic curriculum did some governments initiate programmatic changes to secondary education (Lewis and Lewis, 1985). Vocational-school leavers expected to gain access to more highly-skilled positions in the labor market. When governments' manpower forecasts went unrealized, support for VET programs eroded and interest in academic programs, which seemed a more promising road to stable wage employment, increased. Indeed, the fact that VET programs rarely altered existing employment structures explains in part the qualified and shifting support they received.

In sum, despite the vocational-school fallacy and the many problems associated with VET programs, national and international interest in vocational education remains quite strong. Policies favoring some form of vocationalization have a simple, intuitive logic to them, and they continue to garner financial support—albeit more narrowly targeted—by donor organizations and host governments (World Bank, 1991; Gill et al., 2000). Over the course of the twentieth century, visions of vocational education have invented and re-invented themselves on numerous occasions. They continue to imbue international policy discussions, particularly those that consider the transformation of secondary school systems in less-developed countries (World Bank, 2005). Under very specific economic and institutional conditions, some VET programs became an integral feature of formal secondary schooling. The historical evidence suggests, however, that such programs are being radically transformed. They are less frequently organized around particular jobs and vocations and more often around different types of skill training, increasingly anchored at the upper- and post-secondary levels, increasingly funded by private sources and conducted outside the public education system, and increasingly defined as in-career, rather than pre-career, training. More so than other forms of schooling, cultural orientations and historical legacies have played, and continue to play, a significant role in determining the legitimacy and place of vocational education in postcolonial states (Benavot, 1983).

The Experience of Communist Countries

Unlike most western countries, where major educational transitions resulted from complex and drawn-out historical processes, communist countries often imposed decisive educational reforms in the wake of successful regime change. Newly established socialist governments—including the Soviet Union during the 1920s, China from the late 1950s to the mid-1970s, and Cuba from 1960 to the early 1970s—were deeply committed to educational expansion as well as the promotion of adult literacy through mass campaigns (Bhola, 1984; Arnove and Graff, 1987). Revolutionary leaders "attributed great importance to education as part of the means of achieving social transformation" (Carnoy and Samoff, 1990: 7).

Each of these regimes established new educational frameworks intended to blur the traditional hierarchy between academic and professional studies as well as the separation between school life and the work world. Soviet "factory-run schools and school-run factories" and Chinese work-study programs that encouraged individuals to "work every day and study every day" exemplified the integration of education and labor. In Cuba, academic studies became more utilitarian in character. China highlighted science and technology subjects, especially their application outside the classroom, often carrying out lessons at factories and farm sites (Cheng and Manning, 2003). The polytechnical model, established in the late 1950s and 1960s in the Soviet Union and Eastern Europe, forged new links between school and work by integrating general and vocational education at a national level. At the upper-secondary level, schools sought to strike a balance between theoretical knowledge and practical training in production (UNESCO, 1961: 139–140).

Many of these educational reforms were abruptly reversed in the wake of unmet economic goals and objectives. In the 1930s, the Soviet Union passed a series of decrees that restored aspects of the previous system with the aim of more effectively training technicians, engineers, and administrators. After Mao's death in 1976, Chinese leaders reintroduced college admission examinations and reestablished "key [elite] schools" in every province and city. In Cuba in 1970, weak levels of sugar production—a major economic target of the revolution—led Castro to launch educational reforms stressing grades, discipline, and promotion, thereby undercutting previous initiatives to integrate work and study. In the early 1980s, the establishment of a new elite school system called the School for Exact Sciences launched Cuba's "battle for quality" (Cheng and Manning, 2003). Although leaders abandoned many ambitious educational experiments, communist education systems continued to be inspired by egalitarian ideals and to emphasize technological and scientific study.

Cuba is considered an especially successful example of educational transformation under socialism. According to Padula and Smith, "the revolutionary reforms of Cuban education from 1959–1987...rank as one of the more extraordinary efforts in the history of education" (1988: 135). Education and educational change became a symbol of the revolution itself; mass education became a means of economic participation and mobilization (Carnoy, 1990: 171). Cuba's impressive educational achievements include: universal school enrollment and attendance; comprehensive early childhood education and student health programs; equality of basic educational opportunity, both rural and urban and even in impoverished areas; extensive pre- and in-service training of teachers, who also enjoy relatively high professional status; near-universal adult literacy; expanded non-formal programs for out-of-school youth and adults; and a strong scientific training base (Gasparini, 2000).

Discussion of Cuban educational reform should be framed by two main factors that contributed to its success: the positive influence of certain pre-revolutionary conditions such as relatively high adult literacy rates and a well-organized and educated labor force; and the comprehensive manner in which authorities confronted educational and non-educational problems. Specifically, initiatives sought simultaneously to substantially reduce poverty (Berube, 1984), eliminate adult illiteracy, improve children's health care, increase access to primary and lower-secondary education, raise teachers' status, involve parents and community leaders in school affairs, and bring about important curricular reforms. In addition, community motivation remained strong and was nourished constantly by the politics of mass mobilization.

Recent comparative analyses of mathematics and language achievement among Latin American pupils illustrate the strong performance of Cuban pupils (Willms and Somers, 2001; Carnoy and Marshall, 2005). Indeed, many of Cuba's schools perform at levels similar to those of OECD countries (Gasparini, 2000).

In addition to the aforementioned factors, many scholars discuss how Cuba's state structures and politics have contributed to the outstanding results of its educational system (Carnoy, 1990; Torres, 1991; Carnoy and Marshall, 2005). First, the highly structured educational system depends on a centralized educational administration, which sets national educational policies. Indeed, much political decision making in Cuba is personalistic. Second, the continuity of education strategies has benefited from the stability of political policies over several decades. Third, levels of investment in education have remained high, even during periods of severe resource constraint (Gasparini, 2000). Lastly, community participation in school management has been encouraged, as have parent and student involvement in curriculum reform. Although it is unlikely to be replicated in full, many aspects of Cuba's educational revolution should be carefully considered by other countries that are working to expand and improve their educational systems (MacDonald, 1985).

Conclusion

Concern for equality and equity was not an integral part of the early evolution of national education systems. For centuries, elite education was the norm. Debate in most of Europe and North America initially revolved around the educability of the children of the masses and whether they should be incorporated as citizens in the nascent nation-state through their participation in public schooling. Only in the late nineteenth and early twentieth centuries did the discourse shift from a question of exclusion and inclusion, to a question of the terms of inclusion. In other words, although it was generally accepted that all children should be educated, the debate was over how much schooling, at what ages, and with what objectives and contents in mind (Ramirez, 2003). Even as discourses changed slowly and unevenly, educational realities lagged further behind.

In European colonies and postcolonial states, the issue of whether all children are educable, or need be educated, remained salient well into the twentieth century. In this sense, the educational principles discussed at the International Conferences on Public Education during the inter-War period (Magnin, 2002) and later institutionalized in the UN's Universal Declaration of Human Rights (1948) represented dramatic turning points for children living in dependent territories and former colonies. The idea of free and universal primary education, however elusive its implementation may have been in practice, effectively placed all children of school age into a single category of comparison, in which measures of educational inequalities could be constructed, evaluated, and transformed into objects of policy reform.

As we have seen, secondary education was historically limited in coverage, relatively uniform in structure, and academic in content. Calls to open secondary schools to children from less-privileged backgrounds, and to diversify its traditional purposes, invoked different principles and confronted different realities around the world. The high-status knowledge and elite cultural codes associated with academic secondary schools were deeply ingrained in European history, less so in North America. Many Europeans believed that children of popular origin were incapable of meeting the difficult challenges of academic studies in grammar schools, lycées, and gymnasiums. Expanding access to secondary education meant lowering academic standards. Critics cited the less-than-rigorous demands of American high schools and colleges, in contrast to European ones, as the price of mass secondary education (Resnik, 2001). Moreover, industrial economies demanded more scientists, technicians, and skilled workers. Policies expanding vocational and technological education, on the one hand, and increasing the scientific and technological content of general education, on the other, more effectively addressed the alarming lack of such workers. Thus, to the extent that countries championed policies to increase access to secondary education, they typically advanced these policies within a hierarchical framework of stratified schools and programs of study.

The principle of equality of opportunity and the democratization of secondary education slowly gained momentum in postwar Europe. With high economic growth rates and relatively activist regimes, many European governments inaugurated radical reforms in secondary education: reconfiguring selection criteria, extending compulsory education, establishing clearer markers between lower- and upper-secondary education, transforming vocational education, diversifying curricula, and expanding comprehensive schools. As we have discussed, the evolution towards more democratic secondary education systems involved complex interactions of technological changes, political cultures, educational standards, and cultural and social traditions. In newly independent states, intergovernmental organizations and Western experts played an important role in fostering these new conceptions of education.

By the late 1970s, visions of a more democratic and egalitarian secondary-school sector began to fade. The energy crisis and economic stagnation left egalitarian targets unfulfilled. Notions of equity—a justice-laden concept—began to replace those of equality in educational discourse. Equity-based analyses sought to understand why, despite the seemingly good intentions of educators and planners, education systems continued to produce disappointing results. Equity discourse in Western countries conceptualized and engendered new target groups, such as immigrant children, marginalized populations, and disabled pupils. In international organizations, this discourse addressed indigenous peoples, rural populations, minority groups, and, especially, girls (Chabbott, 2003: 57).

From the mid-1980s, an economic world-competition discourse gradually replaced the economic growth discourse. Shifts in economic and demographic conditions yielded new challenges for education systems in more-developed and less-developed countries alike. There was a pressing need to increase general educational levels in the population, to improve vocational education and skill training, and to provide a solid basis for lifelong learning. Recommendations addressing these challenges were coupled with strategies to reduce education costs, improve efficiency, increase private sector intervention, and decentralize educational governance. As education was increasingly linked to global production needs and the activities of the private sector, many contended that the neoliberal discourse of the New Right had become the dominant model (Kallaway, 1989). Policies endorsed by the World Bank sought to advance these principles without contradicting equity principles. Actions to improve skills training (e.g., macroeconomic strategies, more effective and efficient private sector training, improvements to public skill training) were expected to address equity objectives for the poor and the socially disadvantaged (World Bank, 1991: 17–21). In sum, this new valorizing concept of manual skills permitted the bridging of demands for universal secondary education, more diversified secondary education serving increasingly heterogeneous populations, and the perceived economic imperatives that justify vocational and technical education (Resnik, 2001).

INTERNATIONAL ORGANIZATIONS AND THE INSTITUTIONALIZATION OF THE GLOBAL EDUCATION SYSTEM

Our comparative analytical history of mass schooling has highlighted the influence of transnational and international processes. We contend that the circulation and emulation of foreign educational models are not recent inventions. Rather, what has changed over time is the nature of educational knowledge being discussed and transferred.

The observation and selective borrowing of foreign educational practices has been an integral part of the movement towards compulsory mass education. Scholars interested in new pedagogical approaches, such as that of Pestalozzi (1746–1827), traveled considerable distances to study emergent practices in the eighteenth century. Foreign advisers and educational experts, who served as emissaries of their national governments, came to study the Prussian education system in order to transfer educational knowledge to their countries (Noah and Eckstein, 1969; Cummings, 1980, 1997). From 1830–1850, prominent Americans such as C. Woodbridge and Horace Mann traveled to Western Europe to observe and compare school organization and educational frameworks (Knight, 1955; Fraser, 1969: 1–17). After World War I, John Dewey wrote extensive surveys on prominent educational approaches and practices in Soviet Russia, China, Mexico, and Turkey (Dewey, 1964).

The advent of governmental statistical offices in Europe and North America during the nineteenth century (Desrosières, 1998) contributed to the circulation of more thorough accounts of foreign educational frameworks and heralded the emergence of a world education system (Schriewer, 2000) or world culture (Chabbott, 2003), which expanded rapidly in the twentieth century. Although some studies dealing with education had been carried out by the International Labour Organization prior to the founding of the IBE in 1925, the IBE sought to transform children's education into a scientific field (Magnin, 2002). Beginning in the 1930s, the IBE-sponsored International Conference on [Public] Education brought together leading education proponents and senior officials of ministries of education from around the world. The recommendations of this international forum, which both symbolized and contributed to the growing global education system, "…constitute[d] a kind of international charter or code of public education, a body of educational doctrine of very wide scope and importance" (from the IBE website, accessed June 2003).

Undoubtedly, the establishment of UNESCO after World War II proved to be the most important turning point in the development of this global system (Meyer and Ramirez, 2000; Chabbott, 2003). In addition to its legitimacy as part of the UN system, UNESCO's burgeoning educational agenda was instilled with an unprecedented universalistic moral authority. Education systems around the world came to be considered part of an all-encompassing global framework in which individual units could examine and adapt "proven" or promising educational practices. Beginning in the 1950s, UNESCO launched comparative educational reports, international meetings, and policy declarations, which invested it with further international authority and caused many member states to seriously consider and subsequently apply its recommendations. In addition to UNESCO, intergovernmental organizations such as the

World Bank and OECD became salient channels for the global diffusion of Western standards and educational models through their research reports, policy statements, and project funding. The activities of these organizations resulted in the greater uniformity of educational accounts, a process that has intensified over time (Resnik, 2006b).

The attractiveness of the American educational model also contributed to the adoption of standardized educational recommendations in many international organizations in two significant ways. First, in the aftermath of World War II, the United States emerged as the triumphant superpower and took the lead in a range of economic, political, and cultural arenas. The Allies' victory brought attention to American educational structures and practices, as well as their presumed high technological standards. European scholars were encouraged to travel to U.S. universities in order to absorb ideas from the "New World." Many countries became interested in imitating certain aspects of the American system and in becoming part of global educational networks in which the United States was a central actor (see Paulston, 1968: 100; Hoffman, 1997). Second, the United States was deeply involved in European reconstruction through aid programs, notably the Marshall Plan, and the circulation of professional experts. In the early years after the establishment of UNESCO, Americans held many high-status jobs in the organization. They shaped UNESCO's visions, objectives, and work methods and exposed European leaders cooperating in international organizations (mainly UNESCO, the World Bank, and OECD) to the democratic, egalitarian, and utilitarian worldview dominant in the United States (Pendergast, 1974: 171).

The formation of a global education system and the uniformization of education systems should not be attributed exclusively to pro-U.S. tendencies and American leadership in international organizations. During the First Development Decade (1950–1960) and the Second Development Decade (1960–1970) an "education for development" discourse was constructed in international organizations (Chabbott, 2003: 42–5). The adoption of this "education–economic growth" black box (to use Latour's 1987 term) in international organizations legitimized the empowerment and enlargement of its education departments (Resnik, 2006b). From the late 1950s until the early 1970s, economic growth and modernization theories influenced much of the development thinking of international aid agencies in Europe and North America (Watson, 1984a: 1). Once the United Nations embraced the notion that education is a key factor to economic growth, the idea rapidly gained popularity in international forums and among international policy analysts. The "education–economic growth" black box was perceived as an effective means to accomplish the primary aims of the OECD and UNESCO—that is, to promote the coordination of states, international comparisons, and the global interchange of information among member states. Departments of education in international organizations expanded and their staffs advised and coordinated immense international agendas in both more- and less-developed countries. Member states were expected to increase their educational budgets and were mandated to improve the educational levels of the population. Attempts to realize all these resolutions and recommendations led to the creation of an "education–economic growth" global network (Resnik, 2006b).

The worldwide network encompassed a long list of researchers, economists of education, and planning experts, and recruitment of these individuals intensified. The number of functionaries dealing with educational issues increased considerably in most countries. The global network included many institutions: departments of educational statistics and of educational planning were established in many countries; study groups on education and economic development were organized by UNESCO and OECD; international institutes for promoting education were founded (such as UNESCO's Institute of Education and the International Institute of Educational Planning [IIEP]) or renewed (such as the IBE); comparative scientific educational journals proliferated; and international education forums, such as the IEA (International Association for the Evaluation of Educational Achievement) were founded. This world educational apparatus, in which education units within international organizations were central actors, launched a global campaign stressing Western educational models, in both Europe and in developing countries (Resnik, 2006b).

The faith in economic growth resulting from educational expansion began to fade in the early 1970s (Weiler, 1978; Blakemore and Cooksey, 1981: 281; Fry, 1981). Nevertheless, the adoption of the "education–economic growth" black box in the 1960s had already resulted in a remarkable expansion of education systems through the world. More important, it resulted in the establishment of a global educational apparatus which included, among other things, comparative education reviews and institutions, planning institutions, national institutes of statistics, newly created educational research centers, and partnerships with social sciences and educational sciences at the universities. As the density of interactions

among these entities grew, so too did the standardization of global education descriptions. The uniformization of the global education discourse
influenced educational planning, and transformed educational sciences
into comparative and applied sciences (Resnik, 2006a). Thus, the global
education apparatus developed around techniques of standardized statistics, planning, educational applied research, and comparative education.
As Daston claims, "statistics do not just describe the world, they change
it" (2000: 35). In the 1970s, the ideals of the "education–economic
growth" black box, which had propelled the construction of this enormous educational machine, began to vanish, but the global education system was already widely recognized and institutionalized.

The 1950s and the 1960s were conceived as the golden age of education (Papadopulous, 1994: 37). But, in the mid-1970s, the educational
discourse in international agencies began to change as a result of economic problems caused by the energy crisis. Reductions in educational
expenditures forced developed countries to manage their resources more
efficiently and effectively. These countries developed new indices to monitor their education systems and reduce costs. Donor countries were less
eager to collaborate with costly development projects. In less-developed
countries, this resulted in cutoffs of international educational funding
and in recommendations from international agencies to apply efficiency
and effectiveness norms to their educational administrations. Moreover,
in the 1980s, the debts crisis and the introduction of World Bank and
IMF Structural Adjustment programs forced indebted developing countries to reduce their expenditures in education. Decentralization and local
educational governance became keystones of international discourse,
mainly in the World Bank, as a way to grapple with bloated and inefficient central administrations and to encourage greater community financing of local schools (Kiernan, 2000; Chabbott, 2003: 56). Renewed faith
in market forces, skepticism about state efficiency in providing social
services, and the search for strategies that would enlarge local control and
financing led many donor institutions to favor NGOs as social service
delivery agents, increasing NGO participation in educational projects
(Chabbott, 2003: 46). In the 1990s, the introduction of the Human
Development Index renewed interest in "human resources development," emphasizing the need to increase the participation of girls and
minority children in the education system (Chabbott, 2003: 56–57).

In some international organizations, the drive for educational expansion languished over time. As Chabbott (2003: 62) notes, international

discourse in the last decade of the twentieth century increasingly privileged individual welfare over national growth as the more appropriate measure of development. In other organizations, notably the World Bank, where investments in educational projects grew, faith in education was transformed. No longer simply an engine of economic growth, education became a means of reducing poverty and promoting sustainable development. At UNESCO, where notions of education as a fundamental human right dominated, ambitious large-scale programs to enhance all forms of education were undertaken. The Education for All (EFA) movement, initially launched by UNESCO and other international organizations during the World Education Conference in Jomtien (Thailand) in 1990, placed basic education high on the development agenda. A decade later in Dakar (Senegal), representatives from over 160 countries and NGOs reaffirmed their commitment to EFA and generated a more detailed set of goals, actions, and monitoring mechanisms for achieving educational targets over the coming decades (UNESCO, 2002).

In summary, international discourse on education, in both governmental and nongovernmental organizations, changed substantially over the past four decades. During the 1960s and 1970s, Education for All, Universal Primary Education (UPE), Compulsory and Free Education, and Education for Self Reliance became the rallying cries for governments and donors alike. The World Bank initially emphasized the needs of tertiary education and later highlighted projects that vocationalized secondary education. In the 1970s, the Basic Needs philosophy affected the way in which educational projects and reforms were perceived, while in the 1980s, the Structural Adjustment Programs (SAPs) became the frame through which donor investments in education were evaluated (Kiernan, 2000). The notion of economic growth transformed into economic development; concepts like the "pool of abilities" or equality of oppportunity virtually disappeared from international discourse. The education of minority groups, the cultural rights of aborigines, gender equality and parity, and the emergence of the all-encompassing knowledge society became new themes in international policy papers. Earlier educational recommendations morphed into newer ones—almost all became integrated into world educational culture. Unchanged, however, was the power to initiate, diffuse, and adapt educational discourses, which remained unequal. The adoption of education recommendations, typically formulated in the developed world for international circulation, strongly revolved around national and local considerations in more-industrialized countries. In less-developed countries, by contrast, national contingencies and local conditions took a back seat to the prospect of international aid, thereby reducing degrees of political freedom in adapting recommended reforms.

WHAT CAN BE LEARNED FROM A COMPARATIVE SOCIO-HISTORICAL ANALYSIS OF UNIVERSAL EDUCATION?

The historical development of universal basic education was an uneven and highly contingent process.

The development of universal basic education—compulsory, systemic, integrated, inclusive, diversified, and attuned to discourses advanced by international agencies—was an uneven and highly contingent historical process. This is a major point arising from the comparative socio-historical analysis undertaken in this chapter. The evolution of public systems of primary and secondary schools depended, in different times and places, on changing configurations of local, national, regional, and global conditions. In Europe and North America, state structures and processes of state formation profoundly affected educational expansion and systemization. Late industrializers often linked educational expansion to economic and technological development, and moved more quickly to develop vocational-education frameworks for children destined for positions in industry and manufacturing. In societies with weak aristocratic traditions and less elitist cultural conceptions, there were more determined efforts to prolong compulsory schooling and to expand and diversify secondary education. Compulsory mass schooling emerged from diverse social, economic, and political conditions. In some cases, it invoked nation-building processes and new conceptions of citizenship; in others, it was informed by long-standing conflicts with powerful religious authorities and by social movements supporting secularization; and in still others, it served to weaken the pervasiveness of child labor and gender discrimination.

In Asia, Africa, and Latin America, indigenous educational forms had important historical consequences, not only during the period of European imperialism, but also following political independence. The structures, principles, and practices predominating in colonial and missionary schools left indelible marks on mass education in postcolonial states. Indigenous cultural authorities and foreign actors stimulated distinctive historical legacies, from the varying predominance of ideologies of educational exclusion to the passage and enforcement of educational ordinances, from the strategies used to address religious and private schools to those used to reform of secondary education. Furthermore, transnational and international forces profoundly influenced the development of universal education in newly independent countries. More so than in Europe and North America, in which selective (but limited) cultural borrowing took place, intergovernmental organizations not only circulated prevailing educational models, but also pressured national elites to adopt them. Crucial changes to mass education in these regions depended, in no small measure, on such exogenous forces.

Comparative historical scholarship of the emergence, systemization, and expansion of universal education remains underdeveloped and downplays the diverse origins and meanings of mass schooling.

Even within the narrow confines of the issues addressed in this chapter, there is an acute need for existing social scientific scholarship to reconsider and reevaluate existing studies of the origins and development of mass education. The overemphasis on comparative (usually quantitative) studies of enrollment expansion and isomorphic tendencies has resulted in scholars ignoring or downgrading other aspects of the historical institutionalization of universal education, which is much more diverse and heterogeneous in nature than typically characterized. It is time for comparative researchers to admit long-standing biases in what has (and has not) been studied and to launch new comparative historical studies of mass education, which would extend and enrich the conceptual models that have become accepted truths.

The models, policies, and recommendations of international actors and organizations were de-contextualized from their historical roots.

Another key point to emerge from the comparative analyses in this chapter concerns the problematic flow of Western educational models and practices across space and time. Educational structures in the West resulted from historically diverse national conditions and extensive political debates. In contrast, policies and practices prescribed by transnational agents for developing countries showed relative uniformity and little adaptation to local contexts. Transnational agents often presented these policies as quick solutions to pressing social and economic problems. The educational models flowing to postcolonial states were, by their very nature, de-contextualized. Because these models relied upon research findings framed within Western problematiques and embedded in the institutional configurations of dominant education systems, they lacked an in-depth understanding of the contexts in which they were proffered and transplanted. As Foster (1977) notes, concepts such as social stratification, created to analyze patterns in Western societies, can be misleading if applied uncritically to the non-Western world. Or as Hirschman (1968) points out, modernization theorists institutionalized a model of the development process that was divorced from history and the distinctive features of particular nation-states. Indeed, international educational policies and reforms are rarely grounded in historical configurations.

The longstanding controversy over academic (general) versus vocational (technical) secondary education aptly illustrates the problem of de-contextualization created when exogenous educational models are applied to less-developed countries. In case after case, government initiatives and support for vocational education and training overlooked generic problems and basic fallacies related to the vocational education–employment nexus. These problems included critical public perceptions, poorly trained teachers, outdated facilities, few student incentives, and a paucity of data on actual or future manpower needs (Chapman and Windham, 1985). Vocationalization policies encapsulated a seemingly intuitive logic, which made them attractive to both donor organizations and host governments. Although research indicated that the success of VET was highly context-dependent, it continued to be circulated as a legitimate and attractive policy alternative within a simplified, de-contextualized model.

Another example of this phenomenon can be seen in international recommendations that called on Latin American countries to dismantle the grasp of the federal government or central state over educational provisions. In the 1980s, when such decentralization reforms were implemented in Argentina and Chile, neither greater efficiency nor equity resulted. Instead, private enrollments and socioeconomic segmentation increased (Narodowski and Nores, 2002). As Braslavsky and Gvirtz (2000) contend, decentralization proposals and similar recommendations such as vouchers and school autonomy were conceived in Anglo-Saxon cultures, which could draw upon rich historical experiences of local administration of education prior to reforms. Advocates of decentralization ignored the absence of these experiences in Latin America and minimized the legacy of regressive, elite-driven purposes that school systems had historically served. The adoption of decentralization reforms made a difficult situation even worse, and exacerbated deeply rooted social inequalities.

In short, for prescriptive international policies to thrive, they must consider the richly diverse economic, social, and political contexts in which education systems are embedded (Fagerlind and Saha, 1983: viii).

Religion, cultural diversity, and local institutions are often neglected in policy recommendations.

The educational proposals of international agencies seldom touch upon topics related to cultural patterns and religious traditions, which further contributes to their de-contextualized nature. This restraint might be rationalized in relation to Latin America, owing to its shared Christian traditions and extensive Western influence, but it proves problematic in non-Western states and Muslim societies. The suggestion that educational "best practices" can be transferred indiscriminately from one cultural context to another illustrates the widespread inattention to the cultural grounding of educational policies and processes. In Africa, for example, the roles played by languages of instruction, by indigenous philosophy or gnosis, and by the community in the education of its youth, are scarcely considered in proposals for educational reform (Mudimbe, 1988). Treating these issues as unimportant for the education of African children miseducates, rather than educates, for personal, national, and continental development (Jagusah, 2001).

Many scholars see the adoption of de-contextualized education models as disruptive for their societies. Incorporating implicit Western values through schooling without taking into account indigenous values can prove unproductive and risky in the long run. For example, in Ethiopia, modern schools produced "culturally displaced" individuals who felt at home neither in their own culture nor in the imported foreign culture (Germa, 1982). Schools cultivated scientific attitudes, taught democratic institutions, and transmitted egalitarian values for an imagined society, even though realities on the ground remained pre-scientific, authoritarian, and hierarchical. According to Saqib (1981: 51), the injection of occidental values and lifestyles, mainly through haphazard importation of technology, runs counter to the values promoted by Islam and undermines the morale of their people.

Indigenous African traditions tend to emphasize collectivist orientations rather than individualistic ones (Mazrui and Wagaw, 1985). Patterns of African socialization and training are meant to reflect the values, wisdom, and expectations of the community and wider society. Western forms of schooling, which stress the "intellectual" development of the individual, have been less attentive to community needs, goals, and expectations. Knowledge of the rational, intellectual, and philosophical sciences may be an optional element for a Muslim; knowledge of the religious sciences is obligatory because it is "absolutely essential for man's guidance and salvation" (Naquib al-Attas, 1991: 40). By exclusively focusing on modern secular schooling, policy analysts neglect the potential contributions of Muslim forms of education to national purposes (Fisher, 1969). Despite the centrality of religion in many Muslim nations, educational strategies advanced by Western experts only reluctantly discuss the role of religious studies. Creative accommodations of religious and secular studies—or the lack thereof—may influence parents' willingness to enroll their children, especially girl children, in "modern schools."

Many experts in Africa, the Middle East, and Asia do not believe that the solution to this dilemma lies in abandoning one form of education (indigenous or religious) for another (modern). Public schooling can play a vital societal role if it addresses the cultural, social, and moral challenges, not just political and economic ones, facing local communities. Some scholars refer to this as creating a more domesticated or indigenized education system. For this reason, scholars and policy makers need to become familiar with the historical evolution and contemporary patterns of indigenous education (Bray et al., 1986: 109; Kelly, 2000). In today's multicultural world, a familiarity with both religious and cultural sensibilities and practices, as well as a consideration of ways to incorporate indigenous institutions within educational reform strategies, has considerable relevance.

Political actors and processes, as well as local economic institutions, are disregarded in international educational programs.

In the early 1970s, Heyneman (1971) argued that intergovernmental organizations seldom consider political factors in their recommendations —an argument that is still germane today. Two types of arguments have dominated international reforms, the adaptation and the empirical. The adaptation argument assumes that human nature is social and cooperative, and that the state, party, and nation are logical tools employed by individuals to construct society. The empirical argument is deeply rooted in economic perspectives, which assume the primacy of individual motives and regard the state as neither the most efficient planner nor the best educator (Heyneman, 1971: 7). Both approaches underestimate (or disregard) political considerations and the role of political elites in educational processes, especially in less-developed countries. What and how

schools teach, and which children have access to existing learning opportunities, are, in essence, the outcomes of political processes that involve
multiple, often conflicting, actors and interest groups. Moreover, political
attitudes and positions are likely to be decoupled from actual educational
targets (Meyer and Rowan, 1977). National administrations may agree to
pursue major educational reforms, sometimes based on recommendations
of international agencies, but then dispense with effective implementation mechanisms. Indeed, in less-developed regions, the scarcity of
resources and the enormous gap between the socioeconomic statuses of
the educated and the uneducated turn any educational reform into a con-
tested political issue.

Another problematic aspect of the de-contextualized policies proffered
to less-developed countries, especially in Asia and Africa, is the disregard
of (or inattention to) political outcomes, in contrast to ever-present economic ones. As we have seen, state building and re-conceptions of citizenship played crucial roles in the history of early national education systems.
Coleman (1965: 53) argues that these tasks are no less important for the
education systems of newly independent nations. Political integration and
nurturing a political identity in the young are essential conditions for
national unity and the viability and legitimacy of political institutions. The
construction and preservation of a nation, or a national polity, depend on
effective frameworks of socialization. Nevertheless, the educational agendas of international organizations rarely explicate linkages between specific
educational polices or practices—for example, languages of instruction or
languages taught (Perren, 1969)—and political outcomes such as nation
building, political democratization, or national solidarity.

The absence of the political can also be seen in the neglect of salient
political differences. International policies may focus on a particular geopolitical region, like Sub-Saharan Africa, and then minimize political differences, both past and present, and assume commonalities. Abdi (2003), for
example, shows that variation in the political histories of Somalia, South
Africa, and Nigeria differentially affected educational structures and outcomes (e.g., brain drain). Programs for African education and development, which often lack refinement in these matters, tend to suggest common solutions to the complex educational problems they address. Later,
when policies fail, political explanations (e.g., party infighting, corruption)
are advanced to rationalize lost educational opportunities.

Notwithstanding the deep belief in the power of education, Heyneman (1971: 110) argues that it is misleading to assume that schools can

be the sole agents of social and political change, or even the prime movers of economic and agricultural development. Schools alone are unable to produce widespread changes in rural life. They become effective only when they are part of a broader economic and social plan to make farming more productive (Griffiths, 1965, cited in Heyneman, 1971). As we have seen, vocational education programs or prevocational courses have little influence on local markets and employment conditions. Educational expansion, which produces un-, under-, and mis-employed school graduates, may unintentionally increase social tensions and political instability. In Ethiopia, for instance, the 1974 revolution was spearheaded by disillusioned students who felt uncertain about their future, by young military officers who joined the army after failing at school, by dissatisfied teachers, and by a large number of semi-educated young dropouts (Germa, 1982). The problem of absorbing a large educated labor force is especially salient in Egypt (Bureau for Policy and Program Coordination, 2004). Social and economic inequalities, as well as brutal security structures, have contributed to student radicalism on Egyptian university campuses and to greater Islamic opposition (Bureau for Policy and Program Coordination, 2004: 15). Moreover, the failure of Arab governments to secure the material blessings of modernization sapped their ideological legitimacy and paved the way for an Islamic resurgence.

In short, when educational reforms are treated in isolation from associated changes in economic and political organization, they are unlikely to bring about real social and economic progress.

International educational models are often inadequate and irrelevant in local context.

This chapter has shown that international agencies, which act as independent initiators or catalysts of educational policies and models, shift the foci of their policies according to changing logics and imperatives divorced from local considerations. In the early 1970s, agency interest shifted from higher education to elementary education. Later, there was a change in emphasis from models based on formal education to those based on non-formal education, which stimulated an unprecedented number of studies and projects on non-formal learning supported by the World Bank and UNESCO. Nowadays, international agencies emphasize strategies that integrate school-based and out-of-school learning under the heading of "basic education" or lifelong learning (Bray et al., 1986: 16).

Under conditions of economic dependency, however, the ability of nations to select or adapt educational models is circumscribed. Poor or deeply indebted countries tend to be highly solicitous of aid, grants, loans, or technical assistance from international donors. In order to receive aid and to signal that they are responsible and rational actors, economically weak states construct "frameworks for action," which are consistent with international agendas (Meyer et al., 1997: 153). Thus, economic dependency reduces the possibility of less-developed countries to tailor international educational formulas to national needs and purposes.[13]

Latin American scholars, who have a long history of analyzing structures of external dependency, have been especially sensitive to the imposition of foreign educational models. The *Comisión Económica para América Latina de las Naciónes Unidas* (CEPAL) questioned the utilitarian character of educational planning in international organizations: "Economic growth is a needed condition for human and social development but not a sufficient one. This requires the implementation of adequate institutional and political reforms in the framework of an integral and organic conception of development process" (cited in Gimeno, 1981: 118). At a pivotal UNESCO conference of Latin American and Caribbean ministers of education in 1979, it was argued that the lack of relevance of the region's education systems stemmed from the fact that

> those systems have been created and developed...by following models of countries where the levels and features of development are very different, without any allowance being made for the specific historical context of the education systems....Moreover, imported educational models are inseparable from the development models that have likewise been imported and which have been underscoring the dependent character of the societies and economies of the region. The transplantation of models which are not in keeping with the cultural identity of countries does not foster a sufficiently intensive endogenous effort to identify problems and priorities and to devise types and forms of education that are consonant with actual national needs and capabilities... (UNESCO, 1979b: 24).

---

[13] China represents a contrasting case. Due to its geopolitical position and relative autonomy, China has been able to selectively adapt Western educational models and techniques to its own requirements and capacities (Lewin, 1987: 440).

Education, as stated by the Mexico Declaration, should play a decisive role in creating a new, more balanced style of "authentic" development in which the production of goods and services is in line with "genuine social and national necessities." Education should give a human dimension to development, based on principles of social justice that strengthen awareness, participation, solidarity, and organizational ability, especially among underprivileged groups (UNESCO, 1979c: 69–70). Educational planners in particular should play a mediating role in securing the active participation of different sectors and actors and in helping to preserve cultural identities, redefine development goals, and overcome the forces of external domination (Gimeno, 1981: 128). Education is a population's right and it must be at the service of the whole social life (Terra, 1983).

Recent postcolonial histories of Somalia, South Africa, and Nigeria underscore how traditional models of education and development seldom respond to people's "genuine" needs and expectations (Abdi, 1998, 2003; Nwagwu, 1997; Harber, 1998; Soudien, 1994; Mzamane, 1990; Kallaway, 1984, 1989). The African quest for modernity, based on a different model of development, would eliminate Euro-modernity and gradually integrate indigenous, Afro-Christian, and Afro-Islamic traditions (Mazrui and Wagaw, 1985: 59). African intellectuals are deliberating on new conceptions of education and development, which draw upon non-Western cultures and are not designed for profit-seeking purposes (Devisse, 1995). From a Muslim viewpoint, the many shortcomings of international models are striking: "only Muslim people themselves can change and reform their education system—its entire structure, content, methodology and direction—in a fundamental way" (Khan, 1981: 23). Islamic leaders and Muslim scholars must find ways to adjudicate the competing knowledge claims of religious ideologies and scientific knowledge. International donors and educators should facilitate this critical dialogue (Anzar, 2003).

Final Note

Critiques from the "periphery" appear to have been partially heard by international agencies in the business of circulating educational policy. The discourse of the 1990s has integrated a multitude of new or reworked terms: gender parity, equitable access to appropriate learning and life skills, regionalization of education administration, endogenous education, localization, out-of-school education, flexibility, human development, and competencies. But have educational movers and shakers in Latin America, Asia, and Africa become genuine partners in the elaboration of their educational policies? Or has the lexicon been enhanced without an effect on the basic power inequalities between international educational experts and local decision makers?

Undoubtedly, new actors have consolidated a position that mediates between two poles—the global and the local. The last decade has witnessed the emergence of new transnational advocacy networks in education (Mundy and Murphy, 2004). A diverse range of nongovernmental organizations—for example, associations against child labor and the trafficking of women, aid and relief organizations, teacher and principal unions—have launched campaigns in support of public education for all. The efforts of transnational advocacy networks to link problems of educational access to issues of debt relief, human rights, and global equity, have been realized in recent international policy conferences (e.g., the 2000 World Education Forum held in Dakar). If this form of educational advocacy continues to develop (which seems likely), it may succeed in transforming the process by which international educational policies are generated and circulated (Mundy and Murphy, 2004: 20–21). The creation of such a global civil society may modify the terms of debate, reposition actors in this multi-dimensional system, and give rise to more contextualized educational models.

References

Abdi, Ali. 1998. "Education in Somalia: History, Destruction and Calls for Reconstruction." *Comparative Education* 3 (3): 327–340.

———. 2003. "Searching for Development Education in Africa: Select Perspectives on Somalia, South Africa, and Nigeria." *International Education Journal* 4 (3): 192–200.

Abdulah, Norma. 1981. *The Availability and Utilization of Skills in Guyana.* Trinidad: Institute of Social and Economic Research, University of the West Indies.

Albornoz, Orlando. 1993. *Education and Society in Latin America.* Pittsburgh: University of Pittsburgh Press.

Altbach, Philip, and Gail Kelly, eds. 1984. *Education and Colonial Experience.* 2nd edition. New Brunswick: Transaction.

Anderson, Benedict. 1983. *Imagined Communities.* London, New York: Verso.

Anderson, Perry. 1991. "Nation-states and National Identity." *London Review of Books* 9 (May): 3–8.

Anzar, U. 2003. "Islamic Education: A Brief History of Madrassas with Comments on Curricula and Current Pedagogical Practices." Draft paper presented at the World Bank Diversity and Tolerance Workshop, "Curricula, Textbooks, and Pedagogical Practice, and the Promotion of Peace and Respect for Diversity," Washington, DC, March 24–26.

Arab Human Development Report. 2003. *Building a Knowledge Society.* United Nations Development Programme, Arab Fund for Economics and Social Development.

Archer, Margaret. 1979. *Social Origins of Educational Systems.* London: Sage Publications.

Arnove, Robert, and Harvey Graff, eds. 1987. *National Literacy Campaigns: Historical and Comparative Perspectives.* New York: Plenum Press.

Ashton, David, and Francis Green. 1996. *Education, Training and the Global Economy.* London: Elgar.

Astiz, M. F., A. W. Wiseman, and D. Baker. 2002. "Slouching Towards Decentralization: Consequences of Globalization for Curricular Control in National Education Systems." *Comparative Education Review* 46 (1): 66–88.

Avis, James. 2004. "Work-based Learning and Social Justice: 'Learning to Labour' and the New Vocationalism in England." *Journal of Education and Work* 17 (2): 197–217.

Bailyn, Bernard. 1972 [1960]. *Education in the Forming of American Society.* New York: Norton.

Baker, David. 1999. "Schooling all the Masses: Reconsidering the Origins of American Schooling in the Postbellum Era." *Sociology of Education* 72 (October): 197–215.

Barnard, Henry. 1854. *National Education in Europe: Being an Account of the Organization, Administration, Instruction, and Statistics of Public Schools of Different Grades in Principal States.* Hartford: Frederick Perkins.

Barroso, J. 2001. "L'État et la Régulation Locale de l'Education. Réflexions sur la Situation au Portugal." In *Comment Peut-on Administrer l'Ecole? Pour une Approche Politique de l'Administration de l'Education,* ed. Yves Dutercq. Paris: PUF.

Beckford, George L. 1972. *Persistent Poverty: Underdevelopment in Plantation Economies of the Third World.* New York: Oxford University Press.

Beckwith, Holmes. 1913. "German Industrial Education and Its Lessons for the United States." *United States Bureau of Education Bulletin* no. 19 (whole no. 529). Washington, DC: Government Printing Office.

Benavot, Aaron. 1983. "The Rise and Decline of Vocational Education." *Sociology of Education* 56 (April): 63–76.

———. 2002. "Educational Globalization and the Expansion of Instructional Time in National Education Systems." Background Paper for EFA Global Monitoring Report, 2002. Paris: UNESCO.

Benavot, Aaron, and Cecilia Braslavsky (editors). 2006. *School Knowledge in Comparative and Historical Perspective: Changing Curricula in Primary and Secondary Education.* Hong Kong: The University of Hong Kong Press.

Benavot, Aaron, and Julia Resnik. 2006. "Lessons from the Past: A Comparative Socio-Historical Analysis of Primary and Secondary Education." In *Global Educational Expansion: Historical Legacies and Political Obstacles.* A. Benavot, J. Resnik, and J. Corrales. Cambridge, MA: American Academy of Arts & Sciences.

Benavot, Aaron, and Phyllis Riddle. 1988. "The Expansion of Primary Education, 1870–1940: Trends and Issues." *Sociology of Education* 61: 190–210.

Bendix, Reinhard. 1969. *Nation-Building and Citizenship*. New York: Anchor Books.

Berube, Maurice R. 1984. *Education and Poverty: Effective Schooling in the United States and Cuba*. Westport, CT: Greenwood Press.

Bhola, H. 1984. *Campaigns for Literacy: Eight National Experiences of the Twentieth Century, with a Memorandum to Decision-makers*. Paris: UNESCO.

Blakemore, Kenneth, and Brian Cooksey. 1981. *A Sociology of Education for Africa*. London: George Allen and Unwin.

Blossfeld, Hans Peter, and Yossi Shavit. 1993. "Persistent Barriers: Changes in Educational Opportunities in Thirteen Countries." Pp. 1–24 in *Persistent Inequality*, ed. Y. Shavit and H. P. Blossfeld. Oxford, UK: Westview Press.

Boli, John, and John Meyer. 1978. "The Ideology of Childhood and the State: Rules Distinguishing Children in National Constitutions, 1870–1970." *American Sociological Review* 83: 797–812.

Boli, John, Francisco Ramirez, and John Meyer. 1985. "Explaining the Origins and Expansion of Mass Education." *Comparative Education Review* 29: 145–170.

Bonal, Xavier. 2001. "Expansion of New Vocationalism and Realities of Labour Market: View from the Spanish Periphery." *Journal of Education and Work* 14 (2): 177–187.

Bourdieu, Pierre. 1996. *State Nobility: Elite Schools in the Field of Power*. Translated by Lauretta C. Clough. Cambridge: Polity Press.

Boyd, William. 1961. *The History of Western Education*. London: Adam and Charles Black.

Braslavsky, Cecilia, and Silvina Gvirtz. 2000. "Nuevos Desafíos y Dispositivos en la Política Educacional Latinoamericana de Fin de Siglo." In *Cuadernos Educación Comparada 4, Política y Educación en Iberoamérica*, ed. Manuel de Puelles Benitez, Cecilia Braslavsky, Silvina Gvirtz, Alberto Martinez. Madrid: Organización de los Estados Iberoamericanos (OEI).

Bray, Mark. 1999. "Control of Education: Issues and Tensions in Centralization and Decentralization." Pp. 207–232 in *Comparative Education: The Dialectic of the Global and the Local*, ed. R. Armove and C. Torres. Lanham: Rowman and Littlefield.

Bray, Mark, Peter Clarke, and David Stephens. 1986. *Education and Society in Africa*. London: Edward Arnold.

Breuilly, John. 1982. *Nationalism and the State*. New York: St. Martin's Press.

Brock, Colin, and Witold Tulasiewicz, eds. 2000. *Education in a Single Europe.* 2nd edition. London: Routledge.

Brock-Utne, Birgit. 2000. *Whose Education for All? The Recolonization of the African Mind?* New York/London: Falmer Press.

Bureau for Policy and Program Coordination. 2004. "Strengthening Education in the Muslim World: Countries, Profiles and Analysis." PPC Issue Working Paper No. 1.

Callahan, William. 1992. "Church and State in Spain, 1976–1991." *Journal of Church and State* 34 (3) (Summer): 503–520.

————. 1998. *The Catholic Church in Spain, 1875–1998.* Washington, DC: The Catholic University Press.

Carnoy, Martin. 1974. *Education as Cultural Imperialism.* New York: Longman.

————. 1990a. "Educational Reform and the Social Transformation in Cuba, 1959–1989." Pp.153–208 in *Education and Social Transition in the Third World,* ed. Martin Carnoy and Joel Samoff, with Mary Ann Burris, Anton Johnston, Carlos Alberto Torres. Princeton, NJ: Princeton University Press.

————. 1990b. "Socialist Development and Educational Reform in Cuba, 1959-1980." In *Education From Poverty to Liberty,* ed. Bill Nasson and John Samuel. South Africa: David Philip Publishers, Creda Press.

Carnoy, M., and J. Marshall. 2005. "Cuba's Academic Performance in Comparative Perspective." *Comparative Education Review* 49 (2): 230–261.

Carnoy, Martin, and Joel Samoff. 1990a. *Education and Social Transition in the Third World.* Princeton: Princeton University Press.

————. 1990b. "The Search of a Method." Pp. 5–13 in *Education and Social Transition in the Third World,* ed. Martin Carnoy and Joel Samoff, with Mary Ann Burris, Anton Johnston, and Carlos Alberto Torres. Princeton, New Jersey: Princeton University Press.

Central Education Research Institute. 1967. *Study of Compulsory Education.* Seoul, Korea: Organisation for Economic Co-operation and Development (OECD).

Chabbott, Colette. 2003. *Constructing Education for Development: International Organizations and Education for All.* New York: Routledge Falmer.

Chabbott, Colette, and Francisco Ramirez. 2000. "Development and Education." Pp. 163–187 in *Handbook of the Sociology of Education,* ed. Maureen Hallinan. New York: Kluwer/Plenum.

Chapman, David, and D. M. Windham. 1985. "Academic Program 'Failures' and the Vocational School 'Fallacy.'" *International Journal of Educational Development* 5 (4): 269–81.

Cheng, Yinghong and Patrick Manning. 2003. "Revolution in Education: China and Cuba in Global Context, 1957–76." *Journal of World History* 14 (3): 359–391.

Clark, Victor. 1951. *Compulsory Education in Iraq*. Paris: UNESCO.

Clemens, Michael. 2004. "The Long Walk to School: International Education Goals in Historical Perspective." Working Paper. Center for Global Development, Boston.

Clignet, Remi, and Philip Foster. 1964. "French and British Colonial Education in Africa." *Comparative Education Review* 8 (2): 191–98.

Cohen, Yehudi. 1979. "The State System, Schooling, and Cognitive and Motivational Patterns." Pp. 103–40 in *Social Forces and Schooling*, ed. Nobuo Shimahara and Adam Scrupski. New York: David McKay.

Coleman, James. 1965. "Patterns and Problems of Educational Underdevelopment." Pp. 5–35 in *Education and Political Development*, ed. James Coleman. Princeton: Princeton University Press.

Commission on the Reorganization of Secondary Education. 1918. "*Cardinal Principles of Secondary Education*." Bulletin No. 35. Washington, DC: U.S. Bureau of Education.

Conant, James B. 1959. *The American High School Today: A First Report to Interested Citizens*. New York: McGraw-Hill.

Connell, W.F. 1980. *A History of Education in the Twentieth Century*. New York: Teachers College Press.

Cookson, Peter, Jr., and Caroline Hodges Persell. 1985. *Preparing for Power: America's Elite Boarding Schools*. New York: Basic Books.

Cornell, Francis G. 1956. "Report of the First International Conference on Educational Research, Atlantic City, New Jersey, USA, February 1965." *Educational Studies and Documents* 20.

Cowen, Robert. 1990. "The National and International Impact of Comparative Education Infrastructures." Pp. 321–52 in *Comparative Education: Contemporary Issues and Trends*, ed. W. D. Halls. London and Paris: Jessica Kingsley Publishers and UNESCO.

Craig, John. 1981. "The Expansion of Education." *Review of Research in Education* 9: 151–213.

Cremin, Lawrence. 1970. *American Education: The Colonial Experience.* New York: Harper and Row.

Cross, Michael. 1987. "The Political Economy of Colonial Education: Mozambique, 1930–1975." *Comparative Education Review* 31: 550–569.

Cummings, William. 1980. *Education and Equality in Japan.* Princeton: Princeton University Press.

———. 1997. "An Introduction." Pp. 3–43 in *International Handbook of Education and Development: Preparing Schools, Students, and Nations for the Twenty-First Century,* ed. William Cummings and Noel McGinn. New York/Oxford: Elsevier Science.

———. 2003. *The Institutions of Education: A Comparative Study of Educational Development in Six Core Nations.* Oxford: Symposium Books.

Cummings, William, and Abby Riddell. 1994. "Alternative Policies for the Finance, Control, and Delivery of Basic Education." *International Journal of Educational Research* 21 (8): 751–776.

Daston, Lorraine. 2000. "Why Statistics Tend not only to Describe the World but to Change it." Review of *The Politics of Large Numbers: History of Statistical Reasoning,* by Alain Desrosières (translated by Camille Naish). *London Review of Books* 22 (8): 35.

Demo, Pedro. 1983. "Education and Culture: A Political Perspective." *CEPAL Review* 21 (December): 147–156.

Denison, E. F. 1968. "Measuring the Contribution of Education and the 'Residual' Factor to Economic Growth." Pp. 315–41 in *Readings in the Economics of Education,* ed. J. Vaizey. Paris: UNESCO.

Desrosières, Alain. 1990. "How to Make Things Hold Together: Social Sciences, Statistics, and the State." Pp. 195–218 in *Discourse on Society,* Volume XV, ed. P. Wagner, B. Wittrock, and R. Whitley. Netherlands: Kluwer Academic Publishers.

———. 1998. "L'Administrateur et le Savant. La Métamorphose du Métier de Statisticien." *Courier des Statistiques* 87–88: 71–80.

Devisse J. 1985. "The Development of Education Training in Africa: An Outline for 1930–80." Pp. 91–100 in *The Educational Process and Historiography in Africa,* final report and papers of the symposium organized by UNESCO in Dakar, Senegal, January 25–29, 1982.

Dewey, John. 1916. *Democracy and Education.* New York: MacMillan.

————. 1964. *John Dewey's Impressions of Soviet Russia and the Revolutionary World Mexico-China-Turkey – 1929*. Introduction and notes by William Brickman. New York: Bureau of Publications, Teachers College–Columbia University.

Di Bona, Joseph. 1981. "Indigenous Virtue and Foreign Vice: Alternative Perspectives on Colonial Education." *Comparative Education Review* 25: 202–15.

Dominique, Julia, and Roger Chartier. 1987. "L'École: Traditions et Modernization." Pp. 693–704 in *Transaction of the Seventh International Congress on the Enlightenment*. Oxford: The Voltaire Foundation.

Durkheim, Emile. 1977. *The Evolution of Educational Thought*. Translated by Peter Collins. London: Routledge and Kegan Paul.

Dussel, Ines, Guillermina Tiramonti, and Alejandra Birgin. 2000. "Decentralization and Recentralization: Reshaping Educational Policies in the 1990s in the Argentine Educational Reform." Pp. 155–172 in *Educational Knowledge: Changing Relationships between the State, Civil Society, and the Educational Community*, ed. Thomas Popkewitz. Albany: State University of New York Press.

Dutercq, Y. 2001. *Comment Peut-on Administrer l'École? Pour une Approche Politique de l'Administration de l'Éducation*. Paris: PUF.

Economic Commission for Africa and United Nations Educational, Scientific and Cultural Organization (ECA/UNESCO). 1961. *Final Report of the Conference of African States on the Development of Education in Africa*. Addis Ababa, Ethiopia.

Eklof, Ben, and Edward Dneprov, eds. 1993. *Democracy in the Russian School: The Reform Movement in Education Since 1984*. Boulder, CO: Westview Press.

El Tom, Basheer. 1981. "Education and Society." Pp. 28–44 in *Education and Society in the Muslim World*, ed. Mohammad Wasiullah Khan. Jeddah: Hodder and Soughton, King Abdulaziz University.

Eldering, L. 1996. "Multiculturalism and Multicultural Education in an International Perspective." *Anthropological and Education Quarterly* 27 (3): 315–330.

Evans, Rupert. 1982. *Labor Force Related Outcome, and Public Acceptance of Vocational Education*. Columbus, Ohio: National Center of Research in Vocational Education, Ohio State University.

Fafunwa, Babs A. 1982. "African Education in Perspective." Pp. 9–27 in *Education in Africa: A Comparative Survey*, ed. A. Babs Fafunwa and J. U. Aisiku. London: George Allen and Unwin.

Fagerlind, Ingemar, and Lawrence J. Saha. 1983. *Educational and National Development: A Comparative Perspective*. Oxford, New York: Pergamon Press.

Finegold, D. and S. Soskice. 1988. "The Failure of Training in Britain: Analysis and Description." *Oxford Review of Economic Policy* 4 (3): 21–53.

Fisher, Humphrey. 1969. "Islamic Education and Religious Reform in West Africa." Pp. 247–264 in *Education in Africa: Research and Action*, ed. Richard Jolly. Published for the African Studies Association of the United Kingdom. Nairobi, Kenya: East African Publishing House.

Fortna, Benjamin C. 2002. *Imperial Classroom: Islam, the State and Education in the Late Ottoman Period.* Oxford: Oxford University Press.

Foster, Philip. 1965. "The Vocational School Fallacy in Development Planning." Pp. 142–66 in *Education and Economic Development*, ed. C.A. Anderson and Mary J. Bowman. Chicago: Aldine.

———. 1977. "Education and Social Differentiation in Less Developed Countries." *Comparative Education Review* (June/October): 211–229.

Fraser, Stewart. 1969. "Introduction." Pp. 1–17 in *American Education in Foreign Perspectives: Twentieth Century Essays*, ed. Stewart Fraser. New York: John Wiley and Sons.

Fraser, Stewart and William Brickman. 1968. *A History of International and Comparative Education.* New York: Scott, Foresman and Co.

Fry, Gerald W. 1981. "Schooling, Development and Inequality: Old Myths and New Realities." *Harvard Educational Review* 51 (1): 107–117.

Fuller, Bruce, S. D. Holloway, H. Azuma, R. Hess, and K. Kashiwagi. 1986. "Contrasting Achievement Rules: Socialization of Japanese Children at Home and in School." *Research in Sociology of Education and Socialization* 6: 165–201.

Fuller, Bruce, and Richard Rubinson, eds. 1992. *The Political Construction of Education.* New York: Praeger.

Gale, Laurence. 1969. *Education and Nation Building in Latin America.* New York: Frederick A. Praeger.

Garcia Garrido, Jose Luis. 1986. "Primary Education on the Threshold of the 21st Century." *International Yearbook of Education*, Volume XXXVIII. Paris, Geneva: UNESCO-IBE.

Garnier, Maurice, Jerald Hage, and Bruce Fuller. 1989. "The Strong State, Social Class and Controlled School Expansion in France, 1881–1975." *American Journal of Sociology* 95: 279–306.

Gasperini, Lavinia. 2000. "The Cuban Education System: Lessons and Dilemmas." *Education Reform and Management Publication Series*, vol. I, no. 5 (July). New York: The World Bank.

Gauhar, Syed Altaf. 1981. "Education and Mass Media." Pp. 61–81 in *Education and Society in the Muslim World*, ed. Mohammad Wasiullah Khan. Jeddah: Hodder and Soughton, King Abdulaziz University.

Gellner, Ernest. 1983. *Nations and Nationalism*. Ithaca, New York: Cornell University Press.

Germa, Amare. 1982. "Education in Ethiopia." Pp. 62–97 in *Education in Africa: A Comparative Survey*, ed. A. Babs Fafunwa and J. U. Aisiku. London: George Allen and Unwin.

Gill, Indermit S., Fred Fluitman, and Amit Dar. 2000. *Vocational Education and Training Reform: Matching Skills to Markets and Budgets*. Washington, DC and New York: World Bank/Oxford University Press.

Gimeno, Jose Blat. 1981. *La Educación en América Latina y el Caribe en el Último Terció del Siglo XX*. Paris: UNESCO.

Glenn, Charles Leslie. 1988. *The Myth of the Common School*. Amherst: University of Massachusetts Press.

Goodson, Ivor. 1987. *School Subjects and Curriculum Change*. London: Falmer Press.

Gordon P., R. Aldrich, and D. Dean. 1991. *Education and Policy in England in the Twentieth Century*. London: Woburn Press.

Gorostiaga, Jorge M., Clementina Acedo, and Susana Xifra. 2003. "Secondary Education in Argentina during the 1990s: The Limits of a Comprehensive Reform Effort." *Education Policy Analysis Archives* 11 (17).

Graff, Harvey J. 1987. *The Legacies of Literacy: Continuities and Contradictions in Western Culture and Society*. Bloomington: Indiana University Press.

Grant, Nigel. 1979. *Soviet Education*. 4th edition. New York: Penguin Books.

Green, Andy. 1990. *Education and State Formation: The Rise of Education Systems in England, France and USA*. New York: St. Martin's Press.

———. 1997. *Education, Globalization and the Nation State*. London: Macmillan Press.

Green, Andy, Alison Wolf, and Tom Leney. 1999. *Convergence and Divergence in European Education and Training Systems*. London: Institute of Education, University of London.

Guven, Ismail. 2005. "The Impact of Political Islam on Education: The Revitalization of Islamic Education in the Turkish Educational Setting." *International Journal of Educational Development* 25: 193–208.

Halls, Wilfred. 1990. "Trends and Issues in Comparative Education." Pp. 21–65 in *Comparative Education: Contemporary Issues and Trends,* ed. W. D. Halls. London, Paris: Jessica Kingsley Publishers and UNESCO.

Harber, C. 1998. "Desegregation, Racial Conflict and Education for Democracy in the New South Africa: A Case Study of Institutional Change." *International Review of Education* 4 (5/6): 569–582.

Hawkins, John N. 1974. *Mao Tse-Tung and Education: His Thoughts and Teachings.* Hamden, CT: The Shoe String Press.

Heidenheimer, Arnold. 1981. "Education and Social Security Entitlements in Europe and America." Pp. 269–304 in *The Development of Welfare States in Europe and America,* ed. Peter Flora and A. Heidenheimer. New Brunswick, NJ: Transaction Books.

Heyneman, Stephen P. 1971. *The Conflict Over What is to be Learned in Schools: A History of Curriculum Politics in Africa.* Syracuse, NY: Program of Eastern African Studies, Syracuse University.

Hidalgo, Carlos Otero, Andrés Muñoz Machado, and Carlos J. Fernández Rodríguez. 2002. *Vocational Education and Training in Spain.* Thessaloniki: CEDEFOP (European Centre for the Development of Vocational Training).

Hirschman, A. O. 1968. "Underdevelopment, Obstacles to the Perception of Change, and Leadership." *Daedalus* 97 (3). 925–937.

Hoffmann, Dietrich. 1997. "The Adoption of American Educational Theory in West Germany after 1945 – Heinrich Roth." In special issue, "Mutual Influences on Education: Germany and the United States in the Twentieth Century," ed. Jürgen Heideking, Marc Depaepe, Jürgen Herbst, *Paedagogica Historica* (*International Journal of the History of Education*), New Series XXXIII (1): 277–90.

Holmes, Brian. 1965. *Problems in Education.* London: Routledge and Kegan Paul.

———. 1979. *Guide International des Systèmes d'Éducation.* Paris, Genève: UNESCO-Bureau International d'Éducation.

———. 1981. *Comparative Education.* London: George Allen and Unwin.

Holmes, Beckwith. 1913. "German Industrial Education and its Lessons for the United States." *United States Bureau of Education Bulletin,* no 19 (whole no. 529). Washington, DC: Government Printing Office.

Huq, Muhammad Shamsul. 1954. *Compulsory Education in Pakistan.* Paris: UNESCO.

Hutasott, M. 1954. *Compulsory Education in Indonesia.* Paris: UNESCO.

Hutmacher W. 2001. "Définir et Articuler les Missions du Centre Stratégique d'un Système d'Enseignement Décentralisé. " Pp. 137–160 in *Comment Peut-on Administrer l'École?* ed. Yves Dutercq. Paris: PUF.

Inkeles, Alex, and Larry Sirowy. 1983. "Convergent and Divergent Trends in National Educational Systems." *Social Forces* 62: 303–333.

Institute of Education, University of London. 1951. *The Yearbook of Education 1951.* (Section II). London: Evans Brothers.

International Bureau of Education (IBE). 1932. "Compulsory Schooling." *Bulletin of the International Bureau of Education* 23 (2): 51–53.

———. 2003. *World Data on Education.* 5th edition. Geneva, Switzerland: IBE.

International Labour Office (ILO). 1951. *Vocational Training in Latin America. Studies and Report, New Series*, No. 28. Geneva: ILO.

Isidro, Antonio, J. Canave, P. Manalang, and M. Valdes. 1952. *Compulsory Education in the Philippines.* Paris: UNESCO.

Jagusah, Olivet I. W. 2001. "Educational Policy in Africa and the Issue(s) of Context: The Case of Nigeria and South Africa." *International Education Journal* 2 (5): 113–125.

Japanese National Commission for UNESCO. 1958. *The Making of Compulsory Education in Japan.* Paris: UNESCO.

Johnson, Robert. 1987. "Educational Change in Francophone Africa." *Journal of Negro Education* 56 (3): 265–281.

Jónasson, Jón Torfi. 2003. "Does the State Expand Schooling? A Study Based on Five Nordic Countries." *Comparative Education Review* 47 (2): 160–83.

Jumsai, M. L. Manich. 1951. *Compulsory Education in Thailand.* Paris: UNESCO.

Kach, Nick, and Kas Mazurek. 1993. "Compulsory Schooling as an Instrument of Political and Cultural Hegemony: A Canadian Case Study." Pp. 168–193 in *A Significant Social Revolution: Cross-Cultural Aspects of the Evolution of Compulsory Education*, ed. J. A. Mangan. London: The Woburn Press.

Kaestle, Carl. 1983. *Pillars of the Republic: Common Schools and American Society 1780–1860.* New York: Hill and Wang.

Kallaway, Peter. 1984. "An Introduction to the Study of Education for Blacks in South Africa." Pp. 1–28 in *Apartheid and Education: The Education of Black South Africans*, ed. P. Kallaway. Braamfontein: Ravan Press.

———. 1989. "Privatization as an Aspect of the Educational Politics of the New Right." *British Journal of Educational Studies* 37 (3): 253–278.

Kandel, I. L. 1930. *History of Secondary Education: A Study in the Development of Liberal Education*. Boston: Houghton Mifflin.

Kapcia, Antoni. 2005. *Havana: The Making of Cuban Culture*. London: Berg Publishers.

Keeble, Alexandra, ed. 2002. *In the Spirit of Wandering Teachers: Cuban Literacy Campaign, 1961*. Melbourne, Vic.: Oceanbooks.

Kelly, Gail Paradise (with David Kelly). 2000. *French Colonial Education: Essays on Vietnam and West Africa*. New York: AMS Press.

Kelly, Gail P., and Philip G. Altbach. 1978. "Introduction." In *Education and Colonialism*, ed. Philip G. Altbach and Gail P. Kelly. New York: Longman.

Kerckhoff, Alan. 1995. "Institutional Arrangements and Stratification Processes in Industrial Societies." *Annual Review of Sociology* 15: 323–47.

Khan, Mohammad Wasiullah. 1981. "Introduction." Pp. 1–27 in *Education and Society in the Muslim World*, ed. Mohammad W. Khan. Jeddah: Hodder and Soughton, King Abdulaziz University.

Kiernan, Mike. 2000. "The Role of Donors in Educational Construction and Transformation." Pp. 195–206 in *Globalisation and Educational Transformation and Societies in Transition*, ed. Teame Mebrahtu, Michael Crossley, and David Johnson. United Kingdom: Symposium Books.

King, Kenneth. 1990. "Introduction: Education in Contrasting Societies." Pp. 1–22 in *Handbook of Educational Ideas and Practices*, ed. Noel J. Entwistle. London and New York: Routledge.

Knight, Eleanor G. 1955. "Education in French North Africa." *The Islamic Quarterly* 2: 294–308.

Kwong, Julia. 1979. *Chinese Education in Transition*. Montreal: McGill-Queen's University Press.

———. 1988. *Cultural Revolution in China's Schools*. Stanford: Hoover Institution Press, Stanford University.

Latour, Bruno. 1987. *Science in Action*. Cambridge: Harvard University Press.

Lauglo, J. 1990. "Factors Behind Decentralisation and the Implications for Education: A Comparative Perspective." *Compare* 20 (1): 21–39.

Lee, Thomas H.C. 2000. *Education in Traditional China: A History*. The Netherlands: Brill.

Legrand, Louis. 1988, 1990. *Les Politiques de l'Éducation*. Paris: PUF.

Lerman, Robert I. 2001. *Improving Career Outcomes for Youth: Lessons from the U.S. and OECD experience.* Research and Evaluation Monograph Series OD-1. U.S. Department of Labor.

Lewin, Keith. 1987. "Science Education in China: Transformation and Change in the 1980s." *Comparative Education Review* 31 (3): 419–441.

———. 1993. "Education and Development: The Issues and the Evidence." *Education Research Paper* No. 06, Section 2.3. United Kingdom: Department for International Development.

Lewis, Theodore, and Morgan V. Lewis. 1985. "Vocational Education in the Commonwealth Caribbean and the United States." *Comparative Education* 21 (2): 157–172.

Lillis, Kevin, and Desmond Hogan. 1983. "Dilemmas of Diversification: Problems Associated with Vocational Education in Developing Countries." *Comparative Education* 19 (1): 89–107.

Lindell, Mats. 2004. "From Conflicting Interests to Collective Consent in Advanced Vocational Education." *Journal of Education* 17 (2): 257–277.

Little, Angela. 1998. *Labouring to Learn: Towards a Political Economy of Plantations, People, and Education in Sri Lanka.* London: Macmillan.

MacDonald, Theodore. 1985. *Making a New People: Education in Revolutionary Cuba.* Vancouver: New Start Books.

Maddock, John. 1983. "The Comparative Study of Secondary Education Systems: Lessons to be Learned." *Comparative Education* 19 (3): 245–255.

Magnin, Charles. 2002. "Un Survol de l'Histoire du BIE, de sa Fondation en 1925 jusqu'à Aujourd'hui." Presentation at the 49th Session of the IBE Council, 30 January 2002. http://www.ibe.unesco.org/International/IBEDirector/Council/hismagni.htm.

Makulu, Henry. 1971. *Education, Development and Nation-Building in Independent Africa.* London: SCM Press.

Mangan, J. A., ed. 1994. *A Significant Social Revolution: Cross-Cultural Aspects of the Evolution of Compulsory Education.* London, England and Portland, Oregon: Woburn Press.

Maté, Casely. 1969. "Addis Ababa in Retrospect: An Evaluation since 1961 Conference." Pp. 3–28 in *Education in Africa: Research and Action*, ed. Richard Jolly. Published for the African Studies Association of the United Kingdom. Nairobi, Kenya: East African Publishing House.

Matthews, Mervyn. 1982. *Education in the Soviet Union: Policies and Institutions since Stalin*. London: George Allen and Unwin.

Matthews, Roderic, and Matta Akrawi. 1949. *Education in Arab Countries of the Near East: Egypt, Iraq, Palestine, Transjordan, Syria, Lebanon*. Washington, DC: American Council on Education.

Mayhew, Arthur. 1938. *Education in the Colonial Empire*. London: Longmans, Green and Co.

Maynes, Mary Jo. 1985. *Schooling in Western Europe*. Albany, NY: SUNY Press.

Mazrui, Ali, and Wagaw, T. 1985. "Towards Decolonizing Modernity: Education and Culture Conflict." In *The Educational Process and Historiography in Africa*, final report of a symposium organized by UNESCO, Dakar, Senegal, January 25–29, 1982.

McNeely, Connie. 1995. "Prescribing National Education Policies: The Role of International Organizations." *Comparative Education Review* 39 (4): 483–507.

Meyer, John, John Boli, George M. Thomas, and Francisco O. Ramirez. 1997. "World Society and the Nation State." *American Journal of Sociology* 103: 144–181.

Meyer, John, Joanne Nagel, and Conrad Snyder. 1993. "The Expansion of Mass Education in Botswana: Local and World Society Perspectives." *Comparative Education Review* 37 (November): 454–475.

Meyer, John and Francisco Ramirez. 2000. "The World Institutionalization of Education: Origins and Implications." Pp. 111–132 in *Discourse Formation in Comparative Education*, Comparative Studies Series, vol. 10, ed. Jurgen Schreiwer. Frankfurt a Main: Peter Lange.

Meyer, John, Francisco Ramirez, Richard Rubinson, and John Boli-Bennett. 1977. "The World Educational Revolution, 1950–75." *Sociology of Education* 50: 242–58.

Meyer, John, Francisco Ramirez, and Yasemin Nuhoglu Soysal. 1992. "World Expansion of Mass Education, 1870–1980." *Sociology of Education* 65 (April): 128–149.

Meyer, John, and Brian Rowan. 1977. "Institutionalized Organizations: Formal Structure as Myth and Ceremony." *American Journal of Sociology* 83 (2): 340–63.

Meyer, John, David Tyack, Joanne Nagel, and Audri Gordon. 1979. "Public Education as Nation-building in America." *American Journal of Sociology* 85: 591–613.

Mitch, David. 1992. *The Rise of Popular Vernacular Literacy in Victorian England*. Philadelphia: University of Pennsylvania Press.

Monroe, Paul. 1927. *Essays in Comparative Education*. New York: International Institute, Teachers College, Columbia University.

Morgan, William, and Michael Armer. 1988. "Islamic and Western Educational Accommodation in a West African Society." *American Sociological Review* 53: 634–639.

Mudimbe, Valentin Y. 1988. *The Invention of Africa: Gnosis, Philosophy, and the Order of Knowledge*. Bloomington, IN: Indiana University Press.

Muller, Detlef, Fritz Ringer, and Brian Simon. 1987. *The Rise of the Modern Educational System: Structural Change and Social Reproduction 1870–1920*. London: Cambridge University Press.

Mundy, Karen and Lynn Murphy. 2004. "Transnational Advocacy, Global Society? Emerging Evidence from the Field of Education." http://www.swaray.org/skikshanter/activities_transnational.html.

Mzamane, M. 1990. "Toward a Pedagogy for Liberation: Education for National Culture in South Africa." In *Pedagogy of Domination: Toward Democratic Education in South Africa*, ed. M. Nkomo. Trenton, NJ: Africa World Press.

Naquib al-Attas, Syed Muhammad. 1991. "The Concept of Education in Islam." Pp. 1–46 in *The Concept of Education in Islam: A Framework for an Islamic Philosophy of Education*. Kuala Lumpur, Malaysia: International Institute of Islamic Thought and Civilization.

Narodowski, Mariano, and Milagros Nores. 2002. "Socio-economic Segregation with (without) Competitive Education Policies. A Comparative Analysis of Argentina and Chile." *Comparative Education* 38 (4): 429–451.

Noah, Harold J. 1986. "Education, Employment, and Development in Communist Societies." Pp. 37–58 in *Patriarchy, Party, Population, and Pedagogy*, ed. E.B Gumbert. Atlanta: Georgia State University.

Noah, J. Arnold, and Max Eckstein. 1969. *Towards a Science of Comparative Education*. London: The Macmillan Company.

Nóvoa, António, Luis M. Carvalho, António Correia, Ana Madeira, and Jorge Ramos. 2002. "Flows of Educational Knowledge: The Space-time of Portuguese Speaking Countries." Pp. 212–247 in *Internationalisation: Comparing Educational Systems and Semantics*, ed. Marcelo Caruso and Heinz-Elmar Tenorth. Berlin, New York, Bruxelles: Peter Lang.

Nwagwu, C. 1997. "The Environment of Crisis in the Nigerian Education System." *Comparative Education* 33 (1): 87–95.

Ochs, René. 1997. "L'Éducation et la Société Depuis la Seconde Guerre Mondiale." In *1946 UNESCO 50 Years of Education*. Paris: UNESCO, Education Sector.

Padula, Alfred and Lois M. Smith. 1988. "The Revolutionary Transformation of Cuban Education" Pp. 117–139 in *Making the Future: Politics and Educational Reform in the United States, England, the Soviet Union, China and Cuba*, ed. Edgar B. Gumbert. Atlanta: Georgia State University College of Education, Center of Cross-Cultural Education.

Papadopoulos, George. 1994. *Education 1960–1990. The OECD Perspective*. Paris: OECD.

Parmers, Herbert. 1962. *Forecasting Educational Needs for Economic and Social Development*. The Mediterranean Regional Project. Paris: OECD.

Paulston, Rolland. 1968. *Educational Change in Sweden: Planning and Accepting the Comprehensive School Reforms*. New York: Teachers College Press, Columbia University.

Pendergast, William Richard. 1974. "French Policy in UNESCO." Ph.D. diss., Political Sciences, Columbia University.

Perren, G. E. 1969. "Education through a Second Language: An African Dilemma." Pp. 197–208 in *Education in Africa: Research and Action*, ed. Richard Jolly. Published for the African Studies Association of the United Kingdom. Nairobi, Kenya: East African Publishing House.

Phillips, David, and Kimberly Ochs, eds. 2004. *Educational Policy Borrowing: Historical Perspectives*. Oxford, UK: Symposium Books.

Porter, D. 1970. *Technical and Vocational Education: Six Areas Studies*. Strasbourg: Council for Cultural Co-operation of the Council of Europe.

Pring, Richard. 2004. "The Skills Revolution." *Oxford Review of Education* 30 (1): 105–116.

Psacharopoulos, George. 1987. "To Vocationalize or not to Vocationalize: That is the Curriculum Question." *International Review of Education* 33 (2): 187–211.

———. 1990. *Why Educational Policies Can Fail? An Overview of Selected African Experiences*. Washington, DC: World Bank.

Psacharopoulus, George, and William Loxley. 1985. "Diversified Secondary Education and Development." A report on the Diversified Secondary Curriculum Study (DISCUS). Oxford University Press for the World Bank.

Rabo, Annika. 1986. *Change on the Euphrates: Villagers, Townsmen, and Employees in Northeast Syria*. Stockholm: Studies in Social Anthropology.

Rama, G. W. 1983. "Education in Latin America: Exclusion or Participation." *CEPAL Review* 21: 13–38.

Ramirez, Francisco. 2003. "Toward a Cultural Anthropology of the World?" Pp. 239–254 in *Local Meanings/Global Culture: Anthropology and World Culture Theory*, ed. Kathryn Anderson-Levitt. New York: Palgrave Macmillian.

Ramirez, Francisco, and John Boli. 1982. "Global Patterns of Educational Institutionalization." Pp. 15–38 in *Comparative Education*, ed. Philip Altbach, Robert Arnove, and Gail Kelly. New York: Macmillan.

———. 1987. "The Political Construction of Mass Schooling: European Origins and Worldwide Institutionalization." *Sociology of Education* 60 (January): 2–17.

———. 1993. "The Political Institutionalization of Compulsory Education: The Rise of Compulsory Schooling in the Western Cultural Context." Pp. 1–20 in *A Significant Social Revolution: Cross-Cultural Aspects of the Evolution of Compulsory Education*, ed. J. A. Mangan. London: Woburn.

Ramirez, Francisco, and Yun Kyung Cha. 1990. "Citizenship and Gender: Western Educational Developments in Comparative Perspective." *Research in Sociology of Education and Socialization* 9: 153–73.

Ramirez, Francisco, and Marc Ventresca. 1992. "Building the Institution of Mass Schooling: Isomorphism in the Modern World." Pp. 47–60 in *The Political Construction of Education*, ed. Bruce Fuller and Richard Rubinson. New York: Praeger.

Reisner, Edward. 1927. *Nationalism and Education Since 1789: A Social and Political History of Modern Education*. New York: The Macmillan Company.

Resnik, Julia. 2001. "Globalization of Educational Models: Structural Reforms of the Education System in Israel and France." Ph.D. diss., Department of Sociology and Anthropology, Tel Aviv University.

———. 2006a. "Les Organisations Intergouvernementales et la Diffusion de la Boîte Noire 'Éducation-croissance Économique.'" Pp. 205–232 in *La Société des Savoirs : Trompe-l'œil ou Perspectives*? eds. Michel Carton and Jean-Baptiste Meyer. Paris: Éditions l'Harmattan.

———. 2006b. "International Organizations, The 'Education-Economic Growth' Black Box, and the Development of World Education Culture." *Comparative Education Review* 50: 173–195.

Richardson, John. 1984. "Settlement Patterns and the Governing Structure of Nineteenth-century School Systems." *American Journal of Education* 92: 178–206.

————. 1986. "Historical Sequences and the Origins of Common Schooling in the American States." Pp. 35–64 in *Handbook of Theory and Research for the Sociology of Education*, ed. John Richardson. Westport, CT: Greenwood Press.

Rideout, W., and I. Ural. 1993. *Centralised and Decentralised Models of Education: Comparative Studies.* Halfway House, Development Bank of South Africa.

Ringer, Fritz. 1979. *Education and Society in Modern Europe.* Bloomington: Indiana University Press.

Robert, André. 1999. *Système Éducatif et Réformes.* Paris: Nathan.

Rubinson, Richard, and John Ralph. 1984. "Technical Change and the Expansion of Schooling in the United States, 1890–1970." *Sociology of Education* 57 (July): 134–152.

Saiyidain, K. G., J. Naik, and S. Husain. 1952. *Compulsory Education in India.* Paris: UNESCO.

Saqib, Ghulam Nabi. 1981. "Modernization of Muslim Society and Education: Need for a Practical Approach." Pp. 45–60 in *Education and Society in the Muslim World*, ed. Mohammad Wasiullah Khan. Jeddah: Hodder and Soughton, King Abdulaziz University.

Schleunes, Karl. 1989. *Schooling and Society: The Politics of Education in Prussia and Bavaria, 1750–1900.* Oxford, UK: Berg.

Schmida, Mirjam. 1964. "Assumptions Underlying Major Developments in the System of Universal, Free, Public, Secondary Education in the United States and the High School System of the Municipality of Tel-Aviv with Certain Implications for the Future of Secondary Education in Tel-Aviv." Ed.D. diss., Columbia University.

Schneider, Reinhard. 1982. "Public Education." In *State, Economy, and Society in Western Europe, 1850–1975: A Data Handbook*, ed. P. Flora. Frankfurt: Campus. [Original in German: "Dis bildungsentwitklung in den westeurpaischen staaten 1870–1975" (Development and Expansion of Education in the Western European States, 1870–1975) *Zeitschrift fur Soziologie* 3: 207–226.]

Schriewer, Juergen. 2000. *Discourse Formation in Comparative Education.* Frankfurt: Peter Lang.

Schriewer, Juergen, and Carlos Martinez. 2003. *World Level Ideology or Nation-Specific System-Reflection? Reference Horizons in Educational Discourse.* Lisbon: EDUCA.

Sen, Amartya. 1999. *Development as Freedom.* Oxford: Oxford University Press.

Shimahara, Nobuo. 1979. *Adaptation and Education in Japan*. New York: Praeger.

Smyth, John, ed. 1993. *A Socially Critical View of the Self-Managing School*. London: Falmer.

Soudien, C. 1994. "Equality and Equity in South Africa: Multicultural Education and Change." *Equity and Excellence in Education* 27 (3): 55–60.

Soysal, Yasemin, and David Strange. 1989. "Construction of the First Mass Education Systems in 19th Century Europe." *Sociology of Education* 62: 277–88.

Sutton, Francis. 1965. "Education in the Making of Modern Nations." Pp. 51–74 in *Education and Political Development*, ed. James Coleman. Princeton: Princeton University Press.

Terra, Juan Pablo. 1983. "The Role of Education in Relation to Employment Problems." *CEPAL Review* 21 (December): 81–111.

Tibawi, Abdul Latif. 1972. *Islamic Education*. London: Headley Brothers.

Tillak, Jandhyala. 2002. "Vocational Education and Training in Asia." In *The International Handbook on Educational Research in the Asia-Pacific Region*, ed. John Keeves and Ryo Watanabe. Dordrecht: Kluwer Academic Publishers.

Torres, Carlos Alberto. 1991. "The State, Nonformal Education and Socialism in Cuba, Nicaragua, and Grenada." *Comparative Education Review* 35 (1): 110–130.

Trow, Martin. 1961. "The Second Transformation of American Secondary Education." *International Journal of Comparative Sociology* 2: 144–65.

Tyack, David. 1974. *The One Best System: A History of American Urban Education*. Cambridge: Harvard University Press.

———. 1976. "Ways of Seeing: An Essay on the History of Compulsory Education." *Harvard Educational Review* 46: 355–89.

Tyack, David, and Elisabeth Hansot. 1990. *Learning Together: A History of Coeducation in American Public Schools*. London/New York: Yale University Press.

Tyack, David, Thomas James, and Aaron Benavot. 1987. *Law and the Shaping of Public Education, 1785–1954*. Madison, WI: University of Wisconsin Press.

Ulich, Robert. 1967. *The Education of Nations*. Cambridge, MA: Harvard University Press.

United Nations Educational, Scientific, and Cultural Organization (UNESCO). 1954. *Compulsory Education in South Asia and the Pacific*. Paris: UNESCO.

———. 1956a. *Compulsory Education in the Arab States*. Paris: UNESCO.

————. 1956b. *Report of the First International Conference on Educational Research, Educational Studies and the Documents XX.* (February) Atlantic City, NJ. Paris: UNESCO.

————. 1958. *World Survey of Education II: Primary Education.* Paris: UNESCO.

————. 1961. *World Survey of Education III: Secondary Education.* Paris, UNESCO.

————. 1974. *UNESCO's Revised Recommendation Concerning Technical and Vocational Education.* 19 November. Recommendations adopted by the General Conference of the UNESCO. Paris: UNESCO.

————. 1979a. *Development in Technical and Vocational Education: A Comparative Study.* Trends and Issues in Technical and Vocational Education Series. Paris: UNESCO.

————. 1979b. "Education in the Context of Development in Latin America and the Caribbean." Report 3, Regional Conference of Ministers of Education and Those Responsible for Economic Planning of Member States in Latin America and the Caribbean, Mexico City. December 4–13.

————. 1979c. "Final Report." Regional Conference of Ministers of Education and Those Responsible for Economic Planning of Member States in Latin America and the Caribbean, Mexico City. December 4–13.

————. 1985. *The Educational Process and Historiography in Africa.* Final Report and papers of the symposium organized by the UNESCO in Dakar, Senegal, January 25–29, 1982.

————. 2000. *World Education Report.* Paris: UNESCO.

————. 2002. *Education for All Global Monitoring Report: Is the World on Track?* Paris: UNESCO.

————. 2003/4. *Education for All Global Monitoring Report: The Leap to Equality.* Paris: UNESCO.

UNESCO-International Bureau of Education (UNESCO-IBE). 1977. *International Conference on Education. Recommendations 1934–1977.* Paris: UNESCO.

Uzcategui, Emilio. 1951. *Compulsory Education in Ecuador.* Paris: UNESCO.

Vaizey, John. 1965. "Introduction." In *The Study Group in the Economics of Education: The Residual Factor and the Economic Growth.* Paris: OECD.

van de Stege, Corri. 2003. "The Work-based Learning Route in the Netherlands and in England: Comparing Ideas and Meanings." *Compare* 33 (4): 483–495.

van der Ploeg, Arie. 1977. "Education in Colonial Africa: The German Experience." *Comparative Education Review* 21: 91–109.

van Horn Melton, James. 1988. *Absolutism and the Eighteenth Century Origins of Compulsory Schooling in Prussia and Austria*. New York: Cambridge University Press.

Vaughan, Michalina, and Margaret Scotford Archer. 1971. *Social Conflict and Educational Change in England and France, 1789–1848*. Cambridge: Cambridge University Press.

Vincent, David. 2000. *The Rise of Literacy: Reading and Writing in Modern Europe*. Cambridge: Polity Press.

Waggoner, George, and Barbara Ashton Waggoner. 1971. *Education in Central America*. Lawrence, KS: University Press of Kansas.

Walford, Geoffrey, ed. 1984. *British Public Schools: Policy and Practice*. Lewes and Philadelphia: Falmer Press.

Walters, Pamela Barnhouse, and Philip O'Connell. 1988. "The Family Economy, Work and Educational Participation in the United States, 1890–1940." *American Journal of Sociology* 93 (5): 1116–52.

Waterman, Richard. 1893. "Education Exhibits at World's Fairs." *Educational Review* 5: 120–129; 219–231.

Watson, Keith. 1984a. "Introduction: Dependence and Interdependence and Educational Development." Pp. 1–11 in *Dependence and Interdependence in Education: International Perspectives*, ed. Keith Watson. London: Croom Helm.

———. 1984b. "Some Contemporary Problems and Issues Resulting from Educational Expansion in South East Asia." *Compare* 14 (1): 69–84.

Weiler, Hans N. 1978. "Education and Development: From the Age of Innocence to the Age of Skepticism." *Comparative Education* 14 (3): 179–198.

———. 1983. *Aid and Education: The Political Economy of International Cooperation in Educational Development*. Stanford, CA: Stanford University.

Weiner, Myron. 1991. *The Child and the State in India: Child Labor and Education Policy in Comparative Perspective*. Princeton: Princeton University Press.

Westney, D. E. 1987. *Imitation and Innovation: The Transfer of Western Organizational Patterns to Meiji Japan*. Cambridge: Harvard University Press.

Whitehead, Clive. 1981. "Education in British Colonial Dependencies 1919–1939." *Comparative Education* 17: 71–80.

Whittacer, Cynthia. 1991. *The Origins of Modern Russian Education*. DeKalb, IL: Northern Illinois University Press.

Whitty, Geoff, S. Power, and D. Halpin. 1998. *Devolution and Choice in Education: The School, the State and the Market*. Buckingham: Open University Press.

Willms, J. D., and M-A. Somers. 2001. "Family, Classroom and School Effects on Children's Educational Outcomes in Latin America." *International Journal of School Effectiveness and Improvement* 12 (4): 409–445.

Wittrock, Bjorn, Peter Wagner, and Helmut Hollman. 1991. "Social Sciences and the Modern State: Policy Knowledge and Political Institutions in Western Europe and the United States." Pp. 28–85 in *Social Sciences and Modern States*, ed. P. Wagner, C. H. Weiss, B. Wittrock, and H. Wollmann. Cambridge: Cambridge University Press.

Wolf, Alison. 1998. "Politicians and Economic Panic." *History of Education* 27 (3): 219–234.

Wong, Hoy Kee. 1973. *Comparative Studies in Southeast Asian Education*. Kuala Lumpur, Singapore: Heinemann Educational Books (Asia) Ltd.

World Bank. 1974. *Education: Sector Paper*. Washington, DC: World Bank.

———. 1991. "Vocational and Technical Education Training." *World Bank Policy Paper*. Washington, DC: The World Bank.

———. 2005. *Secondary Education in the 21st Century: New Directions, Challenges, and Priorities*. Washington, DC: The World Bank.

Yates, Barbara. 1984. "Comparative Education and the Third World: The Nineteenth Century Revisited." *Comparative Education Review* 28: 533–549.

Zia, Rukhsana. 2006. "Transmission of Values in Muslim Countries: Religious Education and Moral Development in School Curricula." Pp. 119–135 in *School Knowledge in Comparative and Historical Perspective: Changing Curricula in Primary and Secondary Education*, ed. Aaron Benavot and Cecilia Braslavsky. CERC Studies in Comparative Education Series. Hong Kong: University of Hong Kong Press.

Zine, Jasmin. 2001. "Muslim Youth in Canadian Schools: Education and the Politics of Religious Identity." *Anthropology and Education Quarterly* 32 (4): 399–423.

Zvobgo, R. J. 1994. *Colonialism and Education in Zimbabwe*. Harare, Zimbabwe: Sapes Books.

CHAPTER 3

Political Obstacles to Expanding and Improving Schooling in Developing Countries

JAVIER CORRALES

Expanding education to reach all children is expensive. In the most affluent democracies, where educational coverage is nearly universal, primary and secondary education accounted for an average of approximately 8.7 percent of government expenditures in 1999.[1] Because it absorbs a significant portion of available resources, providing universal education entails high opportunity costs for states. The expansion of state-run or state-financed basic education is also potentially controversial. It entails increasing the influence of the state over society, and this can provoke societal disputes, as different groups argue over who will influence the direction of state expansion (Platt, 1965) and, more contentiously, who will pay (see Weiler, 1984).

Because educational expansion is costly and can be politically contentious, it is highly contingent on the existence of political incentives and pressures. States will expand education only if they face strong enough political incentives and pressures to do so, and if they can overcome political obstacles.

This essay reviews political science literature for the concepts and facts that shed light on the obstacles to educational expansion and ways of removing or circumventing those obstacles. It incorporates theoretical and empirical works—by international relations theorists, comparativists, political economists, as well as historians, anthropologists, and education experts interested in politics—on the incentives and pressures that devel-

---

[1] Based on latest data available in Organisation for Economic Co-operation and Development (OECD) (2002).

oping countries face when deciding whether and how to expand and improve educational coverage. Although the field of political science may not reveal easy solutions to expansion-related conflicts, it can offer insights into the types of conflict that may emerge, the likely actors, and the various opportunities to confront these conflicts.

The central argument of the chapter is straightforward: incentives and pressures for states to expand education and improve educational efficiency, particularly for the poorest and most remote populations, are weak and sometimes perverse. On their own, states in developing countries are unlikely to achieve sufficient institutional capacity and political accountability to establish universal primary and secondary educational coverage. The good news is that weak incentives and pressures can be augmented. For this, states will need extra help and extra funding. The involvement of both external and societal actors seems unavoidable, though potentially polemical.

INCENTIVES, PRESSURES, AND STAGES

The incentives and pressures that drive educational expansion differ as expansion progresses. Mounting evidence suggests that, over time, the expansion of education resembles an S-shaped curve (Clemens, 2004; Wils and Goujon, 1998; Fiala and Lanford, 1987; Meyer et al., 1977). Initially, states procrastinate in the provision of education, as the consolidation of power and neutralization of potential rivals outweigh the need to offer services to the population (Tilly, 1985).

When at a later point in their evolution states begin to provide educational services, the coverage typically expands rapidly. During this second stage, expansion is driven not by political incentives and pressures but by "self-generating" forces: demographic growth among the population of educated individuals; low marginal cost of expansion due in part to economies of scale and installed infrastructure capacity; the effects of state expansion, which include a greater demand for white-collar labor and therefore a greater state interest in educational expansion; savings generated by the decline in teacher salaries relative to per capita gross domestic product (GDP); pressure from organized unions and the already educated; economic growth and rising household incomes; and occupational mobility and anticipatory income (e.g., Clemens, 2004; Mingat and Tan, 2003; Parrado, 1998; Schultz, 1996; Fuller and Rubinson, 1992). Social and political factors such as levels of political participation, date of independence, ethno-linguistic divisions, regime type and international dependence make little or no difference in explaining different rates of educational expansion among countries, at least expansion occurring between 1950 and 1970 (Meyer et al., 1977).

These "self-generating" forces do not continue indefinitely. After reaching another threshold of coverage, educational expansion slows again, possibly stagnating or declining. At this point, the marginal costs of expansion increase steeply. Reaching the last sectors of the population is extraordinarily costly, often because it entails going to geographically remote or sparsely populated regions, or because unenrolled children are the most economically disadvantaged.[2] Unless states find strong incentives and pressures to go forward with educational expansion, progress toward universal education may stall.

VARIATIONS IN COVERAGE AND QUALITY SINCE THE 1960S

Both the speed of progress in the expansion of educational coverage and the quality of education provided vary across countries. In a study focused largely on primary education, Clemens (2004) finds that although after 1960 the typical country took about 28 years to increase from 75 percent net enrollment to 90 percent—significantly faster than was the case prior to the 1960s—there are huge differences in speed across countries (2004: 16). Similarly, Figures 1 and 2 show variation in the speed of expansion of secondary education. Figure 1 shows educational expansion among countries that started with less than 10 percent coverage (using the gross enrollment rate for secondary education) in the 1960s; Figure 2 shows expansion among countries that started with coverage ranging between 10 percent and 20 percent.[3] The achievements of individual countries

---

[2] In every country, completion rates are lowest for children from poor and rural households (Bruns et al., 2003: 32), and in South Asia and the Middle East, completion rates are lower for girls than for boys (Levine et al., 2003).

[3] The gross enrollment rate is calculated by dividing the total number of students enrolled at a particular level of education (regardless of the official age for that level) by the population that, according to national regulations, should be enrolled at this level. The ratio may exceed 100 percent because some enrolled students may be below or above the official primary or secondary school age. The net enrollment ratio is calculated by dividing the total number of enrolled students within the official primary or secondary school age by the population that, according to national regulations, should be enrolled at this level.

Figure 1: Evolution of Gross Enrollment in Secondary Education in Countries with Enrollment Under 10 Percent in 1960

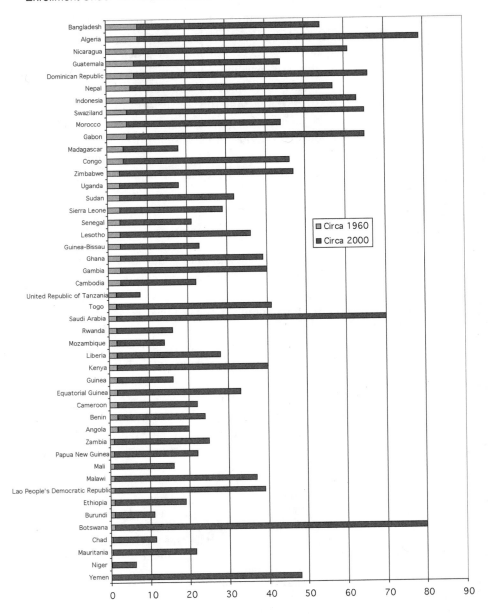

Figure 2: Evolution of Gross Enrollment in Secondary Education in Countries with Enrollment Between 10 Percent and 20 Percent in 1960

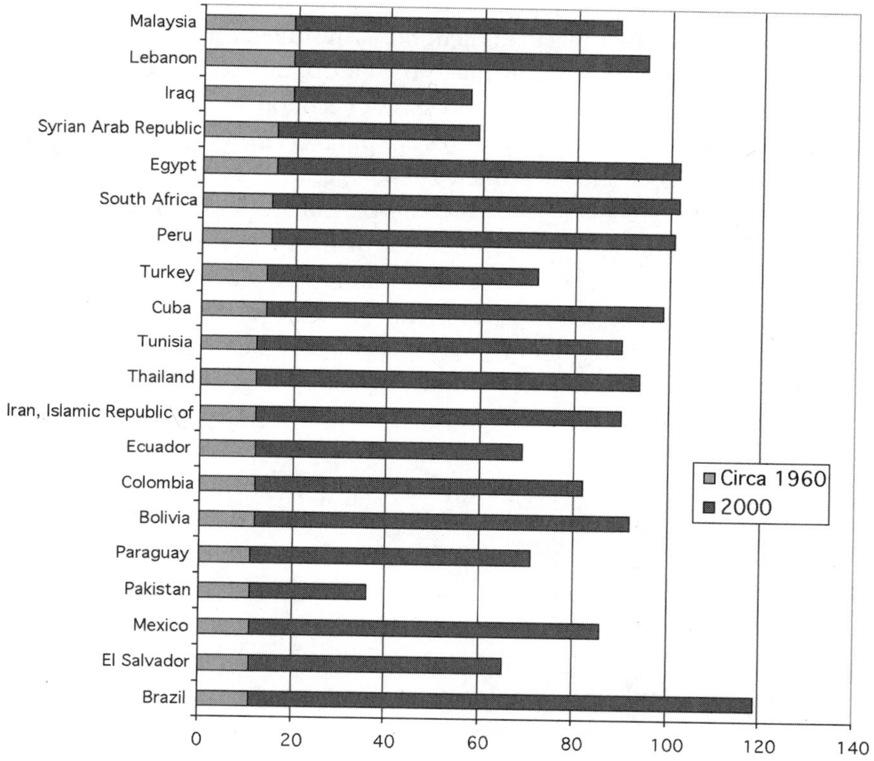

over the same time period vary considerably. Some countries made little progress; others traveled far. The most striking variations occur among the countries that had the lowest starting points in the 1960s.

Among the countries that are close (or on track) to achieving universal coverage, two central issues arise: the efficiency of investment and the quality of instruction. Although these vary across countries, developing countries tend to spend inefficiently, over-investing in inputs that have a limited impact on educational attainment (e.g., salary increases, rather than teaching materials, testing, or infrastructure) (Bruns et al., 2003). Likewise, mounting evidence points to variations in quality across education systems. Standardized tests of academic achievement provide the information most commonly used to indicate or compare quality across countries.[4] These show an abysmal gap between the levels of student attainment in advanced democracies and the levels in developing countries, as well as between the attainment of Asian students and Latin American students (see World Bank, 2003; OECD, 2002). Student performance is not easy to explain on the basis of economic inputs, such as low teacher-pupil ratio or expenditures per pupil (Hanushek, 1995; Kremer, 1995; Simmons and Alexander, 1980). A recent attempt to explain the results of the Trends in International Mathematics and Science Study (TIMSS), a testing program involving more than 40 countries, reveals that school resources play a limited role in explaining variations in achievement. Although the study is based on only 37 cases, the results lead the authors to conclude that "looking beyond simple resource policies appears necessary" (Hanushek and Luque, 2003: 498).

This chapter looks beyond resources by examining the politics of improving educational coverage and quality. No single study has conclusively explained variations in coverage and quality, and this chapter does not attempt to carry out such a task. What follows instead is a synthesis of ideas, as opposed to a solution to the empirical puzzle of why variations in educational performance exist. This chapter highlights arguments from the social sciences that may account for slow expansion or high inefficiency during the last stages of educational expansion.

Scholars who study the development of states (e.g., Tilly, 1992), in particular the rise of state-provided services such as education (e.g., Ginsburg et al., 1990), argue that incentives and pressures emanate from three sources: the international arena (e.g., as a result of the workings of the international economy, the global spread of ideas, or competition with other states), the state (e.g., the desire to promote nationalism or to neutralize domestic rivals), and the society (e.g., the demands for services placed by citizens). I discuss each of these sources.

---

4 The use of test results as indicators of educational quality can be polemical because, among other things, they do not easily allow researchers to distinguish the effect of the education system from individual effort and other non-school-related factors. Nevertheless, test results are often preferred to other indicators of quality (e.g., completion rates, future income of graduates) because tests can be systematically applied across countries.

INTERNATIONAL PRESSURES

States face four types of international pressure to expand education. Three are global in scale: the exigencies of globalization, pressure from multilateral lenders, and the global spread of ideas. One type of pressure is regional, or limited to only a few countries: the desire to emulate or surpass prestigious peers. There is considerable debate about how decisive each of these pressures is, and, in the case of globalization and international lenders, about the direction in which these pressures push.

Globalization and the Role of Firms

Scholars have long recognized that globalization affects the expansion of education, but they disagree about whether its effects are positive or negative. One argument suggests that globalization places a premium on skilled, flexible, and adaptable labor; as a result, nations that wish to compete in the world economy need to develop a highly educated workforce. Employers may conclude that a highly trained workforce will be easier and less costly to train than an uneducated workforce. For example, in a study incorporating interviews with company officials and reviews of internal documents, R. Nelson (2005) finds that high-technology firms consider local levels of educational attainment in choosing investment sites abroad and express this interest to local officials. Another recent study shows that U.S. foreign direct investment in Latin America between 1979 and 1996 gravitated toward countries with higher secondary enrollments, which suggests that education attracts international capital (Tuman and Emmert, 2004). The positive effects of globalization on education may occur through still other mechanisms. In their study of market reforms in Latin America during the 1990s, Stallings and Peres (2000) find that capitalist economies rewarded workers who were more highly skilled, which might increase citizen demand for education. Furthermore, the expansion of trade and capital flows can increase per capita income levels, thus increasing the resources available for education.

Even if globalization does not lead to increased demand by multinational firms for highly skilled workers, it could still lead to competition in the labor market, which might change the expectations of citizens. Facing the anxieties created by market economies, jobseekers might more strongly demand state-provided education as a way to protect themselves from the volatility of markets or to improve their status in comparison to other jobseekers. Although multinational firms may not demand high-level skills, they may nonetheless offer the best wages and working conditions in the country (see Graham, 2000; Moran, 2002). To compete for these better jobs, local citizens may decide to invest in their own education. Individuals pursue education not because it is directly demanded by firms, but because of what it signals to firms—that the worker is self-motivated and more capable of self-improvement than other jobseekers. Insofar as local workers are interested in emigrating, they might pursue education to enhance their chances of admittance into and employment in another country.

This could very well be one of the reasons that Buchmann and Brakewood (2000) find a positive relationship between the growth of the service sector and school enrollment in both Thailand and Kenya. Despite the low-skill nature of service jobs, citizens pursue secondary education to make themselves more competitive in comparison to other job applicants and more attractive to employers in this sector. It has thus been posited that capitalism generates demand for education, on the part of both firms and jobseekers. This might explain why the most globalized economies in the world also have the largest public sectors, of which education is a major component (Garrett, 1999; Rodrik, 1997; Cameron, 1978).

The opposing argument, that globalization has a negative influence on educational expansion, suggests that there are limits to the demand for skilled labor stemming from contemporary capitalism. Although some firms require skilled labor, the preponderance of demand is for cheap and docile labor. Tendler (2002) even finds a "fear of education" among owners and managers of large modern manufacturing firms in the textile, garment, and footwear sectors of northeast Brazil. These firms remained competitive and export-oriented by investing precisely in high-illiteracy zones, and feared that more education would make workers "uppity." A second view argues that, to stay competitive, states and firms need to keep costs low. Capitalism thus discourages spending too much on education. Some critics of globalization hold the contentious view that a global economy diminishes the capacities of nation-states to tax, and thus, to raise revenue for the provision of social services (e.g., Gray, 1998; Tilly, 1995; Cable, 1995). Education could very well be one casualty of this retrenchment.[5]

---

[5] For a summary, see Ginsburg et al., 1990.

Perhaps the best evidence on behalf of the argument for globalization as a positive force is the response of several East Asian countries to a changing global economy. Starting in the 1960s, eight "high performing East Asian economies," to use the World Bank label, significantly expanded primary and secondary schooling and made dramatic improvements in quality and student achievement. For some countries, this educational expansion was a purposeful strategy to achieve international competitiveness by building human capital (Stiglitz, 1996; World Bank, 1993).

However, evidence against the positive-force argument is substantial as well. If capitalism is such an influential driver of education, why is it that only eight countries in the developing world have made great efforts toward and succeeded in the improvement of education? A study by the World Bank (2002) shows that between 1980 and 1997 the 29 "most globalized" nations, despite faster overall economic growth, did not expand secondary enrollments more than other nations (although they did much better in the expansion of primary education).[6] The demands of firms and the self-motivation of citizens, however strong under capitalism, seem insufficient to achieve universal education.

This is in part because international capitalism does not have a uniform global presence. Foreign direct investments vary considerably: although some firms need skilled labor, others do not (e.g., knowledge-based industries versus textiles), and even firms requiring skilled labor may focus on the quality of college graduates with technical degrees rather than overall schooling of the population. The degree to which countries are exposed to global market forces also varies. Kaufman and Segura-Ubiergo (2001) study whether variations in exposure to globalization account for differences in social spending, including spending on education, in fourteen Latin American countries between 1973 and 1997. For social spending generally, their most robust finding is that

---

[6] The World Bank (2002: 35) studied 73 developing countries. The countries were divided into two groups: the 24 most globalized nations, which increased their ratios of trade to GDP by the largest amounts between 1980 and 1997; and the rest. The World Bank excluded the richest economies (i.e., the OECD countries plus Chile, Korea, Singapore, Taiwan, and Hong Kong) from the list of the "most globalized." Although, in comparison to other countries, the most globalized group experienced an impressive expansion in the average years of primary enrollment for adults (from 2.4 to 3.8 versus 2.5 to 3.1), they did not perform any better in terms of secondary enrollment (from 0.8 to 1.3 versus 0.7 to 1.3).

exposure to globalization, measured as the degree of trade integration, negatively affects social spending. Trade in Latin America thus had the opposite effect that it had in Europe: it shrank the public sector.

Kaufman and Segura-Ubiergo also discover that this effect exists only on social security and pension expenditures. The effect of trade on education expenditures is completely different—trade has no significant impact. Rather than economic openness, it is domestic political variables that largely determine spending on human capital: populist governments "squeeze" spending on education to protect pensions, whereas governments in countries transitioning to democracy increase the budget allocations for health and education. It could very well be that more exposure to capitalism prompts governments and constituents to protect education expenditures. In sum, globalization is probably neither a strong nor positive force for educational expansion; it seems less powerful than domestic variables in determining educational spending.

Pressure From Multilateral Organizations

Another set of external incentives and pressures stems from international organizations that specialize in development issues, especially multilateral financial organizations such as the World Bank and the International Monetary Fund (IMF). These organizations offer loans and aid, with strings attached. In 2004, the World Bank financed education projects in 89 low- and middle-income countries.[7] At a minimum, the Bank and other lending organizations require borrowing countries to listen to their technical advice. In theory, borrowers must also agree to conditionalities—implementing certain policies to receive funding. Because countries often resort to multilaterals when they cannot find alternative financing sources, these organizations enjoy bargaining leverage over borrowers.

Critics of multilateral financial organizations make two main arguments about their impact on education: structural-adjustment lending is deleterious to education investments, and pro-education programs sponsored by multilaterals have major leaks, i.e., resources are easily diverted to alternative uses.

The first criticism—typically arising from the left—has seemed less applicable in recent years. The case could be made that prior to the 1990s the World Bank advocated policies that had deleterious side effects on

---

[7] See http://www.worldbank.org/education.

educational expansion, such as reductions in social-sector spending, lower teacher salaries, and a focus on revenue generation. Geo-Jaya and Mangum (2001) document these effects in Nigeria and conclude that World Bank structural adjustment is "the enemy of human development." However, after the 1990s, multilaterals began to stress social spending not only for its role in cushioning the dislocating effects of market-oriented reform, but as an important ingredient for growth (see Hunter and Brown, 2000; Nelson, 1999; Carnoy, 1995; World Bank, 1993). More generous lending for education followed. Between 1970 and 1979, for instance, the World Bank committed an average of $248 million per year for education (in current dollars); today, the annual average is closer to $1.7 billion.[8] Critics still contend, however, that the proportion of education-related lending relative to other sectors has not improved significantly over time and across all regions.

Latin America is a good example of the presumed impact of the new World Bank policies. The region worked closely with the World Bank and the IMF to stabilize economies and open markets in the 1990s. The region, together with Africa, was also the largest recipient of education lending from the World Bank. If the argument that "structural adjustment is bad for education" is correct, we should observe declines in education spending in the region. Instead, seven of nine Latin American countries for which we have data increased spending on education while simultaneously reducing the degree of state control over the economy (see Table 1).

Yet, the relationship suggested by Table 1 should be treated with caution; the numbers do not entirely refute the criticism that structural adjustment hurts education. Most Latin American nations in Table 1 experienced renewed growth in the 1990s, after a decade of stagnation, failed economic stabilization, and declines in social spending. They were bound to experience an expansion in social services in the 1990s. In addition, these examples do not reveal what happens to education when countries are fiscally ill (i.e., undergoing high budget deficits, recession, or capital outflow) and in the midst of implementing structural adjustment programs. Other research shows that when Latin American countries experienced budget deficits, their education spending declined (Huber, Mustillo, and Stephens, 2004). If the initial impact of an IMF stabilization program is a lower gross domestic product (GDP), as some

---

[8] Based on data available at http://devdata.worldbank.org/edstats/wbl_A.asp.

Table 1: Market Reforms and Education Spending in Latin America: the 1980s vs. the 1990s

Country	Change in SOE Economic Activity	Change in SOE Investment	Change in Expenditures on Education
Argentina	-1.4	-6.3	0.52
Bolivia	-2.0	-3.1	2.31
Brazil	-0.3	-4.9	2.1**
Chile	-4.1	-8.8	-0.27
Costa Rica	NA	3.0	-0.64
Ecuador	NA	1.2	2.00
Guatemala	0.1	-1.9	-0.11
Mexico	-1.8	-4.1	1.22
Panama	-0.3	-5.1	0.10
Paraguay	-0.2	-5.7	1.95
Peru	-1.3	-6.2	0.15

Source: Calculated using World Bank (Various Years); SOE data are based on the 2000 edition.

Notes:
Change in SOE (State-owned Enterprise) Economic Activity is the difference between the average percent of GDP accounted for by SOEs in 1985–1990 and the average in the 1990–97 period. **Change in SOE Investment** is the difference between the average SOE investment as a percentage of GDI in 1985–1990 and the average in the 1990–97 period. **Change in Expenditures on Education** is the difference between the average education expenditures in the 1985–90 period and the average in the 1990–97 period.
** Data from Brazil prior to 1994, and from 1996 to 1998, are not available. The reported figure is the difference in percentage points between education spending in 1994 and 2000.

argue (see Vreeland, 2003), then it is not unreasonable to conclude that structural adjustment, at least initially, may hurt education spending insofar as lower growth rates limit spending.

If evidence on the effects of structural adjustment on education is mixed, the second criticism—that loans earmarked for education are hard to control—is increasingly persuasive. Even when multilaterals offer sound pro-education advice and resources, they have few ways of penalizing countries that fail to promote education. They also lack the capacity to monitor implementation. Without the capacity to monitor and sanction, it is hard to believe that multilaterals can exert much pressure on states. As de Moura Castro writes on the use of World Bank money, "all schools are built, most teachers are trained and computers purchased...but the reform component is not implemented" (2002: 395). In addition, although lavish in relation to other forms of aid and in relation to past aid, international aid on education generally accounts for less than 2 percent of the education budget of a recipient country (UNICEF, 1999: 81).

Hunter and Brown (2000) study the impact of World Bank lending on human capital variables in 13 Latin American countries between 1980 and 1992. They concur with de Moura Castro that the World Bank has not had a significant impact on human capital investment in Latin America.[9] They find neither an upward trend in overall education spending corresponding to the beginning of the World Bank's emphasis on education nor any redistribution of resources from tertiary to primary education, which is one of the Bank's most insistent policy recommendations. Local institutional obstacles override the intentions and resources of the World Bank (Hunter and Brown, 2000).

Although important, Hunter and Brown's finding that the World Bank's efforts to promote education have little influence may not be generalizable because the selected cases are idiosyncratic in at least two respects. First, these countries already had devoted substantial resources to education and had relatively high coverage, i.e., they were at the last (flatter) stage of the S-curve. It makes sense to find low levels of World Bank influence at this late stage, when the cost of expanding schooling is high. It remains to be explored whether World Bank lending is more influential in countries at earlier points in the S-curve. This would make intuitive sense; in earlier stages, the cost of expansion is lower and World Bank support—always modest—can have a larger impact. Second, Hunter and Brown's cases were idiosyncratic in terms of the period studied (1980 to 1992) which includes the period of the debt crisis, which Edwards (1995) labels a time of "muddling through" policy-making. Except for Chile and Bolivia, most Latin American countries until the late 1980s eschewed major policy reforms for political reasons—their governments were either unstable dictatorships or nascent democracies fearful of

---

[9] To determine the percentage of World Bank lending, Hunter and Brown divide World Bank lending to Latin America disbursed to a specific country by the home country's economic output, which is expressed as its share of the region's GDP.

generating regime-threatening instability. It could be that under less economically and politically precarious conditions, pro-education lending by the World Bank is more influential. Hunter and Brown's study does not test this proposition.

The conclusion is therefore that poor domestic fiscal health is a worse enemy of education than any external actor. Countries in fiscal trouble require the intervention of external doctors (the IMF and the World Bank) whose medicines (structural adjustment) may depress social spending at first. International organizations now recommend that, once recovery occurs, states expand and reform social services, including education. Financial crises may also encourage states to recruit technical experts with training in economics, a preference for efficiency, and transnational ties (Domínguez, 1997; Grindle, 1996). Insofar as states retain these internationally minded, reform-seeking technical experts, multilaterals retain a window through which they can influence states. In most instances, however, the influence of pro-education World Bank lending may be limited, especially for countries expanding education to the most difficult to reach populations, or those experiencing severe economic crises. It remains to be seen whether World Bank education lending has a more noticeable effect under different conditions, i.e., in countries at the middle stages of the S-curve and those suffering less intense political crises.

The Allure of Ideas

The spread of ideas is another mechanism that may create international pressure to expand education. The idea that education is a public good, in the national interest of every state, is one of the most significant paradigm shifts of the twentieth century (see Coleman, 1965: 3–32). Two centuries ago, most countries in the West considered education a privilege that only those already capable could appreciate and thus receive. Even as recently as the late 1970s, development experts did not agree about the economic benefits of education. As Simmons (1980) documents, some argued that the mass education of rural children would divert resources from investments with higher returns and also depopulate the countryside, creating an employment problem in the agricultural sector and an intractable unemployment problem in cities.[10]

---

[10] I thank Robert Levine for this insight.

Today, most political leaders, activists, and scholars embrace instead the idea that education is both a human right as well as a national good. Part of the reason for the shift in paradigm rests on the influential 1980 World Bank *World Development Report*. The report provided evidence that the expansion of schooling increased agricultural production and reduced fertility and mortality in developing countries. Education, the report showed, leads to smaller, healthier, more productive families in agricultural communities, and by extension, enhances development. Furthermore, research has shown that in lower-income countries, investments in school-related inputs have greater impact on student science test scores than differences in the socioeconomic background of students (Heyneman and Loxley, 1983; Heyneman, 1980). Equally influential has been Psacharopoulos's work since 1973 on the private and social returns on educational investments. He shows that increased education of the labor force explains both increased returns to the individual, especially for the lowest-income individuals, and possibly a substantial part of growth in output, especially in developing countries. Investment in education "behaves in a more or less similar manner as investment in physical capital" (Psacharopoulos and Patrinos, 2004: 118).

Large international organizations and not-so-large non-governmental organizations have also become strong advocates of education as, in the words of the United Nations Children's Fund (UNICEF), both an individual right and a national good. This consensus at the international level is as consequential as two other paradigm shifts in the history of education in the West: the rise of humanism in the sixteenth century, which made erudition a virtue coveted by aristocrats, not just clergy, and the rise of social rights in the nineteenth century (see Marshall, 1964), which compelled European states to accept the idea of providing education services to citizens.

However, it is unclear whether this new consensus at the international level is equally strong within states. To test its presumed spread, Fiala and Lanford (1987) examine "formal expressions of national aims of education" among 125 countries from 1955 and 1965. They find a remarkable convergence: most governments cite the same set of reasons for providing education, top among which are the achievement of "national development," "economic development," and "individual development." For Fiala and Lanford, this is strong evidence of the existence of the new consensus across states. Yet Fiala and Lanford acknowledge that their study cannot prove that the consensus was more than empty promises made for the sake of appearances and that these ideas actually motivated educational expansion.

Ideas may not be all that influential because, to spread change across borders, they need more than just many adherents. It is also necessary that ideas find: 1) transnational institutional mechanisms of diffusion (Slaughter, 2004; Simmons, 2001; Goldstein and Keohane, 1993; Haas, 1992; Keohane and Nye, 1989), 2) institutional penetration in a host country (Jacoby, 2000; Hall, 1989), and 3) strong empirical support, especially in a neighboring country (Weyland, 2005). The idea that education is a "national good" and an "individual right" certainly meets the first criterion (i.e., through the technical missions of international organizations or the openness of Western universities to international students who then return home), but it may not meet the second or third criteria.

For instance, it is not clear that institutional penetration in developing countries has occurred uniformly. Ministries of education are not necessarily staffed with experts committed to education, and even if a ministry of education is duly staffed, other more important ministries, such as finance, might react with skepticism (see Corrales, 1999). This skepticism about the value of education, particularly in ministries of finance, is partly rooted in the third criterion—empirical support. Although UNICEF declares that education "is a matter of morality, justice and economic sense" (1999: 7), there is no worldwide agreement that educational expansion always makes economic sense. Despite its benefits at the individual level, there is still no conclusive empirical evidence that education, in and of itself, is the best antidote for underdevelopment (Easterly, 2002: 71–86). In their review of the literature, Hannum and Buchmann (this volume) observe, "Considerable controversy surrounds the effects of educational expansion on national economic development…Similarly, there is considerable controversy surrounding the effects of educational expansion on the democratization of societies." Even among believers in education, there is enormous disagreement about the most appropriate routes for expanding education (i.e., the proportion of state versus private investment, the proportion of investments in tertiary versus secondary education, and the degree of decentralization). In sum, the political power of international ideas will remain limited as long as ideas remain institutionally homeless and disagreement persists about the economic growth payoffs of education.

Emulating or Surpassing Peers

International relations scholars have long emphasized that the pressures of international political competition may shape domestic outcomes. To some scholars, the presence of an external threat is key, as it may induce nations into "balancing"—attempting to match and surpass the achievements of a rival nation. This may apply to education expansion; some important historical examples of military-political rivalry stimulating education include: 1) educational expansion associated with competition between Protestant and Catholic areas of Europe during the Reformation; 2) the emulation by European nations of Prussia's universal education of soldiers, to which some ascribed Prussia's victory in the 1870–1871 Franco-Prussian War; and, more recently, 3) the expansion of science and engineering education in the United States and the Soviet Union during the Cold War.

However, in developing countries, this type of pressure seems less relevant because external threats stem mostly from neighboring countries over border disputes. This type of dispute places a higher premium on military preparedness than on competition for status, which limits the competitive value of bolstering education.

Emulation may occur, not only among international rivals, but also among mere status-seekers—nations that try to earn acceptance into a prestigious international community or institution (see Walt, 2000). For example, Southern Europe in the 1980s and Eastern Europe in the 1990s boosted education systems with a clear eye to earning the respect of, and thus membership in, the Western European community.

This type of external pressure also seems less applicable to developing countries. For emulation to occur, a nation must come to value membership in a specific international community (see Jacoby, 2000). In addition, the target international community must place a high value on the educational achievements of its members. Even the European Union, the most important example of a prestigious club with many aspiring members, places less emphasis on education than on other policy achievements (e.g., civil rights, human rights, economic development, and macroeconomic discipline). Few developing countries assign a high value to membership in communities that have education achievement as a standard of admission.

In sum, external pressures to expand education that arise from international rivalry or status-seeking seem to be less decisive than external pressures stemming from economic competition, which as discussed previously may not generate pressures for improvements in schooling.

STATE-BASED INCENTIVES

Promoting Nationalism and Loyalty to the State

The creation of loyalty to the state is a primary, if not the most urgent, task of every emerging nation. Since the time of Thomas Hobbes's publication of *Leviathan* in 1651, we have known that states that do not command authority and respect from their citizens risk collapsing, possibly into civil war (see Kohli, 2002). Because they must generate loyalty, states have an interest in controlling the beliefs of citizens (see Pritchett, 2003). States may achieve this by promoting nationalism (see Linz and Stepan, 1996: 16–37) or by undermining the other entities in society that compete for the allegiance of citizens (e.g., religious organizations, tribal strongmen, or simple attachments to tradition or ethnicity). States have often promoted education vigorously because they see education as contributing to both the rise of nationalism and the weakening of rivals (see Benavot and Resnik, this volume).

There is little dispute that the desire to promote nationalism was a fundamental driver of educational expansion in newly independent states in the 1950s and 1960s, especially in Africa (see Sutton, 1965), just as it was in eighteenth- and nineteenth-century Europe. State leaders wanted citizens to develop loyalties to the newly independent state rather than with colonial powers, i.e., to prove to their citizens that they could do better than the colonial powers in the provision of services. During the colonial period, only immigrants from Europe and Asia received high-quality government education in Africa (Makau, 1995); after independence, citizens expected to enjoy the services previously denied to them. Munishi (1995), for instance, argues that after independence the Tanzanian government aggressively pursued social-service expansion despite extremely limited funds. To gain political legitimacy among many different tribes, the Tanzanian government, like other African governments, sought to reduce the authority of NGOs, to promote self-help initiatives, and to expand state services under a "socialist" philosophy akin to populism. The logic behind these initiatives was that citizens would pledge their allegiance to a government that could provide new social services, including education. By fomenting nationalism, the new government would gain legitimacy.

If promoting nationalism at the early stages of state formation is a strong enough incentive to expand education, we should observe more rapid expansion in newly independent states than in other scenarios.

However, Meyer et al. (1977) examine this hypothesis and find no clear evidence that, in general, nations immediately post-independence increase education more vigorously than other countries. This finding does not necessarily negate that nationalism drives education expansion, but it does suggest that nationalism—or controlling beliefs in general—is an insufficient or short-lived source of political energy for the expansion of education, too dependent on bottom-up levels of threat. As the memory of colonial governments recedes, the need to compete with these former colonial powers loses urgency.

Neutralizing Domestic Rivals

When the incentive to promote nationalism is combined with the incentive to neutralize domestic "rivals" such as allegiances to religion, strongmen, or just tradition, the impetus to expand education increases. In Western Europe, a fundamental push for the expansion of education occurred when states prioritized secularization and the modernization of citizens to make them more suitable for industrial life. Another driver in the rise of mass education in nineteenth-century Europe was the desire of "national elites" to compete against local elites for the loyalties of local clients; and, even more fundamentally, the desire to incorporate into society the "vagrant poor"—viewed as always needy and mobile, and thus a potential threat to public security (de Swaan, 2001).

In the postwar period, totalitarian revolutionary regimes (e.g., the Soviet Union and China) combined hyper-nationalism with vigorous efforts to neutralize, even eliminate, strong domestic rivals, and they too expanded education vigorously. Lott (1999) shows that totalitarian regimes—the same regimes that seek to exercise monopoly over the media—spend more on education than other regimes. These regimes do not seem to spend more on health, which suggests a connection between educational expansion and the desire to control a society, rather than a concern for human well-being. Totalitarian states extensively expanded education precisely because of their intense commitment to the control of society and to breaking old allegiances (see Coleman, 1965: 227). Using qualitative methods, Cheng and Manning confirm that the feature that distinguished educational expansion in China and Cuba between 1957 and 1976 from expansion in other post-colonial societies over that period—and what made the effort far more intense—was the state's desire to create a "classless community" and to generate a productivity breakthrough by imposing "voluntary" work on students (2003: 388–389).

Although the incidence of revolutionary impulses has subsided world-wide (except perhaps in the Islamic world), the insight remains that states interested in exacting control over citizens have a stronger motivation to expand education (Pritchett, 2003). This has troubling implications. First, there will be variation in the degree to which states pursue education provision: the more a state seeks to control, the more inclined it will be to pursue expansion.

Second, the extent to which a state wishes to exercise control depends in part on how threatened the state feels by societal groups. The existence of strong domestic rivals to state authority may encourage educational expansion, but this depends on the nature of the rival. If the rival is an armed actor, the state will boost military spending; if the rival is mostly ideological and cultural (i.e., the church, tradition, certain ideologies, surplus immigration), the state might focus more on education than on the military.

Third, where church-state relations are delicate or tense, states seem to pay more attention to education; however, the specific response has varied over time and among countries. For instance, Western European states used education to neutralize the power of the Catholic Church in three ways. One was to placate the religious authorities by granting them complete monopoly over educational services—the prevailing model in Catholic countries for the sixteenth through early eighteenth centuries. In a later model, states offered mass schooling, thereby competing with the Church by providing a presumably cheaper, better, and more accessible education. This was the nineteenth-century model of the expansion of secondary education in Europe. A third option was to antagonize the Church directly by monopolizing education, akin to the secularist, revolutionary, totalitarian route of the twentieth century.

Developing countries that face similar challenges from strong religious groups have sometimes replicated these models (Coleman, 1965: 41–43). However, the most typical approach of these countries has been different: mutual assistance. In the Gulf monarchies, for example, massive educational expansion occurred in a form that was complementary to religious groups. The governments of Bahrain, Kuwait, Oman, Qatar, Saudi Arabia, and the United Arab Emirates officially endorse Islamic education for a number of reasons: it consolidates the partnership between the religious hierarchy and royal families; it allows countries to expand their cultural influence through Islamic university graduates; and it highlights the "pious" character of the state, creating a bulwark against radical Arabism and fundamentalism (Bahgat, 1998). After the September 11 terrorist attacks, U.S. officials became convinced that the proliferation of Islamist schools in Islamic countries, without a commensurate development of secular schools, could pose a threat to international security. This encouraged the U.S. Agency for International Development to increase education-related spending in Islamic countries (Perlez, 2003).

Fourth, states that have less controlling ideologies or limited capabilities may falter in providing education. Specifically, states that feel that they can afford higher degrees of pluralism at home may be less inclined to invest in educational expansion because they are less interested in social control. If this holds true, then democracies, which by definition are more comfortable with dissent and pluralism, may be less driven to expand education than more controlling dictatorships. Universalization in these societies may only occur if societal demand is strong, as discussed below.

Fifth, states may hesitate to expand education out of a fear of generating instability. One common fear centers on the possible sociological outcome of more education, what I call the "Educated-Unemployed-Gramsci" phenomenon. This is the fear that rapid education will produce a mass of educated but unemployed citizens and lead to a plethora of "Gramscis"—a reference to Antonio Gramsci (1891–1937), a well-known Marxist theorist who escaped rural poverty through schooling, including university education, to become one of Italy's most famous political agitators.[11] As LeVine et al. (2001) explain, education plays a dual role in forming citizens. On the one hand, education creates literate citizens who are competent in communication, an outcome that most states would welcome. However, education can also undermine traditionalist norms and empower challengers to the state, outcomes that governments may not welcome.

Another fear centers on the bureaucratic outcome of educational expansion. More education leads to more bureaucracy. Since Max Weber, many political scientists have assumed that bureaucracies are politically functional for rulers. Bureaucracies allow rulers to meet certain societal

---

[11] Fuller and Rubinson illustrate this argument by showing that conservative town council leaders in nineteenth-century France "feared that mass schooling would feed rising social expectations held by the working class and rural peasants" (1992: 9).

demands (see Tilly, 1992), to make societies "more legible"—to use Scott's (1998) term—and thus more pacifiable, or to protect policies from the assaults of political adversaries (McCubbins et al., 1987). Yet there are times when rulers prefer *not* to build bureaucracies because they fear that political rivals will capture the bureaucracy and use it against them. This is precisely what Reno (2000) argues is happening in many African states, especially in Cameroon, Kenya, Zambia, Congo-Kinshasa, Congo-Brazzaville, and Uganda, where rulers are reducing investment in bureaucracies, and thus in education and other social services. Reno's work concludes that, in the context of strong societal adversaries and hopelessly weak states, the rational strategy of rulers is to neglect investments in bureaucracy, because it both takes resources away from other means of dealing with adversaries and because bureaucracies could ultimately be captured by rivals.

In conclusion, the degree of educational expansion may depend on variations in the strength of state capacities and ideologies, as well as the strength of societal rivals. Table 2 summarizes some possible combinations of these variables and the expected educational outcomes, with examples. At the beginning of the twenty-first century, most developing

Table 2: Variations in State and Societal Features: Impact on Educational Expansion

		State Features	
		State vigorously seeks to control civil society (ideology and capabilities are strong)	State refrains from seeking to control civil society (ideology and capabilities are soft)
Societal Features	Strong state challengers	I. Strong education push, driven by state's desire to neutralize societal rivals (e.g., totalitarian-revolutionary regimes of the 20th century)	II. Weak education impulse and possible neglect of bureaucracy (e.g., fragile regimes in Africa)
	Weak/few state challengers	III. Low education drive because states face no political pressure to provide benefits (e.g., stable autocratic regimes in developing countries)	IV. Strong education push *only* if societal demand is strong (e.g., democracies in the 20th century)

countries find themselves in quadrants II or III, where there is low drive for education. The exceptions are democratic Latin American and Asian countries, which might be reaching quadrant IV. In these countries, universalization and improvements in quality depend less on state-based incentives (which are weak in democracies) and more on the strength of societal demand (which varies across and within democracies).

Clientelism

In addition to neutralizing rivals, states must also repay those who provide political support. Rulers have always allowed or encouraged the use of state resources to reward citizens who render useful political services (Bates, 1981; Krueger, 1974; Buchanan and Tullock, 1967). The distribution of valued resources—tangible or intangible—according to political criteria is often called patronage (Pasquino, 1996). When patronage flows from a strong actor toward a weak actor, it is called clientelism (Stokes, 2000; Graziano, 1975; Scott, 1972). When funds or favors are illegally exchanged between economically powerful actors and public officials, misaligning the public interest and the interest of the public official, it is called corruption (see Rose-Ackerman, 1998).

Patronage, clientelism, and corruption are three of the most intense political forces that push states to expand education. It is clear why education lends itself to patronage. As Rose-Ackerman (1998) argues, patronage flourishes around large government activities, such as investments in infrastructure. Education qualifies as a large government activity.

Patronage and clientelism can aid educational expansion also by protecting social spending in poor countries during periods of economic contraction. Brown and Hunter (1999) find that poor democracies of Latin America, which are arguably more susceptible to patronage and clientelism, are less likely than authoritarian regimes to cut social spending when faced with rising debt burdens, slower growth, and budget deficits. These effects dissipate as income rises, however. In more developed countries, there is no clear difference in the extent to which different regime types protect social spending.

However, as a mechanism for expanding education, clientelism carries with it undesirable baggage. It is the main explanation for the tendency of public school systems to be more inefficient (i.e., have a higher input-to-output ratio) than private school systems within the same country: private schools invest more on classroom-based inputs such as instructional

materials and teacher incentives, whereas public schools invest in external
resources such as wages and procurement (Jiménez and Lockheed, 1995).
The latter are typically driven by patronage. Although there are exceptions—mostly in Southeast Asia—of corruption co-existing with relatively
efficient school systems, corruption more frequently goes hand in hand
with misguided educational investment for at least four reasons.

First, clientelism drives the state to expand public employment without demanding that public employees fulfill their responsibilities. In this
way, patronage undermines the legitimacy of government and politicians,
magnifies the power of vested interests, lowers the quality of services provided by the state, and erodes the impact of social policies. Patronage
may protect spending on salaries but not the expenditures necessary for
effective education (e.g., training, facilities, infrastructure maintenance).

Second, corruption may deplete overall resources, leaving less for
investment. In a quantitative study of corruption—a proxy of
patronage[12]—Gupta et al. (2000) find not only that corruption depletes
overall resources, but also that corruption increases the cost of and lowers
the output provided by lower levels of government and social services,
especially in the health and education sectors. By decreasing the quality
of government services, corruption depresses the demand for such services. Combining different indices of corruption (i.e., perceptions among
investors of uncertainty and unpredictability about laws, policies, and
regulations), Gupta et al. find that countries with lower indices of corruption have 26 percent fewer student dropouts at the primary level.

Third, corruption hurts educational expansion because it distorts the
composition of government expenditure. A landmark report by the IMF
showed that corrupt governments, which presumably find it easier to
hide the diversion of funds, spend less on education and more on public
investment; a country that reduces corruption will typically simultaneously raise its spending on education (Mauro, 1996).

Finally, clientelism also operates from the bottom up: local politicians
commit the national government to spend more on education (e.g.,
building more schools) without securing revenue for maintaining the
facilities. The result can be an expansion of physical resources followed by
quick decay of facilities.

---

[12] Like patronage, corruption constitutes the channeling of public resources for
private gains. In addition, patronage and corruption tend to occur simultaneously (see Stokes, 2000; Mainwaring, 1999b).

Several qualitative studies show the close connection between clientelism and inefficient education systems. Plank (1990) shows that in the democratic administration of Brazilian President José Sarney, governors who supported a five-year term for the president were showered with federal monies for their states, while governors who supported a four-year term received little money. Textbook monopolies were granted to specific publishing firms, also as an exchange of favors and not according to a judgment of quality or price bidding. Mainwaring (1999b: 213) finds that in the state of Bahia in northeast Brazil, which has an illiteracy rate of almost 50 percent, an estimated 37,000 teachers on the public payroll as of early 1987 had never taught a single class. A case study of the Indian state of West Bengal shows that political connections dictate whether a teacher will or will not be reprimanded for poor performance and also discourage the government from holding schools accountable (Ruud, 1999). Researchers making unannounced visits to schools in India find that, on average, schoolchildren receive one minute of individual attention per day from a teacher (PROBE Team, 1999) and that one in four teachers is absent on any given day (Kremer et al., 2004). This may be explained by the inability of these schools to monitor or sanction teachers.

In short, patronage and clientelism are double-edged swords. On the one hand, they can be the main drivers of educational expansion in developing countries. On the other hand, except in some Southeast Asian countries, patronage and clientelism—and accompanying corruption—can present major threats to the quality and efficiency of education. These costs may mitigate any gains in educational expansion.

Incentives to Increase Efficiency

Ideally, a government will want not just to expand education, but also to do so efficiently. If patronage is the prevailing incentive to states to provide education, however, the public education system will be plagued by inefficiency and inattention to quality. In a patronage scenario, it is more convenient to expand coverage (e.g., build new schools or add teachers to the payroll), which involves spending money to co-opt political actors, than to fix inefficiencies, which may involve taking resources away from underperforming actors.

Estimating inefficiency rates in a school system is difficult, even if one accepts Simmons's commonsensical definition of efficiency: "the optimum combination of inputs such as teacher training and expenditure per student to achieve at least-cost the desired outcome, such as a certain level of reading achievement" (Simmons, 1980: 10). The problem is that estimates vary depending on the outcome that a school is asked to deliver—a decision that teachers and parents often disagree on—and more important, student or community characteristics, which vary across schools and classrooms. For example, a school whose students are mostly poor, foreign-language speaking, recent immigrants will require more resources than a school with children from middle- or upper-class families, but this does not mean that it is less efficient.

Nevertheless, there is ample evidence dating back to the 1970s that rates of school inefficiency are greater in developing countries than in developed countries. Simmons (1980) reaches this conclusion by examining "wastage rates," which compare the level of investment in relation to several education outputs. These outputs include dropout rates (i.e., desertions based on student's volition), pushout rates (i.e., desertions based on school action), and repetition rates. Although scholars might disagree on the amount of inefficiency, there is agreement that high wastage rates are pervasive in developing countries. This inefficiency probably accounts for the finding by Alesina (1997) that spending on public education—and public health, public employment, and social security—often favors well-off communities, fails to reach the poor, and implies distortions, especially in Latin America, Africa, and rural areas.

One possible incentive for states to increase efficiency in education is the desire to create savings. Cash-strapped states have much to gain by increasing the efficiency of schools, spending less money to achieve similar or better outcomes. In the 1990s, many states developed a historically unusual preference for savings, including lower debts, deficits, and inflation rates. This heightened concern for savings and efficiency in social services, a shift resulting from internationally circulated and accepted ideas, has significantly impacted the propensity of states to pay attention to educational issues. Ministers of finance with a strong preference for savings typically become key political actors pushing for efficiency.

However, pro-efficiency forces at the state level are typically counterbalanced by other state leaders who fear that taking resources away from current beneficiaries will generate political conflict (see Robinson, 1998). These fears, typical of politicians dependent on patronage relationships, can block measures designed to increase efficiency. If ministers of finance do not see a way to maximize efficiency, they may become reluctant to endorse increases in spending in education, which may in turn prevent universalization.

The politics of pushing for efficiency thus involve conflict at the state level, usually pitting three cabinet-level actors against each other: 1) savings-oriented ministers of finance who block education spending unless accompanied by efficiency gains; 2) ministers of education who may desire efficiency, but who also want far more spending than finance ministers allow; and 3) patronage-seeking ministers who care less about generating savings than about keeping crucial political constituents happy with state largess (see Corrales, 2004a; 2004b).

Conflict will not be confined to state actors, and the kind of conflicts and state actors involved will depend on at least two variables: overall GDP, which determines the country's available resources, and the existing level of efficiency. Colclough and Al-Samarrai (2000) offer a useful framework for understanding the relationship between these two factors, as well as their policy implications. In a study of education in Africa and South Asia, they show that countries vary enormously in terms of GDP level and one possible proxy of inefficiency—unit cost of education (measured in terms of spending per student).[13] Although the reason for variation in unit costs (not just within Africa, but across developing countries) remains to be explained, we can nonetheless use Colclough and Al-Samarrai's work to generate some hypotheses about expected political conflicts.

As Colclough and Al-Samarrai note, the ideal policy prescription for a given country depends both on a country's GNP and the unit cost of education (see Table 3).[14] For countries that have high unit costs and relatively high GNP per capita (quadrant I), the policy imperative is to cut costs *and* spend more.[15] If the country has a low GNP per capita (quad-

---

[13] The use of unit cost as a measure of efficiency is open to criticism, as unit costs are blind to variations in the needs of different communities. However, for the purpose of this paper, unit costs serve as a useful measure of efficiency in considering how variations in a country's overall income and efficiency determine the recommended educational policies, and consequently, the expected political conflict.

[14] For higher-income countries, Table 3 could be modified to reflect differences in fiscal health, rather than GNP levels. Fiscally stable countries have more resources to invest in education, and so their politics of education reform will resemble quadrants I and III; countries in fiscal trouble will exhibit the politics of quadrants II and IV.

[15] Again, analysts might disagree with this recommendation. It could very well be that addressing inefficiency may require an increase in investment (e.g., improve infrastructure facilities, provide better training for teachers, etc.), at least in the short term.

Table 3: Unit Costs, GNP levels, and the Politics of Education Reform

		GNP per capita	
		Medium (> US$300) *Modest Financing Need*	**Very small** (<US$300) *Large Financing Need*
Primary Unit Costs as a proportion of GNP per capita	**High** 12% or higher; avg = 21%	I. Policy Imperative: Cut costs, increase spending Examples: Kenya, Senegal, Burkina Faso, Rwanda, Mauritania, Pakistan Expected political problem: Unions	II. Policy imperative: Cut costs, stimulate growth, borrow, and spend more Examples: Burundi, Mozambique, Ethiopia Expected political problem: Unions, politicians, and intra-cabinet
	Low 11% or lower; avg = 7%	III. Policy Imperative: Increase education spending Examples: Zambia, Ghana, Central African Republic Expected political problem: If deficit and debts are large, the IMF and finance ministers will oppose new spending	IV. Policy Imperative: Increase growth and borrow money Examples: Sierra Leone, Uganda, Zaire, Malawi, Chad, Gambia, Tanzania, Bangladesh Expected political problem: Debate among cabinet members about how to stimulate growth

Source: Based on Colclough and Al-Samarrai (2000).

Note: High unit-cost countries include countries whose current primary and pre-primary education spending per pupil is higher than the sub-Saharan Africa average (12 percent of GNP per capita). Low unit-cost countries are those whose current primary and pre-primary education spending per pupil is below the region's average.

rant II) and high unit costs, the policy imperative is to cut costs, of course, and also to stimulate economic growth and borrow more. If the country has low unit costs and high GNP per capita (quadrant III), the policy imperative is simply to spend more (i.e., cutting costs is unnecessary). Finally, a country with low unit costs and low GNP per capita (quadrant IV) will need to focus first on generating economic growth, in order to be able to afford spending on education.

Each of these four policy prescriptions may generate different types of political conflict. Unquestionably, countries that need to cut costs will face the harshest political conflicts. Typically, high unit costs result from relatively high teacher salaries. Because it is often difficult or inadvisable to cut teacher salaries, states must use alternative mechanisms to generate savings, such as increasing the student-teacher ratio or introducing more flexibility in the labor market for teachers. These types of changes are not generally favored by unions, and as a result the politics of cutting costs will likely generate strong conflicts between states and teachers' unions.

If GNP levels happen to be low (quadrant II), conflict will occur, not just between the state and unions but also among leading politicians. The need to generate income and to stimulate growth will cause serious debates throughout the whole political spectrum, as all actors will have different views about the amount of debt to assume and the policies that will produce growth. Tensions between ministries of finance and education, within the ruling party, and between the ruling party and opposition forces are almost guaranteed.

If unit costs are low, politics may be less contentious. This is especially true if GNP per capita is high (quadrant III). However, even in this scenario, the possibility of a serious political conflict may develop between the state and the IMF if an increase in spending hurts macroeconomic stability.

SOCIETY-BASED DEMAND FOR EDUCATION

One of the strongest explanations for the rise of state-provided services—the welfare state—comes from the "politics of contention" school of thought. This school posits that a state will forego the provision of services unless citizens bargain with, and in fact pressure, the state. Some political scientists go as far as to claim that education is mostly a citizen-driven phenomenon (e.g., Craig, 1981). Although this may be an overstatement, there is no question that household demand is crucial for educational expansion, as opposed to services such as health, where demand is universal and context-independent (Levine et al., 2003: 11).

Some of the factors that depress societal demand are intuitive (e.g., competing crises such as crime, unemployment, and corruption can make education less of a priority for citizens; see Kaufman and Nelson, 2004). However, other factors affecting demand are more complex and are related to a society's bargaining capacity. Even when societal actors have a strong preference for more education, demand may falter if societal actors lack the capacity to pressure the state. This section discusses five factors that may shape a society's bargaining capacity: income, organization, information, ideologies, and competitive politics.

Income and Organization as Enablers of Expansion

Income and organization are probably the two most important factors that explain a society's capacity for bargaining, although neither is a sufficient or an unambiguously positive force. Most studies of educational expansion find that income is the most important driver for at least three reasons. First, a higher aggregate income level allows states to invest more in education, although it is important to note that expenditure on education alone is not sufficient to produce universal coverage (UNDP, 2003; World Bank, 2003). Second, as family income increases, the ability or willingness of citizens to temporarily forgo income to continue their education also increases. This explains why higher national income levels lead to increased societal demand for education. Third, income whets the state's appetite for taxes. In the effort to capture more taxes while retaining citizens' loyalty, states might feel more compelled to negotiate with citizens, thereby giving rise to social services.

Low income in general is the most significant barrier to educational expansion; the poorer the country, the more difficult it is for other policy interventions (e.g., increases in public expenditures on education) to compensate for the drag effect of low income (Clemens, 2004).

On an individual level, low-income parents making decisions about their child's education must consider not only the actual cost of schooling but also the opportunity costs, such as the foregone income from a child's labor. The opportunity cost of attending school may be higher in rural areas, but there is no question that poverty—more so than rural lifestyle—is the most significant deterrent of parental demand for schooling and the primary factor leading to desertion. Buchmann and Brakewood (2000) find that impoverished subsistence farmers in Thailand are less likely than wealthier counterparts to send their children to school.

Where attending school is costly, low-income families are often forced to strategize in a way that limits demand for education. In rural Nepal, for example, it is common for poor households to trade the further education of one son for the schooling of other sons (Ashby, 1985). The most promising son pursues a high level of education, while the others forgo school to help with work at home. The educated son is then expected to use his education to benefit his family. In an age-adjusted survey, Ashby finds that, in 83 percent of Nepalese families, at least one son obtained greater schooling than his brothers.

Lack of income can be an obstacle to educational expansion where households derive a significant portion of their income from child labor. Myron Weiner's book on child labor in India makes the alarming argument that in societies ravaged by poverty, where households rely on child labor for income, sending children to school entails substantial foregone income (Weiner, 1991). Parents, therefore, are reluctant to release children from work to send them to school. Fuller and Rubinson (1992) take this argument further. They argue that during the early stages of industrialization, when demand for child labor is large, parental demand for schooling may decline precisely because sending children to school represents forgone income. Where schools are in disrepair, or where education is of poor quality, parental reluctance to send children to school increases (PROBE, 1999), because the perceived economic returns to education are low. The successful provision of two public goods, education and termination of child labor, is constrained by their direct cost to households.

In a chapter that compares India to Western Europe, Weiner develops the argument that educational expansion will occur after societies have undergone a major cultural shift: when parents stop seeing children as assets, generating income for older household members, and begin to consider them more as liabilities, needing income from the older household members (1991: 114). Only households in the latter category are prepared to release their children from child labor to education.

The best sign that this transition—from children being considered assets to being considered liabilities—has occurred is a demographic shift toward smaller families. Weiner's argument leads to the hypothesis that educational expansion is more likely in countries whose fertility rates have declined (which in turn seems more likely in democracies; see Przeworski et al., 2000), not so much because a small student population makes state services less costly, but because the fertility decline is a proxy of parental willingness to send children to school (i.e., a sign that parents have changed how they view children). This argument can explain the enrollment successes of East Asian economies. Between 1965 and 1989, these countries experienced dramatic declines in the school-age population followed by dramatic achievements in secondary enrollment (see Table 4).

The question is, then, what comes first—demographic change or educational expansion? It is possible that the direction of causality changes depending on the stage of educational expansion. In the early stages, minimal provision of education seems necessary to spark demographic

Table 4: Changes in School-Age Population and Enrollment Levels

	School-age (0–14) Population as a Percentage of Total Population		Secondary Enrollment (Percent Gross)
	1965	**1989**	**1990**
East Asian			
Hong Kong	40	22	79.6
Republic of Korea	43	26	89.8
Malaysia	46	37	56.3
Singapore	44	24	68.1
Others			
Bangladesh	43	44	19.0
Kenya	47	51	24.1
Nigeria	46	48	24.9
Pakistan	46	45	22.7

Source: World Bank (1993).

change. Research shows that small increases in the education stock of the population—namely, increases in female literacy rates—generate a substantial decrease in birth rates (see Hannum and Buchmann, this volume). Once this process is underway (i.e., after birth rates have begun to decline rapidly), then the direction of causality changes. Demographic change triggers educational expansion along the lines hypothesized by Weiner, where declining birth rates are associated with greater parental demand for education and lower marginal costs of educational provision.

This two-stage hypothesis linking education and demographic change might explain the education achievements of the Indian state of Kerala. By 1990, Kerala had one of the highest levels of human development, especially literacy, in all of India. One of the reasons for Kerala's success in education could very well be the early expansion of female literacy. By the early 1920s, the three provinces that compose present-day Kerala (Trancavore, Cochin, and Malabar) had achieved female literacy rates that were far above the Indian average (see Table 5). As the two-stage hypothesis would predict, major demographic changes soon followed (see Drèze and Sen, 1995); by the 1950s, birth rates in Kerala were

Table 5: The Possible Link Between Female Literacy and Demographic Change in Kerala, India

Circa	Female Literacy Rates					Birth Rates (per 1,000)	
	India	Kerala*	Trancavore**	Cochin	Malabar	India	Kerala
1891	0.5		3.5	5.5	3.9		
1921	1.9		15.0	9.4	4.9		
1931	2.4		13.9	18.5	7.5	45.2	40
1941	6.9		36.0	30.6	—	39.9	39.8
1951	9.3		37.0**	—	21	41.7	38.9
1961	12.9	38.9					
1971	18.7	54.3				36.8	31.6
1981	24.9	64.5				33.8	25.6

Source: Female literacy rates from Jeffrey (1992: 60); birth rates from Ramachandran (2000: 48).

Notes: * The state Kerala formed in 1956 with the union of Trancavore, Cochin, and Malabar.
** The state Trancavore-Cochin formed in 1949.

declining at a faster rate than the national average. By the early 1970s, the birth rate in Kerala was 31.6 per 1,000 relative to 36.8 per 1,000 for all of India.

The two-stage literacy-demography argument seems plausible for Kerala, but it is not conclusive. In Kerala, the literacy-demography variable coexisted with another social variable that may have had an equally strong impact on schooling: heightened political competition. Competition among religious communities in the nineteenth century, post-independence competition among political parties (the Communist party and the Congress party), and strong societal organizations pressuring the state also contributed to Kerala's strong performance in expanding education (see Jeffrey, 1992).

Raising income levels and reducing the opportunity costs of education, however, might not be necessary to propel the state to provide the needed educational expansion. Even materially deprived citizens can force states to provide services if they become politically organized, for example in political parties, labor unions, or other organizations for parents or communities.

Studying developed countries, Swank (2002) finds that those organized along corporatist lines (i.e., numerous unions with collective negotiations between the government and unions) have resisted the retrenchment of welfare services that may result from the pressures of globalization. In Latin America, scholars attribute the push for education in the region to populist political parties and teachers' unions, which were strong in the postwar period. In Africa, where parties and unions are weaker relative to those in Latin America, societal bargaining leverage vis-à-vis the state has been lower, which explains in part Africa's slower educational expansion. However, the absence of strong parties and unions is not necessarily an insurmountable handicap. Although parties and unions are weak in Africa, parent and community organizations are strong in some countries (e.g., Kenya); this contributes to educational expansion.

In short, states will deliver services when societal actors have the income or the organization to bargain with the state. This argument helps to explain the steepest part of the S-curve. Once the state offers a minimal amount of education, mechanisms that lead to self-sustaining pressures are set in motion. The result is a virtuous cycle: state investments in human capital increase the income of citizens and draw them to cities. Wealthier, more urbanized citizens are then more inclined to organize, which increases pressure on the state to deliver even more education.

This argument might also explain the flattening of the S-curve after a certain income threshold is reached. Because income and urbanization, and thus organization, do not spread across society uniformly—with the persistence of poverty in rural communities and in marginalized ghettos— there will be some demand failures. The poor and the unorganized may fail to strongly petition the state, resulting in large underserved communities. Because the two ingredients needed for the occurrence of effective bargaining—income and organization levels—are typically low or very unevenly distributed in developing countries, societal demand for education may falter. The central tragedy is that those who would profit the most from universal education—i.e., the households who would obtain the highest returns from education, namely, low income groups in low-income countries (see Psacharopoulos and Patrinos, 2004)—are those least likely to be politically organized to make effective demands.

It is important to note that this argument has limits. It cannot explain why some countries, even ones that are comparatively wealthy and that have organized citizens, encounter serious difficulties in providing universal and efficient educational coverage. It also does not account for the underachievers, an indication that there may be a negative side effect to income and organization.

Income and Organization as Obstacles to Expansion

Under certain conditions, income may stand in the way of educational expansion. High-income groups, for instance, can skew public spending on education to the detriment of lower-income groups, because they have either more resources to spend arranging for government benefits or more bargaining power due to the higher level of tax revenue they generate (see Gradstein, 2003). One notable indication of the stranglehold that high-income groups have on educational services in the developing world can be found in the treatment of university systems. In developing countries, universities are frequently overfunded in relation to secondary and primary education and simultaneously underfunded in terms of resources invested in research and development. The result is a heavily subsidized service grant to the middle classes (see UNICEF, 1999: 63; Birdsall, 1996).

As Figure 3 shows, countries with the highest proportion of spending on university education (measured as tertiary education spending per student as a percent of GNP per capita) tend to have the lowest primary completion rates. This suggests that the countries with the greatest need to improve primary education may be constrained by the disproportionate amount they spend on university services. Where this is the case, a country must sacrifice some spending on university services to improve primary coverage. In Latin America, however, beneficiaries of the university system tend to reject the shift in resources (Hunter and Brown, 2000).

Organized interest groups can also obstruct educational expansion. One well-known argument posits that organized groups pursue policies that divert resources to themselves, rather than the public good (Olson, 1965). For example, in developed countries, resistance may come from pensioners. Studies have found correlations between large elderly populations and lower education spending, in part because the elderly are well organized and participate politically to protect their benefits (e.g., Ladd and Murray, 2001; Poterba, 1997; Falch and Rattso, 1997).

This also applies directly to labor unions. McGuire (1999) finds a negative correlation between labor union strength and several human-development indices in East Asia and Latin America, including infant

Figure 3: University Spending versus Primary Completion Rates in Developing Countries, circa 2001

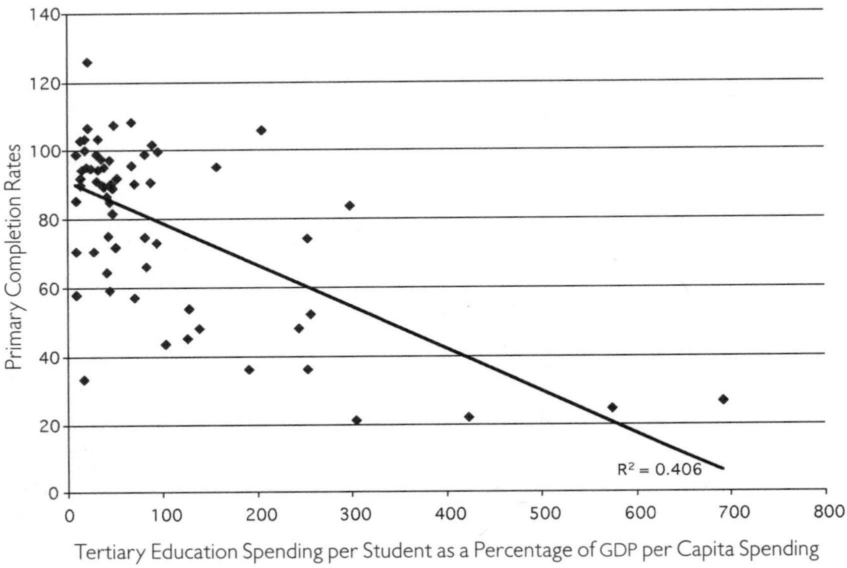

Tertiary Education Spending per Student as a Percentage of GDP per Capita Spending

Source: World Bank (Various Years).
Note: Values are for 2001 or the most recent prior year for which data are available.

survival and life expectancy. Unions, together with actors representing better-off urban groups, often induce governments to enact policies that favor the urban and formal sectors to the detriment of both the rural and urban poor. There is reason to believe that in some instances unions may have a similarly obstructive influence on educational expansion, shifting resources away from inputs that promote education (see Pritchett and Filmer, 1997).

The influence of unions probably depends on how much educational expansion a country has already achieved. Teachers' unions are crucial societal advocates of educational expansion in its early stages. More schools necessitate more teachers, which means stronger, larger unions. This is one reason that unions promote educational expansion, and maybe even better learning (see Zegarra and Ravina, 2003). However, in the latter stages, especially if economic conditions are threatening to unions (e.g., overall austerity, declining wages), their preference for educational expansion is often replaced by a preference for self-protective policies such as limiting spending to teacher wages, rejecting merit pay or teacher evaluations, and opposing changes designed to generate savings (IDB, 2005). The self-protective demands of teachers can lead to strikes, which can in turn block educational expansion, generate inefficiencies, and even hurt student performance (see Murillo et al., 2002).

Scholars have examined the conditions that determine whether teachers' unions become cooperative or obstructionist with reform efforts. An important and consistent finding, based mostly on Latin American cases, is that union cooperation is shaped by three factors: how threatening the context is to the teachers' union, especially salary levels and salary increases (see Umansky, 2005); the loyalty links between unions and parties (see Burgess, 1999); and the level of union professionalization (see Crouch, 2005).

Table 6 shows expected union response under four combinations of different economic contexts and loyalty links to political parties. When the economic context is favorable (e.g., teachers' salaries are increasing) and ties to the ruling political party are strong, unions act cooperatively, focusing mostly on obtaining salary demands (quadrant I). If ties to the ruling party are weak or hostile (quadrant III), state-union cooperation erodes, but not severely. The real problem occurs if the economic and policy contexts are threatening to unions (e.g., austerity measures, stagnated salary levels, or policies that mitigate the power of unions). Under such conditions, if the unions and the ruling party lack historical ties

Table 6: Economic and Policy Context, Links with Ruling Party, and Teachers' Union Response

		Economic Context or Policy Type	
		Non-threatening to Teachers' Unions	Threatening to Teachers' Unions
Links with Ruling Party	**Strong**	I. Cooperation, discussion will focus on wages	II. Conflict, unions may split
	Weak or Hostile	III. Less cooperation, more strikes	IV. Potential for severe political crisis, unions may unite against the state

(quadrant IV), the likely result is confrontation between the state and unions, possibly leading to a paralyzing political crisis in the education sector. If the unions and the ruling party have historical ties, the likely result is a split among labor, which will be divided on how much to negotiate or challenge the state (see Tiramonti, 2001).

Murillo (2001) focuses on the politics of quadrant II. In a threatening economic context (austerity and market reform) in which leading unions have strong ties with the ruling party, two additional variables shape union response: intra-union and inter-union partisan competition. If there is little internal competition for leadership positions, union leaders will be more cooperative. If competition is stiff, union leaders heighten their confrontation with the government.

Information

Generating societal demand for education—among both high-income and low-income groups—often requires public awareness of the effectiveness (or ineffectiveness) of the educational system. In its summary of many years of theoretical work in economics and political science, the World Bank's *World Development Report 2004* makes the compelling argument that both the quantity and quality of social services depend on the accountability relationship between clients (e.g., in the case of education, parents) and the providers (e.g., school administrators). Accountability requires information. Without clear data on the delivery, quality, and outcomes of educational services, it is difficult for users, administrators, and external observers to make fair evaluations, diagnoses, and prescriptions (Bloom, this volume). Users who lack information about educational choices may simply forgo petitioning for needed services or may make weak, unrealistic, or nonspecific demands that are unlikely to be heeded. Evidence suggests that when citizens are informed of the failings of a particular education system, they can compel politicians to pay attention to the education sector (Reimers and McGinn, 1997). In short, without information, demand for more or better education will falter.

One of the most astonishing ironies in the field of development is that education, the area of state activity most concerned with increasing knowledge among the young, is also an area where the state is frequently reluctant to provide information to adults. The UNDP (2003) found that trend data on information as basic as "net primary enrollment ratio" and "children reaching grade five" are lacking in 46 percent and 96 percent of countries, respectively—17 percent and 46 percent of countries, respectively, lack any data whatsoever.[16]

Information is needed on more than just inputs, such as enrollment and attendance (Bloom, this volume). Measuring outputs such as academic attainment is indispensable. A comparison of poor schools in Chile showed that schools with effective diagnostic tests and systematic monitoring of teacher and student performance achieved higher test scores (Raczysnki and Muñoz, 2004). Yet few developing countries offer these diagnostic tests, and even fewer participate in international testing programs or conduct adequate local testing. One region that has made significant progress in measuring student performance is Latin America; in the 1990s, most nations in this region developed specialized agencies to administer, analyze, and disseminate the results of student tests. Some of these agencies acquired a level of institutional strength sufficient to carry out these tasks, in terms of budgets, cadre of technical experts, and legal autonomy (see Ferrer, 2005). However, it seems that for the most part, these institutional efforts have not bolstered societal demand for more or better education. The reason could be that even in these cases, the data released to the public are still somewhat restricted, which makes it impossible for citizens to make use of available information.[17]

Ideological Competition

Educated elites can advocate for underserved populations, stimulating grassroots demand for education. This may occur as a result of the rise of certain ideologies. If Blyth (2003) is correct in arguing that ideas "change interests" and serve as "weapons in political struggles that help agents achieve their ends," then the acceptance of the education-for-all idea matters not so much because it changes the preferences of states, but because it empowers citizens to place greater demands on the state. Paulston (1977) summarizes a number of arguments that emphasize the importance of "cultural revitalization movements." These are movements

---

[16] These include developing countries, Central and Eastern European countries, and members of the Commonwealth of Independent States. A country is defined as having trend data if at least two data points are available—one between 1990 and 1995 and one between 1996 and 2001—and if the two points are at least three years apart.

[17] To the author's knowledge, only Chile provides data that is disaggregated enough (by school) to be useful to parents.

of well-to-do citizens who seek to develop a more "satisfying culture." The premise is that elite citizens become disillusioned with the societal status quo, in particular with inequities in the distribution of benefits, and feel that improvements are both possible and urgent.[18]

If this argument is correct, then one should expect to find that high levels of inequality in a particular society give rise to revitalization ideologies among elites, and thus increase political pressure for universal education. As elites become more outraged at inequality, their demands for attention to the problem increase. This might explain the surprising finding of Clemens (2004) that the more unequally education is distributed in a particular society, the faster the rate of educational expansion tends to be. It is also consistent with the claim of Kaufman and Stallings (1991) that in post-war Latin America the expansion of state spending tends to increase in highly unequal societies. Although this expansion occurs along populist lines and not according to efficiency or need, it is consistent with the finding that inequality compels the "haves" to do something, however flawed, for the "have-nots."

Electoral Politics

Competition for political office may also enhance societal pressures for more and better education. In a democracy, beneficiaries of education and other social services compete among themselves to control state institutions. This competition results in alliances across society, and can make education an electoral issue. Candidates may be forced to make promises on education, and maybe even to deliver on such promises. Jensen (2003) and Shefter (1994) show how electoral competition among U.S. political parties generated expansion of social rights (e.g., services for revolutionary war veterans in the early nineteenth century, and citizenship for immigrants in New York in the 1930s). In theory, then, strong competition for office can generate pressures for the expansion of social services, including education.

---

[18] This may explain why many radical anti-establishment movements often attract elites, including highly educated citizens, to their ranks and leadership positions. For a recent discussion of how contemporary terrorist organizations (the Hezbollah's militant wing and Palestinian suicide bombers) recruit from both advantaged and disadvantaged groups in terms of both income and education levels, see Krueger and Maleãková, 2003.

J. Nelson (2005) reports that, since the late 1990s, more than twenty studies have used cross-section and/or time-series statistical analysis to test the effect of democracy on social sector spending and performance. She finds that most of these studies show that democracy boosts spending on education. The best example of the democracy-favors-education argument may be that of Costa Rica. Unusual among developing countries, Costa Rica has been uninterruptedly democratic since 1949, with fairly competitive electoral politics, stable political parties, and almost negligible military spending. Despite its small size, relatively undiversified economy, modest income levels, and rural-urban inequality (see Muller and Seligson, 1987), Costa Rica achieved an impressive education record early on. By 1990, Costa Rica's literacy and primary enrollment rates were among the highest in the world (see Mesa-Lago, 2000). As of 2000, its literacy rates remained among the highest in Latin American countries and far above the average for countries in its income category (Table 7).

If democracy facilitates educational expansion, then the conditions for achieving universal education are stronger than ever, because the number of democracies is historically high. In 1974, there were fewer than 40 democratic countries in the world. In 2002, there were 121—three of every five countries.

Yet the spread of civil and political liberty has not led to across-the-board improvement in education (World Bank, 2003). Costa Rica, for example, does not have impressive secondary enrollment rates (Table 7). The role of democracy in educational expansion may be limited for two reasons. The first has to do with challenges pertaining to the task of ensuring quality. Improvements in quality usually require changes in the internal organization of education systems, which entail more "reallocating" resources than allocating new resources. However, democracies do not necessarily provide the electoral incentives to generate broad voter coalitions on behalf of reallocation (J. Nelson, 2005).

The second reason has to do with challenges pertaining to democracies, or what Keefer and Khemani (2003) call "political market imperfections." For example, from the point of view of elected officials, the marginal cost of expanding a social service to all citizens—rather than just to the majority needed to win office—may at some point surpass the marginal political benefit obtained by including potential voters. Championing services for the very poor might allow a politician to build a large political base, but to prevail he or she need only obtain the support of the

Table 7: Education Achievements in Costa Rica, Relative to Its Peers, 2000

GDP per capita (Constant 1995 US$)			Years Democratic Since 1940**	Illiteracy Rates (% of people ages 15 and above)			School enrollment, secondary (net enrollment rate)		
Rank*	Country	Value		Rank	Country	Value	Rank	Country	Value
1	Argentina	8173.84	20	1	Trin and Tob	1.71	1	Argentina	79.06
2	Uruguay	6419.96	46	2	Uruguay	2.44	2	Chile	74.52
3	Chile	5304.45	43	3	Argentina	3.17	3	Trin and Tob	72.16
4	Trin and Tob	5270.02	39***	4	Chile	4.24	4	Uruguay	69.93
	Upper-Middle	4888.00		**5**	**Costa Rica**	**4.44**	5	Brazil	69.23
5	Brazil	4626.34	15	6	Paraguay	6.73		Upper Middle	68.61
6	**Costa Rica**	**3911.17**	**51**	7	Venezuela, RB	7.46	6	Bolivia	67.34
7	Mexico	3810.04	3	8	Panama	8.13	7	Peru****	62.00
8	Panama	3483.67	6	9	Colombia	8.37	8	Panama	60.35
9	Venezuela, RB	3301.14	44	10	Ecuador	8.44	9	Mexico	58.22
10	Peru	2334.41	16		Upper-Middle	9.00	10	Colombia	56.54
11	Colombia	2288.99	16	11	Mexico	9.46	11	Venezuela, RB	55.32
12	Dom. Rep.	2053.59	18		Lower-Middle	10.00	**12**	**Costa Rica**	**49.49**
	Middle	1898.00			Middle	10.00	13	Ecuador	48.27
13	Paraguay	1773.14	0	12	Peru	10.15	14	Paraguay	46.79
14	Ecuador	1705.06	21	13	Brazil	13.63	15	Dom. Rep.	40.21
	Lower-Middle	1526.00		14	Bolivia	14.85		Middle	N/A
15	Bolivia	952.71	17	15	Dom. Rep.	16.34		Lower-Middle	N/A

Source: World Development Indicators. For the years democratic from 1940 to 1997, values are derived from Mainwaring (1999a). Mainwaring offers a strict definition of democracy, requiring four conditions: (1) the president and legislature must be chosen in open elections; (2) these authorities must have real governing power and not be over-shadowed by the military; (3) civil liberties must be respected; and (4) the franchise must include a sizable majority of adults. For the years from 1998 to 2000, the classification is based on the author's estimate using Mainwaring's criteria.

Notes: * Refers to GDP per capita ranking within the 15 countries in this table.

** Indicates the number of years country was free of dictatorship between 1930 and 2000.

*** Since year of independence, 1962.

**** Latest figure available is 1998.

majority of voters plus one (or fewer, if there are more than two contenders). It does not pay to spend money to obtain the support of all citizens when the support of a plurality or minimal majority will suffice. At some point, depending on electoral institutions, the extent to which political supporters champion the expansion of services will reach a ceiling (see Persson and Tabellini, 2002). Furthermore, the factors that bring a leader into office might be different from the factors that take him or her out of office. Voters might elect a candidate on the basis of promises to deliver education, but might not necessarily vote him or her out of office for failing to deliver. Much will depend on:

- the strength of monitoring institutions: if they are weak, politicians can hide poor performance;
- the overall performance of incumbents: if politicians have other accomplishments, citizens may accept low performance on education;
- the strength of party alignments: voters may place party loyalty before candidate performance;
- the quality and fragmentation of opponents: the opposition may not offer attractive candidates or programs;
- the themes selected by opinion-makers such as the media, commentators, and party leaders: if opinion-makers ignore the issue of education, voters may not know how to evaluate the government on this issue.

In short, democratic competition seems to facilitate the appearance of education on a political agenda by bringing the issue to light and generating promises from candidates, but is not a guarantee of educational expansion. Elections often do not provide strong sanctioning mechanisms against incumbents who falter on the delivery of education. Further research is needed to specify the particular institutional features of democracy that may promote expansion of social services.

FIVE POSSIBLE POLICIES

From the perspective of state officials, political incentives and pressures to promote universal basic and secondary education are weak. In summary, the most significant impediments to achieving universal primary and secondary schooling fall into five categories: 1) weak societal demand for education, 2) supply-side failures, 3) inefficient use of resources devoted to education, 4) opposition by those who bear the costs of reform, and

5) weak accountability mechanisms for improving the performance of education systems. Advocates of universalized education must continue to think about policies that can overcome these obstacles. Important lessons can be learned from countries that have succeeded in expanding education despite facing one or more of the obstacles above. For example, as argued above, some countries have expanded education to include even citizens who have not demanded it. Some have expanded even as incomes declined and civil society was threatened—i.e., the expansion of education under authoritarian regimes. Clearly, there are means to overcoming even the most substantial obstacles to expansion.

Some promising policy experiments in educational expansion are discussed below, with at least one primary example for each category of political problem. The list is not exhaustive, obviously, and none of the policies discussed is a panacea. Nevertheless, the examples offer reason to be optimistic that more can be done to overcome the political problems discussed in this chapter.

To Boost Demand, Lower the Costs of School Attendance

States can reduce the cost to families of sending children to school, thereby stimulating societal demand. When sending a child to school is expensive (i.e., students are responsible for textbooks, school supplies, school fees, transportation costs, or lunch fees), demand for education weakens, especially among the poorest populations.

In Kenya, the introduction in 1988 of a cost-sharing system, where families were required to contribute to the expense of their child's education, seems to have resulted in high dropout rates and declining enrollments (Bedi et al., 2004; Nafula, 2001). In contrast, Malawi quickly achieved universal primary education in the 1990s when the government eliminated school fees: gross enrollment rates jumped from 66 in 1990 to 135 in 1995 (Colclough and Al-Samarrai, 2000). In Brazil between 1994 and 1999, the proportion of 7–14 year-old children enrolled in school increased from 89 to 96 percent, and the number of illiterate citizens declined from 19.2 million in 1991 to 15.2 million by 1998. More so than other programs, subsidies to parents to send their children to school—and keep them there—led to these results. Brazil has nearly doubled its investment in school lunches since 1995 and has offered subsidies to low-income families that send their children to school (*bolsa escola*). Likewise, when Uganda eliminated primary school tuition fees for up to four children per family in 1996, the impact was "immediate and tremendous"; primary completion rates rose from approximately 40 percent to 65 percent by 2001 (Bruns et al., 2003: 45).

Furthermore, if poor households face formidable barriers to completion—e.g., if poor children have access to primary but not to secondary education, if they tend to have higher repetition rates in primary education, or if local school infrastructure is in shambles—parents (and students) may feel that the investment in primary education is pointless, as the child will not have the opportunity to advance (Levine et al., 2003; see also PROBE, 1999). Expanding access to secondary education, reducing repetition rates in primary levels (typically correlated with income level), and upgrading school infrastructure may help expand household demand for schooling in underserved areas. Finally, new research from Mexico and Brazil shows that providing "conditional cash transfers," in which parents receive a stipend in return for increasing their investment in the human capital of their children, can be an effective strategy for achieving two goals: alleviating poverty and stimulating poor household demand for secondary education (de Janvry and Sadoulet, 2005).

To Bolster the Supply Side (State Efforts), Improve State-Level Expertise and State-Society Links

Most education specialists identify "lack of political will" as a recurrent obstacle to educational expansion. Although "political will" is ubiquitous in the literature, the meaning of this term remains vague. It usually refers to situations in which the executive branch devotes insufficient political attention to education, has a low appetite for conflict (and thus change), or devotes attention to education for reasons unrelated to education such as patronage (see Corrales, 1999). To a certain extent, the argument that low levels of political will lead to stagnant educational services is a truism. The argument is nonetheless intuitive, if difficult to test for lack of a standard way to operationalize low levels of political will.

One way to study political will is to think of it in broader terms. "Will" can be defined as the supply-side strength of education reform, which is composed of various measurable factors. Some factors relate to state characteristics. For instance, high levels of ministerial turnover, intra-cabinet disagreement, failure to incorporate technocrats into the ministry, and weak ties between the ministry of education and multilateral organizations are all indicators of weak supply. As Crouch (2005) explains, positive values on each of these variables explain why Chile was able to introduce far-reaching educational reforms in the 1990s whereas Peru faltered.

State variables are not the only components of the supply side. Also important are state-society links. When reformers form strong political coalitions—especially with political parties—the supply side is enhanced. For instance, Jacoby (2000) shows that, despite prevailing demand for change, secondary education reform failed to take hold in Germany immediately following World War II because reformers did not establish links with political parties. In contrast, reforms took stronger (albeit not perfect) hold in eastern Germany after the 1989 collapse of the Berlin Wall precisely because reformers forged stronger ties with civil society. In a study of Latin American countries, Grindle (2004) shows that countries whose ministers spent considerable time building cross-sectoral alliances were able to push for educational change, even against strong political opponents. Corrales (2004a) shows that the strength of the supply side, defined in terms of state and state-society variables, explains variation in levels of reform in Latin American countries (significant in Central America, moderate in Argentina, insignificant in Peru) where administrations were equally committed to market and state reforms.

Bolstering the supply side of education reform—that is, the political will to reform—involves strengthening both state capacity *and* societal inclusion. Yet inclusion is costly, and not only in terms of time and resources. To include and accommodate a key societal actor, reformers may also need to sacrifice certain policy goals. Furthermore, insistence on societal inclusion can be lethal to a reform—some groups may remain resolutely opposed to change and use inclusion as a way to sabotage policy changes. The determination of an appropriate balance of compromises in policy and social inclusion is a challenge for both scholars and practitioners.

To Improve Efficiency, Generate More Performance Indicators

Traditionally, the role of the state has been to provide services and to mitigate societal inequities. It is also necessary to see the state in a new light—as the generator and disseminator of information. States in general fulfill this role only grudgingly or limitedly. In education, most statistics provided by the state relate to inputs (e.g., coverage and finance). International organizations deserve credit for pressuring states both to collect this information and to adhere to standard methods of measurement. Further work needs to be done in two areas. First, countries need to improve the quantity, accuracy, consistency, and reliability of the basic data on educational inputs that are already collected. Second, states need to collect and disseminate data on other aspects of the education system—indicators of student, teacher, and school performance.

Performance data can play a crucial political role in education reform. By bolstering the empirical foundations of their arguments, data strengthen the political position of reformers. Data can enable specialists to make more precise diagnoses of an education system's failings. Information on school performance can also help citizens to evaluate the validity of claims made by state officials, in turn enhancing the quality of local debates. Performance data are also indispensable for designing teacher incentives (Mizala and Romaguera, 2005), which in turn improve teacher effectiveness and student academic achievement (Vegas and Umansky, 2005).

More can be done to encourage states to generate school, teacher, and student performance information. This will require more testing, which can be difficult to institute, as well as dissemination of results, which is even harder to implement. Political resistance to the dissemination of education data is pervasive at all levels—within bureaucracies, teachers' unions, and schools. Leaders, administrators, and teachers fear that performance information will embarrass them and be used as ammunition to attack them. Because of this resistance, states need assistance from international actors to implement more testing. Newly emerging international nongovernmental organizations that hope to influence education policies could make increased testing a central lobbying issue.

To Contain Opposition, Compensate Threatened Actors

Although educational expansion increases spending, which produces more beneficiaries of government services, it may also involve direct costs to other beneficiaries. Policy-makers may want to consider ways to compensate those who bear the cost (Robinson, 1998) or whose benefits are reduced, in order to reduce opposition to change. In the 1990s, Chilean officials followed this approach by avoiding strict social-spending targets—i.e., they allowed low-middle-income groups, and not just the very poor, to continue to receive state assistance (Ruiz-Tagle, 2000). In doing so, they maintained both social peace and electoral victories.

Educational expansion can also create a cost for teachers if it entails a requirement that teachers increase their productivity. Increasing labor market flexibility and establishing merit pay inject efficiency and accountability into education systems; however, these changes penalize teachers directly, through the loss of benefits such as guaranteed employment and promotions. Some form of protection for teachers, or maybe even compensation, may be necessary to counteract teachers' union opposition.

One policy used to address this cost is to compensate unions with healthy salary increases.[19] This is a tricky issue because recent research by the World Bank, based on data from 47 low-income countries, shows that salary scales for teachers in primary education vary significantly, with some countries paying teachers too much and others paying too little (i.e., many deviate from what the World Bank deems an adequate level—namely, 3.3 percent of GDP) (Bruns et al., 2003). This variation in salary scales creates political complications. In countries where teacher salaries are low, the recommended policy is to raise wages; this gives rise to political difficulties with the ministry of finance and multilateral creditors interested in fiscal austerity. In countries where teachers are overpaid, salaries should not be increased, so as to avoid compounding inefficiencies; this decision infuriates teachers who, like most salaried workers, feel underpaid. Either way, adjusting salaries up or down is politically contentious.

Adjusting salaries is not the only complication. Deciding on the criteria for salary increases might also be of concern. Salary increases that occur independent of performance—the case for salary changes in many developing countries—lead to underperformance. Kremer et al. (2004) find that one in four teachers in India's public primary schools are absent on any given day, and they attribute this to lack of sanctioning mechanisms, poor monitoring, and decaying infrastructure (see also PROBE, 1999). Governments may find it hard to introduce sanctioning mechanisms for teachers, in part because unions will resist, but they could experiment with incentive schemes, infrastructure maintenance, and better accountability mechanisms to encourage improved teacher performance.

To Boost Accountability, Develop New Models of State-Society Cooperation

Given the economic constraints and political disincentives that obstruct universal education—especially during the latter stages of expansion—it is

---

[19] Studying the incidence of teachers' strikes in Argentine provinces, Murillo and Ronconi (2004) find that after "political alignment between the governor and the union," the most significant variable reducing strike activity is "real wage improvement" and "attendance bonuses." Crouch (2005), using evidence from Chile and Peru, argues that differences in salary improvement explain unions' acceptance or rejection of schemes to provide individual, merit-based bonuses for teachers.

unrealistic for the international community to expect states to meet this challenge on their own. The task is formidable, and no state is sufficiently competent or vice-free to achieve this goal without assistance. One of the most innovative developments of the post-war twentieth century was the rise of new international actors willing to assist states in the delivery of education (see Benavot and Resnik, this volume; Weiler, 1984). Although this innovation pushed education to new heights in many countries, it will not be enough to achieve universal education. States need further help.

The only other prospect for assistance is from civil society. Small efforts to incorporate more assistance from civil society have been attempted in the twentieth century, with what seem to be promising results. Although state-society partnerships are complicated and easily corrupted, they can have a positive impact on educational expansion.

One can imagine different combinations of state and societal inputs in an education system. For the sake of simplicity, I consider only two types of input—school management and education finance. Table 8 identifies three possible levels of state input and three possible levels of societal input. Cells A through I provide examples.

Education in secular states is typically conceived as relying on the state to move from cell A, where there is zero education provision, to cell C, where presumably the state meets all of society's educational needs.

Table 8: Different Combinations of State and Society Inputs (with examples of societies where these combinations are prevalent)

		State Involvement		
		Minimum	Medium	High
Society Involvement	**Minimum**	A. No educational provision	B. Minimal schooling (18th and 19th century Europe)	C. Statist Monopoly (Totalitarian Regimes)
	Low	D. Home schooling (poorest African countries; war-torn regions)	E. Modest coverage (less poor African countries)	F. Mostly state schools, with very few private schools (East Asia)
	High	G. Minimally subsidized private education (denominational schools in advanced democracies)	H. Mixed systems with heavily subsidized private education (urban Latin America)	I. Mixed systems with schools of many types; two-way accountability (both state and society actors more engaged in monitoring schools)

However, as argued, states in developing countries seldom have the resources and incentives to travel this far. Furthermore, it is not clear that an exclusively statist system is desirable, given all the problems that arise from excessive statism. Cell C is thus unrealistic and undesirable.

Cell G represents traditional thinking on private education. The state grants nongovernmental organizations the right to offer private education, perhaps with a subsidy. Management, financing, and ownership of the property are private. The main problem with private provision of education is that schools have little incentive to serve needy students.

In moving toward universalization, it makes sense to consider a model of state-society cooperation in which neither exclusive state provision nor exclusive private provision of education predominates. This would entail moving across the two axes by supplementing state efforts with societal efforts (moving from cell C to cells F and I) and by simultaneously supplementing private efforts with more state involvement (moving from cell G to cells H and I).

The benefits for universalization of supplementing state efforts with societal efforts are visible both in southern Africa and Latin America. African countries that nationalized primary education shortly after independence (e.g., Kenya, Tanzania, and Uganda) have made slower progress toward universalization than countries that encouraged supplementary private provision (e.g., Botswana, Lesotho, and Swaziland). The evidence is clearer in Latin America, where states provide most educational services but have allowed a parallel system of private education, which is frequently subsidized by the state (cell H). In 1996, primary and secondary enrollments in private schools in Latin America were 16.4 percent and 23.8 percent (Wolff, 2002: 16); these levels of enrollment save the state some money. Private schools help the state to meet education demand by finding ways to attract students, collect tuition from those who can pay, and save resources for the state by operating more efficiently than public systems (Navarro, 2002). However, as long as these schools remain tuition-driven, with their own particular admission standards, this model of state-society cooperation will not expand coverage universally.

Achieving universal education will require alternative forms of state-society cooperation. Educational systems need to be able to harness greater societal inputs—this is the promise of self-managed or community-managed schools.

"Harambee" groups in Kenya are one notable form of self-managed schools. Harambee groups are self-help communities of rural citizens. These groups mobilize resources, provide infrastructure, and manage schools. The number of Harambee schools grew from zero at the time of independence to 1,497 schools by 1987 (Oguyi, 1995: 127). Most of the expansion of primary and secondary education in Kenya since independence has occurred through the efforts of Harambee groups. Therkildsen and Semboja (1995) compare Kenya with Tanzania and Uganda. All three education systems were, at the time of independence, at similar stages of development. Of these, Kenya had produced the most impressive expansion of coverage by 1990 (Table 9). Tanzania relied exclusively on state-run schools, which allowed the government to make huge inroads, but not nearly to the extent that Kenya did. Tyranny-ridden and war-torn Uganda, which had neither state nor private education (cell E) hardly improved. Kenya's remarkable achievement is all the more surprising given that government spending on education remained stable, and at times declined.

Despite these accomplishments, the model provided by the Kenyan experience ought not be fully emulated. Harambee groups formed and took on educational responsibilities as a result of faltering state initiative. Even in good years, state finance was limited to teachers' salaries as well as some school supplies and milk for students. In other years, the state denied funding even to Harambee groups or tried to control them (Kanyinga, 1995). Harambee groups emerged as a society-based survival effort—in the absence of state help, rural communities organized to meet their educational needs. In this model, society has to finance most education, which is onerous for rural communities and, as most research shows, depresses school attendance. Furthermore, the quality of Harambee schools is inferior to that of government schools.

Table 9: Gross Enrollment Ratios in Primary Education, East Africa, 1960 and 1990

Country	1960	1990	Type of System
Kenya	47	93	Mixed (State and Harambee groups)
Tanzania	25	66	State Monopoly
Uganda	67	71	Low State and Society Inputs

Source: Based on Therkildsen and Semboja (1995).

Another model of state-society partnership is that of self-managed schools, which have emerged in El Salvador, Guatemala, Honduras, and Nicaragua (see Table 10), as well as parts of Brazil, Colombia, and Ecuador in the 1990s. Self-managed schools differ from traditional private schooling in that the state provides the entire operating budget for the school (therefore there is no tuition), and differ from traditional public schooling in that school administration is transferred entirely to local organizations typically composed of parents, teachers, and civilian administrators. These organizations are authorized to spend on infrastructure, and, more significant, to hire and fire teachers, as they see fit. In Nicaragua, these organizations also have authority over curricula. Data show that self-managed schools carry social and academic promise, but also some risks such as corruption and lack of accountability (see Corrales,

Table 10: Alternative Models of State-Society Provision of Education: Latin American Cases in the 1990s

	Public Traditional	**Subsidized** (Chile)	**Self-Managed** (El Salvador, Guatemala, Honduras)	**Self-Managed** (Nicaragua)	**Private Traditional**
Funding	Public (municipal)	Public (central government)	Public	Public (with capacity to raise private funding)	Mostly private (school fees)
Ownership of Establishment	State	Private	Public (in concession to an NGO)	Public	Private
Spending Autonomy (Infrastructure Maintenance)	No	Yes	Yes	Yes	Yes
Personnel Autonomy (Hire and Fire Teaching Staff)	No	Yes	Yes	Yes	Yes
Pedagogy Autonomy (Modify Curriculum and Select Textbooks)	No	Medium	No	Yes	Yes

Source: Based on di Gropello (2004).

2006; di Gropello, 2004; López, 2005). For this reason, this system will work best when the state has the capacity to monitor and sanction communities that mismanage funds, and local communities have strong mechanisms for holding school administrators accountable.

In short, universalization will require highly statist systems to find ways to make room for more societal inputs in the provision of education. Likewise, exclusively private systems must make room for greater state regulation, supervision, and resources. These reforms will give rise to new complications and political conflicts. The task is not to shy away from this, but to find preventive and corrective measures.

CONCLUSION: THE CAUSES AND TRADE-OFFS OF UNIVERSALIZATION

This chapter has argued that some of the incentives and pressures that push states to expand primary and secondary education are relatively weak or perverse in the last stages of educational expansion, particularly in developing countries. At the international level, capitalism exercises an ambiguous influence, or possibly a meager positive pressure; multilaterals do not have effective oversight or sanctioning mechanisms; and international consensus about the value of education does not always change domestic political institutions, especially at the last stages of educational expansion. At the state level, the political and economic conditions that drove states historically to promote education have weakened. Patronage remains one of the strongest incentives to expand education, but it is also at the root of poor quality and inefficiency. The two most important ingredients to boost societal demand—income levels and organization—are often lacking in developing countries and among those who are the last to receive education.

For these reasons, it is unrealistic to expect states—acting alone—to produce universal basic and secondary education. An exclusively state-driven effort to universalize education presents the opportunity for more political vices to enter education systems. International organizations and societal actors are necessary checks against these unwanted outcomes and can help states overcome the institutional obstacles that limit improvements in quality and efficiency.

There are many research questions that remain to be addressed. Cross-country variations in speed of expansion have been well known since the 1970s, but the extent of variations in efficiency is a more recent discovery (see Bruns et al., 2003). These variations in school systems remain largely unexplained. For scholars interested in explaining these variations, this chapter offers a word of caution against the tendency, typical among contemporary social scientists, to insist on identifying the "one key variable" that bests explains all characteristics of a system. Not one factor reviewed in this chapter seems, on its own, either sufficient or necessary to alter speeds of expansion or degrees of efficiency and quality.

Perhaps it is best to think about the intellectual task ahead in terms of what Ragin (2004) calls "multiple conjunctural causation." This is a situation in which the same outcome can emerge through "*different* combinations" of many explanatory variables, depending on the setting (emphasis in the original). For Ragin, multiple conjunctural causal arguments can even take contradictory forms. One example of this was suggested in the section "International Pressures": in relatively stable countries that have not yet approached the flatter part of the S-curve, the influence of the World Bank can be beneficial and significant; however, in less politically and economically stable countries at the latter stages of the S-curve, World Bank influence may be null or negative.

To reach conclusions about multiple conjunctural causation requires, of course, quantitative studies able to test models specifying interactions among variables. However, quantitative studies on cross-country variations in speed of expansion and degree of efficiency are likely to suffer from an unhealthy ratio of too few cases to too many independent variables. For that reason, qualitative studies, which excel at identifying the origins, trajectories, and alternatives within a set of comparable cases, are equally indispensable.

A second open question relates to the possible trade-off between educational expansion and educational quality. A narrow focus on increasing access may result in inattention to quality. Expanding education without worrying about what or whether students learn is tantamount to merely providing day care. Although keeping children in school is valuable, especially in developing countries where street life is precarious, we clearly must strive to provide children with more than day care. It is possible, moreover, that increasing the number of students in school could lead not just to the neglect of quality, but also to its detriment. For instance, governments may be tempted to overpopulate classrooms, to expand coverage through merit-blind hiring of teachers, or to carry out indiscriminate bidding on school infrastructure projects. Educational expansion may be financed by taking resources away from infrastructure maintenance. School facilities decay as a result, which leads to teacher absences (Kremer et al., 2004), less learning, and diminished parental demand for schooling (PROBE, 1999). Or, governments may finance expansion by resisting raises in teachers' salaries, which could produce more teachers' union strikes, which hurt both learning and political stability. There is a danger that universal education may lead, paradoxically, to more education of lesser quality. Research on how best to mitigate this trade-off is needed.

Finally, it is too easy to explain variation in educational attainment by attributing it to family background or the socioeconomic context of the school. In the 1970s and 1980s, research showed the influence of the quality of teaching materials, teacher motivation, and length of instruction, not just family background, on attainment (see Fuller and Heyneman, 1989; Simmons and Alexander, 1980). In the late 1990s, another variable was added to this list: information. Clearly, without adequate information about school performance, no stakeholder in the education system (principal, teacher, bureaucrat, parent, or student) can generate diagnoses about teaching practices that work and don't work. The route to better-educated students could very well be through better-educated adults.

References

Alesina, Alberto. 1997. "The Political Economy of High and Low Growth." In *Annual World Bank Conference on Development Economics 1997*, ed. Boris Pleskovic and Joseph E. Stiglitz. Washington, DC: The World Bank.

Alesina, Alberto, Edward Glaeser, and Bruce Sacerdote. 2001. "Why Doesn't the United States Have a European-Style Welfare State?" *Brookings Papers on Economic Activity* 2: 187–247.

Ashby, Jacqueline. 1985. "Equity and Discrimination Among Children: Schooling Decisions in Rural Nepal." *Comparative Education Review* 29 (2): 68–79.

Bahgat, Gawdat. 1998. "The Silent Revolution: Education and Instability in the Gulf Monarchies." *The Fletcher Forum of World Affairs* 22 (1): 103–112.

Bates, Robert. 1981. *Markets and States in Tropical Africa: The Political Basis of Agricultural Policies*. Berkeley, CA: The University of California Press.

Bedi, Arjun S., Paul K. Kimalu, Damiano Kulundu Mandab, and Nancy Nafula. 2004. "The Decline in Primary School Enrolment in Kenya." *Journal of African Economies* 13 (1): 1–43.

Birdsall, Nancy. 1996. "Public Spending on Higher Education in Developing Countries: Too Much or Too Little?" *Economics of Education Review* 15 (4).

Blyth, Mark. 2003. "Structures Do Not Come with an Instruction Sheet: Interests, Ideas, and Progress in Political Science." *Perspectives on Politics* 1 (4): 695–706.

Brown, David, and Wendy Hunter. 1999. "Democracy and Social Spending in Latin America, 1980–1992." *American Political Science Review* 93 (4): 779–790.

Bruns, Barbara, Alain Mingat, and Ramahatra Rakotomalala. 2003. *A Chance for Every Child: Achieving Universal Primary Education by 2015*. Washington, DC: The World Bank.

Buchanan, James M., and Gordon Tullock. 1962. *The Calculus of Consent: Logical Foundations of Constitutional Democracy*. Ann Arbor: University of Michigan Press.

Buchmann, Claudia, and Dan Brakewood. 2000. "Labor Structures and School Enrollments in Developing Societies: Thailand and Kenya Compared." *Comparative Education Review* 44 (2): 175–204.

Burgess, Katrina. 1999. "Loyalty Dilemmas and Market Reform: Party Union Alliances Under Stress in Mexico, Spain, and Venezuela." *World Politics* 52 (October): 105–134.

Cable, Vincent. 1995. "The Diminished Nation-State: A Study in the Loss of Economic Power." *Daedalus* 124 (2): 23–53.

Cameron, David. 1978. "The Expansion of the Public Economy: A Comparative Analysis." *American Political Science Review* 72: 1243–61.

Carnoy, Martin. 1980. "Can Education Alone Solve the Problem of Unemployment?" In *The Education Dilemma*, ed. John Simmons. Oxford: Pergamon Press.

———. 1995. "Structural Adjustment and the Changing Face of Education." *International Labour Review* 134 (6): 653–673.

Cheng, Yinghong, and Patrick Manning. 2003. "Revolution in Education: China and Cuba in Global Context, 1957–1976." *Journal of World History* 14 (3): 359–391.

Clemens, Michael A. 2004. "The Long Walk to School: International Education Goals in Historical Perspective." Working Paper No. 37 (March). Washington, DC: Center for Global Development.

Colclough, Christopher, and Samer Al-Samarrai. 2000. "Achieving Schooling for All: Budgetary Expenditures on Education in Sub-Saharan Africa and South Asia." *World Development* 28 (11): 1927–1944.

Coleman, James S. 1965. "Introduction: Education and Political Development." In *Education and Political Development*, ed. James S. Coleman. Princeton, NJ: Princeton University Press.

Corrales, Javier. 1999. "The Politics of Education Reform: Bolstering the Supply and Demand; Overcoming Institutional Blocks." *The Education Reform and Management Series*, Vol. 2, No. 1. Washington, DC: The World Bank.

———. 2004a. "The Conflict between Technocracy and Participation." Mimeo. Amherst College.

———. 2004b. "Multiple Preferences, Variable Strengths: The Politics of Education Reform in Argentina." In *Crucial Needs, Weak Incentives: The Politics of Health and Education Reform in Latin America*, ed. Robert R. Kaufman and Joan M. Nelson. Washington, DC and Baltimore, MD: The Woodrow Wilson Center Press and the Johns Hopkins University Press.

———. 2006. "Does Parental Participation in Schools Empower or Strain Civic Society? The Case of Community-Managed Schools in Central America." *Journal of Social Policy and Administration*. Forthcoming.

Craig, John. 1981. "The Expansion of Education." *Review of Research in Education* 9 (1): 151–213.

Crouch, Luis. 2005. "Political Economy, Incentives and Teachers' Unions." In *Incentives to Improve Teaching: Lessons from Latin America*, ed. Emiliana Vegas. Washington, DC: The World Bank.

de Moura Castro, Claudio. 2002. "The World Bank Policies: Dammed If You Do, Damned If You Don't." *Comparative Education* 38 (4): 387–399.

de Janvry, Alain, and Elisabeth Sadoulet. 2005. "Conditional Cash Transfer Programs for Child Human Capital Development: Lessons Derived from Experience in Mexico and Brazil." Washington, DC: World Bank Development Economics Research Group.

de Swaan, Abram. 2001. "Welfare State." In *The Oxford Companion to Politics of the World, Second Edition*, ed. Joel Krieger. New York: Oxford University Press.

di Gropello, Emanuela. 2004. "Education Decentralization and Accountability Relationships in Latin America." World Bank Policy Research Working Paper 3453 (November). Washington, DC: The World Bank.

Drèze, Jean, and Amartya Sen. 1995. *India: Economic Development and Social Opportunity*. Oxford and Delhi: Oxford University Press.

Domínguez, Jorge I., ed. 1997. *Technopols*. University Park: Penn State University Press.

Easterly, William. 2002. *The Elusive Quest for Growth*. Cambridge, MA: The MIT Press.

Edwards, Sebastian. 1995. *Crisis and Reform in Latin America*. New York: Oxford University Press.

Esping-Andersen, Gøsta. 1990. *The Three Worlds of Welfare Capitalism*. Princeton, NJ: Princeton University Press.

Falch, Torberg, and Jorn Rattso. 1997. "Political Economic Determinants of School Spending in Federal States: Theory and Time-series Evidence." *European Journal of Political Economy* 13 (2): 299–314.

Ferrer, Guillermo. 2005. "Estado de Situación de los Sistemas Nacionales de Evaluación de Logros de Aprendizaje en América Latina." PREAL Working Document. Washington, DC: PREAL.

Fiala, Robert, and Audri Gordon Lanford. 1987. "Educational Ideology and the World Educational Revolution, 1950–1970." *Comparative Education Review* 31 (3): 315–332.

Fuller, Bruce, and Stephen P. Heyneman. 1989. "Third World School Quality: Current Collapse, Future Potential." *Educational Researcher* 18 (2): 12–19.

Fuller, Bruce, and Richard Rubinson. 1992. "Does the State Expand Schooling? Review of the Evidence." In *The Political Construction of Education: The State, School Expansion, and Economic Change*, ed. Bruce Fuller and Richard Rubinson. New York: Praeger.

Garrett, G. 1999. "Globalization and Government Spending around the World." Paper presented at the annual meeting of the American Political Science Association, Atlanta, Georgia (September).

Geddes, Barbara. 1996. *Politician's Dilemma: Building State Capacity in Latin America*. Berkeley: University of California Press.

———. 1999. "Institutional Sources of Corruption in Brazil." In *Corruption and Political Reform in Brazil: The Impact of Collor's Impeachment*, ed. Keith S. Rosenn and Richard Downes. Coral Gables, FL: North-South Center at the University of Miami.

Geo-Jaya, Macleans A., and Garth Mangum. 2001. "Structural Adjustment as an Inadvertent Enemy of Human Development in Africa." *Journal of Black Studies* 32 (1): 30–49.

Ginsburg, Mark B, Susan Cooper, Raejeshwari Raghu, and Hugo Zegarra. 1990. "National and World-System Explanations of Educational Reform." *Comparative Education Review* 34 (4): 474–499.

Goldstein, Judith, and Robert Keohane. 1993. *Ideas and Foreign Policy: Beliefs, Institutions and Political Change*. Ithaca, NY: Cornell University Press.

Gradstein, Mark. 2003. "The Political Economy of Public Spending on Education, Inequality and Growth." World Bank Policy Research Working Paper 3162. Washington, DC: The World Bank.

Graham, Edward. 2000. *Fighting the Wrong Enemy: Antiglobal Activists and Multinational Enterprises*. Washington, DC: Institute for International Economics.

Gray, John. 1998. *False Dawn: The Delusions of Global Capitalism*. London: Granta.

Graziano, Luigi. 1975. "A Conceptual Framework for the Study of Clientelism." Western Society Program Occasional Paper, No. 2. Ithaca, NY: Center for International Studies, Cornell University.

Grindle, Merilee. 1996. *Challenging the State*. Cambridge: Cambridge University Press.

———. 2004. *Despite the Odds: The Contentious Politics of Education Reform*. Princeton, NJ: Princeton University Press.

Gupta, Sanjeev, Hamid Davoodi, and Erwin Tiongson. 2001. "Corruption and the Provision of Health Care and Education Services." In *The Political Economy of Corruption*, ed. Arvind K. Jain. London and New York: Routledge.

Haas, Peter. 1992. "Introduction: Epistemic Community and International Policy Coordination." *International Organization* 46 (1): 1–35.

Hall, Peter A. 1989. *The Political Power of Economic Ideas: Keynesianism Across Nations*. Princeton, NJ: Princeton University Press.

Hanushek, Eric A. 1995. "Interpreting Recent Research on Schooling in Developing Countries." *The World Bank Research Observer* 10 (2): 227–46.

Hanushek, Eric A., and Javier A. Luque. 2003. "Efficiency and Equity in Schools Around the World." *Economics of Education Review* 22: 481–502.

Heyneman, Stephen P. 1980. "Differences Between Developed and Developing Countries: Comment on Simmons and Alexander's Determinants of School Achievement." *Economic Development and Cultural Change* 28 (2) (January): 403–406.

Heyneman, Stephen P., and William Loxley. 1983. "The Effect of Primary School Quality on Academic Achievement Across Twenty-Nine High- and Low-Income Countries." *American Journal of Sociology* 88 (6) (May): 1162–1194.

Huber, Evelyne, Thomas Mustillo, and John D. Stephens. 2004. "Determinants of Social Spending in Latin America." Paper Presented at the International Meeting of the Latin American Studies Association, October. Las Vegas, NV.

Hunter, Wendy, and David Brown. 2000. World Bank Directives, Domestic Interests, and the Politics of Human Capital Investment in Latin America." *Comparative Political Studies* 33 (1): 113–141.

Inter-American Development Bank (IDB). 2005. *The Politics of Policies. Economic and Social Progress in Latin America, 2006 Report*. Washington, DC: IDB.

Jacoby, Wade. 2000. *Imitation and Politics: Redesigning Modern Germany*. Ithaca, NY: Cornell University Press.

James, Estelle. 1993. "Why Do Different Countries Choose a Different Public-Private Mix of Educational Services?" *The Journal of Human Resources* 28: 571–592.

Jeffrey, Robin. 1992. *Politics, Women and Well-Being: How Kerala Became a 'Model.'* New Delhi: Oxford University Press.

Jensen, Laura. 2003. *Patriots, Settlers, and the Origins of American Social Policy.* Cambridge: Cambridge University Press.

Jiménez, E., and Lockheed, M. E. 1995. "Public and Private Secondary Education in Developing Countries: A Comparative Study." World Bank Discussion Paper 309. Washington, DC: The World Bank.

Kanyinga, Karuti. 1995. "The Politics of Development Space in Kenya." In *Service Provision under Stress in East Africa: the State, NGOs and People's Organizations in Kenya, Tanzania and Uganda*, ed. Joseph Semboja and Ole Therkildsen. Copenhagen: Centre for Development Research.

Kaufman, Robert, and Joan Nelson, ed. 2004. *Crucial Needs, Weak Incentives: The Politics of Health and Education Reform in Latin America.* Baltimore, MD: Johns Hopkins University Press.

Kaufman, Robert, and Alex Segura-Ubiergo. 2001. "Globalization, Domestic Politics, and Welfare Spending in Latin America: A Time-Series Cross-Section Analysis: 1973–1997." *World Politics* 53 (4): 553–587.

Kaufman, Robert, and Barbara Stallings. 1991. "The Political Economy of Latin American Populism." In *The Macroeconomics of Populism in Latin America*, ed. Rudiger Dornbusch and Sebastian Edwards. Chicago: The University of Chicago Press.

Keefer, Philip, and Stuti Khemani. 2003. "The Political Economy of Public Expenditures." Background paper for *The World Development Report 2004: Making Services Work for Poor People*. Washington, DC: The World Bank.

Keohane, Robert O., and Joseph S. Nye. 1989. *Power and Interdependence*, second edition. Glenview, IL: Harper Collins Publishers.

Knight, Jack. 1992. *Institutions and Social Conflict.* New York: Cambridge University Press.

Kohli, Atul. 2002. "State, Society, and Development." In *Political Science: State of the Discipline*, ed. Ira Katznelson and Helen V. Milner. New York: W. W. Norton and Company.

Kremer, Michael R. 1995. "Research on Schooling: What We Know and What We Don't; A Comment on Hanushek." *The World Bank Research Observer* 10 (2): 247–254.

Kremer, Michael, Nazmul Chaudhury, F. Halsey Rogers, Karthik Muralidharan, and Jeffrey Hammer. 2004. "Teacher Absence in India." Mimeo.

Krueger, Alan B., and Jitka Maleāková. 2003. "Education, Poverty and Terrorism: Is There a Causal Connection?" *Journal of Economic Perspectives* 17 (4): 119–144.

Krueger, Anne. 1974. "The Political Economy of the Rent-Seeking Society." *American Economic Review* 64 (3): 291–303.

Ladd, Helen, and Sheila Murray. 2001. "Intergenerational Conflict Reconsidered: Country Demographic Structure and the Demand for Public Education." *Economics of Education Review* 20: 343–357.

LeVine, Robert A., Sarah E. LeVine, and Beatrice Schnell. 2001. "'Improve the Women': Mass Schooling, Female Literacy, and Worldwide Social Change." *Harvard Educational Review* (Spring): 1–50.

Levine, Ruth, Nancy Birdsall, Amina Ibrahim and Prarthna Dayal. 2003. "Background Paper of the Task Force on Education and Gender Equality: Achieving Universal Primary Education by 2015." Washington, DC: Center for Global Development.

Linz, Juan J., and Alfred Stepan. 1996. *Problems of Democratic Transition and Consolidation*. Baltimore, MD: The Johns Hopkins University Press.

López, Margarita. 2005. "Una Revisión a la Participación Escolar en América Latina." Document prepared for the Task Force on Education Decentralization and School Autonomy (August). Washington, DC: PREAL.

Lott, John R., Jr. 1999. "Public Schooling, Indoctrination, and Totalitarianism." *Journal of Political Economy* 107 (6): 127–157.

Madrid, Raúl L. 2005. "Ideas, Economic Pressures and Pension Privatizations." *Latin American Politics and Society* 47 (2): 23–50.

Mainwaring, Scott P. 1999a. "Democratic Survivability in Latin America." In *Democracy and its Limits: Lessons from Asia, Latin America, and the Middle East*, ed. Hard Handelman and Mark Tessler. Notre Dame: University of Notre Dame Press.

———. 1999b. *Rethinking Party Systems in the Third Wave of Democratization: The Case of Brazil*. Stanford, CA: Stanford University Press.

Makau, B.M. 1995. "Dynamics of Partnership in the Provision of General Education in Kenya." In *Service Provision under Stress in East Africa: the State, NGOs and People's Organizations in Kenya, Tanzania and Uganda*, ed. Semboya and Therkildsen. Copenhagen: Centre for Development Research.

Marques, José, and Ian Bannon. 2003. "Central America: Education Reform in a Post-Conflict Setting, Opportunities and Challenges." Social Development Department Paper No. 4 (April). Washington, DC: The World Bank.

Marshall, T. H. 1964. "Citizenship and Social Class." In *Class, Citizenship and Social Development*, ed. T. H. Marshall. New York: Doubleday and Co.

Mauro, Paolo. 1996. "The Effects of Corruption on Growth, Investment and Government Expenditure." International Monetary Fund (IMF) Working Paper. Washington, DC: IMF.

McCubbins, M., R. Noll, and Barry Weingast. 1987. "Administrative Procedures as Instruments of Political Control." *Journal of Law, Economics and Organization* 3: 243–77.

McGuire, James W. 1999. "Labor Union Strength and Human Development in East Asia and Latin America." *Studies in Comparative International Development* 33 (4): 3–34.

Merritt, Richard, and Fred Coombs. 1977. "Politics and Educational Reform." *Comparative Education Review* 21 (2/3): 247–273.

Mesa-Lago, Carmelo. 2000. *Market, Socialist, and Mixed Economies: Comparative Policy and Performance: Chile, Cuba and Costa Rica.* Baltimore: Johns Hopkins University Press.

Meyer, John W., Francisco O. Ramirez, Richard Rubinson, and John Boli-Bennett. 1977. "The World Educational Revolution, 1950–1970." *Sociology of Education* 50 (4): 242–258.

Mingat, Alain and Jee-Peng Tan. 2003. "On the Mechanics of Progress in Primary Education." *Economics of Education Review* 22: 455–467.

Mizala, Alejandra, and Pilar Romaguera. 2005. "Rendimiento Escolar y Premios por Desempeño: La Experiencia Latinoamericana y el SNED en Chile." In *Uso e Impacto de la Información Educativa en América Latina,* ed. Santiago Cueto. Santiago, Chile: PREAL.

Moran, Theodore. 2002. *Beyond Sweatshops: Foreign Direct Investment and Globalization in Developing Countries.* Washington, DC: Brookings Institution.

Muller, Edward, and Mitchell A. Seligson. 1987. "Inequality and Insurgency." *American Political Science Review* 81 (2): 425–450.

Munishi, Gaspar K. 1995. "Social Services Provision in Tanzania." In *Service Provision under Stress in East Africa: the State, NGOs and People's Organizations in Kenya, Tanzania and Uganda,* ed. Joseph Semboja and Ole Therkildsen. Copenhagen: Centre for Development Research.

Murillo, María Victoria. 2001. *Labor Unions, Partisan Coalitions, and Market Reforms in Latin America.* New York: Cambridge University Press.

Murillo, María Victoria, and Lucas Ronconi. 2004. "Teachers' Strikes in Argentina: Partisan Alignments and Public-sector Labor Relations." *Studies in Comparative International Development* 39 (1): 77–98.

Murillo, María Victoria, Mariano Tommasi, Lucas Ronconi, and J. Sanguinetti. 2002. "The Economic Effects of Unions in Latin America: Teacher's Union and Education in Argentina." Document 56. Washington, DC: Inter-American Development Bank.

Nafula, Nancy. 2001. "Achieving Sustainable Universal Primary Education Through Debt Relief: The Case of Kenya." Paper prepared for Conference on Debt Relief and Poverty Reduction, World Institute for Development Economics Research, Helsinki, Finland, August 17–18.

Navarro, Juan Carlos. 2002. "Resumen y Conclusiones. La Pregunta Original y la Perspective del Análisis." In *Educación Privada y Política Pública en América Latina*, ed. Laurence Wolff, Pablo González, and Juan Carlos Navarro. Washington, DC: PREAL/Inter-American Dialogue.

Nelson, Joan M. 1999. "Reforming Health and Education: The World Bank, the IDB, and Complex Institutional Change." Policy Essay No. 26. Washington, DC: Overseas Development Council.

———. 2005. "Democracy, Social Service Expansion and Institutional Reforms." Mimeo. Woodrow Wilson Center, Washington DC.

Nelson, Roy C. 2005. "Harnessing Globalization: The Promotion of Nontraditional Foreign Direct Investment in Latin America." Mimeo. Thunderbird School of Management, Glendale, AZ.

Oguyi, Walter. 1995. "Service Provision in Rural Kenya: Who Benefits?" In *Service Provision under Stress in East Africa: the State, NGOs and People's Organizations in Kenya, Tanzania and Uganda*, ed. Joseph Semboja and Ole Therkildsen. Copenhagen: Centre for Development Research.

Olson, Mancur. 1965. *The Logic of Collective Action*. Cambridge, MA: Harvard University Press.

Organisation for Economic Co-operation and Development (OECD). 2002. *Education at a Glance 2002*. Paris: OECD.

Parrado, Emilio A. 1998. "Expansion of Schooling, Economic Growth, and Regional Inequalities in Argentina." *Comparative Education Review* 42 (3): 338–364.

Pasquino, Gianfranco. 1996. "Patronage." In *The Social Science Encyclopedia*, 2nd ed., ed. Adam Kuper and Jessica Kuper. New York, NY: Routledge.

Paulston, Rolland. 1977. "Social and Educational Change: Conceptual Frameworks." *Comparative Education Review* 21: 370–395.

Perlez, Jane. 2003. "Enlisting Aid to Education In the War on Terror." *New York Times*, October 12.

Plank, David. 1990. "The Politics of Basic Education Reform in Brazil." *Comparative Education Review* 34 (4): 538–559.

Persson, Torsten, and Guido Tabellini. 2002. "Do Political Institutions Shape Economic Policy?" *Econometrica* 70: 883–905.

Platt, William J. 1965. "Conflicts in Education Planning." In *Education and Political Development*, ed. James S. Coleman. Princeton, NJ: Princeton University Press.

Poterba, J. M. 1997. "Demographic Structure and the Political Economy of Public Education." *Journal of Policy Analysis and Management* 16: 48–66.

Pritchett, Lant, and D. Filmer. 1997. "What Education Production Functions Really Show: A Positive Theory of Education Spending." Policy Research Working Paper 1795. Washington, DC: The World Bank.

Pritchett, Lant. 2003. "When Will They Ever Learn? Why All Governments Produce Schooling." BREAD Working Paper No. 031. Cambridge, MA.

PROBE Team, with the Centre for Development Economics. 1999. *Public Report on Basic Education in India*. New Delhi: Oxford University Press.

Przeworski, Adam, Michael E. Alvarez, José Antonio Cheibub, and Fernando Limongi. 2000. *Democracy and Development: Political Institutions and Well-Being in the World, 1950–1990*. New York: Cambridge University Press.

Psacharopoulos, George, and Harry Anthony Patrinos. 2004. "Returns to Investment in Education: A Further Update." *Education Economics* 12 (2): 111–134.

Raczynski, Dagmar, and Gonzalo Muñoz 2004. "Factores que Desafian los Buenos Resultados Educativos en las Escuelas en Sectores de Pobreza." Santiago, Chile: PREAL/Fondo de Investigaciones Educativas.

Ragin, Charles C. 2004. "Turning the Tables: How Case-Oriented Research Challenges Variable-Oriented Research." In *Rethinking Social Inquiry: Diverse Tools, Shared Standards*, ed. Henry E. Brady and David Collier. Lanham, MD: Rowman and Littlefield Publishers, Inc.

Ramachandran, V. K. 2000. "Human Development Achievements in an Indian State: A Case Study of Kerala." In *Social Development and Public Policy: A Study of Some Successful Experiences*, ed. Dharam Ghai. New York and Geneva, Switzerland: St. Martin's Press and UNRISD.

Reimers, Fernando, and Noel McGinn. 1997. *Informed Dialogue: Using Research to Shape Education Policy Around the World*. Westport, CT: Praeger Press.

Reno, William. 2000. "Clandestine Economies, Violence and States in Africa." *Journal of International Affairs* 53 (2): 433–459.

Robinson, James A. 1998. "Theories of 'Bad Policies.'" *The Journal of Policy Reform* 2 (1): 1–46.

Rodrik, Dani. 1997. *Has Globalization Gone Too Far?* Washington, DC: Institute for International Economics.

Rose-Ackerman, Susan. 1998. "Corruption and Development." In *Annual World Bank Conference on Development Economics 1997*, ed. Boris Pleskovic and Joseph E. Stiglitz. Washington, DC: The World Bank.

Ruiz-Tagle, Jaime. 2000. "Balancing Targeted and Universal Social Policies: The Chilean Experience." In *Social Development and Public Policy: A Study of Some Successful Experiences*, ed. Dharam Ghai. New York and Geneva, Switzerland: St. Martin's Press and UNRISD.

Ruud, Arild Engelsen. 1999. "Embedded Bengal: The Case for Politics." *Forum for Development Studies* 2: 235–259.

Schultz, T. Paul. 1996. "Accounting for Public Expenditures on Education: An International Panel Study." In *Research in Population Economics*, Vol. 8. Greenwich, CT: JAI Press.

Scott, James. 1972. "Patron-Client Politics and Political Change in Southeast Asia." *American Political Science Review* 66 (1): 91–113.

———. 1998. *Seeing Like a State: How Certain Schemes to Improve the Human Condition Have Failed*. New Haven, CT: Yale University Press.

Shefter, Martin. 1994. *Political Parties and the State*. Princeton, NJ: Princeton University Press.

Simmons, Beth. 2001. "The International Politics of Harmonization: The Case of Capital Market Regulation." *International Organization* 55 (Autumn): 589–620.

Simmons, John. 1980. "Policy Issues in the 1980s." In *The Education Dilemma*, ed. John Simmons. Oxford: Pergamon Press.

Simmons, John, and Leigh Alexander. 1980. "Factors Which Promote School Achievement in Developing Countries: A Review of Research. In *The Education Dilemma*, ed. John Simmons. Oxford: Pergamon Press.

Skocpol, Theda. 1992. *Protecting Soldiers and Mothers: The Political Origins of Social Policy in the United States*. Cambridge, MA: Harvard University Press.

Skowronek, Stephen.1982. *Building a New American State.* New York: Cambridge University Press.

Slaughter, Anne-Marie. 2004. *A New World Order.* Princeton, NJ: Princeton University Press.

Stallings, Barbara, and Wilson Peres. 2000. *Growth, Employment, and Equity: The Impact of the Economic Reforms in Latin America and the Caribbean.* Washington DC: Brookings Institution Press.

Stiglitz, Joseph. 1996. "Some Lessons from the East Asian Miracle." *World Bank Research Observer* 11 (2): 151–177.

Stokes, Susan. 2000. "Rethinking Clientelism." Paper presented at the International Congress of the Latin American Studies Association, March.

Sutton, Francis X. 1965. "Education and the Making of Modern Nations." In *Education and Political Development*, ed. James S. Coleman. Princeton, NJ: Princeton University Press.

Swank, Duane H. 2002. *Global Capital, Political Institutions, and Policy Change in Developed Welfare States.* New York: Cambridge University Press.

Tendler, Judith. 2002. "The Fear of Education." Background paper presented at the Fiftieth Anniversary of the Bank of the Northeast and at the Brazilian Development Bank (BNDES), Rio de Janeiro, July.

Therkildsen, Ole and Joseph Semboja. 1995. "A New Look at Service Provision in East Africa." In *Service Provision Under Stress in East Africa: the State, NGOs and People's Organizations in Kenya, Tanzania and Uganda*, ed. Joseph Semboya and Ole Therkildsen. Copenhagen: Centre for Development Research.

Tilly, Charles. 1985. "War-Making and State-Making as Organized Crime." In *Bringing the State Back In*, ed. Peter B. Evans, Dietrich Rueschmeyer, and Theda Skocpol. Cambridge: Cambridge University Press.

———. 1992. *Coercion, Capital, and European States, AD 990–1992.* Cambridge, MA: Blackwell Publishers.

———. 1995. "Globalization Threatens Labor's Rights." *International Labor and Working-Class History* 47 (Spring): 1–23.

Tiramonti, Guillermina. 2001. "Sindicalismo Docente y Reforma Educativa en la América Latina de los '90." In *Sindicalismo Docente y Reforma en América Latina*, ed. Guillermina Tiramonti and Daniel Filmus. Buenos Aires: FLACSO.

Tuman, John P., and Craig F. Emmert. 2004. "The Political Economy of U.S. Foreign Direct Investment in Latin America: A Reappraisal." *Latin American Research Review* 39 (3): 9–28.

Umansky, Ilana. 2005. "A Literature Review of Teacher Quality and Incentives: Theory and Evidence." In *Incentives to Improve Teaching: Lessons from Latin America*, ed. Emiliana Vegas. Washington, DC: The World Bank.

United Nations Children's Fund (UNICEF). 1999. *The State of the World's Children*. UNICEF.

United Nations Development Programme (UNDP). 2003. *Human Development Report. Millennium Development Goals: A Compact Among Nations to End Human Poverty*. New York: Oxford University Press.

Van de Walle, Dominique, and Kimberly Nead. 1995. *Public Spending and the Poor: Theory and Evidence*. Washington, DC and Baltimore, MD: The World Bank and the Johns Hopkins University Press.

Vegas, Emiliana, and Ilana Umansky. 2005. *Improving Teaching and Learning Through Effective Incentives: What We Can Learn from Education Reforms in Latin America*. Washington, DC: The World Bank.

Vreeland, James Raymond. 2003. *The IMF and Economic Development*. New York: Cambridge University Press.

Waldner, David. 2003. "On the Non-Institutional Origins of the Institutional Foundations of Capitalism." Mimeo. University of Virginia, Department of Politics, Charlottesville, VA.

Walt, Stephen M. 2000. "Fads, Fevers, and Firestorms." *Foreign Policy* (November/December): 34–42.

Weiler, Hans N. 1984. "The Political Economy of Education and Development." *Prospects* 14 (4): 467–477.

Weiner, Myron. 1991. *The Child and the State in India: Child Labor and Education Policy in Comparative Perspective*. Princeton, NJ: Princeton University Press.

Weyland, Kurt. 2005. "Theories of Policy Diffusion: Lessons from Latin American Pension Reform." *World Politics* 57 (2): 262–295.

Wils, Annababette, and Anne Goujon. 1998. "Diffusion of Education in Six World Regions: 1960–1980." *Population and Development Review* 24 (2): 357–368.

Wolff, Laurence. 2002. "Introducción." In *Educación Privada y Política Pública en América Latina*, ed. Laurence Wolff, Pablo González, and Juan Carlos Navarro. Santiago, Chile: PREAL/Inter-American Development Bank.

World Bank. 1980. *World Development Report*. Washington, DC: The World Bank.

————. 1993. *The East Asian Miracle: Economic Growth and Public Policy.* New York: Oxford University Press.

————. 1999. "Educational Change in Latin America and the Caribbean." Washington, DC: The World Bank.

————. 2001. *World Development Report 2002: Building Institutions for Markets.* Washington, DC: The World Bank.

————. 2002. *Globalization, Growth and Poverty: Building and Inclusive World Economy.* Washington, DC: The World Bank.

————. 2003. *World Development Report 2004: Making Services Work for Poor People.* Washington, DC: The World Bank.

————. Various Years. *World Development Indicators.* Washington, DC: World Bank.

Zegarra, E., and R. Ravina. 2003. "Teacher Unionization and the Quality of Education in Peru: An Empirical Evaluation Using Survey Data." Research Network Working Paper R-474. Washington, DC: Inter-American Development Bank.

Section III: Improving Education

CHAPTER 4

Using Assessment to Improve Education in Developing Nations

HENRY BRAUN AND ANIL KANJEE

This chapter provides a framework for conceptualizing the various roles assessment plays in education, as well as an overview of educational assessment in the developing world. It undertakes an analysis of some assessment-related issues that arise when planning to expand dramatically educational access and quality. In particular, it suggests how assessment practices and systems can generate relevant and timely information for the improvement of education systems, presents case studies of a number of nations, describes some international efforts, and proposes next steps.

The issues raised in this chapter are especially relevant to the EFA initiatives; in particular, Goal 6 of the Dakar Framework (UNESCO, 2000a: 17) calls for "improving all aspects of the quality of education, and ensuring their excellence so that recognized and measurable learning outcomes are achieved by all, especially in literacy, numeracy and essential life skills." The Dakar Framework also suggests various approaches countries may adopt to attain the goals outlined and proposes that countries "systematically monitor progress towards EFA goals and strategies at the national, regional and international levels" (UNESCO, 2000a: 21).

Our intention in this chapter is not simply to describe how assessment-related initiatives can be extended to the secondary-education sector, but to offer a comprehensive analysis of the roles assessment can—and could —play in educational improvement. This effort is undertaken with humility: most of the sensible things that can be said have been said; nevertheless, many of the sensible things that can be done, have not been done—at least not on a large scale.

The education landscape in many, if not most, developing countries is characterized by a number of patterns:

- There exist substantial disparities in the distribution of opportunity to learn and in achievement. These disparities are associated with factors such as geographic location, race/ethnicity, language, social class, and gender, among others.
- In a particular region (e.g., Latin America or Sub-Saharan Africa), disparities within a country are usually much greater than average differences among countries.[1]
- In general, achievement levels are low, both with respect to a country's own standards and in comparison to the norms established by developed nations.
- There are many impediments to progress, including limited facilities and resources, insufficient capacity, inefficient allocation of available resources, and wastage due to high rates of grade repetition and attrition.

The solutions to these problems are varied and extremely complex, and certainly cannot be addressed only, or even chiefly, through assessment. However, assessment policy and practices are critical to any successful educational improvement strategy; assessment data are essential to teaching and learning and are needed to monitor, evaluate, and improve the education system. Although some assessments serve learners, teachers, parents, and policymakers by providing them with useful information, others focus educational efforts by virtue of the consequences that are attached to learner performance. This dual role leads to the paradox of "high-stakes" assessment as an instrument of change. In the absence of serious consequences, it is difficult for assessment to exert much influence on an education system; however, if performance on an assessment entails serious consequences, it can lead to activities that are educationally unproductive and may actually undermine the integrity of the system.

This paradox is at the heart of the controversy over assessment in educational circles. To some, assessment is a fair and objective way to set and maintain standards, to spearhead reform at the levels of both policy and practice, and to establish a basis for meaningful accountability. To others, it is an instrument for maintaining the status quo, grossly unfair and educationally unproductive. There are of course more balanced positions, such as those of Little (1990) and Noah and Eckstein (1992b). Whatever their position, most observers would agree that assessment is neither an

---

[1] Similar patterns of disparity are also common among developed countries, especially as they relate to language and race.

end in itself nor a panacea for the ills of education. They would likely also accept the proposition that major improvements in assessment systems must be part of a broader educational reform agenda that will be driven by—and constrained by—political, economic, and social considerations (Govinda, 1998; Little, 1992).

The importance of assessment for policy stems, in part, from the widespread recognition that educational indicator systems must include not only inputs but also outputs. A "results agenda" has become increasingly prominent in the planning of international donor agencies (Lockheed, private communication, May 21, 2004). This is complicated, however, by the fact that the assessment data used for policy may be incomplete, of poor quality, or even unreliable or invalid. Furthermore, lack of appropriate sensitivity to contextual issues can make data interpretation and subsequent action problematic. For example, in some regions of a country it may be common for large proportions of learners sitting for an examination to participate in "out-of-school tuition" (N. Postlethwaite, private communication, 15 October 2002) or shadow education (Baker et al., 2002). These practices may raise test scores, but they also distort inferences about the comparative effectiveness of different schools or different regions.

The increased salience of assessment to policy naturally leads to demands that it meet higher standards of quality and validity; this places still greater strains on the assessment capacity of many nations, especially developing countries. Indeed, these will likely have to look beyond available test instruments and consider anew the entire design and development process, in which local and national values and goals play a critical, if often not well articulated, role. At the same time, from a global perspective, there is a wealth of assessment related materials and expertise that developing nations should be able to tap into and adapt to their own needs.

The expectation that assessments aligned to national goals ought to be central to education and thus exert a beneficial influence on the economic and social conditions of the people is not a new one. In 1955, Godfrey Thomson said of the test movement in India (Bhatia, 1955: Foreword):

> It is of the greatest importance to India, and to the world, that her rising generation should be well educated, each in the way best fitted to his or her talents, and that her manpower, in adulthood,

should be helped into those occupations most needed by the nation, most likely to profit by the individual's special abilities, and most likely therefore to make him happy and self-respecting. The object of the test movement...is exactly to forward such aims, not by dictatorial direction but by careful assessment of abilities, general and special, and helpful recommendations based on such assessment.

This chapter focuses on assessment as a tool to improve learning, to monitor and credential students, and to evaluate some aspects of the education system itself. Certainly, assessment data, when appropriately aggregated, can be an important component of a broader educational indicator system. This chapter, however, does not treat the use of assessment for such administrative purposes as the evaluation of teachers, principals, or schools. Lievesley (2001) presents a brief but insightful account of the potential and the pitfalls associated with development indicators.

In this chapter, we first propose a framework through which we conceptualize the role of assessment for improving access, quality, efficiency, and equity within the education system. Next we define assessment, outline the different types of assessment and indicate the various uses to which assessment can be put. We then focus on the considerations particular to the secondary education sector in developing nations and highlight the various factors affecting assessment practices. This is followed by a discussion of ongoing concerns and constraints on improving assessment systems and practices. In addition, we address the role of technology in enhancing the practice of assessment, as well as improving the nature and quality of data collected. This is followed by a review of a number of regional/international assessment initiatives in which developing countries are involved. The chapter concludes with a summary and a presentation of several strategies for moving forward.

CONCEPTUAL FRAMEWORK

In establishing a framework for discussing the role of assessment, we have identified four essential attributes of an education system: Access, Quality, Efficiency, and Equity, which we will refer to by the acronym AQEE (pronounced "a key").[2] Figure 1 illustrates the interdependence among

---

[2] In this framework, the concept of effectiveness has been excluded as it refers more to micro-level factors within any education system.

these various attributes. While recognizing that these attributes are intimately linked, we provide a separate working definition for each. It is important to note that many different meanings and interpretations of the AQEE concepts have been proposed (Ndoye, 2002; Obanya, 2002; UNICEF, 2003). The intent of this review is not to provide universally acceptable definitions. Instead, we

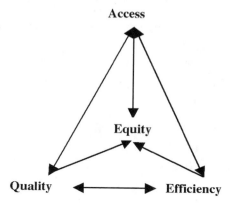

Figure 1: Interdependence of AQEE concepts

offer these attributes as a starting point for systematically examining the uses of assessment in an education system.

Access

The concept of access generally refers to entry into the formal school system and comprises three aspects:

- Getting to school – how learners travel to school, how far they need to travel, and how long it takes
- Getting into school – obstacles to attending schools (e.g., disability, child labor, safety) and admissions policies (e.g., age/grade limits, fees, restriction to specific catchment areas, admissions tests, and availability of places)
- Getting through school – promotion policies and practices, both influenced by the quality of education provided

Quality

The concept of "education quality" has as many different meanings as it has writers, and generally includes the following:

- What learners should know – the goals of the education system as reflected in missions/value statements and elaborated in the curriculum and performance standards
- Where learning occurs – the context in which learning occurs (e.g., class size, level of health and safety of the learning environment, avail-

ability of resources and facilities to support learning such as classrooms, books, learning materials, etc.)
- How learning takes place – the characteristics of learner-teacher interactions (e.g., the roles learners play in their learning, teacher and learner attitudes towards learning, other teacher practices, etc.)
- What is actually learned – the outcomes of education (e.g., the knowledge, skills, competencies, attitudes, and values that learners acquire)

Efficiency

Efficiency refers to the optimal use of educational resources and facilities to improve access to schooling and the quality of education provided. Efficiency generally comprises the following:

- The functioning of the current structures and systems at different levels (e.g., provinces, regions, districts, and schools) – how these are staffed and managed (e.g., district managers, school governing bodies) regarding the formulation, implementation, and monitoring of policy and practice within the system
- The availability, allocation, and use of human and financial resources – how available resources within a system are managed and employed at different levels within the system
- Throughput and repetition rates – the number of learners that enter and leave a system as well as the number of learners that repeat any grades

Equity

The concept of equity is based on the principle that essentially all children can learn and should be provided with an equal opportunity to do so, irrespective of their background. Equity within any education system is generally based on the following principles:

- Inclusivity – the capacity of the education system to address the specific needs of all children irrespective of their language, gender, religion, sexual orientation, (dis)ability, etc.
- Absence of unfair discrimination – the capacity of the education system to actively address unfair discriminatory practices or situations and their consequences for a specific subgroup. (In our view, the use of practices targeted at specific groups to address inequity within the system is both acceptable and necessary; for example, the introduction of additional math and sciences programs specifically for female learners.)

Evidently, there exists a complex interdependence among these attributes. For example, lack of efficiency in the context of limited resources will typically adversely affect access, quality and equity. Similarly, lack of quality, real or perceived, may well reduce access and equity as those families with fewest resources find the returns inadequate to justify the investments in school-related expenses and the opportunity costs incurred.

Systemic Validity

In evaluating the contributions of measurement to an education system, the principle that seems most appropriate is that of "systemic validity" (Frederiksen and Collins, 1989: 28). A systemically valid test is "...one that induces in the education system curricular and instructional changes that foster the development of the cognitive skills that the test is designed to measure." Their notion initially stemmed from a concern that high stakes tests can, and do, cause learners and teachers to focus their efforts on maximizing test scores. Such an effort may not be accompanied by achievement of the intended learning goals if there is a disjuncture between immediate outputs (test scores) and desired outcomes (student learning).

We propose to extend Frederiksen and Collins' definition of systemic validity in the following way:

> Assessment practices and systems are systemically valid if they generate useful information that supports the (continuous) improvement in one or more aspects of AQEE within the education system, without causing undue deterioration in other aspects or at other levels.

We recognize that to make any evaluation of systemic validity requires a judgment about both the nature of any improvement with respect to AQEE and whether particular changes in assessment practices would result in such an improvement.

Our rationale for this revised definition is that, in many instances, assessments can be systemically valid according to Frederiksen and Collins and yet not support educational improvement more broadly. For example, the academic content tested in a school-leaving examination may be suitable for those learners intending to continue their schooling, but not entirely appropriate for those leaving school, who would benefit from a curriculum and a preparation that covered a wider range of skills. There is a conceptual and practical distinction between certifying that a learner has met the standards associated with a given stage of education and determining whether he or she merits advancement to the next stage, and there are few tests that can serve both functions well.

The basic notion of systemic validity is not a new one, even in international education. Heyneman (1987) suggests that national examinations could be used to improve classroom pedagogy while Heyneman and Ransom (1990) suggest that well-designed national examinations could lead to improvements in educational quality. They argue that because these examinations play such an important role in the allocation of life's chances, they have powerful "backwash effects" which can be harnessed to positive ends.[3]

However, existing testing practices often exert deleterious effects on the education system. For example, in a study of public examinations in Sub-Saharan Africa, Kellaghan and Greaney (1992) point out, inter alia, that these practices often result in unwanted narrowing of the curriculum, an unproductive focus on esoteric material, as well as a warping of the teacher's role and, often enough, compromised test results. (It is somewhat ironic that these difficulties are almost identical to the concerns expressed by many observers in the United States, as American states increasingly adopt end-of-grade assessments as a critical element of their own reform efforts.) Likewise, Govinda (1998), in his overview of testing in India over the past half century, offers conclusions on the consequences of mandated testing policies that are consistent with the findings of Kellaghan and Greaney.

The obvious lesson is that assessment is a double-edged sword, with significant departures from systemic validity likely signaling substantial inefficiencies—inefficiencies that the economies of developing nations can ill afford. Unfortunately, achieving systemic validity is not easy. Alignment of the different components of a multi-level education system is a daunting goal. The U.S. assessment initiative alluded to above is intended to be one aspect of accomplishing such a task, but the problems that the United States has encountered and the apparent lack of significant progress are testimony to the difficulties of such an undertaking.

The challenge, then, is how to nurture and develop, even under the manifold constraints characteristic of developing nations, assessment

---

[3] The "backwash effect" refers to the impact of assessment, particularly the uses of assessment results, on learning, teaching, curriculum, learning materials, and education programs.

practices (and systems) that are systemically valid. The constraints range from lack of political will, of human or financial capital and insufficient infrastructure capacity, to the inertia attached to current practice. While these problems may be similar across countries, the specific national (or sub-national) contexts are different enough that it is unlikely that one can formulate meaningful general policy recommendations that will be operationally useful in more than a handful of settings. Accordingly, we subscribe to the aphorism: "Common challenges, local solutions."

Challenges in Implementing Systemically Valid Assessment Practices

The assessment system within the education sector comprises all policies and practices related to conducting assessments and evaluations, as well as the structures and organizations established to ensure effective implementation. Assessment and examination policies, examination structures and practices, national assessments, national standards, classroom assessments, certification bodies, and qualifications frameworks are all components of an assessment system. In practice, the assessment systems of countries vary significantly from each other, both in terms of policies, practices, and structures, as well as the capacity for effective implementation. Thus, it is possible for two seemingly identical assessment systems to have very different outcomes.

The effectiveness of an assessment system is determined not only by how this system (or subsystem) articulates with other facets of education, such as curriculum and instruction, but also by how well the various sectors (primary, secondary, higher) and structures within the education system articulate with one another. In an ideal context, all components of an assessment system would articulate perfectly and function effectively to produce the desired outcomes. However, this is difficult, if not impossible, to attain in practice. Clearly, departures from the ideal lead to various kinds of inefficiencies.

Over and above these structural issues, the operational characteristics of an assessment system are substantially determined by the availability, and appropriate allocation, of both human and financial resources. However, decisions pertaining to the allocation of resources must account for the following: 1) the stage of development of the education system; 2) the form and function of the different assessments, which change from feedback to monitoring and evaluation as one moves up from the classroom to the school, district, and beyond; and 3) the frequency of assessments, which typically tends to decrease as one moves to higher levels of the education system. In general, one can argue that for those education systems that are at an early developmental stage, less frequent assessments, following a baseline assessment, should be sufficient because many of the issues that need to be addressed are known and a number of years are required for detecting substantial improvement. In this case, scarce resources are better devoted to assessments directed at improving learning and teaching, where the returns on investments are likely to be higher (Black and Wiliam, 1998).

In developing nations, the allocation of resources for assessment systems should also account for the specific needs of "vulnerable populations," e.g., the girl child, the out-of-school youth, and the illiterate adult learner. The assessment system should facilitate the collection of data from beyond schools, e.g., household surveys, and allow for the recognition of relevant experiences and skills that many adult learners acquire out of school, especially those who have little or no formal schooling. In this respect, UNICEF has focused on improving the education opportunities of the "girl child" in rural and poor communities as a means of improving the lives of both girls and their communities (UNICEF, 2002). In Brazil, the government has embarked on a national campaign to improve attendance of poor children at school by using financial incentives for poor families as a means of combating the social conditions that force their children to work (Dugger, 2004). In an effort to improve the literacy and numeracy skills of adults in the United States, the National Institute for Literacy has established a set of comprehensive standards to address the question of "what adults need to know and be able to do in the 21st century" (Stein, 2000). These standards are noteworthy in that they cover a broad range of competencies that extend well beyond the usual compendium of academic skills to include the following categories: communication skills, decision-making skills, interpersonal skills, and lifelong learning skills.

WHAT IS ASSESSMENT?

We begin by distinguishing among four related terms (Keeves, 1997; UNESCO, 2000b): measurement, testing, evaluation, and assessment. *Measurement* refers to the process by which a value, usually numerical, is assigned to the attributes or dimensions of some concept or physical object. For example, a thermometer is used to measure temperature while a test is used to measure ability or aptitude. *Testing* refers to the process of administering a test to measure one or more concepts, usually under standardized conditions. For example, tests are used to measure how much a student has learned in a course of mathematics. *Evaluation* refers to the process of arriving at judgments about abstract entities such as programs, curricula, organizations, and institutions. For example, systemic evaluations are conducted to ascertain how well an education system is functioning. In most education contexts, assessments are a vital component of any evaluation. *Assessment* is defined as "the process of obtaining information that is used to make educational decisions about students, to give feedback to the student about his or her progress, strengths and weaknesses, to judge instructional effectiveness and curricular adequacy and to inform policy" (AFT, NCME, NEA, 1990: 1). This process usually involves a range of different qualitative and quantitative techniques. For example, the language ability of learners can be assessed using standardized tests, oral exams, portfolios, and practical exercises.

Assessment plays many roles in education and a single assessment can serve multiple, but quite distinct, roles. For example, results from a selection test can sometimes be used to guide instruction, while a portfolio of learner work culled from assessments conducted during a course of study can inform a decision about whether the learner should obtain a certificate of completion or a degree.[4] Simplifying somewhat, we can posit that from a learner's perspective, there are three main roles for assessments: Choose, Learn, and Qualify. The data from an assessment can be used to choose a program of study or a particular course within a program. Other assessments provide information that can be used by the learner, teacher, or parents to track learner progress or diagnose strengths and weaknesses. Finally, assessments can determine whether learners obtain certificates or other qualifications that enable them to attain their goals. Assessment in the service of individual learning is sometimes referred to as "formative

---

[4] There are hundreds of books and articles on educational assessment (or measurement) with varying levels of comprehensiveness and degrees of association with the different schools of thought. A particularly readable and non-technical introduction to the subject can be found in the UNESCO publication "Status and Trends 2000: Assessing Learning Achievement" and in Black (1998). For a more technical treatment refer to Cronbach (1990).

assessment," in contrast to "summative assessment," which is intended to guide decision-making (see Black and Wiliam, 1998).

From the perspective of the authorities, the three critical functions of assessment are: Select, Monitor, and Hold Accountable. One of the most important functions is to determine which learners are allowed to proceed to the next level of schooling. Assessment results, along with other measurement data (such as those obtained through periodic surveys), are also used to track the functioning of different components of the system (generally referred to as national assessments), and sometimes are used to hold accountable the individuals responsible for those components.

Types of Assessments

To complement our categorization of the different roles of assessment, we present a brief overview of the different types of assessments that are typically employed by most nations. These are described more extensively in a recent report issued by UNESCO (2000).

The most common type of assessment is *school-based*. These assessments are usually devised and administered by class teachers, although some are the work of the school principal or other instructional staff. Typically, they are aligned with the delivered curriculum and may employ a broader array of media (e.g., oral presentations) and address a greater range of topics than is the case with centralized standardized assessments. They have a decided advantage over centralized assessments in that the results are immediately available to the teacher (and, presumably, the learners) and can influence the course of instruction. While these assessments can play an important role in promotion to the next grade, they are rarely used for high-stakes decisions such as admission to the next level of the education system (e.g., university). Black and Wiliam (1998) make a strong case for the potential of school-based assessment to accelerate learning for all students. The key to effective assessment at this level is to devise questions or probes that can elicit learner responses relevant to the learning goals, while ensuring that teachers are capable of interpreting the results in ways that are pedagogically useful and have sufficient resources to guide learners appropriately. They distinguish between perfunctory assessments, the results of which are simply entered into a grade book, and truly formative assessments, meant to guide instruction and focus learner effort.[5]

---

[5] For a specific example of the effective use of formative assessment in a secondary school setting, see Wiliam, Lee, Harrison, and Black (2004).

The second type of assessment, *public examinations,* can fulfill one or more of the following roles: selecting learners for admission to secondary or tertiary education, credentialing learners for the world of work, and/or providing data for holding school staff accountable for their performance. While such examinations are an important component of every nation's education system, they are particularly critical in developing countries, where the number of candidates for advancement is usually many times greater than the number of places available. In many countries, these are standardized multiple choice examinations, while in others they comprise various forms of performance assessment (sometimes in conjunction with multiple choice components). Typically, they are designed, developed, and administered centrally with an almost exclusive focus on academic subjects. There is meager feedback to the school except the scores and/or pass rate, and, as a result, they offer little utility for school improvement programs beyond an exhortation to do better next time. Moreover, as we have already noted, public examination systems often have negative consequences for the general quality of education.

National assessments are studies focused on generating specific information that policymakers need to evaluate various aspects of the educational system. The results can be used for accountability purposes, to make resource allocation decisions, and even to heighten public awareness of education issues. These assessments may be administered to an entire cohort (census testing) or to a statistically chosen group (sample testing) and may also include background questionnaires for different participants (learners, teachers, administrators) to provide a meaningful context for interpreting test results. The utility of the data generated depends on the quality and relevance of the assessment, the thoroughness of the associated fieldwork, as well as the expertise of those charged with the analysis, interpretation, reporting, and dissemination of results.

International assessments assess learners in multiple countries, with the principal aim of providing cross-national comparisons that can illuminate a variety of educational policy issues. As with national assessments, they may also include background questions for different participants (learners, teachers, administrators) to provide a meaningful context for interpreting test results. Such studies are planned and implemented by various organizations, including the IEA (International Association for the Evaluation of Educational Achievement) that conducts TIMSS (Trends in International Mathematics and Sciences Study) and PIRLS (Progress in International Reading Literacy Study), the OECD (Organization for Economic

Co-operation and Development) that is responsible for PISA (Program for International Student Achievement) studies, UNESCO/UNICEF that conducts the MLA (Monitoring Learning Achievement) studies and coordinates regional groupings such as the Latin American Laboratory for Assessment of Quality in Education (Laboratorio),[6] the Southern African Consortium for the Monitoring of Education Quality (SACMEQ), and Program for the Analysis of Educational Systems of the CONFEMEN (Franco-phone Africa) countries (PASEC).[7]

Studies such as TIMSS, PIRLS, and PISA are characterized by high quality assessment instruments, rigorous fieldwork, and sophisticated analyses of results. At their best, they can also provide useful information to those who seek to improve classroom practice. For example, TIMSS included comprehensive surveys of educators and compiled an extensive video library of classes in participating countries. Both have proven to be rich sources of research on cross-national classroom practices and of putative explanations of the differences in results.

As the preceding exposition should make clear, assessment has the potential to contribute to one or more aspects of AQEE, depending on the type of assessment and the context in which it is employed. School-based assessments can enhance efficiency by helping to target the efforts of both learners and teachers. To the extent that they are able to use the information appropriately, the quality of the learning is improved.

Obviously, public examinations for selection or credentialing directly affect access. In principle, they should also enhance equity by providing a "level playing field" for all candidates. In reality, however, differences in "opportunity to learn" mean that not all learners are equally prepared, and this inequality is usually reflected in the outcomes. If these differential rates of success are associated with geographic and/or demographic groupings, there can be political consequences. Despite these failings, public examinations may be the best alternative at a particular time and efforts should be directed at improving education quality for more disadvantaged learners. In the long term, public examinations intended for accountability can lead to improvements in quality and efficiency, provided the results are incorporated into an indicator system that influences policy and resource allocation. The same is true of national and interna-

---

[6] Laboratorio Latinoamericano de Evaluación de la Calidad de la Educación (LLECE).
[7] Programme d'Analyse des Systèmes Educatifs des Pays de la CONFEMEN.

tional assessments—again, provided that the data are relevant and useful to countries and are used productively in planning system improvement.

Standardized Tests

Standardization is a prerequisite for fairness when scores must be comparable. It demands, at a minimum, that the tests be administered under uniform conditions and graded according to a fixed set of rules or rubrics. The degree of standardization is particularly important for school-leaving and selection examinations—and varies considerably from country to country and among regions within a country. In the past, standardization has been best achieved for examinations set by testing agencies, such as the University of Cambridge Local Examination Syndicate that operate internationally. External examinations, set by regional or national authorities, are almost always standardized.

Standardized tests are ordinarily constructed according to one of two models: norm-referenced or criterion-referenced. For the former, a distribution of test scores is established for a reference population. New scores are typically presented in conjunction with the corresponding percentile with respect to that reference distribution. For the latter, two or more ordered categories are defined in terms of fixed thresholds on the score scale, and a new score is labeled in terms of the category into which it falls. The test design process differs according to which model is being used. When the principal interest is in ranking all learners, norm-referenced tests are preferred. When the issue is whether the learner has met a particular standard, criterion-referenced tests are more appropriate.

Typically countries use both norm- and criterion-referenced assessments. Most examinations, e.g., end of school exams, are norm-referenced, while most national assessments are criterion-referenced. For developing nations, criterion-referenced assessments are certainly more useful for obtaining information regarding learner performance against set standards and/or mastery of curriculum objectives. Some examinations are hybrids, with standards set in part by considering substantive criteria but also influenced by normative (often historical) data. One example is the battery of Advanced Placement assessments in the United States.

Test Format and Content

Test designers may use any combination of item types, including multiple choice items, learner constructed response items (solving problems, providing short answers, writing essays), and extended work samples or port-folios. The choice is based, in part, on the appropriateness of the format for the objective to be tested and, in part, on operational issues such as timing and cost. Multiple choice items can be scored much more cheaply (particularly if the scoring is done mechanically) than items that require some degree of human judgment. In addition, learners can usually respond to a larger number of multiple choice items in a given amount of time, so that tests incorporating more of these items tend to give more consistent results.

Test designers must also consider the kinds of cognitive demands elicited by different kinds of items. While it is easy to write items that require factual recall or rote application of procedures, it is more difficult to devise items that demand reasoning, argumentation, and integration. While multiple choice items can be used to test some "higher order skills," many other skills can only be probed by formats that require the learner to produce an uncued response.

Aspects of Technical Quality

The purpose of any assessment is to provide information, which is usually used to support a decision of some sort. By a currently accepted definition, "Validity is an integrated evaluative judgment of the degree to which empirical evidence and theoretical rationales support the adequacy and appropriateness of inferences and actions based on test scores or other modes of assessment" (Messick, 1989: 13).

This definition requires that both developers of assessment instruments and users of assessment results marshal theoretical and empirical arguments to justify a particular application. One does not validate an assessment per se, but, rather, the inferences and implications for action in a specific setting. Thus, the use of an assessment may be quite defensible in one situation but the use of the same assessment – even with the same population – may be problematic in another situation. As we indicated earlier, an assessment that is used to confer high school diplomas may not be suitable for deciding which learners should be admitted to a highly selective college.

From a theoretical perspective, the two main threats to test validity are construct underrepresentation and construct-irrelevant variance (Messick, 1989). As its name suggests, the former refers to a situation in which the assessment does not adequately or fully capture those measurable qualities generally associated by test users with the target construct. For example, if the target construct is general writing ability, then an assessment that requires the learner to write a single essay on a general topic and to complete a set of multiple choice items that focus on grammar would suffer from construct underrepresentation. Construct-irrelevant variance arises when one or more of the sources of systematic (i.e., non-random) individual differences in scores are not closely related to the target construct. To carry the example above a bit further, suppose the learners were required to type their essays using a word processor. If some fraction of the learners had negligible experience with the technology while the rest were quite comfortable with it as a result of substantial use in their schools, the scores of the first group would likely be systematically (and inappropriately) lower than those of the second, even if their writing abilities were equal on average.

These threats to construct validity must be addressed primarily through the design process, although construct-irrelevant variance can also arise through poor control of testing conditions or scoring. Maintaining the integrity of the assessment process is critical. If, for example, some learners are coached by teachers with knowledge (exact or approximate) of the content of the test or, what is worse, the learners have obtained access to the test in advance of the administration, then the validity of the test scores is undermined. This is an extreme example of how fairness is an integral aspect of validity. On the other hand, if some learners have not been exposed to the content of the test, then this differential "opportunity to learn" is a failure of equity. Another, somewhat more technical problem arises when learners who have taken different forms of a test are judged by the same standard. If the test forms have not been carefully constructed to be psychometrically parallel, one group can be advantaged relative to another. In some cases, lack of comparability can be addressed through a process termed "test equating"[8] (Braun and Holland, 1982).

An important empirical characteristic of any assessment is its reliability. Reliability is usually defined as the correlation between sets of scores obtained from a sample of individuals on two occasions. High reliability implies that the ranking of learners would be very similar across different

---

[8] Test equating refers to a statistical method for adjusting raw scores on different tests forms for slight differences in difficulty.

administrations. Reliability is influenced by many factors, including the homogeneity of the items comprising an assessment instrument, the length of the instrument, the nature of the candidate population, and the uniformity of the testing conditions. Reliability is treated in every introductory text on measurement (e.g., Cronbach, 1990). Various extensions, including generalizability theory, are presented in summary fashion in Feldt and Brennan (1989).

There are no absolute standards for acceptable levels of reliability. In high stakes settings, reliabilities above 0.85 are considered desirable. Reliabilities below 0.7 are usually unsatisfactory. Low reliability undermines validity because it implies that a large proportion of the observed variability among scores is due to random error and, consequently, inferences made and actions taken on the basis of those scores are likely to be problematic. On the other hand, for assessments that serve formative purposes, high reliability need not be a priority.

CONSIDERATIONS FOR SECONDARY EDUCATION

Secondary education is critical to improving the quality of life in developing nations. This education sector plays a pivotal role in promoting rapid economic growth by preparing learners to enter the world of work or to pursue further education and training (including teacher training), and by preparing young people and at-risk-youth to participate more fully in their own socio-development and the development of society (Bregman and Stallmeister, 2001; Bhuwanee, 2001). However, despite the key role of secondary education systems, minimal attention has been paid to this sector in the past few years; instead, greater emphases have been placed on the primary and higher education levels of the system (Lewin and Caillods, 2001).

By their very nature, secondary schools face greater challenges than primary schools, given the need for learners at the secondary level to move beyond standard academic content to the acquisition of relevant competencies and skills that would better prepare them to function productively in society. The real challenge is to incorporate relevant knowledge, skills, and experience into the learning and teaching process in a manner that will address the country's specific growth and development needs. This alone is a daunting task for any nation, one that many developed nations also struggle with. Fortunately, a great deal of thought and a fair amount of work has already been devoted to meeting this challenge.

For example, the OECD project on the Definition and Selection of Competencies (Rychen and Salganik, 2003), the Equipped for the Future content standards (Stein, 2000), and the publication on Linking School and Work (Jenkins, 1996; Resnick and Wirt, 1996) provide a number of possible frameworks and examples to address a range of competencies that can require high levels of skills and expertise. These efforts represent valuable sources of ideas, examples, and information that can, at the very least, serve as starting points for addressing the specific challenges facing many developing nations in providing learners with skills appropriate to their society's needs.

Another source of materials and expertise can be found in the national assessments or public examinations conducted by developed countries. For example, in the United States, the National Assessment of Educational Progress (NAEP) is administered to samples of learners in the fourth, eighth, and twelfth grades (Horkay, 1999). The U.S. Department of Education makes available subject frameworks, test items, scoring rubrics, and informational materials for teachers. Similar materials are available from the local examination syndicates in the United Kingdom and (presumably) the testing authorities in other nations as well. At the upper secondary level, the High Schools that Work initiative (Kaufman, Bradby, and Teitelbaum, 2000) focuses on improving the academic skills of U.S. students on the vocational track. Concerns about preparing learners for the world of work and the school-to-work transition are longstanding (Secretary's Commission on Achieving Necessary Skills, 1992; Resnick and Wirt, 1996). We have already mentioned the related activities subsumed under the Equipped for the Future effort (Stein, 2000). For a European perspective, see Jenkins (1996). The point is that, with some diligence, developing nations can harvest guides, frameworks, and materials that can help them to jumpstart their education reform planning and, especially, their assessment strategies. Of course, these resources cannot be simply translated and put to use—a process of critical review, adaptation, and innovation is required. Such a process, especially if it involves diverse stakeholders, can be valuable in itself as an important element of a capacity-building program.

Success in expanding the primary education sector has led to a massive increase in the numbers of learners seeking enrollment at the next level. This section focuses on issues in the secondary education sector that can be addressed by assessment within the framework of AQEE. The information presented is based primarily on our review of developing

African countries, although we cite examples from other developing nations. We also offer some suggestions for how assessment can play a stronger and more constructive role in achieving the goals of AQEE.

What is Being Assessed?

Across the secondary school systems of the developing nations that we surveyed, we found both differences and similarities in what was assessed and how the assessments were conducted. The configuration of assessment practices in different countries naturally depended on how the education systems were structured, as well as the nature and delivery of the curriculum. In the countries surveyed,[9] we found the following:

- Secondary education offers between five and six years of schooling, generally divided into lower secondary (grades seven to nine) and upper secondary (grades ten to twelve).
- In all countries, learners were offered the options of academic, technical, and/or vocational tracks.
- A core curriculum usually includes languages, mathematics, and science, and learners are generally allowed to select additional subjects.
- Some countries specify standards or levels (e.g., the minimum levels of learning in India), while others have no specifications regarding what learners should achieve.
- Criteria for entrance to secondary school vary substantially. In many countries (e.g., South Africa), assessment results from primary schools are used. In some (e.g., Senegal), the results of national examinations at the end of primary school are used, while in others (e.g., Columbia), secondary schools administer their own entrance exams.
- Exit exams are administered at the end of secondary school in all countries surveyed, generally leading to certification. These exams may be administered by the education ministry (e.g., Brazil, China, India, South Africa), by a regional examination board (e.g., the members of the West African Examinations Council—Ghana, Liberia, Nigeria, Sierra Leone, and The Gambia), or outsourced to an international examination board (e.g., Mauritius).
- In all countries, assessment is used primarily for selection of learners into the next grade, while in some countries (e.g., Cuba) assessment is

---

[9] Countries surveyed are: Brazil, Chile, China, Columbia, Cuba, India, Indonesia, Jordan, Mauritius, Mexico, Morocco, Senegal, South Africa, Uganda, Vietnam.

also used for placement of learners into specific programs, such as academic or technical tracks.

- Entrance into higher education institutions also varies among countries. In some countries, school leaving certificates are used for entrance into higher education institutions (e.g., South Africa), while in other countries universities administer their own entrance examinations (e.g., Brazil) or use national entrance examinations (e.g., China). In many countries, additional requirements are often imposed by some universities, or even by faculties or departments within the universities.

Factors Influencing Assessment Practices at the Secondary Education Level

The secondary education sector of many developing nations can be characterized by inappropriate policies, an inexperienced teaching force, inadequate facilities and limited human and financial resources to effect change, relatively low enrollment rates, inappropriate and inadequate systems and structures to address current needs, and examination systems that have a significant impact on the career paths of learners (Bregman and Stallmeister, 2001; Bhuwanee, 2001; Holsinger and Cowell, 2000; Monyooe and Kanjee, 2001). We address each of these six factors below.

Inappropriate policies. In most developing countries, assessment policies (practices) focus primarily on examinations with little or no emphasis on classroom assessment or on monitoring and evaluation of the system (Kellaghan and Greaney, 2001). In instances where specific assessment policies do exist, inadequate attention has been accorded to the impact of assessment on the system. For example, in Chile, where the conduct of national assessments has been a consistent policy of the government for many decades, Schiefelbein (1993) notes that these assessments have not created any improvement in the education system. In South Africa, the implementation of outcomes-based education created greater obstacles for teachers, instead of improving the teaching and learning environment. Fortunately, however, this situation was rectified after the Ministry of Education enacted new policies based on the recommendation of a committee empowered to review the implementation of the new curriculum (DoE, 2000). As Obanya (personal communication, 7 May 2004) argues, we have to consider appropriate policy development and the quality of policy implementation in order to improve our education systems.

Inexperienced teaching force. The shortage of qualified and experienced teachers, as well as the low morale and motivation of the teaching force, has been cited as the key factor for the low performance of the education systems in many developing nations (Bregman and Stallmeister, 2001). The implementation of effective teacher development programs, regarded as vital for improvement in the provision of quality education, has been a characteristic of many systems in the last decade. For example, teacher development comprised a critical feature of the education reform initiatives enacted in 1996 in Brazil (Guimaraes de Castro, 2001b). Similarly, in Indonesia, the government launched a national in-service training program for primary school teachers using the Open University (Moegiadi and Jiyono, 1994).

A key focus of these training programs should be the use of appropriate assessment practices in the classroom and for examination purposes, because most teachers are able neither to conduct adequate assessments in their daily interactions with learners nor to design tests for end-of-year examination or certification purposes. However, limited information is available regarding the content of many teacher development programs.

In South Africa, training programs on the use of Assessment Resource Banks (ARB) to improve teaching have yielded highly successful outcomes (Kanjee, 2003). The ARB comprised a series of assessment tasks, each of which included: 1) the relevant curriculum outcome and assessment standard, 2) assessment items to assess learner performance against specific standards, 3) scoring criteria along with information on interpretation of scores, and 4) a framework for recording scores. Teachers were trained to use the ARB to identify learner strengths and weaknesses, develop relevant intervention programs for specific learners, and record and monitor learner progress. An unintended result was that teachers also used the resource banks for developing lesson plans, writing their own items, and setting homework exercises, indications that the ARB can perhaps be used in teacher development programs.

The lack of proper appraisal systems also contributes to the poor state of teacher qualifications. Appraisal systems focus on evaluating the ability of the teacher to perform his/her job and should, in principle, include teacher competency tests. The application of appraisal systems is vital for recognizing the contributions of individual teachers, rewarding the better teachers while also identifying teachers in need of assistance. Appraisal systems, however, are a contentious issue and are extremely difficult to implement. If these systems are to work, there has to be a consensus on their use by all stakeholders. The system should be based on fair assessment principles and not used for punitive purposes. In Colombia, for example, strong opposition by teacher unions has stymied attempts to introduce such systems (Guzman, personal communication, September 2003).

Inadequate facilities, limited human and financial resources. The lack of adequate facilities and human resources in the education system has had deleterious consequences for many developing nations, and will continue to do so in the near future. For example, the need for more qualified teachers in a number of disciplines adds a burden to the secondary education sector beyond that found in the primary sector. In addition, the education systems of many developing nations are characterized by limited capacity to obtain relevant information for identifying areas in need of intervention, as well as limited financial resources to effect any required change.

In these instances, the use of assessment should be recognized as both a cost effective and efficient way to obtain relevant information pertaining to aspects of AQEE and to identify appropriate interventions for improving both policy and practice. For example, in the MLA Africa study, Chinapah et al. (2000) focused on reporting disparities within countries regarding gender, location (urban/rural), and school type (private/public), rather than on ranking countries by their national mean scores, and on reporting the various factors influencing learner performance in each country. For many countries, this report highlighted areas in need of intervention, information that could be used by policy makers to effect change. Of course, the availability of relevant and useful information does not necessarily mean that the information will be employed in practice.

Technical expertise in conducting such studies is essential to obtaining relevant and reliable information. Assistance and, in some instances, funding to participate in regional or international studies (i.e., MLA, SACMEQ, TIMSS, PISA), is readily available. Most of these studies give priority to developing the capacity of participating countries.

Relatively low enrollment rates. In many developing nations, low secondary enrollment rates are caused by high dropout rates and limited availability of places. Although an obvious solution is to increase access, Bregman and Stallmeister (2001) note that access cannot be expanded rapidly without compromising quality, and caution that with increased access comes additional costs that many developing countries can ill afford. Among other strategies proposed to reduce expenditures, the authors argue for the improvement of internal efficiency by lowering high drop out and repetition rates in secondary schools. In this instance, assessment can be usefully applied. Teachers can be trained to use assessment practices to identify and address learner weaknesses and thus better prepare learners to progress to the next grade. On the assumption that the learners who find school interesting and relevant will not drop out, assessment can also be used to identify learner interests, which should then be incorporated in the daily interaction with learners. This is a good example of how assessment contributes to quality and efficiency, leading in part to improved access.

Inappropriate and inadequate systems and structures. The manner in which components of an education system are structured and articulated across different levels, as well as with the employment sector, affects the pathways by which learners are able to access higher and further education. These systems have to function efficiently in order to make any positive impact. However, in practice, this is difficult to attain. Bregman and Stallmeister (2001) note that support systems and education pathway links are weak or non-existent for many Sub-Saharan schools and advocate the establishment of national frameworks that would provide more rational choices of subject matter for both learners and parents. The authors also argue that the availability of national frameworks would enable learners to map their career pathways, thereby enhancing motivation and reducing dropout rates.

In South Africa, the old curriculum (under apartheid) was replaced by a new curriculum that was aligned with the new National Qualifications Framework (DoE, 1996). The new curriculum and the qualifications framework afforded greater flexibility in obtaining qualifications, allowed for the recognition of prior learning, and encompassed both the formal and non-formal education sectors. Both initiatives required the attainment of specific standards before any qualifications could be obtained. Thus assessment practices were, and still are, critical to successful implementation, especially in regard to the recognition of prior learning and certification of adult learners. However, whether the framework will be able to address the concerns noted by Bregman and Stallmeister is yet to be determined.

At the 2001 Assessment of Mathematics and Science in Africa (AMASA) meeting, participants representing twelve African countries also advocated for the implementation of changes to the assessment system (Monyooe and Kanjee, 2001). Participants noted that the assessment systems in their countries were limited by their focus on selection for the next level of schooling, certification of learners, and the ranking of schools. The participants strongly recommended that assessment systems ought to facilitate effective teaching and learning, diagnose and evaluate the extent to which the countries' educational goals were being met, and direct learners into areas of further study for full self-development. This recommendation attests to the increasing recognition of the potential of assessment to play a stronger role in education reform and to support teachers in improving learning by providing timely and relevant information.

Examination systems. Public examinations play a critical role in determining the career paths of learners in most developing nations. These examinations are used primarily to select learners into the secondary or higher education sector and have a powerful effect on the education system (UNESCO, 2000b). Given the central and critical role of examinations, desirable improvements to the system can possibly be effected through the exam system. As noted by Noah and Eckstein (1992a), changes in examinations have been used as levers to promote change in education and society, to reform the curriculum, to shift effective control of the system away from—or toward—the center, and to achieve specific political goals. Examinations systems can also be used for accountability purposes and for improving the quality of education, especially if the exams replicate what is required in the classroom.

For example, in South Africa, a school-based assessment approach is being used to certify learners at the end of compulsory education (DoE, 2002). This system, known as the Common Tasks of Assessment (CTA) is administered to all ninth grade learners in all subject areas. The assessments are conducted over a number of days for each subject and include standardized as well as performance assessment tasks that encompass a range of appropriate and relevant assessment techniques and activities. The final grades of learners are determined by both their performances throughout the year, as summarized by end-of-year marks, and their performances on the final CTA examination. However, Kellaghan and Greaney (1992) note that public examinations intended to raise quality cannot be the same as those for selection, as the latter generally do not take account of the needs of the majority of learners who are not proceeding to the next level.

Prospects

The establishment of an effective education system, and the accompanying assessment system, to adequately address both the needs of different learners and long term societal requirements is extremely difficult to achieve and requires vast resources. This problem besets education systems in both developing and developed nations. It is especially acute at the secondary level because of the diverse needs and interests of learners. In attempting to address this challenge, Murnane and Levy (1996) argue for restructuring the education system for the teaching of the "new basic skills" to prepare learners to meet the needs of a changing economy. The authors suggest three sets of skills: 1) "hard skills" that include basic mathematics, problem solving, and high level reading; 2) "soft skills" that include the ability to work in groups and to make effective oral and written presentations; and 3) the ability to use personal computers to carry out simple tasks. However, the viability of these suggestions has yet to be demonstrated in practice.

ONGOING CONCERNS

The problematic characteristics of both the technical and substantive aspects of assessments (especially examinations) are a persistent problem in the developing world. The questionable quality of the data collected through the use of unreliable instruments or mediocre administration procedures leads to system inefficiencies and to cynicism among stakeholders. This cynicism is deepened when the integrity of the assessment system is compromised, a widespread phenomenon in many countries. In this section, we highlight a few aspects of assessment that are of particular concern.

One significant difficulty in assessment involves communicating assessment data so that all stakeholders—from education ministry officials to school staff to parents—can make effective use of the results. Although the primary technical goal in test construction is to design instruments that provide valid and reliable data, turning that data into understandable and useable information requires very different skills and is rarely done well, even in the developed world. Yet, without this last step, the potential for assessment to drive system improvements is seriously compromised. These difficulties are exacerbated in some contexts by the natural reluctance of officials at all levels to disseminate information that may reflect poorly on their performance.

Unfortunately, most assessments now in place, especially national assessments in language arts, math, and science, provide little or no information on whether learners have acquired the skills required to function effectively in society. An assessment system should have the capacity to yield information on a broad range of competencies that mark learners as contributing members of their communities. To this end, the relevant competencies should be specified in the curriculum, assessments frameworks, and test specifications. For example, the OECD specified the mathematical, reading, and scientific literacy competencies that young adults (fifteen year olds) should acquire, and implemented a cross national study, PISA, to assess whether these young adults were prepared to meet the challenges of today's knowledge society (OECD, 2000). In the United States, the National Institute for Literacy has developed comprehensive standards for adult learners that focus on the following four categories: communication skills, decision-making skills, interpersonal skills, and life-long learning skills (Stein, 2000). These studies and experiences could prove useful for developing nations to the extent that relevant information can be adapted to the specific context of their learners and their communities.

The cost of developing assessment systems is a critical factor for most decision makers in developing nations. Although there is little debate on the need and value of examinations, the decision to fund national assessments, especially in education systems that lack basic resources, e.g., textbooks or classroom furniture, is extremely difficult to make. A lack of information regarding cost and benefits complicates this decision (Kellaghan and Greaney, 2001; Levin, personal communication, 28 January 2004). In this context, Kellaghan and Greaney (1996) argue that unless decision makers are able to articulate how investments in national assessments will benefit the education system as a whole, resources might be better utilized for other activities.

Of course, there are other sources of unfairness. Inequities in opportunity to learn among different groups are reflected in corresponding disparities in performance (Chinapah, 2000). In some countries, especially those with many language groups, inequities can be exacerbated when the language of instruction and/or assessment is not the learner's native tongue (CAL, 2001). Learners who are more familiar with the language of instruction and assessment will be at considerable advantage. Education systems in countries comprising multiple language communities require greater resources to adequately address the needs of all learners. The technical difficulties in conducting an assessment (especially at the national level, although classroom assessment practices are also affected) increase in this context, as do the possibilities for unfairness. All instruments need to be translated into one or more languages without undue bias against any group, additional analyses are required, and reports must be published in multiple languages. In South Africa, the Grade 3 Systemic Evaluation (national assessment) study was administered in all eleven official languages, as instruction at that level is provided in all of the official languages (DoE, 2003). However, in some countries this may not be possible or feasible. For example, in Papua New Guinea, there are approximately 850 spoken languages of which about 500 are written. In practice, there may be no alternative to the use of a single language but there are ways to mitigate some of the difficulties associated with testing (see Heyneman and Ransom, 1990).

Finally, it bears repeating that high stakes tests can lead to unwanted consequences such as a narrowing of the curriculum and an undue emphasis on test preparation. This is particularly harmful when the learner cohort is heterogeneous with respect to goals. An earlier and more serious narrowing of the curriculum may have already occurred when, for example, schools chose to focus on academic disciplines to the exclusion of more practical subjects, such as typing or woodwork, that are of interest and value to substantial numbers of learners. Ideally, separate examinations should be set for different purposes, but this is usually not practical for developing nations.

CONSTRAINTS ON IMPROVING ASSESSMENT

Any initiative undertaken to improve assessment practice must take account of the formal assessments that are currently in use. Although there is wide variation in both the quality of these assessments and how well they support broad educational improvement, each performs a useful function (at least to some degree), relies on existing capacity, and has some constituency that favors its continued employment. In general, any changes in an assessment system must take into account the broader transformation agenda within the education system and have the support of key constituencies, especially education department officials and teachers.

The proposed introduction of a new school leaving examination, for example, must consider not only how it might influence instruction (an important criterion for systemic validity) but also how it will perform the functions of the current examination. With respect to the latter point, the success of the proposal will depend on its impact "downstream" as well as the potential political repercussions. Heyneman and Ransom (1990) give an example of a failed attempt in Sri Lanka to eliminate the selection function of existing secondary school examinations in favor of the use of a new battery that was better aligned with a new curriculum. Opposition by some universities and the general public forced the government to reverse its decision.

In many countries, attempts at improvement are limited by lack of expertise and inadequate infrastructure. Lack of experience is often accompanied by underestimation of the complexity of the systems and the resources required to support testing functions such as design, development, administration, scoring, analysis, and reporting. Expertise needed in these areas can often be borrowed or bought. Internal capacity, on the other hand, is best built through collegial relationships with assessment professionals in other developing nations and with international experts. Fortunately, a number of successful programs are building needed capacity, even under less than ideal circumstances. Some operate under the auspices of the MLA program. For example, a handbook published by UNESCO (Chinapah, 1997) provides guidance on test and questionnaire design as well as various data analysis methodologies. Relevant activities associated with SACMEQ, PASEC, the Laboratorio, as well as the various IEA studies (TIMSS, PIRLS), have also contributed to the diffusion of expertise among member nations. These and similar initiatives contribute to enhancing the professionalism of testing agency staff.

However successful these efforts may be, corresponding improvements in classroom instruction and learning depend on conveying information back to schools and enhancing the capacity of teachers to make use of this information. Improving classroom-based assessment will probably prove more refractory, because it is so closely tied to the complexities of teacher education and in-service training. Cost is also a perennial problem. Budgets directed specifically at assessment are usually meager and focused on high stakes examinations. Building systemically valid assessments will require substantial additional expenditures. Although some of the required funds could be obtained through targeted grants, we believe the best strategy is to strengthen the connections between assessment and instruction. In the long run, this will permit instructional budgets to be used to support assessment improvement as well.

ROLE OF TECHNOLOGY

There is general agreement that the convergence of computers, multimedia, and broadband communication networks will have a substantial impact on education. In many developed countries, enormous sums have been expended on hardware and software, but evaluations of the consequences for learning have been mixed (Institute for Higher Education Policy, 1999; Angrist and Lavy, 2002). In speaking of the situation in the United States, Braun argues:

> [T]he core functions in most educational systems have not been much affected [by technology]. The reasons include the pace at which technology has been introduced into schools, the organization of technology resources (e.g., computer labs), poor technical support and lack of appropriate professional development for teachers. Accordingly, schools are more likely to introduce applications courses (e.g., word processing, spreadsheets) or "drill-and-kill" activities rather than finding imaginative ways of incorporating technology into classroom practice. While there are certainly many fine examples of using technology to enhance motivation and improve learning, very few have been scaled up to an appreciable degree (2003: 267).

The prospects for developing countries must certainly be dimmer, given the greater disadvantages under which they labor. In seeking ways to apply technology, it will generally be wise to resist the blandishments of complexity in favor of the charms of simplicity. At the same time, specific technological advances such as wireless Internet connections have the potential to greatly enhance access to content and expertise, with implications for both teacher professional development and student learning.

Undoubtedly, the priority for technology investments will be to support instruction. Technology can also be used to enhance the practice of assessment, through the training of teachers in formative assessment and the interpretation of the learner's work. Assessment specialists can also benefit from improved training and access to the latest software. Postlethwaite (private communication, 15 October 2002) cites an example of how staff at the International Institute of Educational Planning (IIEP) in Paris were able to train staff in Vietnam in sampling, data entry, and data cleaning through a series of video conferences. In Pakistan, UNICEF, in cooperation with a local NGO, set up a number of teacher training centers with access to the Internet (UNICEF, 2001) in an effort to improve teacher skills. Teachers were assisted in using these centers to access information, as well as with translations and distributions of materials they found useful and relevant. However, the prospect of technology-based testing itself still seems rather remote, given the infrastructure requirements. This is especially true with respect to classroom practice. Focusing specifically on South America, Gehring (2004) notes that, at the system level, most countries have not been able to harness technology in ways that improve instruction. This is also true for those countries (e.g., Chile, South Africa) where concerted efforts and massive investments have been made to introduce appropriate technology for improving the education system (Gehring, 2004; Zehr, 2004).

In an analysis of technology's impact on assessment, it is important to distinguish between direct and indirect effects. Direct effects refer to the tools and affordances that change how assessment is actually practiced, while indirect effects refer, in part, to the ways in which technology helps to shape the political and economic environment in which decisions about priorities and resource allocation take place. Although the technical literature tends to focus on direct effects, ultimately, funding decisions often have a determining influence on the evolution of assessment. As Braun (2003: 268) points out, "...one can argue that while science and technology give rise to an infinite variety of possible assessment futures, it is the forces at play in the larger environment that determine which of these futures is actually realized."

Technology is changing every aspect of the assessment process, including test delivery (Bennett, 2001), test design (Braun, 2000; Mislevy, 2003), item generation (Irvine, 2002; Bejar, 2002), test assembly (Swanson and Stocking, 1993; van der Linden, 1998) and test scoring (Braun, Bejar, and Williamson, 2006). It is now possible to build large pools of items or problems efficiently, assemble fixed or adaptive forms automatically, deliver assessments over the Internet, receive student responses, score responses (both fixed option and student-constructed) automatically, generate scaled scores, and release reports quickly. Although fully automated processes are still rare, technology-enhanced components are increasingly common across the spectrum of assessment programs with important consequences for both operational efficiencies and validity. These changes are just beginning to influence practices related to international assessments, while activities in developing nations are, for the most part, unaffected as yet.

Significant improvements in the field of psychometrics also have had a profound impact on the areas of instrument development, test analysis, and score reporting. For example, item response theory (IRT) is the underlying technology for most large-scale assessments. It allows test developers to explicitly describe the operating characteristics of individual test items and enables analysts to generate comparable scores for individuals who have possibly taken different sets of items. The latter property is crucial for large-scale assessments, such as cross-national surveys that seek to cover broad domains while keeping individual testing time to a minimum, or for computer adaptive tests that are intended to efficiently determine an individual's level of achievement (see Hambleton et al., 1991 for an overview of IRT, and Wainer et al., 2000 for an overview of Computerized Adaptive Testing).

The consequences have been significant improvements both in the quality and range of the information collected and in the methods of reporting information and comparing trends over time. However, these studies typically require high levels of expertise and considerable experience to be successful. In this regard, technology requirements can be a constraint, especially for those nations that have little or no access to the required expertise. In addition, assessment tools and information must be made available to teachers in order to ensure maximum benefit to learners. The pursuit of more complex technologies for assessment can limit use and often results in tools and data that are psychometrically immaculate but educationally bankrupt. For many developing nations, especially those in the early stages of transforming their education systems, the critical issue is striking a balance between the use of sophisticated hard and soft assessment related technologies and the successful transformation of the system.

Bennett (2001) makes a strong case that rapidly evolving technology, and especially the near-ubiquity of the Internet, will have a substantial impact on testing. Indeed, he argues that it will lead to a reinvention of large-scale assessment just as it has in business practices (and other spheres of activity) around the world. The pervasiveness of technology in developing countries has already facilitated their ability to take advantage of advances in measurement and cognitive science to make testing, in all its roles, more useful and efficient. This argument is further advanced in

Bennett (2001). However, he properly cautions, "The question is no longer whether assessment must incorporate technology. It is how to do it responsibly, not only to preserve the validity, fairness, utility and credibility of the measurement enterprise but, even more so, to enhance it" (Bennett, 2001: 15).

These considerations apply all the more to developing nations that can ill-afford major investments in technology that fail to yield commensurate returns. Accordingly, they have to be strategic and judicious in their planning, taking heed of the hard-won lessons learned by those nations that have gone before.

INTERNATIONAL INITIATIVES

In preparing this chapter, we carried out an extensive review of the education and assessment systems in a number of developing countries.[10] For each region, we selected five countries that reflect the variety of challenges confronting that region's education systems. We judged these countries as being fairly representative of the variation in that region, differing along such dimensions as size, population heterogeneity, and language diversity.

For each country, we provide an introduction, listing relevant demographic information, details pertaining to the structure and management of the education sector in the country, as well as information on education expenditures. We then describe the assessment system, with a brief history, the current assessment capacity, and the uses of assessment within the different levels of the system. Information on those areas integral to the assessment system (i.e., teacher education and curriculum) is also provided, where available. These reviews can be found at http://www.amacad.org/projects/ubase.aspx. We caution against making generalizations given the large differences in the local contexts that shape educational systems of all countries.

The online reviews provide brief descriptions of the various regional and international assessment initiatives that have recently been completed or are currently underway. These initiatives comprise an increasingly

---

[10] The following countries were included in our review: (Africa) Mauritius, Morocco, Senegal, South Africa, Uganda; (Asia and Middle East) China, India, Indonesia, Jordan, Vietnam; (Latin America) Brazil, Chile, Colombia, Cuba, Mexico.

important component of the assessment system in many countries. For each initiative listed, we provide a brief overview, the objectives, areas of focus, and contact information.

The initiatives described are neither a comprehensive catalog nor a representative sample of all such studies. Rather, we selected regional and international initiatives that highlight specific issues, including curriculum coverage, technical approach, capacity development, and reporting practices.

In our review of the literature pertaining to the studies, we noted that all international/regional studies sought to provide countries with relevant information for use by policy makers. However the underlying philosophies and/or approaches varied between and within the different projects depending on circumstances. These approaches can be categorized as follows:

- Emphasis on meeting the highest technical standards (which often means the use of the latest and most sophisticated techniques, methodologies, and software) versus using simpler and more cost-effective approaches to obtain relevant and useful data for the countries involved;
- Use of the curriculum as a basis for assessing learner performance versus assessment of general competencies; and
- Greater emphasis on local capacity development versus attaining project milestones and completion of reports.

In the last decade, an increasing number of countries have begun conducting their own national assessments as well as participating in international assessments (Beaton et al., 1999; Benveniste, 2002). There is limited information on the how these studies have influenced the various national education systems and the cost-benefit tradeoffs (Kellaghan and Greaney, 2001; Levin, personal communication, 28 January 2004). In his study on the reaction of participating countries to the TIMSS 1995 results, Macnab (2000: 12) concludes that while the results of TIMSS study provided participating countries with a valuable opportunity for instituting required reforms, "not all the countries made use of this opportunity; of those that did, not all were prepared to accept what was revealed; and that among those who did accept the verdict of TIMSS, there was not agreement as to the nature and depth of the changes required."

For many countries participating in an international assessment, the most significant benefit, besides the availability of additional information, is the access these studies provide to technical skills and expertise and the opportunity for capacity development. This is especially true for those initiatives where capacity building and sharing is noted as one of the primary objectives, e.g., MLA, SACMEQ, and PASEC (UNESCO, 2000b). Other studies (e.g., the Laboratorio, TIMSS, PIRLS) also provide significant opportunities for professional development, even though capacity building is not a specified objective.

Over the last twenty years, the number and scope of international assessments has increased dramatically, with greater participation by developing nations (Johnson, 1999; Martin et al., 2000). Along with this expansion, there has been significant improvement in the assessment design and methodologies employed, with greater attention paid to capacity development. These studies have also gained greater prominence in many countries and, accordingly, have generally improved the policy discourse. This is not surprising given that international assessments not only provide valuable comparative information but also allow participating countries to benefit from each others' experiences. Results from these studies provide additional insights that would be difficult to obtain from national surveys alone, and are generally viewed as more authoritative than within-country research by both the general public and policy makers (O'Leary, Madaus, and Beaton, 2001; Porter and Gamoran, 2002).

Although there are clear benefits to participation in international surveys, they also bring various challenges that countries should recognize. The most significant issue for policy makers is the degree to which information derived from these studies is relevant to the national context. The actual value of the study will depend not only on the quality of the data but also on the capacity of the country to effectively use the data (Johnson, 1999). Given the large variation in AQEE of participating countries, "the value of international studies may lie more in their potential for generating hypotheses about causal explanations than in their use for testing hypotheses" (Porter and Gamoran, 2002: 15). That is, findings from international studies may only highlight specific issues that would require further investigation by participating countries. Thus, policy makers should understand that participation is only the first step toward developing evidence-based education policy. For example, countries could leverage the experiences and expertise available internationally to mine existing data and develop new assessments in order to generate more detailed in-country information that could be useful to both policy makers and school personnel.

SUMMARY

In this chapter we have identified four essential attributes of an education system—Access, Quality, Efficiency, and Equity—and a general criterion, systemic validity, which addresses the question of whether assessment strategies and instruments contribute constructively toward more fully realizing one or more of the four attributes. After describing different kinds of assessments, as well as the variety of roles assessment can play, we considered a number of relevant issues—from technical aspects of testing to obstacles to improving the quality and efficacy of assessment in developing nations. Specifically, we have recognized that those stakeholders involved in improving secondary education confront special challenges. These are related to the broader curriculum and the greater variety of desired outcomes at that level, both of which contribute to a substantial, and sometimes enormous, gap between needed and available capacity. In particular, current assessments typically take the form of public examinations in academic subjects for high school leaving and/or entrance to tertiary education, while many other possible functions are left unfulfilled.

In our research, we conducted a number of case studies of assessment practices in selected countries. The general picture we drew shows that each country employs a range of assessments in various formats and settings but that, in many respects, the assessment systems do not function optimally. Our review indicates that there has been a global trend toward greater use of assessment. Increasingly, countries are conducting national assessments with the express purpose of obtaining information to improve the quality of education. Concurrently, the range and scope of public examinations are expanding and they continue to dominate the assessment landscape. The principal role of assessment is, still, to determine learner advancement and the awarding of qualifications.

Over the last decade there has been a marked increase in the range and frequency of international assessments spearheaded by both regional initiatives (e.g., SACMEQ, Laboratorio) and international organizations (e.g., IEA, UNESCO/UNICEF, OECD). The results typically have con-

firmed worries about the low levels of achievement attained by learners in
the developing nations. The UNESCO/UNICEF studies and regional initiatives have usually focused on developing nations, with capacity development as one of the primary objectives. In the IEA studies (TIMSS,
PIRLS) and OECD studies (PISA) on the other hand, participants are
mainly drawn from among the more developed nations, although a number of developing nations have also taken part. Although professional
development is not specified as a primary objective, there is evidence that
most developing nations have benefited from participation (Elley, 2002),
which is often funded by third parties such as the World Bank. Elley
(2002) argues that continued support is warranted in view of the quality
of the data obtained, the concomitant increase in technical capacity, and
the opportunity (seized by some countries) to introduce policy reforms
grounded in evidence of the comparative weakness of their education
systems.

The growing global prominence of assessment has led to considerable
investments in establishing improved assessment systems. A number of
developed nations or jurisdictions (e.g., United States, England, and
Wales) have embarked on ambitious assessment programs to spearhead
and reflect education reform strategies. They have recognized the need
to build assessment capacity at all levels of the system and look to international assessments to provide external benchmarks to evaluate their
progress. We can expect developing nations to follow suit, though at a
decidedly slower pace.

At this stage, there is a generally favorable opinion on the value of
participation in international assessments. A balanced analysis is provided
by Rowan (2002), who indicates some of the issues that arise when
developed nations attempt to use assessment results to inform policy. He
and other commentators note the unfortunate tendency to focus on the
"league tables" that present country-level rankings, when there is equal
or greater value in the careful examination of within country differences
and patterns. Johnson (1999) addresses similar issues from the perspective of developing nations. She is generally supportive of their participation, although she does indicate some of the technical and logistical
obstacles they face and, more to the point, the difficulties they have in
making good use of the information gleaned from the raw data.

In the literature on national and international assessments we have
reviewed, there is only passing mention—and almost no serious discus-

sion—of the use of classroom assessments and even less on the inclusion of assessment techniques in either teacher training curricula or teacher professional development programs. (In part, this may be due to the difficulty in obtaining such information from publicly available documents.) Undoubtedly, there has been insufficient attention to helping teachers to use assessment results effectively. For example, diagnostic feedback is not very common, so that test data are not often used to guide improvements in teaching and to enhance learning. This is unfortunate because there is an emerging consensus that formative assessment can be a powerful, cost-effective tool for improving teacher effectiveness (Black and Wiliam, 1998).

We argue, therefore, that there are good reasons for developing nations, and the organizations that assist them, to develop coordinated strategies that will enable these countries to more fully exploit the power of assessment to strengthen their education systems. The next and final section presents some thoughts on the matter.

STRATEGIES FOR MOVING FORWARD

We begin with the premise that essentially all nations seek to enhance their education systems and most consider assessment a legitimate and potentially useful tool in the improvement process. We readily admit that focusing on assessment alone can have only a modest positive impact: meaningful and substantial education reform requires sustained and coordinated changes in all system components. At the same time, risking the accusation of acting like the person with a hammer who sees a world full of nails, we strongly believe that assessment, broadly conceived, should be more prominent in discussions of serious education reform.

A first step is to cultivate among all stakeholders (politicians, policymakers, education bureaucrats, principals, teachers, and parents) a deeper appreciation of the power and cost-effectiveness of assessment. This requires a comprehensive framework to structure discussions about assessment and assessment capacity, as well as case studies that document the (favorable) returns on investment (ROI) yielded by well-planned investments in assessment, often as part of a broader education reform initiative. This is essential to generating needed support for strengthening and reforming assessment so that it can in fact play a more productive role in education improvement.

We believe that the four goals of Access, Quality, Efficiency, and Equity, together with the criterion of systemic validity, offer a starting point for a useful framework. In principle, they can be used to conduct meaningful prospective evaluations of assessment and other education-related reforms. Of course, documenting ROI is very difficult (Levin and McEwen, 2001), and the calculations are necessarily crude. Nonetheless, a start can be made, and as randomized control trials become more prevalent in education policy initiatives, the empirical base for such calculations will become firmer.

To the extent that rational policy development with respect to assessment is consistent with trying to increase systemic validity, nations face a multi-level design problem of great complexity, with goals and constraints at each level. The prerequisites for even a modicum of success are clarity, coherence, and consistency. By clarity we mean that the goals of education at each level, as well as the links between those goals and the relevant assessments, must be explicit, and that the results must be meaningful to all interested parties. By coherence we mean that the assessments at the different levels must articulate properly with one another. Finally, by consistency we mean that the development, implementation, and evolution of the assessment system must be carried out in a disciplined manner over a substantial period of time, at least five to ten years. These are difficult enough to realize for any nation, in the face of the usual bureaucratic inertia and the opposition of entrenched interests. For developing nations, such difficulties are often magnified by other social, economic, and political challenges—not to mention the problem of allocating adequate resources to the education sector.

It is critical to focus on generating more and higher quality data, and then turning those data into the information relevant to improving learning. This will require systematic planning leading to changes in assessment design, development, and reporting. Equally important, the capacity of the system to absorb and use those data effectively must also be enhanced. Among other things, this will involve extensive training of all professionals in the system, with special attention to teachers. As we have argued before, helping teachers to use classroom-based assessments and information from national assessments more effectively can contribute both to their subject matter knowledge and their pedagogy. A number of studies demonstrate that teacher professional development centered on evaluating the work of learners and reflecting on what is valued can be a powerful lever for change (Black and Wiliam, 1998; Wiliam, Lee, Harrison, and Black, 2004).

In addition to such training, the education system (at the school, district, and regional levels) must develop the communication channels, feedback mechanisms, and protocols that characterize data-driven organizations. These are well established in England (Olson, 2004). In the United States, there are a number of efforts focused on helping schools collect, organize, interpret, and use data effectively both for short- and long-term planning. Some, like the "Baldrige in Education Initiative," are modeled on similar undertakings in the corporate world. Their approach to school improvement relies heavily on information generated from assessments and is being used in many school districts across the United States. Other similar initiatives include the "School Information Partnership" and "Just for the Kids." Many related ideas and interesting examples can be found in Senge (2000).

However appealing in principle these data-driven ideas may be, there is no substitute for understanding the political, cultural, social, and commercial context of the hoped for changes at the various levels. Without sensitivity to context, no strategy is likely to be successful. For this reason alone, we expect that regional collaborations like the Laboratorio and SACMEQ, as well as international studies that account for local context, will have a continuing and critical role to play in this effort.

We have already mentioned the extensive participation of developing nations in the UNESCO initiatives and their increasing, but still sporadic, involvement in such international studies as TIMSS, PISA, and PIRLS. Both Johnson (1999) and Elley (2002) discuss the benefits and challenges that developing nations face. Rowan (2002) provides an excellent general treatment but is largely focused on the U.S. perspective. Although we acknowledge that many developing nations can indeed derive substantial value from full participation, we contend that for many others such participation may be of limited utility at this time, given the modest absorptive capacity of their systems. As an alternative, we suggest that the world community should encourage nations in the latter group to develop a strategic plan leading to full participation only after a number of years.

Participation in international studies is essentially a political decision and is not taken lightly, in part because of concern about the consequences of poor performance. One possibility is that nations could apply to join a study consortium as an "associate," with the opportunity to participate in the planning and test development, and then to administer the assessment with a primary focus on addressing specific national issues, as opposed to meeting international criteria. For example, experienced teachers could participate (informally) as part of a professional development program. The results of such a "toe-in-the-water" approach, along with the adaptation of ancillary materials generated by the consortium, could then be used to strengthen curriculum and instruction. Over time, participation could be expanded until the internationally stipulated criteria are reached.

Another possibility is to harness existing networks to take advantage of the valuable resources associated with these international studies. For example, in Africa, a group of nations under the aegis of the International Institute for Capacity-Building in Africa (the AMASA initiative) could organize itself to replicate some aspects of a study, again with a view to building capacity in an incremental but sustainable manner. It could draw on the relevant materials (ordinarily freely available) and invite experts to provide assistance. Each nation would be free to decide on the level of participation and how to employ the results.

Interested entities could also purchase services such as those provided by the Australian Council for Educational Research (ACER). ACER offers "International Benchmark Tests" in mathematics and sciences modeled on the TIMSS assessments. Learner results from these tests could be compared to the results of the different nations that participated in TIMSS. More important, carrying out such an assessment would provide a natural path to drawing on the pedagogical materials and secondary research related to TIMSS. As we indicated in our discussion of considerations for secondary education, there are many national and sub-national assessment programs that make valuable resources available, resources that can easily be adapted to the needs of developing nations.

Universal basic and secondary education means AQEE for all children and adolescents. In this regard, it is fully consistent with the goals that UNESCO has set for its member states (Chinapah, 2001). Under the right circumstances and properly employed, assessment can be a powerful tool for improving access, quality, and efficiency towards developing a more equitable system. But it can also be a crude tool, one that can lead to unintended and deleterious consequences if misapplied. These consequences can generally be avoided when assessment change is part of a comprehensive reform initiative that takes best advantage of what assessment can offer. In the final analysis, all education role players must acknowledge that "testing alone cannot improve learning, nor can it necessarily make education systems more responsive. But it does tune societies and governments alike to the possibilities of their schools and education systems. And, if the past is any guide to the future, well-designed and applied assessments can change the course of education reform and the menu inputs used to promote it" (Schiefelbein and Schiefelbein, 2003: 154).

References

American Federation of Teachers (AFT), National Council on Measurement in Education (NCME), and National Education Association (NEA). 1990. *Standards for Teacher Competence in Educational Assessment of Students.* Washington, DC: American Federation of Teachers.

Angrist, J., and V. Lavy. 2002. "New Evidence on Classroom Computers and Pupil Learning." *The Economic Journal* 112: 735–765.

Baker, D. P., M. Akiba, G. K. LeTendre, and A. W. Wiseman. 2002. "Worldwide Shadow Education: Outside School Learning, Institutional Quality of Schooling and Cross-national Mathematics Achievement." *Educational Evaluation and Policy Analysis* 23 (1): 1–17.

Beaton, A. E., T. N. Postlewaite, K. N. Ross, D. Spearitt, and R. M. Wolf. 1999. *The Benefits and Limitations of International Educational Achievement Studies.* Paris: UNESCO/International Institute for Educational Planning.

Bejar, I. I. 2002. "Generative Testing: From Conception to Implementation." Pp. 199–217 in *Item Generation for Test Development*, ed. S.H. Irvine and P. Kyllonen. Mahwah, NJ: Lawrence Erlbaum.

Bennett, R. E. 2002. "Inexorable and Inevitable: The Continuing Story of Technology and Assessment." *Journal of Technology, Learning, and Assessment* 1 (1). http://www.jtla.org.

———. 2001. "How the Internet Will Help Large-scale Assessment Reinvent Itself." *Education Policy Analysis Archives* 9 (5).

Benveniste, L. 2002. "The Political Structuration of Assessment: Negotiating State Power and Legitimacy." *Comparative Education Review* 46 (1): 89–115.

Bhatia, C. M. 1955. *Performance Tests of Intelligence under Indian Conditions.* Oxford, UK: Oxford University Press.

Bhuwanee, T. 2001. "Concept Paper, Regional Workshop on Secondary Education in Africa." Paper presented at the Regional Workshop on Secondary Education in Africa, Port Louis, Mauritius. December 3–6.

Black, P. 1998. *Testing: Friend or Foe?* London: Falmer Press.

Black, P., and D. Wiliam. 1998. "Inside the Black Box: Raising Standards through Classroom Assessment." Kings College London, School of Education. http://www.kcl.ac.uk/depsta/education/publications/blackbox.html.

Bloom, D. E., and J. E. Cohen. 2002. "Education for All: An Unfinished Revolution." *Daedalus* 131 (3): 84–95.

Bordia, A. 1995. "Indian Education." Pp. 430–439 in *International Encyclopedia of National Systems of Education*, ed. N. Postlethwaite. Oxford/New York/Tokyo: Elsevier Science.

Braun, H. I. 2000. "A Post-modern View of the Problem of Language Assessment." Pp. 263–272 in *Fairness and Validation in Language Assessment*, ed. A. J. Kunnan. Cambridge, UK: Cambridge University Press.

———. 2003. "Assessment and Technology." Pp. 267–288 in *Optimizing New Modes of Assessment*, ed. M. Segers, P. Dochy, and E. Cascallar. Dordrecht, Netherlands: Kluwer.

Braun, H. I., I. I. Bejar, and D. M. Williamson. 2006. "Rule-based Methods for Automated Scoring: Application in a Licensing Context." In *Automated Scoring of Complex Constructed Response Tasks in Computerized Testing*, ed. D. M. Williamson, R. J. Mislevy, and I. I. Bejar. New Jersey: Lawrence Erlbaum Associates.

Braun, H. I., and P. W. Holland. 1982. "Observed-score Test Equating: A Mathematical Analysis of Some ETS Equating Procedures." Pp. 9–49 in *Test Equating*, ed. P.W. Holland, and D.B. Rubin. New York: Academic Press.

Bregman, J., and S. Stallmeister. 2001. "Secondary Education in Africa (SEIA): A Regional Study of the Africa Region of the World Bank." Paper presented at the Regional Workshop on Secondary Education in Africa, Port Louis, Mauritius, December 3–6.

Center for Applied Linguistics (CAL). 2002. *Expanding Educational Opportunity in Linguistically Diverse Societies.* Washington, DC: CAL.

Chinapah, V. 2001. "Quality Education: UNESCO Position Paper." Paper presented at the Regional Workshop on Secondary Education in Africa, Port Louis, Mauritius. December 3–6.

———. 1997. *Handbook on Monitoring Learning Achievement: Towards Capacity Building.* Paris: UNESCO.

Cohen, J. E., and Bloom, D. E. 2005. "Cultivating Minds." *Finance and Development* 42 (2): 8–14.

Chinapah. V., M. H'ddigui, A. Kanjee., W. Falayojo, C. O. Fomba, O. Hamissou, A. Rafalimanana, and A. Byamugisha. 2000. *With Africa for Africa: Towards Quality Education for All.* Pretoria: Human Sciences Research Council.

Cronbach, L. J. 1990. *Essentials of Psychological Testing*, 5th ed. New York: Harper & Row.

Department of Education (DoE). 1996. "Lifelong Learning through a National Qualifications Framework." Report of the Ministerial Committee on the NQF. Pretoria: Department of Education, South Africa.

————. 2000. "A South African Curriculum For The Twenty First Century." Report of the Review Committee On Curriculum 2005. Pretoria: Department of Education, South Africa.

————. 2002. *Guidelines for the Assessment of Learners in Grade 9 in 2002.* Pretoria: Department of Education, South Africa.

————. 2003. *National Report on Systemic Evaluation: Mainstream Education – Foundation Phase.* Pretoria: Department of Education, South Africa.

Dugger, C. W. 2004. "To Help Poor be Pupils, not Wage Earners, Brazil Pays Parents." *The New York Times*, January 3, 2004: A1, A6.

Eckstein, M. A., and H. J. Noah. 1992. *Examinations: Comparative and International Studies.* Oxford: Pergamon Press.

Elley, W. B. 2002. "Evaluating the Impact of TIMSS-R in Low- and Middle-Income Countries: an Independent Report on the Value of World Bank Support for an International Survey of Achievement in Mathematics and Science." World Bank: Unpublished Report.

Feldt, L. S., and R. L. Brennan. 1989. "Reliability." Pp. 105–146 in *Educational Measurement*, 3rd edition, ed. R. L. Linn. New York: American Council on Education & Macmillan.

Feuer, M. J., and K. Fulton. 1994. "Educational Testing Abroad and Lessons for the United States." *Educational Measurement: Issues and Practices* XX (2): 31–39.

Foster, P. J. 1992. "Commentary." Pp. 121–126 in *Examinations: Comparative and International Studies*, ed. M. A. Eckstein, and H. J. Noah. Oxford: Pergamon Press.

Frederiksen, J. and A. Collins. 1989. "A Systems Approach to Educational Testing." *Educational Researcher* 18 (9): 27–32.

Fuller, B. 1987. "What School Factors Raise Achievement in the Third World?" *Review of Educational Research* 57 (3): 255–292.

Gaspirini, L. 2000. "The Cuban Education System: Lessons and Dilemmas." *Country Studies: Education Reform and Management Series* 1 (5): July 2000. Washington, DC: The World Bank.

Gehring, H. 2004. "South America. Technology Counts 2004. Global Links: Lessons from the World." *Education Week* 35: 50–54.

Govinda, R. 1998. *Using Testing as a Tool to Improve School Quality: Reflections on Indian Policies and Practices.* New Delhi: National Institute of Educational Planning and Administration.

Greaney, V., and T. Kellaghan. 1995. *Equity Issues in Public Examinations in Developing Countries.* Washington, DC: World Bank.

———. 1996. *Monitoring the Learning Outcomes of Educational Systems.* Washington, DC: World Bank.

Guimaraes de Castro, M. H. 2001a. "Education Content and Learning Strategies for Living Together in the 21st Century." A Report from the 46th Session of the International Conference on Education, Geneva, Switzerland, UNESCO.

———. 2001b. "Education Assessment and Information Systems in Brazil." Instituto Nacional de Estudos e Pesquisas Educacionais Anísio Teixeira. http://www.inep.gov.br/idiomas/ingles/.

Hallak, J. 2000. "Globalisation and its Impact on Education." Pp. 21–40 in *Globalisation, Educational Transformation and Societies in Transition,* ed. T. Mebrahtu, M. Crossley, and D. Johnson. Oxford, UK: Symposium Books.

Hambleton, R. K., H. Swaminathan, and H. J. Rogers. 1991. *Fundamentals of Item Response Theory.* Newbury Park, CA: Sage Publishers.

Heyneman, S. P. 1987. "Uses of Examinations in Developing Countries: Selection, Research, and Education Sector Management." *International Journal of Educational Development* 7 (4): 251–263.

Heyneman, S. P., and A. W. Ransom. 1990. "Using Examinations and Testing to Improve Educational Quality." *Educational Policy* 4 (3): 177–192.

Holsinger, D. B., and R. N. Cowell. 2000. *Positioning Secondary Education in Developing Nations.* Paris: UNESCO/IIEP.

Horkay, N, ed. 1999. *The NAEP Guide: A Description of the Content and Methods of the 1999 and 2000 Assessments* (NCES 2000-456). U.S. Department of Education. Washington, DC: National Center for Education Statistics.

Institute for Higher Education Policy. 1999. *A Review of Contemporary Research on the Effectiveness of Distance Learning in Higher Education.* Washington, DC: Institute for Higher Education Policy.

Irvine, S. H. 2002. "Item Generation for Test Development: An Introduction." Pp. xv–xxv in *Item Generation for Test Development,* ed. S. H. Irvine, and P. Kyllonen. Mahwah, NJ: Lawrence Erlbaum.

Jenkins, D. 1996. "The Role of Assessment in Educating for High Performance Work: Lessons from Denmark and Britain." Pp. 381–427 in *Linking School and Work: Roles for Standards and Assessment*, ed. L. B. Resnick, and J. G. Wirt. San Francisco, CA: Jossey-Bass Publishers.

Johnson, S. 1999. "International Association for the Evaluation of Educational Achievement Science Assessment in Developing Countries." *Assessment in Education* 6 (1): 57–73.

Kanjee, A. 2003. "Using Assessment Resource Banks to Improve the Teaching and Learning Process." Pp. 59–71 in *Improving the Quality of Primary Education: Good Practices and Emerging Models of District Development*. Pretoria: District Development Support Program/Research Triangle Institute.

Kaufman, P., D. Bradby, and P. Teitelbaum. 2000. "High Schools that Work and Whole School Reform: Raising Academic Achievement of Vocational Completers through the Reform of School Practice." National Center for Research in Vocational Education. http://www.sreb.org/programs/hstw/publications/special/ncrrpt.doc.

Keeves, J. P., ed. 1997. *Educational Research, Methodology and Measurement: An International Handbook*, 2nd ed. New York: Pergamon.

Kellaghan, T. 1992. "Exam Systems in Africa: Between Internationalization and Indigenization." Pp. 95–104 in *Examinations: Comparative and International Studies*, ed. M. A. Eckstein and H. J. Noah. Oxford: Pergamon Press.

———. 1996. "Can Public Examinations be Used to Provide Information for National Assessments." Pp. 33–48 in *National Assessments: Testing the System*, ed. P. Murphy, V. Greany, M. E. Lockheed, and C. Rojas. Washington, DC: World Bank.

Kellaghan, T., and V. Greaney. 1992. *Using Examinations to Improve Education: A Study in Fourteen African Countries*. Washington, DC: World Bank.

———. 2001. *Using Assessment to Improve the Quality of Education*. Paris: UNESCO.

———. 2003. "Monitoring Performance: Assessment and Examinations in Africa." Paper presented at the Association for the Development of Education in Africa (ADEA) Biennial Meeting: Grand Baie, Mauritius, December 3–6.

Kellaghan, T., and P. J. McEwen. 2001. *Cost-effectiveness Analysis*, 2nd ed. Thousand Oaks, CA: Sage.

Levin, H. M., and P. J. McEwan, eds. 2000. *Cost-effectiveness Analysis: Methods and Applications*, 2nd ed. Thousand Oaks, CA: Sage.

Lewin, K., and F. Caillods. 2001. *Financing Secondary Education in Developing Countries: Strategies for Sustainable Growth.* Paris: UNESCO/IIEP.

Lievesley, D. 2001. "Making a Difference: A Role for the Responsible International Statistician." *The Statistician* 50 (4): 367–406.

Little, A. 1990. "The Role of Assessment, Re-examined in International Context." Pp. 9–22 in *Changing Educational Assessment: International Perspectives and Trends,* ed. P. Broadfoot, R. Murphy, and H. Torrance. London: Routledge.

————. 1992. "Decontextualizing Assessment Policy: Does it Make Economic Sense?" Pp. 127–132 in *Examinations: Comparative and International Studies.* M. A. Eckstein, and H. J. Noah. Oxford: Pergamon Press.

Lockheed, M. E. 1995. "Educational Assessment in Developing Countries: The Role of the World Bank." Pp. 133–147 in *International Perspectives on Academic Assessment,* ed. T. Oakland, and R. Hambleton. Boston: Kluwer.

Lockheed, M.E., and H. M. Levin. 1993. "Creating Effective Schools." In *Effective Schools in Developing Countries,* The Stanford Series on Education & Public Policy. Stanford, CA: Stanford University.

Macnab, D. S. 2000. "Forces for Change in Mathematics Education: The Case of TIMSS." *Education Policy Analysis Archives* 8 (15).

Makgmatha, M. 1998. *Assessment Practices in Asia and Oceania: Review of Education System in Indonesia, Malaysia, India, China, Australia, and New Zealand.* Unpublished report. The Education and Training Assessment Studies Unit. Pretoria: Human Sciences Research Council.

Martin, M. O., I. V. S. Mullis, E. J. Gonzales, K. D. Gregory, T. A. Smith, S. J. Chrostowski, R. A. Garden, and K. M. O'Connor. 2000. *TIMSS 1999 International Science Report: Findings from IEA's Repeat of the Third International Mathematics and Science Study at the Eighth Grade.* Chestnut Hill, MA: Boston College.

Messick, S. J. 1989. "Validity." Pp. 13–103 in *Educational Measurement,* 3rd edition, ed. R. L. Linn. New York: American Council on Education & Macmillan.

Ministère de l'Education Nationale et de la Jeunesse. 2003. L'Education au Maroc. http://www.men.gov.ma/, accessed February 2004

Ministry of Education, India. 2003. Central Board of Secondary Education. http://www.education.nic.in, accessed February 2004.

Ministry of Education and Scientific Research. 2004. "National Literacy and Numeracy Strategy." http://www.gov.mu/portal/site/education (See Publications: Reports), accessed February 2004.

Ministry of Education – Jordan. 2003. General Directorate of Examinations and Tests. http://www.moe.gov.jo/ex/eng/IntroductionE.html, accessed February 2004.

Ministerio de Educación Nacional. 2001. *Informe Nacional Sobre el Desarrollo de la Educación en Colombia*. Bogota: Ministerio de Educación Nacional.

Mislevy, R. J. 2003. "On the Structure of Educational Assessments." *Measurement: Interdisciplinary Research and Perspectives* 1: 3–62.

Moegiadi and Jiyono. 1994. "Indonesia: System of Education." Pp. 2784–2792 in *The International Encyclopedia of Education*, ed. T. Husen and T. Postlethwaite. Oxford: Pergamon.

Monyooe, L., and A. Kanjee. 2001. "Final Report." Regional workshop on Assessment of Mathematics and Sciences in Africa (AMASA) held in Johannesburg, South Africa, November 26–30.

Mullis, I. V. S., M. O. Martin, et al., eds. 2002. *PIRLS 2001 Encyclopedia*. Chestnut Hill, MA: International Study Center, Boston College.

Murnane, R. J., and F. Levy. 1996. *Teaching the New Basic Skills: Principles for Educating Children to Thrive in a Changing Economy*. New York: The Free Press.

Ndoye, M. 2002. "Reaching Schools: Where Quality Starts." *ADEA Newsletter* (14) 3. Paris: Association for the Development of Education in Africa.

Noah, H. J., and M. A. Eckstein. 1992a. "Introduction." Pp. 5–6 in *Examinations: Comparative and International Studies*, ed. M. A. Eckstein and H. J. Noah. Oxford: Pergamon.

———. 1992b. "The Two Faces of Examinations: A Comparative and International Perspective." Pp. 147–170 in *Examinations: Comparative and International Studies*, ed. M. A. Eckstein and H. J. Noah. Oxford: Pergamon.

O'Leary, M., G. F. Madaus, and A. E. Beaton. 2001. "Consistency of Findings Across International Surveys of Mathematics and Science Achievement: A Comparison of IAEP 2 and TIMSS." *Education Policy Analysis Archives* (8) 43.

Obanya, P. 2002. *Revitalizing Education in Africa*. Nigeria: Sterling-Horden Publishers.

Olson, L. 2004. "Value Lessons." *Education Week* 23 (May 5): 36–40.

Organisation for Economic Co-operation and Development (OECD). 2000. *Knowledge and Skills for Life: First results from PISA 2000*. http://www1.oecd.org/publications/e-book/9601141E.pdf.

Porter, A. C., and A. Gamoran. 2002. "Progress and Challenges for Large-Scale Studies." Pp. 3–23 in *Methodological Advances in Cross-national Surveys of Educational Achievement*, ed. A.C. Porter and A. Gamoran. Board of International Comparative Studies in Education. Washington, DC: National Academies Press.

Rajput, J. S. 2003. "Towards a Dynamic Evaluation System, National Council of Educational Research and Training." http://ncert.nic.in/icutodyev.htm.

República de Colombia. 1999. *Informe de Países*. Bogotá: Education For All.

Resnick, L. B., and J. G. Wirt, eds. 1996. *Linking School and Work: Roles for Standards and Assessment*. San Francisco, CA: Jossey-Bass Publishers.

Robitaille, D. F., ed. 1997. *National Contexts and Science Education: An Encyclopedia of the Education Systems Participating in TIMSS*. Vancouver: Pacific Educational Press.

Rojas, C., and J. M. Esquivel. 1998. "Los Sistemas de Medición del Logro Académico en Latinoamérica." *LCSHD paper series* 1(25): 7.

Rowan, B. 2002. "Large-scale Cross National Surveys of Educational Achievement: Pitfalls and Possibilities." Pp. 321–349 in *Methodological Advances in Cross-national Surveys of Educational Achievement*, ed. A. C. Porter and A. Gamoran. Board of International Comparative Studies in Education. Washington, DC: National Academies Press.

Rychen D. S., and L. H. Salganik, eds. 2003. *Key Competencies for a Successful Life and a Well-Functioning Society*. Göttingen: Hogrefe & Huber Publishers.

Schiefelbein, E. 1993. "The Use of National Assessments to Improve Primary Education in Chile." Pp. 117–146 in *From Data to Action: Information Systems in Educational Planning*, ed. D. W. Chapman and L. O. Mählck. Paris: UNESCO, International Institute for Educational Planning.

Schieflbein, E., and P. Schiefelbein. 2003. "From Screening to Improving Quality: the Case of Latin America." *Assessment in Education* (10) 2: 141–154.

Secretaría de Educación Publica. 2001. *Educational Development: National Report of Mexico*. Mexico: Secretaría de Educación Publica.

Secretary's Commission on Achieving Necessary Skills. 1992. *Learning A Living: A Blueprint for High Performance—A SCANS Report For America 2000*. Washington, DC: U.S. Department of Labor.

Senge, P. M. 2000. *Schools that Learn: A Fifth Discipline Fieldbook for Educators, Parents, and Everyone Who Cares about Education*. New York: Doubleday.

Stein, S. 2000. *Equipped for the Future Content Standards: What Adults Need to Know and be Able to do in the 21st Century*. Washington, DC: National Institute for Literacy.

Swanson, L., and M. L. Stocking. 1993. "A Model and Heuristic for Solving Very Large Item Selection Problems." *Applied Psychological Measurement* 17: 151–166.

Umar, J. 1996. "Grappling with Heterogeneity: Assessment in Indonesia." Pp. 233–247 in *Assessment in Transition: Learning, Monitoring and Selection in International Perspective,* ed. Little and A. Wolf. Oxford: Pergamon Publishers.

van der Linden, W. J., issue ed. 1998. *Applied Psychological Measurement* 22 (3), Special Issue: Optimal Test Assembly. Thousand Oaks: Sage Publications.

Walberg, H. J., and G. D. Haertel. 1990. *The International Encyclopedia of Educational Evaluation.* Oxford, UK: Pergamon Press.

UNESCO. 1998. "Wasted Opportunities: When Schools Fail." In *Education for All: Status and Trends 1998.* Paris: UNESCO.

———. 2000a. *The Dakar Framework for Action. Education for All: Meeting our Collective Commitments.* Paris: UNESCO.

———. 2000b. *Status and Trends 2000: Assessing learning achievement.* Paris: UNESCO.

UNDP/UNESCO/UNICEF/World Bank. 1990. *World Conference on Education for All, Meeting Basic Education Needs.* Final Report. Paris: UNESCO.

UNICEF. 2001. "Education Technology." *Education Update* 4 (2). New York: Education section, UNICEF.

———. 2002. "Learning Achievement." *Education Update* 5 (3). New York: Education section, UNICEF.

———. 2003. "Girl's Education." http://www.unicef.org/girlseducation/index.html, accessed September 2003.

Wainer, H., ed. 2000. *Computerized Adaptive Testing: A Primer.* Mahwah, NJ: LEA.

Walpole, M., and R. J. Noeth. 2002. *The Promise of Baldrige for K-12 Education.* Iowa City, IA: ACT.

Watkins, K. 2000. *The Oxfam Education Report.* Oxford, UK: Oxfam.

Wiliam, D., C. Lee, C. Harrison, and P. Black. 2004. "Teachers Developing Assessment for Learning: Impact on Student Achievement." *Assessment in Education: Principles, Policy, and Practice* 11 (1): 49–65.

Zehr, M. 2004. "Africa. Technology Counts 2004. Global Links: Lessons from the World." *Education Week* 35: 56–59.

CHAPTER 5

Evaluating Educational Interventions in Developing Countries

ERIC BETTINGER

R andomized experiments are an increasingly popular means of evaluating educational reforms throughout the world. Innovative researchers, policymakers, and foundations have implemented randomized evaluations of programs ranging from educational vouchers in Colombia, to teacher supply in India, to textbook provision and de-worming in Kenya. The use of experimental approaches in the provision of social services is not a new practice; policymakers and researchers have long recognized that experimental approaches can produce reliable evidence of the efficacy (or inefficacy) of social-service provision.

In recent years, the use of randomized implementation and evaluation in the provision of public services has garnered increased support from policy organizations throughout the world. The World Bank, for example, advocates that countries introduce new social programs using random assignment (e.g., Newman, Rawlings, and Gertler, 1994). They argue that "randomized designs are generally the most robust of the evaluation methodologies" (World Bank, 2003). Evidence from randomized experiments is often the most persuasive to policymakers. For example, the "No Child Left Behind" legislation in the United States ties local school funding to "scientifically based research." The act defines scientifically based research, in part, as research that

> ...is evaluated using *experimental or quasiexperimental designs* in which individuals, entities, programs, or activities are assigned to different conditions and with appropriate controls to evaluate the effects of the condition of interest, *with a preference for random-assignment experiments* (PL 107–110: 1965).

Although randomized evaluation can produce persuasive and perhaps conclusive evidence, it also has significant drawbacks. First, implementation of a randomized evaluation may present an ethical dilemma. Inherent in a randomized evaluation is the condition that while one group experiences an innovation (the treatment group) another does not (the control group). Withholding treatment from an individual is difficult to justify, especially when it is believed to be beneficial,[1] and withholding treatment from some groups may be politically unpopular. Furthermore, politicians often have incentives to overstate the effectiveness of their programs or to publish the effects of only successful programs.

Even if researchers and policymakers take care of ethical and political considerations, other problems may remain. For example, randomized evaluation can be expensive and time-consuming, especially in the field of education. Besides the cost of the innovation itself, randomization also entails substantial administrative costs. Researchers and policymakers must administer the randomization and track both treatment and control students over multiple years, as it often takes multiple years of treatment before researchers can gauge the effects of an educational innovation. Likewise, deviations from randomization may limit the validity of subsequent evaluation.

Randomization also presents issues of internal and external validity. If an evaluation has internal validity, then comparisons between treatment and control groups provide meaningful results. In theory, randomization provides an unbiased group through which to gauge the effects of the program on the application pool. Internal validity can be threatened for a number of reasons. For example, if researchers are unable to gather follow-up data for even a portion of the control or treatment groups, then comparisons of the control and treatment groups may not provide accurate estimates of the program's effect. External validity may also be problematic for randomized studies. If an evaluation has external validity, the measured effects of the treatment on the applicant pool will be similar in other populations. Oftentimes, however, researchers apply experimental designs on samples that differ substantially from the overall population. Additionally, many experiments are small, and although they may provide an accurate estimate of the partial equilibrium effect, they may not be

---

[1] See Cook and Panye (2002) for further discussion on the ethicality of random assignment for educational interventions.

able to estimate the general equilibrium effect.[2] The impact of the treatment on a small group, as shown in the partial equilibrium effect, may not hold if substantial changes are required for the expansion of the social service to a more general population. For example, a small voucher program may not affect the supply of schools in a city; however, a large voucher program may provide incentives for the creation of new schools. These schools may be better or worse than the existing schools, but they provide a different quality of education. The voucher may not only affect students directly by allowing them to attend different schools, but it may also affect students by changing the supply of available schools.

Since the early 1970s, economists, education researchers, and education practitioners have studied a range of educational phenomena. Only a few of these educational studies have exploited randomization. This chapter discusses how the few studies with randomization have augmented the larger body of evidence on educational innovations in developing countries.[3] It highlights some of the strengths and weaknesses of randomized evaluations. The study speaks less to the cost-effectiveness of such programs (see Kremer, 2004; also Kremer, this volume) and instead focuses on the knowledge gained from randomized experiments.

This chapter's focus on randomization is not intended to devalue the contributions that other types of studies have made to the field of education research. Randomization is one approach that has gained popularity and, under some conditions, can be more persuasive and compelling than other types of research. However, as this study argues, other types of research have also provided significant insights into educational knowledge. For example, rarely does randomized research comment on ways to improve the quality of implementation. Oftentimes, alternative approaches can complement and provide important synergies to our understanding of the implications of randomized trials. However, in its focus on randomization, this study is narrower in its scope.

The chapter starts by presenting a brief overview of "selection bias" and demonstrates how randomization may help researchers avoid such bias. It then discusses why randomized research is not relied upon more heavily

---

[2] Partial equilibrium refers to the effect of a policy holding the institutions providing the public service and their surrounding infrastructure constant. The general equilibrium effect allows the institutions and the infrastructure to change in response to the program.

[3] Kremer (2003) and Pritchett (2002) also review recent randomized experiments.

and presents a simple model to demonstrate why policymakers may be reluctant to undertake educational projects that rely on randomized evaluation. The second section discusses four types of educational innovations: school infrastructure development, student health, the provision of textbooks and other learning aids, and incentives to schools, teachers, and students. For each type of educational innovation, the chapter reviews both non-experimental and experimental evidence. It also attempts to identify specific cases in which evidence from randomized policies has improved policymakers' and researchers' understanding of educational phenomena.

THE PROMISE OF RANDOMIZATION

Randomized experiments have the potential to produce unbiased estimates of a program.[4] Studies without randomization are susceptible to selection bias, the potential bias arising when participants in a given intervention systematically differ from non-participants. For example, economists have long been interested in knowing how private schooling affects student outcomes relative to public schooling.[5] Studies of private schooling often compare students in public schools to students in private schools. Unfortunately, such comparisons may not be entirely valid. Students who attend private schools typically come from more affluent homes where education may be more highly valued than it is in the homes of students in public schools. Even if private school students were to attend public schools, they might still perform better than other public school students because of a difference in home and family environment.

Typically, researchers using non-experimental research designs must include ample controls for any characteristic that may distinguish the students who participate in the program from the students who do not; yet, even if substantial controls are included in the model, selection bias may not be eradicated. If there is an unobservable characteristic that affects both the likelihood that students participate and their performance in the activity (e.g., ability), then estimates based on non-experimental research designs may still be biased.

---

[4] There are a number of studies that characterize randomized experiments and their technical strengths and weaknesses (e.g., Meyer, 1995; Angrist and Krueger, 2001).

[5] For studies in developing countries, see: Bashir, 1997; Bedi and Garg, 2000; Alderman, Orazem, and Paterno, 2001. In developed countries: Neal, 1997; Evans and Schwab, 1995.

Randomized experiments offer a solution to this problem. Students randomly selected to participate should not differ from students who are randomly not included in the program. Mathematically, it is possible to demonstrate how randomness may eliminate selection bias. For simplicity, consider the example of private schooling. Suppose that there are two types of students, high (H) and low (L) ability. These students attend both private and public schools. The following notation can simplify the following discussion of a hypothetical research program based on test scores:

α_H = Test score effect of being high ability

α_L = Test score effect of being low ability

δ_{pub} = Test score effect of public school

δ_{priv} = Test score effect of private school

These quantities are assumed to exist, although researchers may observe only a test score. For the sake of the example, I will assume that student achievement is a combination of both student ability and a school effect. Hence, if a high-ability student attends private school, her test score would be equal to $\alpha_H + \delta_{priv}$. Similarly, the test score of a low-ability student in public school would be equal to $\alpha_L + \delta_{pub}$.

To demonstrate selection bias, we can further suppose that students perfectly sort by high and low ability into private and public schools respectively. If this is the case, then:

Average Achievement in Public Schools = $\alpha_L + \delta_{pub}$

Average Achievement in Private Schools = $\alpha_H + \delta_{priv}$

A naïve research design would attempt to identify the effects of private schools by looking at the differences in these quantities and attribute this difference to be the "effect of private schooling." However, this comparison is flawed. We cannot distinguish between the effects of private schooling and the effects of ability differences.

To identify the effects of attending public school versus private school, we would ideally like to observe the difference between δ_{priv} and δ_{pub}. We could observe this by comparing the achievement of a student of the same ability in both private and public schools:

Achievement of High Ability in Private School –
Achievement of High Ability in Public School

$$= (\alpha_H + \delta_{priv}) - (\alpha_H + \delta_{pub})$$
$$= \delta_{priv} - \delta_{pub}$$

The problem with perfect sorting is that we do not observe the test score of a high-ability student in public schools. Similarly, we do not observe the test score of a low-ability student in public schools. These hypothetical outcomes are never observed given perfect sorting. Because we cannot observe these outcomes, we cannot deduce the difference in the effect between private and public schools.

However, with randomization, we can produce an unbiased estimate of the difference between private and public schools. Suppose that private schooling was randomly assigned, and that all students applied to private schools. Because of randomization, the number of students attending private or public school should be just equal to the proportion of high-ability students in the population (for simplicity, we will assume that half of students are high ability). With randomization, the average achievement level for private schools will be equal to:

$$\tfrac{1}{2}\,(\alpha_H + \delta_{priv}) + \tfrac{1}{2}\,(\alpha_L + \delta_{priv}) = \tfrac{1}{2}\,(\alpha_H + \alpha_L) + \delta_{priv} \quad (1)$$

The average achievement level for public schools will be equal to:

$$\tfrac{1}{2}\,(\alpha_H + \delta_{pub}) + \tfrac{1}{2}\,(\alpha_L + \delta_{pub}) = \tfrac{1}{2}\,(\alpha_H + \alpha_L) + \delta_{pub} \quad (2)$$

To compare private-school and public-school test scores, we would subtract equation (2) from equation (1). The difference is equal to the effect of private schools relative to the effect of public schools. Hence, randomization can provide unbiased estimates of the effects of private schooling.

Similarly, randomization can provide unbiased estimates of the effects of other interventions, such as class size. For example, in a series of review articles, Hanushek has found no consistently measured effect of class size using research not based on randomization. In evaluating the random assignment of class size in Tennessee, Krueger writes, "A more general point raised by the reanalysis of Hanushek's literature summary is that not all estimates are created equal." He goes on to say that "one good study can be more informative that the rest of the literature." Krueger, quoting Galileo's description of one "Barbary steed" as faster than hundreds of packhorses, concludes that as a result of the sample size and use of randomization "Tennessee's project STAR is the single Barbary steed in the class size literature" (Krueger, 2000: 4).[6]

---

[6] I thank an anonymous referee for providing this quote.

Under-utilization of Randomization

Besides private schooling, there are endless examples of where entry into an educational program is correlated with some unobserved characteristic. All too frequently, students who would have succeeded in the absence of a program are the same people who choose to participate in the program. Randomization can overcome the bias that such participation patterns may create. One might then ask why randomization remains under-utilized.

Eric Hanushek explains, "Although educators are dedicated to teaching students, they are reluctant to submit to the often-painful process of evaluation and learning. Therefore, new ideas are seldom subjected to thorough evaluation, nor are active decisions often made about their success or failure" (1995: 241). He further explains that groups conducting educational experiments produce evaluations that "seldom involve any detailed analytical work that would permit dissemination of new techniques or new organizational forms."

There are a number of reasons that institutions and organizations may be reluctant to engage in randomized experiments in their evaluations. First, there are substantial costs associated with implementing a randomized experiment versus implementing some other intervention. These costs can be financial, political, or technical.

The financial costs can be substantial. Retrospective, nonrandom studies often rely on secondary sources, such as population surveys, to understand the impact on a set of people with certain characteristics in a given region. Randomized studies cannot rely on data collected by others. Certain people participate in the randomization, and those are the people for whom data must be collected. The researcher must track specific individuals over time, which can be extremely costly (e.g., see Ludwig et al., 2001). Some studies have gone so far as to hire expensive private investigators to find study participants (Katz et al., 2000).

There are also significant political costs to implementing randomized evaluations. For example, Colombia recently instituted an educational program similar to Mexico's PROGRESA program. Families were to receive cash stipends if their children attended school and received regular health check-ups. The World Bank strongly encouraged Colombia to implement the program using randomization across cities, but Colombia's central government chose not to do so. At the time, the government was negotiating a cease-fire with guerillas. The educational program provided some political leverage, and the central government implemented the program in selected cities to appease the guerillas.

There are also political costs to evaluation in terms of the long-run viability of a project. For example, Pritchett (2002) provides a model to explain why randomized evaluations are infrequent and when evaluations can be expected. In the model, those who conduct the program face the uncertainty that the program is not generating any useful results. These individuals will experience substantial costs if the program is proved ineffective. In the case of a large-scale project or one that is well funded, knowledge of its efficacy (or lack thereof) could be harmful to its organizers. As Pritchett summarizes, "No advocate would want to engage in research that potentially undermines support for his/her program. Endless, but less than compelling, controversy is preferred to knowing for sure" (Pritchett, 2002: 268).

Finally, the technical costs can also be substantial. Oftentimes, it is difficult to find someone who can accurately manage either the innovation or its implementation. For example, many program managers do not understand what researchers mean by randomization. In one voucher program in the United States, vouchers were initially randomized, but after all voucher winners accepted or rejected the award, there were still awards left over. Rather than randomize again, the voucher organizers "arbitrarily" chose additional students to win. Unfortunately, their "arbitrary" choices were students who had applied to a high-quality private school. There was nothing random about this selection of students (Bettinger, 2001). Other voucher programs, including selected cities involved in Colombia's PACES program, have shown some non-randomness (Angrist et al., 2002).

In other cases, records are not kept or are kept inaccurately. For example, in the Colombian voucher program, many jurisdictions kept lists of lottery winners but not lottery losers. As a result, research could not be conducted because there was not a control group to which the treatment group could be compared. Other jurisdictions deleted records for students who won the voucher lottery but declined to use the voucher. The remaining voucher lottery winners are likely not comparable to the voucher lottery losers, as students using the voucher may differ systematically from students declining the voucher. In yet other jurisdictions, contact information was kept and updated for voucher winners but not for lottery losers. As a result, voucher winners were easier to find and interview than voucher lottery losers. The groups interviewed subsequently differed systematically. In each of these cases, the person maintaining the data did not understand the role and importance of randomization in the assessment, and consequently, expensive innovations could not be accurately evaluated. In each case, the internal validity of the evaluation (discussed below) was threatened.

Many researchers are reluctant to engage in research that identifies effects through randomization because of the difficulty of maintaining internal validity or because of the limitations of external validity. Internal validity refers to the ability of the evaluation to produce accurate estimates of the effects of the innovation while focusing on the people who actually participated in the program. If the randomization is compromised, for example, "treated" students may differ significantly from "control" students. In this situation the true effect of the program cannot be estimated. Besides the examples of administrative errors in randomization cited above, internal validity is often threatened in the data-collection process. Researchers need to be able to identify a specific group of students—the students who participated in the intervention—but sometimes these students are difficult to find or unwilling to participate in the research. If the reluctance to participate is correlated with the treatment (e.g., students who lost the lottery are angry and do not want to participate), then those students receiving the treatment for whom post-experiment/intervention data are available may differ systematically from those not receiving treatment for whom data are available. In sum, not only may the survey effort be costly, but failure to monitor response rates may lead to biased and internally invalid inferences and attrition from the sample may undermine randomization.

One way to avoid the problems that response rates may create is to use administrative data. Recent work by Angrist et al. (forthcoming) uses administrative records to demonstrate the differences between voucher lottery winners and losers. By matching national identification numbers to other databases, the authors are able to follow up with all students who applied for the voucher lottery. This strategy has a lower cost than other means of getting data, although it may not be internally valid if record keeping is not equivalent across winners and losers.[7]

---

[7] In one jurisdiction, as mentioned above, program managers maintained up-to-date records for voucher lottery winners but not for losers. As a result, voucher winners were much more likely to have a valid national identification number and therefore much more likely to match to post-intervention/experiment data.

External validity is another worry of researchers. External validity refers to whether or not the results can be replicated and are relevant for populations besides those participating in the educational intervention. For example, the students who applied to Mexico's PROGRESA program are among the poorest in the nation. As discussed below, the PROGRESA program has improved student enrollment rates amongst these students. The external validity of this result hinges on whether or not this same result would be observed in other populations of students. If the subsidies to families were targeted at middle class or upper class families in the country, would those students also have seen the bump in enrollment rates? The results from PROGRESA shed no light on this question.

Additionally, it is not clear that the PROGRESA results will be externally valid even among students with comparable socioeconomic characteristics. Families in the PROGRESA program had to maintain records and regularly visit doctors, and highly motivated families may be more willing to do these tasks. If these families are more likely to apply to the program, then the observed results may be the effects for "highly motivated" families rather than the effects for all families. In this case, there is an unobservable characteristic (internal motivation) that prompts some families to apply to the program. Comparisons outside of that group may not be valid.

The ability of one country to replicate the programs of another country may threaten external validity. Oftentimes, there are cultural or political barriers preventing reasonable replication. Mexico's PROGRESA program has been implemented in Brazil, Colombia, and other countries. In Colombia, the program was not implemented in a way similar to PROGRESA due to the political environment, and therefore the results may differ significantly. Threats to external validity may occur for regions within a country as well. In the United States, evidence from the Tennessee STAR program on the effectiveness of smaller class sizes led other states (e.g., California) to adopt similar programs. Much like the replication of PROGRESA in other countries, it is not clear that programs in other states experienced the gains from reduced class size that the Tennessee program led to.

Concerns about external validity may be a short-run weakness of randomized evaluation. A single randomized experiment allows researchers to identify a set of conditions under which an intervention may affect student welfare. The question of whether the results from that experiment generalize to a different set of conditions is empirical. By changing the conditions and implementing a similar randomized experiment, researchers can identify a specific intervention's effects in other settings. The duplication of studies under varying conditions allows researchers to draw greater conclusions about the external validity of a particular intervention. In the United States, for example, the implementation of housing subsidies (i.e., Section 8 vouchers) was conducted through a sequential series of randomized experiments. The series of randomizations allowed the U.S. government to identify various conditions affecting the success of housing subsidies.

Finally, most randomized experiments measure a partial equilibrium effect of a program and not the general equilibrium effect. The partial equilibrium effect is the effect of the program on a select group of people under a specific set of circumstances. If the program was deemed successful and expanded to the general population, the set of circumstances that attended the randomized trial may change. For example, studies of voucher programs in the United States frequently focus on the effects for a small group of students attending established schools, typically parochial schools. Where voucher programs have been expanded to larger populations (e.g., Cleveland), numerous new private schools entered the market. These schools have less experience and potentially a different effect on students than the schools participating in the randomized trial. Similar expansions of private school have take place in Colombia and Chile (for Colombia, see Angrist et al., 2002; for Chile, see Hsieh and Urquiola, 2003).

Treatment Intensity and the Interpretation of Effects

One of the inherent difficulties of randomized evaluation is the accurate identification of the effects of an intervention on the people who have actually participated in it. Randomization can almost always identify the effects of an intervention on those to whom policymakers offered the intervention. This is often called the "intention to treat" parameter.[8]

---

[8] Researchers have also attempted to estimate the effect of the "treatment on the treated." This parameter measures the effect on people actually participating in the program as opposed to all people who were invited (or randomly selected) to participate. Under certain assumptions, randomization may provide a suitable instrumental variable for identifying this parameter. Rouse (1998) and Angrist et al. (2002) discuss this possibility and the assumptions necessary to calculate the effect.

However, many who are offered an intervention never enroll. For example, in the Colombian voucher program, not everyone accepted the voucher. In the PROGRESA program, not every family in a participating village chose to participate. Because people who accept the offer to participate in a program may differ systematically from people who decline the offer, and because we cannot observe intent to participate among people who are randomly excluded from participation in the program, it may be difficult to measure accurately the effect on only those who participate in the intervention. Randomization does not facilitate the estimation of such an effect unless everyone offered the intervention utilizes the intervention. Some have argued that the "intention to treat" is the parameter of central interest to policymakers (e.g., Rouse, 1998), because it measures the net effect of the program across people offered the intervention—as opposed to just those people who participate. However, others may want to know the specific effect of the treatment on the people who actually participate in the program.

Finally, the treatment may oftentimes affect the control group as well as the treatment group, making it difficult to compare the two. The most obvious example of this can be found in the results of randomized deworming projects in Kenya. Within schools, students were randomly chosen to receive oral treatments for hookworm, roundworm, and schistosomiasis (Miguel and Kremer 2001); however, because these treatments led to a decrease in contamination in the general population, all students at the school benefited from reduced rates of transmission, even those who had not received these treatments. This made it difficult for researchers to identify the effect of treatment. Similarly, if the control or treatment groups alter behavior as a result of the program, it may bias estimates of the effect of the program. For example, Hoxby (2000) criticizes the Tennessee STAR class-size experiments because teachers participated whether they had a large or small class. Teachers generally prefer small classes, and so participating teachers may have adjusted their behavior to improve the attractiveness of small classes to policymakers.

Political Economy Model of Project Implementation

The appendix shows a simple political economy model that evaluates which types of projects policymakers are likely to implement. The key assumption in the model is that success varies according to the size of a project and the length of time it will take to complete. Some small projects yield immediate short-run benefits, but their long-run impact does not differ substantially from their short-run impact. Other projects may yield few short-run benefits, but have a long-run impact that is much higher than the projects that show short-term benefits. The second type of project is riskier in that it may have higher rewards but may also fail, leading to a large loss of investment. The intuition behind these projects is two-fold: successful programs may take time to produce, and given time, a program can identify and improve upon its weaknesses.

For simplicity, we can assume that there are only these two types of projects. Type A are those that are often large-scale and slow to develop, with small short-run effect and greater long-term effects. Type B projects are easy to implement and can succeed in the short run but may not be as effective in the long run.[9] Figure 1 plots this relationship.

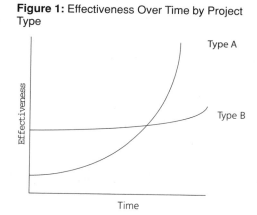

Figure 1: Effectiveness Over Time by Project Type

Time creates an obvious tension in this model. Because individuals are impatient, they will be reluctant to embark on Type A projects. Moreover, not only do Type A projects appear to take too long, but they may not succeed. Because the variance of project success increases in size as a project increases in scale, risk-averse individuals are less likely to embark on large projects. In practice, impatience and risk aversion manifest themselves in both political and academic spheres. For example, politicians may be reluctant to enact important interventions because they will be up for reelection before the results of a long-term intervention will be available. Likewise, researchers—especially those with short tenure clocks—may pursue projects of lesser

---

[9] The designation between Type A and Type B projects is fuzzy at best. Oftentimes, we do not know the true importance of a project until we know its effects. Interventions that appear small may actually provide cost-effective solutions. I use the A/B designation to conceptualize the trade-offs associated with a large-scale intervention like PROGRESA in comparison to a number of smaller projects that may have less overall impact.

importance because results from research on topics of higher importance may take "too long" to obtain.

As discussed above, randomized evaluation can be more costly and more time consuming than other types of evaluation. If you factor these possibilities into the model described in the Appendix, policymakers and researchers may be even more reluctant to implement a program, particularly if randomization increases the time that one must wait for success. However, as Kremer (2004) points out, higher cost need not accompany randomized evaluation. There are numerous examples of inexpensive randomized studies of interventions that have yielded large, long-lasting effects on students. Data on the costs of interventions and evaluations are not commonplace, but when available can provide more detail on the trade-offs associated with different interventions. In addition, the opportunity costs of not undertaking any intervention or not generating new knowledge may be substantial. As Derek Bok is credited with saying, "If you think education is expensive, try ignorance."

The model also suggests that certain conditions (e.g., a longer time horizon or government stability) will improve the likelihood that an organization or government will embark on a randomized experiment. The greater the likelihood that the central leadership will remain in power for a long period of time, the more likely that it may be able to enact a policy. This may be one reason that Mexico was able to implement the PROGRESA program. Also, the more incentives that researchers have to produce more long-term projects, the more likely that they will undertake Type A projects.

CHANGES IN KNOWLEDGE BASE
FROM RANDOMIZED EXPERIMENTS

This chapter shows how randomized experiments have augmented the body of academic knowledge in regard to four types of educational innovations: school infrastructure development, student health, the provision of textbooks and other learning aids, and teacher and student incentives. This chapter attempts to identify the value added by randomized studies in these fields.

Ideally, one would create a complete census of randomized and nonrandomized interventions in education; however, this is impractical for two reasons. First, as the quote from Hanushek (1995) points out above, although many informal experiments are taking place across the world, most are not disseminating their findings. As a result, many experimental studies are lost in dusty cabinets or in library basements. To the extent that it is possible to track down such evaluations, I have attempted to do so. Nonetheless, the set of randomized experiments upon which I focus will be more representative of recent randomized experiments than of the entire body of work in this field.

The second problem is the sheer volume of research regarding these educational topics. Assessing the state of knowledge in the absence of randomized experiments is difficult, especially because there are large discrepancies in the quality of evaluations. For example, there are many non-experimental studies that acknowledge but do not resolve selection bias. There are yet other non-experimental studies that take advantage of "natural experiments" (e.g., changes in a country's policies) and identify the effects of the program using quasi-random variation. There are still other studies that make distributional assumptions and use observable characteristics to provide clues to the nature of the unobservable variables that may cause selection bias.[10] I rely heavily on pre-existing literature reviews to assess academic understanding prior to the recent waves of experimental evidence.

School Infrastructure Development

School construction is an area where all of the promise and problems of randomized experiments are evident. School construction is costly, and it takes a substantial amount of time to actually gauge its effects on student enrollment and attainment. Moreover, building a school in one location may exclude access to students in another, presenting difficult ethical issues. In recent years, two randomized experiments involving school building have taken place.

Before describing these studies, it may be useful to show what economists and researchers actually knew about the effects of school infrastructure prior to the experiments. In the mid-1960s, economists and policy makers were unsure as to the best way to improve access to school. Most agreed that increasing the supply of schools would improve access (Lock-

---

[10] There are a number of studies which analyze randomized experiments as if they are not randomized. For example, Dehejia and Wahba (1998) find that propensity score matching rather than matching based on randomization can yield similar results to randomized studies.

heed and Verspoor, 1991). However, Kindleberger summed up the knowledge as follows, "Work to improve [educational] data and the analysis goes forward to clarify the choices to be made. The need for more education is clear in underdeveloped countries at least, even though the amounts to be sought cannot be quantified" (1965: 115). In a survey of the (non-experimental) literature on school access, Lockheed and Verspoor argued that while there had been an observed increase in enrollment, access remained limited and groups of children were still completely excluded in very low-income countries.

Efforts to improve the supply of schools led to a number of projects. For example, in the late 1960s, Taiwan embarked on an aggressive school-building project, and in the mid-1970s, windfalls from oil revenue in Indonesia led to massive school-building projects. Taiwan and Indonesia's school-building projects were not implemented using randomization. Recent empirical work suggests that these projects could have affected enrollment and attainment. For example, Clark and Hsieh (2000) find that students received almost 0.5 years additional education as a result of Taiwan's school-building project. From 1967 to 1968, Taiwan almost doubled the number of junior high schools in the country. Using national survey data, Clark and Hsieh compare the educational attainment of young men who had already passed junior-high age to the educational attainment of men who had yet to enter junior high in 1968. The males that received the most exposure to the program received 0.42 additional years of schooling compared to the control group.

Although the result suggests that these increases in schooling were an effect of school construction, the results may be confounded by other factors. As Spohr (2003) shows, around this same time, Taiwan introduced mandatory enrollment requirements. The students who were exposed to the junior-high construction project were also exposed to mandatory enrollment requirements. Because of this confounding factor, it is unclear what the true effect of the Taiwan school-building project was on enrollment rates.

Duflo (2000) evaluated the rapid increase in school construction in Indonesia. As in Taiwan, the program was not randomized; however, Duflo shows that the allocation of schools differed by region over time, creating "quasi-randomness" that can be used to evaluate the effects of school construction. She argues that differences in education should be higher not only for younger individuals who were in school when the program began but also for children in regions with more schools built. Duflo shows that the increase in primary-school construction led to both an increase in educational attainment in Indonesia and an increase in wages. Given the regional and temporal variation of school allocation and the corresponding changes in student access, the evidence for the positive effects of school construction is compelling.

Two randomized experiments in school construction, one in Pakistan and the other in Kenya, shed further light on the effects of construction on education. The first study focuses on the creation of private girls' schools under the Urban Girls' Fellowship program, which began in 1995 in Quetta, Pakistan (the capital city of Balochistan). Kim et al. (1998) examine a pilot project that created additional schools. To appease political constituencies, the government of Balochistan guaranteed that each of the ten major urban slum areas would have one school; however, they randomized within neighborhoods as to the location of the school. Kim et al. show that girls' enrollment increased by 33 percentage points and boys' enrollments increased by 27.5 percentage points. The authors suggest this occurred in part because boys were also allowed to attend the new schools. Many parents would not send their daughters to school if they could not also send their sons. One interesting finding was that although the success of the program differed across neighborhoods, it was not necessarily related to the relative wealth of the neighborhood or the education levels of parents. Thus, the authors conclude that this program offers promise for increased enrollments in other poor urban areas.

A similar randomized experiment took place in Kenya. Kremer et al. (2003) evaluated a program that offered funding to seven schools randomly selected from a group of fourteen schools with poor performance. The funding provided for new uniforms and textbooks, as well as for the construction of new classrooms. Not only did the dropout rates fall at the schools where funding increased, but the schools also received an influx of new students. Although class sizes grew, parents still supported the program and were willing to trade off larger classes for the additional funding.

Oftentimes, the key problem for developing countries is not the availability of school buildings but rather the availability of teachers. Student-teacher ratios can be used to illustrate the extent to which teachers are not available. There have been a number of studies that look at the effect of student-teacher ratios on student access and achievement, although few use randomization.

Fuller (1985) examines the effect of student-teacher ratios on achievement and finds little evidence of any effect. Lockheed (1987) looks at the effects of school characteristics on students, particularly the effects of student-teacher ratios on student achievement in Thailand. In her review of the literature on student-teacher ratios, she claims that high student-teacher ratios negatively affect student outcomes. Deaton and Case (1998) look at the effect of student-teacher ratios on educational attainment in South Africa. They find that student-teacher ratios have little effect on student outcomes except in the case of black students. Black students in classes with lower student-teacher ratios advance more quickly and are more likely to be in school than those in classes with higher student-teacher ratios.

There are few studies of student-teacher ratios that rely on randomization. In the most publicized study of student-teacher ratios, Krueger and Whitmore (2002) examine how student-teacher ratios affect student attainment through a randomized experiment in Tennessee. They find that small class size improves student outcomes. In developing countries, there is less evidence to support this finding. Banerjee, Jacob, and Kremer (2002) examine the effect of adding a second teacher in rural schools in Udaipur, India. This second teacher, who was female whenever possible, was randomly assigned to 21 of 42 one-teacher non-formal schools operated by an NGO. The effect of the program was significant and positive on the fraction of girls attending school; however, the authors did not find evidence that the additional teacher affected test scores.

Both random and nonrandom studies conclude that student-teacher ratios and school buildings matter. The studies on school construction provide some evidence as to the precise effect of new schools, although these results may not be externally valid to other scenarios. Interestingly, randomized studies of teacher supply find an enrollment effect but not a corresponding effect on attainment. The results suggest that the effects of teacher supply may also differ by context.

Student Health and Education

A number of randomized experiments in developing countries have focused on improvements in student health. The rationale for many of these programs has been that improving student health may have indirect effects on student education.

Economists have long postulated that there is a direct link between health and education. Enke writes, "Health and education are often joint goods. If children have poor health, they will lose many days from school, so that better health may result in better education... Health and education are alike in that their benefits accrue partly to the individual and partly to others. When a person is cured of tuberculosis there is also a gain for the people whom he might otherwise infect" (1963: 404).

Alderman et al. (1997) investigate the effect of children's health and nutrition on school enrollments in rural Pakistan. They do not rely on randomization. Instead, they use longitudinal data and examine how price shocks to food affected health and nutrition. They identify price shocks that occurred when children were preschool age to determine their health and nutrition stock. They find health and nutrition are three times more important to school-enrollment decisions than suggested by earlier estimates that considered child health and nutrition to be predetermined rather than determined by household decisions. Especially relevant to this study, they find that improvements in nutrition were more pronounced for girls and contributed to reduced gender differences in enrollment. They conclude that improvements in the health and nutrition of preschool children are likely to have long-run productivity effects that result in more schooling and possibly reduce the gender gaps in schooling.

A number of experimental studies have evaluated the effects of health innovations on student outcomes.[11] Miguel and Kremer (2001), for example, study the effects of a de-worming project in 75 primary schools in Kenya. These schools were phased into the program in a randomized order. Miguel and Kremer's research differs from other studies of de-worming by randomizing across schools rather than randomizing across children in the same school. Studies that focus on students within the same school fail to find significant impacts of de-worming (Dickson et al., 2000). Miguel and Kremer find that de-worming programs at the school level led to significantly higher primary-school attendance after two years of medical treatment and that absenteeism fell by almost 25 percent. Miguel and Kremer (2001) also find that de-worming creates large externality benefits by reducing the local incidence of infection within the population not participating in the program. Their study suggests that curbing tropical diseases, especially in Sub-Saharan Africa, can improve school participation.

---

[11] These studies are discussed in more detail in Kremer (this volume).

Bobonis et al. (2003) evaluate efforts to deworm preschool-age children in the urban slums of Delhi, India. Preliminary findings suggest that preschool participation rates increased by 6.3 percentage points for participants and school absenteeism fell by one fifth. Based on these initial findings, the authors advocate the program as a cost-effective way of improving enrollment for children in poor urban areas where the spread of intestinal worms is a problem.

There are a number of interesting lessons that emerge in the comparison of randomized and nonrandomized studies of student health and educational access. First, constructing an appropriate control group for a nonrandomized study is difficult. Researchers must use regional and temporal variation in treatment to construct their studies, and as before, these types of variation can mask confounding factors that may also affect health and/or educational access. In comparison, randomized experiments can provide an accurate estimate of the effect of health interventions on student outcomes. Second, within randomized experiments, the level at which the randomization occurs makes a difference. This is particularly true in health innovations. Treating students within a locale may have external effects on non-treated students (e.g., less incidence of infection). Randomized experiments can be difficult to evaluate if the treatment and control groups are both affected by the intervention. Experimental studies at the individual level within schools could not measure the effects of de-worming because of a decreased incidence of infection within the school, but experimental studies across schools measured a significant effect because they studied populations more isolated from one another.

Student Vouchers and Incentives

Many policymakers have attempted recently to improve educational access by changing the incentives to students. Two policy reforms in particular have been implemented in multiple countries. The first policy reform is a large-scale educational voucher program, such as the programs implemented in Chile and in Colombia. The second policy reform is a set of student subsidies that pay students and families for school attendance, regular health check-ups, and in some cases, student achievement.

Chile established educational vouchers in 1981. The voucher program is a universal program that allows any student to transport the voucher to any participating school. Although many researchers have attempted to measure the effect of the Chilean voucher system on educational access and attainment, there is still no definitive evidence that the voucher system had positive effects on students. A number of studies find positive effects of the voucher (e.g., Carnoy and McEwan, 2001). Other studies find no significant improvement in educational attainment as a result of the voucher program (e.g., Hsieh and Uruquiola, 2003). In their evaluations of the Chilean program, these researchers face the difficulty of constructing a credible control group. As in the studies that investigate school construction, some researchers have compared students who entered the schools prior to the voucher program to those who entered afterward. As before, if there are other systematic changes (e.g., Chile increased teacher pay dramatically after the voucher program started), then it may be unclear whether the effects are due to the voucher program or to other innovations.

Although the voucher program in Colombia was not as large and widely recognized, studies of this program have provided more definitive evidence of the effect of educational vouchers on student outcomes. The key difference between the Chilean and Columbian programs (and as a result, in the research evaluations) is the use of randomization. In the Colombian voucher program, there was a small supply of vouchers, and demand far exceeded supply. Policymakers used randomization to distribute educational vouchers fairly across applicants. Angrist et al. (2002) use this randomized distribution to identify the effects of the educational voucher. They compare students who won the voucher lottery to students who did not. Although they do not find differences in dropout rates after three years, they find that students receiving the voucher were less likely to repeat grades. Subsequent work by Angrist et al. (forthcoming) finds that students who won the voucher lottery were more likely to take and score higher on college entrance exams. Because the randomization only occurs at the level of students applying for the voucher, it is difficult to identify whether the observed effects are the result of private schooling or changes in student incentives. The voucher led to a large increase in the number of students attending private school; however, the voucher changed the students' incentives because students lost their vouchers if they did not maintain academic progress.

Although the randomization in the Colombian voucher program enabled researchers to identify effects of the voucher program, it was only possible to do so in selected cities. Angrist et al. (2002) measured the effect of the educational voucher in Bogotá and Jamundi only. There are a number of other cities for which complete voucher records exist, but in almost every case there appears to be some evidence of nonrandomness. For example, in multiple cities, students with phones and students who were older won the voucher lottery more frequently, suggesting either nonrandomness or differences in record keeping for voucher lottery winners and losers. In one city, there was additional evidence of nonrandomness. Because students could only apply for the voucher after being admitted to a private school, the lottery was random not only among students but among schools as well. In one city, 100 percent of applicants from one school won the lottery, while no other school had above a 20 percent rate of winning the lottery. Even more disconcerting, local citizens claimed that this was the most politically connected school in the city.

Another intervention that affects student incentives is the use of cash payments to reward students for attendance, regular health check-ups, and in some places, achievement. The most widely cited program is the PROGRESA program in Mexico, which was implemented in 1998. In its initial phases, the Mexican government randomly chose 320 out of 506 potential rural villages to take part in the program. Families received a cash payment if their children both attended school and had regular health check ups. There are a number of papers that evaluate PROGRESA (e.g., Schultz, 2002; Bobonis and Finan, 2002). I focus on Behrman et al. (2001). The authors of this study use the randomization to measure the impact of PROGRESA on initial age at entering school, dropout rates, grade repetition rates, and school reentry rates. They find that the program was effective in reducing dropout rates and facilitated "progression through the grades," especially the transition from primary to secondary school. The program also induced a significant number of children who had dropped out prior to the implementation of PROGRESA to re-enter school. Unlike the health experiments, Behrman et al. do not find evidence of strong spillover effects on children who lived in the communities where PROGRESA was implemented, but did not receive subsidies. Behrman et al. (2001) project that PROGRESA might improve secondary school enrollments by as much as 19 percent.

Programs in other countries have also suggested that cash payments may influence educational decisions. In Israel, Angrist and Lavy (2002) found that providing cash-incentives for low-income students could increase *Begrut* (the Israeli high-school matriculation exam) completion, even though the value of the cash-incentive was much less than the actual returns to education. In the United States, Keane and Wolpin (2000) evaluated a 1998 proposal by Robert Reich that would offer cash bonuses to students from low-income families to graduate from high school. Keane and Wolpin found that such an incentive would reduce dropout rates for black students by two-thirds and dropout rates for white students by one-half.

The results of PROGRESA and the voucher programs provide convincing evidence that changing student incentives can alter enrollment and achievement. Still, randomization is not without drawbacks. There were a number of places where additional evidence could have been gathered from the Colombian voucher project, but administrative misunderstanding of the role of randomization and other sources of nonrandomness made it difficult to evaluate a number of settings. This reflects the challenges of internal validity mentioned in the previous section. The Colombian voucher program ended in 1997. The evaluation of its efficacy was published in 2002. This time delay accentuates the length of time it takes to produce accurate research on the effects of educational innovations.

Innovations that Improve Quality of Education

There are a number of educational innovations that focus on better preparing students for future education or the workforce by improving the quality of instruction. Many initiatives have attempted to train teachers to teach more effectively. Other programs have focused on improving classroom instruction through audio-visual materials, particularly computers, and learning aids such as chalkboards, flip charts, and textbooks.

Recent programs have aimed to change incentives to teachers. In many cases, teachers receive substantial bonuses based on their students' performance. Advocates of such programs argue that these programs can increase the incentive for teachers to provide effective instruction, but opponents feel these programs promote "teaching to the test."

Glewwe et al. (2003) report evidence from a randomized evaluation of a program in Kenya that provided primary-school teachers with incentives based on their students' test scores. They find that students in schools where teachers received monetary bonuses for student improvement were more likely to take exams and had higher test scores than students in other schools without the teacher incentive program. However, they do not find support for the hypothesis that these teacher incentives could reduce dropout rates or increase long-run learning. Teachers' attendance rates and the amount of homework assigned were similar across treatment and control schools. The key difference was the increase in test preparation and encouragement for students to take the test in the treatment schools. When the program ended, test score differences across treated and untreated schools disappeared.

The outcome of teacher incentives in this program was consistent with teachers using strategies that increased test scores in the short-run but did not promote long-run learning. Also, given that Kenya's centralized educational system does not provide incentives for teachers to promote long-run learning, alternative programs such as decentralizing control of teachers to the local level or allowing parents to choose schools might prove more effective in improving long-term learning.

Evaluation of the effectiveness of introducing textbooks and other learning aids is an area where randomized experiments have significantly changed our understanding of the educational process. Studies from non-randomized programs suggest positive effects, but recent evidence based on randomized experiments in Kenya suggests that the true effect, if any, may be extremely small.

In his summary of the research on textbook implementation, Fuller (1985) reports that most studies (14 of 22) found that textbooks significantly improved student achievement. Of the 22 studies that Fuller considers, only a few used experimental research designs, and Fuller concludes that these provide the clearest evidence. Lockheed and Hanushek (1987) review evidence from 15 empirical studies concerning the cost-effectiveness of several educational inputs, and find that textbooks are among the more cost-effective inputs.[12] Lockheed and Hanushek discuss the possibility of some heterogeneity in the studies assessing the effectiveness of textbooks. They show that different studies could have reached different conclusions depending on how well matched the level, language, and teacher preparation was for that book in a particular classroom. Like Fuller, they push for more experimental evaluation. They summarize, "Although the firmest conclusions about effectiveness come from experi-

---

12 The most cost effective inputs were textbooks, interactive radio, peer tutoring, and cooperative learning. The least cost-effective interventions included teacher training and technical-vocational schools.

ments, very few true educational experiments have been undertaken in developing countries, particularly on a large scale. Many of what are described as 'experiments' are actually changes in national policy, which, by being implemented uniformly, lack variation. The impact of these 'experiments' on student learning, moreover, are seldom evaluated" (1987: 18).

Glewwe et al. (2004) and Kremer et al. (2000) evaluate a series of efforts to bring flip charts and textbooks to students in Kenya. Glewwe et al. examine the effectiveness of flip charts as a teaching tool. Their sample included 178 schools, of which half received flip charts from a non-government charity. They analyze the data in two comparable ways. First, they do not exploit the randomization and instead compare flip chart schools to all other schools. Using this method, they find that flip charts raised test scores by up to 20 percent of a standard deviation. This number did not change once controls for other educational inputs were added. When they exploit the randomized implementation to evaluate the program's effectiveness, however, they find no evidence that test scores increased with the use of flip charts. They conclude that many retrospective studies of nonrandomized trials would have greatly overestimated the effect of this type of program, and they stress the fact that the results would have been misleading because of omitted-variable bias.

Glewwe et al. (2000) evaluate the effects of textbook provision on student outcomes. A Dutch non-profit organization (Internationaal Christelijk Steunfonds) began a program in 1996 to help 100 primary schools in rural Kenya. In the first year, they randomly selected 25 schools to receive textbooks. In contrast to previous studies of textbook provision, the randomized evaluation of this program produced no evidence that the textbooks had a large positive effect on average test scores nor that the program affected other outcomes such as attendance and dropout rates. Using a variety of methods, the authors compare test scores across students in both treatment and control schools. For all three estimates, after one year, the impact of the textbooks across all subjects and grades is close to zero, and depending upon the estimator used, this estimate is sufficiently precise to reject the hypothesis that the textbooks increased test scores by as little as 0.07 standard deviations. They find the results of the estimates after two and three years to be similar. Because these findings differ from previous studies on textbooks, the importance of other components of textbook use—such as the teacher training for the use of the books and the particular textbook used, as well as family background—come into question. In addition, the findings further illuminate the results from the earlier paper by Glewwe et al. (2000).

CONCLUSION

The use of randomized experiments in the implementation of educational interventions continues to become more prevalent across developed and developing countries. Although randomization has the potential to provide key answers to the types of educational programs that should be implemented and the method of implementation, this study provides some caution on the ways in which randomized experiments should be applied. Although randomization can greatly improve global knowledge about education and its provision, it does not guarantee clear conclusions.

Randomization has many potential pitfalls. It may be costly to conduct, it may require substantial and detailed oversight to ensure the integrity of the randomization, and it may require substantial time to yield meaningful conclusions. In the case of educational vouchers, hundreds of cities in Colombia embarked on ambitious educational voucher initiatives; however, most of these did not yield lessons as to the efficacy of the voucher programs. Poor record-keeping and compromises to the randomization prevented evaluation of a number of sites. Still, although many years elapsed before researchers were able to evaluate the other sites where the randomized evaluation was appropriately conducted, these programs provided conclusive evidence on the efficacy of vouchers in specific settings.

There are other trade-offs that researchers and policymakers must consider in using randomization. Because of the substantial time required to implement and evaluate some of the most important interventions, researchers and policymakers must balance their desire for quick results with their desire for comprehensive and important solutions. Researchers must also consider the costs and benefits of both the intervention and the randomized evaluation.

Has randomization improved global understanding of education and its provision? Undoubtedly. For example, although economists have long suspected relationships between health interventions and educational interventions, randomized experiments in Kenya and other places have demonstrated conclusive evidence that drug treatments can have significant effects on school attendance not only for students receiving them but also on other students (Miguel and Kremer, 2001). The randomized experiments have given us an idea of the magnitude of the effects of such interventions.

There are some educational interventions that may still be evaluated in the absence of randomization. For example, researchers exploiting quasi-randomness in school building projects provide convincing evidence of their effects on student enrollment and attainment (Duflo, 2000). These other approaches both complement randomized evaluations and provide important insights to educational knowledge and the implications of randomized trials. However, in other cases, retrospective evaluations may give misleading results. As Glewwe et al. (2000) illustrate, in some settings, failure to exploit randomization could lead to spurious findings. In the case of flip-chart provision, non-randomized evaluations suggest that flip charts had large effects on student achievement; however, evaluations that took advantage of randomization did not show an effect.

Finally, internal and external validity must also be scrutinized in randomized evaluations. Administrative data may provide comprehensive follow-up and hence improve the internal validity of estimated effects. Systematic ways to improve the external validity of a particular educational reform must be considered when structuring educational reforms. External validity may be an important weakness of random experiments, although it may be overcome through a careful determination of the location and nature of the educational intervention.

Appendix: Political Economy Model of Project Implementation

In this model, consumers implement educational projects. Consumers attempt to maximize their lifetime utility subject to the cost of the project, as equation (4) shows:

$$\max E\left[\sum_{t=1}^{\infty} \beta^t\, u(\tilde{S}(I,t))\right] \text{ subject to } \sum_{t=1}^{\infty} R^t\, C(I,t) \leq C \quad (A1)$$

where $E[\,]$ denotes the expectation operator and _ is the rate of time preference. Individual's utility is a function of the success of a program (), which is drawn from a distribution whose variance increases with the size of a project (I). Success varies by the size of a project and over time. The budget constraint is such that the present discounted value of the cost of the project must be lower than the capacity of the economy to support it.

We can assume that the people's utility increases with the success of a program but at a decreasing rate. This assumption implies that people will be risk averse. We can also make some reasonable assumptions about the nature of the success function. In particular, we can assume that success increases with the time that the program operates, and that the rate of increase in success also increases. Another way to phrase this assumption is that while it takes time to produce a successful program, over time a program can improve upon its weaknesses. We can write these assumptions as follows:

$$u'(S)>0,\ u''(S)<0,\ \frac{\delta E(S)}{dt}>0,\ \frac{\delta_2 E(S)}{dt^2}>0 \quad (A2)$$

For simplicity, we can assume that there are two types of projects—Type A and Type B. Type A projects are often large-scale and slow to develop. They may not have large short-run effects, but their long-run effects may be greater than other projects. Type B projects are easy to implement and can succeed in the short run but may not be as effective in the long-run. Figure 1 in the text plots this relationship.

Time creates an obvious tension in this model. Because individuals are impatient, they will be reluctant to embark on Type A projects. Moreover, because individuals are risk averse and because the variance of project success increases over time, risk-averse individuals are less likely to embark on large projects: not only do they take too long, but there is a greater variance in the likelihood that they will succeed.

References

Alderman, Harold, Jere Behrman, Victor Lavy, and Rekha Menon. 1997. "Child Nutrition, Child Health, and School Enrollment: A Longitudinal Analysis." World Bank Policy Research Working Paper 1700.

Alderman, Harold, Peter Orazem, and Elizabeth Paterno. 2001. "School Quality, School Cost and the Public/Private School Choices of Low-Income Households in Pakistan." *Journal of Human Resources* 36: 304–326.

Angrist, Joshua, Eric Bettinger, Erik Bloom, Michael Kremer, and Elizabeth King. 2002. "The Effects of School Vouchers on Students: Evidence from Colombia." *American Economic Review* 92 (5): 1535–1558.

Angrist, Joshua, Eric Bettinger, and Michael Kremer. Forthcoming. "Evidence from a Randomized Experiment: The Effect of Educational Vouchers on Long-run Educational Outcomes." *American Economic Review.*

Angrist, Joshua, and Alan Krueger. 2001. "Instrumental Variables and the Search for Identification: From Supply and Demand to Natural Experiments." *Journal of Economic Perspectives* 15: 69–85.

Angrist, Joshua, and Victor Lavy. 2002. "The Effect of High School Matriculation Awards: Evidence from Randomized Trials." NBER Working Paper 9389.

Banerjee, Abhijit, Suraj Jacob, and Michael Kremer, with Jenny Lanjouw, and Peter Lanjouw. 2002 " Promoting School Participation in Rural Rajasthan: Results from Some Prospective Trials." Mimeo.

Bashir, Sajitha. 1997. *The Cost Effectiveness of Public and Private Schools: Knowledge Gaps, New Research Methodologies, and an Application in India.* New York: Clarendon Press.

Bedi, Arjun, and Ashish Garg. 2000. "The Effectiveness of Private versus Public Schools: The Case of Indonesia." *Journal of Development Economics* 61: 463–494.

Behrman, Jere, Piyali Sengupta, and Petra Todd. 2001. "Progressing Through PROGRESA: An Impact Assessment of a School Subsidy Experiment."

Bettinger, Eric. 2000. "The Effect of Vouchers on Educational Achievement: Evidence from Michigan." Mimeo. Case Western Reserve.

Bobonis, Gustavo, and Frederica Finan. 2002. "Transfers to the Poor Increase the Schooling of the Non-Poor: The Case of Mexico's PROGRESA Program." Mimeo. University of California, Berkley.

Bobonis, Gustavo, Edward Miguel, and Charu Sharma. 2003. "Child Nutrition and Education: A Randomized Evaluation in India." Mimeo. University of California, Berkeley.

Carnoy, Martin, and Patrick McEwan. 2001. "Privatization Through Vouchers in Developing Countries: The Cases of Chile and Colombia." Pp.151–177 in *Privatizing Education: Can the Marketplace Deliver Choice, Efficiency, Equity, and Social Cohesion?* Boulder: Westview Press.

Clark, Diana, and Chang-Tai Hsieh. 2000. "Schooling and Labor Market Impact of the 1968 Nine-Year Education Program in Taiwan." Mimeo. Princeton University.

Deaton, Angus, and Anne Case. 1998. "School Quality and Educational Outcomes in South Africa." *Papers* 184. Princeton: Woodrow Wilson School-Development Studies.

Dehejia, Rajeev, and Sadek Wahba. 1998. "Propensity Score Matching Methods for Non-experimental Causal Studies." NBER Working Paper Number 6829.

Dickson, Rumona, Shally Awasthi, Paula Williamson, Colin Demellweek, and Paul Garner. 2000. "Effect of Treatment for Intestinal Helminth Infection on Growth and Cognitive Performance in Children: Systematic Review of Randomized Trials." *British Medical Journal* 320 (June 24): 1967–1701.

Duflo, Esther. 2000. "Schooling and Labor Market Consequences of School Construction in Indonesia: Evidence from an Unusual Policy Experiment." *American Economic Review* 91 (4): 795–813.

Enke, Stephen. 1963. *Economics for Development.* New Jersey: Prentice-Hall.

Evans, William, and Robert Schwab. 1995. "Finishing High School and Starting College: Do Catholic Schools Make a Difference?" *Quarterly Journal of Economics* 10: 941–974.

Fuller, Bruce. 1985. "Raising School Quality in Developing Countries: What Investments Boost Learning?" World Bank Discussion Paper Series. Washington, DC: The World Bank.

Glewwe, Paul, Nauman Ilias, and Michael Kremer. 2003. "Teacher Incentives." NBER Working Paper 9671.

Glewwe, Paul, Michael Kremer, and Sylvie Moulin. 2000. "Textbooks and Test Scores: Evidence from a Prospective Evaluation in Kenya." Mimeo. Harvard University.

Glewwe, Paul, Michael Kremer, Sylvie Moulin, and Eric Zitzewitz. 2004. "Retrospective vs. Prospective Analyses of School Inputs: The Case of Flip Charts in Kenya." *Journal of Development Economics* 74 (1): 251–268.

Hanushek, Eric A. 1995. "Interpreting Recent Research on Schooling in Developing Countries." *World Bank Research Observer* 10 (August): 227–246.

Hoxby, Caroline M. 2000. "The Effect of Class Size on Student Achievement: New Evidence from Population Variation." *Quarterly Journal of Economics* 115 (4): 1239–1285.

Hsieh, Chang-Tai, and Miguel Urquiola. 2003. "When Schools Compete, How Do They Compete? An Assessment of Chile's Nationwide School Voucher Program." NBER Working Paper 10008.

Katz, Lawrence, Jeffrey Kling, and Jeffrey Liebman. 2000. "Moving to Opportunity in Boston: Early Results of Randomized Mobility Experiment." NBER Working Paper 7973.

Keane, Michael, and Kenneth Wolpin. 2000. "Eliminating Race Differences in School Attainment and Labor Market Success." *Journal of Labor Economics* 18 (4): 614–653.

Kim, Jooseop, Harold Alderman, and Peter Orazem. 1998. "Can Private Schools Subsidies Increase Schooling for the Poor? The Quetta Urban Fellowship Program." Working Paper Series on the Impact Evaluation of Education Reforms, No 11. Washington, DC: The World Bank.

Kindleberger, Charles. 1965. *Economic Development.* New York: McGraw-Hill.

Kremer, Michael. 2003. "Randomized Evaluations in Developing Countries: Some Lessons." *American Economic Review* 93 (2): 102–106.

Kremer, Michael, Sylvie Moulin, David Myatt, and Robert Namunyu. 1997. "The Quality-Quantity Tradeoff in Education: Evidence from a Prospective Evaluation in Kenya." Working paper.

Kremer, Michael, Sylvie Moulin and Robert Namunyu. 2003. "Decentralization: A Cautionary Tale." Mimeo. Harvard University.

Krueger, Alan. 2000. "Economic Considerations and Class Size." Mimeo. Princeton University.

Krueger, Alan, and Diane Whitmore. 2002. "The Effect of Attending a Small Class in the Early Grades on College-Test Taking and Middle School Test Results: Evidence from Project STAR." NBER Working Paper W7656.

Lockheed, Marlaine. 1987. "School and Classroom Effects on Student Learning Gain: The Case of Thailand." World Bank Discussion Paper Education and Training Series, Report No. EDT 98.

Lockheed, Marlaine, and Eric Hanushek. 1987. "Improving the Efficiency of Education in Developing Countries: Review of the Evidence." World Bank Discussion Paper Series. Washington, DC: The World Bank.

Lockheed, Marlaine, Adriaan Verspoor, and associates. 1991. *Improving Primary Education in Developing Countries.* World Bank Publication. Oxford: Oxford University Press.

Ludwig, Jens, Greg Duncan, and Paul Hirschfield. 2001. "Urban Poverty and Juvenile Crime: Evidence from a Randomized Housing-Mobility Experiment." *Quarterly Journal of Economics* 116: 655–679.

Meyer, Bruce. 1995. "Natural and Quasi-Experiments in Economics." *Journal of Business and Economic Statistics* 13: 151–161.

Miguel, Edward, and Michael Kremer. 2001. "Worms: Education and Health Externalities in Kenya." NBER Working Paper no. 8481.

Neal, Derek. 1997. "The Effects of Catholic Secondary Schooling on Educational Achievement." *Journal of Labor Economics* 15: 98–115.

Newman, John, Laura Rawlings, and Paul Gertler. 1994. "Using Randomized Control Designs in Evaluating Social Sector Programs in Developing Countries." *World Bank Research Observer* 9: 181–201.

No Child Left Behind Act. 2001. http://www.ed.gov/policy/elsec/leg/esea02/107-110.pdf.

Pritchett, Lant. 2002. "It Pays to be Ignorant: A Simple Political Economy of Rigorous Program Evaluation." *Policy Reform* 5 (4): 251–269.

Rouse, Cecilia. 1998. "Private School Vouchers and Student Achievement: An Evaluation of the Milwaukee Parental Choice Program." *Quarterly Journal of Economics* 113: 553–602.

Schultz, T. Paul. 2002. "School Subsidies for the Poor: Evaluating a Mexican Strategy For Reducing Poverty." Yale Economic Growth Center Paper 384.

Spohr, Christopher. 2003. "Formal Schooling and Workforce Participation in a Rapidly Developing Economy: Evidence from 'Compulsory' Junior High School in Taiwan." *Journal of Development Economics* 70: 291–327.

World Bank. 2003. "Evaluation Designs." http://www.worldbank.org/poverty/impact/methods/designs.htm.

CHAPTER 6

Expanding Educational Opportunity on a Budget: Lessons from Randomized Evaluations

MICHAEL KREMER

Although there has been tremendous progress in expanding school enrollments and increasing years of schooling in recent decades, approximately 113 million children of primary school age are still not enrolled in school (UNDP, 2003).[1]

This chapter reviews what has been learned from randomized evaluations of educational programs about how best to increase school participation. I discuss two types of programs that have been found to be extremely cost-effective and that could be implemented even within a very limited budget: school-based health programs and remedial education programs (that take advantage of available inexpensive sources of labor). I then outline a series of programs aimed at lowering the costs of school, or even paying students for attending school, that could be implemented if a higher level of financial support is available, and discuss the possibility of educational reform through school choice, which could be implemented given sufficient political will within a country. The chapter concludes by drawing some general lessons about the contribution of randomized evaluations to understanding the cost-effectiveness of various interventions.

Given the widespread consensus on the importance of education and several existing reviews of the impact of education on income and other outcomes, this chapter focuses not on the effects of education but on issues internal to the education system. The scope of this chapter is also

---

[1] For information on the "Education for All" initiative (which involves numerous organizations including UNESCO, UNICEF, the European Commission, and the World Bank), see UNESCO (2000, 2002).

limited in that it does not address interventions intended to improve the quality of education, such as computer-aided instruction, unless these interventions cut costs and thus free resources that can be used to expand education.

EFFECTIVE PROGRAMS FOR A LIMITED BUDGET

In this section, I outline two categories of programs that have been found to be extremely cost-effective means of making progress towards universal basic education. First, I discuss evidence, gathered from randomized evaluations of school-based health programs in Kenya and India, that suggests that simple and inexpensive treatments for basic health problems such as anemia and intestinal worms can dramatically increase the quantity of schooling that students attain. Second, I discuss the results of the randomized evaluation of a remedial education program in India that has been found to be an extremely cost-effective means of delivering education, particularly for weak students.

It is worth defining the terminology of "school participation" used in this chapter. In developing countries, many pupils attend school erratically and the distinction between a frequently absent pupil and a dropout is often unclear. Attendance rates can vary dramatically among individuals, and thus large differences in the quantity of schooling would be overlooked by considering only years of schooling. One attractive way to incorporate wide variation in attendance when measuring the quantity of schooling is to focus on a more comprehensive measure of schooling, often called "participation." For any child, participation is defined as the proportion of days that he or she is present in school to the number of days that the school is open, over a given period (e.g., Miguel and Kremer, 2004). This can be applied over one or more years, or just for a few days for which reliable data are available. Participation differs from attendance because attendance is usually defined only for children officially enrolled in school, whereas participation includes all children in the appropriate age range.

School-Based Health Programs

Poor health may limit school participation, especially in developing countries. Intestinal helminths (such as hookworm, roundworm, whipworm, and schistosomiasis) affect a quarter of the world's population and are particularly prevalent among school-age children. Moderate-to-severe worm infections can also lead to iron deficiency anemia, protein energy malnutrition, and undernutrition. Below, I review evidence from the evaluations of school-based health programs in Kenya and India.

Available low-cost, single-dose oral therapies can reduce hookworm, roundworm, and schistosomiasis infections by 99 percent (Butterworth et al., 1991; Nokes et al., 1992; Bennett and Guyatt, 2000), and the World Health Organization (WHO) has endorsed mass school-based de-worming programs in areas with high helminth infections. Miguel and Kremer (2004) examine the impact of a twice-yearly primary school de-worming program in western Kenya, where the prevalence of intestinal worms among children is very high (with an estimated 92 percent of pupils having at least one helminth infection). The de-worming program was implemented by a Dutch non-governmental organization (NGO), Internationaal Chistelijk Steunfonds (ICS) Africa, in cooperation with a local District Ministry of Health office. Due to administrative and financial constraints, the health intervention was randomly phased in over several years.

The authors find that child health and school participation improved not only for treated students but also for untreated students at treatment schools (measurable because 22 percent of pupils in treatment schools did not receive de-worming medicine) and untreated students at nearby non-treatment schools due to reduced disease transmission. Previous studies of the impact of de-worming fail to account for potential externalities, and Miguel and Kremer use two approaches to address identification issues that arise in the presence of these disease-reduction externalities. First, randomization at the level of schools allows them to estimate the overall effect of de-worming on a school even if there are treatment externalities among pupils within treatment schools. Second, cross-school externalities—the impact of de-worming for pupils in schools located near treatment schools—are identified using exogenous variation in the local density of treatment-school pupils generated by the school-level randomization.

Using this methodology, the authors find the direct effect of the de-worming program, including within-school health externalities, led to a 7.5 percent average gain in primary school participation in treatment schools, a reduction in absenteeism of at least 25 percent. Including the cross-school externalities, the authors find that de-worming increased schooling by 0.15 years per pupil treated; decomposed into an effect of

the treatment on the students treated and a spillover effect, school participation on average increased by 7.5 percent among pupils in treatment
schools and by 2 percent among pupils in comparison schools. Including
these externality benefits, the cost per additional year of school participation gained is only $3.50, making de-worming an extremely cost-effec-
tive method of increasing school participation.

Bobonis, Miguel, and Sharma (forthcoming) also find evidence that
school-based health programs can have substantial impacts on school participation. Iron deficiency anemia is another of the world's most widespread health problems, affecting approximately 40 percent of children in
African and Asian settings (Hall et al., 2001). Bobonis et al. evaluate the
impact of an NGO project in the slums of Delhi, India that delivers iron
supplementation, de-worming medicine, and vitamin A supplements to
2–6 year old preschool students (an intervention that costs only $1.70
per child per year). Before the start of the project, 69 percent of children
in the sample were anemic and 30 percent suffered from worm infections. Like the Kenyan de-worming program, the Delhi program was
phased in randomly—in this case reaching 200 preschools over two years.
The authors find a sharp increase of 5.8 percent in preschool participation rates, a reduction in preschool absenteeism of roughly one-fifth.
Effects were most pronounced for girls and children in areas of low
socioeconomic status. The study also finds large weight gains (roughly
1.1 pounds on average) within the first five months of the project. In
combination with the findings from the Kenyan de-worming program,
these results provide compelling evidence that school-based health programs can very cost-effectively increase school participation in low-
income countries.

These findings raise an important question: if school health programs
can increase the quantity of schooling, how can such programs best be
implemented in developing countries? Some contend that reliance on
external financing of medicine is not sustainable and instead advocate
health education, water and sanitation improvements, or financing the
provision of medicine through local cost sharing. Kremer and Miguel
(2003) analyze several de-worming interventions, including numerous
"sustainable" approaches, such as cost sharing, health education, verbal
commitments (a mobilization technique), and improvements in sanitation. They examine all except the sanitation efforts using randomized
evaluations. Overall, their results suggest that there may be no alternative

Figure 1: Iron Supplementation and De-worming Program in India: Pre-school Participation Rates Through Time. This table illustrates mean preschool participation rates over time for students in the treatment and comparison groups, respectively. Group I received treatments from January–April 2002 and, as this graph illustrates, experienced a sharp increase in participation rates that remained greater than comparison rates through the end of year one.

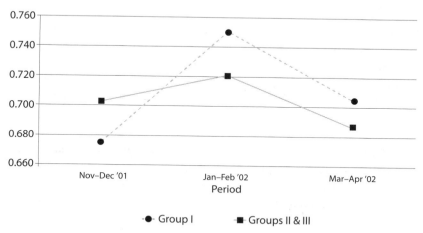

Source: Bobonis, Miguel, and Sharma (forthcoming).

to continued subsidies for de-worming. The "sustainable" public health strategies of health education, community mobilization, and cost recovery were ineffective. For example, a small increase in the cost of the de-worming drugs led to an 80 percent reduction in take-up, relative to free treatment. On the other hand, provision of free de-worming drugs led to high drug take-up and large reductions in serious worm-infection rates. Miguel and Kremer find that the benefits of the health externalities alone are sufficient to justify not only fully subsidizing de-worming treatment, but also paying people to receive treatment.

Miguel and Kremer (2004) find significant disparities between retrospective and prospective estimates of the de-worming project. For example, Miguel and Kremer estimate that students who were moderately or heavily infected in early 1999 had 2.8 percent lower school participation from May 1998 to March 1999. In contrast, an instrumental-variable specification (which imposes the condition that all gains in school participation result from changes in measured worm-infection status) suggests that each moderate-to-heavy infection leads to 20.3 percent lower school participation on average. The authors note several reasons why the instrumental-variable estimates are substantially larger, including recurring infection, complementarities in school participation, and measurement error.

Remedial Education Programs

Many developing countries have substantial numbers of educated, unemployed young people who could be cheaply hired to provide supplemental or alternative instruction in schools. Pratham, an Indian NGO, implemented a remedial education program in 1994 that now reaches over 161,000 children in twenty cities. Motivated by the belief that children often drop out of school because they fall behind and feel lost in class, the program hires young women from the communities to provide remedial education in government schools. These women, the "Balsakhis," have the equivalent of a high school degree and are from the slum communities in which the schools are located. The Balsakhis teach children who have reached grade 2, 3, or 4 but have not mastered the basic grade 1 competencies. Children identified as lagging behind are pulled out of the regular classroom for two hours a day to receive this instruction.

Pratham wanted to evaluate the impact of this program, one of the NGO's flagship interventions, as they looked simultaneously to expand it. Expansion into a new city, Vadodara, provided an opportunity to conduct a randomized evaluation (Banerjee, Cole, Duflo and Linden, 2005). In the first year (1999–2000), the program expanded to forty-nine (randomly selected) of the 123 Vadodara government schools. In the following school year, the program expanded to all schools, but half received a remedial teacher for grade 3, and half received a teacher for grade 4. Grade 3 students in schools that received teachers for grade 4 served as the comparison group for grade 3 students who were directly exposed to the program. A similar intervention was conducted simultaneously in a district of Mumbai, where half the schools received the remedial teachers in grade 2, and half received teachers in grade 3. The program continued for an additional year, with each school switching the grade level to which the teacher was assigned. The program was thus conducted in several grades, in two cities, and with no school feeling that they were deprived of resources relative to others, because all schools participated in the program. After two years the program increased student test scores by 0.39 standard deviations, on average. Moreover, the gains were largest for children at the bottom of the distribution: those in the bottom third gained 0.6 standard deviations after two years. The impact of Pratham's program is increasing over time, and is very similar across cities and regardless of gender. The educational impact of the program, combined with data on the costs of teachers, suggests that hiring remedial education teachers from the community (at a cost of one or two dollars per child per year) appears to be twelve to sixteen times more cost-effective than hiring new teachers.

The positive effects of the program on children's academic achievement is remarkably stable across years and across cities, especially when the instability of the environment is considered—namely, that there was a major riot and catastrophic earthquake while the evaluation was being implemented. In their analysis, the authors carefully take into account these events, as well as their impacts on measures such as attrition, and treat that year of the program as a pilot program.

Table 1: Balsakhi Remedial Education Program in India: Estimated Cost Comparison of Balsakhis and Primary School Teachers in Mumbai. The costs of hiring Balsakhis is notably lower than the costs of hiring primary school teachers, both in terms of cost in rupees per month and in terms of rupees per student.

		Rupees per month	Rupees per student
Balsakhi	Year 1	500	54
	Year 2	750	62
Primary school teachers	Years 1 & 2	7500	1318

Source: Banerjee, Cole, Duflo, and Linden (2005).

PROMISING INVESTMENTS IF ADDITIONAL
RESOURCES ARE AVAILABLE

Several sources of evidence suggest that reducing the costs of education—or paying students to attend school—may significantly improve participation rates. In many developing countries, school fees and required inputs such as uniforms create significant private costs of education for parents. For example, in Kenya parents have historically been required to purchase uniforms that cost about $6, a substantial expense in a country with a per capita income of around $340.

One might assume that a simple way to increase the quantity of school-ing would be to reduce the cost of school or to pay students for school attendance. However, there is significant debate over the desirability of school fees. Proponents argue that fees are necessary to finance inputs, that they increase parental participation in school governance, and that the price elasticity of the demand for schooling is low (Jimenez and Lockheed, 1995). Opponents argue that school fees prevent many students from attending school and cite dramatic estimates from sub-Saharan Africa. When free schooling was introduced in Uganda in 1997, primary school enrollment reportedly doubled from 2.6 to 5.2 million children (Lokshin, Glinskaya, and Garcia, 2000); when primary school fees were eliminated in Tanzania in 2002, initial estimates were that 1.5 million students (pri-marily girls) began attending primary school almost immediately (Coali-tion for Health and Education Rights, 2002); and when Kenyan President Mwai Kibaki eliminated primary school fees in late 2002, the initial response was reportedly a massive influx of new students (Lacey, 2003). Although the elimination of school fees undoubtedly generated large increases in enrollments, the magnitude of the numbers cited in these journalistic accounts should be taken with a grain of salt for a number of reasons: the underlying data on which they are based are often unclear; free schooling is sometimes announced simultaneously with other policy initiatives; and free schooling is often accompanied by a program that replaces school fees with per-pupil grants from the central government, which creates incentives for schools to overreport enrollments.

Evidence from several recent randomized evaluations suggests that programs designed to increase participation rates through a reduction in the costs of schooling, or even payments to students to attend school, can be effective. Below, I review evidence from the Mexican PROGRESA program as well as from a series of educational interventions in Kenya, including a school meals program, a program that provided school uni-forms (among other inputs), and a girls' scholarship program.

Mexico's PROGRESA Program

The PROGRESA program in Mexico[2] distributed cash grants to women, conditional on their children's school attendance and participation in

---

[2] For more information on the PROGRESA program, see http://www.ifpri.org/themes/progresa.htm.

preventative health measures (nutrition supplementation, health care visits, and health education programs). When the program was launched in 1998, officials in the Mexican government took advantage of budgetary constraints that limited their ability to reach the 50,000 potential participant communities of PROGRESA immediately. They started with 506 communities, half of which were randomly selected to receive the program while baseline and subsequent data were collected in the remaining communities (Gertler and Boyce, 2003). This system of implementation had another advantage as well: it increased the probability of the program's continuation through shifts in political power, as proponents of PROGRESA understood that it would require continuous political support to be scaled up successfully.

The task of evaluating the program was given to academic researchers through the International Food Policy Research Institute (IFPRI), who made the data accessible to numerous researchers. A number of papers have been written on PROGRESA's impact, most of which are accessible on the IFPRI web site. The evaluations show that the program was effective in improving both health and education; in a comparison of PROGRESA participants and non-participants, Gertler and Boyce (2003) find that children on average had a 23 percent reduction in the incidence of illness, a 1–4 percent increase in height, and an 18 percent reduction in anemia. Adults experienced a reduction of 19 percent in the number of days lost due to illness. Schultz (2004) finds an average 3.4 percent increase in enrollment for all students in grades 1 through 8; the increase was largest among girls who had completed grade 6, at 14.8 percent.

School Meals Programs

In some contexts, the success of conditional transfers such as those awarded through the PROGRESA program may be undermined if the people administering the program do not enforce the conditionality in practice (Sen, 2002). In these circumstances, school meals may provide a stronger incentive to attend school because children must come to school to participate.

Government-subsidized school meals have been provided in India, Bangladesh, Brazil, Swaziland, and Jamaica to increase both enrollment and attendance (World Food Programme, 2002). Proponents of school meals also claim that school meals can increase both the quantity of schooling and academic performance by improving child nutrition. Critics argue that families may reduce resource allocation to children who receive school meals; however, if this were the case, school meals would still serve as an incentive for families to send children to school. Moreover, a retrospective study (Jacoby, 2002) from the Philippines suggests that parents do not reduce food provided at home in response to school feeding programs (see also Long, 1991, and Powell et al., 1983).

Vermeersch and Kremer (2004) conducted a randomized evaluation of the impact of school meals on participation in Kenyan preschools, and find that school participation was 30 percent greater in the 25 Kenyan preschools where a free breakfast was introduced than in the 25 comparison schools. There is some evidence that the provision of meals cut into instruction time. In schools where the teacher was relatively well trained prior to the program, the meals program led to higher test scores (0.4 of a standard deviation) on academic tests. There were no effects on tests of general cognitive skills, which implies that the school meals program did not improve children's nutritional status and that the academic test-score increases were likely due to the increase in time spent in school.

Provision of School Uniforms

Kremer et al. (2002) conducted a randomized evaluation of a program in rural Kenya in which ICS Africa provided uniforms, textbooks, and classroom construction to seven schools that were randomly selected from a pool of fourteen poorly performing schools. Dropout rates fell considerably in the seven schools that were randomly selected to participate in the program, and after five years pupils in those schools had completed about 15 percent more years of schooling. In addition, many students from nearby schools transferred into program schools, raising class size by 50 percent. This outcome suggests that students and parents were willing to trade substantially larger class sizes for the benefit of free uniforms, textbooks, and improved classrooms. The authors argue that the main reason for the increase in years of schooling was most likely the financial benefit of free uniforms. A separate randomized evaluation of a program which provided textbooks in Kenya (Glewwe et al., 2003) shows that textbooks had almost no impact on the quantity of schooling, and although new classroom construction may have had an impact, the first new classrooms were not built until the second year of the program, whereas dropout rates fell dramatically in the first year. It is possible in theory that anticipation of later classroom construction affected participation, but the authors note that the presence of effects for students in the upper grades,

Figure 2: Kenyan School Uniform, Textbook, and Classroom Construction Program: Program Effect on Grades Advanced and Years Enrolled. Given that the schools receiving the program were randomly selected, this graph illustrates the program effect by reporting the differences between the treatment and comparison groups over time.

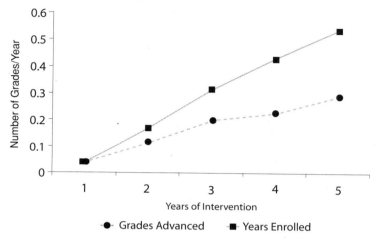

Source: Kremer, Moulin, and Namunyu (2002).

who would have finished school by the time the classrooms were built, casts doubt on this argument.

Girls' Scholarship Programs

In many countries there are significant gender disparities in access to education. It is estimated that about 56 percent of the 113 million school-age children not in school are girls, and in low-income countries there is a 9 percent gender gap in primary gross enrollment rates and a 13 percent gender gap at the secondary level (UNESCO, 2002). Some studies estimate that barely 50 percent of girls in sub-Saharan Africa complete primary school (Carceles, Fredriksen, and Watt, 2001). The question of how to increase enrollment rates of girls in primary and secondary schools in developing countries is often especially important.

There is some evidence that the elasticity of demand for schooling may be higher for girls than for boys, so policies and programs that do not specifically target girls may still result in greater increases in school participation for girls than for boys. Both Schultz (2004) and Morley and Coady (2003) find this trend in the evaluations of PROGRESA.

Table 2: Girls' Scholarship Program: Impact on School Attendance, Busia

		Dependent variable: Attendance in 2001, 2002 (boys and girls)	
Program school		0.05** (0.02)	
		Dependent variable: Attendance in 2001, 2002	
		Girls	Boys
Program impact	*Cohort 1 (2001)*	0.06 (0.04)	0.08* (0.05)
	Cohort 2 (2002)	0.01 (0.02)	-0.03 (0.02)
Post-program impact	*Cohort 1 (2002)*	0.02 (0.02)	0.02 (0.03)
Pre-program impact	*Cohort 2 (2001)*	0.10** (0.05)	0.10* (0.06)
		Dependent variable: Teacher attendance in 2002	
Program school		0.05*** (0.02)	

Source: Kremer, Miguel, and Thornton (2004).

Notes: All estimates are ordinary least squares (OLS) estimates, marked as significantly different than zero at 90 percent (*), 95 percent (**), and 99 percent (***) confidence. Huber robust standard errors are in parentheses.

The alternative is to implement programs that specifically target girls. Kremer, Miguel, and Thornton (2004) conducted a randomized evaluation of the Girls' Scholarship Program, which was introduced in rural Kenya in late 2001 to enhance girls' education. From a set of 128 schools, half were randomly chosen to be eligible for the program. The program consisted of a merit-based scholarship—one portion, intended for school fees, paid directly to the school and a second portion, intended for school supplies and uniforms, paid to the family—that rewarded girls in two districts of Western Kenya who scored in the top 15 percent on tests administered by the Kenyan government.

In the Busia district, the scholarship reduced student absenteeism by approximately 40 percent. Across all districts participating, the program increased the average probability of school attendance by 6 percent among girls in the first cohort of the program. It had a pre-program effect of 10 percent among girls in the second cohort in the year prior to their eligibility for the scholarships, possibly due to anticipation of the future scholarship opportunities or through peer effects. In addition, the test scores of girls eligible for the scholarship increased by 0.2 standard deviations as a result of the program. Moreover, schools offering the scholarship had significantly higher teacher attendance after the program was introduced, and scholarship winners were 7 percent more likely to rate themselves as a "good student" than girls who did not win scholarships.

OTHER EDUCATIONAL REFORMS: SCHOOL CHOICE

Given sufficient political will within a country, another possible educational reform aimed towards increasing enrollment is school choice. Angrist et al. (2002) examine the effects of Colombia's voucher program on education outcomes. The program offered vouchers to attend private secondary schools to over 125,000 students from poor, urban neighborhoods. In most communities the demand for vouchers exceeded the supply, so voucher eligibility was determined by a lottery, generating a natural experiment. Data were collected from 1,600 applicants for the vouchers (primarily from Bogota) three years after they had started high school. The sample was stratified so that half those sampled were lottery winners and half were lottery losers. Angrist and his co-authors find that lottery winners were 15–20 percent more likely to be in private schools, 10 percent more likely to complete grade 8, and that they scored 0.2 standard deviations higher on standardized tests than non-winners, equivalent to a full grade level.

A number of channels could account for the impact of the vouchers. First, lottery winners were more likely to have attended participating private schools, and these schools may be better than public schools. Second, vouchers allowed some pupils who would have attended private schools in the absence of vouchers to attend more expensive schools. Finally, voucher recipients who failed a grade risked losing their voucher, which increased the incentive to these students to devote more effort to school. The authors also find that vouchers affected noneducational outcomes: lottery winners worked less than lottery losers and were less likely to marry or cohabit as teenagers. Analysis of the economic returns to the additional schooling attained by winners after three years of participation suggests that the benefits likely greatly exceeded the $24 per winner additional cost to the government of supplying vouchers instead of public school places.

Table 3: Colombia School Vouchers Program: Effects of the Bogota 1995 Voucher Lottery

Dependent variable	Coefficient on ever having used a private school scholarship (Bogota 1995 voucher lottery)		
	Non-lottery winner's mean	Ordinary least squares (OLS)	Two-stage least squares (2SLS)
Highest grade completed	7.5 (0.965)	0.167** (0.053)	0.196** (0.078)
In school	0.831 (.375)	0.021 (0.021)	0.010 (0.031)
Total repetitions since lottery	0.254 (0.508)	-0.077** (0.029)	-0.100** (0.042)
Finished 8th grade	0.632 (0.483)	0.114** (0.028)	0.151** (0.041)
Test scores (total points)	-0.099 (1.00)	0.379** (0.111)	0.291* (0.153)
Married or living with companion	0.016 (0.126)	-0.009 (0.006)	-0.013 (0.009)

Source: Angrist et al. (2002).

Notes: Results are from models which control for city, year of application, whether applicant had access to a phone, age, type of survey and instrument, strata of residence, and month of interview. Standard deviations are reported in parentheses for the non-lottery winner's means, and robust standard errors are reported in parentheses for the OLS and two-stage least squares (2SLS) columns. As relevant, estimates are marked as significantly different than zero at 90 percent (*) and 95 percent (**).

Angrist, Bettinger, and Kremer (forthcoming) suggest that the vouchers not only had significant effects on the short-run outcomes of recipients, but that their impact also persisted over time. Using administrative records of registration and test scores for a centralized college-entrance examination, the authors find that lottery winners were 7–8 percent more likely to take the university entrance exam (a good predictor of high school graduation given that 90 percent of all high school graduates take the exam), an increase of 15–20 percent in the probability of taking the exam. The authors also find an increase of 0.33 standard deviations in language test scores. Overall, these results point to a substantial gain in both high school graduation rates and achievement as a result of the voucher program. The size and persistence of these impacts suggest the voucher program was cost-effective.

One important concern about school vouchers is the effect of such programs on non-participants. On one hand, pupils left behind in public schools may be hurt by the departure of motivated classmates for private schools. On the other hand, voucher programs may enhance the education of non-participants if public schools may respond positively to increased competition. The available evidence from retrospective evaluations suggests the second effect, namely that public schools may indeed respond positively to increased competition (for evidence from retrospective studies in the United States, see Hoxby, 2000 and Bettinger, 2001). Two recent studies analyze this issue in the context of Chile's nationwide school-choice program. The first study, Hseih and Urquiola (forthcoming), finds that private enrollment rates negatively affect the relative test scores, repetition rates, and socioeconomic status of students in public schools; however, the authors' retrospective fixed-effects estimation strategy is likely problematic given that private schools entered exactly where public schools were weak. The second study, Gallego (2005), analyzes the same Chilean school-choice program using a more credible instrumental variables estimation strategy, and finds that the entry of voucher schools has positive and statistically significant effects on test scores of both public and voucher school students. Such general equilibrium effects cannot be assessed by comparing lottery winners and non-winners, but both authors note that any negative external effects on non-participants would have to be extraordinarily large to outweigh program benefits.

LESSONS

Several broad lessons can be drawn about the role of randomized evaluations in education policy, which I detail below. In addition, I briefly address some critiques of randomized evaluations that are frequently raised.

Costs

As is clear from the examples discussed in this chapter, randomized evaluations are feasible and have been conducted successfully—they are labor intensive and costly, but no more so than other data-collection activities. The randomized evaluations discussed in this chapter were conducted in concert with programs implemented by NGOs, and the cost-benefit estimates discussed include the costs to NGOs of program implementation.

Conducting evaluations in conjunction with NGOs has a variety of benefits. Once an evaluation staff is trained, they can work on multiple projects. Because data collection is the most costly element of these evaluations, crosscutting the sample can also dramatically reduce costs. For example, many of the programs seeking to increase school participation and learning were implemented in the same area, by the same organization. Of course, this approach must consider potential interactions between programs, which can be estimated if the sample is large enough, and may be inappropriate if one program makes the schools atypical. Another advantage of working with NGOs is that conducting a series of studies in the same area (such as the series recently conducted in Kenya) enhances comparability by allowing researchers to compare the cost-effectiveness estimates of different interventions in the same setting.

External Validity

Without a theory to explain why a program has the effect it has, it may be unwarranted to generalize from one well-executed randomized evaluation. However, similar issues of generalizability arise no matter what evaluation technique is used. One way to determine whether a program's effects can be generalized is to encourage adapted replications of randomized evaluations in key domains of interest in several different settings. Although it will always be possible that a program unsuccessful in one context would have been successful in other adapted replications, replication of evaluations, if guided by a theory of why the program was effective, will go a long way toward alleviating concerns about generalizability.

The results of the first phase of a project often may be difficult to interpret because of circumstances that are unique to the first phase. If the project is unsuccessful, it may be because it faced implementation problems that could be avoided in later phases of the project; if the project is successful, it may be because more resources were allocated to it than would have been under a more realistic situation or in a less favorable context. Even if the choice of comparison and treatment groups ensures internal validity of estimates, the external validity of any method of evaluation may be problematic due to the specific circumstances of implementation—the results may not be able to be generalized to other contexts. Problems specific to randomized evaluations include the members of the treatment group changing their behavior (known as the Hawthorne effect) and members of the comparison group having their behavior affected (known as the John Henry effect) as a result of participation in the randomized evaluation.

Some of these concerns can be addressed by implementing adapted replications of successful (and potentially unsuccessful) programs in different contexts. Adapted replications present two advantages: first, in the process of "transplanting" a program, circumstances change, and robust programs will show their effectiveness by surviving these changes; second, obtaining several estimates in different contexts will provide some guidance about whether the impacts of the program are notably different in different groups. Replication of the initial phase of a study in a new context does not necessarily entail a delay in the full-scale implementation of a program if the latter is justified on the basis of existing knowledge. More often than not, the introduction of a program must proceed in stages, and the evaluation only requires that participants be moved into the program in random order. Even within a single study, it is possible to check whether program effects vary with covariates; for example, a program may have differential effects in small and large schools.

One example of adapted replication is the work in India of Bobonis, Miguel, and Sharma (forthcoming) who, as discussed previously, conducted an adapted replication of the de-worming study in Kenya. The baseline revealed that, although present, the levels of worm infection were substantially lower than in Kenya (in India, "only" 27 percent of children suffer from some form of worm infection). However, 70 percent of children had moderate-to-severe anemia; thus, the program was modified to include iron supplementation. The program was administered through a network of preschools in urban India. After one year of treatment, the researchers found a nearly 50 percent reduction in moderate-to-severe anemia, large weight gains, and a 7 percent reduction in absenteeism among 4–6 year olds (but not for younger children). This supports the conclusion of the de-worming research in Kenya (Miguel and Kremer, 2004) that school health programs may be one of the most cost-effective ways of increasing school participation and, importantly, suggests that this conclusion may be relevant in low-income countries outside of Africa. A different external validity issue is that randomized evaluation may be unable to accurately predict the cost of a program if it were implemented on a broader scale. For example, if a program initially implemented by an NGO were scaled up, the relative increase or decrease in costs might be unclear due to issues of corruption, overhead, or supervision.

Issues That Can Affect Both Randomized and Retrospective Evaluations

Sample-selection bias, attrition bias, subgroup variability, and spillover effects can affect both randomized and retrospective evaluations. In the author's opinion, it is often easier to correct for these limitations when conducting randomized evaluations than when conducting retrospective studies.

Sample-selection problems could arise if factors other than random assignment influence program allocation. Even if randomized methods have been employed and the intended allocation of the program was random, the actual allocation may not be. For example, parents may attempt to move their children from a class or school without the program to one with the program. Conversely, individuals allocated to a treatment group may not receive the treatment (for example, because they decide not to take up the program). This problem can be addressed through intention-to-treat (ITT) methods or by using random assignment as an instrument of variables for actual assignment. The problem is much harder to address in retrospective studies because it is often difficult to find factors that plausibly affect exposure to the program that would not affect educational outcomes through other channels.

A second issue affecting both randomized and retrospective evaluations is differential attrition in the treatment and the comparison groups, where participants in the program may be less likely to move or otherwise drop out of the sample than non-participants. At minimum, randomized evaluations can use statistical techniques to bound the potential bias and can attempt to track down individuals who drop out of the sample (e.g., administer tests to students who have dropped out of school), which is often not possible with retrospective evaluations.

A third issue is subgroup variability, the possibility that a program will affect some individuals more than others. The issue of subgroup variability is important, but plausible theoretical mechanisms for its presence often exist. For example, Glewwe et al. (2003) find no evidence that provision of the official textbooks issued by the Kenyan government increased scores for the typical student. However, they do find evidence that textbooks led to higher test scores for the subset of students who scored well on a pretest. The authors note that English, the language both of instruction in Kenyan schools and of the textbooks, was the third language for most pupils. They cite evidence that many weaker pupils likely had difficulty reading the books.

Fourth, programs may create spillover effects on people who have not been treated. These spillovers may be physical, as found for the Kenyan de-worming program. De-worming interferes with disease transmission and thus makes children in treatment schools—and in schools near treatment schools—less likely to have worms, even if they were not themselves given the medicine. Spillovers may also operate through prices: Vermeersch and Kremer (2004) finds that provision of meals in some schools led other schools to reduce school fees. Finally, there might also be learning and imitation effects (Duflo and Saez, 2003; Miguel and Kremer, 2003).

If spillovers are global (for example, due to changes in world prices), identification of total program impacts will be problematic with any methodology. However, if spillovers are local, randomization at the level of groups can allow estimation of the total program effect within groups and can generate sufficient variation in local treatment density to measure spillovers across groups. For example, the solution in the case of the de-worming study was to choose the school (rather than the pupils within a school) as the unit of randomization, and to look at the number of treatment and comparison schools within neighborhoods. Of course, this requires a larger sample size.

One limitation of randomized evaluations is that the evaluation itself may cause the Hawthorne effect or the John Henry effect. Although these effects are specific to randomized evaluations, similar effects can occur in other settings. For example, the provision of inputs could temporarily increase morale among students and teachers, which could improve performance. Although this would create problems for randomized evaluations, it would also create problems for fixed-effect or difference-in-difference estimates.

A final issue is that the program may generate behavioral responses that would not occur if the program were generalized. For example, children may switch into a school that is provided additional inputs. This may affect the original pupils by increasing class size, if class size affects the outcome of interest. Nationwide adoption of the policy would not have this effect.

Although randomized evaluation is not a bulletproof strategy, potential biases are well known and can often be corrected. This stands in contrast to most other types of studies, where the bias due to non-random treatment assignments could be either positive or negative, and cannot be estimated.

AVENUES FOR FURTHER WORK

As illustrated by the substantive examples discussed above, a number of educational interventions have been shown to expand school participation quite effectively. Randomized evaluations of school-based health programs and remedial education programs suggest that these are extraordinarily cost-effective means of increasing the quantity of schooling attained in developing countries. Programs that reduce the cost of schooling or provide incentives for school attendance—whether implicitly, through school meals, or explicitly, through conditional grants—have been shown to have sizable impacts on school participation. Finally, school choice seems to have increased educational attainment in Colombia.

Randomized evaluations of other promising means of increasing school participation rates are needed to promote significant progress towards universal basic and secondary education. For example, a recent study suggests that great potential likely exists through decreasing teacher absenteeism. A new representative survey of primary schools in India indicates that 25 percent of teachers in government primary schools are absent on a typical day. Two key interventions could take advantage of randomized evaluations: increasing community control in various ways (i.e., increasing the powers of parent-teacher associations) and increasing the frequency and quality of inspections, which preliminary evidence suggests can reduce teacher-absence rates.

References

Angrist, Joshua, Eric Bettinger, Erik Bloom, Elizabeth King, and Michael Kremer. 2002. "Vouchers for Private Schooling in Colombia: Evidence from a Randomized Natural Experiment." *American Economic Review* 92 (5): 1535–1558.

Angrist, Joshua, Eric Bettinger, and Michael Kremer. Forthcoming. "Long-term Consequences of Secondary School Vouchers: Evidence from Administrative Records in Colombia." *American Economic Review*.

Banerjee, Abhijit, Shawn Cole, Esther Duflo, and Leigh Linden. 2005. "Remedying Education: Evidence from Two Randomized Experiments in India." National Bureau of Economic Research Working Paper No. 11904. Cambridge, MA; NBER.

Bennett, Andrew, and Helen Guyatt. 2000. "Reducing Intestinal Nematode Infection: Efficacy of Albendazole and Mebendazole." *Parasitology Today* 16 (2): 71–75.

Bettinger, Eric. 2001. "The Effect of Charter Schools on Charter Students and Public Schools." Mimeo. Case Western Reserve University.

Bobonis, Gustavo, Edward Miguel, and Charu Sharma. Forthcoming. "Iron Deficiency Anemia and School Participation." *Journal of Human Resources*.

Buddlemeyer, Hielke, and Emmanuel Skofias. 2003. "An Evaluation on the Performance of Regression Discontinuity Design on PROGRESA." Institute for Study of Labor, Discussion Paper No. 827.

Butterworth, A.E., et al. 1991. "Comparison of Different Chemotherapy Strategies against *Schistosoma mansoni* in Kachakos District, Kenya: Effects on Human Infection and Morbidity." *Parasitology* 103: 339–344.

Carceles, Gabriel, Birger Fredriksen, and Patrick Watt. 2001. "Can Sub-Saharan Africa Reach the International Targets for Human Development?" Africa Region Human Development Working Paper Series. Washington, DC: The World Bank.

Coalition for Health and Education Rights. 2002. "User Fees: The Right to Education and Health Denied." New York: CHER.

Diaz, Juan-Jose, and Sudhanshu Handa. 2003. "Estimating the Evaluation Bias of Matching Estimators Using Randomized-out Controls and Nonparticipants from PROGRESA." Mimeo. University of North Carolina at Chapel Hill.

Duflo, Esther, and Michael Kremer. Forthcoming. "Use of Randomization in the Evaluation of Development Effectiveness." Proceedings of the Conference on Evaluating Development Effectiveness, July 15–16, 2003. Washington, DC: World Bank Operations Evaluation Department (OED).

Duflo, Esther, and Emmanuel Saez. 2003. "The Role of Information and Social Interactions in Retirement Plan Decisions: Evidence from a Randomized Experiment." *Quarterly Journal of Economics* 118 (3): 815–842.

Gallego, Francisco. 2005. "Voucher-School Competition, Incentives, and Outcomes: Evidence from Chile." Mimeo. Massachusetts Institute of Technology.

Gertler, Paul, and Simone Boyce. 2003. "An Experiment in Incentive-based Welfare: The Impact of PROGRESA on Health in Mexico." Royal Economic Society Annual Conference 2003, no. 85. Royal Econometric Society.

Glewwe, Paul, and Michael Kremer. Forthcoming. "Schools, Teachers, and Education Outcomes in Developing Countries." In *Handbook on the Economics of Education*, ed. E. Hanushek and F. Welch.

Glewwe, Paul, Michael Kremer, and Sylvie Moulin. 2003. "Textbooks and Test Scores: Evidence from a Randomized Evaluation in Kenya." Development Research Group, World Bank. Washington, DC: World Bank.

Hall, Andrew, et al. 2001. "Anemia in Schoolchildren in Eight Countries in Africa and Asia." *Public Health Nutrition* 4 (3): 749–756.

Hoxby, Caroline. 2000. "Does Competition among Public Schools Benefit Students and Taxpayers?" *American Economic Review* 90 (5): 1209–1238.

Hseih, Chang-Tai, and Miguel Urquiola. Forthcoming. "The Effects of Generalized School Choice on Achievement and Stratification: Evidence from Chiles's School Voucher Program." *Journal of Public Economics*.

Jacoby, Hanan. 2002. "Is There an Intrahousehold Flypaper Effect? Evidence from a School Feeding Program." *Economic Journal* 112 (476): 196–221.

Jimenez, Emmanuel, and Marianne Lockheed. 1995. "Public and Private Secondary Education in Developing Countries." World Bank Discussion Paper no. 309. Washington, DC: World Bank.

Kremer, Michael. 2003. "Randomized Evaluations of Educational Programs in Developing Countries: Some Lessons." *American Economic Review Papers and Proceedings* 93 (2): 102–115.

Kremer, Michael, and Edward Miguel. 2003. "The Illusion of Sustainability." Mimeo. Harvard University.

Kremer, Michael, Edward Miguel, and Rebecca Thornton. 2004. "Incentives to Learn." Mimeo. University of California, Berkeley.

Kremer, Michael, Sylvie Moulin, and Robert Namunyu. 2002. "Decentralization: A Cautionary Tale." Mimeo. Harvard University.

Lacey, Marc. 2003. "Primary Schools in Kenya, Fees Abolished, Are Filled to Overflowing." *The New York Times*, January 7: A8.

Lokshin, Micahel, Elena Glinskaya, and Marito Garcia. 2000. "The Effect of Early Childhood Development Programs on Women's Labor Force Participation and Older Children's Schooling in Kenya." Policy Research Report on Gender and Development, Working Paper Series no. 15. Washington, DC: World Bank.

Long, Sharon K. 1991. "Do the School Nutrition Programs Supplement Household Food Expenditures?" *The Journal of Human Resources* 26: 654–678.

Miguel, Edward, and Michael Kremer. 2004. "Worms: Identifying Impacts on Education and Health in the Presence of Treatment Externalities." *Econometrica* 72 (1): 159–217.

———. 2003. "Networks, Social Learning, and Technology Adoption: The Case of Deworming Drugs in Kenya." Mimeo. Harvard University.

Morley, Samuel, and David Coady. 2003. *From Social Assistance to Social Development: Education Subsidies in Developing Countries*. Washington, DC: Institute for International Economics.

Nokes, C., S. M. Grantham-McGregor, A. W. Sawyer, E. S. Cooper, B. A. Robinson, and D. A. P. Bundy. 1992. "Moderate-to-heavy Infection of Trichuris richiura Affects Cognitive Function in Jamaican School Children." *Parasitology* 104: 539–547.

Powell, Christine, Sally Grantham-McGregor, and M. Elston. 1983. "An Evaluation of Giving the Jamaican Government School Meal to a Class of Children." *Human Nutrition: Clinical Nutrition* 37C: 381–388.

Schultz, T. Paul. 2004. "School Subsidies for the Poor: Evaluating the Mexican PROGRESA Poverty Program." *Journal of Development Economics* 74: 199–250.

Sen, Amartya. 2002. "The Pratichi Report." Pratichi India Trust.

United Nations Development Programme (UNDP). 2003. *Human Development Report*. New York: UNDP.

United Nations Educational, Scientific, and Cultural Oraganization (UNESCO). 2000. *Informe Final, Foro Mundial Sobre la Educación, Dakar, Senegal*. Paris: UNESCO Publishing.

———. 2002. *Education for All: Is the World On Track?* Paris: UNESCO Publishing.

Vermeersch, Christel, and Michael Kremer. 2004. "School Meals, Educational Achievement, and School Competition: Evidence from a Randomized Evaluation." World Bank Policy Research Working Paper No. 3523. Washington, DC: The World Bank.

World Food Programme. 2002. "Global School Feeding Report 2002." Rome: World Food Programme School Feeding Support Unit.

World Health Organization (WHO). 1992. *Model Describing Information: Drugs Used in Parasitic Diseases.* Geneva: WHO.

Section IV: Costs

CHAPTER 7

Attaining Universal Primary Schooling by 2015: An Evaluation of Cost Estimates

PAUL GLEWWE AND MENG ZHAO

On September 5, 2000, at the United Nations Headquarters in New York City, 189 countries endorsed eight Millennium Development Goals (MDGs) to improve the quality of life in developing countries by the year 2015. The second of these eight goals is to achieve "universal primary education," ensuring that every child finishes primary school. Although the MDGs set clear targets, they do not provide guidance on how to attain these targets.

The intention to attain universal primary education (here referred to as universal primary completion, or UPC), leads to two questions. First, what policy changes can bring about UPC in developing countries? Second, how much additional money will be needed to implement those policies? Several estimates that purport to answer the second question have been published since 2000, but to our knowledge there has been no systematic effort to answer the first. The recent estimates that have been made to answer the second question are based on implicit assumptions about the policies needed to attain UPC. Clearly, the validity of those estimates depends on the accuracy of the implicit policy assumptions.

This chapter examines the state of primary education in developing countries and reviews recent estimates of the cost of attaining UPC. These recent studies are best thought of as estimates of the resources that would be needed if: 1) some policy were implemented that persuaded all parents to enroll their children in primary school, and 2) the decision were made to maintain a particular pupil-teacher ratio (often the existing ratio). In general, these studies assume that the primary barrier to enrollment is lack of a nearby school, or lack of room for new pupils to be admitted at a nearby school. However, there is ample evidence from developing countries that a lack of schools is not the main barrier to enrollment.

Basic data on primary school enrollment in developing countries are presented below, including projections for the year 2015. Data are also presented on current government expenditures on education. The chapter then reviews, and critiques, four recent attempts to calculate the cost of attaining UPC by 2015. It presents some evidence on policies that can boost primary school enrollment in developing countries and what their likely cost would be, although a significant amount of research remains to be done.

UNIVERSAL PRIMARY COMPLETION:
PROGRESS TO DATE AND PROSPECTS FOR 2015

This chapter considers as developing countries all countries that the World Bank (2002) has classified as either low-income or middle-income countries in the year 2000. The list of 151 countries is given in the Appendix. Of these, 66 are classified as low-income countries. Low-income countries are defined as those with an annual income per capita in 2000 (in U.S. dollars) of less than $755. The other 85 are classified as middle-income countries, which have annual per capita incomes in 2000 between $755 and $9265. Table 1 shows the distribution of these countries by geographic region and income level. About 2.5 billion people live in low-income countries and about 2.7 billion people live in middle-income countries. About one half of the population of low-income countries (1.3 billion) are found in South Asia, which primarily reflects India's 1 billion people, and about one fourth (0.6 billion) live in Sub-Saharan Africa. Within middle-income countries, a little more than one half (1.5 billion) live in East Asia, which primarily reflects China's 1.3 billion people, and most of the remainder are found in Latin America and the Caribbean (0.5 billion) or in the Middle East and North Africa (0.35 billion).

For the purposes of this study, it is useful to classify developing countries according to their progress in attaining universal primary school completion (defined as a primary school completion rate of 95 percent or higher) in the year 2000 (see Table 2). A recent report by the World Bank (Bruns et al., 2003) classified three low-income countries (Azerbaijan, Vietnam, and Zimbabwe) and 33 middle-income countries as having attained UPC by or before the year 2000. These countries constitute

Table 1: Distribution of Developing Countries by Income Level and Region

Region	Low Income		Middle Income	
	Number of Countries	Population (millions)	Number of Countries	Population (millions)
Sub-Saharan Africa	39	608	8	50
East Asia and Pacific	9	380	13	1469
South Asia	6	1338	2	19
Europe and Central Asia	9	111	17	297
Latin America and Caribbean	2	13	29	498
Middle East and North Africa	1	18	16	345
Total	66	2468	85	2678

Source: Data from World Bank (2002).
Note: Population data are for the year 2000.

Table 2: Distribution of Developing Countries by Income Level and Progress in Attaining Universal Primary Completion

Progress Status	Low Income		Middle Income	
	Number of Countries	Population (millions)	Number of Countries	Population (millions)
Already Attained	3	99	33	1898
On Track to Attain by 2015	10	246	20	467
Off Track to Attain by 2015	24	1663	19	265
Seriously Off Track	22	340	2	24
Missing Data	7	117	11	36
Total	66	2468	85	2678

Sources: Data from World Bank (2002) and Bruns et al. (2003).
Note: Population data are for the year 2000.

about 4 percent of the population of low-income countries and about 71 percent of the population of middle-income countries (the latter figure largely reflecting China's success in primary education). Another ten low-income countries and twenty middle-income countries are "on track" to achieve UPC by 2015, the target date for the MDGs. "On track" means that a continuation of linear trends from 1990 to 2000 in each of these countries will result in a completion rate of 95 percent or higher by 2015. These countries constitute about 10 percent of the population of low-income countries and about 17 percent of the population of middle-income countries. Thus, only about 14 percent of the population in low-income countries are residents of countries that will attain the goal of UPC by 2015, while about 88 percent of the population in middle-income countries live in countries that will attain this goal.

The remaining countries are either not expected to attain UPC or, for a small number of countries, data to assess their progress are missing. The "off track" countries can be divided into two types. The primary completion rates of "moderately off track" countries are projected to be greater than 50 percent (but less than 95 percent) by 2015, while the primary completion rates of "seriously off track" countries are projected to be 50 percent or lower. In low-income countries, 67 percent of the population live in countries that are "moderately off track" in attaining the goal of UPC, 14 percent live in countries that are "seriously off track," and 5 percent live in countries without reliable data on completion rates. In middle-income countries, 10 percent of the population lives in countries that are off track for attaining UPC by 2015, 1 percent live in countries that are seriously off track, and 1 percent live in countries for which no reliable data are available on completion rates.

The figures in Table 2 may give the impression of a crisis regarding the achievement of UPC in low-income developing countries. Eighty percent of the population in those countries are residents of countries that are off-track or seriously off-track. However, in most of these countries, a majority of children will complete primary school. Table 3 shows primary school completion rates for 2000 and projected primary school completion rates for 2015 in low- and middle-income countries, categorized as they are in Table 2. In 2000, 73 percent of children in "off track" low-income countries completed primary school, and this number is projected to increase to 84 percent by 2015. Only in the countries that are "seriously off track" (a group that is smaller in terms of population size) is the situation bleaker. These countries had a primary completion rate of 35 percent in 2000, a rate that is projected to drop to 25 percent by 2015. In all low-income countries, the overall primary school completion rate is estimated to have been 68 percent in 2000 and is expected to increase to 77 percent in 2015 (if trends from 1990 to 2000 continue). In middle-income countries the completion rate was already 97 percent, and it is projected to hold steady (96 percent).

Little can be done to assess the situation in countries with missing data. Seven low-income countries lack reliable data on primary comple-

Table 3: Primary School Completion Rates by Income Level and Progress in Attaining Universal Primary Completion

	Low Income		Middle Income	
Progress Status	**2000**	**Projection for 2015**	**2000**	**Projection for 2015**
Already Attained	103	100	105	99
On Track to Attain by 2015	71	98	82	100
Off Track to Attain by 2015	73	84	82	79
Seriously Off Track	35	25	57	34
Missing Data	—	—	—	—
Total	68	77	97	96

Sources: Data from World Bank (2002) and Bruns et al. (2003).

tion rates: Kyrgystan, Liberia, Myanmar, North Korea, Somalia, Turkmenistan, and Uzbekistan. Among middle-income countries, data are missing for eleven. Of these, six are small island nations: Kiribati, the Marshall Islands, Micronesia, Palau, Seychelles, and Tonga. The other five are Kazakhstan, Libya, Macedonia, Palestine, and Suriname. The seven low-income countries with missing data constitute 4.7 percent of the population of all low-income countries and the eleven middle-income countries constitute 1.0 percent of the population of all middle-income countries. Thus the omission of these countries will have only a small effect on the results of this study.

This study also excludes the formerly socialist countries of Eastern Europe and Central Asia, for three reasons. First, data are scarce for these countries (Table 4), especially historical data that allow one to determine whether these countries will attain UPC by the year 2015 (this limitation applies to 12.7 percent of the population). Second, the history of these countries is very different from that of the other low- and middle-income countries. Third, most of them have either already attained UPC or are on track to do so. Those that are not (Albania, Armenia, Belarus, Estonia, Georgia, and Tajikistan) constitute only 7 percent of the primary school age population of these countries (another 13 percent live in countries with missing data, but that lack of data also precludes their use in this study). One country in this group, Turkey, is not a former socialist state. For simplicity, this study retains Turkey but assigns it to the category Middle East/North Africa. This reclassification has minimal effect. As

Table 4: Progress in Attaining Universal Primary Completion, by Region

	Low Income		Middle Income	
	Number of Countries	**Population (millions)**	**Number of Countries**	**Population (millions)**
Sub-Saharan Africa				
Already Attained	1	13	4	46
On Track to Attain by 2015	4	38	3	4
Off Track to Attain by 2015	11	231	–	–
Seriously Off Track	21	314	–	–
Missing Data	2	12	1	0.1
Total	39	608	8	50
East Asia and Pacific				
Already Attained	1	79	4	1312
On Track to Attain by 2015	2	17	1	77
Off Track to Attain by 2015	4	214	3	84
Seriously Off Track	–	–	–	–
Missing Data	2	70	5	0.4
Total	9	380	13	1469
South Asia				
Already Attained	–	–	2	19
On Track to Attain by 2015	1	131	–	–
Off Track to Attain by 2015	4	1176	–	–
Seriously Off Track	1	27	–	–
Missing Data	–	–	–	–
Total	6	1338	2	19
Europe and Central Asia				
Already Attained	1	8	9	251
On Track to Attain by 2015	2	54	3	15
Off Track to Attain by 2015	3	15	3	15
Seriously Off Track	–	–	–	–
Missing Data	3	35	2	17
Total	9	111	17	297
Latin America and the Caribbean				
Already Attained	–	–	12	204
On Track to Attain by 2015	1	5	8	242
Off Track to Attain by 2015	1	8	8	53
Seriously Off Track	–	–	–	–
Missing Data	–	–	1	0.4
Total	2	13	29	498
Middle East and North Africa				
Already Attained	–	–	2	69
On Track to Attain by 2015	–	–	5	131
Off Track to Attain by 2015	1	18	5	114
Seriously Off Track	–	–	2	24
Missing Data	–	–	2	8
Total	1	18	16	345

Sources: Data from World Bank (2002) and Bruns et al. (2003).
Note: Population data are for the year 2000.

Turkey is on target to attain UPC by 2015, it is not used in any of the calculations in this study on the cost of attaining UPC by 2015.

Before turning to cost, a few comments should be made about region-specific trends in UPC (Table 4). The most worrisome region is Sub-Saharan Africa. Nearly 90 percent of the population of this region live in countries that are off track to attain UPC by 2015, and nearly half of the population are in countries that are seriously off track. For Sub-Saharan African countries as a group, the primary school completion rate was only 53 percent in 2000. The World Bank projections indicate that it will remain at 53 percent in 2015.

The situation in East Asia is much better. Only about 15 percent of the population live in countries that are off track, and none of the countries (with the possible exception of the few with missing data) is seriously off track. In contrast, almost 90 percent of the population of South Asia live in countries that are off track, which mostly reflects India's weak performance. Yet, unlike Sub-Saharan Africa, only a tiny percent of the population (2–3 percent) live in countries that are seriously off track. For South Asia as a whole, the primary school completion rate in 2000 was 72 percent. The World Bank projection for 2015 is 87 percent.

In Latin America and the Caribbean, the situation is much more hopeful. About 95 percent of the population live in countries that have already achieved UPC, or will achieve it by 2015, and none of the few off-track countries is seriously off track. For the region as a whole, the primary school completion rate in 2000 was 83 percent, and the projected rate for 2015 is 95 percent. The countries of North Africa and the Middle East are between these extremes. About 55 percent of the population live in countries that have already achieved UPC, or will achieve it by 2015. About 35 percent live in countries that are off track, but not seriously off track, and only about 7 percent live in countries that are seriously off track (2–3 percent are in countries with missing data). For the region as a whole, the primary school completion rate in 2000 was 85 percent, and the projected rate for 2015 is 87 percent.

CURRENT COSTS OF PRIMARY EDUCATION

This section presents data from developing countries on current government expenditures on primary education, including both recurrent costs and capital costs. Because detailed data on household expenditures on education are unavailable for many countries, and because proposed programs to achieve UPC inevitably will be financed by governments, only government expenditures are documented here. The section then focuses on countries for which UPC is unlikely to be attained by 2015, presenting data that divide total recurrent costs into teacher costs and other costs.

Total Current Cost

Data on current costs (presented in Table 5) are available for almost all developing countries. This subsection presents those data by region, income level, and on-track versus off-track status.

In the year 2000, Sub-Saharan African countries spent a total of $6.1 billion on 89 million students in primary school, or $68 per pupil per year on average. This average is inflated by five countries (Botswana, Cape Verde, Mauritius, South Africa, and Zimbabwe) that have already attained UPC and spend, on average, $376 per student per year, and by one country, Seychelles, for which data are missing on enrollment but spending per pupil is known to be $650 per student per year. Excluding these countries leaves per student spending rates of $35 for countries that are on track to achieve UPC, $27 for students that are off track, and $31 for countries that are seriously off track. Thus Sub-Saharan countries not only have a substantial number of students who are not finishing primary schooling (39 million), but those who are enrolled attend schools with very low spending per pupil, which suggests low quality education.

The developing region with the lowest spending per primary school pupil is South Asia. Although governments in that region spend slightly more than governments in Sub-Saharan Africa, $6.9 billion, the number of pupils enrolled is much higher, at 149 million. Government spending per pupil in this region is only $46 per year. The two countries that have already attained UPC, the Maldives and Sri Lanka, spend, on average, $80 per pupil, while the one country that is on track to attain UPC by 2015, Bangladesh, spends only $25 per pupil. The remaining countries are all off track. On average they spend $49 per pupil.

East Asia has the largest population of all the regions, with 1.85 billion people. The governments in those countries spend about $21 billion on primary education each year. With 206 million students in primary school, this yields an average of $103 per student per year. This average is very similar across countries, regardless of their UPC status. (One country, Micronesia, has no data on total enrollment but spends $227 per student per year; this country is in the "No Enrollment Data" category for East Asia in Table 5.) In fact, the countries that have already achieved

Table 5: Current Per Year Expenditures on Primary Schooling in Developing Countries

Region	Percent of Population Within Region	All Developing Countries (except Europe & Central Asia)	Spending per Student (US $)	Total Spending (millions US $)	Percent of population with spending data
Sub-Saharan Africa					
Already Attained	9	1	376	3720	94
On Track to Attain	6	1	35	388	100
Off Track	35	5	27	820	100
Seriously Off Track	48	7	31	1160	100
No Enrollment Data	2	0	650	7	1
Total	100	14	68	6100	98
East Asia and Pacific					
Already Attained	75	29	99	15,000	100
On Track to Attain	5	2	101	1620	100
Off Track	16	6	118	4580	100
Seriously Off Track	–	–	–	–	–
No Enrollment Data	4	1	227	18	0
Total	100	38	103	21,200	96
South Asia					
Already Attained	1	0	80	144	99
On Track to Attain	10	3	25	449	100
Off Track	87	25	49	6320	100
Seriously Off Track	–	–	–	–	–
No Enrollment Data	–	–	–	–	–
Total	100	28	46	6910	98
Europe and Central Asia					
Already Attained	63	–	1048	4860	25
On Track to Attain	17	–	264	195	22
Off Track	7	–	268	147	34
Seriously Off Track	–	–	–	–	–
No Enrollment Data	13	–	–	–	–
Total	100	–	878	5210	22
Latin America and the Caribbean					
Already Attained	40	4	608	17,200	95
On Track to Attain	48	5	339	10,500	98
Off Track	12	1	97	466	46
Seriously Off Track	–	–	–	–	–
No Enrollment Data	–	–	–	–	–
Total	100	10	440	28,200	90
Middle East and North Africa					
Already Attained	19	1	226	167	7
On Track to Attain	36	3	972	11,400	75
Off Track	36	3	179	2670	87
Seriously Off Track	7	1	299	13	3
No Enrollment Data	2	0	–	–	0
Total	100	8	519	14,200	60
Total	–	100	151	81,800	88

Sources: Data from World Bank (2002) and Bruns et al. (2003). Averages are weighted by number of pupils, taken from Bruns et al. (2003).

UPC spend slightly less per pupil per year, $99, while those on track to attain UPC in 2015 spend $101, and those that are off track spend $118. The figure of $99 primarily reflects education spending in China.

The other three regions—Europe and Central Asia, the Middle East and North Africa, and Latin America and the Caribbean—spend much more per student per year: $878, $519, and $440, respectively. As explained above, this study does not discuss Europe and Central Asia in detail. Turning to Latin America, greater spending per student coupled with 64 million students in primary school implies that about $28 billion is spent per year in that region.[1] Unlike the lack of correlation between spending per pupil and UPC in East Asia, Latin America's progress in attaining UPC is positively correlated with spending per student. In countries that have already attained UPC, the average spending per primary student is $608, while countries on track spend $339 and countries that are off track spend $97.

Countries in the Middle East and North Africa spend about $14 billion on primary school education each year. Divided among 27 million pupils, this is an average expenditure of $519 per pupil per year. There is no clear relationship between UPC progress and spending per pupil in this region. The two countries that have already attained UPC, Egypt and Jordan, spend (on average, which primarily reflects Egypt) $226 per pupil per year. The five countries that are on track to attain UPC by 2015 (Algeria, Oman, Saudi Arabia, Tunisia, and Turkey) spend much more, an average of $972 per pupil. The six countries that are off track (Bahrain, Iran, Lebanon, Morocco, Syria, and Yemen) spend a relatively low amount, $179, but the two countries that are seriously off track, Djibouti and Iraq, spend (on average, which primarily reflects Iraq) almost twice as much, $299.

In sum, the developing countries of the world for which there are data spent about $82 billion on primary education in 2000. This number varied from only $6 billion in Sub-Saharan Africa, which reflects both the low average expenditure of $68 per pupil per year and low enrollment rates, to $28 billion in Latin America and the Caribbean, which reflects near-universal enrollment and an average expenditure of $440 per pupil per year.

---

[1] The spending per student in Latin America is likely to be underestimated because a relatively large percentage of children attend private school. Because separate data on private school students are often unavailable, the figures in Table 5 divide total government spending on education by all students, public and private.

Teacher Costs and Non-Teacher Costs

The discussion thus far has examined total costs to governments of providing primary education. Ideally, one would consider the major components of these costs, such as teacher and administrator salaries, pedagogical materials, and construction and maintenance. Unfortunately, there are few systematic data on the composition of costs. Although individual country studies break the costs down in more detail, very little disaggregated information is comparable across a wide range of countries.

Bruns et al. (2003) report the limited information that is available on the division of total costs into teacher salaries and non-teacher costs (which includes the salaries of non-teacher staff). Table 6 presents per student costs (in U.S. dollars), disaggregated into teacher salary costs and other costs, for low-income countries only.[2] These countries are grouped according to their prospects for attaining UPC. Data are available for 47 of the 56 low-income countries that have not already achieved UPC (and are not missing any other data).[3] The percent of money spent on teacher salaries varies little. The lowest level is 75 percent, which is in countries that are on track to attain UPC by 2015, and the highest is 80 percent, for countries that are seriously off track. In most educational systems in both developed and developing countries, teacher salaries account for more than half of total costs, so these figures for low-income countries are not very surprising. Without more data and further analysis, it is not possible to say whether these figures strike a good balance between teacher salary costs and other costs.

Table 6: Teacher and Non-Teacher Costs of Primary Education

Status	Teacher costs per pupil (US $)	Non-teacher costs per pupil (US $)	Teacher costs as a percent of total costs
Already Attained	–	–	–
On Track to Attain	14.7	5.2	75
Off Track	32.0	8.4	79
Seriously Off Track	27.5	6.8	80
All	29.0	7.7	79

Source: Bruns et al. (2003).

---

[2] This excludes the three countries that have achieved UPC, for which no data are available.

[3] Data are available for 9 on-track countries, which are dominated by Bangladesh, for 19 off-track countries, which are dominated by India, and for 19 seriously off-track countries.

REVIEW OF PAST ESTIMATES OF UNIVERSAL PRIMARY
ENROLLMENT OR COMPLETION

Three recent studies have attempted to calculate the cost of attaining UPC by 2015. Each is subject to specific criticisms, and a general criticism applies to all three.

An Earlier World Bank Estimate

Before the publication of Bruns et al. (2003), the research staff at the World Bank produced estimates of the costs of attaining all eight Millennium Development Goals (Devarajan et al., 2002). Given the relatively short length of the paper and its objective of calculating the costs of all eight goals, the paper used a simple method to calculate the cost of attaining UPC by 2015.

Devarajan et al. calculated the number of additional children that need to be enrolled in school to attain UPC, about 103 million, and multiplied this by one of four estimates of the cost of enrolling a child in school: 1) the average cost over all developing countries (obtained by dividing total recurrent spending on primary education in all these countries by the number of children enrolled); 2) the median cost per primary school pupil, calculated separately for each region; 3) the average cost per student, calculated separately for each country; and 4) a "target" average cost determined separately for each country, defined as 13 percent of GDP per capita. This procedure ignored population growth from 2000 to 2015 and assumed no economic growth.

With these four methods to calculate the per pupil cost, Devarajan et al. estimated the following annual costs to attain UPC for all developing countries: $11.4 billion, $14.9 billion, $10.4 billion, and $27.6 billion, based on methods 1 through 4, respectively. The fourth scenario is more costly mainly because it implies much higher spending per pupil in East Asia and Latin America compared to the current level of spending, and the additional cost includes not only enrolling new children but also increasing the amount spent on children already enrolled. Because these two regions are already doing well in attaining UPC, this scenario seems inappropriate.

Another World Bank paper (Filmer, 2001) presents some simple estimates of the impact of economic growth on school enrollment from 2000 to 2015. It suggests that growth alone will increase enrollment somewhat, and that the cost to finance the remaining gap will be only 70 percent to

80 percent of the range of estimates in Devarajan et al.[4] Neither of these estimates speculates on how much can be paid by developing countries and how much is needed from donor agencies.

A UNICEF Estimate

Delamonica, Mehrota, and Vandermoortele (2001) calculate the cost of attaining "education for all" (EFA) at the primary level. Their estimates are based on an analysis of net enrollment rates and do not explicitly account for additional costs due to grade repetition (which leads to "overage" children being enrolled in primary school). Their target for achieving EFA is a net enrollment rate of 100 percent. If net enrollment rates were to reach 100 percent and there were no grade repetition, then every child would finish primary school and thus UPC would be attained.[5]

The authors of the UNICEF study make two other simplifying assumptions. First, they assume that per capita income will not change in developing countries between 2000 and 2015. Second, they assume that the cost of providing education to children not in school is the same as the cost of providing education to those currently in school. These assumptions are made for convenience, and the authors state that using more realistic assumptions would greatly complicate the calculations.

Where the study by Devarajan et al. ignored population growth, the UNICEF estimate for the number of new children that must be enrolled in school to attain EFA accounts for both population growth and a gradual increase in the net enrollment rate to 100 percent. The UNICEF study obtained (or in some cases estimated) net enrollment rates for all countries for the year 2000. Estimates of the number of children of primary school age were taken from the United Nations Population Division for every year from 2000 to 2015. The baseline estimate of the number of children in school "under the status quo" for each year from 2000 to

---

[4] Filmer's paper also attempts to estimate (using cross-country data) the response of enrollment rates to government expenditures on primary education, and finds a weak relationship. A rather simplistic simulation based on the this weak relationship gives cost estimates of $131 billion to $369 billion per year, but the paper does not claim that these estimates be taken seriously.

[5] Recall that UPC was defined above as 95 percent or more of all children finishing primary school; this is a slightly lower goal than the 100 percent completion that would be achieved with a net primary enrollment rate of 100 percent and no grade repetition.

2015 is the 2000 net enrollment rate multiplied by the estimate of the number of children of primary school age for that year. An annual increase in the net enrollment rate is set for each country, starting from the 2000 net rate, such that the net enrollment rate reaches 100 percent by 2015. The incremental increase in the net enrollment rate is then multiplied by the number of children of primary school age in that year to calculate the number of children in school for each year if EFA were to be attained. The difference between the baseline estimate of children in school and the second estimate is the gap in enrollment that needs to be filled in order to attain EFA by 2015. The paper estimates the gap to be about 170 million new students.

The cost per new student is calculated separately for each country by dividing the current total spending on primary education by the current number of children in primary school. The total cost for each country is then calculated by multiplying the average cost per child by the number of children that must be enrolled to attain a 100 percent net enrollment rate. This calculation is made separately for recurrent costs and capital costs. Over 15 years, the average annual recurrent cost is about $7 billion. Total capital costs are estimated to be $0.6 billion. An estimate is also made of the cost of increasing school quality, primarily by spending at least 15 percent of recurrent expenditures on items other than teacher salaries; this spending affects all pupils, not just those who have been added to attain universal enrollment. The cost of this additional expenditure is estimated to be $1.1 billion dollars. Another relatively simple calculation to account for improved school quality is to add the cost of hiring enough teachers to attain a pupil-teacher ratio of 40 in countries where the pupil-teacher ratio is higher than 40. This entails an additional cost of about $0.5 billion. Adding these costs together, the total average annual cost from 2000 to 2015 is $9.1 billion. The paper does not divide this amount into the portion that would be borne by the countries and the portion that would need to be financed by donors.

A UNESCO Estimate

An unpublished paper written by UNESCO staff presents a third estimate of the cost of attaining UPC by 2015 (Brossard and Gacougnolle, 2001). The authors begin by forecasting the primary school age population for each country in 2015 using United Nations population estimates. After making a small adjustment to account for the 1–2 percent of primary school age children who are in secondary school, they multiply the net enrollment rate by the forecast of the primary school age population. This determines the number of primary school age children enrolled in primary school in 1997. In developing countries, many children enrolled in primary school are older than the official primary school age. For each country, the authors calculate the proportion of children enrolled in primary school who are of primary school age and use the inverse of this proportion as an "inflation factor" to convert the number of primary school age children enrolled in primary school in 1997 to the total number of children enrolled in primary school, regardless of age.

These calculations generate a formula that expresses total enrollment in primary school as the product of the net enrollment rate, the number of children of primary school age, and the inverse of the proportion of children in primary school who are of primary school age. This formula accounts for grade repetition. That is, because repetition results in secondary school age children still enrolled in primary school, the number of children who will be enrolled in primary school to achieve UPC will exceed the number of primary school age children. The authors forecast that there will be 595 million children of primary school age in developing countries in 2015 but that 693 million children must be enrolled in primary school at that time to achieve UPC.[6] The additional 98 million children are repeaters. The UNESCO data show that 571 million children were enrolled in primary school in 1997, so the authors estimate the cost of increasing total enrollment by 122 million (to reach 693 million) by 2015.[7] To estimate the cost of recurrent educational expenditures, they calculate recurrent expenditure per pupil for each country in 1997. It is possible to decompose recurrent expenditures per pupil into the product of recurrent expenditures per teacher and current teachers per pupil (the inverse of the pupil-teacher ratio). This decomposition is used in one scenario, described below. The authors also incorporate capital costs (unlike the early World Bank estimate), but in a simple manner. They assume that capital costs are a constant proportion of recurrent costs.

Brossard and Gacougnolle consider three scenarios to estimate the cost

---

[6] The figure of 693 million children was obtained by using the formula given above, after setting the net enrollment rate to 100 percent.

[7] It is not clear why this figure is lower than the 170 million figure given in the UNICEF report; neither report provides a comprehensive explanation of data or methodology.

of achieving UPC. The first assumes that spending per pupil is unchanged (and thus that the pupil-teacher ratio is unchanged) and, for each country, multiplies spending per pupil by the number of pupils that need to be added to attain a net primary enrollment rate of 100 percent.[8] Using this scenario, the authors estimate that annual costs must increase by $26 billion (1995 U.S. dollars), from $99 billion in 1997 to $125 billion in 2015 (so the averge annual cost from 1997 to 2015 is $13 billion).

The second scenario adds the quality improvement of reducing the pupil-teacher ratio by 10 percent in each country. This increases the per pupil recurrent cost by about 11 percent, not only for newly added students but also for students currently in school. The total cost for UPC rises to $133 billion, which implies a financing gap of $34 billion. The third scenario includes a cost-savings assumption, where new teachers hired under the second assumption can be paid only 70 percent of what current teachers are paid. This reduces the cost of UPC by $2 billion and thus reduces the financing gap to $32 billion. All cost figures in each of the three scenarios are *annual* figures. If gradual increases begin in 1997, the total amount over the entire 18-year period for each scenario would be $263 billion, $338 billion, and $320 billion, respectively.[9]

Some Problems with these Estimates

All three of these studies needed to make simplifying assumptions to obtain their estimates, and the assumptions made tend to ignore or avoid complicating factors. The more simplifying assumptions made in a study, however, the more likely it is that the estimates are inaccurate. The assumptions of these studies are summarized in Table 7.

The Devarajan et al. study makes the greatest number of simplifying assumptions. It ignores capital costs, economic growth, the spread of AIDS in many Sub-Saharan African countries, private schools, and grade repetition. Four of these five assumptions are likely to lead to underestimation of the cost, the sole exception being the role of private schools. Ignoring capital costs clearly underestimates the total cost. Ignoring the spread of AIDS also underestimates the cost because many teachers with AIDS will be absent for long periods of time, may require medical care,

---

[8] Adding this number of pupils over all developing countries leads to the 122 million figure used in the study.

[9] These figures are calculated by multiplying the annual figures listed in Table 15 of the Brossard and Gacougnolle paper by 18.

Table 7: Selected Characteristics of the Four Cost Studies

	Devarajan	UNICEF	UNESCO	Bruns
Includes capital costs?	No	Yes	Yes	Yes
Allows for economic growth?	No	No	No	Yes
Includes AIDS & orphan costs?	No	No	No	Yes
Adjusts for private schools?	No	No	No	Yes
Accounts for repeaters?	No	No	Yes	Yes
Scenarios to raise school quality?	No	Yes	Yes	Yes
Cost comparison made	Adding new students, relative to current students	Adding new students, relative to current students	Adding new students, relative to current students	Gap in what countries can finance and what is needed
Number of countries included in cost comparison	About 150	151	128	47
Annual cost estimate, billions US$	10–15	9	13–17	0–6

Sources: Authors' summary based on the four studies.

and will die at an early age (which implies that a new teacher must be trained). Although ignoring economic growth may, at first glance, appear to overestimate costs because growing economies have more resources to pay for education, a growing economy also generates higher wages, which leads to an increase in teacher salaries. Ignoring grade repetition underestimates costs because children who repeat grades take more time in school to finish primary schooling, which increases the number of children in school at any point in time. Ignoring the role of private schools, on the other hand, leads to an overestimate of costs. Private schools are financed by parents or private organizations (e.g. churches), so an increased number of students in private schools decreases the financial burden on public schools (and thus on the government budget).

Brossard and Gacougnolle improve on Devarajan et al. by incorporating capital costs (although their method for doing so is not clearly described). They explicitly recognize their omission of additional costs resulting from the spread of AIDS. They ignore economic growth, grade repetition, and private schools. Brossard and Gacougnolle make further improvements. They account for grade repetition and capital costs, but not costs due to AIDS, the impact of economic growth on costs, nor children who attend private schools.

These three studies arrive at estimates of the annual costs of achieving UPC between $9 billion and $17 billion. The narrow range of results is not surprising because these methods have more similarities than differences. A fourth study, the World Bank study by Bruns and her coauthors discussed in more detail below, addresses many of the shortcomings raised in this subsection, though not always convincingly.

The Most Serious Problem with these Estimates

Unfortunately, these three studies and the Bruns et al. study suffer from a shortcoming that will be almost impossible to address at a global level, although data from some countries may allow researchers to address it at the national level. The problem is that they make no attempt to answer the first question raised in the introduction to this chapter: What policy changes can bring about UPC in developing countries?

In the studies discussed, the number of children to be enrolled in school is multiplied by the cost per student, the latter usually based on current average costs per student. Such exercises are useful under two possible scenarios. First, if some policy were developed that persuaded all parents to enroll their primary school age children, the cost of accommodating these students while maintaining current pupil-teacher ratios and other costs would be useful to know. Yet this would only be one part of the cost of attaining UPC, because the policy itself, whatever it may be, would also have a cost. Moreover, the calculation assumes that the (marginal) cost of educating children who are currently not enrolled in school is equal to the average cost for currently enrolled children, which is unlikely to be true.

The second scenario that makes such exercises useful is one in which the main reason that children of primary school age are not enrolled in school is that there are no schools available. Either the nearest school is too far away or the nearest school is full and cannot admit any more students. One way to phrase this scenario is to say, "If you build the schools, they will come."[10]

Unfortunately, the assumption behind this second interpretation is

---

[10] A closely related interpretation would supplement the construction of schools and the hiring of more teachers with enforcement of a compulsory schooling law. This can be paraphrased as "Build the schools and force them to come." In developing countries, however, such laws are rarely, if ever, enforced, because

unlikely to be true in many developing countries. In western Honduras, for example, only about half of all children finish primary school (Glewwe and Olinto, 2004). In a household questionnaire administered in 2000 to 5768 households in 80 municipalities, 50 percent of households reported that the nearest primary school is within a 10 minute walk and 90 percent reported that the nearest primary school is within a 30 minute walk. School access is not a major problem, even in communities where primary school completion rates are low. According to a questionnaire administered in the same municipalities in 2002 (the following figures are from the 20 municipalities that were the control group), among 1525 children age 7–12, 94 percent had started school but 9 percent of these (130 children) had already dropped out and thus would not finish primary school. Parents reported the main reasons their children had dropped out. The three main reasons were: child not interested in school (36 percent), "economic problems" (19 percent), and child must work (9 percent). Only 8 percent reported lack of a nearby school as the problem. In Honduras, although many schools have been built, a substantial fraction of children do not attend.

In India, the primary completion rate was 76 percent in 1999. For most of the population, distance to the nearest primary school in India is very low; in 1993, 94 percent of the rural population lived within one kilometer of a primary school (PROBE Team, 1999).

In Ghana, parents of out-of-school children aged 6 to 21 were asked to report the main reason why their children were not enrolled (World Bank, 2004). The two reasons given most frequently were: school is too expensive or child is needed to work at home (46 percent) and parents view education as having little value (22 percent). Only 7 percent reported that the school is too far away or of low quality. When primary school head teachers were asked the same question, 78 percent responded that the main reason children were not enrolled was that school is too expensive and/or the child is needed at home. Only 2 percent said that the school is too far away or of low quality.

Indonesia may offer a counterexample. Duflo (2001) points out that a major expansion in the number of schools in Indonesia in the 1970s coincided with an increase in the primary enrollment rate from about 69 percent in 1973 to about 83 percent in 1978. Yet school construction

---

governments in those countries have neither the personnel nor the political will to enforce compulsory schooling laws.

was only one aspect of a larger plan to promote education. For example, in 1978 the Indonesian government removed all primary school enrollment fees. Moreover, the massive increase in primary school construction (which doubled the number of primary schools in Indonesia in seven years) still did not lead to 100 percent enrollment rates. Even in countries that continue to have serious problems with school availability (the Indonesian example is quite dated) there is no evidence that building more schools is sufficient to attain UPC.

The unfortunate conclusion to draw about the cost estimates of the studies discussed above, as well as the Bruns et al. study discussed below, is that they either beg the question of how UPC will be achieved or they are based on the grossly inaccurate assumption that the only obstacle to UPC is a shortage of schools. A different method for estimating the cost of attaining UPC for a few countries is presented below, after a discussion of the cost estimates made by Bruns et al.

MECHANICS OF THE NEW WORLD BANK COST ESTIMATES

The most comprehensive estimates of the cost of attaining UPC by 2015 are those developed at the World Bank by Bruns, Mingat, and Rakotomalala (2003). The methodology used in this study is explained in detail below, with emphasis on the assumptions made, and their implications. Although these estimates are still subject to the important criticism made above, they warrant a detailed presentation. In addition to explaining the methodology, some simulations are presented to demonstrate what underlies the estimates produced by this report.

Assumptions

All methods used to estimate the costs of attaining UPC must make some assumptions. Perhaps the most basic assumption is what the population growth rate will be, because that determines how many children of school age there will be in each future year. The World Bank assumes no change in the population growth rate over time. This means that the population growth rate is assumed to remain unchanged between 2000 and 2015.[11] This is a reasonable assumption, given that the projections are made only to the year 2015, and population growth rates change slowly over time.

---

[11] For some countries the population growth rate is not for the year 2000 but for another year, usually 1997, 1998, or 1999.

For developing countries as a whole the population growth rate changed very little from 1980 to 1990, dropping from 1.9 percent to 1.8 percent, although the rate dropped more quickly from 1990 to 2000 (to 1.3 percent).

Another assumption that has important implications for costs is the grade-repetition rate, because this rate determines the actual number of years, on average, that a child spends in primary school. The World Bank presents two scenarios, a "base scenario" for which repetition rates are assumed to be constant from 2000 to 2015, and an "efficiency improvement" scenario. The second scenario assumes no change for countries with a repetition rate below 10 percent and a gradual reduction in grade repetition to 10 percent by 2015 for countries with a rate greater than 10 percent in 2000.

A third assumption concerns economic growth. A country with a growing economy will have more internal resources to pay for education, but a growing economy will also lead to higher incomes and therefore higher teacher salaries, increasing the total cost of UPC. Moreover, forecasting future economic growth is very difficult. The World Bank report assumes, without much explanation, a rate of GDP growth of 5 percent per year. Of course, per capita economic growth will vary according to population growth rates; countries with higher population growth rates will have lower growth rates in per capita GDP.

Equations

The equations used in the World Bank estimates are presented below. Italicized variables are those for which direct assumptions are made (e.g., the population growth rate is assumed to remain unchanged), while variables not in italics are calculated as functions of the direct assumptions (e.g., per capita GDP is calculated based on the assumptions concerning GDP growth and population growth). Thus, each scenario is a set of assumptions about the variables in italics, and these are then used to calculate a number of intermediary cost variables and, eventually, the overall (simulated) cost. The presentation below begins with the equation for overall cost, and works backward toward the underlying assumptions.

In the World Bank estimates, the total cost at time t (tc_t) of primary schooling in a given country is the sum of four distinct costs (all at time t), capital costs (kc_t), recurrent costs (rc_t), costs associated with the prevalence of HIV/AIDS ($hivc_t$), and costs associated with the percentage of children of primary school age who are orphans (orc$_t$), most of whom have become orphans because their parents have died of AIDS:

$$tc_t = kc_t + rc_t + hivc_t + orc_t \quad (1)$$

Capital costs (kc$_t$) result from the construction of new classrooms (often through the construction of new schools) to accommodate an increase in the number of children. Thus capital costs are the product of the new classrooms required (newcls$_t$) and the cost of their construction (*clsc$_t$*):

$$kc_t = newcls_t \times clsc_t \quad (2)$$

The cost of classroom construction (*clsc$_t$*) is in italics to indicate that this variable needs no further calculation; for each country, Bruns et al. set *clsc$_t$* at values that "regional experts consider to be a 'good practice' level" (2003: 143).

To calculate the variable newcls$_t$ in equation (2), the methodology assumes that the costs are incurred in the year before the new classrooms are first used. Thus the number of new classrooms constructed in year t is determined by the increase in the number of students from year t to year t+1, adjusted for pupil-teacher ratios and the number of teachers in each classroom (in many developing countries several classes, each with their own teacher, may meet in the same classroom). The number of new classrooms required depends on changes in the number of teachers (numtch) and changes in the number of teachers per classroom (*tchpcls*), the latter being one indicator of school quality:

$$newcls_t = numtch_{t+1}/tchpcls_{t+1} - numtch_t/tchpcls_t \quad (3)$$

The number of teachers in any year (numtch$_t$) is determined by the number of students in primary school (totstud$_t$) divided by the primary level pupil-teacher ratio (*puptchrat$_t$*):

$$numtch_t = totstud_t/puptchrat_t \quad (4)$$

The number of students is determined by the total population of the country (*totpop$_t$*), the fraction of the population that are of primary school age (*primage%$_t$*), the gross enrollment rate (ger$_t$) and the percent of primary school students who are in private schools (*priv%$_t$*):

$$totstud_t = (primage\%_t \times totpop_t) \times ger_t \times (1 - priv\%_t) \quad (5)$$

The last step is to calculate the gross enrollment rate. If all children enroll in primary school at the standard age (e.g., 6 years old) and there were no grade repetition, it would equal the average, over different ages (6 years, 7 years, etc.) of the number of children enrolled divided by the total number of children of that age. For the first year of primary schooling, this would be the intake rate (*inrate*) into primary school (the proportion of children who eventually enroll in primary school), and for the last year of primary school this would be the primary school completion rate (*comprate*). The World Bank authors make the plausible assumption that the average over all grades is approximately the average over the first and last grades, i.e., (*inrate* + *comprate*)/2. The last issue to consider is grade repetition. Repetition adds to the gross number of children enrolled in primary school, raising the gross enrollment rate:

$$\text{ger}_t = [(inrate_t + comprate_t)/2] \times (1 + reprate_t) \quad (6)$$

The variable *reprate_t* is the repetition rate in primary school. This completes the discussion of the first term in equation (1), capital costs.

The next term in equation (1) is recurrent costs. This can be divided into teacher salary costs ($tsal_t$) and other (non-teacher) costs. Expressing the latter as a multiple of teacher salary costs (*ntc%tsal*) gives:

$$\text{rc}_t = \text{tsal}_t \times (1 + ntc\%tsal) \quad (7)$$

In the simulations below, *ntc%tsal* is set at its value in the year 2000, unless indicated otherwise.

Teacher salary costs are in turn determined by the number of teachers ($numtch_t$) and the average teacher salary, the latter of which can be expressed as the ratio of a teacher's salary as a function of per capita GDP (this ratio will be denoted as *tsal%gdppc_t*) and per capita GDP (*gdppc_t*, which is simply total GDP, denoted as *gdp_t*, divided by total population, *totpop_t*):

$$\text{tsal}_t = numtch_t \times [tsal\%gdppc_t \times gdppc_t]$$
$$= numtch_t \times [tsal\%gdppc_t \times (gdp_t / totpop_t)] \quad (8)$$

Recall that $numtch_t$ was explained in equations (4), (5), and (6).

The third component of total costs in equation (1) is costs due to HIV/AIDS. It is calculated as a percentage increment to teacher salaries,

$$\text{hivc}_t = hiv\%tsal_t \times \text{tsal}_t \quad (9)$$

where $tsal_t$ is derived as in equation (8). The increment (*hiv%tsal_t*) is calculated based on the proportion of teachers with HIV/AIDS (assumed to be the same as that in the general population) and estimates that a teacher with HIV/AIDS will die after about 10 years and during those years will be absent from school (and thus a substitute will need to be hired) for 260 school days over those 10 years.[12] The cost of training new teachers to replace those who die is not incorporated into these cost estimates.

The final component of total costs in equation (1) is orphan costs. This component is calculated as the cost per orphan (*orcpo*) multiplied by the number of students who are orphans (which is the total number of students divided by the percent of students that are orphans, *orphan%*):

$$\text{orc}_t = orcpo_t \times orphan\%_t \times \text{totstud}_t \quad (10)$$

Recall that total students is given above in equation (5). The cost per orphan is in effect the cost of a subsidy given to orphans to support their school expenses, which is assumed to be $50 per month for all countries.

Substituting equations (2) through (10) into equation (1) gives the overall equation for simulating total costs of primary education for each country for each year. The variables in italics are directly determined by the assumptions of the model. Different assumptions will produce different estimates of total cost.

The above equations are used to calculate the total cost of attaining UPC in each country. The final step is to calculate the domestic financial resources that each country can provide, and any gap between this number and the total cost represents a need for international assistance to achieve UPC. Domestic financial resources (domres$_t$) are assumed to be the product of four factors: gross domestic product (*gdp$_t$*), government revenue as a percent of gross domestic product (*gvrv%gdp*), education spending as a percent of government revenue (*edsp%gvrv*), and the percent of government spending on education that is allocated to primary education (*prsp%edsp*):

$$\text{domres}_t = gdp_t \times gvrv\%gdp_t \times edsp\%gvrv_t \times prsp\%edsp_t \quad (11)$$

In the simulations, *gvrv%gdp$_t$* is set at 14 percent for the poorest low-income counties, 16 percent for low-income countries whose per capita GDP is between about $300 and about $500, and 18 percent for low-income countries with a per capita GDP greater than about $500 (this rule was not strictly followed, but it is not clear how the exceptions were made). The percent of government revenue devoted to education

---

[12] For details and references, see Bruns et al., p. 77.

($edsp\%gvrv_t$) was set to 20 percent for all countries, and the percent of education spending allocated to primary education ($prsp\%edsp_t$) was set to 50 percent for countries with a six-year primary cycle and 42 percent for countries with a five-year primary cycle.

Simulations

Using the methodology just described, Bruns and her coauthors present six simulations of the cost of attaining UPC. For each simulation, there are three outcomes: total cost, domestic resources, and the gap between the total cost and domestic resources. These simulations are limited to the 47 low-income countries that are off track. In addition to the simulations done by Bruns, et al., this study undertakes several others to understand better the workings of the methodology.

The first simulation, referred to as Scenario 1, calculates cost, resources, and the gap between cost and resources after gradually increasing the intake rate and the completion rate in equation (6) to be 100 percent.[13] All other parameters (variables in italics) are left unchanged. The total cost over 15 years for the 47 countries in the simulation is $208 billion dollars, and the total resources available is about $170 billion. The financing gap is $38 billion spread over 15 years, which implies a modest donor increase of only $2.5 billion per year. Nearly 80 percent of this gap ($30 billion) is for Sub-Saharan African countries, and most of the rest ($6.6 billion) is for South Asia.

This cost estimate is not comparable to those of the three previous studies. Those studies estimated the *additional* cost of getting unenrolled children into school, which can be calculated as the difference between the total cost calculated in the World Bank Scenario 1 and the total cost of maintaining primary school enrollment at the current number from 2000 to 2015. This was not calculated in the World Bank study but it is given here, in Scenario 13(a). The total in this case is $110 billion, which, when compared to Scenario 1, implies that the incremental cost of attaining UPC by 2015 in these 47 countries will be $98 billion. Divided over 15 years, this implies an incremental cost of $6.5 billion per year. This is smaller than all the cost estimates of the other studies, primarily because it excludes countries that are on track even though they have not

---

[13] The intake rate reaches 100 percent by 2010, and the completion rate reaches 100 percent by 2015.

yet attained UPC.

Scenario 13(a) assumes that, in the absence of a concerted international effort, primary school enrollment will remain the same. One could also argue that "doing nothing" does not mean that enrollment will be fixed for the next 15 years. Two alternative scenarios are: 1) the proportion of children enrolled (relative to the number of school age children) is unchanged; and 2) the enrollment trend from 2000 to 2015 follows the same (linear) trend that it followed from 1990 to 2000. These are Scenarios 13(b) and 13(c), respectively. In each case, the cost suggests a somewhat smaller incremental gap—$74 billion in the former and $86 billion in the latter—which reduces the annual cost to about $5 billion and $5.7 billion, respectively.

The scenario that receives the most attention in the Bruns et al. study is Scenario 5 (see Table 8). This calculates the cost of achieving UPC by 2015 while simultaneously improving school quality,[14] enhancing efficiency,[15] and increasing mobilization of domestic financial resources. Under this scenario, the total cost of attaining UPC by 2015 would increase to $244 billion, but domestic resources would also increase, to $213 billion, so the financing gap is slightly lower, at $31 billion over 15 years (about $2 billion per year).

Scenarios 2, 3, 4, and 6 (see Table 8) are the other scenarios presented in the Bruns et al. book. Scenarios 7–12 are "experiments" that consider what happens to the estimates when some parameters are changed. One potential criticism of the World Bank scenarios is that they assume GDP growth rates of 5 percent, which may be too optimistic, especially for Sub-Saharan African countries. Scenario 7 uses the assumptions of Scenario 5 but assumes that GDP growth from 2000 to 2015 will equal the average GDP growth rate from 1990 to 2000 (instead of assuming 5 percent GDP growth). Very little happens when this assumption is changed. Domestic resources decline slightly, but costs also decline (because teacher salaries, tied to GDP per capita, decline slightly). Scenario 8 uses IMF projections for the GDP growth rate. IMF projections

---

[14] Improvement in school quality is incorporated primarily through a reduction in the pupil-teacher ratio in countries where that number is higher than 40, but also through an increase in teacher salaries and "non-teacher" spending for some countries.

[15] Efficiency enhancement is calculated as a reduction in teacher salaries in countries with relatively high teacher salaries and in raising pupil-teacher ratios to 40 in countries where they are less than 40.

Table 8: Simulation Results Using World Bank Methodology (Bruns et al., 2003)

Region	Total Cost (millions US $)	Domestic Resources (millions US $)	Financing Gap (millions US $)
Scenario 1: Base Estimate			
Sub-Saharan Africa	84,650	54,632	-30,018
South Asia	113,439	106,816	-6623
East Asia and Pacific	874	1094	220
Latin America and Caribbean	1957	1718	-238
Middle East and North Africa	7084	5603	-1480
Total	208,004	169,864	-38,140
Scenario 2: Improve School Quality (reduce student-teacher ratio to 40 and, in some countries, raise teacher salaries and non-teacher spending)			
Sub-Saharan Africa	110,113	54,632	-55,480
South Asia	139,458	106,816	-32,641
East Asia and Pacific	2491	1094	-1397
Latin America and Caribbean	2266	1718	-546
Middle East and North Africa	7948	5603	-2344
Total	262,275	169,864	-92,410
Scenario 3: Improve Quality and Raise Efficiency (reduce teacher salaries in countries with very high salaries, and raise student-teacher ratio to 40 in countries where it is less than 40)			
Sub-Saharan Africa	90,925	54,632	-36,293
South Asia	140,690	106,816	-33,874
East Asia and Pacific	2177	1094	-1083
Latin America and Caribbean	2000	1718	-282
Middle East and North Africa	5884	5603	-281
Total	241,676	169,864	-71,812
*Scenario 4: Improve Quality and Efficiency, and Mobilize Domestic Resources**			
Sub-Saharan Africa	88,132	63,216	-24,916
South Asia	145,677	147,631	1954
East Asia and Pacific	2050	1713	-337
Latin America and Caribbean	2623	2003	-620
Middle East and North Africa	5620	4423	-1197
Total	244,104	218,987	-25,116
*Scenario 5: Improve Quality and Efficiency, and Mobilize Domestic Resources**			
Sub-Saharan Africa	88,132	59,828	-28,304
South Asia	145,677	145,232	-446
East Asia and Pacific	2050	1619	-431
Latin America and Caribbean	2623	1985	-639
Middle East and North Africa	5620	4423	-1197
Total	244,104	213,086	-31,017

Region	Total Cost (millions US $)	Domestic Resources (millions US $)	Financing Gap (millions US $)
Scenario 6: *Improve Quality and Efficiency, and Mobilize Domestic Resources**			
Sub-Saharan Africa	88,132	78,538	-9594
South Asia	145,677	167,999	22,321
East Asia and Pacific	2050	2029	-22
Latin America and Caribbean	2623	2266	-358
Middle East and North Africa	5620	6658	1038
Total	244,104	257,489	13,384
Scenario 7: *Scenario 5, but GDP growth is same as average growth from 1990 to 2000*			
Sub-Saharan Africa	76,738	50,675	-26,063
South Asia	152,798	153,507	709
East Asia and Pacific	2043	1587	-457
Latin America and Caribbean	1789	1287	-501
Middle East and North Africa	5910	4672	-1238
Total	239,278	211,728	-27,550
Scenario 8: *Scenario 5, but GDP growth is assumed to follow IMF projections*			
Sub-Saharan Africa	84,936	57,289	-27,647
South Asia	171,792	173,287	1495
East Asia and Pacific	2427	1932	-495
Latin America and Caribbean	2005	1455	-550
Middle East and North Africa	5549	4359	-1190
Total	266,708	23,833	-28,386
Scenario 9: *Scenario 5, but GDP growth is assumed to be 3 percent*			
Sub-Saharan Africa	76,097	50,321	-25,776
South Asia	123,408	121,451	-1957
East Asia and Pacific	1734	1356	-378
Latin America and Caribbean	2034	1482	-552
Middle East and North Africa	4882	3786	-1096
Total	208,155	178,396	-29,759
Scenario 10: *Scenario 5, but reduce the fraction of students in private schools*			
Sub-Saharan Africa	79,161	50,675	-28,486
South Asia	153,326	153,507	181
East Asia and Pacific	2046	1587	-460
Latin America and Caribbean	1833	1287	-546
Middle East and North Africa	5910	4671	-1238
Total	242,276	211,728	-30,548

Region	Total Cost (millions US $)	Domestic Resources (millions US $)	Financing Gap (millions US $)
Scenario 11: Scenario 1, but teacher salaries are not increased over time			
Sub-Saharan Africa	68,486	54,632	-13,854
South Asia	85,422	106,816	21,394
East Asia and Pacific	675	1094	419
Latin America and Caribbean	1519	1718	200
Middle East and North Africa	5694	5603	-91
Total	161,796	169,864	8068
Scenario 12: Scenario 1, but no new teachers are hired and no classrooms are built (student-teacher ratio increases)			
Sub-Saharan Africa	42,545	50,675	8131
South Asia	112,208	153,507	41,299
East Asia and Pacific	2270	1587	-684
Latin America and Caribbean	1013	1287	274
Middle East and North Africa	5389	4672	-717
Total	163,425	211,727	48,303
Scenario 13(a): Enrollment levels remain at 2000 levels			
Sub-Saharan Africa	34,501	42,171	6770
South Asia	69,211	79,167	9956
East Asia and Pacific	717	823	107
Latin America and Caribbean	1035	1235	200
Middle East and North Africa	3710	4419	709
Total	110,073	127,815	17,742
Scenario 13(b): Enrollment rates stay at 2000 rates			
Sub-Saharan Africa	45,675	42,171	-3503
South Asia	81,277	79,167	-2110
East Asia and Pacific	975	823	-152
Latin America and Caribbean	1335	1235	-101
Middle East and North Africa	4887	4419	-468
Total	134,149	127,815	-6334
Scenario 13(c): Enrollment trends are the same as the trends from 1990 to 2000			
Sub-Saharan Africa	36,479	42,171	5692
South Asia	79,612	79,167	-445
East Asia and Pacific	716	823	107
Latin America and Caribbean	1587	1235	-352
Middle East and North Africa	3619	4419	800
Total	122,013	127,815	5802

Sources: Authors' simulations based on data from World Bank (2002) and Bruns et al. (2003).

* Scenarios 4, 5, and 6 differ only in the assumptions made about the ability of the government to raise domestic resources, with Scenario 5 being the most pessimistic and Scenario 6 being the most optimistic. See Bruns et al. for details.

are optimistic in assuming higher than 5 percent growth in most regions, but the increase in resources is matched by increased costs in teacher salaries, so again there is little effect on the gap. Scenario 9 assumes a more pessimistic GDP growth of only 3 percent. As expected, domestic resources drop, but the drop in domestic costs is almost the same, so that there is very little change in the financing gap compared to Scenario 5. Scenario 10 assumes a smaller fraction of students in private schools, but this has little effect on the simulation results.

A much different picture emerges if teacher salaries are held constant even though GDP growth is 5 percent. Scenario 11 implements the base case of Scenario 1, with one change: teacher salaries are held constant. There is no change in domestic resources, but domestic costs drop by about $46 billion. This results in an overall surplus of about $8 billion, although it is still the case that Sub-Saharan Africa has a financing gap of about $14 billion.

Scenario 12 examines the result if pupil-teacher ratios are allowed to rise as more students are enrolled (all other assumptions are the same as those in Scenario 5). This means that no new schools are built and no new teachers are hired; in effect, more children are crowded into existing class-rooms. Under this scenario, costs are much lower than domestic resources, leading to a financing surplus of $48 billion. Even Sub-Saharan Africa has such a surplus, about $8 billion. However, the implied pupil-teacher ratios are quite high in some regions. For Sub-Saharan Africa, the ratio rises from 47 to 83, and in Latin America it rises from 43 to 88.[16]

MORE CREDIBLE EVIDENCE ON THE COST OF
UNIVERSAL PRIMARY COMPLETION

The assumptions underlying all of the above cost estimates, including the Bruns et al. World Bank estimates, are doubtful. As discussed above, none of the studies considers the reasons why primary school age chil-dren are not enrolled in school. The cost estimates are meaningful only if the main reason that children are not enrolled is that no school is avail-able, but this is unlikely to be the case.

If the main problem is not lack of schools, how might additional

---

[16] The very high figure for Latin America reflects the dramatic increase in Haiti, which is one of only two countries in that region not expected to attain UPC by 2015.

funds be used to increase school enrollment? One possibility is to subsidize schooling by providing payments to parents conditional on their children being enrolled. This subsidy has been offered in several countries (e.g., Bangladesh, Brazil, Chile, Honduras, Mexico, and Nicaragua). In a few of these countries, policies providing subsidies were implemented using randomized trials, which probably provide the best estimates of the impact of such policies on school enrollment. Honduras and Nicaragua provide two recent examples. Glewwe and Olinto (2004) report that subsidies to Honduran parents to enroll their children in school, worth about $50 per year per child (about 3 percent of annual household expenditures), increased enrollment rates about 1–2 percentage points. In Nicaragua, the subsidies were much larger, about $112 per child per year (about 18 percent of annual household expenditures). Maluccio and Flores (2004) report that school enrollment rates increased by 16 percentage points, from about 77 percent to about 93 percent. Estimates reported by Morley and Coady (2003) for Nicaragua suggest that the intervention raises the probability of a Nicaraguan child entering the fifth grade, conditional on starting first grade, from 55 percent to 80 percent. These increases in enrollment in Honduras and Nicaragua were not accompanied by the construction of new schools, although some new teachers may have been hired; thus, it is likely that pupil-teacher ratios increased. However, the evidence from developing countries shows that pupil-teacher ratios have little effect on student learning (Hanushek, 1995), so it may not be necessary to reduce class size to previous levels.

Consider the case of Nicaragua in more detail. Using the World Bank methodology, the assumption that enrollment rates remain constant (the "doing nothing" scenario) implies that operating schools in Nicaragua will cost $979 million over the next 15 years. The cost of reaching UPC under the "build more schools and they will come" assumption, as simulated by Bruns et al. Scenario 1, is $1,050 million. Thus, the incremental cost over 15 years of attaining UPC is about $71 million, or about $5 million per year.

In contrast to this cost estimate, consider the cost of providing subsidies to attend schools in poor rural areas. The total number of primary age children in Nicaragua in 2000 was about 600,000 children, about half from rural areas. The study discussed above suggests that a $112 annual subsidy per child will increase the percentage of children who reach grade 5, conditional on starting school, from about 55 percent to 80 percent.

Under the assumption that half of children in rural areas need assistance to be induced to stay in school, providing the subsidy to about 150,000 Nicaraguan children will cost about $17 million annually. This is 3–4 times higher than the annual cost of achieving UPC implied by the World Bank report, and providing subsidies can be expected to achieve only 80 percent completion of grade 5. This rough calculation suggests that the costs of achieving UPC through such a program will be much higher than the "build the schools and they will come" approach. The data from Honduras, in which a $50 per year subsidy increased the enrollment rate by only 1–2 percentage points, also suggest that using subsidies will be much more expensive than the "build the schools and they will come" approach.

There may be other ways to attract children to school, but there is currently very little research on this subject. An important exception, doubly important because it examines a poor African country (Kenya), is a study by Miguel and Kremer (2004) of the impact that providing medical treatment for intestinal parasites has on school attendance. The study found that providing low-cost (49 cents per student per year) deworming medicine increased school participation (which incorporates both attendance and enrollment) by seven percentage points. While this impact is not very large from the viewpoint of reaching UPC, it highlights one less expensive alternative to subsidies. This particular alternative applies only in settings where a high percentage of children have moderate to heavy levels of intestinal parasites, which is not the case for most developing countries,[17] but it suggests that health may be a significant factor in determining whether children enroll and participate in primary school. It is possible that programs for improving child health will need to be a part of policies to achieve UPC, and therefore the cost of such programs must be incorporated into estimates of the cost of attaining UPC.

The approach used by the studies reviewed in this chapter is based on an incorrect, or at least incomplete, understanding of why many children in developing countries do not complete primary school. No one knows how much it will cost to attain universal primary school completion, because no one knows what policies can achieve that goal. Effective policies to promote universal primary education, and the calculation of its

---

[17] Miguel and Kremer report infection levels of 200 million to 1.3 billion, depending on the type of parasite, compared to a total population in developing countries of about 5 billion, but they also note that most of these infections are "light."

cost, must be based on new research on the determinants of school enrollment in developing countries.

CONCLUSION

Developing countries are making steady progress toward UPC, but at the current rates of improvement it is unlikely that they will attain that goal by 2015. Lagging far behind the rest of the world, Sub-Saharan Africa had an average primary school completion rate of 53 percent in 2000 and this number is projected to remain at 53 percent in 2015. In all other regions, the projected primary completion rate by 2015 is near 90 percent or higher (the lowest being South Asia and the Middle East and North Africa, both of which have a projected rate of 87 percent). The introduction to this chapter posed two questions: What policy changes can bring about UPC in developing countries? How much additional money will be needed to implement those policies?

Though they claim to do so, none of the four recent studies reviewed in this chapter adequately answers the second question, because none identifies policies that can bring about UPC. These studies focus on how much it will cost to build new classrooms and to hire new teachers to accommodate children currently not in school, but building new schools does not always mean that children will come. In many developing countries, schools are available but millions of parents choose not to enroll their children in those schools. Only a thorough investigation of the choices made by parents, especially in the countries of Sub-Saharan Africa, will reveal what is required to persuade parents to enroll their children, and only then will it be possible to calculate the cost of achieving UPC. This research is a critical task for researchers and development agencies. Recent research from Latin America on the use of subsidies suggests that this method can be effective, but the cost may by three to four times higher than the expense of building new classrooms and hiring more teachers. Although there is less evidence from Sub-Saharan Africa on the effectiveness of subsidies on school enrollment, recent rapid increases in primary school enrollment following the removal of primary school fees in three East African countries (Kenya, Tanzania, and Uganda) suggest that monetary incentives are likely to have strong effects in that region (see Stasavage, 2005; IMF, 2003; World Bank, 2004b).

Providing direct monetary incentives to enroll in primary school is only one possible route for attaining UPC. There may be other effective policies. For example, in countries where children have high levels of intestinal parasites, provision of deworming medicines can raise enrollment rates, at least to some extent, for a very low cost. More generally, primary schools must be effective at providing skills, and the return to those skills must be high enough for parents to continue to enroll their children. Ensuring that schools effectively teach skills is the responsibility of ministries of education, while ensuring that skills are rewarded in the labor market is a general task of economic policy. Just as little is known about why some children are not enrolled in school, little is known about how education policies affect learning (see Glewwe, 2002, and Glewwe and Kremer, 2006).

In our view, the research done to date is inadequate to provide a plausible estimate of the cost of attaining UPC. More research is needed on education policies that persuade parents to enroll their children, and on policies that ensure that children learn valuable skills. Randomized trials are arguably the most convincing approach to assessing specific school policies, and donor agencies should encourage and support such evaluations. Given the concentration of the problem in Sub-Saharan Africa, most studies should be undertaken in those countries. Because the causes of non-enrollment are likely to vary across regions within a single country, separate studies may have to be done in each region where a large proportion of children are not completing primary school.

Once effective policies are found, it is usually simple to calculate the costs of implementing those policies. The data needed on expenditure are usually part of the cost of implementing the randomized evaluation, and in many cases, the cost per school does not change when the program is expanded to the national level. The main barrier to increasing the number of randomized evaluations is funding. Most economists would agree that the results from such studies are public goods, which implies that some government agency or agencies should provide funding. International development agencies such as the World Bank and the United Nations are obvious sources for such funding. When those agencies, perhaps in concert with bilateral aid agencies, provide funds for a large number of randomized trials, a key step will have been taken toward calculating the cost of attaining universal primary completion, and ultimately toward attaining that goal itself.

Appendix:

Table A.1: Countries used in the analysis

Country	UPC Status	Income Level	Most Recent PCR	(year)	PCR 2015
Sub-Saharan Africa					
1 Angola	seriously off track	low	—	—	—
2 Benin	off track	low	39	1998	73
3 Botswana	already achieved	middle	102	1996	100
4 Burkina Faso	seriously off track	low	25	1998	38
5 Burundi	seriously off track	low	43	1998	37
6 Cameroon	seriously off track	low	43	1999	18
7 Cape Verde	already achieved	middle	117	1997	100
8 Central African Rep.	seriously off track	low	19	2000	6
9 Chad	seriously off track	low	19	2000	19
10 Comoros	seriously off track	low	33	1993	11
11 Congo	seriously off track	low	44	2000	19
12 Cote D'Ivoire	seriously off track	low	48	1999	55
13 Congo, Democratic Rep.	seriously off track	low	40	2000	28
14 Equatorial Guinea	seriously off track	low	46	1993	—
15 Eritrea	off track	low	35	1999	61
16 Ethiopia	seriously off track	low	24	1999	28
17 Gabon	on track to achieve	middle	80	1995	100
18 Gambia	on track to achieve	low	70	2000	100
19 Ghana	off track	low	64	1999	66
20 Guinea	off track	low	34	2000	61
21 Guinea–Bissau	seriously off track	low	31	2000	50
22 Kenya	seriously off track	low	58	1995	38
23 Lesotho	off track	low	69	1996	85
24 Liberia	no data	low	—	—	—
25 Madagascar	seriously off track	low	26	1998	9
26 Malawi	on track to achieve	low	50	1995	100
27 Mali	off track	low	23	1998	49
28 Mauritania	off track	low	46	1998	72
29 Mauritius	already achieved	middle	111	1997	100
30 Mozambique	off track	low	36	1998	49
31 Namibia	on track to achieve	middle	90	1997	100
32 Niger	seriously off track	low	20	1998	24
33 Nigeria	off track	low	67	2000	60
34 Rwanda	seriously off track	low	40	2000	49
35 Sao Tome & Principe	off track	low	84	2001	—
36 Senegal	seriously off track	low	41	2000	36
37 Seychelles	no data	middle	—	—	—
38 Sierra Leone	seriously off track	low	32	2000	—
39 Somalia	no data	low	—	—	—
40 South Africa	already achieved	middle	98	1995	100
41 Sudan	seriously off track	low	35	1996	—
42 Swaziland	on track to achieve	middle	81	1997	100

Table A.1 continued

Country	UPC Status	Income Level	Most Recent PCR	(year)	PCR 2015
43 Togo	on track to achieve	low	63	1999	100
44 Uganda	on track to achieve	low	65	2001	98
45 Tanzania	off track	low	59	1997	88
46 Zambia	seriously off track	low	83	1995	43
47 Zimbabwe	already achieved	low	113	1997	100
East Asia and Pacific					
1 Cambodia	on track to achieve	low	70	2001	100
2 China	already achieved	middle	108	1996	100
3 Micronesia	no data	middle	—	—	—
4 Fiji	already achieved	middle	95	1992	100
5 Indonesia	off track	low	91	2000	90
6 Kiribati	no data	middle	—	—	—
7 Korea, Dem. Repub.	no data	low	—	—	—
8 Korea, Republic of	already achieved	middle	96	2000	100
9 Laos	on track to achieve	low	69	2000	100
10 Malaysia	off track	middle	90	1994	85
11 Marshall Islands	no data	middle	—	—	—
12 Mongolia	off track	low	82	1998	—
13 Myanmar	no data	low	—	—	—
14 Papua New Guinea	off track	low	59	1995	83
15 Philippines	on track to achieve	middle	92	1996	100
16 Palau	no data	middle	—	—	—
17 Samoa	already achieved	middle	99	1997	100
18 Solomon Islands	off track	low	66	1994	71
19 Thailand	off track	middle	90	2000	86
20 Tonga	no data	middle	—	—	—
21 Vanuatu	off track	middle	86	1992	52
22 Viet Nam	already achieved	low	101	2001	100
Europe and Central Asia					
1 Albania	off track	middle	89	1995	57
2 Armenia	off track	low	82	1996	—
3 Azerbaijan	already achieved	low	100	1998	100
4 Belarus	off track	middle	93	1996	74
5 Bosnia & Herzegovina	on track to achieve	middle	88	1999	—
6 Bulgaria	on track to achieve	middle	92	1996	98
7 Croatia	already achieved	middle	96	2001	100
8 Czech Republic	already achieved	middle	109	1995	100
9 Estonia	off track	middle	88	1995	55
10 Georgia	off track	low	82	1998	—
11 Hungary	already achieved	middle	102	1995	100
12 Kazakhstan	no data	middle	—	—	—
13 Kyrgyzstan	no data	low	—	—	—
14 Latvia	on track to achieve	middle	86	1996	100

Table A.1 continued

	Country	UPC Status	Income Level	Most Recent PCR	(year)	PCR 2015
15	Lithuania	already achieved	middle	95	1996	100
16	Moldova	on track to achieve	low	79	1999	100
17	Poland	already achieved	middle	96	1995	100
18	Romania	already achieved	middle	98	1996	100
19	Russia	already achieved	middle	96	2001	100
20	Serbia & Montenegro	already achieved	middle	96	2000	100
21	Slovakia	already achieved	middle	97	1996	100
22	Tajikistan	off track	low	77	1996	—
23	Macedonia	no data	middle	91	1996	100
24	Turkmenistan	no data	low	—	—	—
25	Ukraine	on track to achieve	low	94	2002	—
26	Uzbekistan	no data	low	—	—	—

Latin America and the Caribbean

	Country	UPC Status	Income Level	Most Recent PCR	(year)	PCR 2015
1	Antigua & Barbuda	already achieved	middle	98	2000	—
2	Argentina	already achieved	middle	96	2000	100
3	Belize	off track	middle	82	1999	69
4	Bolivia	on track to achieve	middle	72	2000	98
5	Brazil	on track to achieve	middle	72	1999	100
6	Chile	already achieved	middle	99	2000	100
7	Colombia	on track to achieve	middle	85	2000	100
8	Costa Rica	on track to achieve	middle	89	2000	100
9	Cuba	already achieved	middle	—	—	—
10	Dominica	already achieved	middle	103	2000	100
11	Dominican Republic	off track	middle	62	2000	—
12	Ecuador	already achieved	middle	96	1999	100
13	El Salvador	on track to achieve	middle	80	2000	100
14	Grenada	already achieved	middle	106	2001	100
15	Guatemala	off track	middle	52	2000	67
16	Guyana	off track	middle	89	2000	85
17	Haiti	off track	low	40	1997	71
18	Honduras	off track	middle	67	2000	69
19	Jamaica	on track to achieve	middle	94	2000	100
20	Mexico	already achieved	middle	100	2000	100
21	Nicaragua	on track to achieve	low	65	2000	95
22	Panama	on track to achieve	middle	94	2000	100
23	Paraguay	on track to achieve	middle	78	2000	98
24	Peru	already achieved	middle	98	2000	100
25	St. Kitts & Nevis	already achieved	middle	110	2001	100
26	St. Lucia	already achieved	middle	106	2001	100
27	St. Vincent & Grenadines	off track	middle	84	2001	—
28	Suriname	no data	middle	—	—	—
29	Trinidad & Tobago	off track	middle	94	2000	94
30	Uruguay	already achieved	middle	98	2000	100
31	Venezuela	off track	middle	78	1999	55

Table A.1 continued

Country	UPC Status	Income Level	Most Recent PCR	(year)	PCR 2015
Middle East and North Africa					
1 Algeria	on track to achieve	middle	91	1996	100
2 Bahrain	off track	middle	91	1996	59
3 Djibouti	seriously off track	middle	30	1999	26
4 Egypt	already achieved	middle	99	1996	100
5 Iran	off track	middle	92	1996	86
6 Iraq	seriously off track	middle	57	1995	33
7 Jordan	already achieved	middle	104	2000	100
8 Lebanon	off track	middle	70	1996	—
9 Libya	no data	middle	—	—	—
10 Morocco	off track	middle	55	1996	85
11 Oman	on track to achieve	middle	76	1996	100
12 Palestine	no data	middle	—	—	—
13 Saudi Arabia	on track to achieve	middle	69	1996	98
14 Syria	off track	middle	90	1996	65
15 Tunisia	on track to achieve	middle	91	1996	100
16 Turkey	on track to achieve	middle	—	—	—
17 Yemen	off track	low	58	2000	—
South Asia					
1 Afghanistan	seriously off track	low	8	1999	0
2 Bangladesh	on track to achieve	low	70	2000	100
3 Bhutan	off track	low	59	2001	—
4 India	off track	low	76	1999	90
5 Maldives	already achieved	middle	112	1993	100
6 Nepal	off track	low	65	2000	85
7 Pakistan	off track	low	59	2000	79
8 Sri Lanka	already achieved	middle	111	2001	100

Source: Bruns et al (2003).

Note:
'already achieved' denotes countries that have already achieved UPC of 95 percent or higher;
'on track to achieve' denotes countries that will achieve UPC of 100 percent by 2015;
'off track' denotes countries whose projected UPC for 2015 is between 50 percent and 100 percent;
'seriously off track' denotes countries whose projected UPC for 2015 is less than 50 percent;
'no data' denotes countries that have not yet achieved UPC and for which no data are available to make projections to 2015.

The 151 countries in this table differ in the following ways from the 155 in the World Bank report by Bruns et al. (2003). First, this list includes Suriname, which appears to have been mistakenly omitted in the World Bank study. Second, this list excludes four high income countries that were included in the World Bank report: Kuwait, Qatar, Slovenia, and the United Arab Emirates. Third, this list excludes East Timor, due to its small size and lack of data. Fourth, low income and middle income in this list is defined according to the World Bank's definition, namely countries with annual income per capita below or above $755, respectively, while the World Bank study defines it in terms of whether or not loans are received from the World Bank's source of funds for low income countries, the International Development Association (IDA).

References

Brossard, Mathieu, and Luc-Charles Gacougnolle. 2001. "Financing Primary Education for All: Yesterday, Today and Tomorrow." Paris: UNESCO.

Bruns, Barbara, Alain Mingat, and Ramahatra Rakotomalala. 2003. *Achieving Universal Primary Education by 2015: A Chance for Every Child.* Washington, DC: The World Bank.

Delamonica, Enrique, Santosh Mehrotra, and Jan Vandemoortele. 2001. "Is EFA Affordable? Estimating the Global Minimum Cost of Education for All." Innocenti Working Paper 87. Florence, Italy: UNICEF.

Devarajan, Shantayana, Margaret Miller, and Eric Swanson. 2002. "Goals for Development: History, Prospects and Costs." Policy Research Working Paper No. 2819. Washington, DC: The World Bank.

Duflo, Esther. 2001. "Schooling and Labor Market Consequences of School Construction in Indonesia: Evidence from an Unusual Policy Experiment." *American Economic Review* 91 (4): 795–813.

Filmer, Deon. 2001. "'Costing' the Goal of Universal Primary Enrollment by 2015: Back of the (Big) Envelope Calculations." Washington, DC: The World Bank.

Glewwe, Paul. 2002. "Schools and Skills in Developing Countries: Education Policies and Socioeconomic Outcomes." *Journal of Economic Literature* 40 (2): 436–482.

Glewwe, Paul, and Michael Kremer. 2006. "Schools, Teachers and Education Outcomes in Developing Countries." In *Handbook of the Economics of Education*, ed. E. Hanushek and F. Welch. Amsterdam: North Holland.

Glewwe, Paul, and Pedro Olinto. 2004. "Evaluating the Impact of Conditional Cash Transfers on Schooling: An Experimental Analysis of Honduras' PRAF Program." University of Minnesota and International Food Policy Research Institute. Mimeo.

Hanushek, Eric. 1995. "Interpreting Recent Research on Schooling in Developing Countries." *World Bank Research Observer* 10 (2): 227–246.

International Monetary Fund (IMF). 2003. "Tanzania: Joint Staff Assessment of the Poverty Reduction Strategy Paper." IMF Country Report No. 03/306. Washington, DC: The International Monetary Fund.

Maluccio, John, and Rafael Flores. 2004. "Impact Evaluation of a Conditional Cash Transfer Program: The Nicaraguan *Red de Protección Social*." Food Consumption and Nutrition Division discussion paper. Washington DC: International Food Policy Research Institute.

Miguel, Edward, and Michael Kremer. 2004. "Worms: Identifying Impacts on Education and Health in the Presence of Treatment Externalities." *Econometrica* 72 (1): 159–217.

Morley, Samuel, and David Coady. 2003. *From Social Assistance to Social Development: Targeted Education Subsidies in Developing Countries*. Washington, DC: Center for Global Development and International Food Policy Research Institute.

PROBE Team. 1999. *Public Report on Basic Education in India*. New Delhi: Oxford University Press.

Stasavage, David. 2005. "On the Role of Democracy in Uganda's Move to Universal Primary Education." *Journal of Modern African Studies* 43 (1): 53–73.

World Bank. 2002. *World Development Indicators 2002*. Washington, DC: The World Bank.

———. 2004a. "Books, Buildings and Learning Outcomes: An Impact Evaluation of World Bank Support to Basic Education in Ghana." Washington, DC: The World Bank.

———. 2004b. "Kenya: Strengthening the Foundation of Education and Training in Kenya." Washington, DC: The World Bank.

CHAPTER 8

The Cost of Providing Universal Secondary Education in Developing Countries

MELISSA BINDER

Low levels of education around the world contribute to continued poverty for millions of people. Nearly 400 million children in developing countries between the ages of 12 and 17 do not attend secondary school. According to an extensive literature, these children will be less economically productive and will have worse health outcomes and higher fertility rates than those with more education.[1] There is some evidence that their low levels of education will inhibit economic growth at the national level for the countries in which they live.[2] In short, low levels of education have high costs, in terms of foregone opportunity and well being.

Since the 1960s, access to primary education worldwide has increased dramatically. As of the year 2000, 96 of 112 reporting low-income countries had primary gross enrollment rates that exceeded 75 percent. Access to secondary schooling, unfortunately, has not followed suit. Of these same countries, only 39 reported similarly high gross enrollment rates for secondary education. Moreover, there is evidence that the expansion of secondary schooling has stagnated in recent years (Bloom, this volume; Lewin and Caillods, 2001; Binder and Woodruff, 2002; IDB, 1998), perhaps in

---

[1] For more on the economic returns to schooling, see Psacharopoulos (1994). For a review of health and fertility effects of education, see Hannum and Buchmann (this volume).

[2] Hannum and Buchmann (this volume) review this literature.

part because of a decline in development aid for secondary schooling during the 1980s.[3]

Given the central role of secondary education in alleviating poverty and promoting economic growth, it is vital that we understand the barriers to its expansion so that they can be overcome. This chapter identifies the likely financial costs of supplying secondary school places to all children in developing countries. The supply-side analysis below includes the costs of teacher salaries, classrooms, materials, and administration.

The study does not consider costs borne by families in sending their children to school. The higher direct costs of secondary schooling in comparison to primary schooling and, even more important, the higher opportunity costs of sending older children to school instead of to work pose significant barriers to enrollment. However, systematic cross-country data on these costs are not available. Estimating the direct costs borne by families requires data on school fees and on the costs of transportation, books, and other school supplies where these are not provided by schools. For some countries, these data are available from consumer-expenditure surveys; however, locating these data was beyond the scope of this project, and the number of countries for which these data are complete would likely be small. Estimating opportunity costs requires wage data disaggregated by age and gender. These are probably available for the dozens of developing countries that collect labor-force information in household surveys, but again, the enormity of the task precludes making use of them in this analysis. In both cases, the poorest countries are unlikely to collect these data. Given these limitations, calculating demand-side costs might best be served by focusing on comprehensive case studies for a small subset of countries.

Finally, this analysis does not consider the additional expense to governments of achieving universal primary education. The estimates provided here therefore cover only part—albeit an important part—of the expense that the achievement of universal secondary education will require.

THE UNIT COST METHOD

I adopt the unit cost method typical of research that assesses the supply costs of educational expansion at the primary level (Delamonica et al.,

---

[3] Spending for secondary education has recovered since the early 1990s (Bloom, this volume; Lewin and Caillods, 2001: 4).

2001; Devarajan et al., 2002). Under this method, the researcher determines the per student cost of the current educational system and then multiplies this unit cost by the number of children not enrolled in school. Although a straightforward calculation, compiling unit costs is complicated considerably by lack of data for many countries. The World Development Indicators (WDI) 2003 data set shows current unit costs for secondary schooling as a percent of per capita income in 1999 for only 60 of the 144 developing countries in this study's sample population. The World Education Indicators (WEI) program of the Organization for Economic Co-operation and Development (OECD) and the UNESCO Institute for Statistics (UNESCO-UIS) provides 1999 unit costs for 15 of the developing countries it tracks, and reports a mean country unit cost of $1127 in purchasing power parity (PPP) US dollars (OECD/UNESCO-UIS, 2003: Table 9). Although the WEI countries with unit cost data are home to 53 percent of the secondary school age population (those 12–17 years old) in developing countries, they represent only 10 percent of developing countries and include only three low-income countries (out of a total of 66) and only one African country. Moreover, providing costs in PPP terms makes it difficult to assess the contribution of external donors. As shown below, the costs appear to be much lower in standard currency-converted dollars, as well as for poorer countries.

In this study, I estimate unit costs according to the following procedure. First, I determine the total public expenditure for secondary schooling. Second, I divide by the number of students, to determine the unit cost. Third, I multiply the unit cost by the number of children not enrolled in school to determine the additional cost of schooling these students. Industrialized countries average 90 percent enrollment of secondary school age children; this study uses the 90 percent enrollment rate as the goal for achieving "universal" secondary education.[4]

The primary data source for this analysis is the WDI; most of the calculations below derive from data for 1998–2000. For some variables, I make use of UNESCO-UIS statistics. WDI provides figures for total public expenditure—which combines current and capital expenditures—on education as a percent of GDP, and UNESCO provides figures for spending on secondary schooling as a percent of total public expenditure on educa-

---

[4] The United States, with an 88 percent enrollment rate, falls short of universal secondary education under this definition.

tion. The product of these figures is public expenditure on secondary education as a percent of GDP, which I multiply by a country's GDP in constant 1995 U.S. dollars (using current exchange rates) to get current total spending in U.S. dollars. I then use the GDP deflator to convert these figures to 2002 dollars. This analysis uses the exchange rate conversion rather than the PPP conversion, as stated earlier, because of a greater interest in knowing the dollar amount of providing school spaces. If the dollar goes further in many countries, then this is so much the better.

WDI reports the gross enrollment rate (GER) in secondary education for 118 developing countries, and the net enrollment rate (NER) in secondary education for 92 of these countries. I use the regional mean of the NER-to-GER ratio to estimate NERs for countries that only report the GER. The GER is the number of students enrolled in secondary education programs (as defined by UNESCO) as a proportion of the population who are of the appropriate age. For most countries, secondary education covers children between the ages of 12 and 17, and this is the population used in the calculations below. The NER is the number of enrolled secondary education students of the appropriate age group as a proportion of the total population of age-appropriate children. Again, this study uses the 12–17 age group. The GER includes students who are outside the expected school-age range due to grade repetition or entrance into the school system older or younger than the standard entry age. It typically exceeds the NER. Although the GER does not indicate how many children of the appropriate age are enrolled, it does provide a measure of the capacity of the school system to absorb these children and is therefore an important indicator.

Multiplying the GER by the population of 12–17 year olds yields the number of students enrolled, and this is the number used to calculate per student costs. Multiplying the NER by the 12–17 year-old population and subtracting this number from the target of 90 percent of the 12–17 year-old population yields the number of school-age children who would need to enroll to achieve a 90 percent enrollment rate. I calculate the total additional cost of providing schooling by multiplying unit costs by the number of children who need to enroll to reach the target enrollment rate. Table 4 of the Appendix delineate these steps.

This method provides a useful starting point for estimating the resources required to achieve universal secondary education. Some caveats apply, however. First, in many countries with low secondary school enrollment, expanding enrollment will involve the construction of new classrooms and schools. The unit cost calculations in this study combine capital and recurring costs, and thus may overestimate the costs in a country experiencing rapid increases in schooling access, because future capital costs will be lower. Likewise, it may underestimate the costs in a country that is not increasing access significantly. Lewin and Caillods (2001) point out that many African countries have barely kept up with demand for secondary schooling—the transition rate from primary to secondary schooling was stable, at least in the 1990s. This does indicate that some expansion occurred as the number of primary graduates increased; however, the expansion required to achieve universal access will likely incur higher capital costs than those indicated in unit costs based on current capital outlays.

One way to estimate these costs would be to look at the experiences of countries that have increased secondary enrollments over a period of time. Unfortunately, time-series data that report capital and recurrent education spending are not consistently available. Nor is it possible to make use of the literature on educational cost functions (Jimenez, 1986; Tsang, 1994) because the information gleaned from the few developing countries for which estimates are available "may be almost totally irrelevant in a different education system" (Verry, 1987: 400). A final possibility is to use an average or preferred classroom size and country or best-practice construction costs to assess the need for and cost of more classrooms (Colclough with Lewin, 1993; Bruns et al., 2003). It was not possible, however, to locate data on construction costs for secondary school classrooms for use in this analysis.

Another set of concerns is presented by the distinction between lower- and upper-secondary schooling. Although WDI provides enrollment data for some countries by secondary schooling level, there are no corresponding expenditure data. The unit costs calculated in this study therefore mix the two levels, likely overestimating the costs of lower-secondary and underestimating the costs of upper-secondary education. The WEI unit cost data report lower- and upper-secondary costs separately for ten countries. On average, country unit costs for upper-secondary exceed lower-secondary costs by 39 percent. This average is skewed by the more than 3.5 times difference between lower- and upper-secondary costs in China. The average differential without China is 10 percent. Although not necessarily representative, the data suggest that it is feasible to assume that countries can offer both levels of secondary schooling at close to the same unit cost. Countries that currently have large discrepancies in costs between these levels could presumably expand secondary education at a lower average cost. Using the average over both levels for these countries would overestimate expansion costs. Nevertheless, because implementing new institutional structures to reduce upper-secondary costs will likely be costly, computing a unit cost for both levels combined results in a figure that is probably not terribly far from the mark.

Finally, the contribution of private-sector education to total educational coverage is likely important in some countries. Ideally, one would calculate unit costs by dividing public spending on secondary schooling by the number of public-school students. Unfortunately, even if the number of students in public institutions is known, some countries provide funding to private schools (Lewin and Caillods, 2001). Excluding private students in these cases will result in an overestimate of unit costs, while including them in countries with no subsidies will lead to an underestimate. Data on private enrollment[5] are available for only 70 countries in the sample. Calculating unit costs over public-school students only in this sample gives a unit cost estimate 7.5 percent higher than the cost calculated over all students. Because limiting the spread of costs to students in public institutions overestimates costs (i.e., some public spending supports private-school students), the actual difference may be smaller. Nevertheless, an increase of 7.5 percent in the estimates of this study would roughly account for the higher costs masked by using total enrollments in the unit cost calculations.

THE STUDY POPULATION

This study provides estimates for the 144 developing countries on the July 2003 World Bank list of countries for which UNESCO also provides population figures for children ages 12–17. (Table 1 in the Appendix arranges these countries by their World Bank classification for region and income group). As Table 1 below shows, estimates for 69 countries (and 67 percent of the 12–17 year-old developing country population) are based on complete country data; estimates for 61 countries (30 percent of the target population) use at least some imputed data in the cost calculations. The remaining 14 countries (3 percent of the target population) had inadequate data for cost calculations and simply receive the regional mean unit cost.

---

[5] Available through the World Bank EDSTATS system: http://www1.worldbank. org/education/edstats.

Table 1: Data Available for Calculating Unit Costs

| | Children 12–17 Years of Age in 2000 | | | | |
| | All | | | Not enrolled | |
	Number of Countries	Number in millions	Percent	Number in millions	Percent
Complete data in at least one year between 1998 and 2000	60	405.5	64.5	198.2	60.9
Complete data in different years between 1998 and 2000	9	16.1	2.6	8.9	2.7
Imputed based on partial data	61	187.9	29.9	107.5	33.1
Insufficient data to impute	14	19.0	3.0	est. 10.6	3.3
TOTAL	144	628.5		325.2	

Source: Author's calculations based on World Development Indicators and UNESCO-UIS and Population Division of the Department of Economic and Social Affairs of the United Nations Secretariat, *World Population Prospects: The 2002 Revision,* and *World Urbanization Prospects: The 2001 Revision.* Available online: http://esa.un.org/unpp.

Note: Population figures for this age group are provided directly by the UN Population Division (see above). The estimate of those not enrolled was derived as follows. First, I estimated the number of children 12–17 who were enrolled in school by multiplying the total population in this age group by the most recently available net enrollment rate between 1998 and 2000 for the 96 countries reporting this statistic directly. I imputed the net enrollment rate for an additional 35 countries that reported the gross enrollment rate, using the predicted value from a regression of the ratio of the net to gross enrollment rate on per capita income, 12–17 year-old population, spending on secondary schooling as a percent of GDP, and five regional dummy variables. For 13 countries with no enrollment data, I used the average regional enrollment rate. Second, I subtracted the estimated number enrolled from the total 12–17 population.

The most common missing variable was percent of total education spending spent at the secondary level. I calculate unit costs for these countries by imputing missing values from a neighboring country with similar income, population, and enrollment rates. Because so few countries in Europe reported complete education data, I rely on education finance data prior to 1998 for some imputations. I am reluctant to do this more generally, because the UNESCO classification of secondary school programs changed between 1997 and 1998. Costs have not been imputed for the 14 countries with no enrollment rates or GDP data, although they have been included in global cost estimates by using regional averages.

Table 2: Summary Statistics by Region, TIMSS Participation, and Income Group

	SSA*	SA*	EA&P*	ME&NA*	LA&C*	E&CA*	ALL		TIMSS	
							Not weighted	Weighted	Not weighted	Weighted
Number of countries										
Total	46	8	19	16	28	27	144		20	
Low income	39	6	10	1	2	8	66		2	
Lower-middle income	4	2	8	10	15	11	50		12	
Upper-middle income	3	—	1	5	11	8	28		6	
Population shares										
Total (% of developing country population 12–17 years of age)	14.8	27.8	32.1	7.1	10.2	8.0	100		15.6	
Low income (% of region or TIMSS)	92.6	98.8	24.3	6.1	3.2	24.1			27.3	
Lower-middle income (% of region or TIMSS)	6.8	1.2	74.4	84.1	27.9	62.2			67.3	
Upper-middle income (% of region or TIMSS)	0.6	—	1.3	9.9	69.0	13.7			5.4	

* SSA=Sub-Saharan Africa, SA=South Asia, EA&P=East Asia and Pacific, ME&NA=Middle East and North Africa, LA&C=Latin America and the Caribbean, E&CA=Europe and Central Asia.

Table 2 (continued)

	SSA*	SA*	EA&P*	ME&NA*	LA&C*	E&CA*	ALL Not weighted	ALL Weighted	TIMSS Not weighted	TIMSS Weighted
Net enrollment rates										
Total	23.1 (15.9)	42.8 (15.3)	51.4 (25.8)	59.2 (17.9)	60.0 (16.0)	79.5 (9.4)	49.5 (26.8)	48.2 (19.0)	70.0 (15.3)	59.8 (13.8)
Low income	17.4 (8.6)	39.5 (11.5)	37.2 (17.2)	37.0 (.)	35.5 (.)	75.9 (9.8)	30.1 (22.5)	37.1 (18.0)	57.9 (14.6)	47.9 (4.0)
Lower-middle income	47.8 (8.7)	49.4 (25.4)	64.9 (27.9)	59.1 (19.6)	54.9 (15.9)	78.4 (10.1)	61.6 (19.8)	57.7 (11.0)	66.9 (16.1)	63.3 (13.5)
Upper-middle income	59.8 (12.6)	—	70.2 (.)	64.9 (12.3)	68.3 (11.8)	84.6 (6.6)	71.8 (13.2)	68.8 (10.9)	80.4 (8.1)	76.8 (8.7)
Unit costs in constant 2002 dollars										
Total	202 (222)	85 (37)	336 (455)	917 (1219)	561 (490)	521 (510)	421 (574)	240 (358)	661 (509)	435 (330)
Low income	128 (87)	86 (42)	136 (139)	249 (.)	122 (142)	125 (72)	128 (90.1)	125 (65)	148 (158)	255 (43)
Lower-middle income	417 (311)	82 (.)	382 (470)	369 (291)	325 (249)	307 (168)	342 (284)	227 (194)	426 (244)	429 (252)
Upper-middle income	820 (82)	—	1417 (.)	2180 (1634)	919 (522)	1157 (394)	1183 (809)	912 (815)	1302 (343)	1415 (255)

Source: WDI; UNESCO-UIS. Unit costs based on author's calculations.

Note: Standard deviations in parentheses.

* SSA=Sub-Saharan Africa, SA=South Asia, EA&P=East Asia and Pacific, ME&NA=Middle East and North Africa, LA&C=Latin America and the Caribbean, E&CA=Europe and Central Asia.

Table 2 provides summary statistics by region and income for the sample as a whole, and for the countries that participated in the 1999 Trends in International Mathematics and Science Study (TIMSS), a project organized by the International Association for the Evaluation of Educational Achievement and sponsored by the United States, the World Bank, and the United Nations, among others. Although only 20 of the study-population countries participated in TIMSS, I use the reported test scores as a direct measure of the effectiveness of an educational system. Table 2 in the Appendix provides a list of TIMSS countries.

Table 2 shows that, within regions, net enrollment rates rise with income. The rates are similar for lower- and upper-middle-income groups across regions, although the region of Europe and Central Asia enjoys particularly high rates and Sub-Saharan Africa has particularly low rates. The lower-middle-income group exhibits considerable variation among regions, with Sub-Saharan Africa and South Asia at the low end. Large standard deviations for most cells indicate that there is a wide range of outcomes, even for countries in the same region and income group.

Unit costs are also quite similar across regions for low-income countries. Note that at the secondary level, unit costs in Sub-Saharan Africa are typical of other regions, in contrast to the primary level, where Africa's costs appear to be considerably higher (Colclough with Lewin, 1993). Costs in the middle-income countries vary more across regions, especially for the upper-middle-income group. The Middle East and North Africa region has particularly high costs—more than double the mean costs estimated for Sub-Saharan Africa and Latin America. Again, large standard deviations suggest considerable variation within income groups and regions.

The mean population-weighted NER is 37 percent for children living in low-income countries, 58 percent in lower-middle-income countries, and 69 percent in upper-middle-income countries. The mean weighted unit cost is $125 for low-income countries, compared with $227 and $912, for lower- and upper-middle-income countries, respectively. These figures suggest that the educational expansion needed to achieve universal access will occur primarily in poorer countries where costs are lower. The figures also indicate that there is an enormous increase in costs moving from lower-middle-income to upper-middle-income countries.

Of the twenty TIMSS countries listed in Appendix Table 2, eleven are in Europe, and all but two are middle income. As noted above, Europe has the highest enrollment rates and fairly typical, although not lower than average, unit costs. The over-representation of European countries in the TIMSS sample may bias the analysis of test-score performance in this study. Table 2 shows that enrollment rates and unit costs are higher for TIMMS countries than for the sample as a whole. Analysis using t-tests indicates that the differences are statistically significant, although not for unit costs compared within income groups, nor for the NER compared within the middle-income group. Nevertheless, the TIMSS sample as a whole clearly over-represents middle-income countries, and includes low-income and upper-middle-income countries with higher-than-average enrollments. Inferences from the TIMSS data will therefore be somewhat limited.

EDUCATION FINANCE, SERVICE DELIVERY, AND SECONDARY SCHOOLING OUTCOMES

Another important question remains: What are the appropriate unit costs to use in estimating the financial resources needed to achieve universal secondary education in developing countries? In the expansion of an educational system, it is relevant to ask whether we want to provide "more of the same" quality or type of education, or whether the system needs reform. This section explores whether countries with better schooling outcomes vary systematically from poorly performing countries in education finance and service delivery.[6]

Ideally, a study would use indicators of educational outcomes to identify countries that provide a high quality education to a high proportion of the age-appropriate population. As might be expected, measures of the quantity side of a system's performance (i.e., enrollment rates) are much more readily available than are measures of the quality side (i.e., test scores or literacy rates). In some sense, however, high enrollment rates do reflect quality—they indicate that a country has been relatively successful not only at creating more schooling places, but also at generating demand for those places. This analysis uses the net enrollment rate to measure quality (high gross enrollment rates alone, which often reflect high repetition rates, are not necessarily a desirable outcome). Performance quality is measured more directly using TIMSS scores. High-performing countries are identified by their outcomes relative to their

[6] This approach is similar to that used by Bruns et al. (2003) for primary education.

Figure 1: NER, Predicted NER, and Log Per Capita GDP

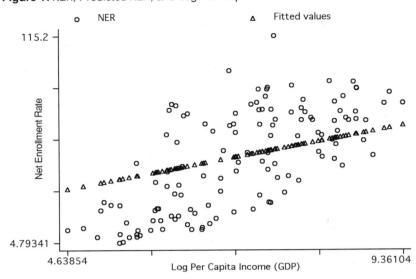

Source: Author's calculations based on enrollment rates and per capita income reported in the World Development Indicators.

incomes because, as demonstrated below, income is very closely associated with both net enrollment rates and TIMSS scores.

Figure 1 illustrates the high positive correlation between per capita income (here illustrated as log per capita income) and net enrollment rates in developing countries. The calculations[7] show that income alone accounts for 87 percent of the total variation of net enrollment rates. Adding region interactions raises this figure to 93 percent. Table 2 in the Appendix lists the countries that perform better than would be predicted by their per capita income and by their income level for their region.[8]

Figure 2 shows that TIMSS scores are also highly correlated with income. The regression line shown excludes the outlier (South Africa, which has a test score below 245); log income explains 97 percent of the

---

[7] Calculations used ordinary least squares (OLS) estimates of the effect of log per capita income on enrollment rates.

[8] Predictions of performance by income level are made according to a regression of net enrollment rates on log per capita income. Predictions by income and region are made according to a regression of net enrollment rates on log per capita income interacted with region.

Figure 2: TIMSS Math Score, Predicted Score, and Log Per Capita GDP

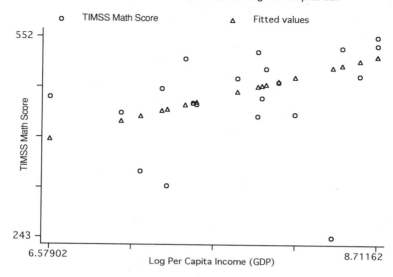

Source: Author's calculations based on test scores from the 1999 Trends in International Mathematics and Science Study (TIMSS) and per capita income reported in the World Development Indicators.

Note: Predictions based on a regression model that uses region and income interactions.

sample variation in test scores, even when South Africa is included. As Table 3 in the Appendix shows, all but one of the countries considered high performing under the TIMSS measure are in Europe. Moreover, six of the low-performing TIMSS countries are considered high performing under the NER measure. This provides further evidence that the TIMSS sample over-represents the better-performing countries.

Table 3 presents enrollment rates, education finance, and service delivery means for high- and low-performing countries under three performance criteria: 1) countries that have higher NER than predicted by income, 2) countries that have higher NER than predicted by income within regions, and 3) countries that have higher TIMSS scores than predicted by income. Statistically significant differences[9] appear in bold. Under both NER criteria, high-performing countries have significantly higher gross and net enrollment rates. The differences are more pro-

---

[9] Significance is determined by t-tests.

Table 3: Education Finance and Service Variables for Countries with Better and Worse Net Enrollment Rates Relative to Income and Region, and Better and Worse 1999 TIMSS Scores Relative to Income

	Net enrollment rates						TIMSS		
	Performance relative to income			Performance relative to income X region			Performance relative to income		
	N	Better	Worse	N	Better	Worse	N	Better	Worse
GER	92	**83.9**	**39.1**	92	**74.2**	**46.5**	20	**85.1**	**74.5**
NER	93	**73.2**	**30.1**	92	**63.3**	**37.8**	20	**77.1**	**62.9**
Public expenditure on education (% GDP)	80	**4.8**	**4.0**	79	**4.8**	**4.0**	20	5.1	4.6
Spending on secondary schooling (% of total education spending)	54	36.4	33.0	54	35.6	35.6	15	**45.4**	**32.4**
Unit cost in 2002 U.S. dollars	91	**$632**	**$342**	91	$538	$414	20	$789	$534
Unit cost as % of per capita income	91	**17.8**	**29.6**	91	**19.1**	**29.2**	20	23.3	18.8
Per capita GDP	93	**$3315**	**$1318**	92	**$2873**	**$1705**	20	$3021	$2888
Transition rate from primary to secondary levels	65	**89.9**	**75.1**	65	**88.4**	**75.2**	10	**94.8**	**84.6**
% of teachers who are trained	25	74.0	68.8	25	70.5	80.5	3	NA	NA
Pupils per teacher	67	**16.8**	**24.1**	66	20.8	19.5	12	**12.9**	**23.4**
Repetition rate	61	**5.3**	**11.0**	61	**6.4**	**10.3**	11	**1.3**	**12.0**

Source: WDI and UNESCO-UIS. Unit costs are author's calculations from these sources.

Note: Significant differences in bold font. Significance using one-tailed tests is at the 5 percent level except for public expenditure on education (GDP share) for net enrollment rate performance and transition rate for TIMSS performance, which are significant at the 10 percent level.

nounced for high-performing countries relative to income alone, reflecting the exceptional performance of European countries in all income groups; when countries are compared within regions, the differences are somewhat attenuated, but still large. High-performing countries devote larger GDP shares to education under the NER criteria, but are not different from low-performing countries in the share of the education budget directed toward secondary schooling.

Unit costs as a percent of per capita income are significantly lower under the NER measures, although absolute unit costs are significantly higher for high performers relative to income alone. Better-performing countries under the NER criteria also have higher per capita income, even though they are judged relative to income. This explains why better performers can have higher unit costs and lower per capita unit costs at the same time. Indeed, this is clearly indicated in Figure 1, where a greater number of higher income countries appear above the regression line. Finally, among the service delivery measures, the repetition rate is 40–50 percent lower for countries with better-than-predicted NERs, and the primary-to-secondary transition rate is significantly higher, compared with countries that had worse-than-predicted enrollments. The number of pupils per teacher is lower for high-performing countries under the income-only criterion.

Because the countries in the TIMSS comparison appear to be a select lot, and a small representation at that, it is interesting that several significant differences emerge under the TIMSS measures. As was true under the NER measures, high-performing TIMSS countries have higher gross and net enrollment rates, higher transition rates between the primary and secondary levels, and considerably lower repetition rates. Similar to outcomes under the NER criterion relative to income only (criterion 1), high-performing TIMSS countries have significantly lower pupil-to-teacher ratios. Unit costs, however, are not significantly different among the TIMSS countries, nor is the GDP share dedicated to education. Unlike better-performing countries under the NER criteria, better-performing TIMSS countries do devote higher shares of their education expenditure to secondary schooling. Finally, higher-income countries do not appear to have an advantage over lower-income countries under the TIMSS criterion, even when middle-income but very low performing South Africa is omitted from the comparison.

A consistent finding under all three performance criteria is that educational systems with successful secondary schooling outcomes have low repetition rates and high transition rates from the primary level. In some sense, these are, in and of themselves, measures of success. High-quality education implies that there will be little need for repetition and high demand for secondary places among primary school graduates. This begs the question of how countries can provide high-quality education; however, the answer requires more complete data than are currently available.

It also appears that better-performing countries have a stronger financial commitment to education, as represented by the share of GDP spent on education, but it is difficult to draw conclusions about the relationship between performance and the other two education finance indicators: spending on secondary schooling as a share of total education spending, and unit costs.

Table 4 investigates whether the association between performance and finance and service delivery variables varies by income. There do appear to be differences among income groups. In particular, within the low-income group, unit costs as a percent of per capita income are significantly lower, transition rates are significantly higher, and repetition rates are significantly lower for high-performing countries. A distinct pattern also emerges for secondary education spending as a share of total education expenditure: high performers among the low-income countries spend a larger share than low performers, while high performers among middle-income countries spend a smaller share than low performers. This pattern likely reflects the growing importance of post-secondary education expenditures as secondary completion rates rise. For low-income countries, the low share of total education expenditure spent on secondary schooling is likely an artifact of the much greater effort involved in achieving universal primary education.

Table 5 repeats the analyses of Tables 3 and 4, using statistical techniques that allow us to consider the joint effects of education finance variables on performance. I regress the residuals from regressions of the NER on income, and on income and region interactions on: 1) education spending in GDP, 2) secondary spending in educational expenditure, 3) the log of unit cost, and 4) the log of unit cost as a percent of per capita income. Because few countries report all education finance variables, the sample is restricted to 52 countries; to include the service delivery variables would restrict the sample even more, so no more elaborate specification is made. For the countries included in the regression analysis, share of GDP in education spending is significantly associated with better outcomes. Performance relative to income improves with higher unit costs, but worsens with higher costs as a percent of per capita income. Performance relative to income and region does not depend on the level of unit costs, but does again worsen for countries with high unit costs as a percent of per capita income. Finally, the last three columns of Table 5 show results of an analysis similar to that in Table 4, where effects are allowed to

Table 4: Education Finance and Service Variables for Countries with Better and Worse than Predicted Net Enrollment Rates Relative to Income and Region, by Income

	Low income			Lower-middle income			Upper-middle income		
	N	Better than predicted	Worse than predicted	N	Better than predicted	Worse than predicted	N	Better than average	Worse than average
GER	38	**48.9**	**29.6**	30	**79.6**	**58.6**	24	**88.0**	79.0
NER	38	**42.8**	**24.6**	30	**66.1**	**47.1**	24	**76.2**	**63.5**
Public expenditure on education (% GDP)	32	4.1	3.5	24	4.9	4.0	23	5.2	5.3
Spending on secondary schooling (% of total education spending)	17	**41.8**	**27.9**	19	**31.1**	**48.1**	18	**34.1**	**40.2**
Unit cost in 2002 U.S. dollars	38	$95	$130	29	$364	$378	24	$1102	$1280
Unit cost as % of per capita income	38	**23.4**	**33.6**	29	16.1	23.2	24	19.3	23.5
Transition rate from primary to secondary levels	26	**90.0**	**62.7**	21	87.5	85.4	18	88.1	91.8
Trained teachers	9	68.1	74.5	8	70.7	86.5	0	NA	NA
Pupils per teacher	22	26.4	24.7	22	**20.9**	**17.2**	22	16.3	14.8
Repetition rate	22	**7.1**	**13.9**	21	6.5	6.7	18	5.8	6.8
Per capita GDP	38	$386	$23	92	**$2150**	**$1678**	24	$5730	$5158

Source: WDI and UNESCO-UIS. Unit costs are author's calculations from these sources.

Note: Significant differences in bold font. Significance using one-tailed tests is at the 5 percent level for all variables except spending on secondary schooling as a share of total education spending for low income and upper-middle-income countries, pupils per teacher for lower-middle-income countries, and GER for upper-middle-income countries, which are all significant at the 10 percent level.

vary by income group. Under this specification, which uses the income and region interactions residuals as the dependent variable, unit costs as a share of per capita income for lower-middle-income countries are the only unit cost measures significantly associated with NER performance.

These analyses do not provide evidence for a strong link between unit costs and performance, making it difficult to choose the "right" unit cost. One option is to use the lowest cost country of those in the high-perform-

Table 5: Ordinary Least Squares Estimates of the Relationship between Education Finance Variables and Enrollment Rate Performance (measured as the residual from a regression of the NER on income and region) and Differences by Income Group

	Basic specification		Differences specification		
	Dependent variable		Dependent variation is residual from income and region interactions		
	Residual from regression on income	Residual from regression on income and region interactions	Main effect	Differences	
			Low income	Lower-middle income	Upper-middle income
GDP share	2.5**	2.2**	2.5**	.8	1.4
	(1.2)	(.9)	(.9)	(2.2)	(4.0)
Secondary share	.5**	-.02	.5**	-.7*	-.5
	(.2)	(.2)	(.2)	(.4)	(.6)
Log unit cost	7.5**	2.1	-4.8	10.9	13.5
	(2.2)	(1.6)	(4.5)	(8.5)	(8.4)
Log of unit cost divided by per capita GDP	-16.9**	-8.5**	-1.3	-20.1**	-17.3
	(3.9)	(2.8)	(4.6)	(9.9)	(18.2)
R²	.43	.27	.39		
N	52	52	52		

Source: Author's calculations based on data from WDI and UNESCO-UIS.

Note: Models include a constant. Standard errors are in parentheses.
**Denotes estimate is significant at the 5 percent level.
*Denotes significance at the 10 percent level.

ing group. This would presumably be the most efficient spending model. Given, however, that it may be difficult (and initially costly) to replicate the most efficient system even if such a system had identifiable elements, and that perhaps some of the very low estimated unit costs derive from measurement error, this analysis instead uses the median-cost country among the high performers. The median-cost country provides a spending level that yields good results, does not require that countries be exemplary in efficiency, and avoids the possibility that the lowest-cost estimate is a mistake. I construct two of these best-practice, reasonable spending-level unit costs: one by income group and one by region and income group.

Notwithstanding this pragmatic decision, several countries apparently have generated excellent secondary schooling outcomes at very low costs.

This suggests that it is possible to achieve universal secondary schooling with less money than even the most optimistic estimates presented here. In-depth case studies are necessary to assess how these low costs are achieved, and whether or not they can be replicated elsewhere.

Despite the uncertain statistical relationship between unit costs and enrollment outcomes, the foregoing analysis suggests a significant link between enrollment and the share of GDP devoted to public spending on education. This study therefore establishes goals for apportioning costs between countries and external donors using best-practice GDP share as the baseline spending for a country. The analyses also indicate that low repetition rates are a feature of successful secondary-education systems. Although it is true that low repetition rates are likely the result of high-quality schooling rather than the cause, this study adopts a low-repetition scenario as a desirable feature when estimating costs. In addition to reflecting improved quality, low repetition rates also generate large cost savings, as described below.

COST CALCULATIONS

The estimates, detailed below, of the amount of spending needed to pro-vide enough school spaces to achieve universal secondary education in developing countries are based on a series of assumptions about unit costs, repetition rates, and time horizons. I consider three unit cost scenarios. The first scenario assumes that present estimated unit costs give a realistic idea of what educational expansion will cost in the future. In this scenario, countries are expected simply to provide more of the same. In the second and third scenarios, I assume that the creation of additional spaces alone does not guarantee a corresponding rise in demand, and that countries also need to boost demand by investing in educational reform. As shown below, the median high-performing country achieves better outcomes at a lower per unit cost than the average country. This suggests that substantial cost savings may be possible if research can determine how some countries are able to do better with less.

Although it is beyond the scope of this study, as mentioned above, understanding cross-country differences in educational finance and out-comes is clearly a priority for future research. This study relies simply on the median unit cost of education in countries with higher-than-predicted —"best practice"—enrollment rates, thereby ascribing a reasonable (and clearly attainable) ideal unit cost also associated with better outcomes.[10] The median is derived for two groups of countries corresponding to the NER criteria developed in the previous section: high performers relative to income, and high performers relative to income and region.

I also consider two alternative absorption scenarios. In the first, repetition rates are unchanged and so new school spaces must be created for all new enrollees, with an allowance for repetition among the new students as well. Under this scenario, unit costs are first multiplied by the number of new students who need to be enrolled to achieve a given net enrollment rate and this number is inflated by the current repetition rate, here defined as the ratio of the gross to the net enrollment rate.[11] Although this seems reasonable, many school systems in developing countries have high repetition rates, with a sizable proportion of over-age students.[12] These school systems already provide more spaces for school-age children than the number of out-of-school children would suggest. A country that reduced or eliminated grade repetition while enrolling new school-age children would therefore incur lower additional costs, because some of the needed spaces would already be available. I therefore consider an absorption scenario in which reduced repetition releases spaces currently occupied by over-age students to new age-appropriate enrollees. The target repetition rate is 7 percent, the mean rate among high-performing low-income countries. I assume no change in the repetition rate for countries already below this target.[13]

---

[10] Using the student-weighted mean cost for high-performing countries results in costs about 5 percent lower for the income standard and 10 percent lower for the income and region standard. This analysis uses the median as a more conservative benchmark, because the required cost reduction is lower.

[11] See Brossard and Gacougnolle (2001) for a similar correction.

[12] The mean primary repetition rate for the 121 developing countries reporting this statistic in the WDI is 9.3 percent, 43 developing countries have repetition rates greater than 10 percent and 17 have rates greater than 20 percent. This compares to an average of 3.5 percent for the 19 reporting high-income countries reporting the statistic, with only one observation greater than 10 percent. UNESCO (2003) provides the secondary repetition rate for 78 developing countries: the mean is 8.9 per cent; 27 countries have rates exceeding 10 percent and eight countries have rates exceeding 20 percent. This compares with a 6.0 percent mean for the 16 reporting high-income countries, and only one high-income country exceeding 10 percent.

[13] See lines 6 and 7 in Table 4 in the Appendix for the formulas used to calculate needed enrollment under each absorption scenario.

Finally, I consider two alternative target dates—2015 and 2025—for achieving universal secondary schooling.

Table 6 presents mean unit costs both for countries and per student, by region and income group for all developing countries. Recall that countries with insufficient data are assigned the regional mean unit cost. Student-weighted costs, which indicate the mean per student cost, are quite similar across the three unit cost scenarios, at $296 using present unit costs, $292 using median cost for best-practice countries by income group, and $268 using median cost for best-practice countries by income group and region. The distribution of students, however, is different from the distribution of out-of-school children, with the latter disproportionately in poorer countries. As a result, one could expect even lower costs for each new enrollee.

Table 7 shows the expense of increasing school spaces so as to achieve instantaneous universal secondary education according to each cost scenario and absorption assumption. Under present costs, and if repetition rates are unchanged and new spaces for unenrolled students (inflated by the repetition rate) need to be created, the per new enrollee cost is $198. Under present costs, but with a reduction in the repetition rate to 7 percent, the cost per new enrollee falls to $172, for total additional spending requirements of $62 billion and $44 billion, respectively. The lower per new enrollee unit costs calculated under the assumption of lower repetition rates points to the fact that the countries with larger discrepancies between the GER and the NER tend to be the lower-cost countries.

Under costs determined according to the median cost of the best-practice countries by income group, the per new enrollee cost falls to $166 and $150, yielding total new spending levels of $52 billion with no change in the repetition rate and $38 billion with a 7 percent repetition rate. Under costs ascribed from the median-cost best-practice countries by income group and region, the per new enrollee costs are lower still, at $151 and $128, with total new spending of $47 billion and $33 billion, depending on the repetition assumptions.

The best-practice spending totals include savings on currently enrolled students in countries where present costs exceed best-practice costs—the case for most countries. In some instances, these savings on current students exceed the spending needed to enroll new students. These countries are not included in the totals, as this would imply that their savings could be used to defray spending in other countries. For

Table 6: Unit Costs (in Constant 2002 U.S. Dollars) under Different Scenarios, by Region and Income Group, per Enrolled Student

	SSA*	SA*	EA&P*	ME&NA*	LA&C*	E&CA*	Total per country	Total per student
Present Unit Costs								
Low Income	$128	$86	$136	$249	$122	$125	$127	$126
Lower-Middle Income	417	82	382	369	325	307	337	244
Upper-Middle Income	820	—	1417	2180	919	1157	1219	884
Country mean	199	85	307	927	544	505	412	—
Mean cost per student	257	117	168	571	577	462	—	296
Best Practice by Income Group								
Low Income	66	66	66	66	66	66	66	66
Lower-Middle Income	290	290	290	290	290	290	290	290
Upper-Middle Income	877	—	877	877	877	877	877	877
Country mean	139	122	203	459	505	398	302	—
Mean cost per student	138	71	247	338	725	329	—	292
Best Practice by Region and Income Group								
Low Income	75	67	23	249	222	93	76	64
Lower-Middle Income	637	82	139	384	312	219	299	221
Upper-Middle Income	785	—	1417	1555	877	902	1014	938
Country mean	171	69	145	741	527	384	336	—
Mean cost per student	231	67	132	492	734	300	—	268

Source: Author's calculations based on data from WDI and UNESCO-UIS.

Note: Best-practice country cost is the median unit cost by income group or region and income group for countries with net enrollment rates higher than predicted by regressions of region and income interactions.

* SSA=Sub-Saharan Africa, SA=South Asia, EA&P=East Asia and Pacific, ME&NA=Middle East and North Africa, LA&C=Latin America and the Caribbean, E&CA=Europe and Central Asia.

Table 7: Additional Spending (in Constant 2002 U.S. Dollars) to Achieve Immediate 90 Percent Net Enrollment Rates at the Secondary Level under Alternative Cost and Absorption Assumptions

	Present costs			Best practice by income group		Best practice by region and income group	
	Population to be enrolled (1000s)	Cost per new enrollee	Total cost (millions)	Cost per new enrollee	Total cost (millions)	Cost per new enrollee	Total cost (millions)
Absorption assumption 1: New spaces for all new enrollees, no change in repetition rates							
SSA*	90,587	$132	$11,965	$76	$6,851	$97	$8,766
SA*	88,222	116	10,270	68	5,958	67	5,923
EA&P*	87,031	153	13,314	219	19,039	113	9,843
ME&NA*	16,559	743	12,307	322	5,325	483	7,992
LA&C*	22,589	472	10,671	564	12,737	578	13,049
E&CA*	7,843	424	3,327	262	2,055	212	1,666
Low income	203,045	123	25,069	65	13,229	68	13,730
Lower-middle income	93,360	217	20,220	276	25,804	204	19,035
Upper-middle income	16,426	1,008	16,565	787	12,932	881	14,475
TOTALS	**312,832**	**$198**	**$61,854**	**$166**	**$51,965**	**$151**	**$47,239**
Absorption assumption 2: Reduction of repetition rate to 7% allows some existing capacity to be used for new enrollees							
SSA*	67,492	$119	$8,016	$69	$4,669	$81	$5,475
SA*	88,321	116	10,285	68	5,964	67	5,928
EA&P*	68,977	154	10,554	233	16,078	117	8,066
ME&NA*	11,659	688	7,792	325	3,789	490	5,708
LA&C*	10,453	388	4,065	541	5,651	560	5,858
E&CA*	7,311	384	2,988	259	1,891	205	1,499
Low income	176,775	123	21,746	66	11,693	68	11,937
Lower-middle income	70,825	202	14,295	290	20,552	193	13,691
Upper-middle income	6,613	1,158	7,660	877	5,797	1,044	6,906
TOTALS	**254,213**	**$172**	**$43,700**	**$150**	**$38,042**	**$128**	**$32,534**

Source: Author's calculations based on data from WDI and UNESCO-UIS.

Note: Totals reflect figures for all new students. The region and income panels are different decompositions of the same underlying totals.

* SSA=Sub-Saharan Africa, SA=South Asia, EA&P=East Asia and Pacific, ME&NA=Middle East and North Africa, LA&C=Latin America and the Caribbean, E&CA=Europe and Central Asia.

other countries, the best-practice costs exceed present costs.[14] These countries face increased costs for students already enrolled. The last row in each panel shows that the amount of spending directed to these students is a sizable share of the total needed to achieve universal secondary schooling.

Table 8 shows the cost requirements for gradually increasing the enrollment rate to universal access by 2015 or 2025, using present cost and best-practice cost by income and region, and reducing repetition rates to 7 percent over the full period. The calculations include additional costs (or cost savings) incurred for existing students under the best-practice scenario. They assume a 1.6 percent annual growth in enrollment rates, which is the median growth rate for all developing countries.[15] Thus, some of the cost savings over an extended time horizon result from expansion that could reasonably have been expected to occur anyway.[16] The predicted decline in the secondary school age population between 2005 and 2011 also moderates costs. The estimates show that increasing school spaces to achieve universal secondary schooling by 2015 would cost $34 billion annually under present costs and repetition rates, and $28 billion annually under best-practice costs. With a gradual reduction in the repetition rate to 7 percent, the average annual costs under the present and best-practice cost structures are $32 and $27 billion, respectively. The difference between the estimate with no change in cost structure and repetition rates and the estimate with best-practice costs and 7 percent repetition is 21 percent.

Under a 25-year time frame, the average annual cost to expand educational systems to achieve universal enrollment is $28 billion, at present

---

[14] For best-practice countries with present costs below the median, I use their present costs as best-practice costs.

[15] Enrollment rate growth is the average annual growth for countries reporting NERs in the 1998–2000 period. Where NERs were unavailable, GERs were used.

[16] Most countries in the sample also can expect to see income growth in the next 15–25 years. I assume that this growth, at the current share of GDP spent on education, will finance the predicted growth in the NER and the expected increases in teacher salaries due to rising standards of living. Typically, teacher salaries rise in absolute terms as national income rises, but decline as a share of per capita income. This suggests that simply maintaining the share of GDP in education will easily cover these costs. Estimates for more rapid expansion than would otherwise occur are thus in addition to the costs that a country will incur under expected rates of school expansion and income growth.

Table 8: Cost Projections for Reaching 90 Percent NER in 15 and 25 years (in Millions of Constant 2002 U.S. Dollars)

Year	Population 12-17 (1000s)	Repetition rates unchanged				Repetition 7% or less			
		15-year horizon		25-year horizon		15-year horizon		25-year horizon	
		Present costs	Best practice costs	Present costs	Best practice costs	Present costs	Best practice costs	Present costs	Best practice costs
2001	649,490	$4141	$10,747	$2042	$9590	$3853	$10,546	$1784	$9383
2002	649,700	8310	13,169	4098	10,795	7731	12,766	3580	10,388
2003	649,910	12,509	15,635	6169	12,016	11,635	15,029	5387	11,406
2004	650,120	16,735	18,131	8254	13,253	15,564	17,317	7204	12,436
2005	650,330	20,990	20,697	10,353	14,503	19,519	19,676	9032	13,477
2006	649,938	25,274	23,172	12,468	15,661	23,496	21,941	10,871	14,436
2007	649,545	29,587	25,657	14,596	16,817	27,498	24,216	12,720	15,396
2008	649,153	33,928	28,137	16,738	18,010	31,524	26,481	14,579	16,375
2009	648,760	38,297	30,678	18,895	19,203	35,573	28,786	16,447	17,357
2010	648,368	42,695	33,222	21,065	20,391	39,654	31,107	18,324	18,332
2011	649,591	47,241	35,991	23,298	21,745	43,859	33,641	20,244	19,453
2012	650,814	51,836	38,776	25,553	23,114	48,105	36,189	22,178	20,628
2013	652,038	56,479	41,580	27,828	24,492	52,391	38,745	24,125	21,759
2014	653,261	61,169	44,400	30,124	25,876	56,717	41,300	26,084	22,983
2015	654,484	65,906	47,238	32,442	27,267	61,082	43,861	28,055	24,101
2016	657,962	64,858	46,727	34,720	28,703	29,090	22,772	29,995	25,264
2017	661,441	63,879	46,259	37,010	30,165	28,228	22,478	31,941	26,471
2018	664,919	62,875	45,778	39,311	31,648	27,435	22,269	33,892	28,188
2019	668,398	61,851	45,265	41,624	33,139	26,629	22,062	35,848	29,314
2020	671,876	60,801	44,734	43,948	34,637	25,815	21,844	37,809	30,441
2021	675,140	59,641	44,147	46,197	36,101	25,022	21,628	39,699	31,535
2022	678,405	58,539	43,543	48,448	37,569	24,222	21,413	41,590	32,636
2023	681,669	57,425	42,927	50,701	39,040	23,667	21,193	43,479	33,733
2024	684,934	56,325	42,298	52,956	40,513	23,138	20,976	45,364	34,824
2025	688,198	55,212	41,655	55,212	41,990	22,592	20,753	47,246	35,915
Cost per year over 25-year period		44,660	34,822	28,162	25,049	29,361	24,760	24,299	22,249
Cost per year over 15-year period		34,340	28,482			31,880	26,773		

Source: Author's calculations based on data from WDI and UNESCO-UIS.

Note: Best-practice costs are the median cost by income group and region for countries performing better than predicted in a regression model of enrollment rates on region and income interactions.

costs and repetition rates. Under best-practice costs and repetition rates, the cost falls to $22 billion, a 21 percent reduction. Over 25 years, but with universal enrollment achieved at 15 years, the same cost comparison is $45 billion and $25 billion, implying a possible 45 percent reduction in costs.

Although it is certain that reduced repetition will lower the cost of secondary school expansion considerably, the "best-practice" scenarios depend on the ability of countries to adopt lower-cost systems. The best-practice simulations and their implications for savings underscore the need for research on the cross-country variation in education costs. At this time, and particularly without an understanding of the mechanics of lower-cost systems, it would be imprudent to suggest that substantial cost reductions are possible. I therefore prefer the estimates based on present costs, which suggest annual costs between $24 billion and $45 billion over the next 25 years, depending on the extent of repetition reduction, and the speed with which universal enrollment occurs.

Table 9 puts these spending levels in perspective by comparing them to current spending, calculating them as a percent of GDP, and determining the finance gap after countries have committed at least the median GDP share to education (based on the GDP share of high-performing countries by income group). This minimum is set at 4.1 percent of GDP for low-income countries, and 5.0 percent for middle-income countries. Not surprisingly, Table 9 shows that achieving universal secondary education imposes a heavy burden on the poorest countries. Under the 25-year time horizon and with present cost structures, low-income countries would need to more than double their current spending on secondary education, at a cost of nearly 2 percent of GDP. If the low-income countries were to increase their spending to the best-practice share of GDP, the annual foreign aid requirement would be $10.5 billion.

Achieving universal secondary schooling in middle-income countries would impose a much smaller financial burden. Under a 15-year horizon and 7 percent repetition rates, lower-middle-income countries would have to increase spending by 7 percent over current spending on secondary education; the increase for upper-middle-income countries would be less than 1 percent. If countries are required to commit a minimum percent of GDP, the estimates suggest external funding requirements of $6.3 billion.

If low-income countries adopt the 25-year horizon and middle-income countries adopt the 15-year horizon, the combined external requirement is $16.8 billion annually. This amount is more than 25 per-

Table 9: Indicators of Median Country Burden and External Aid Requirements for Achieving 90 Percent Net Enrollment Rates, Average Annual Spending over 25 Years (Spending in billions of constant 2002 U.S. dollars)

| | Repetition rates unchanged | | | | Repetition rates 7% or less | | | |
| | 15-year horizon | | 25-year horizon | | 15-year horizon | | 25-year horizon | |
	Present costs	Best practice costs	Present costs	Best practice costs	Present costs	Best practice costs	Present costs	Best practice costs
Low Income Countries								
Total present spending=$15.3								
Additional spending needed	$20.3	$8.6	$13.8	$6.1	$16.9	$7.0	$13.2	$5.9
As factor of present spending	3.2	2.0	2.2	1.3	2.5	1.4	2.2	1.2
As share of GDP	2.8	1.2	2.0	0.6	2.1	0.8	1.9	0.6
Foreign aid required after country spends best practice GDP	$16.9	$6.7	$11.1	$4.7	$13.6	$5.1	$10.5	$4.5
Country burden as factor of present spending after foreign aid paid	0.20	0.08	0.19	0.03	0.16	0.06	0.14	0.02
Lower-Middle Income Countries								
Total present spending=$35.9								
Additional spending needed	$10.9	$13.5	$6.5	$9.6	$6.4	$9.3	$5.4	$8.6
As factor of present spending	0.25	0.12	0.11	0.01	0.11	0.06	0.07	0
As share of GDP	0.3	0.2	0.1	0.1	0.2	0.1	0.1	0.2
Foreign aid required after country spends best practice GDP	$5.3	$5.8	$3.3	$4.1	$2.9	$3.5	$2.7	$3.5
Country burden as factor of present spending after foreign aid paid	<0.01	<0.01	<0.01	<0.01	<0.01	<0.01	<0.01	<0.01
Upper-Middle Income Countries								
Total present spending=$41.8								
Additional spending needed	$13.4	$12.7	$7.9	$9.3	$6.0	$8.5	$5.7	$7.8
As factor of present spending	0.05	0.01	<0.01	<0.01	<0.01	<0.01	<0.01	<0.01
As share of GDP	0.07	0.02	<0.01	<0.01	<0.01	<0.01	<0.01	<0.01
Foreign aid required after country spends best practice GDP	$8.9	$7.7	$4.6	$4.6	$3.4	$4.4	$3.8	$4.2
Country burden as factor of present spending after foreign aid paid	<0.01	<0.01	<0.01	<0.01	<0.01	<0.01	<0.01	<0.01
All Countries								
Total present spending=$93.0								
Additional spending needed	$44.7	$34.8	$28.2	$25.0	$29.4	$24.8	$24.3	$22.2
Foreign aid required after country spends best practice GDP	$31.1	$20.2	$19.0	$13.4	$19.9	$13.0	$17.0	$12.2

Source: Author's calculations based on data from WDI and UNESCO-UIS.

cent of the $65 billion provided by official development assistance in 2002, and is about equal to the aid ear-marked for projects that address the UN's Millennium Development Goals, which include eradicating extreme poverty and hunger, achieving universal primary education, and improving health (UN Millennium Project, 2005). Thus, relative to the current level of external aid, $16.8 billion is a large sum.

ACHIEVING UNIVERSAL SECONDARY EDUCATION

The foregoing discussion suggests that, depending on time horizon, cost structure, and repetition rates, the annual financial burden of providing enough school spaces to achieve universal secondary schooling in developing countries will fall between $22 billion and $45 billion annually. The above calculations reveal a seemingly rich potential in the workings of low-cost, high-performing education systems and in the significant savings that countries can reap if they are able to reduce repetition rates. Both of these tasks would require comprehensive case studies of how some countries produce exemplary outcomes at exceedingly modest costs.

Under present costs and repetition rates, the financial requirements of achieving universal secondary education are particularly onerous for low-income countries. Yet, if countries were to increase the share of their GDP committed to education to the median share adopted by high-performing countries, external finance requirements would fall by about 30 percent under most cost and repetition scenarios. Clearly, some combination of cost reform, repetition rate reduction, and increased national commitment would go a long way in making universal secondary schooling a reality.

Appendix

Table A.1: Study Population Countries by Region, Income Classification, and Population 12–17 Years of Age

	Income group	Population 12–17 Years of Age (1000s)
Sub-Saharan Africa		
Angola	Low	1,703
Benin	Low	939
Botswana	Upper-middle	257
Burkina Faso	Low	1,757
Burundi	Low	1,007
Cameroon	Low	2,170
Cape Verde	Lower-middle	69
Central African Republic	Low	512
Chad	Low	1,074
Comoros	Low	105
Congo, Rep.	Low	482
Cote d'Ivoire	Low	2,427
Democratic Rep. of the Congo	Low	6,975
Equatorial Guinea	Low	60
Eritrea	Low	533
Ethiopia	Low	9,171
Gabon	Upper-middle	175
Gambia	Low	171
Ghana	Low	2,899
Guinea	Low	1,128
Guinea-Bissau	Low	183
Kenya	Low	4,969
Lesotho	Low	283
Liberia	Low	425
Madagascar	Low	2,165
Malawi	Low	1,491
Mali	Low	1,760
Mauritania	Low	355
Mauritius	Upper-middle	117
Mozambique	Low	2,474
Namibia	Lower-middle	251
Niger	Low	1,515
Nigeria	Low	16,379
Rwanda	Low	1,134
Sao Tome and Principe	Low	23
Senegal	Low	1,367
Sierra Leone	Low	590
Somalia	Low	1,224
South Africa	Lower-middle	5,860
Sudan	Low	4,164
Swaziland	Lower-middle	161
Togo	Low	643
Uganda	Low	3,400
United Republic of Tanzania	Low	5,147
Zambia	Low	1,505
Zimbabwe	Low	2,026

Table A.1 continued

	Income group	Population 12–17 Years of Age (1000s)
South Asia		
Afghanistan	Low	2,902
Bangladesh	Low	19,019
Bhutan	Low	295
India	Low	127,056
Maldives	Lower-middle	44
Nepal	Low	3,176
Pakistan	Low	19,830
Sri Lanka	Lower-middle	2,134
East Asia & Pacific		
Cambodia	Low	2,196
China	Lower-middle	132,931
Dem. People's Rep. of Korea	Low	2,228
Fiji	Lower-middle	104
Indonesia	Low	26,201
Lao PDR	Low	739
Malaysia	Upper-middle	2,725
Micronesia, Fed. Sts.	Lower-middle	16
Mongolia	Low	367
Myanmar	Low	5,884
Papua New Guinea	Low	700
Philippines	Lower-middle	10,267
Samoa	Lower-middle	25
Solomon Islands	Low	62
Thailand	Lower-middle	6,738
Timor-Leste	Low	130
Tonga	Lower-middle	14
Vanuatu	Lower-middle	29
Viet Nam	Low	10,534
Middle East & North Africa		
Algeria	Lower-middle	4,370
Djibouti	Lower-middle	89
Egypt	Lower-middle	9,630
Iran, Islamic Rep.	Lower-middle	11,046
Iraq	Lower-middle	3,292
Jordan	Lower-middle	690
Lebanon	Upper-middle	427
Libyan Arab Jamahiriya	Upper-middle	804
Malta	Upper-middle	34
Morocco	Lower-middle	3,930
Oman	Upper-middle	333
Palestinian Autonomous Territories	Lower-middle	443
Saudi Arabia	Upper-middle	2,788
Syrian Arab Republic	Lower-middle	2,631
Tunisia	Lower-middle	1,269
Yemen	Low	2,697

Table A.1 continued

	Income group	Population 12–17 Years of Age (1000s)
Latin America & Caribbean		
Argentina	Upper-middle	3,965
Barbados	Upper-middle	25
Belize	Lower-middle	34
Bolivia	Lower-middle	1,096
Brazil	Upper-middle	21,329
Chile	Upper-middle	1,628
Colombia	Lower-middle	5,055
Costa Rica	Upper-middle	502
Cuba	Lower-middle	989
Dominican Republic	Lower-middle	1,117
Ecuador	Lower-middle	1,623
El Salvador	Lower-middle	787
Guatemala	Lower-middle	1,657
Guyana	Lower-middle	94
Haiti	Low	1,275
Honduras	Lower-middle	919
Jamaica	Lower-middle	328
Mexico	Upper-middle	12,732
Nicaragua	Low	741
Panama	Upper-middle	349
Paraguay	Lower-middle	766
Peru	Lower-middle	3,288
St. Lucia	Upper-middle	19
St. Vincent and the Grenadines	Lower-middle	17
Suriname	Lower-middle	59
Trinidad and Tobago	Upper-middle	169
Uruguay	Upper-middle	310
Venezuela	Upper-middle	3,099
Europe & Central Asia		
Albania	Lower-middle	354
Armenia	Low	382
Azerbaijan	Low	1,052
Belarus	Lower-middle	1,020
Bosnia and Herzegovina	Lower-middle	380
Bulgaria	Lower-middle	649
Croatia	Upper-middle	349
Czech Republic	Upper-middle	791
Estonia	Upper-middle	131
Georgia	Low	514
Hungary	Upper-middle	738
Kazakhstan	Lower-middle	1,934
Kyrgyzstan	Low	665
Latvia	Upper-middle	224
Lithuania	Upper-middle	332
Poland	Upper-middle	3,823
Republic of Moldova	Low	497

Table A.1 continued

	Income group	Population 12–17 Years of Age (1000s)
Romania	Lower-middle	2,056
Russian Federation	Lower-middle	14,623
Serbia and Montenegro	Lower-middle	964
Slovak Republic	Upper-middle	512
Tajikistan	Low	909
Former Yugoslav Rep. of Macedonia	Lower-middle	197
Turkey	Lower-middle	8,566
Turkmenistan	Lower-middle	647
Ukraine	Low	4,591
Uzbekistan	Low	3,562

Income group designated by the following ranges of per capita gross national income calculated using the World Bank Atlas method:

$735 or less—Low income
$736–$2935—Lower-middle-income
$2936–$9075—Upper-middle-income

Source: World Bank 2003 list of developing countries and UNESCO (for population figures).

Table A.2: Study Population Countries Included in TIMSS

	Income group	Region
Bulgaria	Lower-middle	E&CA
Czech Republic	Upper-middle	E&CA
Hungary	Upper-middle	E&CA
Indonesia	Low	EA&P
Iran, Islamic Rep.	Lower-middle	ME&NA
Jordan	Lower-middle	ME&NA
Latvia	Upper-middle	E&CA
Lithuania	Upper-middle	E&CA
Malaysia	Upper-middle	EA&P
Morocco	Lower-middle	ME&NA
Philippines	Lower-middle	EA&P
Republic of Moldova	Low	E&CA
Romania	Lower-middle	E&CA
Russian Federation	Lower-middle	E&CA
Slovak Republic	Upper-middle	E&CA
South Africa	Lower-middle	SSA
Thailand	Lower-middle	EA&P
Former Yugoslav Rep. of Macedonia	Lower-middle	E&CA
Tunisia	Lower-middle	ME&NA
Turkey	Lower-middle	E&CA

Source: 1999 TIMSS and World Bank 2003 list of developing countries.

Table A.3: Best-Practice Countries by Performance Criteria

	Net Enrollment Rate		TIMSS
	High relative to income	High relative to income & region	High relative to income[1]
Sub-Saharan Africa			
Botswana	X	X	
Eritrea		X	
Gambia		X	
Ghana		X	
Liberia		X	
Malawi		X	
Mauritius	X	X	
Namibia		X	
Sierra Leone		X	
South Africa		X	0
Swaziland		X	
Zimbabwe		X	
South Asia			
None			
East Asia & Pacific			
Indonesia			X
Malaysia	X	X	0
Mongolia	X	X	
Philippines	X	X	0
Samoa	X	X	
Tonga	X	X	
Viet Nam	X	X	
Middle East & North Africa			
Algeria	X	X	
Egypt	X	X	
Jordan	X	X	0
Lebanon	X	X	
Malta	X	X	
Tunisia	X	X	0
Latin America & Caribbean			
Argentina	X	X	
Barbados	X	X	
Belize	X	X	
Bolivia	X	X	
Brazil	X	X	
Chile	X	X	
Colombia		X	
Jamaica	X	X	
Nicaragua		X	
Panama	X	X	
Peru	X	X	
St. Lucia	X	X	
Trinidad and Tobago	X	X	
Uruguay	X	.	

Table A.3 continued

	Net Enrollment Rate		TIMSS
	High relative to income	High relative to income & region	High relative to income[1]
Europe & Central Asia			
Albania	X		
Armenia	X		
Azerbaijan	X	X	
Belarus	X		
Bulgaria	X	X	X
Czech Republic			X
Estonia	X		
Georgia	X		
Hungary	X	X	X
Kazakhstan	X	X	
Latvia	X		X
Lithuania	X	X	X
Poland	X	X	
Republic of Moldova	X		X
Romania	X	X	X
Russian Federation			X
Slovak Republic	X		X
Tajikistan	X	X	
The Former Yugoslav Rep. of Macedonia	X		0
Total number of high performing countries	43	45	10

[1] A zero shows that the country has a TIMSS score, but is not a best-practice country.
Source: Author's calculations based on data from WDI and TIMSS.

Table A.4: Derivation of Spending Calculations

Unit Costs

1. Total Education Expenditure = [Share of GDP in Education Spending (current and capital)] X [2000 Country GDP in constant 2002 US dollars]

2. Spending on Secondary Education= [1] X [Share of Total Education Expenditure at Secondary level]

3. Students = GER X [Population 12–17 years of age]

4. Present Unit Cost = [2] / [3]

5. "Best-Practice" Unit Cost = Median cost among countries with better outcomes

Absorption Scenarios

6. Number of Children Who Need to Enroll to Achieve 90%, at Current Repetition = [0.9 – NER] X [Population 12–17 years of age] X GER/NER

7. Number of Children Who Need to Enroll to Achieve 90%, at 7% Repetition = [0.9 – GER(1-.07)] X [Population 12–17 years of age] X 1.07*

Spending Needed to Achieve Universal Secondary Enrollment

8. Present Unit Costs, No Change in Repetition = [4] X [6]

9. Present Unit Costs, Repetition Capped at 7%= [4] X [7]

10. Best-Practice Unit Costs, No Change in Repetition = [5] X [6]

11. Best-Practice Unit Costs, Repetition Capped at 7% = [5] X [7]

*This calculation assumes that places can be converted from over-age to appropriate-age students.

References

Binder, Melissa, and Christopher Woodruff. 2002. "Inequality and Intergenerational Mobility in Schooling: The Case of Mexico." *Economic Development and Cultural Change* 50 (2): 249–67.

Brossard, Mathieu, and Luc-Charles Gacougnolle. 2001. "Financing Primary Education for All: Yesterday, Today and Tomorrow." Paris: UNESCO.

Bruns, Barbara, Alain Mingat, and Ramahatra Rakotomalala. 2003. *Achieving Universal Primary Education by 2015: A Chance for Every Child.* Washington, DC: The World Bank.

Colclough, Christopher, with Keith Lewin. 1993. *Educating All the Children: Strategies for Primary Schooling in the South.* Oxford: Clarendon Press.

Delamonica, Enrique, Santosh Mehrotra, and Jan Vandemoortele. 2001. "Is EFA Affordable? Estimating the Global Minimum Cost of 'Education for All.'" Innocenti Working Paper No. 87. Florence: UNICEF Innocenti Research Center.

Devarajan, Shantayanan, Margaret J. Miller, and Eric V. Swanson. 2002. "Goals for Development: History, Prospects and Costs." World Bank Working Paper. Washington, DC: The World Bank.

Hannum, Emily, and Claudia Buchmann. 2003. *The Consequences of Global Educational Expansion: Social Science Perspectives.* Cambridge, MA: American Academy of Arts and Sciences.

Inter-American Development Bank (IDB). 1998. *Facing Up to Inequality in Latin America: Economic and Social Progress in Latin America, 1998–1999 Report.* Washington, DC: Inter-American Development Bank.

Jimenez, Emmanuel. 1986. "The Structure of Educational Costs: Multiproduct Cost Functions for Primary and Secondary Schools in Latin America." *Economics of Education Review* 5 (1): 25–39.

Lewin, Keith, and Francoise Caillods. 2001. *Financing Secondary Education in Developing Countries: Strategies for Sustainable Growth.* Paris: UNESCO.

Organization of Economic Co-operation and Development (OECD) and UNESCO Institute of Statistics (UNESCO-UIS). 2003. *Financing Education —*

Investments and Returns: Analysis of the World Education Indicators, 2002 Edition. Paris: UNESCO-UIS/OECD.

Psacharopoulos, George. 1994. "Returns to Investment in Education: A Global Update." *World Development* 22 (9): 1325–43.

Tsang, Mun. 1994. "Costs of Education In China: Issues Of Resource Mobilization, Equality, Equity And Efficiency." *Education Economics* 2 (3): 287–312.

UNESCO Institute for Statistics. 2003. *Global Education Digest 2003: Comparing Education Statistics Across the World*. Montreal: UNESCO Institute for Statistics.

UN Millennium Project. 2005. "Resources Required to Finance the Millennium Development Goals." In *Investing in Development: A Practical Plan to Achieve the Millennium Development Goals*. New York: United Nations Development Programme.

Verry, D.W. 1986. "Educational Cost Functions." Pp. 400–409 in *Economics of Education: Research and Studies*, ed. George Psacharopoulos. Oxford: Pergamon Press.

Section V: Consequences

Global Educational Expansion and Socio-Economic Development: An Assessment of Findings from the Social Sciences[*]

EMILY HANNUM AND CLAUDIA BUCHMANN

A mong development agencies, conventional wisdom holds that educational expansion facilitates numerous favorable changes for nations and individuals. Improved economic welfare and health, reduced inequalities, and more democratic political systems are just some of the purported benefits invoked in pleas for the expansion of education throughout the world. A recent World Bank document on the Education for All initiative provides a characteristic example:

> [G]lobal research…has established unequivocally that education increases individual incomes; that it is positively correlated with macroeconomic growth; that it is strongly correlated with reductions in poverty, illiteracy and income inequality; and that it has strong complementary effects on the achievement of…lower infant and child mortality, better nutrition, and the construction of democratic societies. The expansion of educational opportunity, which can simultaneously promote income equality and growth, is a "win win" strategy that in most societies is far easier to implement than the redistribution of other assets, such as land or capital. In short, education is one of the most powerful instruments known for reducing poverty and inequality and for laying the basis for sus-

[*]Reprinted from *World Development* 33 (3), Emily Hannum and Claudia Buchmann, "Global Educational Expansion and Socio-economic Development: An Assessment of Findings from the Social Sciences." Pp. 1–22, © 2004, with permission from Elsevier.

tained economic growth, sound governance, and effective institutions (2002a: v).

Similar rationales for investments in education are readily found in other documents produced by the World Bank, the United Nations Educational, Scientific, and Cultural Organization (UNESCO), the United Nations Children's Fund (UNICEF), and other international organizations supporting greater access to education worldwide (see World Bank, 1999, 2002b, UNESCO 2002; UNICEF 1995).

Just how strong is the empirical foundation for statements, like the one above, that portray education as the panacea for a wide range of social ills? To address this question, we assess the evidence on five related assumptions about the consequences of educational expansion for socio-economic development:

• Human capital stock is central to national economic development, as better-educated citizens are more productive.
• Within societies, the expansion of educational opportunities enables individuals to improve their economic circumstances.
• Educational expansion narrows social inequalities within nations by promoting a meritocratic basis for status attainment in which the talented can achieve appropriate positions in the economy, regardless of social background.
• Countries with better-educated citizens have healthier, slower-growing populations, as educated individuals make better health choices, live longer, and have healthier and fewer children.
• Countries with more educated populations are more democratic, as their citizens are able to make more informed political decisions.

We investigate these statements by drawing on evidence from empirical studies in sociology, demography, economics, political science, and anthropology.[1] Prior reviews of the impact of education have tended to focus on research in a single discipline; in contrast, this paper synthesizes

---

[1] One challenge with this interdisciplinary approach is that different disciplines vary in their ideas about the kinds of research designs that demonstrate evidence of causal relationships. The studies referenced here include a mix of cross-sectional and longitudinal designs; macro- and micro-level analyses; and studies that focus on changes over time. Many of the available studies in this realm involve cross-sectional research; readers may find some designs more convincing than others.

available evidence for a range of outcomes and across the social sciences with the goal of accumulating knowledge from diverse disciplines and promoting interdisciplinary research on the implications of global educational expansion. We also illustrate certain points made in the literature with empirical evidence about links between education and economic, health, demographic, and political outcomes. Note that the term education can refer to a wide range of formal and informal learning programs and processes; for the purposes of this paper, we follow the general convention in development organization documents and use the term to refer to formal schooling.

Our comprehensive assessment of empirical research on the consequences of educational expansion is revealing on several fronts. We find consistent evidence from a range of disciplines for the beneficial effects of educational expansion in the realms of health and demographic change. There is less consensus regarding the effects of educational expansion for economic growth, the erosion of social inequalities, or democratization. Finally, we identify four plausible reasons for inconclusive or ambiguous findings in these domains. These insights should serve to advance future research on the consequences of global educational expansion.

EDUCATION AND NATIONAL ECONOMIC DEVELOPMENT

Human capital stock is central to national economic development, as better-educated citizens are more productive.

On the one hand, there is an obvious coincidence of educational expansion and national economic development: developed countries tend to have more educated populations than less-developed countries. Figure 1 presents an illustration of the relationship, plotting primary, secondary, and tertiary gross enrollment ratios against gross national product (GNP) per capita for 102 countries with complete data in 1995. Data points for individual countries and trend lines for each level of education are included. Figure 1 demonstrates that countries with higher per capita GNPs have higher ratios of educational enrollment, especially at levels beyond primary school.[2] More rigorous evidence supporting the link

---

[2] Correlations between per capita GNP and enrollment ratios derived from the same data provide further illustration: the correlation of per capita GNP with the primary gross enrollment ratio is weak and marginally significant (.16, N=131,

between human capital stock and growth can be found in Barro's (1991) study showing a positive relationship between initial enrollment rates and economic growth in 98 countries. Most recently, in a synthesis of the empirical growth literature, Petrakis and Stamatakis (2002) similarly concluded that economies with a larger stock of human capital experience faster growth.

Also supporting the beneficial consequences of educational expansion for growth is research on the impact of government investments in education. Poot's (2000) synthesis of research on the impact of government policies on long-run growth concludes that the most definitive results relate to the positive impact of education expenditures: eleven of the twelve empirical studies identified showed significant, positive effects of educational expenditures on growth (Poot: Table 4). Sylwester (2000) similarly found a long-term positive effect of educational expenditures on economic growth. [3]

On the other hand, associations between measures of educational expansion and indicators of economic growth are open to interpretation. Scholars do not agree on the best way to isolate causal impacts on national development. Two factors contribute to the controversy: the difficulty of distinguishing the effects of growth on education from the effects of education on growth, and the possibility that other factors drive both educational expansion and economic growth. Moreover, some studies cast doubt on whether a consistent, positive relationship between education and economic growth really exists (e.g., Levine and Renelt, 1992: Table 5; see Krueger and Lindahl, 2000 for a critical review). Emblematic of this line of research is Pritchett's (1996) aptly titled piece, "Where Has All the Education Gone?" Pritchett uses two cross-national time-series data sets spanning the 1960s to the mid-1980s and finds that the rate of growth of educational capital is not significantly related to growth in GDP per worker.

One possible explanation for controversies surrounding the education-growth relationship is a mismatch between education and labor mar-

---

p=0.07), while the correlations with secondary and tertiary gross enrollment ratios are strong and significant (.64, N=121, p= 0.00 for secondary; .63, N=107, p= 0.00 for tertiary).

[3] Sylwester (2000) found that educational expenditures were negatively related with contemporaneous growth, but that previous expenditures were positively related.

Figure 1: Gross Enrollment Ratios by GNP Per Capita

	(1) Total Unemployment Rate[1]	(2) Internet Users per 100 Population[2]	(3) Life Expectancy at Birth[3]	(4) Total Fertility Rate[3]	(5) Infant Mortality Rate (per 1000)[3]	(6) Political Rights Index[4]	(7) Civil Liberties Index[4]
Tertiary Gross Enrollment Ratio[3]	0.07	0.20	0.07	-0.01	-0.25	0.03	0.04
	(2.08)**	(5.66)**	(2.89)**	(1.62)	(2.53)*	(3.81)**	(4.55)**
Secondary Gross Enrollment Ratio[3]	0.03	-0.05	0.10	-0.02	-0.43	0.00	-0.01
	(1.78)*	(2.63)**	(7.76)**	(7.34)**	(7.55)**	(0.93)	(1.46)
Primary Gross Enrollment Ratio[3]	0.01	0.02	0.09	-0.01	-0.68	0.01	0.03
	(0.66)	(1.01)	(6.26)**	(2.41)*	(10.24)**	(2.60)**	(5.15)**
GNP/Capita[3]	0.00	0.00	0.00	0.00	0.00	0.00	0.00
	(0.88)	(4.93)**	(0.02)	(2.53)*	(2.90)**	(1.91)	(1.10)
Population	0.00	0.00	0.00	0.00	0.00	0.00	0.00
	(1.01)	(0.25)	(2.89)**	(5.87)**	(3.13)**	(0.89)	(1.96)
Constant	3.21	-7.00	49.54	5.96	139.90	3.31	1.96
	(1.43)	(2.79)**	(40.17)**	(18.62)**	(23.63)**	(9.64)**	(4.62)**
Number of Observations	431	367	554	661	690	953	953
Range of Years in Estimation Sample[5]	1980-1997	1980-1997	1970-1997	1970-1997	1970-1997	1975-1997	1975-1997
Number of Countries	79	103	142	145	144	151	151
R-squared (Within)	0.09	0.32	0.52	0.33	0.45	0.03	0.07

Source: Created from data in U.S. Agency for International Development. 2000. "Global Education Database (GED) 2000 Edition," http://www.usaid.gov/educ_training/ged.html, accessed June 2002.

Note: Countries are Algeria, Armenia, Australia, Austria, Azerbaijan, Belarus, Belgium, Benin, Botswana, Brunei, Bulgaria, Cambodia, Canada, Chad, Chile, China, Colombia, Comoros, Croatia, Cyprus, Czech Rep., Denmark, Egypt, El Salvador, Eritrea, Estonia, Ethiopia, Finland, France, Georgia, Germany, Greece, Guatemala, Guinea, Guyana, Hungary, Iceland, India, Indonesia, Iran, Ireland, Israel, Italy, Kazakhstan, Kuwait, Kyrgyz Rep., Laos, Latvia, Lebanon, Lesotho, Lithuania, Luxembourg, Macedonia, Madagascar, Malawi, Malaysia, Mali, Malta, Mauritania, Mauritius, Mexico, Moldova, Mongolia, Morocco, Mozambique, Namibia, Nepal, Netherlands, New Zealand, Nicaragua, Norway, Oman, Panama, Papua New Guinea, Paraguay, Peru, Philippines, Poland, Portugal, Qatar, Romania, S. Korea, Saudi Arabia, Singapore, Slovakia, Slovenia, South Africa, Spain, Sri Lanka, Swaziland, Sweden, Tanzania, Thailand, Togo, Trinidad & Tobago, Tunisia, Turkey, Uganda, the United Kingdom, the United States, Vietnam, and Zimbabwe.

ket demands in some countries, if the education system primarily serves to sort individuals to fill slots in the labor market, rather than to help individuals to create new opportunities in the market. To the extent that labor markets are static, the incidence of unemployment may rise with education, and increases in education may reduce total output (Krueger and Lindahl, 2000: 10). For example, column 1 in Table 1 shows fixed-effects panel regressions of total unemployment rates for countries with valid data for years between 1980 and 1997. Net of population size and per capita GNP, the significant, positive coefficients for tertiary enroll-ment suggest that as enrollment ratios at this level increased, unemploy-ment rates increased as well.[4] Marginally significant results at the second-ary level suggest, if weakly, the same inference. The possibility that unemployment rises—or at least fails to fall—with educational expansion may be particularly relevant in countries where those most likely to bene-fit from continued educational expansion, such as the rural poor and, in many cases, women, were historically excluded from wage employment.

Other scholars attribute ambiguous results regarding the relationship between education and economic development to data problems such as measurement error and time-frame limitations. Krueger and Lindahl (2000) maintain that there is considerable measurement error in country-level education data, particularly at secondary and tertiary levels. After accounting for measurement error, they find that increased years of schooling has little short term effect on GDP growth, but positive and statistically significant effects on economic growth over periods of ten to twenty years (2000: 25).[5]

---

[4] We present the results in Table 1 to illustrate temporal associations of education and various national outcomes. This table is not meant to imply that education alone causes the observed changes in the outcome variables.

[5] While much research on education and national development has focused on the issue of growth, an equally important aspect of national economic develop-ment is the distribution of income. Studies suggest beneficial consequences of educational expansion for income distributions. Theoretical work in economics predicts that income inequality declines with support for public education (Glomm and Ravikumar, 1992). In an empirical study of 50 countries, Syl-wester (2002) showed that public education expenditures were associated with a subsequent decrease in the level of income inequality. He argues that costs must be low enough that individuals have enough resources to forego income and attend school. If individuals are too poor to attend school, then promoting public education can cause the distribution of income to become more skewed.

Table 1: Panel Regressions of Seven Outcomes on Gross Enrollment Ratios, 1970–2000

	Total Unemployment Rate[1]	Internet Users per 100 Population[2]	Life Expectancy at Birth[3]	Total Fertility Rate[3]	Infant Mortality Rate (per 1000)[3]	Political Rights Index[4]	Civil Liberties Index[4]
Tertiary Gross Enrollment Ratio[3]	0.07	0.20	0.07	-0.01	-0.25	0.03	0.04
	(2.08)**	(5.66)**	(2.89)**	(1.62)	(2.53)*	(3.81)**	(4.55)**
Secondary Gross Enrollment Ratio[3]	0.03	-0.05	0.10	-0.02	-0.43	0.00	-0.01
	(1.78)*	(2.63)**	(7.76)**	(7.34)**	(7.55)**	(0.93)	(1.46)
Primary Gross Enrollment Ratio[3]	0.01	0.02	0.09	-0.01	-0.68	0.01	0.03
	(0.66)	(1.01)	(6.26)**	(2.41)*	(10.24)**	(2.60)**	(5.15)**
GNP/Capita[3]	0.00	0.00	0.00	0.00	0.00	0.00	0.00
	(0.88)	(4.93)**	(0.02)	(2.53)*	(2.90)**	(1.91)	(1.10)
Population	0.00	0.00	0.00	0.00	0.00	0.00	0.00
	(1.01)	(0.25)	(2.89)**	(5.87)**	(3.13)**	(0.89)	(1.96)
Constant	3.21	-7.00	49.54	5.96	139.90	3.31	1.96
	(1.43)	(2.79)**	(40.17)**	(18.62)**	(23.63)**	(9.64)**	(4.62)**
Number of Observations	431	367	554	661	690	953	953
Range of Years in Estimation Sample[5]	1980-1997	1980-1997	1970-1997	1970-1997	1970-1997	1975-1997	1975-1997
Number of Countries	79	103	142	145	144	151	151
R-squared (Within)	0.09	0.32	0.52	0.33	0.45	0.03	0.07

Note: Absolute value of t statistics are in parentheses; * denotes significance at 10% and ** denotes significance at 5%. Models are estimated using data on outcome y for country i at time t, and allow for different intercepts (ui) for countries, but constrain the slopes (B) to be the same across countries. Models are estimated as $y_{it} = (alpha + u_i) + XB + e_{it}$.

[1] Source: United Nations. 2002. United Nations Common Database, http://unstats.un.org, series 4690: Unemployment Rate [99 countries, 1980-1997], accessed July 2002.

[2] Source: United Nations. 2002. United Nations Common Database, http://unstats.un.org, series 29969: Internet users per 100 population [209 countries, 1980-2001], accessed June 2002.

[3] Source: U.S. Agency for International Development. 2000. Global Education Database (GED) 2000 Edition, http://www.usaid.gov/educ_training/ged.html [1970-1998], accessed June 2002.

[4] Source: Freedom House, Inc. 2000. Annual Survey of Freedom Country Scores 1972-73 to 1999-00. http://www.freedomhouse.org/ratings/index.htm, accessed June 2002.

[5] Years with valid data in these ranges are included in the estimation samples.

GNP per capita is the gross national product, converted to U.S. dollars using the World Bank Atlas method, divided by the mid-year population. GNP is the sum of gross value added by all resident producers plus any taxes (less subsidies) that are not included in the valuation of output plus net receipts of primary income (employee compensation and property income) from nonresident sources. Data are in current U.S. dollars. GNP, calculated in national currency, is usually converted to U.S. dollars at official exchange rates for comparisons across economies, although an alternative rate is used when the official exchange rate is judged to diverge by an exceptionally large margin from the rate actually applied in international transactions. To smooth fluctuations in prices and exchange rates, a special Atlas method of conversion is used by the World Bank. This applies a conversion factor that averages the exchange rate for a given year and the two preceding years, adjusted for differences in rates of inflation between the country and the G-5 countries (France, Germany, Japan, the United Kingdom, and the United States).

A third possible explanation for mixed results is that different levels of schooling simply may not have consistent consequences for growth across countries. Petrakis and Stamatakis (2002) demonstrate that the levels of education that matter for economic development may depend on the nations' level of development: in less developed countries, primary and secondary education may matter more; in more developed countries, tertiary education may matter more.

A final complication is that past studies may tell us less and less about the future, as globalization and technological change modify the imperative for education. Using an index of technological progress constructed of five components (personal computers, Internet hosts, fax machines, mobile phones, and televisions), Rodríguez and Wilson (2000) show that human capital investment is positively related to national technological progress. They argue that there may be particular synergies between technology and human capital, and that high levels of education may be a necessary condition for technological innovation and adaptation. Column 2 in Table 1 shows some suggestive results, regressing Internet users per 100 population on enrollment ratios, population, and per capita GNP. Only tertiary gross enrollment ratios show a significant positive coefficient for Internet use. This example, together with Rodríguez and Wilson's study, suggests that globalization and technological change may be forging new mechanisms to link advanced skills to national development; mechanisms that may modify old relationships.

EDUCATION AND INDIVIDUAL ECONOMIC WELFARE

Within societies, the expansion of educational opportunities enables individuals to improve their economic circumstances.

The supposition that nations with more educated individuals should prosper hinges on the notion that better educated individuals are socialized in ways that increase their productivity and improve their economic standing. Researchers in the fields of sociology and economics have thoroughly investigated these assumptions. Sociologists have examined patterns and trends in individuals' school-to-work transitions and occupational attainment. These studies reveal variations in the links between education and labor markets across industrialized and industrializing countries (see Blau and Duncan, 1967; Shavit and Kraus, 1990; Bills and Haller, 1984; Hannum and Xie, 1998; Treiman et al., 1996; Shavit and

Mueller, 1998). Similarly, in the field of economics, rate-of-return studies show dramatic variations across countries (Nielsen and Westergard-Nielsen, 2001), as well as within countries across levels of schooling, social groups, and time periods (Moll, 1996; Psacharopoulos and Velez, 1992; Demetriades and Psacharopoulos, 1987; Zhang and Zhao, 2006; see Psacharopoulos and Patrinos, 2002, Appendix Table A-4 for an extensive compilation of comparable estimates). Variations notwithstanding, these studies attest to the importance of education as a determinant of individuals' occupational outcomes and subsequent economic status.

The credentialism hypothesis raises questions about such results. This hypothesis states that educational attainment offers credentials that signal underlying abilities, preferences, and privileges that are important for labor outcomes but often unmeasured in empirical studies. In other words, education simply provides a convenient "job queue" for employers, rather than actually improving the productivity of individuals.[6] If education were primarily a process of credentialing, rather than generating, productivity, cross-sectional studies of occupational attainment, or rates-of-return could tell us little about the consequences of further educational expansion. Stated more generally, the fact that education itself reflects social origins, abilities, choices and preferences, and assessments of likely returns complicates the task of interpreting estimates of the consequences of schooling for labor or other outcomes (see Becker, 1967, chapter two for a discussion).

It is likely that the selective function of schooling does play some role in producing the relationships between education and employment observed in many of the studies cited above, but empirical evidence casts doubt on strict credentialist arguments. Studies in a variety of national settings have offered more conservative tests of the beneficial economic consequences of schooling by attempting to address potential biases associated with unmeasured background characteristics such as ability, preferences, or privileged social origins (for example, see Lam and Schoeni, 1993 for Brazil; Duflo, n.d. for Indonesia; Psacharopoulos and Velez, 1992 for Colombia). One particularly convincing approach took advantage of a natural experiment to trace the impact of school construction on earnings in Indonesia. This study estimated wage increases of 1.5 to

---

[6] However, as discussed below, considerable evidence supports a different form of the credentialism argument: that educational credentials often serve to reproduce older forms of social inequality.

2.7 percent for each additional school built per 1,000 children (Duflo, n.d.: 34).

Two recent studies have offered critical assessments of evidence about whether conventional rate of return studies are misleading. In their review of studies that used natural experiments to develop instrumental variables estimates of the returns to schooling, Krueger and Lindahl (2000) concluded that the impact of education persists with ability and other factors controlled. Psacharopoulos and Patrinos (2002) found that rate-of-return estimates based on twins measures or instrumental variables estimates yielded an average rate of return to schooling—10 percent—that was the same as the average based on a much larger compilation of studies that used more conventional rate-of-return estimation techniques. Psacharopoulos and Patrinos (2002) also point out that economists' direct attempts to quantify bias in returns estimates associated with ability have suggested that it does not exceed 10 percent of the estimated schooling coefficients.

Most of the research on returns to education has operationalized education as the amount of time or number of years spent in school. But failure to consider the *quality* of education in addition to the amount of time spent in school can produce misleading conclusions regarding the returns to education. To address this concern, a number of studies have examined the impact of school quality on labor market and other outcomes (Behrman and Birdsall, 1983; Card and Krueger, 1992; Behrman, Birdsall, and Kaplan, 1996; Glewwe, 1999a; Glewwe, 1999b). The measures of school quality used in these studies vary, but are usually comprised of some combination of student-teacher ratios, teacher training or pay, measures of physical aspects of schools, or the availability of resources related to learning (e.g., textbooks or computers). This literature generally concludes that the quality of education an individual receives is as important for labor market outcomes as the quantity of education. Moreover, these studies demonstrate that treating school quality separately from time spent in school affects the inferences about the impact of school quantity; in some cases returns to years of education are lower once school quality is taken into account (Behrman and Birdsall, 1983). These findings suggest that, for labor outcomes, deepening education by increasing its quality is as important as expanding education.

Evidence about the economic benefits of schooling for individuals tells only part of the story. In developing countries, educational expansion, particularly among women, also appears to have significant implications for the human capital of children of the newly educated (Schultz, 2002). Behrman et al. (1999: 682) argue that a component of the significant positive relationship between maternal literacy and child schooling in India reflects the productivity effect of home teaching. This effect, combined with the increase in returns to schooling for men, underlies the expansion of female literacy following the onset of the green revolution.[7]

The mechanisms behind such findings are illuminated in anthropological studies in developing countries. Most notably, Robert and Sarah LeVine's cross-cultural research combining ethnographic methods, survey work and literacy testing in Mexico, Nepal, Zambia, and Venezuela indicates that education, and particularly the acquisition of literacy, helps women develop aspirations, skills, and models of learning that eventually affect their child-bearing, child-rearing behaviors (LeVine et al., 1991; LeVine et al., 2001; LeVine et al., 2004).

These studies attest to the economic benefits of increased schooling for individuals, and to the likely echo effects on their children. Yet, forecasting the specific economic implications of rising educational attainments is extremely complex, absent access to unusual data sources such as those utilized by Duflo (n.d.). Part of the difficulty is that peoples' economic opportunities are linked not only to their own human capital, but also to the contexts in which they find themselves. For example, in Latin America and China, both poverty and non-enrollment are concentrated in poor rural settings where returns to education tend to be lowest (Lopez and Valdez, 2000; Piazza et al., 2001; Zhao, 1997).[8] Lower returns in the poorest rural settings may be partially attributable to lower quality of schooling or lack of ready access to urban labor markets in which educational credentials can directly affect employment. Lower returns may also be attributable to the fact that, among farmers, the

---

[7] These findings may not apply in developed settings, where educational opportunities are relatively expanded. In a study using twins data from the United States, Behrman and Rosenzweig (2002) suggest that the observed positive relationship between the schooling of mothers and their children is substantially biased upward due to correlations between schooling and heritable "ability" and assortative mating. They conclude that in the United States, an increase in women's schooling would not be beneficial in terms of the schooling of children.

[8] These issues have global significance, as some estimates suggest that rural poverty accounts for nearly 63 percent of poverty worldwide (Khan, 2000).

returns to schooling vary in ways likely to be directly related to the level of local development. Where farmers have the possibility to innovate, such as in areas where the agricultural practices are in flux due to techno-logical modernization, returns to schooling tend to be higher (Schultz, 1975: 841). Rosenzweig (1995) observes that returns to education are high when productive learning activities can be exploited, such as during times of technological innovation (for a similar discussion, see Welch, 1970: 47).[9] Where agricultural practices are static, as they are likely to be in the poorest areas, returns to education are smaller or even non-existent (Schultz, 1975: 841). These examples provide an important caution that the implications of education for economic welfare for those remaining outside of the school system may be less favorable, on average, than for those already in the school system.[10]

A second important contextual factor is that the value of an individ-ual's own educational credential depends in part on how it compares to the credentials of the local population. As the average level of schooling in the population increases, the value of a given level of education in the labor market declines, leading to "credential inflation" (e.g., Moll, 1996; Demetriades and Psacharopoulos, 1987; Psacharopoulos and Velez, 1992). Both of these contextual factors are consistent with a global trend of slightly falling returns to education with economic development and educational expansion (Psacharopoulos and Patrinos, 2002).[11]

One unique contribution of sociology to debates about contextual effects on returns to schooling is the insight that the value of a given edu-cational credential depends not only on the average level of education in a population, but also on the institutional structures of national educa-tion systems. Shavit and Mueller's (1998) study of linkages between edu-

---

[9] Welch (1970) credited changing technologies for a trend of rising education without falling rates of return to schooling in the United States.

[10] There are additional factors that suggest other labor market disadvantages for children currently excluded from the school system. Poorer health may be one example. Levine's (2004) review cites studies in Egypt and Tanzania showing that out-of-school children were less healthy than children enrolled in school. It is also likely that those currently excluded from schooling have less access to social networks that can be helpful in the labor market.

[11] There are, however, important exceptions to this trend. Zang and Zhao (2006) have shown that returns to schooling in China have risen in recent years, during a period of educational and economic expansion. In addition, Psacharopoulos and Patrinos (2002) report increases in private returns to terti-ary schooling.

cational qualifications and occupations in thirteen industrialized countries demonstrates this point. In some countries, education is valued for the specific vocational skills it confers; in others, for providing workers with general knowledge; in others still, for sorting students by scholastic ability or potential to learn. Shavit and Mueller (1998) argue that where education's main purpose is to sort students, there is a built-in incentive for young people to acquire more education in order to stay ahead of the queue. As ever-larger proportions of a population obtain a credential, its labor market value declines. In contrast, in countries where vocational qualifications are used by employers to organize jobs and allocate persons among them, the value of a credential derives not from its scarcity, but rather from the specific skills it represents. In such contexts, credential inflation is less of a problem.

Shavit and Mueller's work suggests that the returns to schooling are conditioned both by the existing stock of human capital and by the nature of the credentials conferred. A larger conclusion to be drawn from this section is that, while studies attest to the importance of education as a determinant of individuals' occupational outcomes and subsequent economic status, the rate of return to schooling depends on a number of contextual factors, many of which are not easily incorporated into empirical models.

EDUCATION AND SOCIAL INEQUALITY

Educational expansion narrows social inequalities by promoting a meritocratic basis for status attainment in which the talented can rise to appropriate positions in the economy, regardless of social background.

While returns vary with context, a convergence of evidence suggests that education plays an important role in improving the absolute economic standing of individuals. Whether educational expansion improves the *relative* standing of historically disadvantaged groups such as the poor, women, and ethnic minorities is a different question. Here, we discuss evidence regarding the impact of educational expansion on socioeconomic, gender, and ethnic inequalities. Much of the sociological research attempting to answer this question has been guided by the "industrialism hypothesis," or the idea that industrialization promotes greater social mobility (Treiman, 1970). This theory holds that as societies develop, urbanization, mass communication, and industrialization should lead to greater social openness and a shift from particularistic to universalistic bases of achievement. These changes, in turn, should tighten the link between education and economic mobility. Data constraints have precluded systematic evaluation of the industrialism hypothesis, but existing studies show only mixed support for the notion that development and educational expansion bring increased social mobility (e.g., Kelley and Perlman, 1971; Holsinger, 1975; Bills and Haller, 1984; Mukweso et al., 1984).

Socioeconomic Inequality. Substantial research indicates that educational expansion does not reduce the relative advantages of elite children over children from less-privileged backgrounds. Educational expansion alone does not change the relative position of social groups in the "education queue" and elites manage to maintain their status by getting more education than the masses (Walters, 2000:254). Research from a wide range of societies finds little change in educational opportunities between social strata over the course of educational expansion (e.g., Mare, 1981; Halsey et al., 1980; Smith and Cheung, 1986; Shavit and Blossfeld, 1993). As Walters (2000: 254) notes, these findings highlight the need to consider separately the effects on educational inequality of an overall increase in the size of the educational system (i.e., school expansion) and changes in the rules by which educational opportunities are allocated (i.e., school reform).

Even expansions in education accompanied by reforms designed to modify the allocation of educational opportunities within society do not always reduce educational inequality. Raftery and Hout (1993; see also Hout et al., 1993) argue that a process they call "maximally maintained inequality" explains the seeming puzzle that many sweeping reforms intended to make education more egalitarian have not accomplished their purpose. When advantaged groups are not fully integrated at a given level of education, they strongly support efforts to expand educational participation by eliminating tuition fees and increasing capacity. Expansion at these levels of education does not lead to greater equality between social groups because advantaged groups, who tend to favor education, can garner the largest share of valuable educational credentials (Mare, 1981; Halsey et al., 1980). In such cases, expansion does not alter the effect of social background on educational transitions.

Gender Inequality. Evidence from countries around the world indicates a global, long-term trend toward girls' access to schooling catching up with boys' (King and Hill, 1993; Knodel and Jones, 1996; Shavit and Blossfeld, 1993; Schultz, 1993). In the United States and Europe, in fact, females have made substantial gains in all realms of education and now generally outperform males on several key educational benchmarks. In the United States today, women are more likely than men to persist in college, obtain degrees, and enroll in graduate school (Bae et al., 2000). In the year 2000 in all member states of the European Union, there were more 18–21 year old women than men of the same age group enrolled in tertiary education (Eurostat, 2002). Likewise, a recent analysis of survey data from 18 countries in Latin America showed that girls in most of the countries receive more education than boys (Andersen, 2000). Researchers are just beginning to examine this shift toward a female advantage in education in some countries.

In contrast, in South Asia and the Middle East, expanding education overall has occurred in the context of extreme gender gaps that continue to favor boys (King and Hill, 1993). For example, in Nepal, during a period when entrance and completion rates rose for girls, rates for boys also rose, such that gender gaps did not substantially narrow (Stash and Hannum, 2001). Sometimes the persistence of gender gaps that disadvantage females is linked to cultural norms surrounding women's roles in society, particularly women's access to paid employment.

Further, norms about female labor force participation can condition the consequences of educational expansion among girls. Female gains in education are not always mirrored by female gains in employment and income. For example, a study of five Asian nations using World Fertility Survey data showed that in the 1970s, higher levels of educational attainment had little impact on female labor force participation in Korea, the most developed and highly educated of the societies under study (Cameron et al., 2001). Similar research comparing Taiwan and Korea found very different education-employment relationships for women in the two societies. In Taiwan, higher levels of education increased women's probability of employment; in Korea, highly educated women were less likely to be employed. The difference was likely due to the fact that an adequate supply of educated males offered Korean employers few incentives to reduce barriers to married women's employment, while in Taiwan, an inadequate male labor force pressured employers to alter "patriarchal preferences" (Brinton et al., 1995: 1111). Finally, research on South Africa and Israel in the 1980s concluded that, despite relatively egalitarian patterns of educational attainment by gender, women lagged behind men in occupational attainment (Mickelson et al., 2001).

Ethnic Inequality. Because of the close link between education and occupational outcomes, increased absolute levels of education are likely to benefit disadvantaged ethnic groups. However, it is not safe to assume that expansion in access to education will allow disadvantaged minorities to "catch up" with initially advantaged ethnic groups, at least in the short run. For example, in Nepal, patterns of access to formal education have closely mirrored traditional caste-ethnic hierarchies, despite rapid educational expansion (Stash and Hannum, 2001). Likewise, Shavit and Kraus (1990) show that in Israel, from the 1940s to the 1970s, the effects of ethnicity declined in the transition from primary to secondary schooling but remained constant for subsequent educational transitions. In China, analysis of data through the early 1990s showed that considerable ethnic disparities persisted, with progress toward equity at the stage of primary entrance offset by increasing disparities at the junior high school stage (Hannum, 2002).

The effects of educational expansion on ethnic inequalities in occupational status are also mixed. In Brazil, Telles (1994) showed that industrialization and educational expansion were associated with decreased racial inequality across the full occupational distribution, but greater racial inequality in professional and white-collar sectors. In northwest China, rising ethnic disparities in occupational status in the 1980s could be explained by rising ethnic differences in education, despite dramatic improvements in access to schooling for both minorities and ethnic Chinese (Hannum and Xie, 1998). Similarly, in South Africa, despite educational expansion, educational disparities played an important role in maintaining race-based differences in occupational status in the 1980s (Mickelson et al., 2001) and 1990s (Treiman et al., 1996; Powell and Buchmann, 2002).

In short, while educational expansion offers new economic opportunities to both advantaged and disadvantaged groups, its implications for reducing inequality associated with socioeconomic status, gender, and ethnicity are decidedly mixed. While human capital disparities can be an important cause of occupational and income disparities across social groups, there are often important contextual causes, outside of education, as well. Further, as education becomes more central to occupations and incomes, those who are otherwise able but lack appropriate credentials are excluded from high wage jobs, and those who gain credentials later may have a harder time turning their credentials into high-status or high-wage employment. Yet, to maintain a balanced perspective on these

Figure 2: Under-5 Mortality Rates in 10 Years Preceding Survey by Mother's Educational Attainment, DHS Countries with 2000 or later Survey Dates

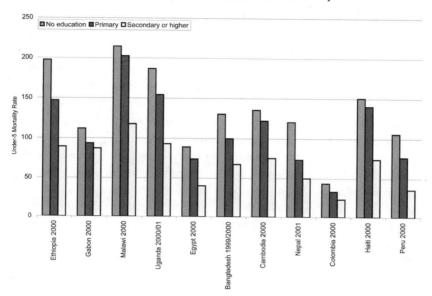

Source: Created from data in MEASURE DHS+.ND. "Demographic and Health Surveys Stat Compiler," http://www.measuredhs.com/data/indicators/, accessed June 2002.

findings, it is important to bear in mind that continued relative deprivation loses some of its significance if absolute deprivation is eased significantly by educational expansion.

EDUCATION, HEALTH, AND DEMOGRAPHIC CHANGE

Countries with better-educated citizens have healthier, slower-growing populations, as educated individuals make more informed health choices, live longer, and have healthier and fewer children.

Across many fields of research, there are important linkages between education, health, fertility decline, and, subsequently, slowing population growth. Beginning with the education-health relationship, recent cross-national research has shown that the education of children, especially girls, is associated with significantly longer life expectancies and lower death rates (Hadden and London, 1996; Buchmann, 1996; Schultz,

2002). According to the within-country, over-time estimates provided in Table 1, a 10 percent rise in primary enrollment ratios is associated with an average 0.9 year increase in life expectancy. A 10 percent increase in secondary enrollment ratios relates to an average one year increase in life expectancy; for tertiary enrollment ratios, the figure is 0.7 years (column 3). Similarly, increases in enrollment ratios at all levels are associated with significant reductions in infant mortality per 1,000 live births (column 5). Of course, because educational investments and investments in expanding health systems may occur concurrently, it is difficult to separate the influence of investments in education from those in health care.

Nonetheless, micro-level data suggest that, whether on its own or in conjunction with improving health care systems, education does have an impact. For example, Figure 2 graphs under-five mortality rates by mothers' education for countries with recent Demographic and Health Surveys (hereafter DHS) data (2000 or later).[12] Consistent with the aggregate findings just described, DHS data indicate that children of better-educated mothers have lower mortality rates. The relationship between maternal education and child health persists across empirical studies that employ controls for other dimensions of socio-economic status (see reviews in Jejeebhoy, 1996 and Schultz, 2002).

The mechanisms driving the relationship have yet to be fully understood. However, many studies suggest that, rather than specific health or scientific knowledge gleaned from the school curriculum, it is a general set of skills and orientations that enables educated women to obtain the knowledge or services that they need, or that empower them to act effectively.[13] Research suggests that women with more education, even when that education was of dubious quality, were better able to process information about health (LeVine et al., 2004). In Nepal, both survey-based regression estimates and ethnographic fieldwork point to the enhancing effect of women's literacy on concrete health-related skills, such as ability

---

[12] Armenia and Turkmenistan both had surveys in 2000, but are excluded here due to implausible data.

[13] The focus of research in the US is somewhat different, but also emphasizes empowerment. Recent research in sociology linking individuals' education and health in the United States emphasizes the key mediating roles played by psycho-social factors such as level of personal control, sense of agency, self-concept, and stress (Williams, 1990; Williams and Collins, 1995; House et al., 1994; Mirowsky and Ross, 1998; Ross and Mirowsky, 1999).

Figure 3: Immunization Rates by Mother's Educational Attainment, DHS Countries with 2000 or later Survey Dates

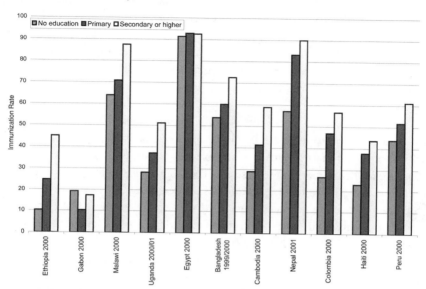

Source: Created from data in MEASURE DHS+.ND. "Demographic and Health Surveys Stat Compiler," http://www.measuredhs.com/data/indicators/, accessed June 2002.

to comprehend health messages in print and over the radio, to understand medical instructions, and to explain health problems in a comprehensible manner (Levine et al., 2004). Similarly, Glewwe's (1999c) research in Morocco highlights the importance of general literacy and numeracy skills acquired in school that enabled mothers to obtain health knowledge not taught in schools. Health knowledge, in turn, was an important predictor of child height-for-age.

Finally, other research suggests that, compared to mothers with no schooling, educated mothers were more informed about preventive health care practices such as immunizations, less fatalistic about disease, and more likely to adopt innovative behaviors related to children's health (Jejeebhoy, 1996; Cleland and van Ginnekin, 1988). One illustrative example comes through clearly in recent DHS surveys. Figure 3 shows that in most of the countries participating in the DHS since the year 2000, children of better-educated mothers have higher immunization rates.

Better health is an end in itself, but better health also carries implications for demographic change. Improved infant and child survival enables parents to plan their family size and, therefore, contributes to declines in fertility (e.g., London, 1992; Subbarao and Raney, 1995). Using data from 23 African countries, Kirk and Pillet (1998) show that countries with higher rates of female schooling and lower child mortality experienced substantial reductions in fertility and desired family size. Lower infant mortality may also extend the period of lactation and postpartum infecundability, thus reducing the time women are at risk of conceiving additional children.

Because access to non-familial employment expands with higher levels of education, better-educated women are more likely to delay or forego childbearing, in part because the opportunity costs associated with childbearing and childrearing increase and the time available for parenting declines.[14] Evidence from 20 countries participating in the World Fertility Survey indicated that female participation in the labor force was consistently associated with reduced fertility (Rodriguez and Cleland, 1981). While the authors acknowledge that data limitations precluded statistically convincing causal interpretations, they argue that in societies where fertility norms were rapidly changing, it is reasonable to interpret this pattern as evidence that participation in the labor market is perceived as an alternative to childbearing, and thus influences fertility decisions.

Education and employment may increase women's decision-making authority and receptiveness to innovation—changes that lead not only to greater utilization of health resources and improved child health, as described above, but also to increased family planning. For example, in nine Latin American countries, while fertility preferences varied little across education levels, achieved fertility levels varied substantially (Castro Martin and Juarez, 1995). In Vietnam, better-educated women (and women with better-educated husbands) were more likely to use contraceptives (Dang, 1995). In Sub-Saharan Africa, Lloyd et al. (2002) find that the onset of mass education, defined as the point at which 75 percent of 15–19 year-olds completed at least four grades of school, was linked to increased contraceptive practice.[15] Even the behavior of individ-

---

[14] Of course, as noted above, the degree to which the extension of educational opportunities to girls translates to gender equity in the labor market varies across societies.

[15] Note that innovative behavior is not always demographically favorable. Education can lead to unfavorable demographic outcomes such as the erosion of traditional norms regarding postpartum sexual abstinence or breast-feeding, thus

Figure 4: Average Number (Mean) Children Ever Born to Women Ages 40–49 by Educational Attainment, DHS Countries with 2000 or later Survey Dates

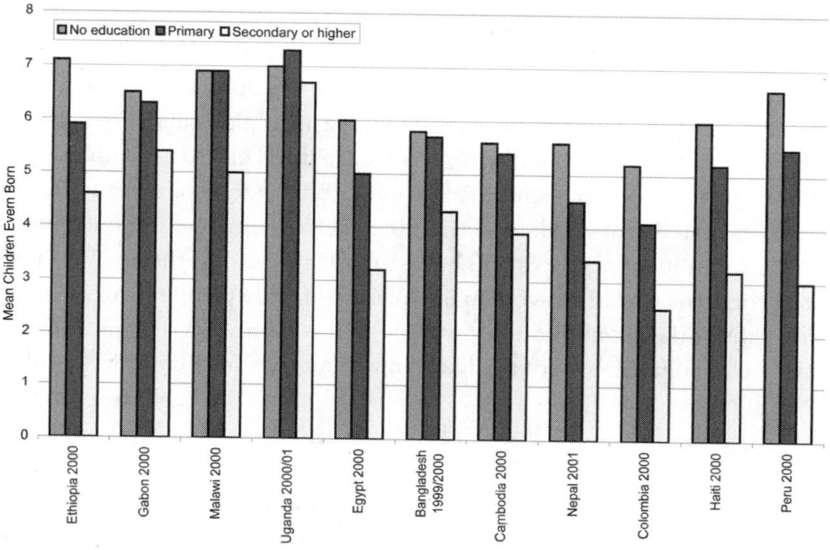

Source: Created from data in MEASURE DHS+.ND. "Demographic and Health Surveys Stat Compiler," http://www.measuredhs.com/data/indicators/, accessed June 2002.

uals who themselves do not attend school may be affected, as educational expansion speeds cultural change and creates new values (Caldwell, 1980). In Nepal, Axinn and Barber (2001) show that women's proximity to schools during childhood dramatically increased their contraceptive use in adulthood. Women who had lived near a school had 39 percent higher annual odds of adopting a permanent contraceptive method, given that they had not already done so.[16] This finding was largely independent

---

contributing to increased fertility (e.g., Oni, 1985). Further, some scholars have warned that education may also confer more liberal attitudes toward high-risk behaviors and thus indirectly increase the incidence of HIV/AIDS (Krull, 1994).

[16] This finding offers an example of the kind of potential "spillover" effect of schooling that makes assessing the full range of benefits of investing in education difficult to quantify. Psacharopoulos and Patrinos (2002: 3) review studies that attempt to quantify externalities of schooling, and characterize these studies as inconclusive (for a similar assessment, see Foster and Rosenzweig, 1995: 1176–1177).

of whether the woman subsequently attended school, her husband attended school, she lived near a school in adulthood, or she sent her children to school.

Finally, educational expansion reduces the economic benefits associated with childbearing, through increasing the pressures on parents to invest in their children and through reducing a child's availability for working inside and outside the home (see Caldwell, 1980). Axinn's (1993) analysis of microdemographic data from a rural community in Nepal indicated that children's schooling exerted a strong influence on parents' fertility preferences and behavior. Ogawa and Retherford (1993) cited concerns voiced by women in a national family planning survey in Japan about the economic and psychological costs involved in educating children as an indication of the likely importance of such considerations in fertility decisions.

Together, these influences lead to a consistent and regular association between education and fertility. Figure 4 shows the average number of children born to women ages 40–49 by educational attainment for recent DHS countries. These graphs show a regular pattern in which women with education, especially secondary and higher education, had substantially fewer children by the end of their childbearing years. The negative relationship between education and fertility is also evident in national aggregate data. Estimates in Table 1 indicate that a 10 percent expansion in primary gross enrollment ratios leads to an average reduction in the total fertility rate of 0.1 children; the corresponding increase in secondary enrollment ratios is associated with a reduction of 0.2 children (column 4).

Such relationships ultimately imply slowed population growth. Lutz and colleagues (1998) illustrate the significance of links between education and demographic change by including educational fertility and mortality differentials into population projections. Using data from Tunisia, Sudan, and Austria, the authors conclude that under the conditions of large age differentials in educational attainment and significant education-related fertility and mortality differentials that characterize many developing countries, the explicit inclusion of education in population projections significantly impacts population size. Their projections indicate that short-term investments in education will produce long-term effects on population size.

Beyond its effects through health and fertility, education also may slow population growth through encouraging a later age at marriage (Jejeebhoy, 1996). Later marriage typically increases the mean length of a generation, or the time a cohort takes to replace itself, and thus slows population growth even at constant fertility levels. Weinberger's (1987) analysis of World Fertility Survey data indicated that the mean age at marriage was four years later for women with at least seven years of education than for uneducated women. In a study of five Asian societies, Hirschman (1985) showed that women's schooling had a strong effect on the timing of family formation, with the largest effect at the secondary level.

Of course, as in the case of conventional rate-of-return studies, studies that do not account for factors that determine education itself may overstate the causal impact of education. For example, one study conducted in the Philippines compared three-stage least square and OLS estimates of the effect of schooling on age at marriage, and concluded that OLS estimates were inflated by 40 percent due to heterogeneity and the endogenous response of schooling to attributes valued in the marriage market (Boulier and Rosenzweig, 1984: 727). Even so, the authors raised doubts about whether the estimates were statistically significantly distinct, and substantively, the difference was small: a year of schooling in their OLS estimation increased age at marriage by 0.3 years, compared to 0.2 years in three-stage least squares estimates. While this example suggests caution about the precise magnitude of education effects on age at marriage in research that adopts simple model specifications, it supports the notion that education is associated with later age at marriage.

EDUCATION AND POLITICAL CHANGE

Countries with more educated populations are more democratic, as their citizens are able to make more informed political decisions.

In the debate over the "requisites" of political democratization, education is just one of many factors deemed important. Research has also examined the role of economic factors (economic development, income inequality, dependence on foreign aid, position in the world economy), and non-economic factors (ethnic heterogeneity, experience with colonialism, religious orientation) as they relate to the rise and stability of democratic institutions. While many scholars have emphasized the positive role of educational expansion in facilitating political development, there are fewer empirical analyses of the impact of educational expansion than there are analyses of these other potential factors (Benavot, 1996: 377).

Of the research that has investigated this issue, two theoretical perspectives offer somewhat different views on the processes linking education with democratization. The political modernization perspective sees a
strong causal linkage between an educated citizenry and democracy.
Schools produce "modern" individuals who have a greater desire and
ability to participate in political decisions and national concerns (Inkeles
and Smith, 1974). Indeed, early cross-national studies (Lipset, 1963;
Cutright, 1969) found strong correlations between mass literacy and the
presence of democratic political systems, as well as between the expansion
of primary education and degree of political development. In their survey
of six countries, Inkeles and Smith (1974) showed that people with more
schooling tended to be more individualistic, more informed and activist-
oriented, and less parochial than those with little education.

Of course, one weakness of these studies was that their emphasis on
correlations said little about the issue of causality. Later studies that
approximated a longitudinal design through the use of panel data
reported more ambiguous results. According to the political modernization perspective, the "aggregate effects of mass education expansion on
democracy are largely achieved via education's socializing influences on
individuals" (Benavot, 1996: 384). Moreover, this view assumes that
education has linear effects on individuals that are beneficial for the
development and retention of democracy (Kamens, 1988).

The institutional perspective differs on both fronts. First, in contrast
to modernization arguments, the institutional perspective focuses on the
macro-level impact of educational expansion. Educational systems are
part of a broader process in the social and political construction of society, in which highly institutionalized social roles and categories are created and legitimated (Benavot, 1996: 385). Thus, educational expansion
affects the political development of society not only through its impact
on individuals, but through the wider meanings attributed to given levels
of educational attainment. Meyer (1977) refers to this as the "charter-
ing" role of education, and suggests that the organization of education
may have as important an effect on political development as the expansion of education. Moreover, whether or not education is beneficial for
the development and retention of democracy depends on how education
and educated elites are incorporated into the political system of a nation.
In societies where graduates of tertiary education become representatives
of the nation state, the result may be a decline in the independent author-

ity of other collectives (Kamens, 1988: 119). For example, Ramirez et al. (1973) found that the level of political incorporation of higher education had statistically significant negative effects on the introduction and retention of democracy between 1950 and 1968.

These perspectives also differ in their views regarding how expansion of different levels of education should influence political development. Political modernization views all levels of schooling as beneficial for the building of democracy, but emphasizes mass schooling—primary and secondary levels—as most important. For reasons explained above, institutionalists emphasize the importance of tertiary education.

The results presented in Table 1 do not resolve this debate, but they indicate a positive relationship between educational and democracy. The final two columns of Table 1 show regressions of two commonly used scales, political rights and civil liberties, taken from Freedom House scores (Freedom House, Inc., 2000). Both primary and tertiary enrollment ratios have significant, positive effects on both indicators of democracy, with much larger effects at the tertiary level.

Benavot (1996) provided a more sophisticated examination of the consequences of educational expansion at primary, secondary and tertiary levels for four measures of democracy prevalent in the literature.[17] He investigated the effect of educational expansion over two periods (1965–80 and 1980–88), controlling for economic development, colonial heritage, date of independence, ethnic homogeneity, and region, and found no impact of educational expansion on political democracy in the early period. In the 1980–88 period, educational expansion at the tertiary

---

[17] The four measures capture slightly different elements of democracy, but are highly correlated. The index designed by Ken Bollen (1980) captures the extent of political liberties and popular sovereignty and is considered highly reliable and valid cross-nationally. The measure designed by Zehra Arat (1991) captures 4 dimensions of democracy: degree of popular participation in political decision making, the lack of restrictiveness in the franchise, the degree of competitiveness in the political system, and the extent of civil liberties. A third measure, developed by Tatu Vanhanen (1990), combines a measure of political competition (the smaller parties' share of votes in either parliamentary or presidential elections) and the degree of public participation (the percentage of the population that voted). The fourth measure of democracy is based on an annual cross-national survey coordinated by Raymond Gastile (1987) and sponsored by the Freedom House. In this measure each nation is ranked on two seven-point scales according to the extent to which political rights and civil liberties are respected.

level had strong positive effects on both measures of political democracy available for that time period, while primary and secondary expansion had negligible effects on the same measures. Benavot contends that the contrast of these results with earlier studies (that find positive effects of lower levels of schooling on democracy) is due to the superior methods and data used in his study.

At the individual level, abundant research from a wide range of contexts shows a strong relationship between education and political participation (Almond and Verba, 1963; Inglehart, 1977; Nie et al., 1979). Most of this research focuses on already democratic societies where citizens have rights to participate in political processes through voting and opposition or protest. Studies show that educated citizens are more likely to vote (Nie et al., 1996) and voice more tolerant attitudes and democratic values.[18] The assumption is that schools are responsible for transmitting these outlooks, but exactly how schools promote these outlooks is unclear (Chabott and Ramirez, 2000). Some arguments emphasize curriculum (Torney et al., 1976); others stress the institutional influence of the school (Meyer, 1977; Kamens, 1988).

Several caveats regarding research on the relationship between education and democracy are noteworthy. First, many of the studies that attempt to measure individual political views and values use paper and pencil tests to determine democratic orientations. It is possible that more educated individuals are better able to guess the "appropriate" answers to questions about political norms. This raises questions about the nature of the relationship between education and political orientations. Second, the rapid expansion of education in the absence of growth in labor market opportunities may create a crash in returns to schooling. Certainly, the presence of educated, unemployed youth may have a negative impact on political stability (Huntington, 1968; Lipset, 1985).

Finally, it is very important to consider the content of education. Cuba and pre-reform-era China are important examples of socialist countries where periods of rapid expansion of "revolutionary" schooling were not characterized by obvious shifts toward political democratization, as conventionally defined in the West. Similarly, high levels of state control

---

[18] The empirical evidence regarding the relationship between education and tolerance is mixed. For example, Weil (1985) shows that the relationship between individual level of education and degree of political tolerances varies across countries.

over tertiary education may undermine the support of democratic political institutions because, in such cases, graduates are more likely to become state civil servants and representatives of the nation state.

CONCLUSION

This paper has discussed the empirical foundations for widely held expectations about the consequences of educational expansion. We find that two of the assumptions listed at the outset of this paper are well supported by empirical research. First and most strikingly, substantial research spanning disciplinary boundaries attests to the health and demographic benefits of improved educational composition: Countries with better-educated citizens indeed have healthier populations, as educated individuals make more informed health choices, live longer, and have healthier children. The populations of countries with more educated citizens are likely to grow more slowly, as educated people tend to marry later and have fewer children. Second, educational opportunities enhance, but do not necessarily ensure, the future economic security of the world's most vulnerable children. Consistent results spanning many years and several social science disciplines guided by diverse research paradigms suggest that these benefits can be reasonably anticipated from further educational expansion.

In other areas, empirical support for the assumed benefits of education is more ambiguous. Considerable controversy surrounds the effects of educational expansion on national economic development. Many empirical studies find a positive relationship, but other studies cast doubt on it. Reverse causality, time frame limitations and measurement error have often been blamed for the disparate results. In short, statements of the benefits of educational expansion for economic growth are still based on mixed evidence, as research has not established a consensus regarding findings or the best ways to address complex conceptual, methodological, and data challenges.

For other hypothesized consequences, important lines of research in the fields of sociology and political science contradict the rhetoric common in development organizations. For example, numerous empirical studies in sociology have indicated that while educational expansion tends to offer absolute benefits to disadvantaged groups, it is less likely to erode social inequalities rapidly, except perhaps for inequalities associated with gender. Inequalities associated with economic origins or ethnicity often prove resistant to educational expansion, as educational access often expands faster for advantaged than disadvantaged groups. In short, decades of empirical research in social stratification and mobility offer evidence that educational expansion does not necessarily narrow social inequalities between advantaged and disadvantaged groups.

Similarly, there is considerable controversy surrounding the effects of educational expansion on the democratization of societies, though expansions of primary and secondary education are likely to improve the informed citizenship of individuals. Obvious concerns with this line of research include measurement issues related to the challenge of developing valid and reliable measures of democratization. An additional concern is that democratization, perhaps more so than other outcomes, may hinge directly on the hard-to-measure content of education. This possibility is suggested in studies that find larger effects of tertiary education than lower levels of education. The consequences of expanding basic and secondary education for political democratization remain an empirical question.

In areas where research is inconclusive or contradictory, four general points are worth considering. First, much of the research discussed above underscores the importance of a long-term perspective. The observed relationship between educational expansion and economic growth is stronger over longer time periods (Krueger and Lindahl, 2000). Studies also show echo-effects of parental education for children's human capital (e.g., Behrman et al., 1999; LeVine et al., 2001), suggesting future economic payoffs for current expansions. Lutz et al. (1998) emphasize that ambiguities in the research on short-term national-level benefits of education may be attributable, in part, to the lag time between improving enrollments of children and changes in the overall human capital stock of the population. As data for longer time periods become available, the ambiguities of current research may be clarified with the improved ability to incorporate appropriate time lags into such studies.

Second, the expansion of different levels of education seems to have different consequences. For example, tertiary enrollments in particular appear to be linked significantly to democratization and technological change, while educational expansion through the secondary level appears to be extremely important for reaping many health and demographic benefits. These differences may be linked to qualitative differences in what individuals learn at these different stages in education.

Third, the "quality" of education, the organizational structures of education, linkages between education and the labor market, and the specific content of education all matter for education's impacts on various outcomes. While this point seems obvious, at present, widely available measures of education systems and schools are insufficient for revealing critical mechanisms that link education to various outcomes. Hence, with the exception of rate-of-return studies on school quality, little research incorporates these nontrivial elements of education into empirical strategies. There is an urgent need to develop data collection strategies that allow more detailed empirical descriptions of what education means in different national contexts, and thus enable investigations of the attributes of education that facilitate outcomes across a variety of realms.

This point is as applicable to data collected from individuals as it is to data collected about schools and school systems. Our understanding of the potential consequences of schooling could be much improved by knowing more about those aspects of individuals' skills that are enhanced by education. The concept of human capital stock has occupied a central role in research on educational expansion, but few researchers have tried to develop direct measures of the aspects of human capital thought to be most important. One way that research can make progress in this direction is by incorporating new literacy and life-skills assessments into studies of the consequences of education. The recent International Adult Literacy Survey (IALS) initiative (OECD and HRDC, 1997; OECD, 2000) is an important step toward developing international standards for measuring productivity-related skills. A parallel initiative sponsored by UNESCO explores how adult literacy, numeracy, and life skills can be best measured in developing countries.[19] The measures being developed by these initiatives seem particularly suited to the task of uncovering the links between education, skills, and the positive social changes of interest to development agencies. Combined with appropriate survey data, such measures would allow direct investigation of the competencies acquired in the school system, and their consequences for economic welfare, health and family change, and citizenship.

A final contributor to contradictory findings, and an important caveat even in areas where consistent results have emerged, is the point that

---

[19] For a summary of key guidelines emerging from the UNESCO project, see ILI and UNESCO (1999).

educational impacts are sensitive to context. The human capital perspective implicit in much of the research on educational investments is inherently individualistic, assuming that education will offer the same enabling capacities to individuals regardless of the contexts in which they function. This perspective often fails to acknowledge that within the global economy, within nations, within local communities, and within school systems, social structures shape and constrain the impact of expanding education. For example, effects of educational expansion on economic development may be conditioned by national political stability or by a nation's position in the global trade system. Within countries, the economic benefits to those educated later may be smaller than the benefits to those educated earlier, because as a national population's educational composition improves, the value of a given educational credential in the labor market declines. As education expands to reach individuals from increasingly disadvantaged or isolated groups, these individuals may have a harder time than others turning credentials into high-status, high-wage employment. The health benefits of education may be more evident in societies where the sanitation infrastructure is weak, or less evident in societies with universal access to health care. These examples emphasize that educational expansion should be viewed as one of many important elements in economic and social development. Reasonable forecasts of the consequences of further expansions intended to reach the world's most disadvantaged populations need to consider the diverse social contexts in which these expansions will occur.

References

Almond, G., and S. Verba. 1963. *The Civic Culture*. NJ: Princeton University Press.

Andersen, L. E. 2000. "How is Social Mobility Related to Education Policy in Latin America? A Schooling Gap Regression Analysis." La Paz, Bolivia: Instituto de Investigaciones Socio-Económicas (IISEC), Universidad Católica Boliviana.

Arat, Z. 1991. *Democracy and Human Rights in Developing Countries*. Boulder: Lynne Reinner.

Axinn, W. G. 1993. "The Effects of Children's Schooling on Fertility Limitation." *Population Studies* 47: 481–93.

Axinn, W. G., and J. S. Barber. 2001. "Mass Education and Fertility Transition." *American Sociological Review* 66 (4): 481–505.

Bae, Y., S. Choy, C. Geddes, J. Sable, and T. Snyder. 2000. *Trends in Educational Equity of Girls and Women*. Washington, DC: National Center for Education Statistics.

Barro, R. J. 1991. "Economic Growth in a Cross-Section of Countries." *Quarterly Journal of Economics* 106: 407–443.

Becker, G. S. 1967. "Human Capital and the Personal Distribution of Income: An Analytical Approach." University of Michigan Woytinsky Lecture, Ann Arbor. Republished, pp. 94–117 in *Human Capital*, 2nd edition, Gary S. Becker, Cambridge, MA: NBER, 1975.

Behrman, J. R. and N. Birdsall. 1983. "The Quality of Schooling: Quantity Alone is Misleading." *American Economic Review* 73: 928–46.

Behrman, J. R., N. Birdsall, and R. Kaplan. 1996. "The Quality of Schooling and Labor Market Outcomes in Brazil: Some Further Explorations." Pp. 245–66 in *Opportunity Foregone: Education in Brazil*, ed. Nancy Birdsall and Richard Sabot. Baltimore: Johns Hopkins.

Behrman, J. R., Foster, A. D., Rosenzweig, M. R., and Vashishtha, P. 1999. "Women's Schooling, Home Teaching, and Economic Growth." *The Journal of Political Economy* 107: 682–714.

Behrman, J. R., and Rosenzweig, M. R. 2002. "Does Increasing Women's Schooling Raise the Schooling of the Next Generation?" *American Economic Review* 92: 323–34.

Benavot, A. 1996. "Education and Political Democratization: Cross-National and Longitudinal Findings." *Comparative Education Review* 40: 377–403.

Bills, D. B., and A. O. Haller. 1984. "Socio-economic Development and Social Stratification: Reassessing the Brazilian Case." *Journal of Developing Areas* 19: 59–70.

Blau, P. M., and O. D. Duncan. 1967. *The American Occupational Structure*. New York: Wiley.

Bollen, K. 1980. "Issues in the Comparative Measurement of Political Democracy." *American Sociological Review* 45: 370–90.

Boulier, B. L. and M. R. Rosenzweig. 1984. "Schooling, Search and Spouse Selection: Testing Economic Theories of Marriage and Household Behavior." *Journal of Political Economy* 92 (4) (August): 712–732.

Brinton, M. C., Y. J. Lee, and W. Parish. 1995. "Married Women's Employment in Rapidly Industrializing Societies: Examples from East Asia." *American Journal of Sociology* 100: 1099–132.

Buchmann, C. 1996. "The Debt Crisis, Structural Adjustment and Women's Education: Implications for Status and Social Development." *International Journal of Comparative Sociology* 37: 5–30.

Caldwell, J. C. 1980. "Mass Education as a Determinant of the Timing of Fertility Decline." *Population and Development Review* 6: 225–55.

Cameron, L. A., J. M. Dowling, and C. Worswick. 2001. "Education and Labor Market Participation of Women in Asia: Evidence from Five Countries." *Economic Development and Cultural Change* 49: 460–77.

Card, D., and A. B. Krueger. 1992. "Does School Quality Matter? Returns to Education and the Characteristics of Public Schools in the United States." *Journal of Political Economy* 100: 1–40.

Castro Martin, T., and F. Juarez. 1995. "The Impact of Women's Education on Fertility in Latin America: Searching for Explanations." *International Family Planning Perspectives* 21: 52–57, 80.

Chabott, C., and F. O. Ramirez. 2000. "Development and Education." Pp. 163–87 in *Handbook of the Sociology of Education*, ed. Maureen Hallinan. New York: Kluwer Academic.

Cleland, J., and J. van Ginnekin. 1988. "Maternal Education and Child Survival in Developing Countries: The Search for Pathways of Influence." *Social Science and Medicine* 27: 1357–68.

Cutright, P. 1969. "National Political Development: Measurement and Analysis." Pp. 367–83 in *Scientific Investigations in Comparative Education*, ed. Max Eckstein and Harold Noah. New York: MacMillan.

Dang, A. 1995. "Differentials in Contraceptive Use and Method Choice in Vietnam." *International Family Planning Perspectives* 21: 2–5.

Demetriades, E. L., and G. Psacharopoulos. 1987. "Educational Expansion and the Returns to Education: Evidence from Cyprus." *International Labor Review* 126: 597–603.

Duflo, E. n.d. "Schooling and Labor Market Consequences of School Construction of Indonesia: Evidence from an Unusual Policy Experiment."

Eurostat. 2002. *The Life of Women and Men in Europe: A Statistical Portrait.* Luxembourg: Eurostat.

Foster, A. D., and M. R. Rosenzweig. 1995. "Learning by Doing and Learning from Others: Human Capital and Technical Change in Agriculture." *Journal of Political Economy* 103: 1176–1209.

Freedom House, Inc. 2000. "Annual Survey of Freedom Country Scores 1972–73 to 1999–00." http://www.freedomhouse.org/ratings/index.htm, accessed June 2002.

Gastile, R. 1987. *Freedom in the World: Political Rights and Civil Liberties, 1986–1987.* New York: Greenwood.

Glewwe, P. 1999a. *The Economics of School Quality Investments in Developing Countries: An Empirical Study of Ghana.* New York: St. Martin's.

———. 1999b. "School Quality, Student Achievement, and Fertility in Developing Countries." Pp. 105–37 in *Critical Perspectives on Schooling and Fertility in the Developing World*, ed. Caroline H. Bledsoe et al. Washington, DC: National Academy Press.

———. 1999c. "Why does Mother's Schooling Raise Child Health in Developing Countries? Evidence from Morocco." *The Journal of Human Resources* 34: 124–59.

Glomm, G., and B. Ravikumar. 1992. "Public versus Private Investment in Human Capital: Endogenous Growth and Income Inequality." *Journal of Political Economy* 100: 818–34.

Hadden, K., and B. London. 1996. "Educating Girls in the Third World: the Demographic, Basic Needs and Economic Benefits." *International Journal of Comparative Sociology* 37: 31–46.

Halsey, A. H., A. F. Heath, and J. M. Ridge. 1980. "Chapter 11, Retrospect and Prospect." Pp. 194–219 in *Origins and Destinations: Family, Class, and Education in Modern Britain*. Oxford: Clarendon Press.

Hannum, E. 2002. "Ethnic Differences in Basic Education in Reform-Era Rural China." *Demography* 39 (1): 95–117.

Hannum, E., and Y. Xie. 1998. "Ethnic Stratification in Northwest China: Occupational Differences between Han Chinese and National Minorities in Xinjiang, 1982–1990." *Demography* 35: 323–33.

Hirschman, C. 1985. "Premarital Socioeconomic Roles and the Timing of Family Formation: A Comparative Study of Five Asian Societies." *Demography* 22: 35–59.

Holsinger, D. B. 1975. "Education and the Occupational Attainment Process in Brazil." *Comparative Education Review* 19: 267–75.

House, J. S., J. M. Lepkowski, A. M. Kinney, R. P. Mero, R. C. Kessler, and A. R. Herzog. 1994. "The Social Stratification of Aging and Health." *Journal of Health and Social Behavior* 35: 213–34.

Hout, M., A. E. Raftery, and E. O. Bell. 1993. "Making the Grade: Educational Stratification in the United States, 1925–1989." Pp. 25–49 in *Persistent Inequality: Changing Educational Attainment in Thirteen Countries*, ed. Y. Shavit and H.P. Blossfeld. Boulder, CO: Westview.

Huntington, S. 1968. *Political Order in Changing Societies*. New Haven: Yale University.

Inglehart, R. 1977. *The Silent Revolution*. Princeton: Princeton University.

Inkeles, A., and D. Smith. 1974. *Becoming Modern*. Cambridge MA: Harvard University.

International Literacy Institute (ILI) and UNESCO. 1999. *Basic Learning Competencies Among the Youth Population in Developing Countries: A Survey Design and Analytical Framework*, Final Report on Expert Workshop for EFA 2000 (Philadelphia: ILI).

Jejeebhoy, S. 1996. "Women's Education, Autonomy, and Reproductive Behavior: Assessing What We Have Learned. Paper prepared for the conference on The Status of Women and Demographic Change: Assessing What We Have Learned," sponsored by the Rockefeller Foundation and the East-West Center.

Kamens, D. 1988. "Education and Democracy: A Comparative Institutional Analysis." *Sociology of Education* 61: 114–27.

Kelley, J., and M. L. Perlman. 1971. "Social Mobility in Toro: Some Preliminary Results from Western Uganda." *Economic Development and Cultural Change* 19: 204–21.

Khan, M. H. 2000. "Rural Poverty in Developing Countries—Issues and Policies." IMF Working Paper no. WP/00/78. Washington DC: International Monetary Fund, p. 6.

King, E. M., and M. A. Hill. 1993. *Women's Education in Developing Countries: Barriers, Benefits, and Policies.* Baltimore, Maryland: The Johns Hopkins University Press.

Kirk, D., and B. Pillet. 1998. "Fertility Levels, Trends, and Differentials in Sub-Saharan Africa in the 1980s and 1990s." *Studies in Family Planning* 29: 1–22.

Knodel, J., and G. Jones. 1996. "Post-Cairo Population Policy: Does Promoting Girls' Schooling Miss the Mark?" *Population and Development Review* 22: 683–702.

Krueger, A. B., and M. Lindahl. 2000. "Education for Growth: Why and For Whom?" NBER Working Paper no. 7591.

Krull, C. D. 1994. "Level of Education, Sexual Promiscuity, and AIDS." *Alberta Journal of Educational Research* 40: 7–20.

Lam, D., and R. F. Schoeni. 1993. "Effects of Family Background on Earnings and Returns to Schooling: Evidence from Brazil." *Journal of Political Economy* 101: 710–41.

Levine, R. 2004. "Better Health through More Education: Getting to Win-Win Policy." Working paper. American Academy of Arts and Sciences, Cambridge, MA.

Levine, R., and D. Renelt. 1992. "A Sensitivity Analysis of Cross-Country Growth Regressions." *American Economic Review* 82: 942–963.

LeVine, R. A., S. E. LeVine, M. L. Rowe, and B. Schnell-Anzola. 2004. "Maternal Literacy and Health Behavior: A Nepalese Case Study." *Social Science and Medicine* 58: 863–877.

LeVine, R. A., S. E. LeVine, and B. Schnell. 2001. "Improve the Women: Mass Schooling, Female Literacy, and Worldwide Social Change." *Harvard Education Review* 71: 1–50.

LeVine, R. A., S. E. LeVine, A. Richman, F. M. T. Uribe, C. S. Correa, and P. M. Miller. 1991. "Women's Schooling and Child Care in the Demographic Transition: A Mexican Case Study." *Population and Development Review* 17: 459–496.

Lipset, S. M. 1963. *The First New Nation.* NY: Doubleday.

———. 1985. *Consensus and Conflict: Essays in Political Sociology.* New Brunswick, NJ: Transaction.

Lloyd, C., C. Kaufman, and P. Hewett. 2002. "The Spread of Primary Schooling in Sub-Saharan Africa: Implications for Fertility Change." *Population and Development Review* 26: 483–515.

London, B. 1992. "School-Enrollment Rates and Trends, Gender, and Fertility: A Cross-National Analysis." *Sociology of Education* 65: 306–16.

Lopez, R., and A. Valdez. 2000. "Fighting Rural Poverty in Latin America: New Evidence of the Effects of Education, Demographics, and Access to Land." *Economic Development and Cultural Change* 49: 197–211.

Lutz, W., A. Goujon, and G. Doblhammer-Reiter. 1998. "Demographic Dimensions in Forecasting: Adding Education to Age and Sex." Pp. 42–58 in *Frontiers of Population Forecasting,* ed. W. Lutz, J. W. Vaupel and D. A. Ahlburg, *Population and Development Review* (Supplement to Volume 24).

Mare, R. 1981. "Change and Stability in Educational Stratification." *American Sociological Review* 46: 72–87.

MEASURE DHS+. ND. Demographic and Health Surveys Stat Compiler, http://www.measuredhs.com/data/indicators/, accessed June 2002.

Meyer, J. W. 1977. "The Effects of Education as an Institution." *American Journal of Sociology* 63: 55–77.

Mickelson, R., M. Nkomo, and S. Smith. 2001. "Education, Ethnicity, Gender and Social Transformation in Israel and South Africa." *Comparative Education Review* 45: 1–28.

Mirowsky, J., and C. Ross. 1998. "Education, Personal Control, Lifestyle and Health: A Human Capital Hypothesis." *Research on Aging* 20: 415–49.

Moll, P. G. 1996. "The Collapse of Primary Schooling Returns in South Africa 1960–90." *Oxford Bulletin of Economics and Statistics* 58: 185–209.

Mukweso, M., G. J. Papgiannis, and S. Milton. 1984. "Education and Occupational Attainment from Generation to Generation: the Case of Zaire." *Comparative Education Review* 28: 52–68.

Nie, N. H., J. Junn, and K. Stehlick-Barry. 1996. *Education and Democratic Citizenship in America.* Chicago: University of Chicago Press.

Nie, N. H., S. Verba, and J. Petocik. 1979. *The Changing American Voter*. Cambridge, MA: Harvard University Press.

Nielsen, H. S., and N. Westergard-Nielsen. 2001. "Returns to Schooling in Less Developed Countries: New Evidence from Zambia." *Economic Development and Cultural Change* 49: 365–94.

Ogawa, N., and R. D. Retherford. 1993. "The Resumption of Fertility Decline in Japan: 1973–92." *Population and Development Review* 19: 703–41.

Oni, G. A. 1985. "Effects of Women's Education on Postpartum Practices and Fertility in Urban Nigeria." *Studies in Family Planning* 16: 321–31.

Organization for Economic Co-Operation and Development (OECD). 2000. "Literacy in the Information Age: Final Report of the International Adult Literacy Project." Paris: OECD.

OECD and Human Resources Development Canada (HRDC) 1997. *Literacy Skills for the Knowledge Society*. Paris: OECD.

Petrakis, P.E., and D. Stamakis. 2002. "Growth and Education Levels: A Comparative Analysis." *Economics of Education Review* 21: 513–521.

Piazza, A., J. Li, G. Su, T. McKinley, E. Cheng, C. Saint-Pierre, T. Sicular, B. Trangmar, and R. Weller. 2001. *China: Overcoming Rural Poverty*. World Bank Country Study no. 22137. Washington, DC: World Bank.

Poot, J. 2000. "A Synthesis of Empirical Research on the Impact of Government on Long-Run Growth." *Growth and Change* 31: 516–47.

Powell, T. A., and C. Buchmann. 2002. "Racial Inequality of Occupational Status in South Africa: The Effect of Local Opportunity Structures on Occupational Outcomes." Paper presented at the International Sociological Association Research Committee on Stratification (RC28) Conference, Oxford, U.K. April.

Pritchett, L. 1996. "Where has All the Education Gone?" World Bank Policy Research Working Paper no. 1581. Washington DC: World Bank.

Psacharopoulos, G., and Patrinos, H. 2002. "Returns to Investment in Education: A Further Update." World Bank Policy Research Working Paper 2881. (September). Washington, D.C.: World Bank.

Psacharopoulos, G., and E. Velez. 1992. "Schooling, Ability, and Earnings in Colombia, 1988." *Economic Development and Cultural Change* 40: 629–44.

Raftery, A. E., and M. Hout. 1993. "Maximally Maintained Inequality: Expansion, Reform and Opportunity in Irish Education, 1921–1975." *Sociology of Education* 66: 41–62.

Ramirez, F., R. Rubinson, and J. Meyer. 1973. "National Educational Expansion and Political Development: Causal Interrelationships, 1950–1970." Paper presented at the SEADAG Seminar on Education and National Development, Singapore.

Rodríguez, F., and E. J. Wilson. 2000. "Are Poor Countries Losing the Information Revolution?" InfoDev Working Paper, http://www.infodev.org/library/working.htm, accessed February 2002.

Rodriguez, G., and J. Cleland. 1981. "The Effects of Socioeconomic Characteristics on Fertility in 20 Countries." *International Family Planning Perspectives* 7 (3): 93–101.

Rosenzweig, Mark R. 1995. "Why are there Returns to Schooling?" *American Economic Review* 85 (2) (May): 153–158.

Ross, C., and J. Mirowsky. 1999. "Refining the Relationship Between Education and Health: The Effects of Quantity, Credential, and Selectivity." *Demography* 36 (4): 445–460.

Schultz, T. P. 1993. "Returns to Women's Education." In *Women's Education in Developing Countries: Barriers, Benefits, and Policies*, ed. Elizabeth M. King and M. A. Hill. Baltimore, MD: The Johns Hopkins University Press.

———. 2002. "Why Governments Should Invest More to Educate Girls." *World Development* 30: 207–225.

Schultz, T. W. 1975. "The Value of the Ability to Deal with Disequilibria." *Journal of Economic Literature* 13 (3): 827–846.

Shavit, Y., and H. P. Blossfeld. 1993. *Persistent Inequality: Changing Educational Attainment in Thirteen Countries*. Boulder, CO: Westview.

Shavit, Y., and V. Kraus. 1990. "Educational Transitions in Israel: A Test of the Industrialization and Credentialism Hypotheses." *Sociology of Education* 63: 133–41.

Shavit, Y., and W. Mueller. 1998. *From School to Work: A Comparative Study of Educational Qualifications and Occupational Destinations*. New York: Oxford University Press.

Smith, H. L., and P. L. Cheung. 1986. "Trends in the Effects of Family Background on Educational Attainment in the Philippines." *American Journal of Sociology* 9: 1387–408.

Stash, S., and E. Hannum. 2001. "Who Goes to School? Educational Stratification by Gender, Caste and Ethnicity in Nepal." *Comparative Education Review* 45: 354–378.

Subbarao, K., and L. Raney. 1995. "Social Gains from Female Education: A Cross-National Study." *Economic Development and Cultural Change* 44: 105–128.

Sylwester, K. 2000. "Income Inequality, Education Expenditures, and Growth." *Journal of Development Economics* 63: 379–398.

———. 2002. "Can Educational Expenditures Reduce Income Inequality?" *Economics of Education Review* 21: 43–52.

Telles, E. 1994. "Industrialization and Racial Inequality in Employment: The Brazilian Example." *American Sociological Review* 59: 46–63.

Torney, J., A. M. Oppenheim, and R. F. Farnen. 1976. *Civic Education in Ten Countries: An Empirical Study.* New York: Wiley.

Treiman, D. J. 1970. Industrialization and Social Stratification. Pp. 207–34 in *Social Stratification: Research and Theory for the 1970s,* ed. E.O. Laumann. Indianapolis: Bobbs-Merrill.

Treiman, D. J., M. McKeever, and E. M. Fodor. 1996. "Racial Differences in Occupational Status and Income in South Africa, 1980 and 1991." *Demography* 33: 111–32.

United Nations. 2002. "United Nations Common Database," http://unstats.un.org, accessed July 2002.

United Nations Children's Fund (UNICEF). 1995. "UNICEF Strategies in Basic Education." http://www.unicef.org/programme/education/board95.htm, accessed August 2002.

United Nations Educational, Scientific and Cultural Organization (UNESCO). 2002. "Global Campaign For Education Briefing Paper For The Johannesburg World Summit, 2002." http://www.unesco.org/education/efa/news_en/26.08.02_globalcampaign.shtml, accessed August 2002.

United States Agency for International Development (USAID). 2000. "Global Education Database (GED) 2000 Edition," http://www.usaid.gov/educ_training/ged.html, accessed June 2002.

Vanhanen, T. 1990. *The Process of Democratization.* New York: Crane Russak.

Walters, P. B. 2000. "The Limits of Growth: School Expansion and School Reform in Historical Perspective." Pp. 163–87 in *Handbook of the Sociology of Education,* ed. Maureen Hallinan. New York: Kluwer Academic.

Weil, F. 1985. "The Variable Effect of Education on Liberal Attitudes: A Comparative Historical Analysis of Anti-Semitism Using Public Opinion Survey Data." *American Sociological Review* 50: 458–75.

Weinberger, M. B. 1987. "The Relationship between Women's Education and Fertility: Selected Findings from the World Fertility Surveys." *International Family Planning Perspectives* 13: 35–46.

Welch, Finis. 1970. "Education in Production." *Journal of Political Economy* 78: 35–59.

Williams, D. R. 1990. "Socio-Economic Differentials in Health: Review and Redirection." *Social Psychology Quarterly* 53: 81–99.

Williams, D. R., and C. Collins. 1995. "US Socioeconomic and Racial Differences in Health: Patterns and Explanations." *Annual Review of Sociology* 21: 349–86.

World Bank. 1999. *Education Sector Strategy.* http://www1.worldbank.org/education/strategy.asp.

———. 2002a. *Achieving Education for All by 2015: Simulation Results for 47 Low-Income Countries.* http://www1.worldbank.org/education/pdf/EFA%20 Complete%20Draft.pdf, accessed August 2002.

———. 2002b. *Education and Development.* http://www1.worldbank.org/education/pdf/EducationBrochure.pdf, accessed August 2002.

Zhang, Junsen and Yaohui Zhao. 2006. "Rising Schooling Returns in Urban China." *Education and Reform in China*, ed. Emily Hannum and Albert Park. London: Routledge (Forthcoming).

CHAPTER 10

Education, Health, and Development[*]

DAVID E. BLOOM

The separate roles of education and health in promoting human development have been extensively studied and discussed. As the impressive social and economic performance of East Asian tigers seems to show, strong education and health systems are vital to economic growth and prosperity (Asian Development Bank, 1997; World Bank, 1993). Moreover, the Millennium Development Goals adopted by member states of the United Nations in September 2000 are evidence of an international consensus regarding human development: five of the eight goals relate to education or health. Recent research that links education and health suggests novel ways to enhance development policy by taking advantage of the ways in which the two interact.

Development is a complex process involving multiple interactions among different components. In addition to health and education, the most important drivers of development include governance and other political factors, geography and climate, cultural and historical legacies, a careful openness to trade and foreign investment, labor policies that promote productive employment, good macroeconomic management, some protection against the effects of environmental shocks, overall economic orientation, and the actions of other countries and international organizations.

The interactions among these factors carry important implications for our understanding of the development process as well as for policy. It is now clear that increased access to education, although of great importance, is by itself no magic bullet. Its positive effects on development may

---

[*] This chapter is a revised, updated, and expanded version of an article published earlier as the introduction to a special issue of *Comparative Education Review* 49 (4) November 2005.

be limited by a lack of job opportunities that require high-level skills and therefore enable people to use education to their economic advantage. And, as healthy but poor Cuba and the state of Kerala in India show, the impacts of good health on development are limited without concomitant advances in other areas.

The connections between education and health and their impacts on development have received relatively little attention.[1] This paper discusses these connections and briefly outlines some central issues. The first part of the paper discusses why interactions between health and education are important. The second part describes how the links might work, looking at conceptual channels between them. Part three reviews the literature to establish whether there is evidence for these channels and concludes that there is.

WHY DO INTERACTIONS MATTER?

Better education and better health are important goals in themselves. Each can improve an individual's quality of life and his or her impact on others. There is an extensive literature on the importance of education and health as indicators and as instruments of human development (See Sen, 1999).

Education

Educational indicators are of various types, and those that are monitored relate primarily to inputs—that is, investments in education in terms of resources and time. UNESCO, for example, collects data on numerous inputs such as enrollment numbers and rates, repetition rates, and pupil/teacher ratios (Bloom, chapter 1 of this volume). On outputs—the direct results of the education process—UNESCO measures literacy rates and education stocks. The Organization for Economic Co-operation and

---

[1] One of the more useful and extensive studies to date is United Nations (2005). *World Population Monitoring 2003: Population, Education and Development.* This work reviews some relevant studies and provides data on education, health, and development. The report asserts that education has been found to be closely associated with better overall health, and that this association is supported consistently, using a range of indicators. In general, the report considers education to be a lever for improving health, although the exact relationships that underlie this connection are acknowledged to be unclear. For children's health, the education of their mothers is particularly important.

Development (OECD) and the International Association for the Evaluation of Educational Achievement collect other output data on average years of schooling and test scores in mathematics, science, and reading.

Education is recognized as a basic human right, and better education improves people's welfare. As an instrument of development, education fosters and enhances work skills and life skills such as confidence and sociability. These skills in individuals promote economic growth on a societal level via increased productivity and, potentially, better governance (Hannum and Buchmann, this volume).

Health

The World Health Organization defines health as "a state of complete physical, mental and social well-being and not merely the absence of disease or infirmity."[2] Health indicators produced by the World Health Organization and other UN bodies include infant and child mortality rates, life expectancy, morbidity data, burden of disease, and disability-adjusted life years (DALYs). Improvements in these measures reflect improvements in quality of life.

Good health not only promotes human development. It also allows people to attend work regularly, to be productive at work, and to work for more years. Healthy individuals also contribute to the good health of those around them because they do not spread infection, and they have the physical and mental strength to look after others. Robust health can often serve as a platform for progress in other areas, given a suitable policy environment.

Good health can also alter the population growth rate in ways that promote development. Health improvements often have the greatest effect on those who are most vulnerable, children in particular. Advances in medicine and nutrition increase the likelihood that a child will survive into adulthood, and parents therefore need to bear fewer children to attain their ideal family size. High fertility, still prevalent in much of the developing world, tends to decline when child survival improves (Stark and Rosenzweig, 2006).

---

[2] Preamble to the Constitution of the World Health Organization as adopted by the International Health Conference, New York, 19–22 June, 1946; signed on 22 July 1946 by the representatives of 61 states (Official Records of the World Health Organization, no. 2, p. 100) and entered into force on 7 April 1948.

Reduced fertility means parents can concentrate investments of time and money on a few children rather than spreading these resources across many, thus enhancing their children's prospects of leading healthier and better-educated lives. Reduced infant and child mortality lessens emotional stress on families, potentially increasing family cohesion, and gives parents more time to devote to productive activities as the need to care for sick infants decreases. Lower fertility also improves mothers' health, as early and frequent childbirth, particularly in developing countries where health systems are weak and often unsafe, poses serious health risks. Maternal mortality is a major problem in the developing world; in some parts of Africa, 2 percent of live births result in the mother's death (UN Statistics Division, 2004).

Fertility declines also change population structure, with positive effects on development. In the time lag between increased child survival and parents' subsequent decision to bear fewer children, a "boom" generation is created, which is larger than both the preceding and the succeeding generations. As this generation reaches working age, it can strongly boost an economy if economic policies encourage job creation. This "demographic dividend" accounted for as much as one-third of East Asia's "economic miracle," and has also had strong effects in Ireland (Bloom et al., 2002; Bloom and Canning, 2003).

Health and Education

Certain effects of health and education on development are well established. There may also be synergies between these two, in which case we are likely underestimating their impacts. Understanding the links between health and education is important for social policy as well as academic knowledge.

The recent success stories of East and Southeast Asia and Ireland suggest that development requires a combination of factors, such as those listed earlier (Bloom and Canning, 2003). Interactions among the many relevant factors have the potential to set off virtuous development spirals and to halt vicious spirals (Agosín et al., 2006). Understanding how different drivers of development affect one another can translate into better policy. A description of the interactions between education and health may provide a useful model for these other factors.

Most governments treat health and education separately, via separate ministries for health and education. Collaboration between these ministries is often patchy, with spending decisions on education rarely taking account of impacts on health, and vice versa. In all settings, but particularly in developing countries where funds are especially scarce, maximizing the return on investments is critical. An intervention that improves health will have some impact on human development, but one that improves health and education simultaneously may be a more effective use of resources. In contexts where trade-offs are inevitable, the knowledge that an intervention in one area is likely to spark improvement in other areas could have a major influence on policy.

Ignoring these interactions in policy making is wasteful. It may also be damaging. If they are to succeed, policy interventions intended to spur development must adequately address the range of factors that can impede a country's progress. Funds invested in teacher training, for example, may be squandered if teachers receive no advice or assistance with HIV prevention. AIDS has decimated the education workforce in parts of Sub-Saharan Africa, triggering a vicious spiral whereby poor health in teachers hinders the education of children. This leaves children, through their lack of knowledge, more vulnerable to HIV infection themselves.

Figure 1 suggests that health and education are linked. The figure plots infant mortality against adult literacy for all countries for which data are available, and shows the resulting linear regression lines for both 1970 and 2000. Countries with low infant mortality tend to have high literacy levels, although the range of adult literacy is wide at all levels of infant mortality. Both health status and educational indicators have improved somewhat since 1970, but the relationship between them has remained relatively stable (and this is true for indicators beyond those shown here). However, as we discuss in more detail below, we cannot infer causality from these data: education could affect health, or vice versa, or both could be affected by other factors.

Understanding causality is a key to unlocking the potential for improvement in infant health suggested by Figure 1. Examination (via case studies) of the countries that do not conform to the general trend may also be instructive. The Maldives, for example, had a high literacy rate (88 percent) but also a high infant mortality rate (157 per thousand live births) in 1970. By 2000, its infant mortality rate had improved greatly (to 59 per thousand). Did education have a delayed effect on health or was education in 1970 not of the right type or quality to have

Figure 1: Infant Mortality and Adult Literacy, 1970 and 2000

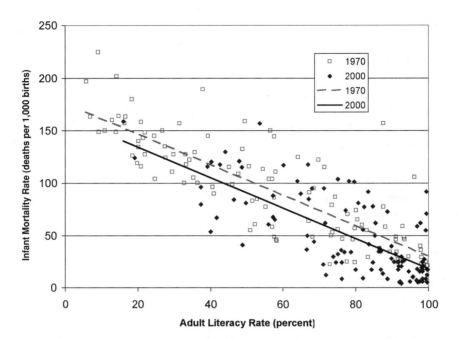

an effect on health knowledge or behaviors? Alternatively, did non-educational factors, such as a lack of access to technology or medicine, hinder health improvement? An assessment of why health lagged education and how the Maldives made such huge strides in cutting infant mortality could provide lessons for policy makers facing similar challenges.

CONCEPTUAL CHANNELS:
HOW EDUCATION AND HEALTH COULD BE LINKED

In this section, I look first at the reasons to expect that better health leads to better or more education, and then at the reasons to expect effects in the reverse direction. Although there are numerous possible channels, not all occur as described below, particularly because government policy and actions influence these potential interactions between education and health.

Health to Education

Different theoretical channels from improved health to better education occur over the course of an individual's life. Good health as an infant enhances cognitive development, allowing healthy children to derive greater benefit from schooling. At school age, good health means that children can attend school more frequently and pay better attention in class. Good attendance, enabled by good health, is more likely to lead to higher attainment through secondary and post-secondary education and, in adulthood, to increase the mental agility needed for lifelong learning. The health of other family members also affects educational enrollment, as healthy siblings and parents alleviate the pressure on older children to care for others at home. Maternal health, closely connected with child health, is likely to be linked to children's educational outcomes.

Good health also makes investment in education more likely. Healthy parents are likely to be economically better off, and thus better able to afford education (or better education). Parents of healthy children, moreover, receive a greater return on the investment in their children's education than do parents of sick children who may not survive to adulthood.[3] The same is true for governments considering investments in schools: in countries with relatively healthy populations, government investment in education will yield a higher return in economic growth and other social benefits. Health improvements thus make it more likely that children will attend school for long periods and that the schools they attend will have the resources to teach them well.

Just as good health can strengthen education, bad health can weaken it. At a national level, major health shocks divert public funds from schooling (among other government investments). They also damage the human capital needed to run education systems and teach in schools, as in the case of HIV/AIDS in southern Africa. At the family level, health shocks may divert assets from education. Sick children need medicine and care, both of which consume a family's time and financial resources. Sick

---

[3] This argument, of course, is based on the idea that parents will act in their children's long-term interests. This assumption, generally reasonable, underlies much thinking about development. However, there is a possibility for this assumption to be off the mark in some cases, as parents' interests are not identical to those of their children, and they may choose, or be forced, to make decisions based on their own shorter-term interests, which could diminish the effect of good health on education.

parents cannot work to fund their children's schooling, and they may require children to withdraw from school to look after them or to earn income for the family.

Education to Health

There are numerous conceptual links from education to improved health. Direct effects occur if schools provide health services such as vaccines or treatment for illness, or if they supply nutritious meals that students would not receive at home. A negative direct effect of school attendance may be increased exposure to illness; however, if short-term sicknesses are overcome, children can build up immunity against diseases that may be dangerous, or at least time-consuming, if caught in adulthood.

Many less-direct links also exist. Educated individuals have readier access to health information than those without education. The skills gained through schooling can help children absorb health information and adopt health-seeking behavior, although it is unclear whether health is most improved by health-specific education or general education. Many schools provide lessons on hygiene, nutrition, and sex education, and also encourage health-seeking behaviors such as washing hands before meals (families, of course, also provide much of this information to children). Good education nurtures inquisitiveness and teaches the links between cause and effect, with possible positive consequences for health outcomes as evidenced by the impact of maternal education on child health (LeVine, 1987; Buor, 2003; Caldwell, 1979). Educated children may have a more concrete understanding of how various behaviors affect health outcomes. A better understanding of symptoms may also make interactions with physicians more effective.

Education also indirectly affects health through education's effect on incomes. Educated children tend to earn higher incomes in adulthood and, therefore, are more likely to have the money and time to visit medical practitioners. Children in school—and their parents—have more to lose financially in taking health risks (such as smoking, having unprotected sex, making poor dietary choices, and failing to exercise) than those who are unenrolled. These factors may encourage health-seeking behavior. In adulthood, higher incomes allow people to eat better food (although in some cases wealth can also lead to their eating too much food), live in more secure dwellings, protect themselves against environmental shocks, and purchase better health care. The educated may, as a consequence, be more resilient to health setbacks and better able to respond to them.

Higher income also affects mental health. People with higher incomes have more effective support networks than the poor, and they are less likely to feel and to be socially excluded. Wealth enables greater control of one's circumstances than poverty, and stress levels are therefore likely to be lower. The combination of social exclusion and stress could make the less educated more vulnerable to mental illness and its physical effects.

Through its positive effects on wage rates, education can also contribute to fertility decline. Higher wages increase the opportunity cost for women of raising children full-time, and in most countries increased wages have been associated with falls in fertility. As discussed above, fertility declines allow parents to concentrate resources in fewer children, increasing the likelihood that children will be healthy.

Perhaps most important, the broader context matters in facilitating the links between education and health. If, for example, large numbers of people are unemployed, then increasing education levels will not raise incomes and the health benefits that would otherwise follow from raised incomes are foregone. In this circumstance, there is no consequent health improvement to feed back to better or more education.

THE EVIDENCE

The Big Questions

Despite a growing body of academic work[4] on the links between health and education, many key questions about their interaction remain unanswered. A search of the Rockefeller University library's Evidence-Based Medicine database uncovers over 1,000 items discussing both health and education. However, few of these studies are based on randomized trials, and many overlook the effect of external variables on education and health improvements. Although associations are often found between advances in health and education, causality is more often implied than proved, with ad hoc studies prevailing over more robust longitudinal data and data from randomized controlled trials.

---

[4] See, for example, "Education and Public Health: Mutual Challenges Worldwide," Special Issue of *Comparative Education Review* 49 (4) (November 2005), and the works cited therein.

To deepen academic understanding of the links and to strengthen policy decisions, a core set of questions should be addressed. Regarding channels leading from health to education, we might first ask, "Whose health, if anyone's, is important to a child's educational outcomes?" The health of many parties may be important. The nutritional status and overall health of a young child may affect his or her ability to learn. Maternal physical and mental health before, during, and after pregnancy plays an important role. If a child's father is the breadwinner, the father's health could be crucial to the child's education. If a child has siblings, their illness can divert resources away from a child's education. The health of teachers, too, may be relevant to children's educational outcomes.

We also need to investigate what types of health interventions improve schooling outcomes. Such interventions might include dietary improvements (e.g., school lunches and micronutrient and vitamin supplements), immunization programs, and school-based clinics. They might also include public health information campaigns that target children or their family members.

Regarding channels from education to health, we need to ask, "Whose education benefits whose health?" In particular, we need to better understand what role mothers' education plays in maternal, infant, spousal, and child health. Similarly, what are the effects of a father's education? Other questions in this area include: Do educated children bring health benefits to uneducated parents or siblings? Do the effects of education on male health and female health differ? Do impacts vary by country or region? To what extent are policy lessons transferable from one location to another?

We have some knowledge about how education improves health, but we do not know enough about exactly how this works. With a dearth of randomized experiments, our understanding has room to develop. It is plausible that attending school promotes health-seeking behaviors such as exercise, good hygiene, avoidance of alcohol and smoking, and delay of sexual initiation/pregnancy, but we do not know enough about these interactions. For example, some have suggested that education is like a "social vaccine" for HIV/AIDS prevention.[5] To what extent is this true, and

---

[5] "Ministries of education increasingly recognise that education is an effective 'social vaccine' against HIV/AIDS, but that the impact of the epidemic is compromising their ability to deliver this vaccine" (Donald Bundy, of the World Bank, quoted in http://siteresources.worldbank.org/CSO/Resources/Learning_to_Survive_by_Oxfam.pdf).

do particular levels of education have different effects? Are some health problems—say, infectious diseases or mental health issues—more responsive to education than others? We also need to know when education might pose a threat to health, for example, by increasing exposure to disease.

We need to understand how different types of education counter risks and maximize health benefits. For example, primary schooling may be a key for some disease prevention efforts but not others. Health education per se has been the subject of numerous studies, but more work is needed to understand the means and extent of any impact.

The Evidence – Research Methods

Empirical research on the links between health and education takes various forms, including randomized studies, retrospective studies, ethnographic work, and case studies.

Few studies on the links between health and education have employed randomized designs (Bettinger, this volume) although these are often the most compelling way of establishing causal connections.[6] Evaluating health and education interventions requires evidence of causality. Studies that look at retrospective data, as valuable and often necessary as they are, do not necessarily construct valid groups for comparison—groups that are statistically similar but for the single difference of interest. The validity of the results may be colored by unexamined differences, making inferences of causality unreliable (Moffitt, 2005). A finding that children who attend school are healthier than those who do not may reflect the inability of unhealthy children to attend school, or it may result from the variety of ways that factors such as family income, parental health knowledge, or diet influence health and education status.

---

[6] However, such trials can be quite costly to conduct and they sometimes raise difficult ethical issues. Denying a control group of children access to schooling is not politically or morally feasible. Similarly, offering an intervention to only one group of students or one set of schools, when that intervention seems likely to be beneficial, is also very problematic. This ethical problem is mitigated, however, by the consideration that if no students receive the intervention, none of them will be better off, nor will anyone learn whether the intervention is definitely effective or cost-effective. Obviously, such trials must be carefully designed and reviewed before they are initiated. One additional possibility is sequential staging, in random order, of an intervention that cannot be delivered everywhere at once to solve the ethical problem while permitting statistically valid comparisons.

Although multivariate analysis can, in principle, eliminate the confounding effects of factors that are included in the analysis, multivariate analysis cannot eliminate the effects of unknown confounding variables. It may be difficult to be confident of the impact of schooling unless confounding factors are reasonably spread across treatment and control groups, and only randomization can ensure such comparability.

In randomized tests, randomly selected treatment and control groups are likely to be similar to each other on average and are therefore valid groups for comparison. Any changes occurring after programs are implemented may be more reliably attributed to the intervention. Because randomized trials can be costly to implement and results can take several years to emerge, especially in areas with long-term effects such as health and education, they tend to be underutilized. Strong skills in research design and implementation are needed for trials to be effective, and these skills are often insufficient in developing countries.[7] However, as the INDEPTH network[8] of demographic surveillance sites in Africa, Asia, and Latin America demonstrates, investing in randomized studies can help build up local research capacity and inform national policy.

In terms of wasted policy opportunities, the cost of *not* conducting randomized trials may be much higher than that incurred by conducting them. As an example, a randomized community health study by the Navrongo Demographic Surveillance Site in northern Ghana found that moving nurses into communities and mobilizing community volunteers to assist the nurses reduced overall mortality in treatment areas by 30 percent. The program is now part of Ghana's national health care policy and has sparked international interest.

Novel combinations of research methods will make possible new and stronger findings, as illustrated by two examples. First, the relationship between health and education can be investigated using micro-data, such as those from surveys or randomized trials, or macro-data where the typical unit of observation is a nation, such as those supplied by the World Bank's *World Development Indicators*. Asking the same question via these two very different methods may yield consistent or contradictory results. To the best of my knowledge, this type of comparison has not been carried out very often, if at all, and may be a fruitful direction for research. Second, qualitative research methods may offer another fruitful approach.

---

[7] Bettinger (this volume) offers a detailed discussion of these challenges.
[8] http://www.indepth-network.net/

Randomized studies do not try to explain *why* people act as they do. Focus groups, case studies, and ethnographic techniques are required to generate useful hypotheses about the dynamics of a situation that can sometimes be tested using quantitative research methods. Such qualitative designs are often complementary to quantitative ones.

The Evidence – Health to Education

In this subsection, I summarize some studies covering channels from health to education and the reverse. Although this summary is not an exhaustive review of the literature, most of the studies are prominent or recent. These studies indicate that education and health have mutually reinforcing interactions.

The most persuasive evidence that good health leads to good education has come from randomized studies. These studies examine the effects on school children (absenteeism, test scores) of de-worming programs, iron supplementation, and the provision of school meals in developing countries.

A 2004 study by Miguel and Kremer examines the effect of de-worming programs on primary school children in Kenya. The investigation, which was randomized over 75 schools, finds that de-worming reduced absenteeism from school by one-quarter in the treatment group and also improved health and school participation in students who were not included in the program, both in the treatment school and beyond it (Miguel and Kremer, 2004). The study finds no impact of the de-worming program on academic test scores, however. A similar study by Bobonis, Miguel, and Sharma (n.d.) in the slums of Delhi, India, finds that delivering iron supplementation and de-worming drugs to children attending pre-school reduced absenteeism by one-fifth in the first five months of the program. The authors could not maintain randomized groups for comparison when they extended the study over a further year, as parents who were aware of the program self-selected their children into treatment schools (highlighting a potential problem with randomized trials).

In addition to increasing attendance, treatment of health problems may also improve cognition and learning abilities. Nokes and others (1992) test the impact of whipworm infection on the cognitive abilities of 9–12 year-old children in Jamaica. The study includes a treatment group, a group that received a placebo, and a control group of uninfected children. It finds that curing whipworm led to significantly improved scores in short-term and long-term memory tests, and that treated children caught up with uninfected children in these tests after nine weeks. A similar study by Bhargava et al. in Kenya provides further evidence of the effect of health on cognitive development, finding that both height and hemoglobin concentration are significant predictors of scores on achievement tests (Bhargava et al., 2005).

School meals provide a strong incentive for students to attend school, although no evidence shows that improved nutrition enhances learning. A randomized test in Kenya finds that school meals improved school attendance and test scores. School attendance by the treatment group was 36 percent, while in the control group it was 27 percent. Test scores improved only in schools where teachers were more experienced. According to the authors, "what seems crucial is that the children who had better scores attended school more often and had a teacher with more experience" (Vermeersch and Kremer, 2004). A non-randomized study in Pakistan by Alderman and others finds that health and nutrition had significant positive effects on school enrollment and that these effects were stronger for girls than boys (Alderman et al., 2001). As noted above, however, the results of non-randomized studies may be less conclusive due to biases in the data.

Several non-randomized studies consider the effect of HIV/AIDS on students and teachers. An analysis of case studies of 49 families infected with HIV/AIDS in Zambia finds that among 215 children, over one-quarter had had to withdraw from school (Haworth et al., 1991). A further Zambian study finds that the number of AIDS-related teacher deaths in the first ten months of 1998 was equivalent to two-thirds of the country's newly qualified teaching pool each year (UNICEF, 2000). Kobiané and others (2005) investigate the effect of adult deaths on the education of young children by studying the educational participation of orphans. This issue is particularly salient in the face of the HIV/AIDS crisis in Africa. The study finds that orphans are less likely to enter school than their non-orphan peers, and this effect is more pronounced in rural areas, among the poor, and for girls.

Not all randomized studies supported the health-to-education link. A study by Dickson et al. (2000) reviews 30 earlier studies covering 15,000 children to determine whether treating children infected with worms improved their cognitive performance. This meta-analysis finds no connection, but various problems with the data compromise the study's ability to do so. Likewise, Madhavan and Thomas (2005) find that although childbearing would seem to be an impediment to a girl's completion of formal education (and most data support this supposition), it does not necessarily signal the end of schooling. The analysis by Madhavan and Thomas suggests that certain household-level attributes might enable young mothers to complete their education.

In sum, although there is evidence that health affects education, the overall picture is not entirely clear. Many questions remain unanswered, and many health interventions that may affect education have not been tested in randomized trials. More research is needed before health interventions can be most effectively incorporated into education policy.

The Evidence – Education to Health

It is possible to test educational interventions to improve the health of children using randomized trials, but most work to determine the effect of education on health has been carried out using other research methods.

Studies have investigated the impact of education on broad indicators of health, such as mortality and functional ability. To determine whether the association between education and health is causal, Adriana Lleras-Muney (2005) examines the health of individuals who had grown up with differing compulsory education laws; those who were subject to such laws would have had more education than those who were not, even if other socioeconomic factors were equal across such groups. Her study concludes that education reduces adult mortality and that the effect is larger than previously thought. A study by Scott J. Adams (2002) uses econometric modeling of U.S. Health and Retirement Study data to demonstrate that increased educational attainment promotes improved health among adults. Using functional ability as an indicator for health and controlling for family background, the study finds education to have a significant positive effect on almost all indicators, with a stronger effect for women than for men. Another study in four different U.S. locations finds that education was associated with lower mortality rates in adults in men, but not in women (Bassuk et al., 2002).

Other studies consider more specific health effects. Berger and Leigh (1989) use econometric modeling to eliminate the impact of self-selection bias on findings that education improves health. They find that increased schooling was associated with lower blood pressure and lower likelihood of reporting disabilities or functional impairments, even after accounting for background variables such as age, initial health, and ability. A study based on data from Brazil, Ghana, and the United States finds that parental education influenced children's height, which is often seen as a proxy for health. In particular, a father's educational level had a bigger effect on his son's height than on his daughter's, and a mother's level affected her daughters' height more than her sons' height (Thomas, 1994).[9] Donald Kenkel (1991) uses U.S. Health Interview Survey data to show that schooling was associated with increased health-seeking behavior in terms of refraining from smoking, partaking in exercise, and reducing alcohol consumption. The study does not establish causality, however, and does not rule out the possibility that variables other than schooling had a greater effect.

Maternal education is strongly associated with improved health outcomes for children and with reduced fertility. Studies reported by Robert A. LeVine (1987) use survey data and ethnographic observations in Mexico to show that maternal education is negatively associated with fertility and with infant mortality after controlling for socioeconomic factors. Educated mothers were more likely to take sick children to clinics, and their fertility rates were lower even after taking into account the effect of attending school or work on age of marriage. "The pathways from school to reduced fertility," the author reports, "do not run through postponed marriage and improved job opportunities but through the apparent psychosocial influence of school on a woman and her marriage to a man more likely to share her lower fertility goals" (LeVine 1987).

---

[9] One reviewer asked whether this study had "...[considered] the possibility that parental physical vigor and intelligence were a common causal factor responsible for both high levels of parental education and greater height of their offspring;" and, "Instead of education causing health, it could be that both parental education and child height result from a common antecedent, parental 'fitness.'" In private correspondence related to this point, Duncan Thomas wrote: "First, it may be that parental education is proxying for resource. . . [T]he evidence on parental education being positively associated with child height is robust to controlling parental resources (measured with income, wealth or consumption). Second, it is possible that there are other unmeasured factors that drive parental education and child height. To the extent these do not vary with the gender of the child, and as long as their influence on child height is linear and additive, then models that include household fixed effects will absorb their impact on child height. The evidence you cite is robust to including household fixed effects. This amounts to comparing the influence of father's education on sons, relative to daughters, and doing the same for mother's education.

The findings reported in LeVine's summary are supported by other research. Janet Currie and Enrico Moretti (2003) construct longitudinal panel data from U.S. Vital Statistics natality files to measure the effect of mothers' education on child health. They find that schooling in mothers reduces the incidence of low birth weight, premature birth, and fertility. Cynthia Lloyd and others (2000) use Demographic and Health Survey (DHS) data to study the link between primary schooling and fertility in Sub-Saharan Africa. All nine countries that had achieved mass primary schooling began their fertility transitions soon after. As with other studies, however, causality is not addressed.

A particularly intriguing study in Ghana by Benefo (2006) finds that, independent of a woman's own level of education, her interest in modern methods of contraception and in having fewer children increases when the level of education of other women in her community increases. This result suggests that education may have greater ability to influence reproductive health in rural Africa than has previously been thought.

Other studies suggest the links from education to health are either negligible or negative. A study of the effect of years of schooling on cigarette smoking in the United States analyzes survey data of high-school age students and includes follow-up interviews of a sample of the survey respondents seven years later. The authors find no correlation between additional years of schooling and propensity to smoke (Farrell and Fuchs, 1982). A Tanzanian study comparing children enrolled in primary school with those not enrolled found no consistent difference in levels of parasitic infection. The study, which relied on survey data and blood and urine samples, finds some positive correlation between school enrollment and malnutrition and anemia (Beasley et al., 2000). A review of 27 studies on the effect of education on HIV infection finds that in Africa the more educated had an increased rate of infection (although it appeared that this pattern might be changing), whereas in Thailand education was associated with a lower risk of HIV (Hargreaves and Glynn, 2002). A 1994 sentinel surveillance study in Zambia supports the Africa finding. A 1997 study finds a positive correlation between education and HIV levels among women aged 25–29 (Flykesnes et al., 1997). Later on in the epidemic, however, the strength of this relationship weakened, and in some African countries it reversed (Vandemoortele and Delamonica, 2000).

Evidence for differences in health effects of general education versus health-specific education is difficult to find. Education by itself, as opposed to health-specific education, may be a key driver of health improvements. A study by Nayga (2001) uses U.S. Diet and Health Knowledge Survey data to examine the effect of schooling on obesity. Among a randomly selected sample of 1,579 survey respondents, education was linked to significantly reduced obesity in women and men, even after controlling for health knowledge, suggesting that schooling's association with lower obesity was not due to health knowledge. The author does not examine other factors that may account for the link, but the study points to a significant benefit of general education for health.

Other studies indicate the importance of maternal education in child health. A regression analysis of survey data in Morocco shows that although the health knowledge mothers obtain as a result of schooling was associated with significantly better health for their children, fathers' schooling had no relationship with child health (Glewwe, 1997). The channels from mothers' education to their children's health appear to work through the acquisition at school of skills in reading and basic mathematics. These skills enabled girls to acquire health knowledge after leaving school, which they used to improve their children's health. Direct health education of girls in schools might have improved their children's health further, but the study does not test this idea.

The proposed pathway from maternal education to child health is supported by the work of Rowe and others (2005) on education's effect on maternal health practices in Nepal. Their work shows that general education enables mothers to benefit from health-specific education. As in some other relatively isolated countries, the dissemination of information about health practices that improve the life chances of children is hampered in Nepal by illiteracy, by within-country geographical barriers, and by longstanding child-raising practices that do not benefit from knowledge gained in other parts of the world. Rowe et al. show that the health-related knowledge and practices of mothers is affected not only by their schooling, but by subsequent use of their literacy skills and also by their exposure to media.

Health education occurring outside of formal schooling may have positive effects on health-seeking behavior. Lee and Mason (2005) find that mothers who used prenatal care had a higher subsequent likelihood of immunizing their children.

The effects of health-specific education on student health are not clear. A UNAIDS literature review assesses the impact of HIV/AIDS and sexual health education on the sexual behavior of young people. The review finds that of 53 studies that evaluate interventions, 27 report no change in recipients' sexual behavior. Twenty-two studies report reductions in behaviors linked with a higher risk of HIV infection, such as the number of sexual partners, unplanned pregnancy, and sexually transmitted disease. However, the authors admit that "the interpretative value of this research was somewhat compromised . . . because of inadequacies in study design, analytic techniques, outcome indicators, and reporting of statistics"(UNAIDS, 1997). Responding to studies that cast doubt on the efficacy of education initiatives in promoting health, Pridmore and Yates (2005) argue that a different type of education may be more effective in confronting the HIV/AIDS crisis. They advocate that governments embrace open learning systems and new, more flexible means of educating youth, and suggest that young people should be involved in encouraging communities to confront AIDS.

A particularly interesting study by Curtin and Nelson (1999) finds that the benefits of improved health that are expected to result from primary education only come about when children also receive post-primary education. The authors attribute longstanding beliefs in the higher returns (both for income and health improvements) from investments in primary education (as opposed to secondary or tertiary education) as stemming from flawed World Bank methodology.

Although few of the studies described above provide decisive evidence of causality, they do identify the possible impacts of education on health, and these are consistent with the intuitive reasons for their occurrence. Uncertainties abound, even on basic questions. Mothers' education appears to be particularly strongly associated with better health outcomes for their children, but clarifying the effect of a child's schooling on his or her own health has proved more difficult. Whether health education and general education have different effects is unclear, as is knowledge of what type of health education is most effective under what circumstances and for what purposes. Differences in the specific health impacts of primary, secondary, and tertiary schooling have yet to be determined, although the study by Curtin and Nelson does shed light on a possible important difference between the effects of primary and post-primary education on health. There is also considerable uncertainty about the effects of education on male health versus female health. Nevertheless, with the balance of studies suggesting there are links from education to better health, establishing how these links work is critical for designing policies to take advantage of them.

The effects of education on health could vary from one context to another. For example, in a country that trades extensively with a large neighbor, the effect of education on health might be different from that in a country whose economy is more isolated. Without the opportunities that arise from proximity to a behemoth, an isolated country may have fewer development options, so the need for education to facilitate health improvements may be stronger. Similarly, the effects of education on health can vary over time. In Africa, individuals with more education were at first more likely to become infected with HIV. As those with education became more aware of how HIV spreads, uneducated people became the ones more likely to become infected.

CONCLUSION

Although the evidence is far from complete, it appears that the interactions between education and health can promote virtuous development spirals. Good health boosts school attendance and improves learning. Good education, particularly of mothers, boosts child health, and the effects can last into adulthood. Policies that take advantage of the interactions between health and education should be developed and implemented. They should also avoid potential pitfalls. A case study in Karnataka, India, finds that a disproportionate share of subsidies for education and health benefited the well-off, and relatively little went to women, people in rural areas, or other individuals with low levels of health and education (Mahal, 2000).

Because key questions remain unanswered, policy-makers have only slim evidence on which to formulate plans. More research is needed. Randomized studies should be an important focus of efforts, but different research designs have different strengths that may be beneficial to research efforts. Retrospective quantitative studies can draw on large amounts of data and benefit from experiences in a wide array of situations. Qualitative studies can both provide seminal insights and lead to critical, testable hypotheses. Effective policy requires strong evidence, and a robust mix of studies may have the potential to push our understanding forward faster than any single research strategy.

References

Adams, Scott J. 2002. "Educational Attainment and Health: Evidence from a Sample of Older Adults." *Education Economics* 10 (1): 97–109.

Agosín, Manuel R., David E. Bloom, Georges Chapelier, and Jagdish Saigal, eds. Forthcoming 2006. *Solving the Riddle of Globalization and Development*. United Kingdom: Routledge.

Alderman, Harold, Jere Behrman, Victor Lavy, and Rekha Menon. 2001. "Child Health and School Enrollment: A Longitudinal Analysis." *Journal of Human Resources*, 36 (1): 185–205.

Asian Development Bank. 1997. *Emerging Asia: Changes and Challenges*. Manila: Asian Development Bank.

Bassuk, Shari S., Lisa F. Berkman, and Benjamin C. Amick III. 2002. "Socioeconomic Status and Mortality Among the Elderly: Findings from Four US Communities." *American Journal of Epidemiology* 155 (6).

Beasley, N. M., A. Hall, A. M. Tomkins, C. Donnelly, P. Ntimbwa, J. Kivuga, C. M. Kihamia, W. Lorri, D. A. Bundy. 2000. "The Health of Enrolled and Non-Enrolled Children of School Age in Tanga, Tanzania." *Acta Tropica* 76 (3) (October): 223–229.

Benefo, Kofi D. 2006. "The community-level effects of women's education on reproductive behavior in rural Ghana." *Demographic Research*. 14. Article 20. pp. 485–508. June 2. Available at http://www.demographic-research.org/Volumes/Vol14/20/

Berger, Mark C., and J. P. Leigh. 1989. "Schooling, Self-Selection, and Health." *Journal of Human Resources* 24: 433–455.

Bhargava, Alok, Matthew Jukes, Damaris Ngorosho, Charles Khilma, and Donald A.P. Bundy. 2005. "Modeling the Effects of Health Status and the Educational Infrastructure on the Cognitive Development of Tanzanian Schoolchildren." *American Journal of Human Biology* 17: 280–292.

Bloom, David E., and David Canning. 2003. "Contraception and the Celtic Tiger." *Economic and Social Review* 34 (3) (Winter): 229–247.

Bloom, David E., David Canning, and Jaypee Sevilla. 2002. *The Demographic Dividend: A New Perspective on the Economic Consequences of Population Change.* Santa Monica, California: RAND, MR-1274.

Bobonis, G. J., E. Miguel, and C. P Sharma. n.d. "Iron Deficiency Anemia and School Participation." Poverty Action Lab Paper no. 7.

Buor, Daniel. 2003. "Mothers' Education and Childhood Mortality in Ghana." *Health Policy* 64 (3) (June): 297–309.

Caldwell, J. C. 1979. "Education as a Factor in Mortality Decline: An Examination of Nigerian Data." *Population Studies* 3: 395–414.

Currie, Janet, and Enrico Moretti. 2003. "Mother's Education and the Intergenerational Transmission of Human Capital: Evidence from College Openings and Longitudinal Data." *The Quarterly Journal of Economics* 118 (4) (November).

Curtin, T.R.C. and E.A.S. Nelson. 1999. "Economic and health efficiency of education funding policy." *Social Science & Medicine* 48: 1599–1611.

Dickson, Rumona, Shally Awasthi, Paula Williamson, Colin Demellweek, and Paul Garner. 2000. "Effects of Treatment for Intestinal Helminth Infection on Growth and Cognitive Performance in Children: Systematic Review of Randomised Trials." *British Medical Journal* 320: 1697–1701.

Farrell, Phillip, and Victor R. Fuchs. 1982. "Schooling and Health: The Cigarette Connection." *Journal of Health Economics* 1 (3) (December): 217–230.

Fylkesnes, K., R. M. Musonda, K. Kasumba, Z. Ndhlovu, F. Mluanda, L. Kaetano, C. C. Chipaila. 1997. "The HIV Epidemic in Zambia: Socio-demographic Prevalence Patterns and Indications of Trends among Childbearing Women." *AIDS* 11: 339–345.

Glewwe, Paul. 1997. "How Does Schooling of Mothers Improve Child Health? Evidence From Morocco." LSMS Working Paper Number 128. The World Bank, Washington DC.

Haworth, A., K. Kalumba, P. Kwapa, E. Van Praag, and C. Hamavhwa. 1991. "The Impact of HIV/AIDS in Zambia: General Socio-Economic Impact." Paper presented to the VII International Conference on AIDS, Florence.

Hargreaves, James R., and Judith R. Glynn. 2002. "Educational Attainment and HIV Infection in Developing Countries: A Systematic Review." *Tropical Medicine and International Health* 7 (6): 489–498.

Kenkel, Donald S. 1991. "Health Behavior, Health Knowledge, and Schooling." *Journal of Political Economy* 99 (April): 287–305.

Kobiané, Jean-François, Anne-Emmanuèle Calvès, and Richard Marcoux. 2005. "Parental Death and Children's Schooling in Burkina Faso." *Comparative Education Review* 49 (4) (November): 468–489.

Lee, Sang-Hyop, and Andrew Mason. 2005. "Mother's Education, Learning-by-Doing, and Child Health Care in Rural India." *Comparative Education Review* 49 (4): 534–551.

LeVine, Robert A. 1987. "Women's Schooling, Patterns of Fertility, and Child Survival." *Educational Researcher* 16 (9) (December): 21–27.

Lleras-Muney, Adriana. 2005. "The Relationship Between Education and Adult Mortality in the United States." *Review of Economic Studies* 72: 189–221.

Lloyd, C., C. E. Kaufman, and P. Hewett. 2000. "The Spread of Primary Schooling in Sub-Saharan Africa: Implications for Fertility Change." *Population and Development Review* 26 (3): 483–515.

Madhavan, Sangeetha, and Kevin J. A. Thomas. 2005. "Childbearing and Schooling: New Evidence from South Africa." *Comparative Education Review* 49 (4): 452–467.

Mahal, Ajay. 2000. "Policy Implications of the Distribution of Public Subsidies on Health and Education: The Case of Karnataka, India." *Comparative Education Review* 49 (4) (November): 552–574.

Miguel, Edward, and Michael Kremer. 2004. "Worms: Identifying Impacts on Education and Health the Presence of Treatment Externalities." *Econometrica* 72 (1): 159–217.

Moffitt, Robert. 2004. "Remarks on the Analysis of Causal Relationships in Population Research." *Demography* 42 (1) (February): 91–108.

Nayga R.M., Jr. 2001. "Effect of Schooling on Obesity: Is Health Knowledge a Moderating Factor?" *Education Economics* 9 (2) (August): 129–137.

Nokes, C., S. M. Grantham-McGregor, A. W. Sawyer, E. S. Cooper, B. A. Robinson, and D. A. P. Bundy. 1992. "Moderate-to-Heavy Infection of Trichuris trichiura Affects Cognitive Function in Jamaican School Children." *Parasitology* 104: 539–547.

Pridmore, Pat, and Chris Yates. 2005. "Combating AIDS in South Africa and Mozambique: The Role of Open, Distance, and Flexible Learning (ODFL)." *Comparative Education Review* 49 (4) (November): 490–511.

Rowe, Meredith L., Bijaya Kumar Thapa, Robert Levine, Sarah Levine, and Sumon K. Tuladhar. 2005. "How Does Schooling Influence Maternal Health Practices? Evidence from Nepal." *Comparative Education Review* 49 (4) (November): 512–533.

Sen, Amartya. 1999. *Development as Freedom*. New York: Alfred A. Knopf.

Stark, O. and M. R. Rosenzweig, eds. 2006. *Handbook of Population and Family Economics*. North Holland: Elsevier.

Thomas, Duncan. 1994. "Like Father, Like Son; Like Mother, Like Daughter: Parental Resources and Child Height." *Journal of Human Resources* 29 (4) (Autumn): 950–988.

UNAIDS. 1997. "Impact of HIV and Sexual Health Education on the Sexual Behaviour of Young People: A Review Update." UNAIDS/97.4.

United Nations Children's Fund (UNICEF). 2000. *The Progress of Nations 2000*. Geneva: UNICEF.

United Nations Statistics Division. 2004. Millennium Indicators Database. Available at http://millenniumindicators.un.org/unsd/mi/mi_goals.asp.

Vandemoortele, J. and E. Delamonica. 2000. "The 'Education Vaccine' against HIV/AIDS." *Current Issues in Comparative Education* 3 (1) (December).

Vermeersch, Christel, and Michael Kremer. 2004. "School Meals, Educational Achievement, and School Competition: Evidence from a Randomized Evaluation." World Bank Policy Research Working Paper No. 3523. November.

World Bank. 1993. *The East Asian Miracle: Economic Growth and Public Policy*. New York: Oxford University Press.

Contributors

AARON BENAVOT is a Senior Policy Analyst at UNESCO (Paris) working on the Global Monitoring Report on Education for All and a senior lecturer (on leave) at the Hebrew University of Jerusalem in Israel. His research has examined the effects of education on economic development and democratization, the origins and expansion of mass education, and worldwide patterns of school curricula. In addition to co-authoring *School Knowledge for the Masses* (with John Meyer and David Kamens) and *Law and the Shaping of Public Education* (with David Tyack and Thomas James), he recently co-edited (with Cecilia Braslavsky) *School Knowledge in Comparative Historical Perspective*. He has carried out consultancy work for the World Bank, the International Bureau of Education, and the European Union.

ERIC BETTINGER is an associate professor in the department of economics at Case Western Reserve University. He is also a faculty research fellow at the National Bureau of Economic Research. His work focuses on determinants of student success in primary and secondary school. He has written several papers on the effects of educational vouchers on student outcomes in Colombia. He has also written on the academic and non-academic effects of educational vouchers in the United States. His most recent work focuses on the determinants of dropping out of college and the effectiveness of remediation in reducing dropout behavior.

MELISSA BINDER is an associate professor in the department of economics at the University of New Mexico. Much of her research focuses on education decisions in the United States and Mexico. She has also written on the relationship between education and the motherhood wage gap in the United States. At the University of New Mexico, Binder teaches courses on labor economics and Latin American development.

DAVID E. BLOOM is Clarence James Gamble Professor of Economics and Demography and chair of the Department of Population and International Health at the Harvard School of Public Health. His recent work has focused on primary, secondary, and higher education in developing countries and on the links among population health, demographic change, and economic growth. He has been on the faculty of the public policy school at Carnegie Mellon University and the economics departments of Harvard University and Columbia University. He is a fellow of the American Academy of Arts and Sciences and is co-director of its project on Universal Basic and Secondary Education.

HENRY BRAUN is a distinguished presidential appointee at the Educational Testing Service (ETS) and served as vice-president for research management at ETS from 1990–1999. He has published in the areas of mathematical statistics and stochastic modeling, the analysis of large-scale assessment data, test design, expert systems, and assessment technology. His current interests include the interplay of testing and education policy. He has investigated such issues as the structure of the Black-White achievement gap, the relationship between state education policies and state education outputs, and the effectiveness of charter schools. He is a co-winner of the Palmer O. Johnson award from the American Educational Research Association (1986), and a co-winner of the National Council for Measurement in Education award for Outstanding Technical Contributions to the Field of Educational Measurement (1999). He is a fellow of the American Statistical Association (1991) and has served on a number of national and international advisory panels.

CLAUDIA BUCHMANN is Associate Professor of Sociology at the Ohio State University. Her research interests include social stratification, education, family dynamics, and comparative sociology. Her current research focuses on race, class, and gender inequalities in the United States and institutional variations of educational systems in industrialized societies and their impact on youths' educational aspirations. In other research she has examined processes related to education stratification in developing societies and the consequences of globalization and worldwide educational expansion for economic and social development.

JOEL E. COHEN is the Abby Rockefeller Mauzé Professor of Populations at the Rockefeller University and Professor of Populations at Columbia University. He heads the Laboratory of Populations at Rockefeller and Columbia Universities. His research deals mainly with the demography, ecology, population genetics, epidemiology, and social organization of human and nonhuman populations and with mathematical concepts useful in these fields. He is author of numerous books and articles, including *How Many People Can the Earth Support?* (Princeton, 1995). He is a fellow of the American Academy of Arts and Sciences and co-director of the project on Universal Basic and Secondary Education.

JAVIER CORRALES is an associate professor of political science at Amherst College in Amherst, Massachusetts. In the spring of 2005, he was a Fulbright Scholar in Caracas, Venezuela, and in the fall, a visiting lecturer at the Center for Documentation and Research on Latin America (CEDLA) in Amsterdam, the Netherlands. His publications include *Presidents without Parties* (Penn State University Press, 2002) and the article "Political Regimes and the Digital Divide" (forthcoming in *International Studies Quarterly*). He obtained his Ph.D. in political science in 1996 from Harvard University, specializing in the politics of economic and social policy reform in Latin America.

HELEN ANNE CURRY is a graduate student in history at Yale University. Her research interests include the history of ecology and the life sciences. From 2004 until 2006, she was a program assistant at the American Academy of Arts and Sciences, where she worked extensively with the UBASE project.

PAUL GLEWWE is a professor in the department of applied economics at the University of Minnesota. Previously he was a senior economist in the Development Research Group at the World Bank. His research focuses almost exclusively on developing countries and includes the following topics: education, child health, inequality and poverty, and the design of household surveys. He has worked in and conducted research on many countries in Africa, Asia, Latin America, and the Middle East. At the University of Minnesota he teaches courses on econometrics, the microeconomics of economic development, and demand theory.

EMILY HANNUM is Assistant Professor of Sociology at the University of Pennsylvania. Her research focuses on education, child welfare, and social inequality, particularly in China. She co-directs the Gansu Survey of Children and Families, a study of family, school, and community factors that support children's education and healthy development in rural Northwest China. Recent publications include "Market Transition, Educational Disparities, and Family Strategies in Rural China: New Evidence on Gender Stratification and Development" (*Demography*, 2005) and "Children's Social Welfare in Post-Reform China: Access to Health Insurance and Education, 1989–1997" (*The China Quarterly*, 2005, with Jennifer Adams).

ANIL KANJEE is an executive director at the Human Sciences Research Council, South Africa and head of the National Education Quality Initiative. His research centers on education quality improvement in developing nations, the development and use of education indicators, the monitoring and evaluation of education systems, and the application of Item Response Theory for test development and reporting scores. He has extensive experience in national and international studies and has authored numerous publications on education assessment and evaluation.

MICHAEL KREMER is Gates Professor of Developing Societies at Harvard University, senior fellow at the Brookings Institution, and a non-resident fellow at the Center for Global Development. He founded and was the first executive director of WorldTeach, a non-profit organization that places two hundred volunteer teachers annually in developing countries (1986–1989). He previously served as a teacher in Kenya. Kremer received the MacArthur Fellowship in 1997, and his research interests include AIDS and infectious diseases in developing countries, economics of developing countries, education and development, and mechanisms for encouraging research and development. He is a fellow of the American Academy of Arts and Sciences.

MARTIN B. MALIN is director of the Academy's program on Science and Global Security and staff director of the UBASE project at the American Academy of Arts and Sciences. His writing has focused on American foreign policy, international relations in the Middle East, and arms control. He has taught at Columbia University, Barnard College, and Rutgers University. Prior to joining the staff of the American Academy, he served as a consultant to the Social Science Research Council with the SSRC-MacArthur Program on International Peace and Security.

JULIA RESNIK is an assistant professor in the School of Education of the Hebrew University of Jerusalem. Her main research interests include cultural globalization, national identity, and the educational incorporation of immigrant children. Her recent publications, based on her doctoral dissertation (earned at Tel Aviv University in 2002), deal with the diffusion of education models and reforms; in particular, the role played by scholars, experts, and international organizations in setting educational agenda and influencing educational realities since 1945. Her present research focuses on migrant workers' children, multicultural schools, and international education. She teaches courses on "State, education and civil society" and "Globalization and education."

GENE SPERLING is Director of the Center for Universal Education at the Council on Foreign Relations and serves as U.S. chair of the Global Campaign for Education. Previously, Mr. Sperling served as National Economic Advisor to President Clinton from 1997–2001, and led the United States delegation to the 2000 UN World Education Forum in Dakar, Senegal. He is co-author of *What Works in Girls' Education: Evidence and Policies from the Developing World*, and he has written several essays calling for a strong global compact on education in such publications as *Foreign Affairs, New York Times, Washington Post, Financial Times*, and *Finance and Development*. Mr. Sperling currently serves as a member of the FTI Task Team on Education in Fragile States. He is also a Senior Fellow at the Center for American Progress and a Contributing Editor and Columnist for Bloomberg News.

MENG ZHAO is a Ph.D. student in the department of applied economics at the University of Minnesota. Her research focuses on development economics with special interest in education, health, and agriculture in China. She has also worked as a consultant for the World Bank, analyzing longitudinal survey data collected in rural China and cross-country data on education in Africa.

Index

THE AMERICAN ACADEMY OF ARTS AND SCIENCES

Founded in 1780, the American Academy of Arts and Sciences is an international learned society composed of the world's leading scientists, scholars, artists, business people, and public leaders. With a current membership of 4,000 American Fellows and 600 Foreign Honorary Members, the Academy has four major goals:

- Promoting service and study through analysis of critical social and intellectual issues and the development of practical policy alternatives;

- Fostering public engagement and the exchange of ideas with meetings, conferences, and symposia bringing diverse perspectives to the examination of issues of common concern;

- Mentoring a new generation of scholars and thinkers through the newly established Visiting Scholars Program;

- Honoring excellence by electing to membership men and women in a broad range of disciplines and professions.